## ALSO BY WILLIAM J. BENNETT

*Counting by Race: Equality from the Founding Fathers to Bakke* (with Terry Eastland)

*Our Children and Our Country: Improving America's Schools and Affirming the Common Culture*

*The De-Valuing of America: The Fight for Our Culture and Our Children*

*Edited,*
*with Commentary, by*

# William J. Bennett

Simon & Schuster Paperbacks

*New York London Toronto Sydney*

# The Book *of* Virtues™

*A Treasury of Great Moral Stories*

*SIMON & SCHUSTER PAPERBACKS*

*Rockefeller Center*
*1230 Avenue of the Americas*
*New York, New York 10020*



*For information about special discounts for bulk purchases, please contact Simon & Schuster Special Sales:*
*1-800-456-6798 or business@simonandschuster.com.*

*Designed by Karolina Harris*
*Manufactured in the United States of America*

*20 19*

*The Library of Congress has cataloged the hardcover edition as follows:*
*The Book of virtues : a treasury of great moral stories / [compiled] by William J. Bennett.*
*p. cm.*
*Includes index.*
*Summary: Well-known works including fables, folklore, fiction, drama, and more, by such authors as Aesop, Dickens, Tolstoy, Shakespeare, and Baldwin, are presented to teach virtues, including compassion, courage, honesty, friendship, and faith.*
*1. Literature—Collections. 2. Conduct of life—Literary collections. [1. Conduct of life—Literary collections.] I. Bennett, William John, 1943–*
*PN6014.B695 1993*
*808.8'038—dc20*
*93-8981*
*CIP*
*AC*

*ISBN-13: 978-0-671-68306-1*
*ISBN-10: 0-671-68306-3*
*ISBN-13: 978-0-684-83577-8 (Pbk)*
*ISBN-10: 0-684-83577-0 (Pbk)*

*To the families of America from my family:*
*Bill, Elayne, John, and Joseph Bennett.*

# Contents

**211**

**Very Difficult**

**Time**

# 212

**Very Difficult**

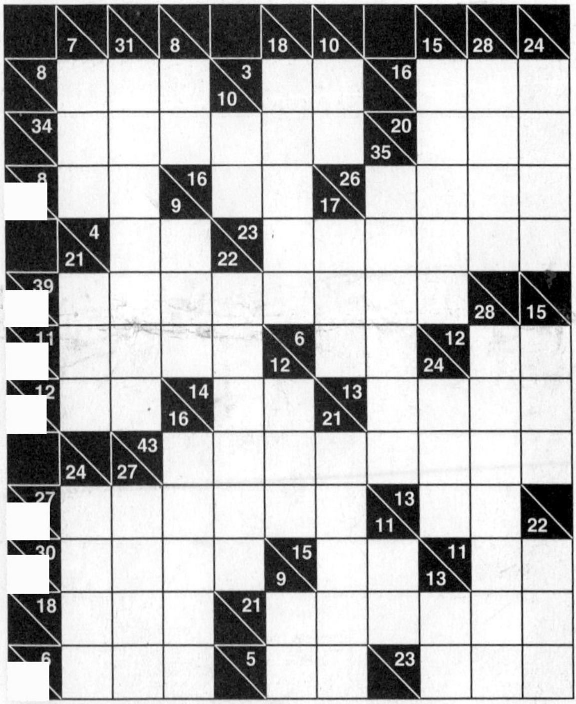


**Time**

# Introduction

This book is intended to aid in the time-honored task of the moral education of the young. Moral education—the training of heart and mind toward the good—involves many things. It involves rules and precepts—the *dos* and *don'ts* of life with others—as well as explicit instruction, exhortation, and training. Moral education *must* provide training in good habits. Aristotle wrote that good habits formed at youth make all the difference. And moral education must affirm the central importance of moral example. It has been said that there is nothing more influential, more determinant, in a child's life than the moral power of quiet example. For children to take morality seriously they must be in the presence of adults who take morality seriously. And with their own eyes they must see adults take morality seriously.

Along with precept, habit, and example, there is also the need for what we might call moral literacy. The stories, poems, essays, and other writing presented here are intended to help children achieve this moral literacy. The purpose of this book is to show parents, teachers, students, and children what the virtues look like, what they are in practice, how to recognize them, and how they work.

This book, then, is a "how to" book for moral literacy. If we want our children to possess the traits of character we most admire, we need to teach them what those traits are and why they deserve both admiration and allegiance. Children must learn to identify the forms and content of those traits. They must achieve at least a minimal level of moral literacy that will enable them to make sense of what they see in life and, we may hope, help them live it well.

Where do we go to find the material that will help our children in this task? The simple answer is we don't have to reinvent the wheel. We have a wealth of material to draw on—material that virtually all schools and homes and churches once taught to students for the sake of shaping character. That many no longer do so is something this book hopes to change.

The vast majority of Americans share a respect for certain fundamental traits of character: honesty, compassion, courage, and perseverance. These are virtues. But because children are not born with this knowledge, they need to learn what these virtues are. We can help them gain a grasp and appreciation of these traits by giving children material to read about them. We can invite our students to discern the moral dimensions of stories, of historical events, of famous lives. There are many wonderful stories of virtue and vice with which our children should be familiar. This book brings together some of the best, oldest, and most moving of them.

Do our children know these stories, these works? Unfortunately, many do not. They do not because in many places we are no longer teaching them. It is time we take up that task again. We do so for a number of reasons.

First, these stories, unlike courses in "moral reasoning," give children some specific reference points. Our literature and history are a rich quarry of moral literacy. We should mine that quarry. Children must have at their disposal a stock of examples illustrating what we see to be right and wrong, good and bad—examples illustrating that, in many instances, what is morally right and wrong can indeed be known and promoted.

Second, these stories and others like them are fascinating to children. Of course, the pedagogy (and the material herein) will need to be varied according to students' levels of comprehension, but you can't beat these stories when it comes to engaging the attention of a child. Nothing in recent years, on television or anywhere else, has improved on a good story that begins "Once upon a time . . ."

Third, these stories help anchor our children in their culture, its history and traditions. Moorings and anchors come in handy in life; moral anchors and moorings have never been more necessary.

Fourth, in teaching these stories we engage in an act of renewal. We welcome our children to a common world, a world of shared ideals, to the community of moral persons. In that common world we invite them to the continuing task of preserving the principles, the ideals, and the notions of goodness and greatness we hold dear.

The reader scanning this book may notice that it does not discuss issues like nuclear war, abortion, creationism, or euthanasia. This may come as a disappointment to some. But the fact is that the formation of character in young people is educationally a different task from, and a prior task to, the discussion of the great, difficult ethical controversies of the day. First things first. And planting the ideas of virtue, of good traits in the young, comes first. In the moral life, as in life itself, we take one step at a time. Every field has its complexities and controversies. And so too does ethics. And every field has its basics. So too with values. This is a book in the basics. The tough issues can, if teachers and parents wish, be taken up later. And, I would add, a person who is morally literate will be immeasurably better equipped than a morally illiterate person to reach a reasoned and ethically defensible position on these tough issues. But the formation of character and the teaching of moral literacy come first, in the early years; the tough issues come later, in senior high school or after.

Similarly, the task of teaching moral literacy and forming character is not political in the usual meaning of the term. People of good character are not all going to come down on the same side of difficult political and social issues. Good people—people of character and moral literacy—can be conservative, and good people can be liberal. We must not permit our disputes over thorny political questions to obscure the obligation we have to offer instruction to all our young people in the area in which we have, as a society, reached a consensus: namely, on the importance of good character, and on some of its pervasive particulars. And that is what this book provides: a compendium of great stories, poems, and essays from the stock of human history and literature. It embodies common and time-honored understandings of these virtues. It is for everybody—all children, of all political and religious backgrounds, and it speaks to them on a more fundamental level than race, sex, and gender. It addresses them as human beings—as moral agents.

Every American child ought to know at least some of the stories and poems in this book. Every American parent and teacher should be familiar with some of them, too. I know that some of these stories will strike some contemporary sensibilities as too simple, too corny, too old-fashioned. But they will not seem so to the child, especially if he or she has never seen them before. And I believe that if adults take this book and read it in a quiet place, alone, away from distorting standards, they will find themselves enjoying some of this old, simple, "corny" stuff. The stories we adults used to know and forgot—or the stories we never did know but perhaps were supposed to know—are here. (Quick!—what did Horatius do on the bridge? What is the sword of Damocles? The answers are in this book.) This is a book of lessons and reminders.

In putting this book together I learned many things. For one, going through the material was a mind-opening and encouraging rediscovery for me. I recalled great stories that I had forgotten. And thanks to the recommendations of friends, teachers, and the able prodding of my colleagues in this project, I came to know stories I had not known before. And, I discovered again how much books and education have changed in thirty years. In looking at this "old stuff" I am struck by how different it is from so much of what passes for literature and entertainment today.

Most of the material in this book speaks without hesitation, without embarrassment, to the inner part of the individual, to the moral sense. Today we speak about values and how it is important to "have them," as if they were beads on a string or marbles in a pouch. But these stories speak to morality and virtues not as something to be possessed, but as the central part of human nature, not as something to have but as something to be, the most important thing to be. To dwell in these chapters is to put oneself, through the imagination, into a different place and time, a time when there was little doubt that children are essentially moral and spiritual beings and that the central task of education is virtue. This book reminds the reader of a time—not so long ago—when the verities were the moral verities. It is thus a kind of antidote to some of the distortions of the age in which we now live. I hope parents will discover that reading this book with or to children can deepen their own, and their children's, understanding of life and morality. If the book reaches that high purpose it will have been well worth the effort.

A few additional notes and comments are in order. Although the book is titled *The Book of Virtues*—and the chapters are organized by virtues—it is also very much a book of vices. Many of the stories and poems illustrate a virtue in reverse. For children to know about virtue they must know about its opposite.

In telling these stories I am interested more in the moral than the historic lesson. In some of the older stories—Horatius at the bridge, William Tell, George Washington and the cherry tree—the line between legend and history has been blurred. But it is the instruction in the moral that matters. Some of the history that is recounted here may not meet the standards of the exacting historian. But we tell these familiar stories as they were told before, in order to preserve their authenticity.

Furthermore, I should stress that this book is by no means a definitive collection of great moral stories. Its contents have been defined in part by my attempt to present some material, most of which is drawn from the corpus of Western Civilization, that American schoolchildren, once upon a time, knew by heart. And the project, like any other, has faced several practical limitations such as space and economy (the rights to reprint recent stories and translations can be very expensive, while older material often lies in the public domain). The quarry of wonderful literature from our culture and others is deep, and I have barely scratched the surface. I invite readers to send me favorite stories not printed here, in case I should attempt to renew or improve this effort sometime in the future.

This volume is not intended to be a book one reads from cover to cover. It is, rather, a book for browsing, for marking favorite passages, for reading aloud to family, for memorizing pieces here and there. It is my hope that parents and teachers will spend some time wandering through these pages, discovering or rediscovering some moral landmarks, and in turn pointing them out to the young. The chapters can be taken in any order; on certain days we need reminding of some virtues more than others. A quick look at the Contents will steer the reader in the sought-after direction.

The reader will notice that in each chapter the material progresses from the very easy to the more difficult. The early material in each chapter can be read aloud to, or even by, very young children. As the chapter progresses greater reading and conceptual proficiency are required. Nevertheless we urge younger readers to work their way through as far as possible. As children grow older they can reach for the more difficult material in the book. They can grow up (and perhaps even grow better!) with this book.

Finally, I hope this is an encouraging book. There is a lot we read of or experience in life that is not encouraging. This book, I hope, does otherwise. I hope it encourages; I hope it points us to "the better angels of our nature." This book reminds us of what is important. And it should help us lift our eyes. St. Paul wrote, "Whatever is true, whatever is honorable, whatever is right, whatever is pure, whatever is lovely, whatever is of good repute, if there is any excellence and anything worthy of praise, let your mind dwell on these things."

I hope readers will read this book and dwell on those things.

I am indebted to Bob Asahina, my able editor at Simon and Schuster, for his encouragement, advice, and usual sober judgment. Sarah Pinckney, also of Simon and Schuster, kept the train running on time with her always-on-target and always-gracious answers, solutions, and suggestions. Robert Barnett, my agent, provided sound counsel and enthusiasm for this venture. My two colleagues in this project deserve special mention. Steven Tigner was judicious, knew where to find things and how best to describe virtues. He promised to help and he did; he's a man of virtue. As to John Cribb, I cannot thank him enough for his efforts to make this book a reality. Unfailingly and constantly he "mined the quarry" at the Library of Congress, in cartons of old books, in piles of dog-eared magazines. He came to love the stories and the idea of this book. He was "miner," scout, archivist, researcher, and critic. I owe him a great deal; I am grateful for the example of his friendship.

Finally, my wife, Elayne, always thought this was *my* book, the one book I *had* to do. And she was, as usual, right. She read, reviewed, guided, and recommended. As with everything else in my life, this, too, was made better because of her touch. And ironically enough I owe her thanks because on many nights long after I fell asleep, tired from a day of doing a lot of things—including putting this book together—she was the one still awake and reading good stories like these to our boys.

You know that the beginning is the most important part of any work, especially in the case of a young and tender thing; for that is the time at which the character is being formed and the desired impression is more readily taken. . . . Shall we just carelessly allow children to hear any casual tales which may be devised by casual persons, and to receive into their minds ideas for the most part the very opposite of those which we should wish them to have when they are grown up?

We cannot. . . . Anything received into the mind at that age is likely to become indelible and unalterable; and therefore it is most important that the tales which the young first hear should be models of virtuous thoughts. . . .

Then will our youth dwell in a land of health, amid fair sights and sounds, and receive the good in everything; and beauty, the effluence of fair works, shall flow into the eye and ear, like a health-giving breeze from a purer region, and insensibly draw the soul from the earliest years into likeness and sympathy with the beauty of reason.

There can be no nobler training than that.

—PLATO'S *Republic*

# 1

# Self-Discipline

In self-discipline one makes a "disciple" of oneself. One is one's own teacher, trainer, coach, and "disciplinarian." It is an odd sort of relationship, paradoxical in its own way, and many of us don't handle it very well. There is much unhappiness and personal distress in the world because of failures to control tempers, appetites, passions, and impulses. "Oh, if only I had stopped myself" is an all too familiar refrain.

The father of modern philosophy, René Descartes, once remarked of "good sense" that "everybody thinks he is so well supplied with it, that even the most difficult to please in all other matters never desire more of it than they already possess." With self-discipline it is just the opposite. Rare indeed is the person who doesn't desire more self-discipline and, with it, the control that it gives one over the course of one's life and development. That desire is itself, as Descartes might say, a further mark of good sense. We *do* want to take charge of ourselves. But what does that mean?

The question has been at or near the center of Western philosophy since its very beginnings. Plato divided the soul into three parts or operations—reason, passion, and appetite—and said that right behavior results from harmony or control of these elements. Saint Augustine sought to understand the soul by ranking its various forms of love in his famous *ordo amoris*: love of God, neighbor, self, and material goods. Sigmund Freud divided the psyche into the id, ego, and superego. And we find William Shakespeare examining the conflicts of the soul, the struggle between good and evil called the *psychomachia*, in immortal works such as *King Lear, Macbeth, Othello,* and *Hamlet.* Again and again, the problem is one of the soul's proper balance and order. "This was the noblest Roman of them all," Antony says of Brutus in *Julius Caesar.* "His life was gentle, and the elements so mixed in him that nature might stand up and say to all the world, 'This was a man!' "

But the question of correct order of the soul is not simply the domain of sublime philosophy and drama. It lies at the heart of the task of successful everyday behavior, whether it is controlling our tempers, or our appetites, or our inclinations to sit all day in front of the television. As Aristotle pointed out, here our habits make all the difference. We learn to order our souls the same way we learn to do math problems or play baseball well—through practice.

Practice, of course, is the medicine so many people find hard to swallow. If it were easy, we wouldn't have such modern-day phenomena as multimillon-dollar diet and exercise industries. We can enlist the aid of trainers, therapists, support groups, step programs, and other strategies, but in the end, it's practice that brings self-control.

The case of Aristotle's contemporary Demosthenes illustrates the point. Demosthenes had great ambition to become an orator, but suffered natural limitations as a speaker. Strong desire is essential, but by itself is insufficient. According to Plutarch, "His inarticulate and stammering pronunciation he overcame and rendered more distinct by speaking with pebbles in his mouth." Give yourself an even greater challenge than the one you are trying to master and you will develop the powers necessary to overcome the original difficulty. He used a similar strategy in training his voice, which "he disciplined by declaiming and reciting speeches or verses when he was out of breath, while running or going up steep places." And to keep himself studying without interruption "two or three months together," Demosthenes shaved "one half of his head, that so for shame he might not go abroad, though he desired it ever so much." Thus did Demosthenes make a kind of negative support group out of a general public that never saw him!

# Good and Bad Children

*Robert Louis Stevenson*

Children, you are very little,
And your bones are very brittle;
If you would grow great and stately,
You must try to walk sedately.

You must still be bright and quiet,
And content with simple diet;
And remain, through all bewild'ring,
Innocent and honest children.

Happy hearts and happy faces,
Happy play in grassy places—
That was how, in ancient ages,
Children grew to kings and sages.

But the unkind and the unruly,
And the sort who eat unduly,
They must never hope for glory—
Theirs is quite a different story!

Cruel children, crying babies,
All grow up as geese and gabies,
Hated, as their age increases,
By their nephews and their nieces.

# Please

*Alicia Aspinwall*

*Webster's* defines our manners as our "morals shown in conduct." Good people stick to good manners, as this story from a turn-of-the-century reader reminds us.

There was once a little word named "Please," that lived in a small boy's mouth. Pleases live in everybody's mouth, though people often forget they are there.

Now, all Pleases, to be kept strong and happy, should be taken out of the mouth very often, so they can get air. They are like little fish in a bowl, you know, that come popping up to the top of the water to breathe.

The Please I am going to tell you about lived in the mouth of a boy named Dick; but only once in a long while did it have a chance to get out. For Dick, I am sorry to say, was a rude little boy; he hardly ever remembered to say "Please."

"Give me some bread! I want some water! Give me that book!" —that is the way he would ask for things.

His father and mother felt very bad about this. And, as for the poor Please itself, it would sit up on the roof of the boy's mouth day after day, hoping for a chance to get out. It was growing weaker and weaker every day.

This boy Dick had a brother, John. Now, John was older than Dick—he was almost ten; and he was just as polite as Dick was rude. So his Please had plenty of fresh air, and was strong and happy.

One day at breakfast, Dick's Please felt that he must have some fresh air, even if he had to run away. So out he ran—out of Dick's mouth—and took a long breath. Then he crept across the table and jumped into John's mouth!

The Please-who-lived-there was very angry.

"Get out!" he cried. "You don't belong here! This is *my* mouth!"

"I know it," replied Dick's Please. "I live over there in that brother mouth. But alas! I am not happy there. I am never used. I never get a breath of fresh air! I thought you might be willing to let me stay here for a day or so—until I felt stronger."

"Why, certainly," said the other Please, kindly. "I understand. Stay, of course; and when my master uses me, we will both go out together. He is kind, and I am sure he would not mind saying 'Please' twice. Stay, as long as you like."

That noon, at dinner, John wanted some butter; and this is what he said:

"Father, will you pass me the butter, please—please?"

"Certainly," said the father. "But why be so *very* polite?"

John did not answer. He was turning to his mother, and said,

"Mother, will you give me a muffin, please—please?"

His mother laughed.

"You shall have the muffin, dear; but why do you say 'please' twice?"

"I don't know," answered John. "The words seem just to jump out, somehow. Katie, please—please, some water!"

This time, John was almost frightened.

"Well, well," said his father, "there is no harm done. One can't be too 'pleasing' in this world."

All this time little Dick had been calling, "Give me an egg! I want some milk. Give me a spoon!" in the rude way he had. But now he stopped and listened to his brother. He thought it would be fun to try to talk like John; so he began,

"Mother, will you give me a muffin, m-m-m-?"

He was trying to say "please"; but how could he? He never guessed that his own little Please was sitting in John's mouth. So he tried again, and asked for the butter.

"Mother, will you pass me the butter, m-m-m-?"

That was all he could say.

So it went on all day, and everyone wondered what was the matter with those two boys. When night came, they were both so tired, and Dick was so cross, that their mother sent them to bed very early.

But the next morning, no sooner had they sat down to breakfast than Dick's Please ran home again. He had had so much fresh air the day before that now he was feeling quite strong and happy. And the very next moment, he had another airing; for Dick said,

"Father, will you cut my orange, please?" Why! the word slipped out as easily as could be! It sounded just as well as when John said it—John was saying only *one* "please" this morning. And from that time on, little Dick was just as polite as his brother.

# Rebecca,

*Who Slammed Doors for Fun and Perished Miserably.*

*Hilaire Belloc*

Aristotle would have loved this poem and the one that follows it. The first illustrates excess, the second deficiency. The trick to finding correct behavior is to strike the right balance. (See the passage from Aristotle's *Ethics,* later in this chapter.)

A trick that everyone abhors
In Little Girls is slamming Doors.
A Wealthy Banker's Little Daughter
Who lived in Palace Green, Bayswater
(By name Rebecca Offendort),
Was given to this Furious Sport.
She would deliberately go
And Slam the door like Billy-Ho!
To make her Uncle Jacob start.
She was not really bad at heart,
But only rather rude and wild:
She was an aggravating child. . . .

It happened that a Marble Bust
of Abraham was standing just
Above the Door this little Lamb
Had carefully prepared to Slam,
And Down it came! It knocked her flat!
It laid her out! She looked like that.

Her Funeral Sermon (which was long
And followed by a Sacred Song)
Mentioned her Virtues, it is true,
But dwelt upon her Vices too,
And showed the Dreadful End of One
Who goes and slams the Door for Fun.

The children who were brought to hear
The awful Tale from far and near
Were much impressed, and inly swore
They never more would slam the Door.
—As often they had done before.

---

## Godfrey Gordon Gustavus Gore

*William Brighty Rands*

Godfrey Gordon Gustavus Gore—
No doubt you have heard the name before—
Was a boy who never would shut a door!

The wind might whistle, the wind might roar,
And teeth be aching and throats be sore,
But still he never would shut the door.

His father would beg, his mother implore,
"Godfrey Gordon Gustavus Gore,
We really *do* wish you would shut the door!"

Their hands they wrung, their hair they tore;
But Godfrey Gordon Gustavus Gore
Was deaf as the buoy out at the Nore.

When he walked forth the folks would roar,
"Godfrey Gordon Gustavus Gore,
Why don't you think to shut the door?"

They rigged out a Shutter with sail and oar,
And threatened to pack off Gustavus Gore
On a voyage of penance to Singapore.

But he begged for mercy, and said, "No more!
Pray do not send me to Singapore
On a Shutter, and then I will shut the door."

"You will?" said his parents; "then keep on shore!
But mind you do! For the plague is sore
Of a fellow that never will shut the door,
Godfrey Gordon Gustavus Gore!"

---

# The Lovable Child

*Emilie Poulsson*

We meet the well-behaved child (whom everybody loves).

Frisky as a lambkin,
  Busy as a bee—
That's the kind of little girl
  People like to see.

Modest as a violet,
  As a rosebud sweet—
That's the kind of little girl
  People like to meet.

Bright as is a diamond,
  Pure as any pearl—
Everyone rejoices in
  Such a little girl.

Happy as a robin,
  Gentle as a dove—
That's the kind of little girl
  Everyone will love.

Fly away and seek her,
  Little song of mine,
For I choose that very girl
  As my Valentine.

# John, Tom, and James

We meet three ill-behaved children (whom nobody likes).

John was a bad boy, and beat a poor cat;
Tom put a stone in a blind man's hat;
James was the boy who neglected his prayers;
They've all grown up ugly, and nobody cares.

---

# There Was a Little Girl

We meet the child who, like most, is sometimes well behaved and sometimes not. And we face a hard, unavoidable fact of life: if we cannot control our own behavior, eventually someone will come and control it for us in a way we probably will not like. This poem is sometimes attributed to Henry Wadsworth Longfellow.

There was a little girl,
And she had a little curl
Right in the middle of her forehead.
When she was good
She was very, very good,
And when she was bad she was horrid.

One day she went upstairs,
When her parents, unawares,
In the kitchen were occupied with meals,
And she stood upon her head
In her little trundle-bed,
And then began hooraying with her heels.

Her mother heard the noise,
And she thought it was the boys
A-playing at a combat in the attic;
But when she climbed the stair,
And found Jemima there,
She took and she did spank her most emphatic.

---

## My Own Self

*Retold by Joseph Jacobs*

Sometimes fortune offers us close calls we should take as warnings. Heaving a sigh of relief is not enough; if we're smart, we'll change our behavior. Self-discipline is learned in the face of adversity, as this old English fairy tale reminds us.

In a tiny house in the North Countrie, far away from any town or village, there lived not long ago, a poor widow all alone with her little son, a six-year-old boy.

The house door opened straight on to the hillside, and all around about were moorlands and huge stones, and swampy hollows; never a house nor a sign of life wherever you might look, for their nearest neighbors were the fairies in the glen below, and the "will-o'-the-wisps" in the long grass along the path-side.

And many a tale the widow could tell of the "good folk" calling to each other in the oak trees, and the twinkling lights hopping on to the very windowsill, on dark nights; but in spite of the loneliness, she lived on from year to year in the little house, perhaps because she was never asked to pay any rent for it.

But she did not care to sit up late, when the fire burned low, and no one knew what might be about. So, when they had had their supper she would make up a good fire and go off to bed, so that if anything terrible *did* happen, she could always hide her head under the bedclothes.

This, however, was far too early to please her little son; so when she called him to bed, he would go on playing beside the fire, as if he did not hear her.

He had always been bad to do with since the day he was born, and his mother did not often care to cross him. Indeed, the more she tried to make him obey her, the less heed he paid to anything she said, so it usually ended by his taking his own way.

But one night, just at the fore-end of winter, the widow could not make up her mind to go off to bed, and leave him playing by the fireside. For the wind was tugging at the door, and rattling the windowpanes, and well she knew that on such a night, fairies and such like were bound to be out and about, and bent on mischief. So she tried to coax the boy into going at once to bed:

"It's safest to bide in bed on such a night as this!" she said. But no, he wouldn't go.

Then she threatened to "give him the stick," but it was no use.

The more she begged and scolded, the more he shook his head; and when at last she lost patience and cried that the fairies would surely come and fetch him away, he only laughed and said he wished they *would,* for he would like one to play with.

At that his mother burst into tears, and went off to bed in despair, certain that after such words something dreadful would happen, while her naughty little son sat on his stool by the fire, not at all put out by her crying.

But he had not long been sitting there alone, when he heard a fluttering sound near him in the chimney, and presently down by his side dropped the tiniest wee girl you could think of. She was not a span high, and had hair like spun silver, eyes as green as grass, and cheeks red as June roses.

The little boy looked at her with surprise.

"Oh!" said he, "what do they call ye?"

"My own self," she said in a shrill but sweet little voice, and she looked at him too. "And what do they call ye?"

"Just my own self too," he answered cautiously; and with that they began to play together.

She certainly showed him some fine games. She made animals out of the ashes that looked and moved like life, and trees with green leaves waving over tiny houses, with men and women an inch high in them, who, when she breathed on them, fell to walking and talking quite properly.

But the fire was getting low, and the light dim, and presently the little boy stirred the coals with a stick, to make them blaze, when out jumped a red-hot cinder, and where should it fall, but on the fairy child's tiny foot!

Thereupon she set up such a squeal, that the boy dropped the stick, and clapped his hands to his ears. But it grew to so shrill a screech, that it was like all the wind in the world, whistling through one tiny keyhole!

There was a sound in the chimney again, but this time the little boy did not wait to see what it was, but bolted off to bed, where he hid under the blankets and listened in fear and trembling to what went on.

A voice came from the chimney speaking sharply:

"Who's there, and what's wrong?" it said.

"It's my own self," sobbed the fairy child, "and my foot's burned sore. O-o-h!"

"Who did it?" said the voice angrily. This time it sounded nearer, and the boy, peeping from under the clothes, could see a white face looking out from the chimney opening!

"Just my own self too!" said the fairy child again.

"Then if ye did it your own self," cried the elf mother shrilly, "what's the use o' making all this fuss about it?"—and with that she stretched out a long thin arm, and caught the creature by its ear, and, shaking it roughly, pulled it after her, out of sight up the chimney!

The little boy lay awake a long time, listening, in case the fairy mother should come back after all. And next evening after supper, his mother was surprised to find that he was willing to go to bed whenever she liked.

"He's taking a turn for the better at last!" she said to herself. But he was thinking just then that, when next a fairy came to play with him, he might not get off quite so easily as he had done this time.

---

## To the Little Girl Who Wriggles

*Laura E. Richards*

In which we learn to sit still.

Don't wriggle about anymore, my dear!
I'm sure all your joints must be sore, my dear!
It's wriggle and jiggle, it's twist and it's wiggle,
Like an eel on a shingly shore, my dear,
Like an eel on a shingly shore.

Oh! how do you think you would feel, my dear,
If you should turn into an eel, my dear?
With never an arm to protect you from harm,
And no sign of a toe or a heel, my dear,
No sign of a toe or a heel?

And what do you think you would do, my dear,
Far down in the water so blue, my dear,
Where the prawns and the shrimps,
with their curls and their crimps,
Would turn up their noses at you, my dear,
Would turn up their noses at you?

The crab he would give you a nip, my dear,
And the lobster would lend you a clip, my dear.
And perhaps if a shark should come by in the dark,
Down his throat you might happen to slip, my dear,
Down his throat you might happen to slip.

Then try to sit still on your chair, my dear!
To your parents 'tis no more than fair, my dear.
For we really don't feel like inviting an eel
Our board and our lodging to share, my dear,
Our board and our lodging to share.

---

# Jim,

*Who ran away from his Nurse, and was eaten by a Lion.*

*Hilaire Belloc*

In which we discover the kind of gruesome end that comes to children who dart away from their mothers into streets, run away from their fathers at crowded ball parks, dash screaming down grocery store aisles, and who in general cannot bring themselves to hold on to the hand they are told to hold.

There was a Boy whose name was Jim;
His Friends were very good to him.
They gave him Tea, and Cakes, and Jam,
And slices of delicious Ham,
And Chocolate with pink inside,
And little Tricycles to ride,
And read him Stories through and through,
And even took him to the Zoo—
But there it was the dreadful Fate
Befell him, which I now relate.

You know—at least you *ought* to know,
For I have often told you so—
That Children never are allowed
To leave their Nurses in a Crowd;
Now this was Jim's especial Foible,
He ran away when he was able,
And on this inauspicious day
He slipped his hand and ran away!
He hadn't gone a yard when—Bang!
With open Jaws, a Lion sprang,
And hungrily began to eat
The Boy: beginning at his feet.

Now just imagine how it feels
When first your toes and then your heels,
And then by gradual degrees,
Your shins and ankles, calves and knees,
Are slowly eaten, bit by bit.
No wonder Jim detested it!
No wonder that he shouted "Hi!"
The Honest Keeper heard his cry,
Though very fat he almost ran
To help the little gentleman.
'Ponto!" he ordered as he came
(For Ponto was the Lion's name),
"Ponto!" he cried, with angry Frown.
"Let go, Sir! Down, Sir! Put it down!"
The Lion made a sudden Stop,
He let the Dainty Morsel drop,
And slunk reluctant to his Cage,

Snarling with Disappointed Rage.
But when he bent him over Jim,
The Honest Keeper's Eyes were dim.
The Lion having reached his Head,
The Miserable Boy was dead!

When Nurse informed his Parents, they
Were more Concerned than I can say:
His Mother, as She dried her eyes,
Said, "Well—it gives me no surprise,
He would not do as he was told!"
His Father, who was self-controlled,
Bade all the children round attend
To James' miserable end,
And always keep a-hold of Nurse
For fear of finding something worse.

---

## The Duel

*Eugene Field*

In which we discover the unfortunate consequences of fighting.

The gingham dog and the calico cat
Side by side on the table sat;
'Twas half past twelve, and (what do you think!)
Nor one nor t'other had slept a wink!
  The old Dutch clock and the Chinese plate
  Appeared to know as sure as fate
There was going to be a terrible spat.
    (*I wasn't there; I simply state*
    *What was told to me by the Chinese plate!*)

The gingham dog went "bow-wow-wow!"
And the calico cat replied "mee-ow!"
The air was littered an hour or so,
With bits of gingham and calico.
While the old Dutch clock in the chimney place
Up with its hands before its face,
For it always dreaded a family row!
(*Now mind; I'm only telling you*
*What the old Dutch clock declares is true!*)

The Chinese plate looked very blue,
And wailed, "Oh, dear! what shall we do!"
But the gingham dog and the calico cat
Wallowed this way and tumbled that,
Employing every tooth and claw
In the awfullest way you ever saw—
And, oh! how the gingham and calico flew!
(*Don't fancy I exaggerate—*
*I got my news from the Chinese plate!*)

Next morning, where the two had sat
They found no trace of dog or cat;
And some folks think unto this day
That burglars stole that pair away!
But the truth about the cat and pup
Is this: they ate each other up!
Now what do you really think of that!
(*The old Dutch clock it told me so,*
*And that is how I came to know.*)

# Let Dogs Delight to Bark and Bite

*Isaac Watts*

Let dogs delight to bark and bite,
  For God hath made them so;
Let bears and lions growl and fight,
  For 'tis their nature too.

But, children, you should never let
  Such angry passions rise;
Your little hands were never made
  To tear each other's eyes.

---

# The King and His Hawk

*Retold by James Baldwin*

Thomas Jefferson gave us simple but effective advice about controlling our temper: count to ten before you do anything, and if very angry, count to a hundred. Genghis Khan (c.1162–1227), whose Mongol empire stretched from eastern Europe to the Sea of Japan, could have used Jefferson's remedy in this tale.

Genghis Khan was a great king and warrior.

He led his army into China and Persia, and he conquered many lands. In every country, men told about his daring deeds, and they said that since Alexander the Great there had been no king like him.

One morning when he was home from the wars, he rode out into the woods to have a day's sport. Many of his friends were with him. They rode out gayly, carrying their bows and arrows. Behind them came the servants with the hounds.

It was a merry hunting party. The woods rang with their shouts and laughter. They expected to carry much game home in the evening.

On the king's wrist sat his favorite hawk, for in those days hawks were trained to hunt. At a word from their masters they would fly high up into the air, and look around for prey. If they chanced to see a deer or a rabbit, they would swoop down upon it swift as any arrow.

All day long Genghis Khan and his huntsmen rode through the woods. But they did not find as much game as they expected.

Toward evening they started for home. The king had often ridden through the woods, and he knew all the paths. So while the rest of the party took the nearest way, he went by a longer road through a valley between two mountains.

The day had been warm, and the king was very thirsty. His pet hawk had left his wrist and flown away. It would be sure to find its way home.

The king rode slowly along. He had once seen a spring of clear water near this pathway. If he could only find it now! But the hot days of summer had dried up all the mountain brooks.

At last, to his joy, he saw some water trickling down over the edge of a rock. He knew that there was a spring farther up. In the wet season, a swift stream of water always poured down here; but now it came only one drop at a time.

The king leaped from his horse. He took a little silver cup from his hunting bag. He held it so as to catch the slowly falling drops.

It took a long time to fill the cup; and the king was so thirsty that he could hardly wait. At last it was nearly full. He put the cup to his lips, and was about to drink.

All at once there was a whirring sound in the air, and the cup was knocked from his hands. The water was all spilled upon the ground.

The king looked up to see who had done this thing. It was his pet hawk.

The hawk flew back and forth a few times, and then alighted among the rocks by the spring.

The king picked up the cup, and again held it to catch the trickling drops.

This time he did not wait so long. When the cup was half full, he lifted it toward his mouth. But before it had touched his lips, the hawk swooped down again, and knocked it from his hands.

And now the king began to grow angry. He tried again, and for the third time the hawk kept him from drinking.

The king was now very angry indeed.

"How do you dare to act so?" he cried. "If I had you in my hands, I would wring your neck!"

Then he filled the cup again. But before he tried to drink, he drew his sword.

"Now, Sir Hawk," he said, "this is the last time."

He had hardly spoken before the hawk swooped down and knocked the cup from his hand. But the king was looking for this. With a quick sweep of the sword he struck the bird as it passed.

The next moment the poor hawk lay bleeding and dying at its master's feet.

"That is what you get for your pains," said Genghis Khan.

But when he looked for his cup, he found that it had fallen between two rocks, where he could not reach it.

"At any rate, I will have a drink from that spring," he said to himself.

With that he began to climb the steep bank to the place from which the water trickled. It was hard work, and the higher he climbed, the thirstier he became.

At last he reached the place. There indeed was a pool of water; but what was that lying in the pool, and almost filling it? It was a huge, dead snake of the most poisonous kind.

The king stopped. He forgot his thirst. He thought only of the poor dead bird lying on the ground below him.

"The hawk saved my life!" he cried, "and how did I repay him? He was my best friend, and I have killed him."

He clambered down the bank. He took the bird up gently, and laid it in his hunting bag. Then he mounted his horse and rode swiftly home. He said to himself,

"I have learned a sad lesson today, and that is, never to do anything in anger."

# Anger

*Charles and Mary Lamb*

Anger in its time and place
May assume a kind of grace.
It must have some reason in it,
And not last beyond a minute.
If to further lengths it go,
It does into malice grow.
'Tis the difference that we see
'Twixt the serpent and the bee.
If the latter you provoke,
It inflicts a hasty stroke,
Puts you to some little pain,
But it *never stings again*.
Close in tufted bush or brake
Lurks the poison-swelled snake
Nursing up his cherished wrath;
In the purlieus of his path,
In the cold, or in the warm,
Mean him good, or mean him harm,
Wheresoever fate may bring you,
The vile snake will *always sting you*.

# Dirty Jim

*Jane Taylor*

Why should we bother to practice cleanliness? Aside from some very good practical considerations, Francis Bacon reminded us why: "For cleanness of body was ever esteemed to proceed from a due reverence to God, to society, and to ourselves."

There was one little Jim,
'Tis reported of him,
And must be to his lasting disgrace,
That he never was seen
With hands at all clean,
Nor yet ever clean was his face.

His friends were much hurt
To see so much dirt,
And often they made him quite clean;
But all was in vain,
He got dirty again,
And not at all fit to be seen.

It gave him no pain
To hear them complain,
Nor his own dirty clothes to survey;
His indolent mind
No pleasure could find
In tidy and wholesome array.

The idle and bad,
Like this little lad,
May love dirty ways, to be sure;
But good boys are seen,
To be decent and clean,
Although they are ever so poor.

---

## Washing

Dear Lord, sometimes my hair gets quite
Untidy, rough, and mussy;
And when my Mother makes it right
I'm apt to think she's fussy.
My hands get black with different dirts,
And when no one is present,
I don't half wash; I think it hurts
To make myself more pleasant.

Please make me feel that Cleanliness
Is just a proper virtue,
And that cold water's here to bless,
And never here to hurt you.
Please show me how I always can
Do simple things, that lead to
The making of a gentleman,
And *wash,* because I need to.

## Table Rules for Little Folks

In which we learn how to take our daily bread.

In silence I must take my seat,
And give God thanks before I eat;
Must for my food in patience wait,
Till I am asked to hand my plate;
I must not scold, nor whine, nor pout,
Nor move my chair nor plate about;
With knife, or fork, or napkin ring,
I must not play, nor must I sing.
I must not speak a useless word,
For children should be seen, not heard;
I must not talk about my food,
Nor fret if I don't think it good;
I must not say, "The bread is old,"
"The tea is hot," "The coffee's cold";
My mouth with food I must not crowd,
Nor while I'm eating speak aloud;
Must turn my head to cough or sneeze,
And when I ask, say "If you please";
The tablecloth I must not spoil,
Nor with my food my fingers soil;
Must keep my seat when I have done,
Nor round the table sport or run;
When told to rise, then I must put

My chair away with noiseless foot;
And lift my heart to God above,
In praise for all his wondrous love.

## The Little Gentleman

Take your meals, my little man,
Always like a gentleman;
Wash your face and hands with care,
Change your shoes, and brush your hair;
Then so fresh, and clean and neat,
Come and take your proper seat;
Do not loiter and be late,
Making other people wait;
Do not rudely point or touch:
Do not eat and drink too much:
Finish what you have before
You even ask or send for more:
Never crumble or destroy
Food that others might enjoy;
They who idly *crumbs* will waste
Often want a loaf to taste!
Never spill your milk or tea,
Never rude or noisy be;
Never choose the daintiest food,
Be content with what is good:
Seek in all things that you can
To be a little gentleman.

## Our Lips and Ears

In which we learn how to conduct our conversation.

If you your lips would keep from slips,
Five things observe with care:
Of whom you speak, to whom you speak,
And how and when and where.

If you your ears would save from jeers,
These things keep meekly hid:
Myself and I, and mine and my,
And how I do and did.

---

## Little Fred

In which we learn how to retire for the evening.

When little Fred
Was called to bed,
He always acted right;
He kissed Mama,
And then Papa,
And wished them all good night.

He made no noise,
Like naughty boys,
But gently up the stairs
Directly went,
When he was sent,
And always said his prayers.

# The Story of Augustus, Who Would Not Have Any Soup

*Heinrich Hoffmann*

In which we see the inevitable result of not eating enough of the right stuff.

Augustus was a chubby lad;
Fat, ruddy cheeks Augustus had;
And everybody saw with joy
The plump and hearty, healthy boy.
He ate and drank as he was told,
And never let his soup get cold.

But one day, one cold winter's day,
He screamed out—"Take the soup away!
O take the nasty soup away!
I won't have any soup today."

Next day begins his tale of woes;
Quite lank and lean Augustus grows.
Yet, though he feels so weak and ill,
The naughty fellow cries out still—

"Not any soup for me, I say:
O take the nasty soup away!
I won't have any soup today."

The third day comes; O what a sin!
To make himself so pale and thin.
Yet, when the soup is put on table,
He screams, as loud as he is able—
"Not any soup for me, I say:
O take the nasty soup away!
I won't have any soup today."

Look at him, now the fourth day's come!
He scarcely weighs a sugarplum;
He's like a little bit of thread,
And on the fifth day, he was—dead!

---

## The Vulture

*Hilaire Belloc*

This one belongs on the refrigerator door.

The Vulture eats between his meals,
  And that's the reason why
He very, very rarely feels
  As well as you or I.
His eye is dull, his head is bald,
  His neck is growing thinner.
Oh, what a lesson for us all
  To only eat at dinner.

---

## The Boy and the Nuts

*Aesop*

One good, practical reason for controlling our cravings is that if we grasp for too much, we may end up getting nothing at all.

A little boy once found a jar of nuts on the table.

"I would like some of these nuts," he thought. "I'm sure Mother would give them to me if she were here. I'll take a big handful." So he reached into the jar and grabbed as many as he could hold.

But when he tried to pull his hand out, he found the neck of the jar was too small. His hand was held fast, but he did not want to drop any of the nuts.

He tried again and again, but he couldn't get the whole handful out. At last he began to cry.

Just then his mother came into the room. "What's the matter?" she asked.

"I can't take this handful of nuts out of the jar," sobbed the boy.

"Well, don't be so greedy," his mother replied. "Just take two or three, and you'll have no trouble getting your hand out."

"How easy that was," said the boy as he left the table. "I might have thought of that myself."

---

## The Goose That Laid the Golden Eggs

*Aesop*

Here is Aesop's classic fable about plenty not being enough, about what happens when "having it all" becomes the motto of the day.

A man and his wife had the good fortune to possess a goose that laid a golden egg every day. Lucky though they were, they soon began to think they were not getting rich fast enough, and, imagining the bird must be made of gold inside, they decided to kill it in order to secure the whole store of precious metal at once. But when they cut it open they found it was just like any other goose. Thus, they neither got rich all at once, as they had hoped, nor enjoyed any longer the daily addition to their wealth.

Much wants more and loses all.

# The Flies and the Honey Pot

*Aesop*

A jar of honey chanced to spill
Its contents on the windowsill
In many a viscous pool and rill.

The flies, attracted by the sweet,
Began so greedily to eat,
They smeared their fragile wings and feet.

With many a twitch and pull in vain
They gasped to get away again,
And died in aromatic pain.

*Moral*

O foolish creatures that destroy
Themselves for transitory joy.

---

# Mr. Vinegar and His Fortune

*Retold by James Baldwin*

A runaway appetite is just about the surest ticket to never getting anywhere. The English philosopher John Locke put it this way: "He that has not a mastery over his inclinations; he that knows not how to resist the importunity of present pleasure or pain, for the sake of what reason tells him is fit to be done, wants the true principle of virtue and industry, and is in danger of never being good for anything." Meet Mr. Vinegar, who is in such danger.

A long time ago there lived a poor man whose real name has been forgotten. He was little and old, and his face was wrinkled; and that is why his friends called him Mr. Vinegar.

His wife was also little and old, and they lived in a little old cottage at the back of a little old field.

One day when Mrs. Vinegar was sweeping, she swept so hard that the little old door of the cottage fell down.

She was frightened. She ran out into the field and cried, "John! John! The house is falling down. We shall have no shelter over our heads."

Mr. Vinegar came and looked at the door.

Then he said, "Don't worry about that, my dear. Put on your bonnet and we will go out and seek our fortune."

So Mrs. Vinegar put on her hat, and Mr. Vinegar put the door on his head and they started.

They walked and walked all day. At night they came to a dark forest where there were many tall trees.

"Here is a good place to lodge," said Mr. Vinegar.

So he climbed a tree and laid the door across some branches. Then Mrs. Vinegar climbed the tree, and the two laid themselves down on the door.

"It is better to have the house under us than over us," said Mr. Vinegar. But Mrs. Vinegar was fast asleep, and did not hear him.

Soon it was pitch dark, and Mr. Vinegar also fell asleep. At midnight he was awakened by hearing a noise below him.

He started up. He listened.

"Here are ten gold pieces for you, Jack," he heard someone say. "And here are ten pieces for you, Bill. I'll keep the rest for myself."

Mr. Vinegar looked down. He saw three men sitting on the ground. A lighted lantern was near them.

"Robbers!" he cried in great fright, and sprang to a higher branch.

As he did this he kicked the door from its resting place. The door fell crashing to the ground, and Mrs. Vinegar fell with it.

The robbers were so badly scared that they took to their heels and ran helter-skelter into the dark woods.

"Are you hurt, my dear?" asked Mr. Vinegar.

"Ah, no!" said his wife. "But who would have thought that the door would tumble down in the night? And here is a beautiful lantern, all lit and burning, to show us where we are."

Mr. Vinegar scrambled to the ground. He picked up the lantern to look at it. But what were those shining things that he saw lying all around?

"Gold pieces! Gold pieces!" he cried. And he picked one up and held it to the light.

"We've found our fortune! We've found our fortune!" cried Mrs. Vinegar. And she jumped up and down for joy.

They gathered up the gold pieces. There were fifty of them, all bright and yellow and round.

"How lucky we are!" said Mr. Vinegar.

"How lucky we are!" said Mrs. Vinegar.

Then they sat down and looked at the gold till morning.

"Now, John," said Mrs. Vinegar, "I'll tell you what we'll do. You must go to the town and buy a cow. I will milk her and churn butter, and we shall never want for anything."

"That is a good plan," said Mr. Vinegar.

So he started off to the town, while his wife waited by the roadside.

Mr. Vinegar walked up and down the street of the town, looking for a cow. After a time a farmer came that way, leading one that was very pretty and fat.

"Oh, if I only had that cow," said Mr. Vinegar, "I would be the happiest man in the world."

"She is a very good cow," said the farmer.

"Well," said Mr. Vinegar, "I will give you these fifty gold pieces for her."

The farmer smiled and held out his hand for the money. "You may have her," he said. "I always like to oblige my friends."

Mr. Vinegar took hold of the cow's halter and led her up and down the street. "I am the luckiest man in the world," he said, "for only see how all the people are looking at me and my cow."

But at one end of the street he met a man playing bagpipes. He stopped and listened. Tweedle-dee, tweedle-dee!

"Oh, that is the sweetest music I ever heard," he said. "And just see how all the children crowd around the man and give him pennies! If I only had those bagpipes, I would be the happiest man in the world."

"I will sell them to you," said the piper.

"Will you? Well then, since I have no money, I will give you this cow for them."

"You may have them," answered the piper. "I always like to oblige a friend."

Mr. Vinegar took the bagpipes, and the piper led the cow away.

"Now we will have some music," said Mr. Vinegar. But try as hard as he might, he could not play a tune. He could get nothing out of the bagpipes but "squeak! squeak!"

The children, instead of giving him pennies, laughed at him. The day was chilly, and, in trying to play the pipes his fingers grew very cold. He wished that he had kept the cow.

He had just started for home when he met a man who had warm gloves on his hands. "Oh, if I only had those pretty gloves," he said, "I would be the happiest man in the world."

"How much will you give for them?" asked the man.

"I have no money, but I will give you these bagpipes," answered Mr. Vinegar.

"Well," said the man, "you may have them, for I always like to oblige a friend."

Mr. Vinegar gave him the bagpipes and drew the gloves on over his half-frozen fingers. "How lucky I am!" he said, as he trudged homeward.

His hands were soon quite warm, but the road was rough and the walking hard. He was very tired when he came to the foot of a steep hill.

"How shall I ever get to the top?" he said.

Just then he met a man who was walking the other way. He had a stick in his hand which he used as a cane to help him along.

"My friend," said Mr. Vinegar, "if I only had that stick of yours to help me up this hill, I would be the happiest man in the world."

"How much will you give me for it?" asked the man.

"I have no money, but I will give you this pair of warm gloves," said Mr. Vinegar.

"Well," said the man, "you may have it, for I always like to oblige a friend."

Mr. Vinegar's hands were now quite warm. So he gave the gloves to the man and took the stout stick to help him along.

"How lucky I am," he said, as he toiled upward.

At the top of the hill he stopped to rest. But as he was thinking of all his good luck that day, he heard someone calling his name. He looked up and saw only a green parrot sitting in a tree.

"Mr. Vinegar! Mr. Vinegar!" it cried.

"What now?" asked Mr. Vinegar.

"You're a dunce! You're a dunce!" answered the bird. "You went to seek your fortune, and you found it. Then you gave it for a cow, and the cow for some bagpipes, and the bagpipes for some gloves, and the gloves for a stick which you might have cut by the roadside. Hee! hee! hee! hee! hee! You're a dunce! You're a dunce!"

This made Mr. Vinegar very angry. He threw the stick at the bird with all his might. But the bird only answered, "You're a dunce! You're a dunce!" and the stick lodged in the tree where he could not get it again.

Mr. Vinegar went on slowly, for he had many things to think about. His wife was standing by the roadside, and as soon as she saw him she cried out, "Where's the cow? Where's the cow?"

"Well, I don't just know where the cow is," said Mr. Vinegar; and then he told her the whole story.

I have heard she said some things he liked even less than what the bird had said, but that is between Mr. and Mrs. Vinegar, and really nobody's business but theirs.

"We are no worse off than we were yesterday," said Mr. Vinegar. "Let us go home and take care of our little old house."

Then he put the door on his head and trudged onward. And Mrs. Vinegar followed him.

## The Frogs and the Well

*Aesop*

The prudent person looks before leaping.

Two frogs lived together in a marsh. But one hot summer the marsh dried up, and they left it to look for another place to live in, for frogs like damp places if they can get them. By and by they came to a deep well, and one of them looked down into it, and said to the other, "This looks a nice cool place. Let us jump in and settle here." But the other, who had a wiser head on his shoulders, replied, "Not so fast, my friend. Supposing this well dried up like the marsh, how should we get out again?"

Think twice before you act.

# The Fisherman and His Wife

*Retold by Clifton Johnson*

The ancient Greeks had a famous saying: "Nothing overmuch." The maxim calls not for total abstinence, but rather reminds us to avoid excess. We should know that too much of anything, even a good thing, may prove to be our undoing, as this old tale shows. We need to recognize when enough is enough.

There was once a fisherman who lived with his wife in a poor little hut close by the sea. One day, as the fisherman sat on the rocks at the water's edge fishing with his rod and line, a fish got caught on his hook that was so big and pulled so stoutly that he captured it with the greatest difficulty. He was feeling much pleased that he had secured so big a fish when he was surprised by hearing it say to him, "Pray let me live. I am not a real fish. I am a magician. Put me in the water and let me go."

"You need not make so many words about the matter," said the man. "I wish to have nothing to do with a fish that can talk."

Then he removed it from his hook and put it back into the water. "Now swim away as soon as you please," said the man, and the fish darted straight down to the bottom.

The fisherman returned to his little hut and told his wife how he had caught a great fish, and how it had told him it was a magician, and how, when he heard it speak, he had let it go.

"Did you not ask it for anything?" said the wife.

"No," replied the man. "What should I ask for?"

"What should you ask for!" exclaimed the wife. "You talk as if we had everything we want, but see how wretchedly we live in this dark little hut. Do go back and tell the fish we want a comfortable house."

The fisherman did not like to undertake such an errand. However, as his wife had bidden him to go, he went; and when he came to the sea the water looked all yellow and green. He stood on the rocks where he had fished and said,

"Oh, man of the sea!
Come listen to me;
For Alice my wife,
The plague of my life,
Hath sent me to beg a gift of thee!"

Then the fish came swimming to him and said, "Well, what does she want?"

"Ah," answered the fisherman, "my wife says that when I had caught you I ought to have asked you for something before I let you go. She does not like living any longer in our little hut. She wants a comfortable house."

"Go home then," said the fish. "She is in the house she wants already."

So the man went home and found his wife standing in the doorway of a comfortable house, and behind the house was a yard with ducks and chickens picking about in it, and beyond the yard was a garden where grew all sorts of flowers and fruits. "How happily we shall live now!" said the fisherman.

Everything went right for a week or two, and then the wife said, "Husband, there is not enough room in this house, and the yard and garden are a great deal smaller than they ought to be. I would like to have a large stone castle to live in. So go to the fish again and tell him to give us a castle."

"Wife," said the fisherman, "I don't like to go to him again, for perhaps he will be angry. We ought to be content with a good house like this."

"Nonsense!" said the wife. "He will give us a castle very willingly. Go along and try."

The fisherman went, but his heart was heavy, and when he came to the sea the water was a dark gray color and looked very gloomy. He stood on the rocks at the water's edge and said,

"Oh, man of the sea!
Come listen to me;
For Alice my wife,
The plague of my life,
Hath sent me to beg a gift of thee!"

Then the fish came swimming to him and said, "Well, what does she want now?"

"Ah," replied the man very sorrowfully, "my wife wants to live in a stone castle."

"Go home then," said the fish. "She is at the castle already."

So away went the fisherman and found his wife standing before a great castle. "See," said she, "is not this fine?"

They went into the castle, and many servants were there, and the rooms were richly furnished with handsome chairs and tables; and behind the castle was a park half a mile long, full of sheep and goats and rabbits and deer.

"Now," said the man, "we will live contented and happy in this beautiful castle for the rest of our lives."

"Perhaps so," responded the wife. "But let us consider and sleep on it before we make up our minds." And they went to bed.

The next morning when they awoke it was broad daylight, and the wife jogged the fisherman with her elbow and said, "Get up, husband; bestir yourself, for we must be king and queen of all the land."

"Wife, wife," said the man, "'why should we wish to be king and queen? I would not be king even if I could be."

"Well, I will be queen, anyway," said the wife. "Say no more about it; but go to the fish and tell him what I want."

So the man went, but he felt very sad to think that his wife should want to be queen. The sea was muddy and streaked with foam as he cried out,

"Oh, man of the sea!
Come listen to me;
For Alice my wife,
The plague of my life,
Hath sent me to beg a gift of thee!"

Then the fish came swimming to him and said, "Well, what would she have now?"

"Alas!" said the man. "My wife wants to be queen."

"Go home," said the fish. "She is queen already."

So the fisherman turned back and presently he came to a palace, and before it he saw a troop of soldiers, and he heard the sound of drums and trumpets. Then he entered the palace and there he found his wife sitting on a throne, with a golden crown on her head, and on each side of her stood six beautiful maidens.

"Well, wife," said the fisherman, "are you queen?"

"Yes," she replied, "I am queen."

When he had looked at her for a long time he said, "Ah, wife, what a fine thing it is to be queen! Now we shall never have anything more to wish for."

"I don't know how that may be," said she. "Never is a long time. I am queen, 'tis true, but I begin to be tired of it. I think I would like to be pope next."

"Oh, wife, wife!" the man exclaimed. "How can you be pope? There is but one pope at a time in all Christendom."

"Husband," said she, "I will be pope this very day."

"Ah, wife!" responded the fisherman. "The fish cannot make you pope and I would not like to ask for such a thing."

"What nonsense!" said she. "If he can make a queen, he can make a pope. Go and try."

So the fisherman went, and when he came to the shore the wind was raging and the waves were dashing on the rocks most fearfully, and the sky was dark with flying clouds. The fisherman was frightened, but nevertheless he obeyed his wife and called out,

"Oh, man of the sea!
Come listen to me;
For Alice my wife,
The plague of my life,
Hath sent me to beg a gift of thee!"

Then the fish came swimming to him and said, "What does she want this time?"

"Ah," said the fisherman, "my wife wants to be pope."

"Go home," commanded the fish. "She is pope already."

So the fisherman went home and found his wife sitting on a throne that was a hundred feet high, and on either side many candles of all sizes were burning, and she had three great crowns on her head one above the other and was surrounded by all the pomp and power of the church.

"Wife," said the fisherman, as he gazed at all this magnificence, "are you pope?"

"Yes," she replied, "I am pope."

"Well, wife," said he, "it is a grand thing to be pope. And now you must be content, for you can be nothing greater."

"We will see about that," she said.

Then they went to bed; but the wife could not sleep because all night long she was trying to think what she should be next. At last morning came and the sun rose. "Ha!" cried she. "I was about to sleep, had not the sun disturbed me with its bright light. Cannot I prevent the sun rising?" and she became very angry and said to her husband, "Go to the fish and tell him I want to be lord of the sun and moon."

"Alas, wife," said he, "can you not be content to be pope?"

"No," said she, "I am very uneasy, and cannot bear to see the sun and moon rise without my leave. Go to the fish at once!"

The man went, and as he approached the shore a dreadful storm arose so that the trees and rocks shook, and the sky grew black, and the lightning flashed, and the thunder rolled, and the sea was covered with vast waves like mountains. The fisherman trembled so that his knees knocked together, and he had hardly strength to stand in the gale while he called to the fish:

"Oh, man of the sea!
Come listen to me;
For Alice my wife,
The plague of my life,
Hath sent me to beg a gift of thee!"

Then the fish came swimming to him and said, "What more does she want?"

"Ah," said the man, "she wants to be lord of the sun and moon."

"Go home to your hut again," said the fish.

So the man returned, and the palace was gone, and in its place he found the dark little hut that had formerly been his dwelling, and he and his wife have lived in that little hut to this very day.

---

# The Magic Thread

Too often, people want what they want (or what they *think* they want, which is usually "happiness" in one form or another) *right now*. The irony of their impatience is that only by learning to wait, and by a willingness to accept the bad with the good, do we usually attain those things that are truly worthwhile. "He that can have patience, can have what he will," Benjamin Franklin told us, and this French tale bears him out.

Once there was a widow who had a son called Peter. He was a strong, able boy, but he did not enjoy going to school and he was forever daydreaming.

"Peter, what are you dreaming about this time?" his teacher would say to him.

"I'm thinking about what I'll be when I grow up," Peter replied.

"Be patient. There's plenty of time for that. Being grown up isn't all fun, you know," his teacher said.

But Peter found it hard to enjoy whatever he was doing at the moment, and was always hankering after the next thing. In winter he longed for it to be summer again, and in summer he looked forward to the skating, sledging, and warm fires of winter. At school he would long for the day to be over so that he could go home, and on Sunday nights he would sigh, "If only the holidays would come." What he enjoyed most was playing with his friend Liese. She was as good a companion as any boy, and no matter how impatient Peter was, she never took offense. "When I grow up, I shall marry Liese," Peter said to himself.

Often he wandered through the forest, dreaming of the future. Sometimes he lay down on the soft forest floor in the warm sun, his hands behind his head, staring up at the sky through the distant treetops. One hot afternoon as he began to grow sleepy, he heard someone calling his name. He opened his eyes and sat up. Standing before him was an old woman. In her hand she held a silver ball, from which dangled a silken golden thread.

"See what I have got here, Peter," she said, offering the ball to him.

"What is it?" he asked curiously, touching the fine golden thread.

"This is your life thread," the old woman replied. "Do not touch it and time will pass normally. But if you wish time to pass more quickly, you have only to pull the thread a little way and an hour will pass like a second. But I warn you, once the thread has been pulled out, it cannot be pushed back in again. It will disappear like a puff of smoke. The ball is for you. But if you accept my gift you must tell no one, or on that very day you shall die. Now, say, do you want it?"

Peter seized the gift from her joyfully. It was just what he wanted. He examined the silver ball. It was light and solid, made of a single piece. The only flaw in it was the tiny hole from which the bright thread hung. He put the ball in his pocket and ran home. There, making sure that his mother was out, he examined it again. The thread seemed to be creeping very slowly out of the ball, so slowly that it was scarcely noticeable to the naked eye. He longed to give it a quick tug, but dared not do so. Not yet.

The following day at school, Peter sat daydreaming about what he would do with his magic thread. The teacher scolded him for not concentrating on his work. If only, he thought, it was time to go home. Then he felt the silver ball in his pocket. If he pulled out a tiny bit of thread, the day would be over. Very carefully he took hold of it and tugged. Suddenly the teacher was telling everyone to pack up their books and to leave the classroom in an orderly fashion. Peter was overjoyed. He ran all the way home. How easy life would be now! All his troubles were over. From that day forth he began to pull the thread, just a little, every day.

One day, however, it occurred to him that it was stupid to pull the thread just a little each day. If he gave it a harder tug, school would be over altogether. Then he could start learning a trade and marry Liese. So that night he gave the thread a hard tug, and in the morning he awoke to find himself apprenticed to a carpenter in town. He loved his new life, clambering about on roofs and scaffolding, lifting and hammering great beams into place that still smelled of the forest. But sometimes, when payday seemed too far off, he gave the thread a little tug and suddenly the week was drawing to a close and it was Friday night and he had money in his pocket.

Liese had also come to town and was living with her aunt, who taught her housekeeping. Peter began to grow impatient for the day when they would be married. It was hard to live so near and yet so far from her. He asked her when they could be married.

"In another year," she said. "Then I will have learned how to be a capable wife."

Peter fingered the silver ball in his pocket.

"Well, the time will pass quickly enough," he said, knowingly.

That night Peter could not sleep. He tossed and turned restlessly. He took the magic ball from under his pillow. For a moment he hesitated; then his impatience got the better of him, and he tugged at the golden thread. In the morning he awoke to find that the year was over and that Liese had at last agreed to marry him. Now Peter felt truly happy.

But before their wedding could take place, Peter received an official-looking letter. He opened it in trepidation and read that he was expected to report at the army barracks the following week for two years' military service. He showed the letter to Liese in despair.

"Well," she said, "there is nothing for it, we shall just have to wait. But the time will pass quickly, you'll see. There are so many things to do in preparation for our life together."

Peter smiled bravely, knowing that two years would seem a lifetime to him.

Once Peter had settled into life at the barracks, however, he began to feel that it wasn't so bad after all. He quite enjoyed being with all the other young men, and their duties were not very arduous at first. He remembered the old woman's warning to use the thread wisely and for a while refrained from pulling it. But in time he grew restless again. Army life bored him with its routine duties and harsh discipline. He began pulling the thread to make the week go faster so that it would be Sunday again, or to speed up the time until he was due for leave. And so the two years passed almost as if they had been a dream.

Back home, Peter determined not to pull the thread again until it was absolutely necessary. After all, this was the best time of his life, as everyone told him. He did not want it to be over too quickly. He did, however, give the thread one or two very small tugs, just to speed along the day of his marriage. He longed to tell Liese his secret, but he knew that if he did he would die.

On the day of his wedding, everyone, including Peter, was happy. He could hardly wait to show Liese the house he had built for her. At the wedding feast he glanced over at his mother. He noticed for the first time how gray her hair had grown recently. She seemed to be aging so quickly. Peter felt a pang of guilt that he had pulled the thread so often. Henceforward he would be much more sparing with it and only use it when it was strictly necessary.

A few months later Liese announced that she was going to have a child. Peter was overjoyed and could hardly wait. When the child was born, he felt that he could never want for anything again. But whenever the child was ill or cried through the sleepless night, he gave the thread a little tug, just so that the baby might be well and happy again.

Times were hard. Business was bad and a government had come to power that squeezed the people dry with taxes and would tolerate no opposition. Anyone who became known as a troublemaker was thrown into prison without trial and rumor was enough to condemn a man. Peter had always been known as one who spoke his mind, and very soon he was arrested and cast into jail. Luckily he had his magic ball with him and he tugged very hard at the thread. The prison walls dissolved before him and his enemies were scattered in the huge explosion that burst forth like thunder. It was the war that had been threatening, but it was over as quickly as a summer storm, leaving behind it an exhausted peace. Peter found himself back home with his family. But now he was a middle-aged man.

For a time things went well and Peter lived in relative contentment. One day he looked at his magic ball and saw to his surprise that the thread had turned from gold to silver. He looked in the mirror. His hair was starting to turn gray and his face was lined where before there had not been a wrinkle to be seen. He suddenly felt afraid and determined to use the thread even more carefully than before. Liese bore him more children and he seemed happy as the head of his growing household. His stately manner often made people think of him as some sort of benevolent ruler. He had an air of authority as if he held the fate of others in his hands. He kept his magic ball in a well-hidden place, safe from the curious eyes of his children, knowing that if anyone were to discover it, it would be fatal.

As the number of his children grew, so his house became more overcrowded. He would have to extend it, but for that he needed money. He had other worries too. His mother was looking older and more tired every day. It was of no use to pull the magic thread because that would only hasten her approaching death. All too soon she died, and as Peter stood at her graveside, he wondered how it was that life passed so quickly, even without pulling the magic thread.

One night as he lay in bed, kept awake by his worries, he thought how much easier life would be if all his children were grown up and launched upon their careers in life. He gave the thread a mighty tug, and the following day he awoke to find that his children had all left home for jobs in different parts of the country, and that he and his wife were alone. His hair was almost white now and often his back and limbs ached as he climbed the ladder or lifted a heavy beam into place. Liese too was getting old and she was often ill. He couldn't bear to see her suffer, so that more and more he resorted to pulling at the magic thread. But as soon as one trouble was solved, another seemed to grow in its place. Perhaps life would be easier if he retired, Peter thought. Then he would no longer have to clamber about on drafty, half-completed buildings and he could look after Liese when she was ill. The trouble was that he didn't have enough money to live on. He picked up his magic ball and looked at it. To his dismay he saw that the thread was no longer silver but gray and lusterless. He decided to go for a walk in the forest to think things over.

It was a long time since he had been in that part of the forest. The small saplings had all grown into tall fir trees, and it was hard to find the path he had once known. Eventually he came to a bench in a clearing. He sat down to rest and fell into a light doze. He was woken by someone calling his name, "Peter! Peter!"

He looked up and saw the old woman he had met so many years ago when she had given him the magic silver ball with its golden thread. She looked just as she had on that day, not a day older. She smiled at him.

"So, Peter, have you had a good life?" she asked.

"I'm not sure," Peter said. "Your magic ball is a wonderful thing. I have never had to suffer or wait for anything in my life. And yet it has all passed so quickly. I feel that I have had no time to take in what has happened to me, neither the good things nor the bad. Now there is so little time left. I dare not pull the thread again for it will only bring me to my death. I do not think your gift has brought me luck."

"How ungrateful you are!" the old woman said. "In what way would you have wished things to be different?"

"Perhaps if you had given me a different ball, one where I could have pushed the thread back in as well as pulling it out. Then I could have relived the things that went badly."

The old woman laughed. "You ask a great deal! Do you think that God allows us to live our lives twice over? But I can grant you one final wish, you foolish, demanding man."

"What is that?" Peter asked.

"Choose," the old woman said. Peter thought hard.

At length he said, "I should like to live my life again as if for the first time, but without your magic ball. Then I will experience the bad things as well as the good without cutting them short, and at least my life will not pass as swiftly and meaninglessly as a day-dream."

"So be it," said the old woman. "Give me back my ball."

She stretched out her hand and Peter placed the silver ball in it. Then he sat back and closed his eyes with exhaustion.

When he awoke he was in his own bed. His youthful mother was bending over him, shaking him gently.

"Wake up, Peter. You will be late for school. You were sleeping like the dead!"

He looked up at her in surprise and relief.

"I've had a terrible dream, Mother. I dreamed that I was old and sick and that my life had passed like the blinking of an eye with nothing to show for it. Not even any memories."

His mother laughed and shook her head.

"That will never happen," she said. "Memories are the one thing we all have, even when we are old. Now hurry and get dressed. Liese is waiting for you and you will be late for school."

As Peter walked to school with Liese, he noticed what a bright summer morning it was, the kind of morning when it felt good to be alive. Soon he would see his friends and classmates, and even the prospect of lessons didn't seem so bad. In fact he could hardly wait.

---

# The Golden Touch

*Adapted from Nathaniel Hawthorne*

This retelling of the famous Greek tale about lust for gold is adapted from Nathaniel Hawthorne's version in his *Wonder Book*. The Midas of mythology is usually identified by scholars with a king of ancient Phrygia (now Turkey) who ruled in the eighth century B.C. The early Greeks believed Phrygia to be a land of fabulous wealth.

Once upon a time there lived a very rich king whose name was Midas. He had more gold than anyone in the whole world, but for all that, he thought it was not enough. He was never so happy as when he happened to get more gold to add to his treasure. He stored it away in great vaults underneath his palace, and many hours of each day were spent counting it over.

Now King Midas had a little daughter named Marygold. He loved her devotedly, and said: "She shall be the richest princess in all the world!"

But little Marygold cared nothing about it all. She loved her garden, her flowers and the golden sunshine more than all her father's riches. She was a lonely little girl most of the time, for her father was so busy planning new ways to get more gold, and counting what he had, that he seldom told her stories or went for walks with her, as all fathers should do.

One day King Midas was down in his treasure room. He had locked the heavy doors and had opened up his great chests of gold. He piled it on the table and handled it as if he loved the touch of it. He let it slip through his fingers and smiled at the clink of it as if it had been sweet music. Suddenly a shadow fell over the heap of gold. Looking up, he saw a stranger dressed in shining white smiling down at him. King Midas started up in surprise. Surely he had not failed to lock the door! His treasure was not safe! But the stranger continued to smile.

"You have much gold, King Midas," he said.

"Yes," said the king, "but think how little this is to all the gold there is in the world!"

"What! Are you not satisfied?" asked the stranger.

"Satisfied?" said the king. "Of course I'm not. I often lie awake through the long night planning new ways to get more gold. I wish that everything I touch would turn to gold."

"Do you really wish that, King Midas?"

"Of course I wish it. Nothing could make me so happy."

"Then you shall have your wish. Tomorrow morning when the first rays of the sun fall through your window you shall have the golden touch."

When he had finished speaking, the stranger vanished. King Midas rubbed his eyes. "I must have dreamed it," he said, "but how happy I should be if it were only true!"

The next morning King Midas woke when the first faint light came into his room. He put out his hand and touched the covers of his bed. Nothing happened. "I knew it could not be true," he sighed. Just at that moment the first rays of the sun came through the window. The covers on which King Midas's hand lay became pure gold. "It's true, it's true!" he cried joyfully.

He sprang out of bed and ran about the room touching everything. His dressing gown, his slippers, the furniture, all became gold. He looked out of the window through Marygold's garden.

"I'll give her a nice surprise," he said. He went down into the garden touching all of Marygold's flowers, and changing them to gold. "She will be so pleased," he thought.

He went back into his room to wait for his breakfast; and took up his book which he had been reading the night before, but the minute he touched it, it was solid gold. "I can't read it now," he said, "but of course it is far better to have it gold."

Just then a servant came through the door with the king's breakfast. "How good it looks," he said. "I'll have that ripe, red peach first of all."

He took the peach in his hand, but before he could taste it, it became a lump of gold. King Midas put it back on the plate. "It's very beautiful, but I can't eat it!" he said. He took a roll from the plate, but that, too, became gold. He took a glass of water in his hand, but that, too, became gold. "What shall I do?" he cried. "I am hungry and thirsty, I can't eat or drink gold!"

At that moment the door was opened and in came little Marygold. She was crying bitterly, and in her hand was one of her roses.

"What's the matter, little daughter?" said the king.

"Oh, Father! See what has happened to all my roses! They are stiff, ugly things!"

"Why, they are golden roses, child. Do you not think they are more beautiful than they were?"

"No," she sobbed, "they do not smell sweet. They won't grow anymore. I like roses that are alive."

"Never mind," said the king, "eat your breakfast now."

But Marygold noticed that her father did not eat, and that he looked very sad. "What is the matter, Father dear?" she said, and she ran over to him. She threw her arms about him, and he kissed her. But he suddenly cried out in terror and anguish. When he touched her, her lovely little face became glittering gold, her eyes could not see, her lips could not kiss him back again, her little arms could not hold him close. She was no longer a loving, laughing little girl; she was changed to a little golden statue.

King Midas bowed his head and great sobs shook him.

"Are you happy, King Midas?" he heard a voice say. Looking up he saw the stranger standing near him.

"Happy! How can you ask? I am the most miserable man living!" said the king.

"You have the golden touch," said the stranger. "Is that not enough?"

King Midas did not look up or answer.

"Which would you rather have, food and a cup of cold water or these lumps of gold?" said the stranger.

King Midas could not answer.

"Which would you rather have, O King—that little golden statue, or a little girl who could run, and laugh, and love you?"

"Oh, give me back my little Marygold and I'll give up all the gold I have!" said the king. "I've lost all that was worth having."

"You are wiser than you were, King Midas," said the stranger. "Go plunge in the river which runs at the foot of your garden, then take some of its water and sprinkle whatever you wish to change back as it was." The stranger vanished.

King Midas sprang up and ran to the river. He plunged into it, and then he dipped up a pitcher of its water and hurried back to the palace. He sprinkled it over Marygold, and the color came back into her cheeks. She opened her blue eyes again. "Why, Father!" she said. "What happened?"

With a cry of joy King Midas took her into his arms.

Never after that did King Midas care for any gold except the gold of the sunshine, and the gold of little Marygold's hair.

---

# The Fox and the Crow

*Aesop*

Vanity is largely a matter of self-control, or lack thereof. Others may try to feed our ego, but it is up to us to constrain it.

A coal-black crow once stole a piece of meat. She flew to a tree and held the meat in her beak.

A fox, who saw her, wanted the meat for himself, so he looked up into the tree and said, "How beautiful you are, my friend! Your feathers are fairer than the dove's.

"Is your voice as sweet as your form is beautiful? If so, you must be the queen of birds."

The crow was so happy in his praise that she opened her mouth to show how she could sing. Down fell the piece of meat.

The fox seized upon it and ran away.

# King Canute on the Seashore

*Adapted from James Baldwin*

Canute the Second, who reigned during the eleventh century, was the first Danish king of England. In this famous tale, he proves to be a man who knows how to control his pride. It is a good lesson for all who aspire to high office.

Long ago, England was ruled by a king named Canute. Like many leaders and men of power, Canute was surrounded by people who were always praising him. Every time he walked into a room, the flattery began.

"You are the greatest man that ever lived," one would say.

"O king, there can never be another as mighty as you," another would insist.

"Your highness, there is nothing you cannot do," someone would smile.

"Great Canute, you are the monarch of all," another would sing. "Nothing in this world dares to disobey you."

The king was a man of sense, and he grew tired of hearing such foolish speeches.

One day he was walking by the seashore, and his officers and courtiers were with him, praising him as usual. Canute decided to teach them a lesson.

"So you say I am the greatest man in the world?" he asked them.

"O king," they cried, "there never has been anyone as mighty as you, and there never will be anyone so great, ever again!"

"And you say all things obey me?" Canute asked.

"Absolutely!" they said. "The world bows before you, and gives you honor."

"I see," the king answered. "In that case, bring me my chair, and we will go down to the water."

"At once, your majesty!" They scrambled to carry his royal chair over the sands.

"Bring it closer to the sea," Canute called. "Put it right here, right at the water's edge." He sat down and surveyed the ocean before him. "I notice the tide is coming in. Do you think it will stop if I give the command?"

His officers were puzzled, but they did not dare say no. "Give the order, O great king, and it will obey," one of them assured him.

"Very well. Sea," cried Canute, "I command you to come no further! Waves, stop your rolling! Surf, stop your pounding! Do not dare touch my feet!"

He waited a moment, quietly, and a tiny wave rushed up the sand and lapped at his feet.

"How dare you!" Canute shouted. "Ocean, turn back now! I have ordered you to retreat before me, and now you must obey! Go back!"

And in answer another wave swept forward and curled around the king's feet. The tide came in, just as it always did. The water rose higher and higher. It came up around the king's chair, and wet not only his feet, but also his robe. His officers stood about him, alarmed, and wondering whether he was not mad.

"Well, my friends," Canute said, "it seems I do not have quite so much power as you would have me believe. Perhaps you have learned something today. Perhaps now you will remember there is only one King who is all-powerful, and it is he who rules the sea, and holds the ocean in the hollow of his hand. I suggest you reserve your praises for him."

The royal officers and courtiers hung their heads and looked foolish. And some say Canute took off his crown soon afterward, and never wore it again.

---

# Ozymandias

*Percy Bysshe Shelley*

Ozymandias is the Greek name for the Egyptian King Rameses the Second, who ruled about 1290 to 1223 B.C. and carried out (or took credit for) many great construction projects. The colossal stone head of a statue of Rameses lies on the ground at his mortuary temple in western Thebes, and the ancient Greek historian Diodorus Siculus described a funeral temple bearing an inscription much like the lines in Shelley's poem. Remembering Ozymandias is a great way to control our vanity, especially as we climb the ladder of success. It makes a striking contrast with the story of King Canute.

I met a traveler from an antique land
Who said: Two vast and trunkless legs of stone
Stand in the desert . . . Near them, on the sand,
Half sunk, a shattered visage lies, whose frown,
And wrinkled lip, and sneer of cold command,
Tell that its sculptor well those passions read
Which yet survive, stamped on these lifeless things,
The hand that mocked them, and the heart that fed:
And on the pedestal these words appear:
"My name is Ozymandias, king of kings:
Look on my works, ye Mighty, and despair!"
Nothing beside remains. Round the decay
Of that colossal wreck, boundless and bare
The lone and level sands stretch far away.

---

# Phaeton

*Adapted from Thomas Bulfinch*

The feeling of youth, Joseph Conrad said, is the feeling of being able to "last forever, outlast the sea, the earth, and all men." Somehow, as we all know from having been there, youth cannot recognize the illusion of invincibility. Here is one of Ovid's grandest stories. It tells of the rashness of youth and reminds us of the need for the governing prudence of parents.

Phaeton was the son of Phoebus Apollo and the nymph Clymene. One day a schoolfellow laughed at the idea of his being the offspring of a god, and Phaeton went in rage and shame to his mother.

"If I am indeed of heavenly birth," he said, "give me some proof of it."

"Go and ask your father yourself," Clymene replied. "It will not be hard. The land of the Sun lies next to ours."

Full of hope and pride, Phaeton traveled to the regions of the sunrise. The palace of the Sun stood reared on lofty columns, glittering with gold and precious stones, while polished ivory formed the ceilings, and silver the doors. Upon the walls Vulcan had represented earth, sea, and skies with their inhabitants. In the sea were the nymphs, some sporting in the waves, some riding on the backs of fishes, while others sat upon the rocks and dried their sea-green hair. The earth had its towns and forests and rivers and rustic divinities. Over all was carved the likeness of the glorious heaven, and on the silver doors were the twelve signs of the zodiac, six on each side.

Clymene's son climbed the steep ascent and entered the halls of his father. He approached the chamber of the Sun, but stopped at a distance, for the light was more than he could bear. Phoebus, arrayed in a purple vesture, sat on a throne, which glittered as with diamonds. On his right hand and his left stood the Day, the Month, and the Year, and, at regular intervals, the Hours. Spring stood with her head crowned with flowers. Summer stood with garment cast aside and a garland formed of spears of ripened grain. And there too were Autumn, her feet stained with grape juice, and icy Winter, his hair stiffened with hoarfrost.

Surrounded by these attendants, the Sun, with the eye that sees everything, beheld the youth dazzled with the novelty and splendor of the scene.

"What is the purpose of your errand?" he asked.

"Oh light of the boundless world," the youth replied, "I beseech you, give me some proof that I am indeed your son."

He ceased, and his father, laying aside the beams that shone all around his head, bade him approach.

"You are my son," he said, embracing him. "What your mother has told you is true. To put an end to your doubts, ask what you will, and the gift shall be yours. I call to witness the dreadful river Styx, which we gods swear by in our most solemn engagements."

Many times Phaeton had watched the Sun riding across the sky, and he had dreamed of what it would be like to drive his father's chariot, urging the winged horses along their heavenly course. Now he realized his dream could come true.

"I want to take your place for a day, Father," he cried at once. "Just for one day, I want to drive your chariot across the sky and bring light to the world."

Instantly the Sun realized the foolishness of his promise, and he shook his radiant head in warning. "I have spoken rashly," he said. "This is the only request I would deny, and I beg you to withdraw it. You ask for something not suited to your youth and strength, my son. Your lot is mortal, and you ask what is beyond a mortal's power. In your ignorance, you aspire to do what even the other gods themselves may not do. None but myself may drive the flaming car of Day. Not even Jupiter, whose terrible right arm hurls the thunderbolts, would try it.

"The first part of the way is steep," the Sun continued, "so steep that even when the horses are fresh in the morning, they can hardly make the climb. The middle part of the journey takes me high up in the heavens, and I can scarcely look down without alarm and behold the earth and sea stretched beneath me. The last part of the road descends rapidly, and requires the most careful driving. Tethys, the Ocean's wife, who is waiting to receive me, often trembles for me lest I should fall headlong. Add to all this, the heaven is all the time turning round and carrying the stars with it. I have to be perpetually on my guard lest that movement, which sweeps everything else along, should also hurry me away.

"Suppose I should lend you the chariot. What would you do? Could you keep your course while the sphere was revolving under you? Perhaps you think there are forests and cities, the abodes of gods, and palaces and temples along the way. On the contrary, the road runs through the midst of frightening monsters. You pass by the horns of the Bull, in front of the Archer, and near the Lion's jaws, and where the Scorpion stretches its arms in one direction and the Crab in another. Nor will you find it easy to guide those horses, who snort fire from their mouths and nostrils. I can scarcely govern them myself when they resist the reins.

"Beware, my son, lest I be the donor of a fatal gift. Recall your request while yet you may. Do you want proof that you are sprung from my blood? I give you proof in my fears for you. Look at my face—I would that you could look into my heart, and there you would see a father's cares.

"Look about you, and ask for anything from all the riches of the earth or sea. Ask and you shall have it! But I beg you not to ask this one thing. It is destruction, not honor, you seek. You shall have it if you persist. I swore the oath, and it must be kept. But I beg you to choose more wisely."

He ended, but his warning did no good, and Phaeton held to his demand. So, having resisted as long as he could, Phoebus at last led the way to where the lofty chariot stood. Its wheels were made of gold, its spokes of silver. Along the yoke every kind of jewel reflected the brightness of the sun. While the boy gazed in admiration, the early Dawn threw open the purple doors of the east, and showed the pathway strewn with roses.

Phoebus, when he saw the Earth beginning to glow, and the Moon preparing to retire, ordered the Hours to harness the horses. They obeyed, and led the steeds from the lofty stalls, well fed with rich ambrosia. Then the Sun rubbed his son's face with a magic lotion which made him able to endure the brightness of the flame. He placed the crown of rays on his head and sighed.

"If you insist on doing this," he said, "at least heed my advice. Spare the whip and hold the reins tight. The steeds need no urging, but you must labor to hold them back. Do not take the straight road through the five circles of Heaven, but turn off to the left. Avoid the northern and southern zones, but keep within the limit of the middle one. You will see the marks of the wheels, and they will guide you. The sky and the earth both need their due share of heat, so do not go too high, or you will burn the heavenly dwellings, nor too low, or you will set the earth on fire. The middle course is the safest and best.

"Now I leave you to Fortune, who I hope will plan better for you than you have for yourself. Night is passing out of the western gates, and we can delay no longer. Take the reins. Or better yet, take my counsel and let me bring light to the world while you stay here and watch in safety."

But even as he was speaking, the boy sprang into the chariot, stood erect, and grasped the reins with delight, pouring out thanks to his reluctant parent. The horses filled the air with their fiery snortings and stamped the ground impatiently. The barriers were let down, and suddenly the boundless plain of the universe lay open before them. They darted forward and sliced through the clouds, into the winds from the east.

It wasn't long before the steeds sensed that the load they drew was lighter than usual. As a ship without ballast careens and rolls off course on the sea, so the chariot was dashed about as if empty. The horses rushed headlong and left the traveled road. Phaeton began to panic. He had no idea which way to turn the reins, and even if he knew, he had not the strength. Then, for the first time, the Big Bear and the Little Bear were scorched with heat, and would have plunged into the water if possible. The Serpent, which lies coiled around the pole, torpid and harmless in the chill of the heavens, grew hot and writhed in angry fury.

When the unhappy Phaeton looked down upon the earth, now spreading in the vast expanse beneath him, he grew pale, and his knees shook with terror. In spite of the glare all around him, the sight of his eyes grew dim. He wished he had never touched his father's horses. He was borne along like a vessel driven before a storm, when the pilot can do no more than pray. Much of the heavenly road was behind him, but much more still lay ahead. He found himself stunned and dazed, and did not know whether to hold the reins or drop them. He forgot the names of the horses. He was horrified at the sight of the monstrous forms scattered across the heaven. The Scorpion, for instance, reached forward with its two great claws, while its poisonous stinger stretched behind. Phaeton's courage failed, and the reins fell from his hands.

The horses, when they felt the reins loose on their backs, dashed headlong into the unknown regions of the sky. They raced among the stars, hurling the chariot over pathless places, now up in the high heaven, now down almost to earth. The Moon saw with astonishment her brother's chariot running beneath her own. The clouds began to smoke, and the mountain tops caught fire. Fields grew parched with heat, plants withered, and harvests went up in flames. Cities perished, with their walls and towers, and whole nations turned to ashes.

Phaeton beheld the world on fire, and felt the intolerable heat. The air was like the blast of a furnace, full of soot and sparks. The chariot glowed white-hot and veered one way, then another. Forests turned to deserts, rivers ran dry, and the earth cracked open. The sea shrank and threatened to become a dry plain. Three times Neptune tried to raise his head above the surface, and three times he was driven back by the fiery heat.

Then Earth, amid the smoking waters, screening her face with her hand, looked up to heaven, and in a trembling voice called on Jupiter.

"O ruler of the gods," she cried, "if I have deserved this treatment, and it is your will that I perish with fire, why withhold your thunderbolts? Let me at least fall by your hand. Is this the reward of my fertility? Is it for this that I have given fodder for cattle, and fruits for men, and incense for your altars? And what has my brother Ocean done to deserve such a fate? And look at your own skies. The very poles are smoking, and if they topple, your palace will fall. If sea, earth, and heaven perish, we fall into ancient Chaos. Save what remains from the devouring flame. Take thought, and deliver us from this awful moment!"

And overcome with heat and thirst, Earth could say no more. But Jupiter heard her, and saw that all things would perish if he did not quickly help. He climbed the highest tower of heaven, where often he had spread clouds over the world and hurled his mighty thunder. He brandished a lightning bolt in his hand, and flung it at the charioteer. At once the car exploded. The mad horses broke the reins, the wheels shattered, and the wreckage scattered across the stars.

And Phaeton, his hair on fire, fell like a shooting star. He was dead long before he left the sky. A river god received him and cooled his burning frame.

---

## George Washington's Rules of Civility

In the late nineteenth century, a school notebook entitled "Forms of Writing" was discovered at Mount Vernon, Virginia, George Washington's plantation home on the Potomac River. The notebook apparently dates from about 1745, when George was fourteen years old and attending school in Fredericksburg, Virginia. Inside, in George's own handwriting, we find the foundation of a solid character education for an eighteenth-century youth: some 110 "Rules of Civility in Conversation Amongst Men." Historical research has shown that young George probably copied them from a 1664 English translation of an even older French work. Most of the rules are still delightfully applicable as a modern code of personal conduct. On the assumption that what was good enough for the first president of the United States is good enough for the rest of us, here are fifty-four of George Washington's "Rules of Civility."

1. Every action in company ought to be with some sign of respect to those present.

2. In the presence of others sing not to yourself with a humming voice, nor drum with your fingers or feet.

3. Speak not when others speak, sit not when others stand, and walk not when others stop.

4. Turn not your back to others, especially in speaking; jog not the table or desk on which another reads or writes; lean not on anyone.

5. Be no flatterer, neither play with anyone that delights not to be played with.

6. Read no letters, books, or papers in company; but when there is a necessity for doing it, you must ask leave. Come not near the books or writings of anyone so as to read them unasked; also look not nigh when another is writing a letter.

7. Let your countenance be pleasant, but in serious matters somewhat grave.

8. Show not yourself glad at the misfortune of another, though he were your enemy.

9. They that are in dignity or office have in all places precedency, but whilst they are young, they ought to respect those that are their equals in birth or other qualities, though they have no public charge.

10. It is good manners to prefer them to whom we speak before ourselves, especially if they be above us, with whom in no sort we ought to begin.

11. Let your discourse with men of business be short and comprehensive.

12. In visiting the sick do not presently play the physician if you be not knowing therein.

13. In writing or speaking give to every person his due title according to his degree and the custom of the place.

14. Strive not with your superiors in argument, but always submit your judgment to others with modesty.

15. Undertake not to teach your equal in the art he himself professes; it savors of arrogancy.

16. When a man does all he can, though it succeeds not well, blame not him that did it.

17. Being to advise or reprehend anyone, consider whether it ought to be in public or in private, presently or at some other time, also in what terms to do it; and in reproving show no signs of choler, but do it with sweetness and mildness.

18. Mock not nor jest at anything of importance; break no jests that are sharp or biting; and if you deliver anything witty or pleasant, abstain from laughing thereat yourself.

19. Wherein you reprove another be unblamable yourself, for example is more prevalent than precept.

20. Use no reproachful language against anyone, neither curses nor revilings.

21. Be not hasty to believe flying reports to the disparagement of anyone.

22. In your apparel be modest, and endeavor to accommodate nature rather than procure admiration. Keep to the fashion of your equals, such as are civil and orderly with respect to time and place.

23. Play not the peacock, looking everywhere about you to see if you be well decked, if your shoes fit well, if your stockings set neatly and clothes handsomely.

24. Associate yourself with men of good quality if you esteem your own reputation, for it is better to be alone than in bad company.

25. Let your conversation be without malice or envy, for it is a sign of tractable and commendable nature; and in all causes of passion admit reason to govern.

26. Be not immodest in urging your friend to discover a secret.

27. Utter not base and frivolous things amongst grown and learned men, nor very difficult questions or subjects amongst the ignorant, nor things hard to be believed.

28. Speak not of doleful things in time of mirth nor at the table; speak not of melancholy things, as death and wounds; and if others mention them, change, if you can, the discourse. Tell not your dreams but to your intimate friends.

29. Break not a jest when none take pleasure in mirth. Laugh not aloud, nor at all without occasion. Deride no man's misfortunes, though there seem to be some cause.

30. Speak not injurious words, neither in jest or earnest. Scoff at none, although they give occasion.

31. Be not forward, but friendly and courteous, the first to salute, hear and answer, and be not pensive when it is time to converse.

32. Detract not from others, but neither be excessive in commending.

33. Go not thither where you know not whether you shall be welcome or not. Give not advice without being asked; and when desired, do it briefly.

34. If two contend together, take not the part of either unconstrained, and be not obstinate in your opinion; in things indifferent be of the major side.

35. Reprehend not the imperfection of others, for that belongs to parents, masters, and superiors.

36. Gaze not on the marks or blemishes of others, and ask not how they came. What you may speak in secret to your friend deliver not before others.

37. Speak not in an unknown tongue in company, but in your own language; and that as those of quality do, and not as the vulgar. Sublime matters treat seriously.

38. Think before you speak; pronounce not imperfectly, nor bring out your words too hastily, but orderly and distinctly.

39. When another speaks, be attentive yourself, and disturb not the audience. If any hesitate in his words, help him not, nor prompt him without being desired; interrupt him not, nor answer him till his speech be ended.

40. Treat with men at fit times about business, and whisper not in the company of others.

41. Make no comparisons; and if any of the company be commended for any brave act of virtue, commend not another for the same.

42. Be not apt to relate news if you know not the truth thereof. In discoursing of things you have heard, name not your author always. A secret discover not.

43. Be not curious to know the affairs of others, neither approach to those that speak in private.

44. Undertake not what you cannot perform; but be careful to keep your promise.

45. When you deliver a matter, do it without passion and indiscretion, however mean the person may be you do it to.

46. When your superiors talk to anybody, hear them; neither speak or laugh.

47. In disputes be not so desirous to overcome as not to give liberty to each one to deliver his opinion, and submit to the judgment of the major part, especially if they are judges of the dispute.

48. Be not tedious in discourse, make not many digressions, nor repeat often the same matter of discourse.

49. Speak no evil of the absent, for it is unjust.

50. Be not angry at table, whatever happens; and if you have reason to be so show it not; put on a cheerful countenance, especially if there be strangers, for good humor makes one dish a feast.

51. Set not yourself at the upper end of the table; but if it be your due, or the master of the house will have it so, contend not, lest you should trouble the company.

52. When you speak of God or his attributes, let it be seriously, in reverence and honor, and obey your natural parents.

53. Let your recreations be manful, not sinful.

54. Labor to keep alive in your breast that little spark of celestial fire called conscience.

---

# Boy Wanted

*Frank Crane*

This "want ad" appeared in the early part of this century.

WANTED—A boy that stands straight, sits straight, acts straight, and talks straight;

A boy whose fingernails are not in mourning, whose ears are clean, whose shoes are polished, whose clothes are brushed, whose hair is combed, and whose teeth are well cared for;

A boy who listens carefully when he is spoken to, who asks questions when he does not understand, and does not ask questions about things that are none of his business;

A boy that moves quickly and makes as little noise about it as possible;

A boy who whistles in the street, but does not whistle where he ought to keep still;

A boy who looks cheerful, has a ready smile for everybody, and never sulks;

A boy who is polite to every man and respectful to every woman and girl;

A boy who does not smoke cigarettes and has no desire to learn how;

A boy who is more eager to know how to speak good English than to talk slang;

A boy that never bullies other boys nor allows other boys to bully him;

A boy who, when he does not know a thing, says, "I don't know," and when he has made a mistake says, "I'm sorry," and when he is asked to do a thing says, "I'll try";

A boy who looks you right in the eye and tells the truth every time;

A boy who is eager to read good books;

A boy who would rather put in his spare time at the YMCA gymnasium than to gamble for pennies in a back room;

A boy who does not want to be "smart" nor in any wise to attract attention;

A boy who would rather lose his job or be expelled from school than to tell a lie or be a cad;

A boy whom other boys like;

A boy who is at ease in the company of girls;

A boy who is not sorry for himself, and not forever thinking and talking about himself;

A boy who is friendly with his mother, and more intimate with her than anyone else;

A boy who makes you feel good when he is around;

A boy who is not goody-goody, a prig, or a little pharisee, but just healthy, happy, and full of life.

This boy is wanted everywhere. The family wants him, the school wants him, the office wants him, the boys want him, the girls want him, all creation wants him.

---

## The Cattle of the Sun

*Retold by Andrew Lang*

Times of plenty call for one kind of self-discipline (as in the story of the goose that laid the golden eggs). Times of hardship call for other sorts of self-restraint. During tough times, people are tempted to put aside social and moral codes. In this episode from Homer's *Odyssey*, the crew of Odysseus (Ulysses) does not have the self-control to pass a tough test.

The ship swept through the roaring narrows between the rock of Scylla and the whirlpool of Charybdis, into the open sea, and the men, weary and heavy of heart, bent over their oars, and longed for rest.

Now a place of rest seemed near at hand, for in front of the ship lay a beautiful island, and the men could hear the bleating of sheep and the lowing of cows as they were being herded into their stalls. But Ulysses remembered that, in the Land of the Dead, the ghost of the blind prophet had warned him of one thing. If his men killed and ate the cattle of the Sun, in the sacred island of Thrinacia, they would all perish. So Ulysses told his crew of this prophecy, and bade them row past the island. Eurylochus was angry and said that the men were tired, and could row no further, but must land, and take supper, and sleep comfortably on shore. On hearing Eurylochus, the whole crew shouted and said that they would go no further that night, and Ulysses had no power to compel them. He could only make them swear not to touch the cattle of the Sun God, which they promised readily enough, and so went ashore, took supper, and slept.

In the night a great storm arose: the clouds and driving mist blinded the face of the sea and sky, and for a whole month the wild south wind hurled the waves on the coast, and no ship of these times could venture out in the tempest. Meanwhile the crew ate up all the stores in the ship, and finished the wine, so that they were driven to catch seabirds and fishes, of which they took but few, the sea being so rough upon the rocks. Ulysses went up into the island alone, to pray to the gods, and when he had prayed he found a sheltered place, and there he fell asleep.

Eurylochus took the occasion, while Ulysses was away, to bid the crew seize and slay the sacred cattle of the Sun God, which no man might touch, and this they did, so that, when Ulysses wakened, and came near the ship, he smelled the roast meat, and knew what had been done. He rebuked the men, but, as the cattle were dead, they kept eating them for six days; and then the storm ceased, the wind fell, the sun shone, and they set the sails, and away they went. But this evil deed was punished, for when they were out of sight of land, a great thundercloud overshadowed them, the wind broke the mast, which crushed the head of the helmsman, the lightning struck the ship in the center; she reeled, the men fell overboard, and the heads of the crew floated a moment, like cormorants, above the waves.

But Ulysses had kept hold of a rope, and, when the vessel righted, he walked the deck till a wave stripped off all the tackling, and loosened the sides from the keel. Ulysses had only time to lash the broken mast with a rope to the keel, and sit on this raft with his feet in the water, while the South Wind rose again furiously, and drove the raft back till it came under the rock where was the whirlpool of Charybdis. Here Ulysses would have been drowned, but he caught at the root of a fig tree that grew on the rock, and there he hung, clinging with his toes to the crumbling stones till the whirlpool boiled up again, and up came the timbers. Down on the timbers Ulysses dropped, and so sat rowing with his hands, and the wind drifted him at last to a shelving beach of an island.

# David and Bathsheba

*Retold by Jesse Lyman Hurlbut*

Of all the vices, lust is the one many people seem to find the most difficult to control. The story of David and Bathsheba is from the second book of Samuel in the Bible.

When David first became king he went with his army upon the wars against the enemies of Israel. But there came a time when the cares of his kingdom were many, and David left Joab, his general, to lead his warriors, while he stayed in his palace on Mount Zion.

One evening, about sunset, David was walking upon the roof of his palace. He looked down into a garden nearby, and saw a woman who was very beautiful. David asked one of his servants who this woman was, and he said to him, "Her name is Bathsheba, and she is the wife of Uriah."

Now Uriah was an officer in David's army, under Joab; and at that time he was fighting in David's war against the Ammonites, at

Rabbah, near the desert, on the east of Jordan. David sent for Uriah's wife, Bathsheba, and talked with her. He loved her, and greatly longed to take her as one of his own wives—for in those times it was not thought a sin for a man to have more than one wife. But David could not marry Bathsheba while her husband, Uriah, was living. Then a wicked thought came into David's heart, and he formed a plan to have Uriah killed, so that he could then take Bathsheba into his own house.

David wrote a letter to Joab, the commander of his army. And in the letter he said, "When there is to be a fight with the Ammonites, send Uriah into the middle of it, where it will be the hottest; and manage to leave him there, so that he may be slain by the Ammonites."

And Joab did as David had commanded him. He sent Uriah with some brave men to a place near the wall of the city, where he knew that the enemies would rush out of the city upon them; there was a fierce fight beside the wall; Uriah was slain, and other brave men with him. Then Joab sent a messenger to tell King David how the war was being carried on, and especially that Uriah, one of his brave officers, had been killed in the fighting.

When David heard this, he said to the messenger, "Say to Joab, 'Do not feel troubled at the loss of the men slain in battle. The sword must strike down some. Keep up the siege; press forward, and you will take the city.' "

And after Bathsheba had mourned over her husband's death for a time, then David took her into his palace, and she became his wife. And a little child was born to them, whom David loved greatly. Only Joab, and David, and perhaps a few others, knew that David has caused the death of Uriah; but God knew it, and God was displeased with David for this wicked deed.

Then the Lord sent Nathan, the prophet, to David to tell him that, though men knew not that David had done wickedly, God had seen it, and would surely punish David for his sin. Nathan came to David, and he spoke to him thus:

"There were two men in one city; one was rich, and the other poor. The rich man had great flocks of sheep and herds of cattle; but the poor man had only one little lamb that he had bought. It grew up in his home with his children, and drank out of his cup, and lay upon his lap, and was like a little daughter to him.

"One day a visitor came to the rich man's house to dinner. The rich man did not take one of his own sheep to kill for his guest. He robbed the poor man of his lamb, and killed it, and cooked it for a meal with his friend."

"When David heard this, he was very angry. He said to Nathan, "The man who did this thing deserves to die! He shall give back to his poor neighbor fourfold for the lamb taken from him. How cruel to treat a poor man thus, without pity for him!"

And Nathan said to David, "You are the man who has done this deed. The Lord made you king in place of Saul, and gave you a kingdom. You have a great house, and many wives. Why, then, have you done this wickedness in the sight of the Lord? You have slain Uriah with the sword of the men of Ammon; and you have taken his wife to be your wife. For this there shall be a sword drawn against your house; you shall suffer for it, and your wives shall suffer, and your children shall suffer, because you have done this."

When David heard all this, he saw, as he had not seen before, how great was his wickedness. He was exceedingly sorry; and said to Nathan, "I have sinned against the Lord."

And David showed such sorrow for his sin that Nathan said to him, "The Lord has forgiven your sin; and you shall not die on account of it. But the child that Uriah's wife has given to you shall surely die."

Soon after this the little child of David and Bathsheba, whom David loved greatly, was taken very ill. David prayed to God for the child's life; and David took no food, but lay in sorrow, with his face upon the floor of his house. The nobles of his palace came to him, and urged him to rise up and take food, but he would not. For seven days the child grew worse and worse, and David remained in sorrow. Then the child died; and the nobles were afraid to tell David, for they said to each other, "If he was in such grief while the child was living, what will he do when he hears that the child is dead?"

But when King David saw the people whispering to one another with sad faces, he said, "Is the child dead?"

And they said to him, "Yes, O king, the child is dead."

Then David rose up from the floor where he had been lying. He washed his face, and put on his kingly robes. He went first to the house of the Lord, and worshipped; then he came to his own house, and sat down to his table, and took food. His servants wondered at this, but David said to them, "While the child was still alive, I fasted, and prayed, and wept; for I hoped that by prayer to the Lord, and by the mercy of the Lord, his life might be spared. But now that he is dead, my prayers can do no more for him. I cannot bring him back again. He will not come back to me, but I shall go to him."

And after this God gave to David and to Bathsheba, his wife, another son, whom they named Solomon. The Lord loved Solomon, and he grew up to be a wise man.

After God had forgiven David's great sin, David wrote the Fifty-first Psalm, in memory of his sin and of God's forgiveness. Some of its verses are these:

Have mercy upon me, O God,
According to thy loving kindness:
According to the multitude of thy tender mercies
Blot out my transgressions.
Wash me thoroughly from mine iniquity,
And cleanse me from my sin.
For I acknowledge my transgressions:
And my sin is ever before me.
Against thee, thee only, have I sinned,
And done that which is evil in thy sight:
. . . . . . . . .

Hide thy face from my sins,
And blot out all mine iniquities.
Create in me a clean heart, O God,
And renew a right spirit within me.
Cast me not away from thy presence;
And take not thy holy spirit from me.
Restore unto me the joy of thy salvation;
And uphold me with a free spirit.
Then will I teach transgressors thy ways;
And sinners shall be converted unto thee.
. . . . . . . . .

For thou delightest not in sacrifice; else would I give it:
Thou hast no pleasure in burnt offering.
The sacrifices of God are a broken spirit:
A broken and a contrite heart, O God, thou will not despise.

# Vaulting Ambition, Which O'erleaps Itself

*William Shakespeare*

Here is unbridled, "vaulting" ambition at work in Shakespeare's *Macbeth*. The scene is the courtyard of Inverness, Macbeth's castle, where Macbeth and Lady Macbeth prepare to murder Duncan, king of Scotland, and thereby gain the throne. As Macbeth himself points out, his victim is his guest, his kinsman, and his king. But even these claims are not enough to stop the voracity of uncontrolled aspiration. Lady Macbeth urges her husband to "screw your courage to the sticking place" when he seems on the verge of faltering—and so we see that a degree of self-mastery is required to conclude their plot. But it's the wrong kind of self-control, driven only by runaway ambitions.

*Macb.* If it were done when 'tis done, then 'twere well
It were done quickly: if the assassination
Could trammel up the consequence, and catch,
With his surcease, success; that but this blow
Might be the be-all and the end-all here,
But here, upon this bank and shoal of time,
We'ld jump the life to come. But in these cases
We still have judgment here; that we but teach
Bloody instructions, which being taught return
To plague the inventor: this even-handed justice
Commends the ingredients of our poison'd chalice
To our own lips. He's here in double trust:
First, as I am his kinsman and his subject,
Strong both against the deed; then, as his host,
Who should against his murderer shut the door,
Not bear the knife myself. Besides, this Duncan
Hath borne his faculties so meek, hath been
So clear in his great office, that his virtues
Will plead like angels trumpet-tongued against
The deep damnation of his taking-off;

And pity, like a naked new-born babe,
Striding the blast, or heaven's cherubim horsed
Upon the sightless couriers of the air,
Shall blow the horrid deed in every eye,
That tears shall drown the wind. I have no spur
To prick the sides of my intent, but only
Vaulting ambition, which o'erleaps itself
And falls on the other.

*Enter* LADY MACBETH

How now! what news?

*Lady M.* He has almost supp'd: why have you left the chamber?
*Macb.* Hath he ask'd for me?
*Lady M.* Know you not he has?
*Macb.* We will proceed no further in this business:
He hath honor'd me of late; and I have bought
Golden opinions from all sorts of people,
Which would be worn now in their newest gloss,
Not cast aside so soon.
*Lady M.* Was the hope drunk
Wherein you dress'd yourself? hath it slept since?
And wakes it now, to look so green and pale
At what it did so freely? From this time
Such I account thy love. Art thou afeard
To be the same in thine own act and valor
As thou art in desire? Wouldst thou have that
Which thou esteem'st the ornament of life,
And live a coward in thine own esteem,
Letting "I dare not" wait upon "I would,"
Like the poor cat i' the adage?
*Macb.* Prithee, peace
I dare do all that may become a man;
Who dares do more is none.
*Lady M.* What beast was't then
That made you break this enterprise to me?
When you durst do it, then you were a man;
And, to be more than what you were, you would
Be so much more the man. Nor time nor place
Did then adhere, and yet you would make both:
They have made themselves, and that their fitness now
Does unmake you. I have given suck, and know

How tender 'tis to love the babe that milks me:
I would, while it was smiling in my face,
Have pluck'd my nipple from his boneless gums,
And dash'd the brains out, had I so sworn as you
Have done to this.

*Macb.* If we should fail?

*Lady M.* We fail!
But screw your courage to the sticking-place,
And we'll not fail. When Duncan is asleep—
Whereto the rather shall his day's hard journey
Soundly invite him—his two chamberlains
Will I with wine and wassail so convince,
That memory, the warder of the brain,
Shall be a fume, and the receipt of reason
A limbec only: when in swinish sleep
Their drenched natures lie as in a death,
What cannot you and I perform upon
The unguarded Duncan? what not put upon
His spongy officers, who shall bear the guilt
Of our great quell?

*Macb.* Bring forth men-children only;
For thy undaunted mettle should compose
Nothing but males. Will it not be received,
When we have mark'd with blood those sleepy two
Of his own chamber, and used their very daggers,
That they have done't?

*Lady M.* Who dares receive it other,
As we shall make our griefs and clamor roar
Upon his death?

*Macb.* I am settled, and bend up
Each corporal agent to this terrible feat.
Away, and mock the time with fairest show:
False face must hide what the false heart doth know.

*Exeunt.*

# How Much Land Does a Man Need?

*Leo Tolstoy*

This story by Leo Tolstoy (1828–1910), written in 1886, in its fundamental physical action is a marvelous metaphor for the need for us to set definite boundaries on our own appetites.

There once was a peasant named Pahom who worked hard and honestly for his family, but who had no land of his own, so he always remained as poor as the next man. "Busy as we are from childhood tilling mother earth," he often thought, "we peasants will always die as we are living, with nothing of our own. If only we had our own land, it would be different."

Now, close to Pahom's village there lived a lady, a small landowner, who had an estate of about three hundred acres. One winter the news got about that the lady was going to sell her land. Pahom heard that a neighbor of his was buying fifty acres and that the lady had consented to accept one half in cash and to wait a year for the other half.

"Look at that," Pahom thought. "The land is being sold, and I shall get none of it." So he spoke to his wife. "Other people are buying it, and we must also buy twenty acres or so. Life is becoming impossible without land of our own."

So they put their heads together and considered how they could manage to buy it. They had one hundred rubles laid by. They sold a colt, and one half of their bees, hired out one of their sons as a laborer, and took his wages in advance. They borrowed the rest from a brother-in-law, and so scraped together half the purchase money. Having done this, Pahom chose a farm of forty acres, some of it wooded, and went to the lady and bought it.

So now Pahom had land of his own. He borrowed seed, and sowed it, and the harvest was a good one. Within a year he had managed to pay off his debts to the lady and his brother-in-law. So he became a landowner, plowing and sowing his own land, making hay on his own land, cutting his own trees, and feeding his cattle on his own pasture. When he went out to plow his fields, or to look at his growing corn, or at his meadows, his heart would fill with joy. The grass that grew and the flowers that bloomed there seemed to him unlike any that grew elsewhere. Formerly, when he had passed by that land, it had appeared the same as any other land, but now it seemed quite different.

Then one day Pahom was sitting at home when a peasant, passing through the village, happened to stop in. Pahom asked him where he came from, and the stranger answered that he came from beyond the Volga, where he had been working. One word led to another, and the man went on to say that much land was for sale there, and that many people were moving there to buy it. The land was so good, he said, that the rye sown on it grew as high as a horse, and so thick that five cuts of a sickle made a sheaf. One peasant, he said, had brought nothing with him but his bare hands, and now he had six horses and two cows of his own.

Pahom's heart was filled with desire. "Why should I suffer in this narrow hole," he thought, "if one can live so well elsewhere? I will sell my land and my homestead here, and with the money I will start fresh over there and get everything new."

So Pahom sold his land and homestead and cattle, all at a profit, and moved his family to the new settlement. Everything the peasant had told him was true, and Pahom was ten times better off than he had been. He bought plenty of arable land and pasture, and could keep as many head of cattle as he liked.

At first, in the bustle of building and settling down, Pahom was pleased with it all, but when he got used to it he began to think that even here he was not satisfied. He wanted to sow more wheat, but had not enough land of his own for the purpose, so he rented extra land for three years. The seasons turned out well and the crops were good, so that he began to lay money by. He might have gone on living comfortably, but he grew tired of having to rent other people's land every year, and having to scramble to pay for it.

"If it were all my own land," Pahom thought, "I should be independent, and there would not be all this unpleasantness."

Then one day a passing land dealer said he was just returning from the land of Bashkirs, far away., where he had bought thirteen thousand acres of land, all for only one thousand rubles.

"All one need do is to make friends with the chiefs," he said. "I gave away about one hundred rubles' worth of dressing gowns and carpets, besides a case of tea, and I gave wine to those who would drink it, and I got the land for less than twopence an acre."

"There now," thought Pahom, "out there I can get more than ten times as much land as I have now. I must try it."

So Pahom left his family to look after the homestead and started on the journey, taking his servant with him. They stopped at a town on their way, and bought a case of tea, some wine, and other presents, as the tradesman had advised him. On and on they went until they had gone more than three hundred miles, and on the seventh day they came to a place where the Bashkirs had pitched their tents.

As soon as they saw Pahom, they came out of their tents and gathered around their visitor. They gave him tea and kumiss, and had a sheep killed, and gave him mutton to eat. Pahom took presents out of his cart and distributed them, and told them he had come about some land. The Bashkirs seemed very glad, and told him he must talk to their chief about it. So they sent for him and explained to him why Pahom had come.

The chief listened for a while, then made a sign with his head for them to be silent, and addressing himself to Pahom, said:

"Well, let it be so. Choose whatever piece of land you like. We have plenty of it."

"And what will be the price?" asked Pahom.

"Our price is always the same: one thousand rubles a day."

Pahom did not understand.

"A day? What measure is that? How many acres would that be?"

"We do not know how to reckon it out," said the chief. "We sell it by the day. As much as you can go round on your feet in a day is yours, and the price is one thousand rubles a day."

Pahom was surprised.

"But in a day you can get round a large tract of land," he said.

The chief laughed.

"It will all be yours!" said he. "But there is one condition: if you don't return on the same day to the spot whence you started, your money is lost."

"But how am I to mark the way that I have gone?"

"Why, we shall go to any spot you like, and stay there. You must start from that spot and make your round, taking a spade with you. Wherever you think necessary, make a mark. At every turning, dig a hole and pile up the turf; then afterward we will go round with a plow from hole to hole. You may make as large a circuit as you please, but before the sun sets you must return to the place you started from. All the land you cover will be yours."

Pahom was delighted. It was decided to start early next morning. They talked awhile, and after drinking some more kumiss and eating some more mutton, they had tea again, and then the night came on. They gave Pahom a featherbed to sleep on, and the Bashkirs dispersed for the night, promising to assemble the next morning at daybreak and ride out before sunrise to the appointed spot.

Pahom lay on the featherbed, but could not sleep. He kept thinking about the land.

"What a large tract I will mark off!" thought he. "I can easily do thirty-five miles in a day. The days are long now, and within a circuit of thirty-five miles what a lot of land there will be! I will sell the poorer land, or let it to peasants, but I'll pick out the best and farm it. I will buy two ox teams, and hire two more laborers. About a hundred and fifty acres shall be plow land, and I will pasture cattle on the rest."

Looking round he saw through the open door that the dawn was breaking.

"It's time to wake them up," thought he. "We ought to be starting."

He got up, roused his man (who was sleeping in his cart), bade him harness; and went to call the Bashkirs.

"It's time to go to the steppe to measure the land," he said.

The Bashkirs rose and assembled, and the chief came too. Then they began drinking kumiss again, and offered Pahom some tea, but he would not wait.

"If we are to go, let us go. It is high time," said he.

The Bashkirs got ready and they all started: some mounted on horses, and some in carts. Pahom drove in his own small cart with his servant, and took a spade with him. When they reached the steppe, the morning red was beginning to kindle. They ascended a hillock and, dismounting from their carts and their horses, gathered in one spot. The chief came up to Pahom and stretched out his arm toward the plain.

"See," said he, "all this, as far as your eye can reach, is ours. You may have any part of it you like."

Pahom's eyes glistened: it was all virgin soil, as flat as the palm of your hand, as black as the seed of a poppy, and in the hollows different kinds of grasses grew breast high.

The chief took off his fox fur cap, placed it on the ground and said:

"This will be the mark. Start from here, and return here again. All the land you go round shall be yours."

Pahom took out his money and put it on the cap. Then he

took off his outer coat, remaining in his sleeveless undercoat. He unfastened his girdle and tied it tight below his stomach, put a little bag of bread into the breast of his coat, and tying a flask of water to his girdle, he drew up the tops of his boots, took the spade from his man, and stood ready to start. He considered for some moments which way he had better go—it was tempting everywhere.

"No matter," he concluded, "I will go toward the rising sun."

He turned his face to the east, stretched himself, and waited for the sun to appear above the rim.

"I must lose no time," he thought, "and it is easier walking while it is still cool."

The sun's rays had hardly flashed above the horizon, before Pahom, carrying the spade over his shoulder, went down into the steppe.

Pahom started walking neither slowly nor quickly. After having gone a thousand yards he stopped, dug a hole, and placed pieces of turf one on another to make it more visible. Then he went on; and now that he had walked off his stiffness he quickened his pace. After a while he dug another hole.

Pahom looked back. The hillock could be distinctly seen in the sunlight, with the people on it, and the glittering tires of the cart wheels. At a rough guess Pahom concluded that he had walked three miles. It was growing warmer; he took off his undercoat, flung it across his shoulder, and went on again. It had grown quite warm now; he looked at the sun, it was time to think of breakfast.

"The first shift is done, but there are four in a day, and it is too soon yet to turn. But I will just take off my boots," said he to himself.

He sat down, took off his boots, stuck them into his girdle, and went on. It was easy walking now.

"I will go on for another three miles," thought he, "and then turn to the left. This spot is so fine, that it would be a pity to lose it. The further one goes, the better the land seems."

He went straight on for a while, and when he looked round, the hillock was scarcely visible and the people on it looked like black ants, and he could just see something glistening there in the sun.

"Ah," thought Pahom, "I have gone far enough in this direction, it is time to turn. Besides I am in a regular sweat, and very thirsty."

He stopped, dug a large hole, and heaped up pieces of turf. Next he untied his flask, had a drink, and then turned sharply to the left. He went on and on; the grass was high, and it was very hot.

Pahom began to grow tired: he looked at the sun and saw that it was noon.

"Well," he thought, "I must have a rest."

He sat down, and ate some bread and drank some water; but he did not lie down, thinking that if he did he might fall asleep. After sitting a little while, he went on again. At first he walked easily: the food had strengthened him; but it had become terribly hot, and he felt sleepy; still he went on, thinking: "An hour to suffer, a lifetime to live."

He went a long way in this direction also, and was about to turn to the left again, when he perceived a damp hollow: "It would be a pity to leave that out," he thought. "Flax would do well there." So he went on past the hollow, and dug a hole on the other side of it before he turned the corner. Pahom looked toward the hillock. The heat made the air hazy: it seemed to be quivering, and through the haze the people on the hillock could scarcely be seen.

"Ah!" thought Pahom, "I have made the sides too long; I must make this one shorter." And he went along the third side, stepping faster. He looked at the sun: it was nearly halfway to the horizon, and he had not yet done two miles of the third side of the square. He was still ten miles from the goal.

"No," he thought, "though it will make my land lopsided, I must hurry back in a straight line now. I might go too far, and as it is I have a great deal of land."

So Pahom hurriedly dug a hole, and turned straight toward the hillock.

Pahom went straight toward the hillock, but he now walked with difficulty. He was done up with the heat, his bare feet were cut and bruised, and his legs began to fail. He longed to rest, but it was impossible if he meant to get back before sunset. The sun waits for no man, and it was sinking lower and lower.

"Oh dear," he thought, "if only I have not blundered trying for too much! What if I am too late?"

He looked toward the hillock and at the sun. He was still far from his goal, and the sun was already near the rim.

Pahom walked on and on; it was very hard walking, but he went quicker and quicker. He pressed on, but was still far from the place. He began running, threw away his coat, his boots, his flask, and his cap, and kept only the spade which he used as a support.

"What shall I do," he thought again. "I have grasped too much, and ruined the whole affair. I can't get there before the sun sets."

And this fear made him still more breathless. Pahom went on running, his soaking shirt and trousers stuck to him, and his mouth was parched. His breast was working like a blacksmith's bellows, his heart was beating like a hammer, and his legs were giving way as if they did not belong to him. Pahom was seized with terror lest he should die of the strain.

Though afraid of death, he could not stop. "After having run all that way they will call me a fool if I stop now," thought he. And he ran on and on, and drew near and heard the Bashkirs yelling and shouting to him, and their cries inflamed his heart still more. He gathered his last strength and ran on.

The sun was close to the rim, and cloaked in mist looked large, and red as blood. Now, yes now, it was about to set! The sun was quite low, but he was also quite near his aim. Pahom could already see the people on the hillock waving their arms to hurry him up. He could see the fox fur cap on the ground, and the money on it, and the chief sitting on the ground holding his sides.

"There is plenty of land," thought he, "but will God let me live on it? I have lost my life, I have lost my life! I shall never reach that spot!"

Pahom looked at the sun, which had reached the earth; one side of it had already disappeared. With all his remaining strength he rushed on, bending his body forward so that his legs could hardly follow fast enough to keep him from falling. Just as he reached the hillock it suddenly grew dark. He looked up—the sun had already set! He gave a cry: "All my labor has been in vain," thought he, and was about to stop, but he heard the Bashkirs still shouting, and remembered that though to him, from below, the sun seemed to have set, they on the hillock could still see it. He took a long breath and ran up the hillock. It was still light there. He reached the top and saw the cap. Before it sat the chief laughing and holding his sides. Pahom uttered a cry: his legs gave way beneath him, he fell forward and reached the cap with his hands.

"Ah, that's a fine fellow!" exclaimed the chief. "He has gained much land!"

Pahom's servant came running up and tried to raise him, but he saw that blood was flowing from his mouth. Pahom was dead!

The Bashkirs clicked their tongues to show their pity.

His servant picked up the spade and dug a grave long enough for Pahom to lie in, and buried him in it. Six feet from his head to his heels was all he needed.

# Terence, This Is Stupid Stuff

*A. E. Housman*

With wry irony, Alfred Edward Housman (1859–1936) advises preparing oneself for a world that may contain "much good, but much less good than ill." Escapist solutions such as drink (Burton-on-Trent, mentioned in the second stanza, is a famous English brewing town) offer only the false answer of illusion. The best tack, Housman says, is to "train for ill and not for good," and thereby steel oneself against all the unfairness life has to offer. And so he suggests as a model Mithridates, king of ancient Pontus in Asia Minor, who made himself immune to poison by swallowing small doses every day. There's a bit of cynicism in this poem, but there's also a good measure of hard truth: we must practice bracing ourselves for all of life's contingencies.

"Terence, this is stupid stuff:
You eat your victuals fast enough;
There can't be much amiss, 'tis clear,
To see the rate you drink your beer.
But oh, good Lord, the verse you make,
It gives a chap the bellyache.
The cow, the old cow, she is dead;
It sleeps well, the hornéd head:
We poor lads, 'tis our turn now
To hear such tunes as killed the cow.
Pretty friendship 'tis to rhyme
Your friends to death before their time
Moping melancholy mad:
Come, pipe a tune to dance to, lad."

Why, if 'tis dancing you would be,
There's brisker pipes than poetry.
Say, for what were hopyards meant,
Or why was Burton built on Trent?

Oh many a peer of England brews
Livelier liquor than the Muse,
And malt does more than Milton can
To justify God's ways to man.
Ale, man, ale's the stuff to drink
For fellows whom it hurts to think:
Look into the pewter pot
To see the world as the world's not.
And faith, 'tis pleasant till 'tis past:
The mischief is that 'twill not last.
Oh I have been to Ludlow fair
And left my necktie God knows where,
And carried halfway home, or near,
Pints and quarts of Ludlow beer:
Then the world seemed none so bad,
And I myself a sterling lad;
And down in lovely muck I've lain,
Happy till I woke again.
Then I saw the morning sky.
Heigho, the tale was all a lie;
The world, it was the old world yet,
I was I, my things were wet,
And nothing now remained to do
But begin the game anew.

Therefore, since the world has still
Much good, but much less good than ill,
And while the sun and moon endure
Luck's a chance, but trouble's sure,
I'd face it as a wise man would,
And train for ill and not for good.
'Tis true the stuff I bring for sale
Is not so brisk a brew as ale:
Out of a stem that scored the hand
I wrung it in a weary land.
But take it: if the smack is sour,
The better for the embittered hour;
It should do good to heart and head
When your soul is in my soul's stead;
And I will friend you, if I may,
In the dark and cloudy day.

There was a king reigned in the East:
There, when kings will sit to feast,
They get their fill before they think
With poisoned meat and poisoned drink.
He gathered all that springs to birth
From the many-venomed earth;
First a little, thence to more,
He sampled all her killing store;
And easy, smiling, seasoned sound,
Sate the king when healths went round.
They put arsenic in his meat
And stared aghast to watch him eat;
They poured strychnine in his cup
And shook to see him drink it up:
They shook, they stared as white's their shirt.
Them it was their poison hurt.
—I tell the tale that I heard told.
Mithridates, he died old.

---

# Plato on Self-Discipline

*From the* Gorgias

The right and wrong uses of rhetoric are technically the themes of Plato's *Gorgias,* but, as with all Platonic dialogues, the true end is the examination of how life should be lived. Here we find Callicles boldly asserting "what the rest of the world think, but do not like to say": leading the Good Life means having what you want, as much as you want, whenever you want. In short, the life of the rich and famous is the truly happy life. Socrates replies with his telling image of a leaky vessel as a metaphor for the intemperate soul. He insists that the ordered soul is the only truly happy one, the only one capable of living the Good Life.

*Socrates.* Every man is his own ruler; but perhaps you think that there is no necessity for him to rule himself; he is only required to rule others?

*Callicles.* What do you mean by his "ruling over himself"?

*Soc.* A simple thing enough; just what is commonly said, that a man should be temperate and master of himself, and ruler of his own pleasures and passions.

*Cal.* What innocence! you mean those fools—the temperate?

*Soc.* Certainly: anyone may know that to be my meaning.

*Cal.* Quite so, Socrates; and they are really fools, for how can a man be happy who is the servant of anything? On the contrary, I plainly assert, that he who would truly live ought to allow his desires to wax to the uttermost, and not to chastise them; but when they have grown to their greatest he should have courage and intelligence to minister to them and to satisfy all his longings. And this I affirm to be natural justice and nobility. To this however the many cannot attain; and they blame the strong man because they are ashamed of their own weakness, which they desire to conceal, and hence they say that intemperance is base. As I have remarked already, they enslave the nobler natures, and being unable to satisfy their pleasures, they praise temperance and justice out of their own cowardice. For if a man had been originally the son of a king, or had a nature capable of acquiring an empire or a tyranny or sovereignty, what could be more truly base or evil than temperance—to a man like him, I say, who might freely be enjoying every good, and has no one to stand in his way, and yet has admitted custom and reason and the opinion of other men to be lords over him?—must not he be in a miserable plight whom the reputation of justice and temperance hinders from giving more to his friends than to his enemies, even though he be a ruler in his city? Nay, Socrates, for you profess to be a votary of the truth, and the truth is this: that luxury and intemperance and license, if they be provided with means, are virtue and happiness—all the rest is a mere bauble, agreements contrary to nature, foolish talk of men, worth nothing.

*Soc.* There is a noble freedom, Callicles, in your way of approaching the argument; for what you say is what the rest of the world think, but do not like to say. And I must beg of you to persevere, that the true rule of human life may become manifest. Tell me, then: you say, do you not, that in the rightly developed man the passions ought not to be controlled, but that we should let them grow to the utmost and somehow or other satisfy them, and that this is virtue?

*Cal.* Yes; I do.

*Soc.* Then those who want nothing are not truly said to be happy?

*Cal.* No indeed, for then stones and dead men would be the happiest of all.

*Soc.* But surely life according to your view is an awful thing. . . . Let me request you to consider how far you would accept this as an account of the two lives of the temperate and intemperate in a figure: There are two men, both of whom have a number of casks; the one man has his casks sound and full, one of wine, another of honey, and a third of milk, besides others filled with other liquids, and the streams which fill them are few and scanty, and he can only obtain them with a great deal of toil and difficulty; but when his casks are once filled he has no need to feed them anymore, and has no further trouble with them or care about them. The other, in like manner, can procure streams, though not without difficulty; but his vessels are leaky and unsound, and night and day he is compelled to be filling them, and if he pauses for a moment, he is in an agony of pain. Such are their respective lives: And now would you say that the life of the intemperate is happier than that of the temperate? Do I not convince you that the opposite is the truth?

*Cal.* You do not convince me, Socrates, for the one who has filled himself has no longer any pleasure left; and this, as I was just now saying, is the life of a stone: he has neither joy nor sorrow after he is once filled; but the pleasure depends on the superabundance of the influx.

*Soc.* But the more you pour in, the greater the waste; and the holes must be large for the liquid to escape.

*Cal.* Certainly.

*Soc.* The life which you are now depicting is not that of a dead man, or of a stone, but of a cormorant; you mean that he is to be hungering and eating?

*Cal.* Yes.

*Soc.* And he is to be thirsting and drinking?

*Cal.* Yes, that is what I mean; he is to have all his desires about him, and to be able to live happily in the gratification of them. . . .

*Soc.* Listen to me, then, while I recapitulate the argument: Is the pleasant the same as the good? Not the same. Callicles and I are agreed about that. And is the pleasant to be pursued for the sake of the good? or the good for the sake of the pleasant? The pleasant is to be pursued for the sake of the good. And that is pleasant at the presence of which we are pleased, and that is good at the presence of which we are good? To be sure. And we are good, and all good things whatever are good when some virtue is present in us or them? That, Callicles, is my conviction. But the virtue of each thing, whether body or soul, instrument or creature, when given to them in the best way comes to them not by chance but as the result of the order and truth and art which are imparted to them: Am I not right? I maintain that I am. And is not the virtue of each thing dependent on order or arrangement? Yes, I say. And that which makes a thing good is the proper order inhering in each thing? Such is my view. And is not the soul which has an order of her own better than that which has no order? Certainly. And the soul which has order is orderly? Of course. And that which is orderly is temperate? Assuredly. And the temperate soul is good? No other answer can I give, Callicles dear; have you any?

*Cal.* Go on, my good fellow.

*Soc.* Then I shall proceed to add, that if the temperate soul is the good soul, the soul which is in the opposite condition, that is, the foolish and intemperate, is the bad soul. Very true.

And will not the temperate man do what is proper, both in relation to the gods and to men; for he would not be temperate if he did not? Certainly he will do what is proper. In his relation to other men he will do what is just; and in his relation to the gods he will do what is holy; and he who does what is just and holy must be just and holy? Very true. And must he not be courageous? For the duty of a temperate man is not to follow or to avoid what he ought not, but what he ought, whether things or men or pleasures or pains, and patiently to endure when he ought; and therefore, Callicles, the temperate man, being, as we have described, also just and courageous and holy, cannot be other than a perfectly good man, nor can the good man do otherwise than well and perfectly whatever he does; and he who does well must of necessity be happy and blessed, and the evil man who does evil, miserable: now this latter is he whom you were applauding—the intemperate who is the opposite of the temperate. Such is my position, and these things I affirm to be true. And if they are true, then I further affirm that he who desires to be happy must pursue and practice temperance and run away from intemperance as fast as his legs will carry him: he had better order his life so as not to need punishment; but if either he or any of his friends, whether private individual or city, are in need of punishment, then justice must be done and he must suffer punishment, if he would be happy. This appears to me to be the aim which a man ought to have, and toward which he ought to direct all the energies both of himself and of the state, acting so that he may have temperance and justice present with him and be happy, not suffering his lusts to be unrestrained, and in the never-ending desire to satisfy them leading a robber's life. Such a one is the friend neither of God nor man, for he is incapable of communion, and he who is incapable of communion is also incapable of friendship. And philosophers tell us, Callicles, that communion and friendship and orderliness and temperance and justice bind together heaven and earth and gods and men, and that this universe is therefore called Cosmos or order, not disorder or misrule, my friend.

---

# Aristotle on Self-Discipline

## *From the* Nicomachean Ethics

We are the sum of our actions, Aristotle tells us, and therefore our habits make all the difference. Moral virtue, we learn in this discussion from the *Nicomachean Ethics,* comes with practice, just like the mastery of any art or mechanical skill. And what is the best way to practice? Aristotle's answer lies in his explanation of "the mean." In his view, correct moral behavior in any given situation lies at the midway point between the extremes of two vices. We must practice hitting the mean by determining which vice we tend toward and then consciously moving toward the other extreme, until we reach the middle.

Virtue, then, is of two kinds, intellectual and moral. Intellectual virtue springs from and grows from teaching, and therefore needs experience and time. Moral virtues come from habit. . . . They are in us neither by nature, nor in despite of nature, but we are furnished by nature with a capacity for receiving them, and we develop them through habit. . . . These virtues we acquire by first exercising them, as in the case of other arts. Whatever we learn to do, we learn by actually doing it: men come to be builders, for instance, by building, and harp players, by playing the harp. In the same way, by doing just acts we come to be just; by doing self-controlled acts, we come to be self-controlled; and by doing brave acts, we become brave. . . .

How we act in our relations with other people makes us just or unjust. How we face dangerous situations, either accustoming ourselves to fear or confidence, makes us brave or cowardly. Occasions of lust and anger are similar: some people become self-controlled and patient from their conduct in such situations, and others uncontrolled and passionate. In a word, then, activities produce similar dispositions. Therefore we must give a certain character to our activities. . . . In short, the habits we form from childhood make no small difference, but rather they make all the difference.

Moral virtue is a mean that lies between two vices, one of excess and the other of deficiency, and . . . it aims at hitting the mean both in feelings and actions. So it is hard to be good, for surely it is hard in each instance to find the mean, just as it is difficult to find the center of a circle. It is easy to get angry or to spend money—anyone can do that. But to act the right way toward the right person, in due proportion, at the right time, for the right reason, and in the right manner—this is not easy, and not everyone can do it.

Therefore he who aims at the mean should make it his first care to keep away from that extreme which is more contrary than the other to the mean. . . . For one of the two extremes is always more erroneous than the other. And since hitting the mean exactly is difficult, one must take the next best course, and choose the least of the evils as the safest plan. . . .

We should also take notice of the errors into which we naturally tend to fall. They vary in each individual's case, and we will discover ours by the pleasure or pain they give us. Having discovered our errors, we must force ourselves off in the opposite direction. For we shall arrive at the mean by moving away from our failing, just as if we were straightening a bent piece of wood. But in all cases we should guard most carefully against what is pleasant, and pleasure itself, because we are not impartial judges of it. . . .

This much, then, is plain: in all our conduct, the mean is the most praiseworthy state. But as a practical matter, we must sometimes aim a bit toward excess and sometimes toward deficiency, because this will be the easiest way of hitting the mean, that is, what is right.

# Go Forth to Life

*Samuel Longfellow*

Go forth to life, oh! child of Earth.
Still mindful of thy heavenly birth;
Thou art not here for ease or sin,
But manhood's noble crown to win.

Though passion's fires are in thy soul,
Thy spirit can their flames control;
Though tempters strong beset thy way,
Thy spirit is more strong than they.

Go on from innocence of youth
To manly pureness, manly truth;
God's angels still are near to save,
And God himself doth help the brave.

Then forth to life, oh! child of Earth,
Be worthy of thy heavenly birth,
For noble service thou art here;
Thy brothers help, thy God revere!

---

# For Everything There Is a Season

*From* Ecclesiastes

For every thing there is a season, and a time for every purpose under the heaven:

A time to be born, and a time to die; a time to plant, and a time to pluck up that which is planted;

A time to kill, and a time to heal; a time to break down, and a time to build up;

A time to weep, and a time to laugh; a time to mourn, and a time to dance;

A time to cast away stones, and a time to gather stones together; a time to embrace, and a time to refrain from embracing;

A time to get, and a time to lose; a time to keep, and a time to cast away;

A time to rend, and a time to sew; a time to keep silence, and a time to speak;

A time to love, and a time to hate; a time of war, and a time of peace.

# 2

# Compassion

JUST as courage takes its stand *by* others in challenging situations, so compassion takes its stand *with* others in their distress. Compassion is a virtue that takes seriously the reality of other persons, their inner lives, their emotions, as well as their external circumstances. It is an active disposition toward fellowship and sharing, toward supportive companionship in distress or in woe.

The seeds of compassion are sown in our very nature as human beings. "There is some benevolence, however small, infused into our bosom, some spark of friendship for human kind, some particle of the dove kneaded into our frame, along with the elements of the wolf and serpent," as David Hume once put it. His contemporary Jean-Jacques Rousseau agreed: "compassion is a natural feeling, which, by moderating the violence of love of self in each individual, contributes to the preservation of the whole species. It is this compassion that hurries us without reflection to the relief of those who are in distress."

Happily, this eighteenth-century view is in fashion once again. It is our twentieth-century understanding that human infants do not distinguish between their own distress and that of others. One baby's cries in the nursery are frequently picked up by the rest, and together they form a natural choral symphony of sympathetic woe. Compassion seeks to retain our hold on this very early awareness that we are all in the same boat, that "but for the grace of God there go I."

Compassion thus comes close to the very heart of moral awareness, to seeing in one's neighbor another self. The American philosopher Josiah Royce gave memorable expression to this insight more than a hundred years ago. "What then is thy neighbor?" he asks in his quaint but compelling way. And the answer he gives, in part, is that one's neighbor "is a mass of states, of experiences, thoughts, and desires, just as real as thou art. . . . Does thou believe this? Art thou sure what it means? This is for thee the turning-point of thy whole conduct towards him."

How does one cultivate a compassionate nature in children? Helpful stories and maxims abound. And fortunately in this case, compassion is as close to a "natural" disposition as any of the virtues. The main task—though this can be really formidable—is to see that neither animosity nor prejudice stunts its natural growth. The divisive "isms" are major obstacles here: racism, sexism, chauvinism, and the rest. And very important in this case, as in so much of the rest of moral upbringing, is the power of consistent example. Treat *no one* with callous disregard. Children know when they are being taken seriously by others, and they imitate what they see. Therein lies both our hope and our peril.

# Kindness to Animals

Compassion may be first learned through kindness to all creatures great and small.

Little children, never give
Pain to things that feel and live;
Let the gentle robin come
For the crumbs you save at home;
As his meat you throw along
He'll repay you with a song.
Never hurt the timid hare
Peeping from her green grass lair,
Let her come and sport and play
On the lawn at close of day.
The little lark goes soaring high
To the bright windows of the sky,
Singing as if 'twere always spring,
And fluttering on an untired wing—
Oh! let him sing his happy song,
Nor do these gentle creatures wrong.

## The Lion and the Mouse

*Aesop*

Here is one of the oldest and best-loved stories of kindness paid and repaid. From it we learn that compassion lies within the power of both the mighty and the meek. Kindness is not a feeble virtue.

One day a great lion lay asleep in the sunshine. A little mouse ran across his paw and wakened him. The great lion was just going to eat him up when the little mouse cried, "Oh, please, let me go, sir. Some day I may help you."

The lion laughed at the thought that the little mouse could be of any use to him. But he was a good-natured lion, and he set the mouse free.

Not long after, the lion was caught in a net. He tugged and pulled with all his might, but the ropes were too strong. Then he roared loudly. The little mouse heard him, and ran to the spot.

"Be still, dear Lion, and I will set you free. I will gnaw the ropes."

With his sharp little teeth, the mouse cut the ropes, and the lion came out of the net.

"You laughed at me once," said the mouse. "You thought I was too little to do you a good turn. But see, you owe your life to a poor little mouse."

---

## Little Sunshine

*Retold by Etta Austin Blaisdell*
*and Mary Frances Blaisdell*

Bestowing compassion is like offering most other gifts. Often it's the thought that counts.

Once there was a little girl named Elsa. She had a very old grandmother, with white hair, and wrinkles all over her face.

Elsa's father had a large house that stood on a hill.

Each day the sun peeped in at the south windows. It made everything look bright and beautiful.

The grandmother lived on the north side of the house. The sun never came to her room.

One day Elsa said to her father, "Why doesn't the sun peep into Grandma's room? I know she would like to have him."

"The sun cannot look in at the north windows," said her father.

"Then let us turn the house around, Papa."

"It is much too large for that," said her father.

"Will Grandma never have any sunshine in her room?" asked Elsa.

"Of course not, my child, unless you can carry some to her."

After that Elsa tried and tried to think how she could carry the sunshine to her grandmother.

When she played in the fields she saw the grass and the flowers nodding their heads. The birds sang sweetly as they flew from tree to tree.

Everything seemed to say, "We love the sun. We love the bright, warm sun."

"Grandma would love it, too," thought the child. "I must take some to her."

When she was in the garden one morning she felt the sun's warm rays in her golden hair. Then she sat down and she saw them in her lap.

"I will take them in my dress," she thought, "and carry them to Grandma's room." So she jumped up and ran into the house.

"Look, Grandma, Look! I have some sunshine for you," she cried. And she opened her dress, but there was not a ray to be seen.

"It peeps out of your eyes, my child," said her grandmother, "and it shines in your sunny, golden hair. I do not need the sun when I have you with me."

Elsa did not understand how the sun could peep out of her eyes. But she was glad to make her dear grandmother happy.

Every morning she played in the garden. Then she ran to her grandmother's room to carry the sunshine in her eyes and hair.

# A Child's Prayer

*M. Bentham-Edwards*

God make my life a little light,
  Within the world to glow;
A tiny flame that burneth bright
  Wherever I may go.

God make my life a little flower,
  That giveth joy to all,
Content to bloom in native bower,
  Although its place be small.

God make my life a little song,
  That comforteth the sad;
That helpeth others to be strong,
  And makes the singer glad.

God make my life a little staff,
  Whereon the weak may rest,
That so what health and strength I have
  May serve my neighbors best.

---

# Diamonds and Toads

*Retold by Charles Perrault*

In this story we learn the old lesson that to speak kindly does not hurt the tongue. To speak with anger and disagreeableness, however, may bring unhappiness.

Once upon a time there was a woman who had two daughters. The elder daughter was very much like her mother in face and manner. They were both so disagreeable and so proud that there was no living with them.

The younger daughter was like her father, for she was good and sweet-tempered, and very beautiful. As people naturally love their own likeness, the mother was very fond of her elder daughter, and at the same time had a great dislike for the younger. She made her eat in the kitchen, and work all the time.

Among other things, this poor child was obliged to go twice a day to draw a pitcherful of water from the spring in the woods, two miles from the house.

One day, when she reached the spring, a poor woman came to her and begged for a drink.

"Oh yes! With all my heart, ma'am," said this pretty little girl, and she took some clear, cool water from the spring, and held up the pitcher so that the woman might drink easily.

When she had finished, the woman said, "You are so very pretty, my dear, so good and so kind, that I cannot help giving you a gift."

Now this was a fairy, who had taken the form of a poor country woman to see how this pretty girl would treat her. "I will give you for a gift," continued the fairy, "that at every word you speak, either a flower or a jewel shall come out of your mouth."

When the girl reached home, her mother scolded her for staying so long at the spring. "I beg your pardon, Mamma," said the poor girl, "for not making more haste." And as she spoke, there came out of her mouth two roses, two pearls, and two large diamonds.

"What is it I see there?" said her mother, very much surprised. "I think I see pearls and diamonds come out of the girl's mouth! How does this happen, my child?" This was the first time she had ever called her "my child," or spoken kindly to her.

The poor child told her mother all that had happened at the spring, and of the old woman's promise. All the time jewels and flowers fell from her lips.

"This is delightful," cried the mother. "I must send my dearest child to the spring. Come, Fanny, see what comes out of your sister's mouth when she speaks! Would you not be glad, my dear, to have the same gift given to you? All you will have to do is to take the pitcher to the spring in the wood. When a poor woman asks you for a drink, give it to her."

"It would be a fine thing for me to do," said the selfish girl. "I will not go to draw water! The child can give me her jewels. She does not need them."

"Yes, you shall," said the mother, "and you shall go this minute."

At last the elder daughter went, grumbling and scolding all the way, and taking with her the best silver pitcher in the house.

She had no sooner reached the spring than she saw a beautiful lady coming out of the wood, who came up to her and asked her for a drink. This was, you must know, the same fairy who had met her sister, but who had now taken the form of a princess.

"I did not come out here to serve you with water," said the proud, selfish maid. "Do you think I brought this silver pitcher so far just to give you a drink? You can draw water from the spring as well as I."

"You are not very polite," said the fairy. "Since you are so rude and so unkind, I give you for a gift that at every word you speak, toads and serpents shall come out of your mouth."

As soon as the mother saw her daughter coming, she cried out, "Well, my dear child, did you see the good fairy?"

"Yes, Mother," answered the proud girl, and as she spoke, two serpents and two toads fell from her mouth.

"What is this that I see?" cried the mother. "What have you done?"

The girl tried to answer, but at every word toads and serpents came from her lips.

And so it was forever after. Jewels and flowers fell from the lips of the younger daughter, who was so good and kind, but the elder daughter could not speak without a shower of serpents and toads.

---

# Old Mr. Rabbit's Thanksgiving Dinner

*Carolyn Sherwin Bailey*

It is a discovery we make again and again, as if by accident each time: it gives us greater satisfaction to be helpful than helped. For a child this discovery when made the first time is one of the important lessons that takes one beyond the confines of the self.

Old Man Rabbit sat at the door of his little house, eating a nice, ripe, juicy turnip. It was a cold, frosty day, but Old Man Rabbit was all wrapped up, round and round, with yards and yards of his best red wool muffler, so he didn't care if the wind whistled through his whiskers and blew his ears up straight. Old Man Rabbit had been exercising, too, and that was another reason why he was so nice and warm.

Early in the morning he had started off, lippity, clippity, down the little brown path that lay in front of his house and led to Farmer Dwyer's corn patch. The path was all covered with shiny red leaves. Old Man Rabbit scuffled through them and he carried a great big bag over his back. In the corn patch he found two or three fat, red ears of corn that Farmer Dwyer had missed, so he dropped them into his bag. A little farther along he found some purple turnips and some yellow carrots and quite a few russet apples that Farmer Dwyer had arranged in little piles in the orchard. Old Man Rabbit went in the barn, squeezing under the big front door by making himself very flat, and he filled all the chinks in his bag with potatoes, and he took a couple of eggs in his paws, for he thought he might want to stir up a little pudding for himself before the day was over.

Then Old Man Rabbit started off home again down the little brown path, his mouth watering every time his bag bumped against his back, and not meeting anyone on the way because it was so very, very early in the morning.

When he came to the little house he emptied his bag and arranged all his harvest in piles in his front room—the corn in one pile, the carrots in one pile, the turnips in another pile, and the apples and potatoes in the last pile. He beat up his eggs and stirred some flour with them and filled it full of currants to make a pudding. And when he had put his pudding in a bag and set it boiling on the stove, he went outside to sit a while and eat a turnip, thinking all the time what a mighty fine old rabbit he was, and so clever, too.

Well, while Old Man Rabbit was sitting there in front of his little house, wrapped up in his red muffler and munching the turnip, he heard a little noise in the leaves. It was Billy Chipmunk traveling home to the stone wall where he lived. He was hurrying and blowing on his paws to keep them warm.

"Good morning, Billy Chipmunk," said Old Man Rabbit. "Why are you running so fast?"

"Because I am cold, and I am hungry," answered Billy Chipmunk. "It's going to be a hard winter, a very hard winter—no apples left. I've been looking all the morning for an apple and I couldn't find one."

And with that, Billy Chipmunk went chattering by, his fur standing straight out in the wind.

No sooner had he passed than Old Man Rabbit saw Molly Mouse creeping along through the little brown path, her long gray tail rustling the red leaves as she went.

"Good morning, Molly Mouse," said Old Man Rabbit.

"Good morning," answered Molly Mouse in a weak little voice.

"You look a little unhappy," said Old Man Rabbit, taking another bite of his turnip.

"I have been looking and looking for an ear of corn," said Molly Mouse in a sad little chirping voice. "But the corn has all been harvested. It's going to be a very hard winter, a very hard winter."

And Molly Mouse trotted by out of sight.

Pretty soon Old Man Rabbit heard somebody else coming along by his house. This time it was Tommy Chickadee hopping by and making a great to-do, chattering and scolding as he came.

"Good morning, Tommy Chickadee," said Old Man Rabbit.

But Tommy Chickadee was too much put out about something to remember his manners. He just chirped and scolded, because he was cold and he couldn't find a single crumb or a berry or anything at all to eat. Then he flew away, his feathers puffed out with the cold until he looked like a round ball, and all the way he chattered and scolded more and more.

Old Man Rabbit finished his turnip, eating every single bit of it, even to the leaves. Then he went in his house to poke the fire in his stove and to see how the pudding was cooking. It was doing very well indeed, bumping against the pot as it bubbled and boiled, and smelling very fine indeed.

Old Man Rabbit looked around his house at the corn and the carrots and the turnips and the apples and the potatoes, and then he had an idea. It was a very funny idea, different from any other idea Old Man Rabbit had ever had before in all his life. It made him scratch his head with his left hind foot, and think and wonder. But it pleased him, too—it was such a very funny idea.

First he took off his muffler, and then he put on his gingham apron. He took his best red tablecloth from the drawer and put it on his table, and then he set the table with his gold-banded china dinner set. By the time he had done all this, the pudding was boiled, so he lifted it, all sweet and steaming, from the kettle and set it in the middle of the table. Around the pudding Old Man Rabbit piled heaps and heaps of corn and carrots and turnips and apples and potatoes, and then he took down his dinner bell that was all rusty, because Old Man Rabbit had very seldom rung it before, and he stood in his front door and he rang it very hard, calling in a loud voice:

"Dinner's ready! Come to dinner, Billy Chipmunk, and Molly Mouse, and Tommy Chickadee!"

They all came, and they brought their friends with them. Tommy Chickadee brought Rusty Robin, who had a broken wing and had not been able to fly south for the winter. Billy Chipmunk brought Chatter-Chee, a lame squirrel, whom he had invited to share his hole for a few months, and Molly Mouse brought a young gentleman Field Mouse, who was very distinguished-looking because of his long whiskers. When they all tumbled into Old Man Rabbit's house and saw the table with the pudding in the center they forgot their manners and began eating as fast as they could, every one of them.

It kept Old Man Rabbit very busy waiting on them. He gave all the currants from the pudding to Tommy Chickadee and Rusty Robin. He selected juicy turnips for Molly Mouse and her friend, and the largest apples for Billy Chipmunk. Old Man Rabbit was so busy that he didn't have any time to eat a bite of dinner himself, but he didn't mind that, not one single bit. It made him feel so warm and full inside just to see the others eating.

When the dinner was over, and not one single crumb was left on the table, Tommy Chickadee hopped up on the back of his chair and chirped:

"Three cheers for Old Man Rabbit's Thanksgiving dinner!"

"Hurrah! Hurrah!" they all twittered and chirped and chattered. And Old Man Rabbit was so surprised that he didn't get over it for a week. You see, he had really given a Thanksgiving dinner without knowing that it really and truly was Thanksgiving Day.

# Androcles and the Lion

*Retold by James Baldwin*

This ancient story is another, more slightly complicated version of the fable of the Lion and the Mouse. Here the human element is introduced. Its appeal lies in the fact that Androcles the slave can feel compassion at another's pain even though he himself has been so cruelly mistreated. It is a unique human capacity, to be able to put oneself in the place and point of view of another. In the end, his own kindness sets him free.

In Rome there was once a poor slave whose name was Androcles. His master was a cruel man, and so unkind to him that at last Androcles ran away.

He hid himself in a wild wood for many days. But there was no food to be found, and he grew so weak and sick that he thought he would die. So one day he crept into a cave and lay down, and soon he was fast asleep.

After a while a great noise woke him up. A lion had come into the cave, and was roaring loudly. Androcles was very much afraid, for he felt sure that the beast would kill him. Soon, however, he saw that the lion was not angry, but that he limped as though his foot hurt him.

Then Androcles grew so bold that he took hold of the lion's lame paw to see what was the matter. The lion stood quite still, and rubbed his head against the man's shoulder. He seemed to say "I know that you will help me."

Androcles lifted the paw from the ground, and saw that it was a long, sharp thorn which hurt the lion so much. He took the end of the thorn in his fingers; then he gave a strong, quick pull, and out it came. The lion was full of joy. He jumped about like a dog, and licked the hands and feet of his new friend.

Androcles was not at all afraid after this. And when night came, he and the lion lay down and slept side by side.

For a long time, the lion brought food to Androcles every day, and the two became such good friends that Androcles found his new life a very happy one.

One day some soldiers who were passing through the wood found Androcles in the cave. They knew who he was, and so took him back to Rome.

It was the law at that time that every slave who ran away from his master should be made to fight a hungry lion. So a fierce lion was shut up for a while without food, and a time was set for the fight.

When the day came, thousands of people crowded to see the sport. They went to such places at that time very much as people now go to see a circus show, or a game of baseball.

The door opened, and poor Androcles was brought in. He was almost dead with fear, for the roars of the lion could already be heard. He looked up, and saw that there was no pity in the thousands of faces around him.

Then the hungry lion rushed in. With a single bound he reached the poor slave. Androcles gave a great cry, not of fear, but of gladness. It was his old friend, the lion of the cave.

The people, who had expected to see the man killed by the lion, were filled with wonder. They saw Androcles put his arms around the lion's neck; they saw the lion lie down at his feet, and lick them lovingly; they saw the great beast rub his head against the slave's face as though he wanted to be petted. They could not understand what it all meant.

After a while they asked Androcles to tell them about it. So he stood up before them, and, with his arm around the lion's neck, told how he and the beast had lived together in the cave.

"I am a man," he said, "but no man has ever befriended me. This poor lion alone has been kind to me and we love each other as brothers."

The people were not so bad that they could be cruel to the poor slave now. "Live and be free!" they cried. "Live and be free!"

Others cried, "Let the lion go free too! Give both of them their liberty!"

And so Androcles was set free, and the lion was given to him for his own. And they lived together in Rome for many years.

# Little Thumbelina

This story is a shortened version of Hans Christian Andersen's "Thumbling." Like the fable of the Lion and the Mouse, it teaches little children how to have big hearts.

Once upon a time there was a little girl no bigger than her Mother's thumb, and so they called her "Thumbelina."

Thumbelina did not sleep in a little white bed, as you do; her bed was half of a walnut shell. Her Mother covered her with pink rose leaves for blankets when she curled up for a cozy nap. By and by, when Thumbelina had grown large enough to run about wherever she wished to go, she started for a walk one beautiful sunshiny morning. She had not gone very far when she heard something coming hoppity-skip, hoppity-skip behind her. She turned around, and there she saw a great big green Grasshopper.

"How do you do, Thumbelina?" he said. "Wouldn't you like to go for a ride this morning?"

"I should like it very much," said Thumbelina.

"Very well, hop up on my back," said the Grasshopper. So Thumbelina hopped up on his back, and away they went, hoppity-skip, hoppity-skip, through the grass. Thumbelina thought it was the finest ride she had ever had. After a while the Grasshopper stopped and let her get down off his back.

"Thank you, Mr. Grasshopper," said Thumbelina. "It was very good of you to take me for a ride."

"I'm glad you enjoyed it," said the Grasshopper. "You may go again some day. Goodbye." And away he went, hoppity-skip, hoppity-skip, through the grass, while Thumbelina went on her walk.

She walked on and on until she came to a river, and as she stood on the bank, looking down into the shining water, a Fish came swimming up.

"How do you do, Thumbelina?" he said.

"How do you do, Mr. Fish?" said Thumbelina.

"Wouldn't you like to go for a sail this morning?" asked the Fish.

"Yes, indeed," said Thumbelina, "but there is no boat."

"Wait a moment," said the Fish, and he flirted his tail, and darted away through the water. Presently he came swimming back to the bank, and in his mouth he held the stem of a lily leaf.

"Step down on this; it will make a fine boat."

Thumbelina stepped down on the lily leaf and sat carefully in the middle of it. The Fish kept the stem in his mouth, and swam away down the stream. Overhead the birds were singing, along the bank the flowers were blooming, and over the edge of the leaf Thumbelina could see the fishes darting here and there through the water.

So they sailed and sailed down the river. But at last the Fish took her back to the bank again.

"Thank you for the sail, Mr. Fish," Thumbelina said as she stepped off onto the bank. "I never had such a good time in all my life."

"I'm glad you enjoyed it, Thumbelina. Goodbye for today."

The Fish darted away through the water, and Thumbelina turned to go home. Just then Mrs. Mouse came running up.

"How do you do, Thumbelina?" she said. "Won't you come home with me and see my babies?"

"I'd love to," said Thumbelina, and she clapped her hands in glee.

Mrs. Mouse's home was quite a way down under the ground. Thumbelina crept through the long dark passageway to the cozy room in which Mrs. Mouse and her three babies lived. They all ran races up and down the long passageway, and Thumbelina tasted the dried peas which Mrs. Mouse had brought home with her.

"I think I must go home now," Thumbelina said at last. "My Mother will be wondering where I am." So she said goodbye to them all and started off home.

She had not walked very far along the path through the field when she heard something saying "Peep, peep" in a weak, sick little voice. Thumbelina looked, and there close beside her in the grass she saw a little Bird. His eyes were shut, and he looked very sick.

"Why, what's the matter, little Bird?" said Thumbelina.

"Oh, I have a thorn in my foot, and it does hurt so."

"Let me see," said Thumbelina. "Perhaps I can help you."

She looked carefully, and there she saw the thorn sticking in the poor Bird's foot. She took her little fingers and pulled it out, as gently as she could. Then she fetched some clear, cold water and bathed the wounded foot. The Bird felt so much better that he opened his eyes.

"Why, it is Thumbelina!" he said.

"How did you know my name?" said Thumbelina, in surprise.

"That's easy to explain," said the Bird. "My nest is up in a tree, close beside your window. I often hear your Mother calling you. But are you not a long way from home?"

"Yes, I am," said Thumbelina. "I was hurrying home when I found you."

"Well," said the Bird, "if you climb up on my back, I'll take you there, far more quickly than you can run." So Thumbelina climbed up on the Birdie's back.

"Hold on tight," he said, as he spread his wings and flew swiftly up above the treetops.

He went so high that sometimes they skimmed along through the clouds, and so fast that Thumbelina could hardly get her breath; but still she thought it was very wonderful, and she was not a bit afraid. Soon the Bird lit right in the window of Thumbelina's own room. She climbed down off his back, and thanked him for bringing her home. Then she ran away to find her Mother, and tell her all about the wonderful things which had been happening to her that day.

---

## The Legend of the Dipper

*Retold by J. Berg Esenwein and Marietta Stockard*

This story suggests to the child that a kind and compassionate act is often its own reward.

There had been no rain in the land for a very long time. It was so hot and dry that the flowers were withered, the grass was parched and brown, and even the big, strong trees were dying. The water dried up in the creeks and rivers, the wells were dry, the fountains stopped bubbling. The cows, the dogs, the horses, the birds, and all the people were *so* thirsty! Everyone felt uncomfortable and sick.

There was one little girl whose mother grew very ill. "Oh," said the little girl, "if I can only find some water for my mother I'm sure she will be well again. I must find some water."

So she took a tin cup and started out in search of water. By and by she found a tiny little spring away up on a mountainside. It was almost dry. The water dropped, dropped, ever so slowly from under the rock. The little girl held her cup carefully and caught the drops. She waited and waited a long, long time until the cup was full of water. Then she started down the mountain holding the cup very carefully, for she didn't want to spill a single drop.

On the way she passed a poor little dog. He could hardly drag himself along. He was panting for breath and his tongue hung from his mouth because it was so dry and parched.

"Oh, you poor little dog," said the little girl, "you are so thirsty. I can't pass you without giving you a few drops of water. If I give you just a little there will still be enough for my mother."

So the little girl poured some water into her hand and held it down for the little dog. He lapped it up quickly and then he felt so much better that he frisked and barked and seemed almost to say, "Thank you, little girl." And the little girl didn't notice—but her tin dipper had changed into a silver dipper and was just as full of water as it had been before.

She thought about her mother and hurried along as fast as she could go. When she reached home it was late in the afternoon, almost dark. The little girl pushed the door open and hurried up to her mother's room. When she came into the room the old servant who helped the little girl and her mother, and had been working hard all day taking care of the sick woman, came to the door. She was so tired and so thirsty that she couldn't even speak to the little girl.

"Do give her some water," said the mother. "She has worked hard all day and she needs it much more than I do."

So the little girl held the cup to her lips and the old servant drank some of the water. She felt stronger and better right away and she went over to the mother and lifted her up. The little girl didn't notice that the cup had changed into a gold cup and was just as full of water as it was before!

Then she held the cup to her mother's lips and she drank and drank. Oh, she felt so much better! When she had finished there was still some water left in the cup. The little girl was just raising it to her own lips when there came a knock at the door. The servant opened it and there stood a stranger. He was very pale and all covered with dust from traveling. "I am thirsty," he said. "Won't you give me a little water?"

The little girl said, "Why, certainly I will, I am sure that you need it far more than I do. Drink it all."

The stranger smiled and took the dipper in his hand, and as he took it, it changed into a diamond dipper. He turned it upside down and all the water spilled out and sank into the ground. And where it spilled a fountain bubbled up. The cool water flowed and splashed —enough for the people and all the animals in the whole land to have all the water they wanted to drink.

As they watched the water they forgot the stranger, but presently when they looked he was gone. They thought they could see him just vanishing in the sky—and there in the sky, clear and high, shone the diamond dipper. It shines up there yet, and reminds people of the little girl who was kind and unselfish. It is called the Big Dipper.

---

# The Little Match Girl

*Hans Christian Andersen*

To feel another's anguish—this is the essence of compassion. Here is a Hans Christian Andersen masterpiece, a simple, tragic story that stirs pity in every child's heart.

It was dreadfully cold; it was snowing fast, and was almost dark, as evening came on—the last evening of the year. In the cold and the darkness, there went along the street a poor little girl, bareheaded and with naked feet. When she left home she had slippers on, it is true; but they were much too large for her feet—slippers that her mother had used till then, and the poor little girl lost them in running across the street when two carriages were passing terribly fast. When she looked for them, one was not to be found, and a boy seized the other and ran away with it, saying he would use it for a cradle some day, when he had children of his own.

So on the little girl went with her bare feet, that were red and blue with cold. In an old apron that she wore were bundles of matches, and she carried a bundle also in her hand. No one had bought so much as a bunch all the long day, and no one had given her even a penny.

Poor little girl! Shivering with cold and hunger she crept along, a perfect picture of misery.

The snowflakes fell on her long flaxen hair, which hung in pretty curls about her throat; but she thought not of her beauty nor of the cold. Lights gleamed in every window, and there came to her the savory smell of roast goose, for it was New Year's Eve. And it was this of which she thought.

In a corner formed by two houses, one of which projected beyond the other, she sat cowering down. She had drawn under her little feet, but still she grew colder and colder; yet she dared not go home, for she had sold no matches and could not bring a penny of money. Her father would certainly beat her; and, besides, it was cold enough at home, for they had only the house roof above them, and though the largest holes had been stopped with straw and rags, there were left many through which the cold wind could whistle.

And now her little hands were nearly frozen with cold. Alas! a single match might do her good if she might only draw it from the bundle, rub it against the wall, and warm her fingers by it. So at last she drew one out. Whisht! How it blazed and burned! It gave out a warm, bright flame like a little candle, as she held her hands over it. A wonderful little light it was. It really seemed to the little girl as if she sat before a great iron stove with polished brass feet and brass shovel and tongs. So blessedly it burned that the little maiden stretched out her feet to warm them also. How comfortable she was! But lo! the flame went out, the stove vanished, and nothing remained but the little burned match in her hand.

She rubbed another match against the wall. It burned brightly, and where the light fell upon the wall it became transparent like a veil, so that she could see through it into the room. A snow-white cloth was spread upon the table, on which was a beautiful china dinner service, while a roast goose, stuffed with apples and prunes, steamed famously and sent forth a most savory smell. And what was more delightful still, and wonderful, the goose jumped from the dish, with knife and fork still in its breast, and waddled along the floor straight to the little girl.

But the match went out then, and nothing was left to her but the thick, damp wall.

She lighted another match. And now she was under a most beautiful Christmas tree, larger and far more prettily trimmed than the one she had seen through the glass doors at the rich merchant's. Hundreds of wax tapers were burning on the green branches, and gay figures, such as she had seen in shop windows, looked down upon her. The child stretched out her hands to them; then the match went out.

Still the lights of the Christmas tree rose higher and higher. She saw them now as stars in heaven, and one of them fell, forming a long trail of fire.

"Now someone is dying," murmured the child softly; for her grandmother, the only person who had loved her, and who was now dead, had told her that whenever a star falls a soul mounts up to God.

She struck yet another match against the wall, and again it was light; and in the brightness there appeared before her the dear old grandmother, bright and radiant, yet sweet and mild, and happy as she had never looked on earth.

"Oh, Grandmother," cried the child, "take me with you. I know you will go away when the match burns out. You, too, will vanish, like the warm stove, the splendid New Year's feast, the beautiful Christmas tree." And lest her grandmother should disappear, she rubbed the whole bundle of matches against the wall.

And the matches burned with such a brilliant light that it became brighter than noonday. Her grandmother had never looked so grand and beautiful. She took the little girl in her arms, and both flew together, joyously and gloriously, mounting higher and higher, far above the earth; and for them there was neither hunger, nor cold, nor care—they were with God.

But in the corner, at the dawn of day, sat the poor girl, leaning against the wall, with red cheeks and smiling mouth—frozen to death on the last evening of the old year. Stiff and cold she sat, with the matches, one bundle of which was burned.

"She wanted to warm herself, poor little thing," people said. No one imagined what sweet visions she had had, or how gloriously she had gone with her grandmother to enter upon the joys of a new year.

# Beauty and the Beast

*Retold by Clifton Johnson*

This longtime favorite is a story of love growing from compassion. Children are fascinated by the affection between Beauty and the Beast, a kindness made wondrous by their great physical difference. The story is an unforgettable lesson in how appearances can be deceiving, and how character lies beneath the skin. The French fairy tale comes in many versions. This one dates from the turn of the century.

There was once a wealthy merchant who had six children, three sons and three daughters. He loved his children more than he loved his riches and was always trying to make them happy. The three daughters were very handsome, but the youngest was the most attractive of all. While she was little she was called Beauty, and when she grew up she still kept the same name—and she was as good as she was beautiful. She spent much of her time studying, and when not engaged with her books she was busy doing all she could to make her home pleasant for her father. The older sisters were not like Beauty. They were proud of their riches and cared little for study, and they were constantly driving in the parks or attending balls, operas, and plays.

Thus things went along until misfortunes began to overtake the merchant in his business, and one evening he came home and told his family that storms at sea had destroyed his ships, and fire had burned his warehouses. "My riches are gone," said he, "and I have nothing I can call my own but a little farm off in the country. To that little farm we must all go, now, and earn our daily living with our hands."

The daughters wept at the idea of leading such a different life, and the older ones said they would not go, for they had plenty of friends who would invite them to stay in the town. But they were mistaken. Their friends, who were numerous when the family was rich, now kept away and said one to the other, "We are sorry for the merchant and his family, of course. However, we have cares of our own, and we couldn't be expected to help them; and, really, if those two older girls are having their pride humbled it is no more than they deserve. Let them go milk the cows and mind their dairy and see how they like it."

So the family went to live on the little farm in the country, and the merchant and his sons plowed and sowed the fields, and Beauty rose at four o'clock every morning to get breakfast for them. After the breakfast things were out of the way she busied herself about the other housework, and when there was nothing else to do she would sit at her spinning wheel, singing as she spun, or perhaps would take a little time for reading. The work was hard at first, yet when she became used to it she enjoyed it, and her eyes were brighter and her cheeks more rosy than ever before.

Her two sisters did not change their habits so easily, and they were wretched. They were always thinking of the wealth they had lost, and they did not get up till ten o'clock and did very little work after they were up, but spent most of the time sauntering about and complaining.

A year passed and then the merchant received news that one of his ships which he had believed to be lost had come safely into port with a rich cargo. This news nearly turned the heads of the two eldest daughters, who thought that now they could soon leave the little farm and return to the gay city. As soon as their father made ready to go to the port to attend to the unloading and sale of the ship's cargo, they begged him to buy them new gowns and hats and all manner of trinkets.

Then the merchant said, "And what shall I bring you, Beauty?"

"The only thing I wish for is to see you come home safely," she answered.

Her father was pleased, but he thought she ought to tell him of something he might bring her from the town. "Well, dear father," said she, "as you insist, I would like to have you bring me a rose, for I have not seen one since we came here."

The good man now set out on his journey, but when he reached the port he found that a former partner had taken charge of the ship's goods and disposed of them. The man would not turn over the money he had received to the merchant, and the merchant was obliged to sue for it in the courts. But what he recovered barely paid the costs, and at the end of six months of trouble and expense he started for his little farm as poor as when he came.

He traveled day after day until he was within thirty miles of home, and he was thinking of the pleasure he would have in seeing his children again when he lost his way in a great forest through which he had to pass. Night came on cold and rainy, and the poor man grew faint with hunger. But presently he saw bright lights shining through the trees, and he turned his horse toward them and soon came into a long avenue of great oaks. This led to a splendid palace that was lit from top to bottom. Yet when the merchant entered the courtyard no one met him, and when he halooed he received no answer. His horse kept on toward an open stable door, and he dismounted and led the creature inside and hitched it to a manger that was full of hay and oats.

The merchant now sought the castle and went into a large hall where he found a good fire, and a table plentifully set with food, but not a soul did he see. While he stood by the fire drying himself he said, "How fortunate I am to find such shelter, for I should have perished this stormy night out in the forest. But I can't imagine where the people of this house can be, and I hope its master will excuse the liberty I have taken."

He waited for some time and the clock struck eleven. No one came, and then, weak for want of food, he sat down at the table and ate heartily; yet all the while he was fearful that he was trespassing and might be severely dealt with for his presumption. After he had finished eating he felt less timid and he concluded he would look for a chamber. So he left the hall and passed through several splendid rooms till he came to one in which was a comfortable bed, and there he spent the night.

On awaking the following morning he was surprised to find a new suit of clothes laid out for him on a chair by the bedside, marked with his name, and with ten gold pieces in every pocket. His own clothes, which were much the worse for wear and had been wet through by the storm, had disappeared. "Surely," said he, "this palace belongs to some kind fairy who has seen and pitied my distresses."

In the hall where he had supped the night before he found the table prepared for his breakfast, and after he had eaten he went out into a great garden full of beautiful flowers and shrubbery. As he walked along he passed under a bower of roses. "Ah," said he stopping. "I had no money when I left the town to buy the gifts my older daughters wanted, and my mind has been so full of my troubles that I have not thought of the rose for which Beauty asked, until this moment. She shall have one of these." And he reached up and plucked one.

No sooner had he done this than a great beast came suddenly forth from a side path where he had been hidden by a high hedge and stood before the merchant. "This place is mine," said the beast in his deep, gruff voice. "Why do you pick my flowers?"

"Forgive me, my lord," begged the merchant, throwing himself on his knees before the beast. "I did not know I was giving offense. I only wanted to carry a rose to one of my daughters."

"You have daughters, have you?" said the beast. "Now, listen! This palace is lonely and I want one of your daughters to come here and live."

"Oh, sir!" cried the merchant. "Do not ask that."

"Nothing else will appease me," the beast responded. "I promise no harm will be done her. So take the rose you have picked and go at once and tell your daughters what I have said; and in case not one of them will come you must return yourself and be prisoned for the rest of your days in the palace dungeon."

"My lord," replied the merchant, "I shall not let a child of mine suffer for me, and you may as well lock me up in your dungeon now as later."

"No," the beast said, "you go home and consult with your daughters first."

"I am in your power," said the merchant, "and I can only obey you."

Then he went to the stable and mounted his horse and by night he reached home. His children ran out to greet him, but instead of receiving their caresses with pleasure the tears rolled down his cheeks, and he handed the rose to Beauty, saying, "Little do you think how dear that will cost your poor father." And he related all the sad adventures that had befallen him. "Tomorrow," said the merchant in closing, "I shall return to the beast."

"I can't let you do that, dear father," said Beauty. "I am going in your stead."

"Not so, sister," cried her three brothers. "We will seek out the monster and either kill him or die ourselves."

"You could accomplish nothing," declared the merchant, "for he lives in an enchanted palace and has invisible helpers with whom you could not hope to contend successfully."

"How unfortunate it all is!" said the older girls. "What a pity, Beauty, that you did not do as we did and ask for something sensible."

"Well," said Beauty, "who could have guessed that to ask for a rose would cause so much misery? However, the fault is plainly mine, and I shall have to suffer the consequences."

Her father tried to dissuade her from her purpose, but she insisted, and the next morning he mounted his horse and, with Beauty sitting behind him, he started for the beast's palace. They arrived late in the afternoon and rode down the long avenue of oaks and into the silent courtyard to the door of the stable where the horse had been kept before. Then they dismounted, and after the merchant had led the horse into the stable and seen it comfortably housed for the night they went into the palace.

A cheerful fire was blazing in the big hall and the table was daintily spread with most delicious food. They sat down to this repast, but were too sad to eat much and were soon through. Just then the beast came in and addressed the merchant. "Honest man," said he, "I am glad that you could be trusted. I was rude and threatening toward you yesterday, but it seemed necessary. However, in the end, I think you will have nothing to regret. Spend the night here and tomorrow go your way."

"This is my daughter Beauty," said the merchant.

The beast bowed and said, "My lady, I am very grateful to you for coming, and I beg you to remember that I am not what you think me. But I cannot tell you what I really am, for I am under a spell. This spell I hope you will be able to remove."

So saying, the beast withdrew and left the merchant and his daughter sitting by the fire. "What the beast means," said the merchant, "I do not know. But he talks very courteously."

Then they sat long in silence, but at last arose and they each hunted up a chamber and retired to try to sleep.

On the morrow they found breakfast prepared for them in the hall, and after they had eaten, the merchant bade his daughter an affectionate farewell. He went to the stable for his horse. It was all ready for him to mount, and to his surprise the saddlebags were full of gold. "Ah, well!" said he. "Here is wealth once more, but it cannot make up for the loss of my dear daughter."

Beauty watched him ride away. As soon as he was gone she threw herself down on a cushioned window seat and cried till she fell asleep; and while she slept she dreamed she was walking by a brook bordered with trees and lamenting her sad fate, when a young prince, handsomer than any man she had ever seen, came to her and said, "Ah, Beauty, you are not so unfortunate as you suppose. You will have your reward."

She awoke late in the day a good deal refreshed and comforted, and after a little she decided she would walk about and see something of the palace in which she was to live. She found much to admire and presently came to a door on which was written:

BEAUTY'S ROOM

She opened the door and entered a splendidly furnished apartment where there were a multitude of books and pictures, a harpsichord, and many comfortable chairs and couches. She picked up a book that lay on a table, and on the flyleaf she found written in golden letters these words:

"Your wishes and commands shall be obeyed. You are here the queen over everything."

"Alas!" she thought. "My chief wish just at this moment is to see what my poor father is about."

While she was thinking this she perceived some movement in a mirror on the wall in front of her, and when she looked into the mirror she saw her father arriving home and her sisters and brothers meeting him. The vision faded quickly away, but Beauty felt very thankful she had been allowed such a pleasure. "This beast shows a great deal of kindness," said she, glancing about the attractive room. "He must be a far better creature than we have imagined."

She did not see the beast until evening, and then he came and asked if he might sup with her, and she replied that he could. But she would much rather have eaten alone, for she could not help trembling in his presence. As long as they sat at the table, soft, beautiful music was played, though whence it came or who were the musicians she could not discover. The beast talked to Beauty with great politeness and intelligence, yet his gruff voice startled her every time he spoke. When they had nearly finished he said, "I suppose you think my appearance extremely ugly."

"Yes," said Beauty, "for I cannot tell a lie, but I think you are very good."

"You show a most gracious spirit," said the beast, "in not judging me wholly by my uncouth exterior. I will do anything I can to make you happy here."

"You are very kind, Beast," she replied. "Indeed, when I think of your good heart, you no longer seem to me so ugly."

As they rose from the supper table, the beast said, "Beauty, do you think you could ever care enough for me to kiss me?"

She faltered out, "No, Beast," and he turned and left the room sighing so deeply that she pitied him.

In the days and weeks which followed Beauty saw no one save the beast, yet there were invisible servants who did everything possible for her comfort and pleasure. She and the beast always had supper together, and his conversation never failed to be entertaining and agreeable. By degrees she grew accustomed to his shaggy ugliness and learned to mind it less and to think more of his many amiable qualities. The only thing that pained her was that when he was about to leave her at the end of supper he was sure to ask if she thought she could sometime care enough for him to kiss him.

Three months passed, and one day Beauty looked in her mirror and saw a double wedding at her father's cottage. Her sisters were being married to two gentlemen of the region. Not long afterward her mirror showed her that her three brothers had enlisted for soldiers and her father was left alone. A few days more elapsed and she saw that her father was sick. The sight made her weep, and in the evening she told the beast what her mirror had revealed to her and that she wished to go and nurse her father.

"And will you return at the end of a week if you go?" asked the beast.

"Yes," she replied.

"I cannot refuse anything you ask," said he. "I will have a swift horse ready for you at sunrise tomorrow."

The next day at sunrise Beauty found the swift horse saddled for her in the courtyard, and away she went like the wind through the forest toward her father's cottage. When she arrived, the old merchant was so overjoyed at seeing her that his sickness quickly left him and the two spent a most happy week together.

As soon as the seven days were past she returned to the castle of the beast, which she reached late in the afternoon. Supper time came and the food was served as usual, but the beast was absent and Beauty was a good deal alarmed. "Oh, I hope nothing has happened to him," she said. "He was so good and considerate."

After waiting a short time she went to look for the beast. She ran hastily through all the apartments of the palace, but the beast was not there. And then in the twilight she hurried out to the garden, and by the borders of a fountain she found the beast lying as if dead.

"Dear, dear Beast," she cried, dropping on her knees beside him, "what has happened?" And she leaned over and kissed his hairy cheek.

At once a change came over the beast, and on the grass beside the fountain lay a handsome prince. He opened his eyes and said feebly, "My lady, I thank you. A wicked magician had condemned me to assume the form of an ugly beast until some beautiful maiden consented to kiss me. But I think you are the only maiden in the world kindhearted enough to have had affection for me in the ugly form the magician had given me. When you went away to your father I was so lonely I could no longer eat or amuse myself, and I became so weak that today, when I was walking here in the garden, I fell and could not rise."

Then Beauty filled a cup with water from the fountain and lifted him up so that he could drink. That revived him somewhat and with her help he rose to his feet. The enchantment had been removed from the palace as well as from the prince, and the servants were no longer invisible.

"Call for help," said the prince. And when she called, several men instantly came to their aid and carried the prince to the palace. Once there, warmth, food, and happiness went far toward restoring him. The next morning he sent for Beauty's father to come and make his home with them, and not long afterward Beauty and the prince were married and they lived with great joy and contentment in their palace ever after.

## Beautiful

Socrates believed beauty is a thing that "slips in and permeates our souls." That idea lives in this simple little poem, which generations of young Americans memorized from *McGuffey's Second Reader*.

Beautiful faces are they that wear
The light of a pleasant spirit there;
Beautiful hands are they that do
Deeds that are noble, good and true;
Beautiful feet are they that go
Swiftly to lighten another's woe.

# As Rich as Croesus

*Retold by James Baldwin*

This story comes from the Greek historian Herodotus. Croesus (560–546 B.C.), king of Lydia in Asia Minor, was a ruler of proverbial wealth. How Cyrus spared his life is a legendary example of mercy becoming the crown of justice. The story also offers important lessons about money and power's real bearing on happiness.

Some thousands of years ago there lived in Asia a king whose name was Croesus. The country over which he ruled was not very large, but its people were prosperous and famed for their wealth. Croesus himself was said to be the richest man in the world, and so well known is his name that, to this day, it is not uncommon to say of a very wealthy person that he is "as rich as Croesus."

King Croesus had everything that could make him happy—lands and houses and slaves, fine clothing to wear, and beautiful things to look at. He could not think of anything that he needed to make him more comfortable or contented. "I am the happiest man in the world," he said.

It happened one summer that a great man from across the sea was traveling in Asia. The name of this man was Solon, and he was the lawmaker of Athens in Greece. He was noted for his wisdom and, centuries after his death, the highest praise that could be given to a learned man was to say, "He is as wise as Solon."

Solon had heard of Croesus, and so one day he visited him in his beautiful palace. Croesus was now happier and prouder than ever before, for the wisest man in the world was his guest. He led Solon through his palace and showed him the grand rooms, the fine carpets, the soft couches, the rich furniture, the pictures, the books. Then he invited him out to see his gardens and his orchards and his stables, and he showed him thousands of rare and beautiful things that he had collected from all parts of the world.

In the evening as the wisest of men and the richest of men were dining together, the king said to his guest, "Tell me now, O Solon, who do you think is the happiest of all men?" He expected that Solon would say, "Croesus."

The wise man was silent for a minute, and then he said, "I have in mind a poor man who once lived in Athens and whose name was Tellus. He, I doubt not, was the happiest of all men."

This was not the answer that Croesus wanted, but he hid his disappointment and asked, "Why do you think so?"

"Because," answered his guest, "Tellus was an honest man who labored hard for many years to bring up his children and to give them a good education. And when they were grown and able to do for themselves, he joined the Athenian army and gave his life bravely in the defense of his country. Can you think of anyone who is more deserving of happiness?"

"Perhaps not," answered Croesus, half choking with disappointment. "But who do you think ranks next to Tellus in happiness?" He was quite sure now that Solon would say, "Croesus."

"I have in mind," said Solon, "two young men whom I knew in Greece. Their father died when they were mere children, and they were very poor. But they worked manfully to keep the house together and to support their mother, who was in feeble health. Year after year they toiled, nor thought of anything but their mother's comfort. When at length she died, they gave all their love to Athens, their native city, and nobly served her as long as they lived."

Then Croesus was angry. "Why is it," he asked, "that you make me of no account and think that my wealth and power are nothing? Why is it that you place these poor working people above the richest king in the world?"

"O king," said Solon, "no man can say whether you are happy or not until you die. For no man knows what misfortunes may overtake you, or what misery may be yours in place of all this splendor."

Many years after this there arose in Asia a powerful king whose name was Cyrus. At the head of a great army he marched from one country to another, overthrowing many a kingdom and attaching it to his great empire of Babylon. King Croesus with all his wealth was not able to stand against this mighty warrior. He resisted as long as he could. Then his city was taken, his beautiful palace was burned, his orchards and gardens were destroyed, his treasures were carried away, and he himself was made prisoner.

"The stubbornness of this man Croesus," said King Cyrus, "has caused us much trouble and the loss of many good soldiers. Take him and make an example of him for other petty kings who may dare to stand in our way."

Thereupon the soldiers seized Croesus and dragged him to the marketplace, handling him pretty roughly all the time. Then they built up a great pile of dry sticks and timber taken from the ruins of his once beautiful palace. When this was finished they tied the unhappy king in the midst of it, and one ran for a torch to set it on fire.

"Now we shall have a merry blaze," said the savage fellows. "What good can all his wealth do him now?"

As poor Croesus, bruised and bleeding, lay upon the pyre without a friend to soothe his misery, he thought of the words that Solon had spoken to him years before: "No man can say whether you are happy or not until you die," and he moaned, "O Solon! O Solon! Solon!"

It so happened that Cyrus was riding by at that very moment and heard his moans. "What does he say?" he asked of the soldiers.

"He says, 'Solon, Solon, Solon!' " answered one.

Then the king rode nearer and asked Croesus, "Why do you call on the name of Solon?"

Croesus was silent at first. But after Cyrus had repeated his question kindly, he told all about Solon's visit at his palace and what he had said.

The story affected Cyrus deeply. He thought of the words, "No man knows what misfortunes may overtake you, or what misery may be yours in place of all this splendor." And he wondered if sometime he, too, would lose all his power and be helpless in the hands of his enemies.

"After all," said he, "ought not men to be merciful and kind to those who are in distress? I will do to Croesus as I would have others do to me." And he caused Croesus to be given his freedom, and ever afterward treated him as one of his most honored friends.

# The Sin of Omission

*Margaret E. Sangster*

Kindness is not immune to procrastination. We need to guard against "slow compassion" as we tend to our affairs.

It isn't the thing you do, dear,
  It's the thing you leave undone
That gives you a bit of a heartache
  At setting of the sun.
The tender word forgotten,
  The letter you did not write,
The flowers you did not send, dear,
  Are your haunting ghosts at night.

The stone you might have lifted
  Out of a brother's way;
The bit of heartsome counsel
  You were hurried too much to say;
The loving touch of the hand, dear,
  The gentle, winning tone
Which you had no time nor thought for
  With troubles enough of your own.

Those little acts of kindness
  So easily out of mind,
Those chances to be angels
  Which we poor mortals find—
They come in night and silence,
  Each sad, reproachful wraith,
When hope is faint and flagging,
  And a chill has fallen on faith.

For life is all too short, dear,
And sorrow is all too great,
To suffer our slow compassion
That tarries until too late;
And it isn't the thing you do, dear,
It's the thing you leave undone
Which gives you a bit of a heartache
At the setting of the sun.

---

# Moses in the Bulrushes

*Retold by J. Berg Esenwein and Marietta Stockard*

This story, from the book of Exodus, describes one of the most moving acts of compassion in the Bible and all of literature. The decision of the pharaoh's daughter to adopt the baby Moses transcends cultural and class barriers, and ultimately leads to the founding of the Hebrew nation.

The children of Israel lived for many years in the land of Egypt. Year by year, the Israelites grew stronger, richer, and more powerful. At last the Egyptians grew jealous of them.

"These strangers have the best of our land," they complained. "They are growing so many and so powerful that they will soon take the whole land and will rule over us."

At last, King Pharaoh sent out a proclamation that every boy born in the home of a Hebrew should be put to death. He thought that in this cruel way he would stop the growth of these people. The poor mothers wept bitterly, and hid their children from the officers of the king.

Now, about this time, there was born in the home of one of the Hebrews a little boy who was a strong and beautiful child. His mother kept him hidden until he was three months old. Then she grew afraid that the cruel Egyptians might come to her home and find him, so she went down to the river and gathered bulrushes. These she wove into a basket, or ark, and daubed it with mud and pitch, so the water could not come into it; then she took her baby boy and laid him carefully in it. She took the ark and hid it in the rushes on the edge of the river. His little sister stood afar off and kept watch to see what would happen to the child.

By and by, the daughter of Pharaoh and her maidens came down to the river to bathe. As the princess walked along the riverside she saw the ark hidden in the rushes and she sent her maidens to fetch it. She opened the ark of rushes and the child stretched out his arms to her. The princess lifted him from the ark and held him close to her heart. As she looked into his baby face, she was filled with pity and love for the beautiful boy.

"This is one of the Hebrews' children," she said. "Some poor mother has hidden him here. He is a splendid child; I will take him and bring him up as my own son."

Just then the little sister drew near and heard what the princess said. Her heart was filled with joy.

"Shall I go and call a nurse of the Hebrew women that she may nurse the child for thee?"

The princess smiled. "Go," she said.

The girl ran swiftly to her mother and told her all that had happened. Trembling with joy, the mother hurried to the princess, and the child was placed into the arms of his own mother.

"Nurse this child for me and I will give thee thy wage," said the princess. "His name shall be called Moses, because I drew him out of the water."

So, loved and tended by his own mother, Moses grew up in the palace of the king, and he was treated as the son of the princess. He grew to be strong and powerful, but he never turned from his own people, the Hebrews. Long years after, when he had grown wise enough to be a great leader, he took his people out of Egypt, back into their own land.

# The Good Samaritan

*Retold by Jesse Lyman Hurlbut*

Jesus, who taught that we should love our neighbor as we love ourselves, told the parable of the Good Samaritan (Luke 10:29–37) in response to a question: "Who is my neighbor?" To understand the story fully, it is important to know that a "Good Samaritan" would have been a contradictory term for most Jews in Jesus' time because of a long-standing hostility between Jews and Samaritans. The traveler who comes to the wounded man's aid here is the least likely to show sympathy.

Jesus gave the parable or story of "The Good Samaritan." He said, "A certain man was going down the lone road from Jerusalem to Jericho and he fell among robbers, who stripped him of all that he had, and beat him, and then went away, leaving him almost dead. It happened that a certain priest was going down that road, and when he saw the man lying there, he passed by on the other side. And a Levite also, when he came to the place, and saw the man, he, too, went by on the other side. But a certain Samaritan, as he was going down, came where this man was, and as soon as he saw him, he felt a pity for him. He came to the man and dressed his wounds, pouring oil and wine into them. Then he lifted him up and set him on his own beast of burden, and walked beside him to an inn. There he took care of him all night. And the next morning he took out from his purse two shillings, and gave them to the keeper of the inn, and said, 'Take care of him, and if you need to spend more than this, do so. When I come again I will pay it to you.'

"Which one of these three do you think showed himself a neighbor to the man who fell among the robbers?"

The scribe said, "The one who showed mercy on him."

Then Jesus said to him, "Go and do thou likewise."

By this parable Jesus showed that "our neighbor" is the one who needs the help that we can give him, whoever he may be.

# Song of Life

*Charles MacKay*

The Roman statesman Seneca wrote that wherever there is a human being, there is an opportunity for a kindness. No selfless act is insignificant. (Try reading this poem aloud.)

A traveler on a dusty road
  Strewed acorns on the lea;
And one took root and sprouted up,
  And grew into a tree.
Love sought its shade at evening time,
  To breathe its early vows;
And Age was pleased, in heights of noon,
  To bask beneath its boughs.
The dormouse loved its dangling twigs,
  The birds sweet music bore—
It stood a glory in its place,
  A blessing evermore.

A little spring had lost its way
  Amid the grass and fern;
A passing stranger scooped a well
  Where weary men might turn.
He walled it in, and hung with care
  A ladle on the brink;
He thought not of the deed he did,
  But judged that Toil might drink.
He passed again; and lo! the well,
  By summer never dried,
Had cooled ten thousand parched tongues,
  And saved a life beside.

A nameless man, amid the crowd
   That thronged the daily mart,
Let fall a word of hope and love,
   Unstudied from the heart,
A whisper of the tumult thrown,
   A transitory breath,
It raised a brother from the dust,
   It saved a soul from death.
O germ! O fount! O word of love!
   O thought at random cast!
Ye were but little at the first,
   But mighty at the last.

---

## Grandmother's Table

*Adapted from the Brothers Grimm*

It may be that the older we get, the more this story will mean to us. But we should learn it while we are young, for the sake of the generation coming before us.

Once there was a feeble old woman whose husband died and left her all alone, so she went to live with her son and his wife and their own little daughter. Every day the old woman's sight dimmed and her hearing grew worse, and sometimes at dinner her hands trembled so badly the peas rolled off her spoon or the soup ran from her cup. The son and his wife could not help but be annoyed at the way she spilled her meal all over the table, and one day, after she knocked over a glass of milk, they told each other enough was enough.

They set up a small table for her in the corner next to the broom closet and made the old woman eat her meals there. She sat all alone, looking with tear-filled eyes across the room at the others. Sometimes they spoke to her while they ate, but usually it was to scold her for dropping a bowl or a fork.

One evening just before dinner, the little girl was busy playing on the floor with her building blocks, and her father asked her what she was making. "I'm building a little table for you and mother," she smiled, "so you can eat by yourselves in the corner someday when I get big."

Her parents sat staring at her for some time and then suddenly both began to cry. That night they led the old woman back to her place at the big table. From then on she ate with the rest of the family, and her son and his wife never seemed to mind a bit when she spilled something every now and then.

---

# The Angel of the Battlefield

*Joanna Strong and Tom B. Leonard*

Clara Barton (1821–1912) was known as the Angel of the Battlefield for her work among the wounded during the Civil War. As the founder of the American Red Cross, she holds a place among our greatest pioneers of philanthropy.

When the agonizing pain receded a bit, Jack Gibbs was able to think again. "I'll never make it home," he groaned. "Not in one piece, anyway."

He sighed and tried to shift his body to a more comfortable position on the cold, rocky ground. But the movement caused another warm gush, and he knew that if he were to live at all, he must lie still.

"By the time they cart me back to the hospital behind the lines," he thought, "I'll either have bled to death or I'll be in such rotten shape they'll have to take my leg off. And what kind of a husband would I be for Sue? A man with one leg!"

A black cloud swept over him, and he lay unconscious.

When he opened his eyes again, Jack was sure he had died and gone to heaven. A woman was bending over him. That just couldn't happen on a battlefield of the Civil War. No woman ever came on the field. No woman would want to! *No woman would be allowed to!*

But there *was* a woman on the battlefield. Her name was Clara Barton.

With the help of two soldiers, she lifted Jack onto a cot that the men removed from a horse-drawn van. She took some bandages out of her kit and bound up his leg. Then she gave him a pain-killing draft. Jack weakly sipped it down, and the men put him in a crude-looking ambulance.

Clara Barton had been doing this kind of work all day long. She had succored hundreds of the wounded, allayed their fears, relieved their pain, cleansed their wounds.

Ever since the dreadful war had begun, Clara Barton had been worried about the men fighting at the front. She knew that wounded men were left lying on the field until the battle was over. She knew that only then were they collected and taken to hospitals—hospitals far behind the lines. She knew that if they survived this delay, the rough jolting of the wagons might well cause their unbound wounds to open. She knew that they often bled to death before they reached the hospital.

Heartsick at this state of affairs, she determined to bring aid to the men *right on the field.* First, she procured a van. Then she equipped it with medicine and first-aid supplies. And then she went to see the general.

She was a slender little woman. To the commanding officer, she didn't look exactly like battlefield material. In fact, her pet idea horrified him.

"Miss Barton," he said, "what you are asking is absolutely impossible."

"But General," she insisted, "Why is it impossible? I myself will drive the van and give the soldiers what relief I can."

The general shook his head. "The battlefield is no place for a woman. You couldn't stand the rough life. Anyway, we are now doing everything that can be done for our soldiers. No one could do more."

*"I* could," Clara Barton declared. And then, as if she had just entered the room for the first time, she described all over again to the general her plans for first aid on the field.

This interview was repeated again and again, but constant refusal did not deter her. Finally, the commanding officer gave in. Clara Barton received a pass that would let her though the lines.

During the entire course of the Civil War, she ministered to all she could reach. She labored unceasingly. Once she worked with scant rest for five days and nights in a row. Her name became a byword in the army, spoken of with love and gratitude.

As the government saw what she was actually accomplishing, it gradually afforded her more and more cooperation. The army supplied more vans and more men to drive them. More medical supplies were made available. But it was nevertheless an uphill battle all the way for the courageous Miss Barton.

When the war ended, Clara Barton might have been expected to take a well-earned rest. Instead, she was haunted by the thought of the agony of those unfortunate folks who did not know for sure what had happened to their husbands, their fathers, their brothers. She determined to learn the fates of these missing soldiers, and to send the information to their families. She worked at this task for a long time.

Now she knew war at first-hand. She knew what it did to men on the battlefield, and she knew what it did to the families they left behind. When she heard that there was a man in Switzerland, by the name of Jean Henry Dunant, who had a plan to help soldiers in wartime, she immediately went to Switzerland to lend her aid. Dunant formed an organization called the Red Cross. Workers of this organization were to wear a red cross on a white background so that they could easily be identified. They were to be allowed free access to battlefields, so that they might help *all* soldiers, no matter what their nationality, race, or religion.

Here was an idea that fired Clara Barton. She came back to America and convinced the United States Government that it should join with the twenty-two other member nations to give money and supplies to an International Red Cross, organized to help soldiers in wartime.

But Clara Barton added another idea to this great Red Cross plan. It was called *"The American Amendment."*

"There are many other calamities that befall mankind," she said. "Earthquakes, floods, forest fires, epidemics, tornadoes. These disasters strike suddenly, killing and wounding many, leaving others homeless and starving. The Red Cross should stretch out a hand of help to all such victims, no matter where such disasters befall."

Today, the International Red Cross brings succor to millions of people all over the world. This was Clara Barton's wonderful idea. Her great courage, great love, and great charity will ever be revered.

# If I Can Stop One Heart from Breaking

*Emily Dickinson*

Emily Dickinson (1830–1886) reminds us that acts of compassion add meaning to our lives.

If I can stop one heart from breaking,
I shall not live in vain;
If I can ease one life the aching,
Or cool one pain,
Or help one fainting robin
Unto his nest again,
I shall not live in vain.

---

# The Wisdom of Solomon

*Retold by Jesse Lyman Hurlbut*

This is one of the most famous stories of the proverbial wisdom of Solomon, who reigned in Israel for forty years during the tenth century B.C. Solomon's decision at first seems cruel, but in fact turns out to be the brilliant strategy of a leader who must be not only kind but just in a difficult situation. He is wise enough to "smoke out" the guilty party by relying on the power of true compassion. The story is from 1 Kings 3:16–28 in the Bible.

Two women came before King Solomon with two little babies, one dead and the other living. Each of the two women claimed the living child as her own, and said that the dead child belonged to the other woman. One of the women said, "O my lord, we two women were sleeping with our children in one bed. And this woman in her sleep lay upon her child, and it died. Then she placed her dead child beside me while I was asleep, and took my child. In the morning I saw that it was not my child, but she says it is mine, and the living child is hers. Now, O king, command this woman to give me my own child."

Then the other woman said, "That is not true. The dead baby is her own, and the living one is mine, which she is trying to take from me."

The young king listened to both women. Then he said, "Bring me a sword."

They brought a sword, and then Solomon said, "Take this sword, and cut the living child in two, and give half of it to each one."

Then one of the women cried out, and said, "O my lord, do not kill my child! Let the other woman have it, but let the child live!"

But the other woman said, "No, cut the child in two, and divide it between us!"

Then Solomon said, "Give the living child to the woman who would not have it slain, for she is its mother."

And all the people wondered at the wisdom of one so young, and they saw that God had given him understanding.

---

# A Legend of the Northland

*Phoebe Cary*

In which we learn what happens to us when we cannot bring ourselves to share with those in need.

Away, away in the Northland,
  Where the hours of the day are few,
And the nights are so long in winter
  That they cannot sleep them through;

Where they harness the swift reindeer
  To the sledges, when it snows;
And the children look like bears' cubs
  In their funny, furry clothes;

They tell them a curious story—
  I don't believe 'tis true;
And yet you may learn a lesson
  If I tell the tale to you.

Once, when the good Saint Peter
  Lived in the world below,
And walked about it, preaching,
  Just as he did, you know,

He came to the door of a cottage,
  In traveling round the earth,
Where a little woman was making cakes,
  And baking them on the hearth;

And being faint with fasting,
  For the day was almost done,
He asked her, from her store of cakes,
  To give him a single one.

So she made a very little cake,
  But as it baking lay,
She looked at it, and thought it seemed
  Too large to give away.

Therefore she kneaded another,
  And still a smaller one;
But it looked, when she turned it over,
  As large as the first had done.

Then she took a tiny scrap of dough,
  And rolled and rolled it flat;
And baked it thin as a wafer—
  But she couldn't part with that.

For she said, "My cakes that seem too small
  When I eat them of myself,
Are yet too large to give away."
  So she put them on the shelf.

Then good Saint Peter grew angry,
  For he was hungry and faint;
And surely such a woman
  Was enough to provoke a saint.

And he said, "You are far too selfish
  To dwell in a human form,
To have both food and shelter,
  And fire to keep you warm.

"Now, you shall build as the birds do,
  And shall get your scanty food
By boring, and boring, and boring,
  All day in the hard, dry wood."

Then up she went through the chimney,
  Never speaking a word,
And out of the top flew a woodpecker,
  For she was changed to a bird.

She had a scarlet cap on her head,
  And that was left the same,
But all the rest of her clothes were burned
  Black as a coal in the flame.

And every country schoolboy
  Has seen her in the wood,
Where she lives in the trees till this very day,
  Boring and boring for food.

And this is the lesson she teaches:
  Live not for yourself alone,
Lest the needs you will not pity
  Shall one day be your own.

Give plenty of what is given to you,
  Listen to pity's call;
Don't think the little you give is great,
  And the much you get is small.

Now, my little boy, remember that,
  And try to be kind and good,
When you see the woodpecker's sooty dress,
  And see her scarlet hood.

You mayn't be changed to a bird though you live
  As selfishly as you can;
But you will be changed to a smaller thing—
  A mean and selfish man.

---

# The Quality of Mercy

*William Shakespeare*

In perhaps the most famous lines from *The Merchant of Venice,* Portia, the heiress of Belmont, argues that mercy is a divine attribute, and that we make ourselves closer to God when we exercise it. The scene is a Venetian courtroom. Portia, disguised as a lawyer, is trying to convince the moneylender Shylock to give up his legal claim to a pound of Antonio's flesh.

The quality of mercy is not strain'd.
It droppeth as the gentle rain from heaven
Upon the place beneath. It is twice blest:
It blesseth him that gives, and him that takes.
'Tis mightiest in the mightiest; it becomes
The throned monarch better than his crown.
His scepter shows the force of temporal power,
The attribute to awe and majesty,
Wherein doth sit the dread and fear of kings;
But mercy is above this sceptered sway;

It is enthroned in the hearts of kings;
It is an attribute to God himself;
And earthly power doth then show likest God's
When mercy seasons justice.

---

# Echo and Narcissus

*Retold by Thomas Bulfinch*

In Greek mythology, Narcissus was a beautiful youth, the son of the river god Cephisus and the nymph Leiriope. His vanity and heartlessness have made his name forever synonymous with intense self-infatuation. Self-absorption often makes compassion impossible, and vice versa. The retelling of his story is from Thomas Bulfinch's classic *Age of Fable*.

Echo was a beautiful nymph, fond of the woods and hills, where she devoted herself to woodland sports. She was a favorite of Diana, and attended her in the chase. But Echo had one failing; she was fond of talking, and whether in chat or argument, would have the last word. One day Juno was seeking her husband, who, she had reason to fear, was amusing himself among the nymphs. Echo by her talk contrived to detain the goddess till the nymphs made their escape. When Juno discovered it, she passed sentence upon Echo in these words: "You shall forfeit the use of that tongue with which you have cheated me, except for that one purpose you are so fond of —*reply*. You shall still have the last word, but no power to speak first."

This nymph saw Narcissus, a beautiful youth, as he pursued the chase upon the mountains. She loved him and followed his footsteps. O how she longed to address him in the softest accents, and win him to converse! But it was not in her power. She waited with impatience for him to speak first, and had her answer ready. One day the youth, being separated from his companions, shouted aloud, "Who's here?" Echo replied, "Here." Narcissus looked around, but seeing no one, called out, "Come." Echo answered, "Come." As no one came,

Narcissus called again, "Why do you shun me?" Echo asked the same question. "Let us join one another," said the youth. The maid answered with all her heart in the same words, and hastened to the spot, ready to throw her arms about his neck. He started back, exclaiming, "Hands off! I would rather die than you should have me!" "Have me," said she; but it was all in vain. He left her, and she went to hide her blushes in the recesses of the woods. From that time forth she lived in caves and among mountain cliffs. Her form faded with grief, till at last all her flesh shrank away. Her bones were changed into rocks and there was nothing left of her but her voice. With that she is still ready to reply to anyone who calls her, and keeps up her old habit of having the last word.

Narcissus's cruelty in this case was not the only instance. He shunned all the rest of the nymphs, as he had done poor Echo. One day a maiden who had in vain endeavored to attract him uttered a prayer that he might sometime or other feel what it was to love and meet no return of affection. The avenging goddess heard and granted the prayer.

There was a clear fountain, with water like silver, to which the shepherds never drove their flocks, nor the mountain goats resorted, nor any of the beasts of the forests; neither was it defaced with fallen leaves or branches; but the grass grew fresh around it, and the rocks sheltered it from the sun. Hither came one day the youth, fatigued with hunting, heated and thirsty. He stooped down to drink, and saw his own image in the water; he thought it was some beautiful water spirit living in the fountain. He stood gazing with admiration at those bright eyes, those locks curled like the locks of Bacchus or Apollo, the rounded cheeks, the ivory neck, the parted lips, and the glow of health and exercise over all. He fell in love with himself. He brought his lips near to take a kiss; he plunged his arms in to embrace the beloved object. It fled at the touch, but returned again after a moment and renewed the fascination. He could not tear himself away. He lost all thought of food or rest, while he hovered over the brink of the fountain gazing upon his own image. He talked with the supposed spirit. "Why, beautiful being, do you shun me? Surely my face is not one to repel you. The nymphs love me, and you yourself look not indifferent upon me. When I stretch forth my arms you do the same; and you smile upon me and answer my beckonings with the like." His tears fell into the water and disturbed the image. As he saw it depart, he exclaimed, "Stay, I entreat you! Let me at least gaze upon you, if I may not touch you." With this, and much more of the same kind, he cherished the flame that consumed him, so that by degrees he lost his color, his vigor, and the beauty which formerly had so charmed the nymph Echo. She kept near him, however, and when he exclaimed, "Alas! Alas!" she answered him with the same words. He pined away and died; and when his shade passed the Stygian river, it leaned over the boat to catch a look of itself in the waters. The nymphs mourned for him, especially the water nymphs; and when they smote their breasts Echo smote hers also. They prepared a funeral pyre and would have burned the body, but it was nowhere to be found; but in its place a flower, purple within, and surrounded with white leaves, which bears the name and preserves the memory of Narcissus.

---

## Marley's Ghost

*Charles Dickens*

Every young person embarking on a career should take along the remembrance of Marley's Ghost, who cautions us that mankind is our business. Charles Dickens (1812–1870) wrote *A Christmas Carol,* from which this famous scene is taken, in 1843. We see it in many versions on television each year, but the tale's spirit is best known by reading it.

Scrooge fell upon his knees, and clasped his hands before his face.

"Mercy!" he said. "Dreadful apparition, why do you trouble me?"

"Man of the worldly mind!" replied the Ghost. "Do you believe in me or not?"

"I do," said Scrooge. "I must. But why do spirits walk the earth, and why do they come to me?"

"It is required of every man," the Ghost returned, "that the spirit within him should walk abroad among his fellow men, and travel far and wide; and, if that spirit goes not forth in life, it is condemned to do so after death. It is doomed to wander through the world—oh, woe is me!—and witness what it cannot share, but might have shared on earth, and turned to happiness!"

Again the specter raised a cry, and shook its chain and wrung its shadowy hands.

"You are fettered," said Scrooge, trembling. "Tell me why?"

"I wear the chain I forged in life," replied the Ghost. "I made it link by link, and yard by yard; I girded it on of my own free will, and of my own free will I wore it. Is its pattern strange to *you?*"

Scrooge trembled more and more.

"Or would you know," pursued the Ghost, "the weight and length of the strong coil you bear yourself? It was full as heavy and as long as this seven Christmas Eves ago. You have labored on it since. It is a ponderous chain!"

Scrooge glanced about him on the floor, in the expectation of finding himself surrounded by some fifty or sixty fathoms of iron cable; but he could see nothing.

"Jacob!" he said imploringly. "Old Jacob Marley, tell me more! Speak comfort to me, Jacob!"

"I have none to give," the Ghost replied. "It comes from other regions, Ebenezer Scrooge, and it is conveyed by other ministers, to other kinds of men. Nor can I tell you what I would. A very little more is all permitted to me. I cannot rest, I cannot stay,. I cannot linger anywhere. My spirit never walked beyond our counting house —mark me—in life my spirit never roved beyond the narrow limits of our money-changing hole; and weary journeys lie before me!"

It was a habit with Scrooge, whenever he became thoughtful, to put his hands in his breeches pockets. Pondering on what the Ghost had said, he did so now, but without lifting up his eyes, or getting off his knees.

"You must have been very slow about it, Jacob," Scrooge observed in a businesslike manner, though with humility and deference.

"Slow!" the Ghost repeated.

"Seven years dead," mused Scrooge. "And traveling all the time?"

"The whole time," said the Ghost. "No rest, no peace. Incessant torture of remorse."

"You travel fast?" said Scrooge.

"On the wings of the wind," replied the Ghost.

"You might have got over a great quantity of ground in seven years," said Scrooge.

The Ghost, on hearing this, set up another cry, and clanked its chain so hideously in the dead silence of the night, that the Ward would have been justified in indicting it for a nuisance.

"Oh! Captive, bound, and double-ironed," cried the phantom, "not to know that ages of incessant labor, by immortal creatures, for this earth must pass into eternity before the good of which it is susceptible is all developed! Not to know that any Christian spirit working kindly in its little sphere, whatever it may be, will find its mortal life too short for its vast means of usefulness! Not to know that no space of regret can make amends for one life's opportunities misused! Yet such was I! Oh, such was I!"

"But you were always a good man of business, Jacob," faltered Scrooge, who now began to apply this to himself.

"Business!" cried the Ghost, wringing its hands again. "Mankind was my business. The common welfare was my business; charity, mercy, forbearance, and benevolence were, all, my business. The dealings of my trade were but a drop of water in the comprehensive ocean of my business!"

It held up its chain at arm's length, as if that were the cause of all its unavailing grief, and flung it heavily upon the ground again.

"At this time of the rolling year," the specter said, "I suffer most. Why did I walk through crowds of fellow beings with my eyes turned down, and never raise them to that blessed Star which led the Wise Men to a poor abode? Were there no poor homes to which its light would have conducted *me?*"

Scrooge was very much dismayed to hear the specter going on at this rate, and began to quake exceedingly.

"Hear me!" cried the Ghost. "My time is nearly gone."

"I will," said Scrooge. "But don't be hard upon me! Don't be flowery, Jacob! Pray!"

"How it is that I appear before you in a shape that you can see, I may not tell. I have sat invisible beside you many and many a day."

It was not an agreeable idea. Scrooge shivered, and wiped the perspiration from his brow.

"That is no light part of my penance," pursued the Ghost. "I am here tonight to warn you that you have yet a chance and hope of escaping my fate. A chance and hope of my procuring, Ebenezer."

"You were always a good friend to me," said Scrooge. "Thankee!"

"You will be haunted," resumed the Ghost, "by Three Spirits."

Scrooge's countenance fell almost as low as the Ghost's had done.

"Is that the chance and hope you mentioned, Jacob?" he demanded in a faltering voice.

"It is."

"I—I think I'd rather not," said Scrooge.

"Without their visits," said the Ghost, "you cannot hope to shun the path I tread. Expect the first tomorrow when the bell tolls one."

"Couldn't I take 'em all at once, and have it over, Jacob?" hinted Scrooge.

"Expect the second on the next night at the same hour. The third, upon the next night when the last stroke of twelve has ceased to vibrate. Look to see me no more; and look that, for your own sake, you remember what has passed between us!"

When it had said these words, the specter took its wrapper from the table, and bound it around its head as before. Scrooge knew this by the smart sound its teeth made when the jaws were brought together by the bandage. He ventured to raise his eyes again, and found his supernatural visitor confronting him in an erect attitude, with its chain wound over and about its arm.

The apparition walked backward from him; and, at every step it took, the window raised itself a little, so that, when the specter reached it, it was wide open. It beckoned Scrooge to approach, which he did. When they were within two paces of each other, Marley's Ghost held up its hand, warning him to come no nearer. Scrooge stopped.

Not so much in obedience as in surprise and fear; for, on the raising of the hand, he became sensible of confused noises in the air; incoherent sounds of lamentation and regret; wailings inexpressibly sorrowful and self-accusatory. The specter, after listening for a moment, joined in the mournful dirge; and floated out upon the bleak, dark night.

Scrooge followed to the window, desperate in his curiosity. He looked out.

The air was filled with phantoms, wandering hither and thither in restless haste, and moaning as they went. Every one of them wore chains like Marley's Ghost; some few (they might be guilty governments) were linked together; none were free. Many had been personally known to Scrooge in their lives. He had been quite familiar with one old ghost in a white waistcoat, with a monstrous iron safe attached to its ankle, who cried piteously at being unable to assist a wretched woman with an infant, whom it saw below upon a doorstep. The misery with them all was clearly, that they sought to interfere, for good, in human matters, and had lost the power forever.

Whether these creatures faded into mist, or mist enshrouded them, he could not tell. But they and their spirit voices faded together; and the night became as it had been when he walked home.

Scrooge closed the window, and examined the door by which the Ghost had entered. It was double-locked, as he had locked it with his own hands, and the bolts were undisturbed. He tried to say "Humbug!" but stopped at the first syllable. And being, from the emotions he had undergone, or the fatigues of the day, or his glimpse of the Invisible World, or the dull conversation of the Ghost, or the lateness of the hour, much in need of repose, went straight to bed without undressing, and fell asleep on the instant.

---

## Where Love Is, God Is

*Leo Tolstoy*

This is a reworking of an old Christian folk tale. Its charm lies in its simplicity, and it remains a favorite Tolstoy selection despite its moralism.

In a little town in Russia there lived a cobbler, Martin Avedéitch by name. He had a tiny room in a basement, the one window of which looked out on to the street. Through it one could see only the feet of those who passed by, but Martin recognized the people by their boots. He had lived long in the place and had many acquaintances. There was hardly a pair of boots in the neighborhood that had not been once or twice through his hands, so he often saw his own handiwork through the window. Some he had re-soled, some patched, some stitched up, and to some he had even put fresh uppers. He had plenty to do, for he worked well, used good material, did not charge too much, and could be relied on. If he could do a job by the day required, he undertook it; if not, he told the truth and gave no false promises. So he was well known and never short of work.

Martin had always been a good man, but in his old age he began to think more about his soul and to draw nearer to God.

From that time Martin's whole life changed. His life became peaceful and joyful. He sat down to his task in the morning, and when he had finished his day's work he took the lamp down from the wall, stood it on the table, fetched his Bible from the shelf, opened it, and sat down to read. The more he read the better he understood, and the clearer and happier he felt in his mind.

It happened once that Martin sat up late, absorbed in his book. He was reading Luke's Gospel, and in the sixth chapter he came upon the verses:

> To him that smiteth thee on the one cheek offer also the other; and from him that taketh away thy cloak withhold not thy coat also. Give to every man that asketh thee; and of him that taketh away thy goods ask them not again. And as ye would that men should do to you, do ye also to them likewise.

He thought about this, and was about to go to bed, but was loath to leave his book. So he went on reading the seventh chapter—about the centurion, the widow's son, and the answer to John's disciples—and he came to the part where a rich Pharisee invited the Lord to his house. And he read how the woman who was a sinner anointed his feet and washed them with her tears, and how he justified her. Coming to the forty-fourth verse, he read:

> And turning to the woman, he said unto Simon, "Seest thou this woman? I entered into thine house, thou gavest me no water for my feet, but she hath wetted my feet with her tears, and wiped them with her hair. Thou gavest me no kiss, but she, since the time I came in, hath not ceased to kiss my feet. My head with oil thou didst not anoint, but she hath anointed my feet with ointment."

He read these verses and thought: "He gave no water for his feet, gave no kiss, his head with oil he did not anoint. . . ." And Martin took off his spectacles once more, laid them on his book, and pondered.

"He must have been like me, that Pharisee. He too thought only of himself—how to get a cup of tea, how to keep warm and comfortable, never a thought of his guest. He took care of himself, but for his guest he cared nothing at all. Yet who was the guest? The Lord himself! If he came to me, should I behave like that?"

Then Martin laid his head upon both his arms and, before he was aware of it, he fell asleep.

"Martin!" He suddenly heard a voice, as if someone had breathed the word above his ear.

He started from his sleep. "Who's there?" he asked.

He turned around and looked at the door; no one was there. He called again. Then he heard quite distinctly: "Martin, Martin! Look out into the street tomorrow, for I shall come."

Martin roused himself, rose from his chair and rubbed his eyes, but did not know whether he had heard these words in a dream or awake. He put out the lamp and lay down to sleep.

The next morning he rose before daylight, and after saying his prayers he lit the fire and prepared his cabbage soup and buckwheat porridge. Then he lit the samovar, put on his apron, and sat down by the window to his work. He looked out into the street more than he worked, and whenever anyone passed in unfamiliar boots he would stoop and look up, so as to see not only the feet but the face of the passerby as well. A house-porter passed in new felt boots, then a water-carrier. Presently an old soldier of Nicholas's reign came near the window, spade in hand. Martin knew him by his boots, which were shabby old felt once, galoshed with leather. The old man was called Stepánitch. A neighboring tradesman kept him in his house for charity, and his duty was to help the house-porter. He began to clear away the snow before Martin's window. Martin glanced at him and then went on with his work.

After he had made a dozen stitches he felt drawn to look out of the window again. He saw that Stepánitch had leaned his spade against the wall, and was either resting himself or trying to get warm. The man was old and broken down, and had evidently not enough strength even to clear away the snow.

"What if I called him in and gave him some tea?" thought Martin. "The samovar is just on the boil."

He stuck his awl in its place, and rose, and putting the samovar on the table, made tea. Then he tapped the window with his fingers. Stepánitch turned and came to the window. Martin beckoned to him to come in, and went himself to open the door.

"Come in," he said, "and warm yourself a bit. I'm sure you must be cold."

"May God bless you!" Stepánitch answered. "My bones do

ache, to be sure." He came in, first shaking off the snow, and lest he should leave marks on the floor he began wiping his feet. But as he did so he tottered and nearly fell.

"Don't trouble to wipe your feet," said Martin. "I'll wipe up the floor—it's all in the day's work. Come, friend, sit down and have some tea."

Filling two tumblers, he passed one to his visitor, and pouring his own tea out into the saucer, began to blow on it.

Stepánitch emptied his glass and, turning it upside down, put the remains of his piece of sugar on the top. He began to express his thanks, but it was plain that he would be glad of some more.

"Have another glass," said Martin, refilling the visitor's tumbler and his own. But while he drank his tea Martin kept looking out into the street.

"Are you expecting anyone?" asked the visitor.

"Am I expecting anyone? Well, now, I'm ashamed to tell you. It isn't that I really expect anyone, but I heard something last night which I can't get out of my mind. Whether it was a vision, or only a fancy, I can't tell. You see, friend, last night I was reading the Gospel, about Christ the Lord, how he suffered, and how he walked on earth. You have heard tell of it, I dare say."

"I have heard tell of it," answered Stepánitch. "But I'm an ignorant man and not able to read."

"Well, you see, I was reading how he walked on earth. I came to that part, you know, where he went to a Pharisee who did not receive him well. Well, friend, as I read about it, I thought how that man did not receive Christ the Lord with proper honor. Suppose such a thing could happen to such a man as myself, I thought, what would I not do to receive him! But that man gave him no reception at all. Well, friend, as I was thinking of this, I began to doze, and as I dozed I heard someone call me by name. I got up, and thought I heard someone whispering, 'Expect me. I will come tomorrow.' This happened twice over. And to tell you the truth, it sank so into my mind that, though I am ashamed of it myself, I keep on expecting him, the dear Lord!"

Stepánitch shook his head in silence, finished his tumbler, and laid it on its side, but Martin stood it up again and refilled it for him.

"Thank you, Martin Avedéitch," he said. "You have given me food and comfort both for soul and body."

"You're very welcome. Come again another time. I am glad to have a guest," said Martin.

Stepánitch went away, and Martin poured out the last of the tea and drank it up. Then he put away the tea things and sat down to his work, stitching the back seam of a boot. And as he stitched he kept looking out of the window, and thinking about what he had read in the Bible. And his head was full of Christ's sayings.

Two soldiers went by: one in Government boots, the other in boots of his own; then the master of a neighboring house, in shining galoshes; then a baker carrying a basket. All these passed on. Then a woman came up in worsted stockings and peasant-made shoes. She passed the window, but stopped by the wall. Martin glanced up at her through the window, and saw that she was a stranger, poorly dressed, and with a baby in her arms. She stopped by the wall with her back to the wind, trying to wrap the baby up though she had hardly anything to wrap it in. The woman had only summer clothes on, and even they were shabby and worn. Through the window Martin heard the baby crying, and the woman trying to soothe it, but unable to do so. Martin rose, and going out of the door and up the steps he called to her. "My dear, I say, my dear!"

The woman heard, and turned around.

"Why do you stand out there with the baby in the cold? Come inside. You can wrap him up better in a warm place. Come this way!"

The woman was surprised to see an old man in an apron, with spectacles on his nose, calling to her, but she followed him in.

They went down the steps, entered the little room, and the old man led her to the bed.

"There, sit down, my dear, near the stove. Warm yourself, and feed the baby."

"Haven't any milk. I have eaten nothing myself since early morning," said the woman, but still she took the baby to her breast.

Martin shook his head. He brought out a basin and some bread. Then he opened the oven door and poured some cabbage soup into the basin. He took out the porridge pot also, but the porridge was not yet ready, so he spread a cloth on the table and served only the soup and bread.

"Sit down and eat, my dear, and I'll mind the baby. Why, bless me, I've had children of my own; I know how to manage them."

The woman crossed herself, and sitting down at the table began to eat, while Martin put the baby on the bed and sat down by it.

Martin sighed. "Haven't you any warmer clothing?" he asked.

"How could I get warm clothing?" said she. "Why, I pawned my last shawl for sixpence yesterday."

Then the woman came and took the child, and Martin got up.

He went and looked among some things that were hanging on the wall, and brought back an old cloak.

"Here," he said, "though it's a worn-out old thing, it will do to wrap him up in."

The woman looked at the cloak, then at the old man, and taking it, burst into tears. Martin turned away, and groping under the bed brought out a small trunk. He fumbled about in it, and again sat down opposite the woman. And the woman said, "The Lord bless you, friend."

"Take this for Christ's sake," said Martin, and gave her sixpence to get her shawl out of pawn. The woman crossed herself, and Martin did the same, and then he saw her out.

After a while Martin saw an apple-woman stop just in front of his window. On her back she had a sack full of chips, which she was taking home. No doubt she had gathered them at someplace where building was going on.

The sack evidently hurt her, and she wanted to shift it from one shoulder to the other, so she put it down on the footpath and, placing her basket on a post, began to shake down the chips in the sack. While she was doing this, a boy in a tattered cap ran up, snatched an apple out of the basket, and tried to slip away. But the old woman noticed it, and turning, caught the boy by his sleeve. He began to struggle, trying to free himself, but the old woman held on with both hands, knocked his cap off his head, and seized hold of his hair. The boy screamed and the old woman scolded. Martin dropped his awl, not waiting to stick it in its place, and rushed out of the door. Stumbling up the steps and dropping his spectacles in his hurry, he ran out into the street. The old woman was pulling the boy's hair and scolding him, and threatening to take him to the police. The lad was struggling and protesting, saying, "I did not take it. What are you beating me for? Let me go!"

Martin separated them. He took the boy by the hand and said, "Let him go, Granny. Forgive him for Christ's sake."

"I'll pay him out, so that he won't forget it for a year! I'll take the rascal to the police!"

Martin began entreating the old woman.

"Let him go, Granny. He won't do it again."

The old woman let go, and the boy wished to run away, but Martin stopped him.

"Ask the Granny's forgiveness!" said he. "And don't do it another time. I saw you take the apple."

The boy began to cry and to beg pardon.

"That's right. And now here's an apple for you," and Martin took an apple from the basket and gave it to the boy, saying, "I will pay you, Granny."

"You will spoil them that way, the young rascals," said the old woman. "He ought to be whipped so that he should remember it for a week."

"Oh, Granny, Granny," said Martin, "that's our way—but it's not God's way. If he should be whipped for stealing an apple, what should be done to us for our sins?"

The old woman was silent.

And Martin told her the parable of the lord who forgave his servant a large debt, and how the servant went out and seized his debtor by the throat. The old woman listened to it all, and the boy, too, stood by and listened.

"God bids us forgive," said Martin, "or else we shall not be forgiven. Forgive everyone, and a thoughtless youngster most of all."

The old woman wagged her head and sighed.

"It's true enough," said she, "but they are getting terribly spoiled."

"Then we old ones must show them better ways," Martin replied.

"That's just what I say," said the old woman. "I have had seven of them myself, and only one daughter is left." And the old woman began to tell how and where she was living with her daughter, and how many grandchildren she had. "There, now," she said, "I have but little strength left, yet I work hard for the sake of my grandchildren; and nice children they are, too. No one comes out to meet me but the children. Little Annie, now, won't leave me for anyone. It's 'Grandmother, dear grandmother, darling grandmother.' " And the old woman completely softened at the thought.

"Of course, it was only his childishness," said she, referring to the boy.

As the old woman was about to hoist her sack on her back, the lad sprang forward to her, saying, "Let me carry it for you, Granny. I'm going that way."

The old woman nodded her head, and put the sack on the boy's back, and they went down the street together, the old woman quite forgetting to ask Martin to pay for the apple. Martin stood and watched them as they went along talking to each other.

When they were out of sight Martin went back to the house. Having found his spectacles unbroken on the steps, he picked up his awl and sat down again to work. He worked a little, but soon could not see to pass the bristle through the holes in the leather, and presently, he noticed the lamplighter passing on his way to light the street lamps.

"Seems it's time to light up," thought he. So he trimmed his lamp, hung it up, and sat down again to work. He finished off one boot and, turning it about, examined it. It was all right. Then he gathered his tools together, swept up the cuttings, put away the bristles and the thread and the awls, and, taking down the lamp, placed it on the table. Then he took the Gospels from the shelf. He meant to open them at the place he had marked the day before with a bit of morocco, but the book opened at another place. As Martin opened it, his yesterday's dream came back to his mind, and no sooner had he thought of it than he seemed to hear footsteps, as though someone were moving behind him. Martin turned round, and it seemed to him as if people were standing in the dark corner, but he could not make out who they were. And a voice whispered in his ear: "Martin, Martin, don't you know me?"

"Who is it?" muttered Martin.

"It is I," said the voice. And out of the dark corner stepped Stepánitch, who smiled and vanishing like a cloud was seen no more.

"It is I," said the voice again. And out of the darkness stepped the woman with the baby in her arms, and the woman smiled and the baby laughed, and they too vanished.

"It is I," said the voice once more. And the old woman and the boy with the apple stepped out and both smiled, and then they too vanished.

And Martin's soul grew glad. He crossed himself, put on his spectacles, and began reading the Gospel just where it had opened. And at the top of the page he read:

> I was hungry, and ye gave me meat. I was thirsty, and ye gave me drink. I was a stranger, and ye took me in.

And at the bottom of the page he read:

> Inasmuch as ye did it unto one of these my brethren, even these least, ye did it unto me.

And Martin understood that his dream had come true, and that the Savior had really come to him that day, and he had welcomed him.

# The Gift of the Magi

*O. Henry*

William Sydney Porter (1862–1910), better known as O. Henry, shows us that loving compassion sometimes makes us act foolishly. But what is foolish for the head may be wise for the heart. O. Henry wrote "The Gift of the Magi" in 1905.

One dollar and eighty-seven cents. That was all. And sixty cents of it was in pennies. Pennies saved one and two at a time by bulldozing the grocer and the vegetable man and the butcher until one's cheeks burned with the silent imputation of parsimony that such close dealing implied. Three times Della counted it. One dollar and eighty-seven cents. And the next day would be Christmas.

There was clearly nothing to do but flop down on the shabby little couch and howl. So Della did it. Which instigates the moral reflection that life is made up of sobs, sniffles, and smiles, with sniffles predominating.

While the mistress of the home is gradually subsiding from the first stage to the second, take a look at the home. A furnished flat at $8 per week. It did not exactly beggar description, but it certainly had that word on the lookout for the mendicancy squad.

In the vestibule below was a letter box into which no letter would go, and an electric button from which no mortal finger could coax a ring. Also appertaining thereunto was a card bearing the name "Mr. James Dillingham Young."

The "Dillingham" had been flung to the breeze during a former period of prosperity when its possessor was being paid $30 per week. Now, when the income was shrunk to $20, the letters of "Dillingham" looked blurred, as though they were thinking seriously of contracting to a modest and unassuming D. But whenever Mr. James Dillingham Young came home and reached his flat above he was called "Jim" and greatly hugged by Mrs. James Dillingham Young, already introduced to you as Della. Which is all very good.

Della finished her cry and attended to her cheeks with the powder rag. She stood by the window and looked out dully at a gray cat walking a gray fence in a gray backyard. Tomorrow would be Christmas Day and she had only $1.87 with which to buy Jim a present. She had been saving every penny she could for months, with this result. Twenty dollars a week doesn't go far. Expenses had been greater than she had calculated. They always are. Only $1.87 to buy a present for Jim. Her Jim. Many a happy hour she had spent planning for something nice for him. Something fine and rare and sterling—something just a little bit near to being worthy of the honor of being owned by Jim.

There was a pier glass between the windows of the room. Perhaps you have seen a pier glass in an $8 flat. A very thin and very agile person may, by observing his reflection in a rapid sequence of longitudinal strips, obtain a fairly accurate conception of his looks. Della, being slender, had mastered the art.

Suddenly she whirled from the window and stood before the glass. Her eyes were shining brilliantly, but her face had lost its color within twenty seconds. Rapidly she pulled down her hair and let it fall to its full length.

Now, there were two possessions of the James Dillingham Youngs in which they both took a mighty pride. One was Jim's gold watch that had been his father's and his grandfather's. The other was Della's hair. Had the Queen of Sheba lived in the flat across the airshaft, Della would have let her hair hang out the window someday to dry just to depreciate Her Majesty's jewels and gifts. Had King Solomon been the janitor, with all his treasures piled up in the basement, Jim would have pulled out his watch every time he passed, just to see him pluck at his beard from envy.

So now Della's beautiful hair fell about her, rippling and shining like a cascade of brown waters. It reached below her knee and made itself almost a garment for her. And then she did it up again nervously and quickly. Once she faltered for a minute and stood still while a tear or two splashed on the worn red carpet.

On went her old brown jacket; on went her old brown hat. With a whirl of skirts and with the brilliant sparkle still in her eyes, she fluttered out the door and down the stairs to the street.

Where she stopped the sign read: "Mme. Sofronie. Hair Goods of All Kinds." One flight up Della ran, and collected herself, panting. Madame, large, too white, chilly, hardly looked the "Sofronie."

"Will you buy my hair?" asked Della.

"I buy hair," said Madame. "Take yer hat off and let's have a sight at the looks of it."

Down rippled the brown cascade.

"Twenty dollars," said Madame, lifting the mass with a practiced hand.

"Give it to me quick," said Della.

Oh, and the next two hours tripped by on rosy wings. Forget the hashed metaphor. She was ransacking the stores for Jim's present.

She found it at last. It surely had been made for Jim and no one else. There was no other like it in any of the stores, and she had turned all of them inside out. It was a platinum fob chain simple and chaste in design, properly proclaiming its value by substance alone and not by meretricious ornamentation—as all good things should do. It was even worthy of The Watch. As soon as she saw it she knew that it must be Jim's. It was like him. Quietness and value—the description applied to both. Twenty-one dollars they took from her for it, and she hurried home with the 87 cents. With that chain on his watch Jim might be properly anxious about the time in any company. Grand as the watch was, he sometimes looked at it on the sly on account of the old leather strap that he used in place of a chain.

When Della reached home her intoxication gave way a little to prudence and reason. She got out her curling irons and lighted the gas and went to work repairing the ravages made by generosity added to love. Which is always a tremendous task, dear friends—a mammoth task.

Within forty minutes her head was covered with tiny, close-lying curls that made her look wonderfully like a truant schoolboy. She looked at her reflection in the mirror long, carefully, and critically.

"If Jim doesn't kill me," she said to herself, "before he takes a second look at me, he'll say I look like a Coney Island chorus girl. But what could I do—oh! what could I do with a dollar and eighty-seven cents?"

At 7 o'clock the coffee was made and the frying pan was on the back of the stove hot and ready to cook the chops.

Jim was never late. Della doubled the fob chain in her hand and sat on the corner of the table near the door that he always entered. Then she heard his step on the stair away down on the first flight, and she turned white for just a moment. She had a habit of saying little silent prayers about the simplest everyday things, and now she whispered: "Please God, make him think I am still pretty."

The door opened and Jim stepped in and closed it. He looked thin and very serious. Poor fellow, he was only twenty-two—and to be burdened with a family! He needed a new overcoat and he was without gloves.

Jim stepped inside the door, as immovable as a setter at the scent of quail. His eyes were fixed upon Della, and there was an expression in them that she could not read, and it terrified her. It was not anger, nor surprise, nor disapproval, nor horror, nor any of the sentiments that she had been prepared for. He simply stared at her fixedly with that peculiar expression on his face.

Della wriggled off the table and went for him.

"Jim, darling," she cried, "don't look at me that way. I had my hair cut off and sold it because I couldn't have lived through Christmas without giving you a present. It'll grow out again—you won't mind, will you? I just had to do it. My hair grows awfully fast. Say 'Merry Christmas!' Jim, and let's be happy. You don't know what a nice—what a beautiful, nice gift I've got for you."

"You've cut off your hair?" asked Jim, laboriously, as if he had not arrived at that patent fact yet even after the hardest mental labor.

"Cut it off and sold it," said Della. "Don't you like me just as well, anyhow? I'm me without my hair, ain't I?"

Jim looked about the room curiously.

"You say your hair is gone?" he said, with an air almost of idiocy.

"You needn't look for it," said Della. "It's sold, I tell you—sold and gone, too. It's Christmas Eve, boy. Be good to me, for it went for you. Maybe the hairs on my head were numbered," she went on with a sudden serious sweetness, "but nobody could ever count my love for you. Shall I put the chops on, Jim?"

Out of his trance Jim seemed quickly to wake. He enfolded his Della. For ten seconds let us regard with discreet scrutiny some inconsequential object in the other direction. Eight dollars a week or a million a year—what is the difference? A mathematician or a wit would give you the wrong answer. The magi brought valuable gifts, but that was not among them. This dark assertion will be illuminated later on.

Jim drew a package from his overcoat pocket and threw it upon the table.

"Don't make any mistake, Dell," he said, "about me. I don't think there's anything in the way of a haircut or a shave or a shampoo that could make me like my girl any less. But if you'll unwrap that package you may see why you had me going a while at first."

White fingers and nimble tore at the string and paper. And then an ecstatic scream of joy; and then, alas! a quick feminine change to hysterical tears and wails, necessitating the immediate employment of all the comforting powers of the lord of the flat.

For there lay The Combs—the set of combs, side and back, that Della had worshipped for long in a Broadway window. Beautiful combs, pure tortoiseshell, with jeweled rims—just the shade to wear in the beautiful vanished hair. They were expensive combs, she knew, and her heart had simply craved and yearned over them without the least hope of possession. And now, they were hers, but the tresses that should have adorned the coveted adornments were gone.

But she hugged them to her bosom, and at length she was able to look up with dim eyes and a smile and say: "My hair grows so fast, Jim!"

And then Della leaped up like a little singed cat and cried, "Oh, oh!"

Jim had not yet seen his beautiful present. She held it out to him eagerly upon her open palm. The dull precious metal seemed to flash with a reflection of her bright and ardent spirit.

"Isn't it a dandy, Jim? I hunted all over town to find it. You'll have to look at the time a hundred times a day now. Give me your watch. I want to see how it looks on it."

Instead of obeying, Jim tumbled down on the couch and put his hands under the back of his head and smiled.

"Dell," said he, "let's put our Christmas presents away and keep 'em a while. They're too nice to use just at present. I sold the watch to get the money to buy your combs. And now suppose you put the chops on."

The magi, as you know, were wise men—wonderfully wise men—who brought gifts to the Babe in the manger. They invented the art of giving Christmas presents. Being wise, their gifts were no doubt wise ones, possibly bearing the privilege of exchange in case of duplication. And here I have lamely related to you the uneventful chronicle of two foolish children in a flat who most unwisely sacrificed for each other the greatest treasures of their house. But in a last word to the wise of these days let it be said that of all who give gifts these two were the wisest. Of all who give and receive gifts, such as they are wisest. Everywhere they are wisest. They are the magi.

# Count That Day Lost

*George Eliot*

We can look back on each day as being either lost or spent. Mary Ann Evans, better known as George Eliot (1819–1880), shows us how to tell the difference, and what is worth a day's expense.

If you sit down at set of sun
And count the acts that you have done,
  And, counting, find
One self-denying deed, one word
That eased the heart of him who heard,
  One glance most kind
That fell like sunshine where it went—
Then you may count that day well spent.

But if, through all the livelong day,
You've cheered no heart, by yea or nay—
  If, through it all
You've nothing done that you can trace
That brought the sunshine to one face—
  No act most small
That helped some soul and nothing cost—
Then count that day as worse than lost.

---

# Aristotle on Pity

*From the* Rhetoric

Aristotle argues that pity is a kind of pain felt from a realization that a similar misfortune might at any time affect us or our loved ones. The definition may seem distastefully self-centered, but one should bear in mind that in the *Rhetoric,* Aristotle is teaching the reader, in part, how to play on an audience's emotions. His underlying observation is still worth our attention: Pity arises from some fundamental recognition that suffering is an unavoidable part of every human existence.

Pity may be defined as a pain for apparent evil, destructive or painful, befalling a person who does not deserve it, when we might expect such evil to befall ourselves or some of our friends and when, moreover, it seems near. Plainly, the man who is to pity must be such as to think himself or his friends liable to suffer some ill, and ill of such a sort as has been defined, or of a like or comparable sort. Hence pity is not felt by the utterly lost, for they think that they cannot suffer anything further; they *have* suffered; nor by those who think themselves supremely prosperous, rather they are insolent; for, if they think that they have all goods, of course they think that they have exemption from suffering ill, this being a good. The belief that they may possibly suffer is likely to be felt by those who have already suffered and escaped, by elderly persons, on account of their good sense and experience, by the weak and especially by the rather timid, by the educated, for they are reasonable. By those, too, who have parents, children, or wives; for these are their own, and are liable to the sufferings above-named. And by those who are not possessed by a courageous feeling, such as anger or boldness, for these feelings take no account of the future, and by those who are not in an insolent state of mind, as such are reckless of prospective suffering: pity is felt by those who are in the intermediate states. And by those, again, who are not in great fear, for the panic-stricken do not pity, because they are busied with their own feeling. Men pity, too, if they think that there are some people who may be reckoned good; for he who thinks no one good will think all worthy of evil. And, generally, a man pities when he is in a position to remember that like things have befallen himself or his friends, or to expect that they may. . . .

Again, men pity when the danger is near themselves. And they pity those like them in age, in character, in moral state, in rank, in birth; for all these examples make it more probable that the case may become their own; since here, again, we must take it as a general maxim that all things which we fear for ourselves, we pity when they happen to others.

# The Ride of Collins Graves

*John Boyle O'Reilly*

Here is heroic compassion. On May 16, 1874, the Mill River dam in Hampshire County, Massachusetts, gave way, flooding some 124 acres to an average depth of twenty-four feet. Nearly 200 people from the villages of Williamsburg, Skinnerville, Haydenville, and Leeds perished in the disaster. This old New England ballad tells the story of Collins Graves, who rode through the towns to warn residents of the coming danger.

No song of a soldier riding down
To the raging fight of Winchester town;
No song of a time that shook the earth
With the nation's throe at a nation's birth;
But the song of a brave man free from fear
As Sheridan's self or Paul Revere;
Who risked what they risked—free from strife
And its promise of glorious pay—his life.

The peaceful valley has waked and stirred,
And the answering echoes of life are heard;
The dew still clings to the trees and grass,
And the early toilers smiling pass,
As they glance aside at the white-walled homes,
Or up the valley where merrily comes
The brook that sparkles in diamond rills
As the sun comes over the Hampshire hills.

What was it passed like an ominous breath?
Like a shiver of fear, or a touch of death?
What was it? The valley is peaceful still,
And the leaves are afire on the top of the hill;
It was not a sound, nor a thing of sense,
But a pain, like a pang in the short suspense
That wraps the being of those who see
At their feet the gulf of eternity.

The air of the valley has felt the chill;
The workers pause at the door of the mill;
The housewife, keen to the shivering air,
Arrests her foot on the cottage stair,
Instinctive taught by the mother-love,
And thinks of the sleeping ones above.

Why start the listeners? Why does the course
of the mill-stream widen? It is a horse—
"Hark to the sound of the hoofs!" they say—
That gallops so wildly Williamsburg way?
God! what was that like a human shriek
From the winding valley? Will nobody speak?
Will nobody answer those women who cry
As the awful warnings thunder by?

Whence come they? Listen! and now they hear
The sound of the galloping horse-hoofs near;
They watch the trend of the vale, and see
The rider who thunders so menacingly,
With waving arms and warning scream
To the home-filled banks of the valley stream
He draws no rein, but he shakes the street
With a shout and the ring of the galloping feet,
And this the cry that he flings to the wind,
*"To the hills for your lives! The flood is behind!"*
He cries and is gone, but they know the worst—
The treacherous Williamsburg dam has burst!
The basin that nourished their happy homes
Is changed to a demon. It comes! it comes!
A monster in aspect, with shaggy front
Of shattered dwellings to take the brunt
Of the dwellings they shatter; white-maned and hoarse
The merciless terror fills the course
Of the narrow valley, and rushing raves
With death on the first of its hissing waves,
Till cottage and street and crowded mill
Are crumbled and crushed. But onward still,
In front of the roaring flood, is heard
The galloping horse and the warning word.

Thank God that the brave man's life is spared!
From Williamsburg town he nobly dared
To race with the flood, and to take the road
In front of the terrible swath it mowed.
For miles it thundered and crashed behind,
But he looked ahead with a steadfast mind:
*"They must be warned!"* was all he said,
As away on his terrible ride he sped.

When heroes are called for, bring the crown
To this Yankee rider; send him down
On the stream of time with the Curtius old;
His deed, as the Roman's, was brave and bold;
And the tale can as noble a thrill awake,
For he offered his life for the people's sake!

---

# Vigil Strange I Kept on the Field One Night

*Walt Whitman*

True compassion runs deeper than the kind of grief in which we know only our own pain from another's death. True compassion seeks to understand, or at least recognize, the tragedy dealt to a life suddenly lost.

Walt Whitman (1819–1892) traveled to the Virginia battlefront in 1862 to tend to his wounded brother. Afterwards, he worked in Washington, D.C., as a volunteer nurse in army hospitals. From those experiences came *Drum-Taps,* a collection of poems about the Civil War.

Vigil strange I kept on the field one night;
When you my son and my comrade dropt at my side that day,
One look I but gave which your dear eyes return'd with a look I shall never forget.
One touch of your hand to mine O boy, reach'd up as you lay on the ground,

Then onward I sped in the battle, the even-contested battle,
Till late in the night reliev'd to the place at last again I made my
way,
Found you in death so cold dear comrade, found your body son of
responding kisses, (never again on earth responding,)
Bared your face in the starlight, curious the scene, cool blew the
moderate night-wind,
Long there and then in vigil I stood, dimly around me the battlefield
spreading,
Vigil wondrous and vigil sweet there in the fragrant silent night,
But not a tear fell, not even a long-drawn sigh, long, long I gazed,
Then on the earth partially reclining sat by your side leaning my
chin in my hands,
Passing sweet hours, immortal and mystic hours with you dearest
comrade—not a tear, not a word.
Vigil of silence, love and death, vigil for you my son and my soldier,
As onward silently stars aloft, eastward new ones upward stole,
Vigil final for you brave boy, (I could not save you, swift was your
death,
I faithfully loved you and cared for you living, I think we shall surely
meet again,)
Till at latest lingering of the night, indeed just as the dawn appear'd,
My comrade I wrapt in his blanket, envelop'd well his form,
Folded the blanket well, tucking it carefully over head and carefully
under feet,
And there and then and bathed by the rising sun, my son in his
grave, in his rude-dug grave I deposited,
Ending my vigil strange with that, vigil of night and battlefield dim,
Vigil for comrade swiftly slain, vigil I never forget, how as day
brighten'd,
I rose from the chill ground and folded my soldier well in his
blanket,
and buried him where he fell.

# Abraham Lincoln Offers Consolation

*Abraham Lincoln*

President Lincoln wrote this letter after an aide told him about a Boston widow whose five sons had been killed fighting for the Union armies. As Carl Sandburg wrote, "More darkly than the Gettysburg speech the letter wove its awful implication that human freedom so often was paid for with agony." Here is an American president understanding that agony, sharing it, and performing a heartfelt rite, as Sandburg put it, "as though he might be a ship captain at midnight by lantern light, dropping black roses into the immemorial sea for mystic remembrance and consecration."

Executive Mansion
Washington, Nov. 21, 1864

To Mrs. Bixby, Boston, Mass.
Dear Madam,

I have been shown in the files of the War Department a statement of the Adjutant General of Massachusetts that you are the mother of five sons who have died gloriously on the field of battle. I feel how weak and fruitless must be any word of mine which should attempt to beguile you from the grief of a loss so overwhelming. But I cannot refrain from tendering you the consolation that may be found in the thanks of the republic they died to save. I pray that our Heavenly Father may assuage the anguish of your bereavement, and leave you only the cherished memory of the loved and lost, and the solemn pride that must be yours to have laid so costly a sacrifice upon the altar of freedom.

Yours very sincerely and respectfully,
A. Lincoln

As a historical footnote, we now know that Lincoln had in fact been misinformed: two of Mrs. Bixby's sons had been killed in action, one was taken prisoner, and two deserted. The error does not stand in the way of the letter's deserved fame. Mrs. Bixby's loss and sacrifice hardly could have been greater.

# O Captain! My Captain!

*Walt Whitman*

Here Walt Whitman mourns for the fallen Abraham Lincoln. To the poet, the assassination was a terrible blow to the American democratic comradeship he celebrated in so much of his verse.

O Captain! my Captain! our fearful trip is done;
The ship has weather'd every rack, the prize we sought is won;
The port is near, the bells I hear, the people all exulting,
While follow eyes the steady keel, the vessel grim and daring:
But O heart! heart! heart!
O the bleeding drops of red,
Where on the deck my Captain lies,
Fallen cold and dead.

O Captain! my Captain! rise up and hear the bells;
Rise up—for you the flag is flung—for you the bugle trills;
For you bouquets and ribbon'd wreaths—for you the shores a-crowding;
For you they call, the swaying mass, their eager faces turning:
Here Captain! dear father!
This arm beneath your head!
It is some dream that on the deck,
You've fallen cold and dead.

My Captain does not answer, his lips are pale and still;
My father does not feel my arm, he has no pulse nor will;
The ship is anchor'd safe and sound, its voyage closed and done;
From fearful trip, the victor ship comes in with object won:
Exult, O shores, and ring, O bells!
But I, with mournful tread,
Walk the deck my Captain lies,
Fallen cold and dead.

# The New Colossus

*Emma Lazarus*

Emma Lazarus (1849–1887) wrote "The New Colossus" in 1883 as part of a project by artists and writers to raise funds to build the pedestal of the Statue of Liberty, a gift from France to the United States. The poem's title refers to the Colossus of Rhodes, one of the seven wonders of the ancient world, a giant bronze statue of the sun god Helios that had overlooked the Greek city's harbor. Lazarus's poem, like the Statue of Liberty, came to popularize America's mission as a refuge for immigrants. Here is compassion as a national policy, one of America's great national policies.

Not like the brazen giant of Greek fame,
With conquering limbs astride from land to land;
Here at our sea-washed, sunset gates shall stand
A mighty woman with a torch, whose flame
Is the imprisoned lightning, and her name
Mother of Exiles. From her beacon-hand
Glows world-wide welcome; her mild eyes command
The air-bridged harbor that twin cities frame.

"Keep, ancient lands, your storied pomp!" cries she
With silent lips. "Give me your tired, your poor,
Your huddled masses yearning to breathe free,
The wretched refuse of your teeming shore.
Send these, the homeless, tempest-tost to me.
I lift my lamp beside the golden door!"

# The Influence of Democracy

*Alexis de Tocqueville*

In 1831, the French government sent twenty-six-year-old Alexis de Tocqueville (1805–1859) to the United States to study its penal system. The result was *Democracy in America,* a voluminous masterpiece in which Tocqueville assessed the promises and pitfalls of democracy. In this excerpt, he examines equality's effects on compassion. The accuracy of Tocqueville's observations are, of course, open to debate. Nevertheless, we are forced to ask ourselves: how does modern America measure up to the portrait he painted more than a century and a half ago?

We perceive that for several ages social conditions have tended to equality, and we discover that in the course of the same period the manners of society have been softened. Are these two things merely contemporaneous, or does any secret link exist between them, so that the one cannot go on without making the other advance? Several causes may concur to render the manners of a people less rude; but, of all these causes, the most powerful appears to me to be the equality of conditions. Equality of conditions and growing civility in manners are then, in my eyes, not only contemporaneous occurrences, but correlative facts. . . .

When all the ranks of a community are nearly equal, as all men think and feel in nearly the same manner, each of them may judge in a moment of the sensations of all the others: he casts a rapid glance upon himself, and that is enough. There is no wretchedness into which he cannot readily enter, and a secret instinct reveals to him its extent. It signifies not that strangers or foes be the sufferers; imagination puts him in their place: something like a personal feeling is mingled with his pity, and makes himself suffer while the body of his fellow creature is in torture.

In democratic ages men rarely sacrifice themselves for one another; but they display general compassion for the members of the human race. They inflict no useless ills; and they are happy to relieve the griefs of others, when they can do so without much hurting themselves; they are not disinterested, but they are humane.

Although the Americans have in a manner reduced egotism to a social and philosophical theory, they are nevertheless extremely open to compassion. . . .

When men feel a natural compassion for their mutual sufferings—when they are brought together by easy and frequent intercourse, and no sensitive feelings keep them asunder, it may readily be supposed that they will lend assistance to one another whenever it is needed. When an American asks for the cooperation of his fellow citizens it is seldom refused, and I have often seen it afforded spontaneously and with great good will. If an accident happens on the highway, everybody hastens to help the sufferer; if some great and sudden calamity befalls a family, the purses of a thousand strangers are at once willingly opened, and small but numerous donations pour in to relieve their distress.

It often happens among the most civilized nations of the globe, that a poor wretch is as friendless in the midst of a crowd as the savage in his wilds: this is hardly ever the case in the United States. The Americans, who are always cold and often coarse in their manners, seldom show insensibility; and if they do not proffer services eagerly, yet they do not refuse to render them.

All this is not in contradiction to what I have said before on the subject of individualism. The two things are so far from combating each other, that I can see how they agree. Equality of conditions, while it makes men feel their independence, shows them their own weakness: they are free, but exposed to a thousand accidents; and experience soon teaches them, that although they do not habitually require the assistance of others, a time almost always comes when they cannot do without it.

We constantly see in Europe that men of the same profession are ever ready to assist each other; they are all exposed to the same ills, and that is enough to teach them to seek mutual preservatives, however hard-hearted and selfish they may otherwise be. When one of them falls into danger, from which the others may save him by a slight transient sacrifice or a sudden effort, they do not fail to make the attempt. Not that they are deeply interested in his fate; for if, by chance, their exertions are unavailing, they immediately forget the object of them, and return to their own business; but a sort of tacit and almost involuntary agreement has been passed between them, by which each one owes to the others a temporary support which he may claim for himself in turn.

Extend to a people the remark here applied to a class, and you will understand my meaning. A similar covenant exists in fact between all the citizens of a democracy: they all feel themselves subject to the same weakness and the same dangers; and their interest, as well as their sympathy, makes it a rule with them to lend each other mutual assistance when required. The more equal social conditions become, the more do men display this reciprocal disposition to oblige each other. In democracies no great benefits are conferred, but good offices are constantly rendered: a man seldom displays self-devotion, but all men are ready to be of service to one another.

---

## The Choir Invisible

*George Eliot*

George Eliot once asked, "What do we live for, if it is not to make life less difficult to each other?" Here she asks for the same power even after life has ended. The compassion we show now will surely inspire others after we are gone.

O, may I join the choir invisible
Of those immortal dead who live again
In minds made better by their presence; live
In pulses stirred to generosity,
In deeds of daring rectitude, in scorn
Of miserable aims that end with self,
In thoughts sublime that pierce the night like stars,
And with their mild persistence urge men's minds
To vaster issues. . . .
May I reach
That purest heaven—be to other souls
The cup of strength in some great agony,
Enkindle generous ardor, feed pure love,
Beget the smiles that have no cruelty,
Be the sweet presence of good diffused,
And in diffusion ever more intense!
So shall I join the choir invisible,
Whose music is the gladness of the world.

# 3

# Responsibility

TO "respond" is to "answer." Correspondingly, to be "responsible" is to be "answerable," to be *accountable.* Irresponsible behavior is immature behavior. Taking responsibility—being responsible—is a sign of maturity. When we strive to help our children become responsible persons we are helping them toward maturity. James Madison delimited the parameters of responsibility with characteristic clarity in *Federalist* No. 63. "Responsibility, in order to be reasonable, must be limited to objects within the power of the responsible party, and in order to be effectual, must relate to operations of that power." Persons who have not reached maturity have not yet come into full ownership of their powers.

It is a truism that everything which has ever been *done* in the history of the world has been done *by somebody;* some person has exercised some power to *do* it. Our share of the responsibility for what we do individually or in concert with others varies with the social and political structures within which we operate, but it characteristically increases with maturity. It was an immature Adam in the Garden of Eden who, when discovered to have eaten of the forbidden fruit, laid the responsibility on Eve. And it was an immature Eve who in turn laid it on the beguiling serpent. "She made me do it"/"He made me do it" is an archetypal drama reenacted in every generation where siblings and playmates are called upon to answer for their misdoings.

But it doesn't stop there. An unwitting acknowledgment of this sort of immaturity commonly continues on into adulthood. Nearly everyone has an excuse when things go wrong. In Washington, D.C., common parlance makes ample use of the passive voice to avoid blame: "mistakes were made." But there is no rush to take responsibility. There is no shortage of persons ready to claim credit for contributing to an enterprise that goes well, however, even though a maxim familiar to persons in public service observes that "There is no end to the good you can do if you don't care who gets credit for it."

In the end, we are answerable for the kinds of persons we have made of ourselves. "That's just the way I am!" is not an excuse for inconsiderate or vile behavior. Nor is it even an accurate description, for we are never *just* what we are. As Aristotle was among the first to insist, we *become* what we are as persons by the decisions that we ourselves make. British philosopher Mary Midgley points out in *Beast and Man* that "the really excellent and central point of Existentialism [is] the acceptance of responsibility for being as we have made ourselves, the refusal to make bogus excuses."

Søren Kierkegaard, one of Existentialism's nineteenth-century pioneers, deplored the damaging effects of crowds and gangs on our *sense* of responsibility. "A crowd," as he wrote in *The Point of View for My Work as an Author,* "in its very concept is the untruth, by reason of the fact that it renders the individual completely impenitent and irresponsible, or at least weakens his sense of responsibility by reducing it to a fraction." In his *Confessions* St. Augustine made this weakened sense of responsibility under peer pressure a central feature of his meditation upon the vandalism of his youth, "all because we are ashamed to hold back when others say 'Come on! Let's do it!' " But he was as insistent as Aristotle and the Existentialists on recognizing personal responsibility for what he had done. A weakened *sense* of responsibility does not weaken the *fact* of responsibility.

Responsible persons are mature people who have taken charge of themselves and their conduct, who *own* their actions and *own up* to them—who *answer* for them. We help foster a mature sense of responsibility in our children in the same way that we help cultivate their other desirable traits: by practice and by example. Household chores, homework, extracurricular activities, after-school jobs, and volunteer work all contribute to maturation if parental example and expectations are clear, consistent, and commensurate with the developing powers of the child.

# Over in the Meadow

*Olive A. Wadsworth*

This poem shows us parents' first responsibility: the nurture of the young.

Over in the meadow,
   In the sand, in the sun,
Lived an old mother toad
   And her little toadie one.
"Wink," said the mother;
   "I wink," said the one;
So she winked and she blinked
   In the sand, in the sun.

Over in the meadow,
   Where the stream runs blue,
Lived an old mother fish
   And her little fishes two.
"Swim," said the mother;
   "We swim," said the two;
So they swam and they leaped
   Where the stream runs blue.

Over in the meadow,
In a hole in a tree,
Lived an old mother bluebird
And her little birdies three.
"Sing," said the mother;
"We sing," said the three;
So they sang and were glad,
In the hole in the tree.

Over in the meadow,
In the reeds on the shore,
Lived a mother muskrat
And her little ratties four.
"Dive," said the mother;
"We dive," said the four;
So they dived and they burrowed
In the reeds on the shore.

## The Three Little Kittens

*Eliza Lee Follen*

Children should learn early the practical lesson that responsibility leads to reward, which leads to further responsibility. We must keep track of our mittens if we expect pie, and then we must wash them if we expect ever to have any more dessert.

Three little kittens lost their mittens;
And they began to cry,
"Oh, mother dear,
We very much fear
That we have lost our mittens."
"Lost your mittens!
You naughty kittens!
Then you shall have no pie!"
"Mee-ow, mee-ow, mee-ow."
"No, you shall have no pie."
"Mee-ow, mee-ow, mee-ow."

The three little kittens found their mittens;
And they began to cry,
"Oh, mother dear,
See here, see here!
See, we have found our mittens!"
"Put on your mittens,
You silly kittens,
And you may have some pie."
"Purr-r, purr-r, purr-r,
Oh, let us have the pie!
Purr-r, purr-r, purr-r."

The three little kittens put on their mittens,
And soon ate up the pie;
"Oh, mother dear,
We greatly fear
That we have soiled our mittens!"
"Soiled your mittens!
You naughty kittens!"
Then they began to sigh,
"Mee-ow, mee-ow, mee-ow."
Then they began to sigh,
"Mee-ow, mee-ow, mee-ow."

The three little kittens washed their mittens,
And hung them out to dry;
"Oh, mother dear,
Do not you hear
That we have washed our mittens?"
"Washed your mittens!
Oh, you're good kittens!
But I smell a rat close by,
Hush, hush! Mee-ow, mee-ow."
"We smell a rat close by,
Mee-ow, mee-ow, mee-ow."

# Little Orphant Annie

*James Whitcomb Riley*

In which we learn what may happen to little girls and boys who don't do what they are supposed to do.

Little Orphant Annie's come to our house to stay,
An' wash the cups and saucers up, an' brush the crumbs away,
An' shoo the chickens off the porch, an' dust the hearth, an' sweep,
An' make the fire, an' bake the bread, an' earn her board-an'-keep;
An' all us other children, when the supper things is done,
We set around the kitchen fire an' has the mostest fun
A-list'nin' to the witch-tales 'at Annie tells about,
An' the Gobble-uns 'at gits you
Ef you
Don't
Watch
Out!

Onc't they was a little boy wouldn't say his pray'rs—
An' when he went to bed at night, away up-stairs,
His mammy heerd him holler, an' his daddy heerd him bawl,
An' when they turn't the kivvers down, he wasn't there at all!
An' they seeked him in the rafter-room, an' cubby-hole, an' press,
An' seeked him up the chimbly flue, an' ever'wheres, I guess;
But all they ever found was thist his pants an' roundabout!
An' the Gobble-uns'll git you
Ef you
Don't
Watch
Out!

An' one time a little girl 'ud allus laugh an' grin,
An' make fun of ever' one, an' all her blood-an'-kin,
An' onc't when they was "company," an' ole folks was there,
She mocked 'em an' shocked 'em, an' said she didn't care!
An' thist as she kicked her heels, an' turn't to run an' hide,
They was two great big Black Things a-standin' by her side,
An' they snatched her through the ceilin' 'fore she knowed what she's about!
An' the Gobble-uns'll git you
Ef you
Don't
Watch
Out!

An' little Orphant Annie says, when the blaze is blue,
An the lampwick sputters, an' the wind goes woo-oo!
An' you hear the crickets quit, an' the moon is gray,
An' the lightnin'-bugs in dew is all squenched away,—
You better mind yer parents, an' yer teachers fond an' dear,
An' churish them 'at loves you, an' dry the orphant's tear,
An' he'p the pore an' needy ones 'at clusters all about,
Er the Gobble-uns'll git you
Ef you
Don't
Watch
Out!

## Rebecca

*Eleanor Piatt*

Play is the work of children and entirely suitable as an arena in which to develop habits of responsibility.

I have a doll, Rebecca,
She's quite a little care,
I have to press her ribbons
And comb her fluffy hair.

I keep her clothes all mended,
  And wash her hands and face,
And make her frocks and aprons,
  All trimmed in frills and lace.

I have to cook her breakfast,
  And pet her when she's ill;
And telephone the doctor
  When Rebecca has a chill.

Rebecca doesn't like that,
  And says she's well and strong;
And says she'll try—oh! very hard,
  To be good all day long.

But when night comes, she's nodding;
  So into bed we creep
And snuggle up together,
  And soon are fast asleep.

I have no other dolly,
  For you can plainly see,
In caring for Rebecca,
  I'm busy as can be!

---

## St. George and the Dragon

*Retold by J. Berg Esenwein and Marietta Stockard*

"Somewhere perhaps there is trouble and fear," St. George says in this story before riding off to "find work which only a knight can do." Here we see the course of a morally ambitious conscience, habitually searching to aid others. Such people who go out of their way to help are sometimes called knights, saints, and philanthropists; sometimes they are called ministers, teachers, coaches, policemen, and parents.

Long ago, when the knights lived in the land, there was one knight whose name was Sir George. He was not only braver than all the rest, but he was so noble, kind, and good that the people came to call him Saint George.

No robbers ever dared to trouble the people who lived near his castle, and all the wild animals were killed or driven away, so the little children could play even in the woods without being afraid.

One day St. George rode throughout the country. Everywhere he saw the men busy at their work in the fields, the women singing at work in their homes, and the little children shouting at their play.

"These people are all safe and happy. They need me no more," said St. George.

"But somewhere perhaps there is trouble and fear. There may be someplace where little children cannot play in safety, some woman may have been carried away from her home—perhaps there are even dragons left to be slain. Tomorrow I shall ride away and never stop until I find work which only a knight can do."

Early the next morning St. George put on his helmet and all his shining armor, and fastened his sword at his side. Then he mounted his great white horse and rode out from his castle gate. Down the steep, rough road he went, sitting straight and tall, and looking brave and strong as a knight should look.

On through the little village at the foot of the hill and out across the country he rode. Everywhere he saw rich fields filled with waving grain, everywhere there was peace and plenty.

He rode on and on until at last he came into a part of the country he had never seen before. He noticed that there were no men working in the fields. The houses which he passed stood silent and empty. The grass along the roadside was scorched as if a fire had passed over it. A field of wheat was all trampled and burned.

St. George drew up his horse, and looked carefully about him. Everywhere there was silence and desolation. "What can be the dreadful thing which has driven all the people from their homes? I must find out, and give them help if I can," he said.

But there was no one to ask, so St. George rode forward until at last far in the distance he saw the walls of a city. "Here surely I shall find someone who can tell me the cause of all this," he said, so he rode more swiftly toward the city.

Just then the great gate opened and St. George saw crowds of people standing inside the wall. Some of them were weeping, all of them seemed afraid. As St. George watched, he saw a beautiful maiden dressed in white, with a girdle of scarlet about her waist, pass through the gate alone. The gate clanged shut and the maiden walked along the road, weeping bitterly. She did not see St. George, who was riding quickly toward her.

"Maiden, why do you weep?" he asked as he reached her side.

She looked up at St. George sitting there on his horse, so straight and tall and beautiful. "Oh, Sir Knight!" she cried, "ride quickly from this place. You know not the danger you are in!"

"Danger!" said St. George. "Do you think a knight would flee from danger? Besides, you, a fair girl, are here alone. Think you a knight would leave you so? Tell me your trouble that I may help you."

"No! No!" she cried, "hasten away. You would only lose your life. There is a terrible dragon near. He may come at any moment. One breath would destroy you if he found you here. Go! Go quickly!"

"Tell me more of this," said St. George sternly. "Why are you here alone to meet this dragon? Are there no *men* left in yon city?"

"Oh," said the maiden, "my father, the King, is old and feeble. He has only me to help him take care of his people. This terrible dragon has driven them from their homes, carried away their cattle, and ruined their crops. They have all come within the walls of the city for safety. For weeks now the dragon has come to the very gates of the city. We have been forced to give him two sheep each day for his breakfast.

"Yesterday there were no sheep left to give, so he said that unless a young maiden were given him today he would break down the walls and destroy the city. The people cried to my father to save them, but he could do nothing. I am going to give myself to the dragon. Perhaps if he has me, the Princess, he may spare our people."

"Lead the way, brave Princess. Show me where this monster may be found."

When the Princess saw St. George's flashing eyes and great, strong arm as he drew forth his sword, she felt afraid no more. Turning, she led the way to a shining pool.

"There's where he stays," she whispered. "See, the water moves. He is waking."

St. George saw the head of the dragon lifted from the pool. Fold on fold he rose from the water. When he saw St. George he gave a roar of rage and plunged toward him. The smoke and flames flew from his nostrils, and he opened his great jaws as if to swallow both the knight and his horse.

St. George shouted and, waving his sword above his head, rode at the dragon. Quick and hard came the blows from St. George's sword. It was a terrible battle.

At last the dragon was wounded. He roared with pain and plunged at St. George, opening his great mouth close to the brave knight's head.

St. George looked carefully, then struck with all his strength straight down through the dragon's throat, and he fell at the horse's feet—dead.

Then St. George shouted for joy at his victory. He called to the Princess. She came and stood beside him.

"Give me the girdle from about your waist, O Princess," said St. George.

The Princess gave him her girdle and St. George bound it around the dragon's neck, and they pulled the dragon after them by that little silken ribbon back to the city so that all of the people could see that the dragon could never harm them again.

When they saw St. George bringing the Princess back in safety and knew that the dragon was slain, they threw open the gates of the city and sent up great shouts of joy.

The King heard them and came out from his palace to see why the people were shouting.

When he saw his daughter safe he was the happiest of them all.

"O brave knight," he said, "I am old and weak. Stay here and help me guard my people from harm."

"I'll stay as long as ever you have need of me," St. George answered.

So he lived in the palace and helped the old King take care of his people, and when the old King died, St. George was made King in his stead. The people felt happy and safe so long as they had such a brave and good man for their King.

# The Boy We Want

A boy that is truthful and honest
And faithful and willing to work;
But we have not a place that we care to disgrace
With a boy that is ready to shirk.

Wanted—a boy you can tie to,
A boy that is trusty and true,
A boy that is good to old people,
And kind to the little ones too.

A boy that is nice to the home folks,
And pleasant to sister and brother,
A boy who will try when things go awry
To be helpful to father and mother.

These are the boys we depend on—
Our hope for the future, and then
Grave problems of state and the world's work await
Such boys when they grow to be men.

---

# King Alfred and the Cakes

*Adapted from James Baldwin*

Alfred the Great was king of the West Saxons in England during the ninth century. His determination to protect England from Danish conquest and his emphasis on literacy and education for his people have lifted him into the ranks of England's most popular rulers. This famous story reminds us that attention to little duties prepares us to meet larger ones. It also reminds us that leadership and responsibility walk hand in hand and that truly great leaders do not disdain small responsibilities.

In England many years ago there ruled a king named Alfred. A wise and just man, Alfred was one of the best kings England ever had. Even today, centuries later, he is known as Alfred the Great.

The days of Alfred's rule were not easy ones in England. The country was invaded by the fierce Danes, who had come from across the sea. There were so many Danish invaders, and they were so strong and bold, that for a long time they won almost every battle. If they kept on winning, they would soon be masters of the whole country.

At last, after so many struggles, King Alfred's English army was broken and scattered. Every man had to save himself in the best way he could, including King Alfred. He disguised himself as a shepherd and fled alone through the woods and swamps.

After several days of wandering, he came to the hut of a woodcutter. Tired and hungry, he knocked on the door and begged the woodcutter's wife to give him something to eat and a place to sleep.

The woman looked with pity at the ragged fellow. She had no idea who he really was. "Come in," she said. "I will give you some supper if you will watch these cakes I am baking on the hearth. I want to go out and milk the cow. Watch them carefully, and make sure they don't burn while I'm gone."

Alfred thanked her politely and sat down beside the fire. He tried to pay attention to the cakes, but soon all his troubles filled his mind. How was he going to get his army together again? And even if he did, how was he going to prepare it to face the Danes? How could he possibly drive such fierce invaders out of England? The more he thought, the more hopeless the future seemed, and he began to believe there was no use in continuing to fight. Alfred saw only his problems. He forgot he was in the woodcutter's hut, he forgot about his hunger, and he forgot all about the cakes.

In a little while, the woman came back. She found her hut full of smoke and her cakes burned to a crisp. And there was Alfred sitting beside the hearth, gazing into the flames. He had never even noticed the cakes were burning.

"You lazy, good-for-nothing fellow!" the woman cried. "Look what you've done! You want something to eat, but you don't want to work for it! Now none of us will have any supper!" Alfred only hung his head in shame.

Just then the woodcutter came home. As soon as he walked through the door, he recognized the stranger sitting at his hearth.

"Be quiet!" he told his wife. "Do you realize who you are scolding? This is our noble ruler, King Alfred himself."

The woman was horrified. She ran to the king's side and fell to her knees. She begged him to forgive her for speaking so harshly.

But the wise King Alfred asked her to rise. "You were right to scold me," he said. "I told you I would watch the cakes, and then I let them burn. I deserved what you said. Anyone who accepts a duty, whether it be large or small, should perform it faithfully. I have failed this time, but it will not happen again. My duties as king await me."

The story does not tell us if King Alfred had anything to eat that night. But it was not many days before he had gathered his men together again, and soon he drove the Danes out of England.

## For Want of a Horseshoe Nail

*Adapted from James Baldwin*

This famous legend and rhyme are based on the demise of England's King Richard III, whose defeat at the Battle of Bosworth Field in 1485 has been immortalized by Shakespeare's famous line: "A horse! A horse! My kingdom for a horse!" The story is a nice foil for "King Alfred and the Cakes." It reminds us that little duties neglected bring great downfalls.

King Richard the Third was preparing for the fight of his life. An army led by Henry, Earl of Richmond, was marching against him. The contest would determine who would rule England.

The morning of the battle, Richard sent a groom to make sure his favorite horse was ready.

"Shoe him quickly," the groom told the blacksmith. "The king wishes to ride at the head of his troops."

"You'll have to wait," the blacksmith answered. "I've shoed the king's whole army the last few days, and now I've got to go get more iron."

"I can't wait," the groom shouted impatiently. "The king's

enemies are advancing right now, and we must meet them on the field. Make do with what you have."

So the blacksmith bent to his task. From a bar of iron he made four horseshoes. He hammered and shaped and fitted them to the horse's feet. Then he began to nail them on. But after he had fastened three shoes, he found he did not have enough nails for the fourth.

"I need one or two more nails," he said, "and it will take some time to hammer them out."

"I told you I can't wait," the groom said impatiently. "I hear the trumpets now. Can't you just use what you've got?"

"I can put the shoe on, but it won't be as secure as the others."

"Will it hold?" asked the groom.

"It should," answered the blacksmith, "but I can't be certain."

"Well, then, just nail it on," the groom cried. "And hurry, or King Richard will be angry with us both."

The armies clashed, and Richard was in the thick of the battle. He rode up and down the field, cheering his men and fighting his foes. "Press forward! Press forward!" he yelled, urging his troops toward Henry's lines.

Far away, at the other side of the field, he saw some of his men falling back. If others saw them, they too might retreat. So Richard spurred his horse and galloped toward the broken line, calling on his soldiers to turn and fight.

He was barely halfway across the field when one of the horse's shoes flew off. The horse stumbled and fell, and Richard was thrown to the ground.

Before the king could grab at the reins, the frightened animal rose and galloped away. Richard looked around him. He saw that his soldiers were turning and running, and Henry's troops were closing around him.

He waved his sword in the air. "A horse!" he shouted. "A horse! My kingdom for a horse!"

But there was no horse for him. His army had fallen to pieces, and his troops were busy trying to save themselves. A moment later Henry's soldiers were upon Richard, and the battle was over.

And since that time, people have said,

For want of a nail, a shoe was lost,
For want of a shoe, a horse was lost,
For want of a horse, a battle was lost,
For want of a battle, a kingdom was lost,
And all for the want of a horseshoe nail.

---

## Sir Walter Raleigh

*Retold by James Baldwin*

Goethe said that there is no outward sign of true courtesy that does not rest on a deep moral foundation. This tale about the English explorer and courtier Sir Walter Raleigh (1554–1618) is one of our most famous examples of that kind of everyday responsibility called chivalry.

There once lived in England a brave and noble man whose name was Walter Raleigh. He was not only brave and noble, but he was also handsome and polite. And for that reason the queen made him a knight, and called him Sir Walter Raleigh.

I will tell you about it.

When Raleigh was a young man, he was one day walking along a street in London. At that time the streets were not paved, and there were no sidewalks. Raleigh was dressed in very fine style, and he wore a beautiful scarlet cloak thrown over his shoulders.

As he passed along, he found it hard work to keep from stepping in the mud, and soiling his handsome new shoes. Soon he came to a puddle of muddy water which reached from one side of the street to the other. He could not step across. Perhaps he could jump over it.

As he was thinking what he should do, he happened to look up. Who was it coming down the street, on the other side of the puddle?

It was Elizabeth, the Queen of England, with her train of gentlewomen and waiting maids. She saw the dirty puddle in the street. She saw the handsome young man with the scarlet cloak, standing by the side of it. How was she to get across?

Young Raleigh, when he saw who was coming, forgot about himself. He thought only of helping the queen. There was only one thing that he could do, and no other man would have thought of that.

He took off his scarlet cloak, and spread it across the puddle. The queen could step on it now, as on a beautiful carpet.

She walked across. She was safely over the ugly puddle, and her feet had not touched the mud. She paused a moment, and thanked the young man.

As she walked onward with her train, she asked one of the gentlewomen, "Who is that brave gentleman who helped us so handsomely?"

"His name is Walter Raleigh," said the gentlewoman.

"He shall have his reward," said the queen.

Not long after that, she sent for Raleigh to come to her palace.

The young man went, but he had no scarlet cloak to wear. Then, while all the great men and fine ladies of England stood around, the queen made him a knight. And from that time he was known as Sir Walter Raleigh, the queen's favorite.

# Etiquette in a Nutshell

This little list of rules comes from a late-nineteenth-century book entitled *Correct Manners, a Complete Handbook of Etiquette.* These are some of the day-to-day commonplace obligations that allow us to get along with one another. They never go out of style.

Never break an engagement when one is made, whether of a business or social nature. If you are compelled to do so, make an immediate apology either by note or in person.

Be punctual as to time, precise as to payment, honest and thoughtful in all your transactions, whether with rich or poor.

Never look over the shoulder of one who is reading, or intrude yourself into a conversation in which you are not invited or expected to take part.

Tell the truth at all times and in all places. It is better to have a reputation for truthfulness than one for wit, wisdom, or brilliancy.

Avoid making personal comments regarding a person's dress, manners, or habits. Be sure you are all right in these respects, and you will find you have quite enough to attend to.

Always be thoughtful regarding the comfort and pleasure of others. Give the best seat in your room to a lady, an aged person, or an invalid.

Ask no questions about the affairs of your friend unless he wants your advice. Then he will tell you all he desires to have you know.

A true lady or gentleman, one who is worthy of the name, will never disparage one of the other sex by word or deed.

Always remember that a book that has been loaned you is not yours to loan to another.

Mention your wife or your husband with the greatest respect, even in your most familiar references.

If you have calls to make, see that you attend to them punctually. Your friends may reasonably think you slight them when you fail to do so.

Be neat and careful in your dress, but take care not to overdress. The fop is almost as much of an abomination as the slovenly man.

If wine or liquors are used on your table or in your presence, never urge others to use them against their own inclinations.

---

# The Chest of Broken Glass

Responsibilities of parents and children toward each other change with age, particularly old age. "Old men are children for a second time," the Greek dramatist Aristophanes said. This tale is about that time in life when caring about someone means *taking care* of them. The obligation to "honor thy father and mother" does not end when father and mother grow old.

Once there was an old man who had lost his wife and lived all alone. He had worked hard as a tailor all his life, but misfortunes had left him penniless, and now he was so old he could no longer work for himself. His hands trembled too much to thread a needle, and his vision had blurred too much for him to make a straight stitch. He had three sons, but they were all grown and married now, and they were so busy with their own lives, they only had time to stop by and eat dinner with their father once a week.

Gradually the old man grew more and more feeble, and his sons came by to see him less and less. "They don't want to be around me at all now," he told himself, "because they're afraid I'll become a burden." He stayed up all night worrying what would become of him, until at last he thought of a plan.

The next morning he went to see his friend the carpenter, and asked him to make a large chest. Then he went to see his friend the locksmith, and asked him to give him an old lock. Finally he went to see his friend the glassblower, and asked for all the old broken pieces of glass he had.

The old man took the chest home, filled it to the top with broken glass, locked it up tight, and put it beneath his kitchen table. The next time his sons came for dinner, they bumped their feet against it.

"What's in this chest?" they asked, looking under the table.

"Oh, nothing," the old man replied, "just some things I've been saving."

His sons nudged it and saw how heavy it was. They kicked it and heard a rattling inside. "It must be full of all the gold he's saved over the years," they whispered to one another.

So they talked it over, and realized they needed to guard the treasure. They decided to take turns living with the old man, and that way they could look after him, too. So the first week the youngest son moved in with his father, and cared and cooked for him. The next week the middle son took his place, and the week afterward the eldest son took a turn. This went on for some time.

At last the old father grew sick and died. The sons gave him a very nice funeral, for they knew there was a fortune sitting beneath the kitchen table, and they could afford to splurge a little on the old man now.

When the service was over, they hunted through the house until they found the key, and unlocked the chest. And of course they found it full of broken glass.

"What a rotten trick!" yelled the eldest son. "What a cruel thing to do to your own sons!"

"But what else could he have done, really?" asked the middle son sadly. "We must be honest with ourselves. If it wasn't for this chest, we would have neglected him until the end of his days."

"I'm so ashamed of myself," sobbed the youngest. "We forced

our own father to stoop to deceit, because we would not observe the very commandment he taught us when we were young."

But the eldest son tipped the chest over to make sure there was nothing valuable hidden among the glass after all. He poured the broken pieces onto the floor until it was empty. Then the three brothers silently stared inside, where they now read an inscription left for them on the bottom: HONOR THY FATHER AND MOTHER.

---

## Which Loved Best?

*Joy Allison*

Through dedication to duties we show devotion to the ones we love.

"I love you, Mother," said little John;
Then, forgetting his work, his cap went on,
And he was off to the garden swing,
And left her the water and wood to bring.
"I love you, Mother," said rosy Nell—
"I love you better than tongue can tell";
Then she teased and pouted full half the day,
Till her mother rejoiced when she went to play.
"I love you, Mother," said little Fan;
"Today I'll help you all I can;
How glad I am that school doesn't keep!"
So she rocked the babe till it fell asleep.

Then, stepping softly, she fetched the broom,
And swept the floor and tidied the room;
Busy and happy all day was she,
Helpful and happy as child could be.
"I love you, Mother," again they said,
Three little children going to bed;
How do you think that mother guessed
Which of them really loved her best?

# Cain and Abel

*Retold by Jesse Lyman Hurlbut*

Here, according to the Bible, is the story of the first murder. Just as God sought out Adam and Eve in the Garden of Eden when they fell ("What is this that thou hast done?"), he seeks Cain after Abel's death. Just as Adam and Eve tried to avoid blame ("The serpent beguiled me"), Cain denies his crime. Whether or not one believes in original sin or divine reconciliation, there is certainly no denying our age-old struggle to accept responsibility for our own trespasses.

Adam and Eve went out into the world to live and to work. For a time they were all alone, but after a while God gave them a little child of their own, the first baby that ever came into the world. Eve named him Cain; and after a time another baby came, whom she named Abel.

When the two boys grew up, they worked, as their father worked before them. Cain chose to work in the fields, and to raise grain and fruits. Abel had a flock of sheep and became a shepherd.

While Adam and Eve were living in the Garden of Eden, they could talk with God, and hear God's voice speaking to them. But now that they were out in the world, they could no longer talk with God freely, as before. So when they came to God, they built an altar of stones heaped up, and upon it they laid something as a gift to God, and burned it, to show that it was not their own, but was given to God, whom they could not see. Then before the altar they made their prayer to God, and asked God to forgive their sins—all that they had done that was wrong—and prayed God to bless them and do good to them.

Each of these brothers, Cain and Abel, offered upon the altar to God his own gift. Cain brought the fruits and the grain which he had grown. And Abel brought a sheep from his flock, and killed it and burned it upon the altar. For some reason God was pleased with Abel and his offering, but was not pleased with Cain and his offering. Perhaps Cain's heart was not right when he came before God.

And God showed that he was not pleased with Cain, and Cain,

instead of being sorry for his sin, and asking God to forgive him, was very angry with God, and angry also toward his brother Abel. When they were out in the field together, Cain struck his brother Abel and killed him. So the first baby in the world grew up to be the murderer of his own brother.

And the Lord said to Cain, "Where is Abel your brother?"

And Cain answered, "I do not know. Am I my brother's keeper?"

Then the Lord said to Cain, "What is this that you have done? Your brother's blood is like a voice crying to me from the ground. Do you see how the ground has opened, like a mouth, to drink your brother's blood? As long as you live, you shall be under God's curse for the murder of your brother. You shall wander over the earth, and shall never find a home, because you have done this wicked deed."

And Cain said to the Lord, "My punishment is greater than I can bear. Thou hast driven me out from among men, and thou hast hid thy face from me. If any man finds me he will kill me, because I shall be alone, and no one will be my friend."

And God said to Cain, "If anyone harms Cain, he shall be punished for it." And the Lord God placed a mark on Cain, so that whoever met him should know him, and should know also that God had forbidden any man to harm him. Then Cain and his wife went away from Adam's home, to live in a place by themselves, and there they had children. And Cain's family built a city in that land, and Cain named the city after his first child, whom he had called Enoch.

---

# The Ten Commandments

Western morality may be said to begin with these ten very old, very good rules for living.

1. I am the Lord thy God. Thou shalt have no other gods before me.
2. Thou shalt not make unto thee any graven image.
3. Thou shalt not take the name of the Lord thy God in vain.
4. Remember the sabbath day, to keep it holy.

5. Honor thy father and thy mother.
6. Thou shalt not kill.
7. Thou shalt not commit adultery.
8. Thou shalt not steal.
9. Thou shalt not bear false witness against thy neighbor.
10. Thou shalt not covet.

# If You Were

This little poem reminds us whose responsibilities we should take care of first.

If you were busy being kind,
Before you knew it, you would find
You'd soon forget to think 'twas true
That someone was unkind to you.

If you were busy being glad,
And cheering people who are sad,
Although your heart might ache a bit,
You'd soon forget to notice it.

If you were busy being good,
And doing just the best you could,
You'd not have time to blame some man
Who's doing just the best he can.

If you were busy being right,
You'd find yourself too busy quite
To criticize your neighbor long
Because he's busy being wrong.

# The Bell of Atri

*Retold by James Baldwin*

This old story reminds us that the essence of what we know as justice in civil affairs is people living up to their obligations toward one another.

Atri is the name of a little town in Italy. It is a very old town, and is built halfway up the side of a steep hill.

A long time ago, the King of Atri bought a fine large bell, and had it hung up in a tower in the marketplace. A long rope that reached almost to the ground was fastened to the bell. The smallest child could ring the bell by pulling upon this rope.

"It is the bell of justice," said the king.

When at last everything was ready, the people of Atri had a great holiday. All the men and women and children came down to the marketplace to look at the bell of justice. It was a very pretty bell, and was polished until it looked almost as bright and yellow as the sun.

"How we should like to hear it ring!" they said.

Then the king came down the street.

"Perhaps he will ring it," said the people. And everybody stood very still, and waited to see what he would do.

But he did not ring the bell. He did not even take the rope in his hands. When he came to the foot of the tower, he stopped, and raised his hand.

"My people," he said, "do you see this beautiful bell? It is your bell. But it must never be rung except in case of need. If any one of you is wronged at any time, he may come and ring the bell. And then the judges shall come together at once, and hear his case, and give him justice. Rich and poor, old and young, all alike may come. But no one must touch the rope unless he knows that he has been wronged."

Many years passed by after this. Many times did the bell in the marketplace ring out to call the judges together. Many wrongs were righted, many ill-doers were punished. At last the hempen rope was almost worn out. The lower part of it was untwisted; some of the strands were broken; it became so short that only a tall man could reach it.

"This will never do," said the judges one day. "What if a child should be wronged? It could not ring the bell to let us know it."

They gave orders that a new rope should be put upon the bell at once—a rope that should hang down to the ground, so that the smallest child could reach it. But there was not a rope to be found in all Atri. They would have to send across the mountains for one, and it would be many days before it could be brought. What if some great wrong should be done before it came? How could the judges know about it, if the injured one could not reach the old rope?

"Let me fix it for you," said a man who stood by.

He ran into his garden, which was not far away, and soon came back with a long grapevine in his hands.

"This will do for a rope," he said. And he climbed up, and fastened it to the bell. The slender vine, with its leaves and tendrils still upon it, trailed to the ground.

"Yes," said the judges, "it is a very good rope. Let it be as it is."

Now, on the hillside above the village, there lived a man who had once been a brave knight. In his youth he had ridden through many lands, and he had fought in many a battle. His best friend through all that time had been his horse—a strong, noble steed that had borne him safe through many a danger.

But the knight, when he grew older, cared no more to ride into battle; he cared no more to do brave deeds; he thought of nothing but gold; he became a miser. At last he sold all that he had, except his horse, and went to live in a little hut on the hillside. Day after day he sat among his moneybags, and planned how he might get more gold. And day after day his horse stood in his bare stall, half starved, and shivering with cold.

"What is the use of keeping that lazy steed?" said the miser to himself one morning. "Every week it costs me more to keep him than he is worth. I might sell him, but there is not a man that wants him. I cannot even give him away. I will turn him out to shift for himself, and pick grass by the roadside. If he starves to death, so much the better."

So the brave old horse was turned out to find what he could among the rocks on the barren hillside. Lame and sick, he strolled along the dusty roads, glad to find a blade of grass or a thistle. The boys threw stones at him, the dogs barked at him, and in all the world there was no one to pity him.

One hot afternoon, when no one was upon the street, the horse chanced to wander into the marketplace. Not a man nor child was there, for the heat of the sun had driven them all indoors. The gates were wide open; the poor beast could roam where he pleased. He saw the grapevine rope that hung from the bell of justice. The leaves and tendrils upon it were still fresh and green, for it had not been there long. What a fine dinner they would be for a starving horse!

He stretched his thin neck, and took one of the tempting morsels in his mouth. It was hard to break it from the vine. He pulled at it, and the great bell above him began to ring. All the people in Atri heard it. It seemed to say,

Someone has done me wrong!
Someone has done me wrong!
Oh! come and judge my case!
Oh! come and judge my case!
For I've been wronged!

The judges heard it. They put on their robes, and went out through the hot streets to the marketplace. They wondered who it could be who would ring the bell at such a time. When they passed through the gate, they saw the old horse nibbling at the vine.

"Ha!" cried one, "it is the miser's steed. He has come to call for justice. For his master, as everybody knows, has treated him most shamefully."

"He pleads his cause as well as any dumb brute can," said another.

"And he shall have justice!" said the third.

Meanwhile a crowd of men and women and children had come into the marketplace, eager to learn what cause the judges were about to try. When they saw the horse, all stood still in wonder. Then everyone was ready to tell how they had seen him wandering on the hills, unfed, uncared for, while his master sat at home counting his bags of gold.

"Go bring the miser before us," said the judges.

And when he came, they bade him stand and hear their judgment.

"This horse has served you well for many a year," they said. "He has saved you from many a peril. He has helped you gain your wealth. Therefore we order that one half of all your gold shall be set aside to buy him shelter and food, a green pasture where he may graze, and a warm stall to comfort him in his old age."

The miser hung his head, and grieved to lose his gold. But the people shouted with joy, and the horse was led away to his new stall and a dinner such as he had not had in many a day.

---

# Icarus and Daedalus

This famous Greek myth reminds us exactly why young people have a responsibility to obey their parents—for the same good reason parents have a responsibility to guide their children: there are many things adults know that young people do not. The ancient Greek dramatist Aeschylus put it this way: "Obedience is the mother of success and is wedded to safety." Safe childhoods and successful upbringings require a measure of obedience, as Icarus finds out the hard way.

Daedalus was the most skillful builder and inventor of his day in ancient Greece. He built magnificent palaces and gardens, and created wonderful works of art throughout the land. His statues were so beautifully crafted they were taken for living beings, and it was believed they could see and walk about. People said someone as cunning as Daedalus must have learned the secrets of his craft from the gods themselves.

Now across the sea, on the island of Crete, lived a king named Minos. King Minos had a terrible monster that was half bull and half man called the Minotaur, and he needed someplace to keep it. When he heard of Daedalus's cleverness, he invited him to come to his country and build a prison to hold the beast. So Daedalus and his young son, Icarus, sailed to Crete, and there Daedalus built the famous Labyrinth, a maze of winding passages so tangled and twisted that whoever went in could never find the way out. And there they put the Minotaur.

When the Labyrinth was finished, Daedalus wanted to sail back to Greece with his son, but Minos had made up his mind to keep them in Crete. He wanted Daedalus to stay and invent more wonderful devices for him, so he locked them both in a high tower beside the sea. The king knew Daedalus was clever enough to escape from the tower, so he also ordered that every ship be searched for stowaways before sailing from Crete.

Other men may have given up, but not Daedalus. From his high tower he watched the seagulls drifting on the ocean breezes. "Minos may control the land and the sea," he said, "but he does not rule the air. We'll go that way."

So he summoned all the secrets of his craft, and he set to work. Little by little, he gathered a great pile of feathers of all sizes. He fastened them together with thread, and molded them with wax, and at last he had two great wings like those of the seagulls. He tied them to his shoulders, and after one or two clumsy efforts, he found that by waving his arms he could rise into the air. He held himself aloft, wavering this way and that with the wind, until he taught himself how to glide and soar on the currents as gracefully as any gull.

Next he built a second pair of wings for Icarus. He taught the boy how to move the feathers and rise a few feet into the air, and then let him fly back and forth across the room. Then he taught him how to ride the air currents, climbing in circles, and hang in the winds. They practiced together until Icarus was ready.

Finally the day came when the winds were just right. Father and son strapped on their wings and prepared to fly home.

"Remember all I've told you," Daedalus said. "Above all, remember you must not fly too high or too low. If you fly too low, the ocean sprays will clog your wings and make them too heavy. If you fly too high, the heat of the sun will melt the wax, and your wings will fall apart. Stay close to me, and you'll be fine."

Up they rose, the boy after his father, and the hateful ground of Crete sank far beneath them. As they flew the plowman stopped his work to gaze, and the shepherd leaned on his staff to watch them, and people came running out of their houses to catch a glimpse of the two figures high above the treetops. Surely they were gods—Apollo, perhaps, with Cupid after him.

At first the flight seemed terrible to both Daedalus and Icarus. The wide, endless sky dazed them, and even the quickest glance down made their brains reel. But gradually they grew used to riding among the clouds, and they lost their fear. Icarus felt the wind fill his wings and lift him higher and higher, and began to sense a freedom he had never known before. He looked down with great excitement at all the islands they passed, and their people, and at the broad blue sea spread out beneath him, dotted with the white sails of ships. He soared higher and higher, forgetting his father's warning. He forgot everything in the world but joy.

"Come back!" Daedalus called frantically. "You're flying too high! Remember the sun! Come down! Come down!"

But Icarus thought of nothing but his own excitement and glory. He longed to fly as close as he could to the heavens. Nearer and nearer he came to the sun, and slowly his wings began to soften. One by one the feathers began to fall and scatter in the air, and suddenly the wax melted all at once. Icarus felt himself falling. He fluttered his arms as fast as he could, but no feathers remained to hold the air. He cried out for his father, but it was too late—with a scream he fell from his lofty height and plunged into the sea, disappearing beneath the waves.

Daedalus circled over the water again and again, but he saw nothing but feathers floating on the waves, and he knew his son was gone. At last the body came to the surface, and he managed to pluck it from the sea. With a heavy burden and broken heart Daedalus slowly flew away. When he reached land, he buried his son and built a temple to the gods. Then he hung up his wings, and never flew again.

# The Sword of Damocles

*Adapted from James Baldwin*

This is one of our oldest "if you can't stand the heat, get out of the kitchen" stories. It is a great reminder that if we aspire to any kind of high office or job, we must be willing to live with all the burdens that come with it.

There once was a king named Dionysius who ruled in Syracuse, the richest city in Sicily. He lived in a fine palace where there were many beautiful and costly things, and he was waited upon by a host of servants who were always ready to do his bidding.

Naturally, because Dionysius had so much wealth and power, there were many in Syracuse who envied his good fortune. Damocles was one of these. He was one of Dionysius's best friends, and he was always saying to him, "How lucky you are! You have everything anyone could wish for. You must be the happiest man in the world."

One day Dionysius grew tired of hearing such talk. "Come now," he said, "do you really think I'm happier than everyone else?"

"But of course you are," Damocles replied. "Look at the great treasures you possess, and the power you hold. You have not a single worry in the world. How could life be any better?"

"Perhaps you would like to change places with me," said Dionysius.

"Oh, I would never dream of that," said Damocles. "But if I could only have your riches and your pleasures for one day, I should never want any greater happiness."

"Very well. Trade places with me for just one day, and you shall have them."

And so, the next day, Damocles was led to the palace, and all the servants were instructed to treat him as their master. They dressed him in royal robes, and placed on his head a crown of gold. He sat down at a table in the banquet hall, and rich foods were set before him. Nothing was wanting that could give him pleasure. There were costly wines, and beautiful flowers, and rare perfumes, and delightful music. He rested himself among soft cushions, and felt he was the happiest man in all the world.

"Ah, this is the life," he sighed to Dionysius, who sat at the other end of the long table. "I've never enjoyed myself so much."

And as he raised a cup to his lips, he lifted his eyes toward the ceiling. What was that dangling above him, with its point almost touching his head?

Damocles stiffened. The smile faded from his lips, and his face turned ashy pale. His hands trembled. He wanted no more food, no more wine, no more music. He only wanted to be out of the palace, far away, he cared not where. For directly above his head hung a sword, held to the ceiling by only a single horsehair. Its sharp blade glittered as it pointed right between his eyes. He started to jump up and run, but stopped himself, frightened that any sudden move might snap the thin thread and bring the sword down. He sat frozen to his chair.

"What is the matter, my friend?" Dionysius asked. "You seem to have lost your appetite."

"That sword! That sword!" whispered Damocles. "Don't you see it?"

"Of course I see it," said Dionysius. "I see it every day. It always hangs over my head, and there is always the chance someone or something may cut the slim thread. Perhaps one of my own advisors will grow jealous of my power and try to kill me. Or someone may spread lies about me, to turn the people against me. It may be that a neighboring kingdom will send an army to seize this throne. Or I might make an unwise decision that will bring my downfall. If you want to be a leader, you must be willing to accept these risks. They come with the power, you see."

"Yes, I do see," said Damocles. "I see now that I was mistaken, and that you have much to think about besides your riches and fame. Please take your place, and let me go back to my own house."

And as long as he lived, Damocles never again wanted to change places, even for a moment, with the king.

## The Silent Couple

This tale appears in different versions all over the world, from Sri Lanka to Scotland. This version warns us that pettiness can cause us to forget our obligations.

There was once a young man who was said to be the most pigheaded fellow in town, and a young woman who was said to be the most mule-headed maiden, and of course they somehow managed to fall in love and be married. After the wedding ceremony, they had a grand feast at their new house, which lasted all day.

Finally all the friends and relatives could eat no more, and one by one they went home. The bride and groom collapsed from exhaustion, and were just getting ready to take off their shoes and relax, when the husband noticed that the last guest to leave had failed to close the door.

"My dear," he said, "would you mind getting up and shutting the door? There's a draft coming in."

"Why should I shut it?" yawned the wife. "I've been on my feet all day, and I just sat down. You shut it."

"So that's the way it's going to be!" snapped the husband. "Just as soon as you get the ring on your finger, you turn into a lazy good-for-nothing!"

"How dare you!" shouted the bride. "We haven't even been married a day, and already you're calling me names and ordering me around! I should have known this is the kind of husband you'd turn out to be!"

"Nag, nag, nag," grumbled the husband. "Must I listen to your complaining forever?"

"And must I always listen to your carping and whining?" asked the wife.

They sat glaring at each other for a full five minutes. Then an idea popped into the bride's head.

"My dear," she said, "neither of us wants to shut the door, and both of us are tired of hearing the other's voice. So I propose a contest. The one who speaks first must get up and close the door."

"It's the best idea I've heard all day," replied the husband. "Let us begin now."

So they made themselves comfortable, each on a chair, and sat face-to-face without saying a word.

They had been that way for about two hours when a couple of thieves with a cart passed by and saw the open door. They crept into the house, which seemed perfectly deserted, and began to steal everything they could lay their hands on. They took tables and chairs, pulled paintings off the walls, even rolled up carpets. But the newlyweds neither spoke nor moved.

"I can't believe this," thought the husband. "They'll take everything we own, and she won't make a sound."

"Why doesn't he call for help?" the wife asked herself. "Is he just going to sit there while they steal whatever they want?"

Eventually the thieves noticed the silent, motionless couple and, mistaking them for wax figures, stripped them of their jewelry, watches, and wallets. But neither husband nor wife uttered a sound.

The robbers hurried away with their loot, and the newlyweds sat through the night. At dawn a policeman walked by and, noticing the open door, stuck in his head to ask if everything was all right. But, of course, he couldn't get an answer out of the silent couple.

"Now, see here!" he yelled, "I'm an officer of the law! Who are you? Is this your house? What happened to all your furniture?" And still getting no response, he raised his hands to box the man's ears.

"Don't you dare!" cried the wife, jumping to her feet. "That's my new husband, and if you lay a finger on him, you'll have to answer to me!"

"I won!" yelled the husband, clapping his hands. "Now go and close the door."

# The Athenian Oath

This oath was taken by the young men of ancient Athens when they reached the age of seventeen.

We will never bring disgrace on this our City by an act of dishonesty or cowardice.
We will fight for the ideals and Sacred Things of the City both alone and with many.
We will revere and obey the City's laws, and will do our best to incite a like reverence and respect in those above us who are prone to annul them or set them at naught.
We will strive increasingly to quicken the public's sense of civic duty.
Thus in all these ways we will transmit this City, not only not less, but greater and more beautiful than it was transmitted to us.

---

# The Duties of a Scout

Here are the rules every Boy Scout and Girl Scout promises to live by. Other than the Ten Commandments, it is hard to imagine a better list of virtuous aims for the young.

### The Boy Scout Oath

On my honor I will do my best
To do my duty to God and my country
and to obey the Scout Law;
To help other people at all times;
To keep myself physically strong,
mentally awake, and morally straight.

## The Girl Scout Promise

On my honor, I will try:
To serve God and my country,
To help people at all times,
And to live by the Girl Scout Law.

## The Boy Scout Law

A Scout is Trustworthy
A Scout is Loyal
A Scout is Helpful
A Scout is Friendly
A Scout is Courteous
A Scout is Kind
A Scout is Obedient
A Scout is Cheerful
A Scout is Thrifty
A Scout is Brave
A Scout is Clean
A Scout is Reverent

## The Girl Scout Law

I will do my best:

- to be honest
- to be fair
- to help where I am needed
- to be cheerful
- to be friendly and considerate
- to be a sister to every Girl Scout
- to respect authority
- to use resources wisely
- to protect and improve the world around me
- to show respect for myself and others through my words and actions.

# The American's Creed

*William Tyler Page*

In 1917, William Tyler Page of Maryland won a nationwide contest for "the best summary of American political faith." The U.S. House of Representatives accepted the statement as the American's Creed on April 3, 1918. Its two paragraphs remind us that responsibilities are the source of rights. It deserves to be read and recited. Today very few people have even heard of it.

I believe in the United States of America as a Government of the people, by the people, for the people; whose just powers are derived from the consent of the governed; a democracy in a republic; a sovereign Nation of many sovereign States; a perfect union, one and inseparable; established upon those principles of freedom, equality, justice, and humanity for which American patriots sacrificed their lives and fortunes.

I therefore believe it is my duty to my country to love it; to support its Constitution; to obey its laws; to respect its flag, and to defend it against all enemies.

---

# Respecting the Flag

The United States Code states that "the flag represents a living country and is itself considered a living thing." Here are a few rules for respecting the U.S. flag. They are taken from a booklet entitled *Our Flag* published by Congress. Students of recent politics will be interested in the last rule.

- When the flag is displayed during rendition of the National Anthem or recital of the Pledge of Allegiance, all present except those in uniform should stand at attention facing the flag with the right hand over the heart.
- It is the universal custom to display the flag only from sunrise to

sunset on buildings and on stationary flagstaffs in the open. However, when a patriotic effect is desired, the flag may be displayed twenty-four hours a day if properly illuminated during the hours of darkness.

- The flag should be hoisted briskly and lowered ceremoniously.
- The flag should not be displayed on days when the weather is inclement, except when an all-weather flag is displayed.
- The flag should be displayed daily on or near the main administration building of every public institution.
- The flag should be displayed in or near every polling place on election days.
- The flag should be displayed during school days in or near every schoolhouse.
- The flag of the United States of America should be at the center and at the highest point of the group when a number of flags of states or localities, or pennants of societies, are grouped and displayed from staffs.
- The flag should never be displayed with the union down, except as a signal of dire distress in instances of extreme danger to life or property.
- The flag should never touch anything beneath it, such as the ground, the floor, water, or merchandise.
- The flag should never be carried flat or horizontally, but always aloft and free.
- The flag should never be used as wearing apparel, bedding, or drapery.
- The flag, when it is in such condition that it is no longer a fitting emblem for display, should be destroyed in a dignified way, preferably by burning.

# The Charge of the Light Brigade

*Alfred Tennyson*

Tennyson based this famous poem on the Battle of Balaklava, fought on October 25, 1854, during the Crimean War, in which a small force of British cavalry made a daring but disastrous assault against a Russian artillery line. After the attack, only 195 of the 673 men in the Light Brigade answered muster call. Some find it fashionable to ridicule this poem as a glorification of war and paean to those who blindly, and stupidly, follow orders. But the fact is that there are times when obedient acts of self-sacrifice and courage merit both admiration and profound gratitude.

Half a league, half a league,
   Half a league onward,
All in the valley of Death
   Rode the six hundred.

"Forward, the Light Brigade!
Charge for the guns!" he said:
Into the valley of Death
   Rode the six hundred.

"Forward, the Light Brigade!"
Was there a man dismay'd?
Not tho' the soldier knew
   Someone had blunder'd:
Theirs not to make reply,
Theirs not to reason why,
Theirs but to do and die:
Into the valley of Death
   Rode the six hundred.

Cannon to right of them,
Cannon to left of them,
Cannon in front of them
   Volley'd and thunder'd;
Storm'd at with shot and shell,
Boldly they rode and well,
Into the jaws of Death,
Into the mouth of Hell
   Rode the six hundred.

Flash'd all their sabers bare,
Flash'd as they turn'd in air
Sab'ring the gunners there,
Charging an army, while
   All the world wonder'd:
Plunged in the battery smoke
Right thro' the line they broke;
Cossack and Russian
Reel'd from the saber stroke
   Shatter'd and sunder'd.
Then they rode back, but not
   Not the six hundred.

Cannon to right of them,
Cannon to left of them,
Cannon behind them
   Volley'd and thunder'd:
Storm'd at with shot and shell,
While horse and hero fell,
They that had fought so well
Came through the jaws of death
Back from the mouth of hell,
All that was left of them—
   Left of six hundred.

When can their glory fade?
Oh, the wild charge they made!
   All the world wonder'd.
Honor the charge they made!
Honor the Light Brigade—
   Noble six hundred!

# The Bridge Builder

*Will Allen Dromgoole*

This poem speaks of each generation's responsibilities to its successors.

An old man, going a lone highway,
Came, at the evening, cold and gray,
To a chasm, vast, and deep, and wide,
Through which was flowing a sullen tide.
The old man crossed in the twilight dim;
The sullen stream had no fears for him;
But he turned, when safe on the other side,
And built a bridge to span the tide.
"Old man," said a fellow pilgrim, near,
"You are wasting strength with building here;
*Your* journey will end with the ending day;
You never again must pass this way;
You have crossed the chasm, deep and wide—
Why build you the bridge at the eventide?"

The builder lifted his old gray head:
"Good friend, in the path I have come," he said,
"There followeth after me today
A youth, whose feet must pass this way.
This chasm, that has been naught to me,
To that fair-haired youth may a pitfall be.
He, too, must cross in the twilight dim;
Good friend, I am building the bridge for *him*."

# What a Baby Costs

*Edgar Guest*

It is never too early to begin impressing upon our children, by both word and deed, the responsibilities of parenthood. Part of the job of raising children is raising them to be successful parents themselves.

"How much do babies cost?" said he
The other night upon my knee;
And then I said: "They cost a lot;
A lot of watching by a cot,
A lot of sleepless hours and care,
A lot of heartache and despair,
A lot of fear and trying dread,
And sometimes many tears are shed
In payment for our babies small,
But every one is worth it all.

"For babies people have to pay
A heavy price from day to day—
There is no way to get one cheap.
Why, sometimes when they're fast asleep
You have to get up in the night
And go and see that they're all right.
But what they cost in constant care
And worry, does not half compare
With what they bring of joy and bliss—
You'd pay much more for just a kiss.

"Who buys a baby has to pay
A portion of the bill each day;
He has to give his time and thought
Unto the little one he's bought.
He has to stand a lot of pain
Inside his heart and not complain;
And pay with lonely days and sad
For all the happy hours he's had.
All this a baby costs, and yet
His smile is worth it all, you bet."

---

# F. Scott Fitzgerald to His Daughter

In this letter we see the molding of character: a father gently but explicitly telling his daughter what her duties are.

*Dear Pie:*
I feel very strongly about your doing duty. Would you give me a little more documentation about your reading in French? I am glad you are happy—but I never believe much in happiness. I never believe in misery either. Those are things you see on the stage or the screen or the printed page, they never really happen to you in life.

All I believe in in life is the rewards for virtue (according to your talents) and the *punishments* for not fulfilling your duties, which are doubly costly. If there is such a volume in the camp library, will you ask Mrs. Tyson to let you look up a sonnet of Shakespeare's in which the line occurs *Lilies that fester smell far worse than weeds*.

Have had no thoughts today, life seems composed of getting up a *Saturday Evening Post* story. I think of you, and always pleasantly; but if you call me "Pappy" again I am going to take the White Cat out and beat his bottom *hard, six times for every time you are impertinent*. Do you react to that?

I will arrange the camp bill.

Halfwit, I will conclude. Things to worry about:

Worry about courage
Worry about cleanliness
Worry about efficiency
Worry about horsemanship . . .

Things not to worry about:

Don't worry about popular opinion
Don't worry about dolls
Don't worry about the past
Don't worry about the future
Don't worry about growing up
Don't worry about anybody getting ahead of you
Don't worry about triumph
Don't worry about failure unless it comes through your own fault
Don't worry about mosquitoes
Don't worry about flies
Don't worry about insects in general
Don't worry about parents
Don't worry about boys
Don't worry about disappointments
Don't worry about pleasures
Don't worry about satisfactions

Things to think about:

What am I really aiming at?
How good am I in comparison to my contemporaries in regard to:

(a) Scholarship
(b) Do I really understand about people and am I able to get along with them?
(c) Am I trying to make my body a useful instrument or am I neglecting it?

*With dearest love*

# The Hiltons' Holiday

*Sarah Orne Jewett*

This story is about the most fundamental of parental responsibilities: spending time with children. Here we find two parents doing their best to instruct their daughters in matters of right conduct. We find the teaching through example of civility, politeness, remembrance of old friends, and thoughtfulness for loved ones. And we discover that in the observance of these daily duties, we win happiness. According to Willa Cather, this was Sarah Orne Jewett's (1849–1909) favorite story.

## I

There was a bright, full moon in the clear sky, and the sunset was still shining faintly in the west. Dark woods stood all about the old Hilton farmhouse, save down the hill, westward, where lay the shadowy fields which John Hilton, and his father before him, had cleared and tilled with much toil—the small fields to which they had given the industry and even affection of their honest lives.

John Hilton was sitting on the doorstep of his house. As he moved his head in and out of the shadows, turning now and then to speak to his wife, who sat just within the doorway, one could see his good face, rough and somewhat unkempt, as if he were indeed a creature of the shady woods and brown earth, instead of the noisy town. It was late in the long spring evening, and he had just come from the lower field as cheerful as a boy, proud of having finished the planting of his potatoes.

"I had to do my last row mostly by feelin'," he said to his wife. "I'm proper glad I pushed through, an' went back an' ended off after supper. 'Twould have taken me a good part o' tomorrow mornin', an' broke my day."

" 'Tain't no use for ye to work yourself all to pieces, John," answered the woman quickly. "I declare it does seem harder than ever that we couldn't have kep' our boy; he'd been comin' fourteen years old this fall, most a grown man, and he'd work right 'longside of ye now the whole time."

" 'Twas hard to lose him; I do seem to miss little John," said the father sadly. "I expect there was reasons why 'twas best. I feel able an' smart to work; my father was a girt strong man, an' a monstrous worker afore me. 'Tain't that; but I was thinkin' by myself today what a sight o' company the boy would ha' been. You know, small's he was, how I could trust to leave him anywheres with the team, and how he'd beseech to go with me wherever I was goin'; always right in my tracks I used to tell 'em. Poor little John, for all he was so young he had a great deal o' judgment; he'd ha' made a likely man."

The mother sighed heavily as she sat within the shadow.

"But then there's the little girls, a sight o' help an' company," urged the father eagerly, as if it were wrong to dwell upon sorrow and loss. "Katy, she's most as good as a boy, except that she ain't very rugged. She's a real little farmer, she's helped me a sight this spring; an' you've got Susan Ellen, that makes a complete little housekeeper for ye as far as she's learnt. I don't see but we're better off than most folks, each on us having a workmate."

"That's so, John," acknowledged Mrs. Hilton wistfully, beginning to rock steadily in her straight, splint-bottomed chair. It was always a good sign when she rocked.

"Where be the little girls so late?" asked their father. " 'Tis gettin' long past eight o'clock. I don't know when we've all set up so late, but it's so kind o' summerlike an' pleasant. Why, where be they gone?"

"I've told ye; only over to Becker's folks," answered the mother. "I don't see myself what keeps 'em so late; they beseeched me after supper till I let 'em go. They're all in a dazzle with the new teacher; she asked 'em to come over. They say she's unusual smart with 'rethmetic, but she has a kind of a gorpen look to me. She's goin' to give Katy some pieces for her doll, but I told Katy she ought to be ashamed wantin' dolls' pieces, big as she's gettin' to be. I don't know's she ought, though; she ain't but nine this summer."

"Let her take her comfort," said the kindhearted man. "Them things draws her to the teacher, an' makes them acquainted. Katy's shy with new folks, more so'n Susan Ellen, who's of the business kind. Katy's shy-feelin' and wishful."

"I don't know but she is," agreed the mother slowly. "Ain't it sing'lar how well acquainted you be with that one, an' I with Susan Ellen? 'Twas always so from the first. I'm doubtful sometimes our Katy ain't one that'll be like to get married—anyways not about here. She lives right with herself, but Susan Ellen ain't nothin' when she's alone, she's always after company; all the boys is waitin' on her a'ready. I ain't afraid but she'll take her pick when the time comes. I expect to see Susan Ellen well settled—she feels grown up now—but Katy don't care one mite 'bout none o' them things. She wants to be rovin' out-o'-doors. I do believe she'd stand an' hark to a bird the whole forenoon."

"Perhaps she'll grow up to be a teacher," suggested John Hilton. "She takes to her book more 'n the other one. I should like one of 'em to be a teacher same's my mother was. They're good girls as anybody's got."

"So they be," said the mother, with unusual gentleness, and the creak of her rocking chair was heard, regular as the ticking of a clock. The night breeze stirred in the great woods, and the sound of a brook that went falling down the hillside grew louder and louder. Now and then one could hear the plaintive chirp of a bird. The moon glittered with whiteness like a winter moon, and shone upon the low-roofed house until its small windowpanes gleamed like silver, and one could almost see the colors of a blooming bush of lilac that grew in a sheltered angle by the kitchen door. There was an incessant sound of frogs in the lowlands.

"Be you sound asleep, John?" asked the wife presently.

"I don't know but what I was a'most," said the tired man, starting a little. "I should laugh if I was to fall sound asleep right here on the step; 'tis the bright night, I expect, makes my eyes feel heavy, an' 'tis so peaceful. I was up an' dressed a little past four an' out to work. Well, well!" and he laughed sleepily and rubbed his eyes. "Where's the little girls? I'd better step along an' meet 'em."

"I wouldn't just yet; they'll get home all right, but 'tis late for 'em certain. I don't want 'em keepin' Mis' Becker's folks up neither. There, le's wait a few minutes," urged Mrs. Hilton.

"I've be'n a-thinkin' all day I'd like to give the child'n some kind of a treat," said the father, wide awake now. "I hurried up my work 'cause I had it so in mind. They don't have the opportunities some do, an' I want 'em to know the world, an' not stay right here on the farm like a couple o' bushes."

"They're a sight better off not to be so full o' notions as some is," protested the mother suspiciously.

"Certain," answered the farmer; "but they're good, bright child'n, an' commencin' to take a sight o' notice. I want 'em to have all we can give 'em. I want 'em to see how other folks does things."

"Why, so do I"—here the rocking chair stopped ominously—"but so long's they're contented—"

"Contented ain't all in this world; hopper-toads may have that quality an' spend all their time a-blinkin'. I don't know's bein' contented is all there is to look for in a child. Ambition's somethin' to me."

"Now you've got your mind on to some plot or other." (The rocking chair began to move again.) "Why can't you talk right out?"

" 'Tain't nothin' special," answered the good man, a little ruffled; he was never prepared for his wife's mysterious powers of divination. "Well there, you do find things out the master! I only thought perhaps I'd take 'em tomorrow, an' go off somewhere if 'twas a good day. I've been promisin' for a good while I'd take 'em to Topham Corners; they've never been there since they was very small."

"I believe you want a good time yourself. You ain't never got over bein' a boy." Mrs. Hilton seemed much amused. "There, go if you want to an' take 'em; they've got their summer hats an' new dresses. I don't know o' nothin' that stands in the way. I should sense it better if there was a circus or anythin' to go to. Why don't you wait an' let the girls pick 'em some strawberries or nice ros'berries, and then they could take an' sell 'em to the stores?"

John Hilton reflected deeply. "I should like to get me some good yellow-turnip seed to plant late. I ain't more'n satisfied with what I've been gettin' o' late years o' Ira Speed. An' I'm goin' to provide me with a good hoe; mine's gettin' wore out an' all shackly. I can't seem to fix it good."

"Them's excuses," observed Mrs. Hilton, with friendly tolerance. "You just cover up the hoe with somethin', if you get it—I would. Ira Speed's so jealous he'll remember it of you this twenty year, your goin' an' buyin' a new hoe o' anybody but him."

"I've always thought 'twas a free country," said John Hilton soberly. "I don't want to vex Ira neither; he favors us all he can in trade. 'Tis difficult for him to spare a cent, but he's as honest as daylight."

At this moment there was a sudden sound of young voices, and a pair of young figures came out from the shadow of the woods into the moonlighted open space. An old cock crowed loudly from his perch in the shed, as if he were a herald of royalty. The little girls were hand in hand, and a brisk young dog capered about them as they came.

"Wa'n't it dark gittin' home through the woods this time o' night?" asked the mother hastily, and not without reproach.

"I don't love to have you gone so late; Mother an' me was timid about ye, and you've kep' Mis' Becker's folks up, I expect," said their father regretfully. "I don't want to have it said that my little girls ain't got good manners."

"The teacher had a party," chirped Susan Ellen, the elder of the two children. "Goin' home from school she asked the Grover boys, an' Mary an' Sarah Speed. An' Mis' Becker was real pleasant to us: she passed round some cake, an' handed us sap sugar on one of her best plates, an' we played games an' sung some pieces too. Mis' Becker thought we did real well. I can pick out most of a tune on the cabinet organ; teacher says she'll give me lessons."

"I want to know, dear!" exclaimed John Hilton.

"Yes, an' we played Copenhagen, an' took sides spellin', an' Katy beat everybody spellin' there was there."

Katy had not spoken; she was not so strong as her sister, and while Susan Ellen stood a step or two away addressing her eager little audience, Katy had seated herself close to her father on the doorstep. He put his arm around her shoulders, and drew her close to his side, where she stayed.

"Ain't you got nothin' to tell, daughter?" he asked, looking down fondly; and Katy gave a pleased little sigh for answer.

"Tell 'em what's goin' to be the last day o' school, and about our trimmin' the schoolhouse," she said; and Susan Ellen gave the program in most spirited fashion.

" 'Twill be a great time," said the mother, when she had finished. "I don't see why folks wants to go traipsin' off to strange places when such things is happenin' right about 'em." But the children did not observe her mysterious air. "Come, you must step yourselves right to bed!"

They all went into the dark, warm house; the bright moon shone steadily all night, and the lilac flowers were shaken by no breath of wind until the early dawn.

## II

The Hiltons always waked early. So did their neighbors, the crows and song sparrows and robins, the light-footed foxes and squirrels in the woods. When John Hilton waked, before five o'clock, an hour later than usual because he had sat up so late, he opened the house door and came out into the yard, crossing the short green turf hurriedly as if the day were too far spent for any loitering. The magnitude of the plan for taking a whole day of pleasure confronted him seriously, but the weather was fair, and his wife, whose disapproval could not have been set aside, had accepted and even smiled upon the great project. It was inevitable now that he and the children should go to Topham Corners. Mrs. Hilton had the pleasure of waking them, and telling the news.

In a few minutes they came frisking out to talk over the great plans. The cattle were already fed, and their father was milking. The only sign of high festivity was the wagon pulled out into the yard, with both seats put in as if it were Sunday; but Mr. Hilton still wore his everyday clothes, and Susan Ellen suffered instantly from disappointment.

"Ain't we goin', Father?" she asked complainingly; but he nodded and smiled at her, even though the cow, impatient to get to pasture, kept whisking her rough tail across his face. He held his head down and spoke cheerfully, in spite of this vexation.

"Yes, sister, we're goin' certain', an' goin' to have a great time too." Susan Ellen thought that he seemed like a boy at that delightful moment, and felt new sympathy and pleasure at once. "You go an' help Mother about breakfast an' them things; we want to get off quick's we can. You coax Mother now, both on ye, an' see if she won't go with us."

"She said she wouldn't be hired to," responded Susan Ellen. "She says it's goin' to be hot, an' she's laid out to go over an' see how her aunt Tamsen Brooks is this afternoon."

The father gave a little sigh; then he took heart again. The truth was that his wife made light of the contemplated pleasure, and, much as he usually valued her companionship and approval, he was sure that they should have a better time without her. It was impossible, however, not to feel guilty of disloyalty at the thought. Even though she might be completely unconscious of his best ideals, he only loved her and the ideals the more, and bent his energies to satisfying her indefinite expectations. His wife still kept much of that youthful beauty which Susan Ellen seemed likely to reproduce.

An hour later the best wagon was ready, and the great expedition set forth. The little dog sat apart, and barked as if it fell entirely upon him to voice the general excitement. Both seats were in the wagon, but the empty place testified to Mrs. Hilton's unyielding disposition. She had wondered why one broad seat would not do, but John Hilton meekly suggested that the wagon looked better with both. The little girls sat on the back seat dressed alike in their Sunday hats of straw with blue ribbons, and their little plaid shawls pinned neatly about their small shoulders. They wore gray thread gloves, and sat very straight. Susan Ellen was half a head the taller, but otherwise, from behind, they looked much alike. As for their father, he was in his Sunday best—a plain black coat, and a winter hat of felt, which was heavy and rusty-looking for that warm early summer day. He had it in mind to buy a new straw hat at Topham, so that this with the turnip seed and the hoe made three important reasons for going.

"Remember an' lay off your shawls when you get there an' carry them over your arms," said the mother, clucking like an excited hen to her chickens. "They'll do to keep the dust off your new dresses goin' an' comin'. An' when you eat your dinners don't get spots on you, an' don't point at folks as you ride by, an' stare, or they'll know you come from the country. An', John, you call into Cousin Ad'line Marlow's an' see how they all be, an' tell her I expect her over certain to stop awhile before hayin'. It always eases her phthisic to git up here on the high land. An' don't come home all wore out; an', John, don't you go an' buy me no kickshaws to fetch home. I ain't a child, an' you ain't got no money to waste. I expect you'll go, like's not, an' buy you some kind of a foolish boy's hat; do look an' see if it's reasonable good straw, an' won't splinter all off round the edge. An' you mind, John—"

"Yes, yes, hold on!" cried John impatiently; then he cast a last affectionate, reassuring look at her face, flushed with the hurry and responsibility of starting them off in proper shape. "I wish you was goin' too," he said, smiling. "I do so!" Then the old horse started, and they went out at the bars, and began the careful long descent of the hill. The young dog, tethered to the lilac bush, was frantic with piteous appeals; the little girls piped their eager goodbyes again and again, and their father turned many times to look back and wave his hand. As for their mother, she stood alone and watched them out of sight.

There was one place far out on the high road where she could catch a last glimpse of the wagon, and she waited what seemed a very long time until it appeared and then was lost to sight again behind a low hill. "They're nothin' but a pack o' child'n together," she said aloud; and then felt lonelier than she expected. She even stooped and petted the unresigned little dog as she passed him, going into the house.

The occasion was so much more important than anyone had

foreseen that both the little girls were speechless. It seemed at first like going to church in new clothes; or to a funeral; they hardly knew how to behave at the beginning of a whole day of pleasure. They made grave bows at such persons of their acquaintance as happened to be straying in the road. Once or twice they stopped before a farmhouse, while their father talked an inconsiderately long time with someone about the crops and the weather, and even dwelt upon town business and the doings of the selectmen, which might be talked of at any time. The explanations that he gave of their excursion seemed quite unnecessary. It was made entirely clear that he had a little business to do at Topham Corners, and thought he had better give the little girls a ride; they had been very steady at school, and he had finished planting, and could take the day as well as not. Soon, however, they all felt as if such an excursion were an everyday affair, and Susan Ellen began to ask eager questions, while Katy silently sat apart, enjoying herself as she never had done before. She liked to see the strange houses, and the children who belonged to them; it was delightful to find flowers that she knew growing all along the road, no matter how far she went from home. Each small homestead looked its best and pleasantest, and shared the exquisite beauty that early summer made—shared the luxury of greenness and floweriness that decked the rural world. There was an early peony or a late lilac in almost every dooryard.

It was seventeen miles to Topham. After a while they seemed very far from home, having left the hills far behind, and descended to a great level country with fewer tracts of woodland, and wider fields where the crops were much more forward. The houses were all painted, and the roads were smoother and wider. It had been so pleasant driving along that Katy dreaded going into the strange town when she first caught sight of it, though Susan Ellen kept asking with bold fretfulness if they were not almost there. They counted the steeples of four churches, and their father presently showed them the Topham Academy, where their grandmother once went to school, and told them that perhaps someday they would go there too. Katy's heart gave a strange leap; it was such a tremendous thing to think of, but instantly the suggestion was transformed for her into one of the certainties of life. She looked with solemn awe at the tall belfry, and the long rows of windows in the front of the academy, there where it stood high and white among the clustering trees. She hoped that they were going to drive by, but something forbade her taking the responsibility of saying so.

Soon the children found themselves among the crowded village houses. Their father turned to look at them with affectionate solicitude.

"Now sit up straight and appear pretty," he whispered to them. "We're among the best people now, an' I want folks to think well of you."

"I guess we're as good as they be," remarked Susan Ellen, looking at some innocent passersby with dark suspicion, but Katy tried indeed to sit straight, and folded her hands prettily in her lap, and wished with all her heart to be pleasing for her father's sake. Just then an elderly woman saw the wagon and the sedate party it carried, and smiled so kindly that it seemed to Katy as if Topham Corners had welcomed and received them. She smiled back again as if this hospitable person were an old friend, and entirely forgot that the eyes of all Topham had been upon her.

"There, now we're coming to an elegant house that I want you to see; you'll never forget it," said John Hilton. "It's where Judge Masterson lives, the great lawyer; the handsomest house in the county, everybody says."

"Do you know him, Father?" asked Susan Ellen.

"I do," answered John Hilton proudly. "Him and my mother went to school together in their young days, and were always called the two best scholars of their time. The Judge called to see her once; he stopped to our house to see her when I was a boy. An' then, some years ago—you've heard me tell how I was on the jury, an' when he heard my name spoken he looked at me sharp, and asked if I wa'n't the son of Catharine Winn, an' spoke most beautiful of your grandmother, an' how well he remembered their young days together."

"I like to hear about that," said Katy.

"She had it pretty hard, I'm afraid, up on the old farm. She keepin' school in our district when Father married her—that's the main reason I backed 'em down when they wanted to tear the old schoolhouse all to pieces," confided John Hilton, turning eagerly. "They all say she lived longer up here on the hill than she could anywhere, but she never had her health. I wa'n't but a boy when she died. Father an' me lived alone afterward till the time your mother come; 'twas a good while, too; I wa'n't married so young as some. 'Twas lonesome, I tell you; Father was plumb discouraged losin' of his wife, an' her long sickness an' all set him back, an' we'd work all day on the land an' never say a word. I s'pose 'tis bein' so lonesome early in life that makes me so pleased to have some nice girls growin' up round me now."

There was a tone in her father's voice that drew Katy's heart toward him with new affection. She dimly understood, but Susan Ellen was less interested. They had often heard this story before, but to one child it was always new and to the other old. Susan Ellen was apt to think it tiresome to hear about her grandmother, who, being dead, was hardly worth talking about.

"There's Judge Masterson's place," said their father in an everyday manner, as they turned a corner, and came into full view of the beautiful old white house standing behind its green trees and terraces and lawns. The children had never imagined anything so stately and fine, and even Susan Ellen exclaimed with pleasure. At that moment they saw an old gentleman, who carried himself with great dignity, coming slowly down the wide box-bordered path toward the gate.

"There he is now, there's the judge!" whispered John Hilton excitedly, reining his horse quickly to the green roadside. "He's goin' downtown to his office; we can wait right here an' see him. I can't expect him to remember me; it's been a good many years. Now you are goin' to see the great Judge Masterson!"

There was a quiver of expectation in their hearts. The judge stopped at his gate, hesitating a moment before he lifted the latch, and glanced up the street at the country wagon with its two prim little girls on the back seat, and the eager man who drove. They seemed to be waiting for something; the old horse was nibbling at the fresh roadside grass. The judge was used to being looked at with interest, and responded now with a smile as he came out to the sidewalk, and unexpectedly turned their way. Then he suddenly lifted his hat with grave politeness, and came directly toward them.

"Good morning, Mr. Hilton," he said. "I am very glad to see you, sir"; and Mr. Hilton, the little girls' own father, took off his hat with equal courtesy, and bent forward to shake hands.

Susan Ellen cowered and wished herself away, but little Katy sat straighter than ever, with joy in her father's pride and pleasure shining in her pale, flowerlike little face.

"These are your daughters, I am sure," said the old gentleman kindly, taking Susan Ellen's limp and reluctant hand; but when he looked at Katy, his face brightened. "How she recalls your mother!" he said with great feeling. "I am glad to see this dear child. You must come to see me with your father, my dear," he added, still looking at her. "Bring both the little girls, and let them run about the old garden; the cherries are just getting ripe," said Judge Masterson hospitably. "Perhaps you will have time to stop this afternoon as you go home?"

"I should call it a great pleasure if you would come and see us again some time. You may be driving our way, sir," said John Hilton.

"Not very often in these days," answered the old judge. "I thank you for the kind invitation. I should like to see the fine view again from your hill westward. Can I serve you in any way while you are in town? Goodbye, my little friends!"

Then they parted, but not before Katy, the shy Katy, whose hand the judge still held unconsciously while he spoke, had reached forward as he said goodbye, and lifted her face to kiss him. She could not have told why, except that she felt drawn to something in the serious, worn face. For the first time in her life the child had felt the charm of manners; perhaps she owned a kinship between that which made him what he was, and the spark of nobleness and purity in her own simple soul. She turned again and again to look back at him as they drove away.

"Now you have seen one of the first gentlemen in the county," said their father. "It was worth comin' twice as far"—but he did not say any more, nor turn as usual to look in the children's faces.

In the chief business street of Topham a great many country wagons like the Hiltons' were fastened to the posts, and there seemed to our holidaymakers to be a great deal of noise and excitement.

"Now I've got to do my errands, and we can let the horse rest and feed," said John Hilton. "I'll slip his headstall right off, an' put on his halter. I'm goin' to buy him a real good treat o' oats. First we'll go an' buy me my straw hat; I feel as if this one looked a little past to wear in Topham. We'll buy the things we want, an' then we'll walk all along the street, so you can look in the windows an' see the han'some things, same's your mother likes to. What was it Mother told you about your shawls?"

"To take 'em off an' carry 'em over our arms," piped Susan Ellen, without comment, but in the interest of alighting and finding themselves afoot upon the pavement the shawls were forgotten. The children stood at the doorway of a shop while their father went inside, and they tried to see what the Topham shapes of bonnets were like, as their mother had advised them; but everything was exciting and confusing, and they could arrive at no decision. When Mr. Hilton came out with a hat in his hand to be seen in a better light, Katy whispered that she wished he would buy a shiny one like Judge Masterson's; but her father only smiled and shook his head, and said that they were plain folks, he and Katy. There were dry-goods for sale in the same shop, and a young clerk who was measuring linen kindly pulled off some pretty labels with gilded edges and gay pictures, and gave them to the little girls, to their exceeding joy. He may have had small sisters at home, this friendly lad, for he took pains to find two pretty blue boxes besides, and was rewarded by their beaming gratitude.

It was a famous day; they even became used to seeing so many people pass. The village was full of its morning activity, and Susan Ellen gained a new respect for her father, and an increased sense of her own consequence, because even in Topham several persons knew him and called him familiarly by name. The meeting with an old man who had once been a neighbor seemed to give Mr. Hilton the greatest pleasure. The old man called to them from a house doorway as they were passing, and they all went in. The children seated themselves wearily on the wooden step, but their father shook his old friend eagerly by the hand, and declared that he was delighted to see him so well and enjoying the fine weather.

"Oh, yes," said the old man, in a feeble, quavering voice. "I'm astonishin' well for my age. I don't complain, John, I don't complain."

They talked long together of people whom they had known in the past, and Katy, being a little tired, was glad to rest, and sat still with her hands folded, looking about the front yard. There were some kinds of flowers that she never had seen before.

"This is the one that looks like my mother," her father said, and touched Katy's shoulder to remind her to stand up and let herself be seen. "Judge Masterson saw the resemblance; we met him at his gate this morning."

"Yes, she certain does look like your mother, John," said the old man, looking pleasantly at Katy, who found that she liked him better than at first. "She does, certain; the best of young folks is, they remind us of the old ones. 'Tis nateral to cling to life, folks say, but for me, I git impatient at times. Most everybody's gone now, an' I want to be goin'. 'Tis somethin' before me, an' I want to have it over with. I want to be there 'long o' the rest o' the folks. I expect to last quite awhile, though; I may see ye couple o' times more, John."

John Hilton responded cheerfully, and the children were urged to pick some flowers. The old man awed them with his impatience to be gone. There was such a townful of people about him, and he seemed as lonely as if he were the last survivor of a former world. Until that moment they had felt as if everything were just beginning.

"Now I want to buy somethin' pretty for your mother," said Mr. Hilton, as they went soberly away down the street, the children keeping fast hold of his hands. "By now the old horse will have eat his dinner and had a good rest, so pretty soon we can jog along home. I'm goin' to take you round by the academy, and the old North Meetinghouse where Dr. Barstow used to preach. Can't you think o' somethin' that your mother'd want?" he asked suddenly, confronted by a man's difficulty of choice.

"She was talkin' about wantin' a new pepper box, one day; the top o' the old one won't stay on," suggested Susan Ellen, with delightful readiness. "Can't we have some candy, Father?"

"Yes, ma'am," said John Hilton, smiling and swinging her hand to and fro as they walked. "I feel as if some would be good myself. What's all this?" They were passing a photographer's doorway with its enticing array of portraits. "I do declare!" he exclaimed excitedly, "I'm goin' to have our pictures taken; 'twill please your mother more 'n a little."

This was, perhaps, the greatest triumph of the day, except the delightful meeting with the judge; they sat in a row, with the father in the middle, and there was no doubt as to the excellence of the likeness. The best hats had to be taken off because they cast a shadow, but they were not missed, as their owners had feared. Both Susan Ellen and Katy looked their brightest and best; their eager young faces would forever shine there; the joy of the holiday was mirrored in the little picture. They did not know why their father was so pleased with it; they would not know until age had dowered them with the riches of association and remembrance.

Just at nightfall the Hiltons reached home again, tired out and happy. Katy had climbed over into the front seat beside her father, because that was always her place when they went to church on Sundays. It was a cool evening, there was a fresh sea wind that brought a light mist with it, and the sky was fast growing cloudy. Somehow the children looked different; it seemed to their mother as if they had grown older and taller since they went away in the morning, and as if they belonged to the town now as much as to the country. The greatness of their day's experience had left her far behind; the day had been silent and lonely without them, and she had their supper ready, and been watching anxiously, ever since five o'clock. As for the children themselves they had little to say at first—they had eaten their luncheon early on the way to Topham. Susan Ellen was childishly cross, but Katy was pathetic and wan. They could hardly wait to show the picture, and their mother was as much pleased as everybody had expected.

"There, what did make you wear your shawls?" she exclaimed a moment afterward, reproachfully. "You ain't been an' wore 'em all day long? I wanted folks to see how pretty your new dresses was, if I did make 'em. Well, well! I wish more 'n ever now I'd gone an' seen to ye!"

"An' here's the pepper box!" said Katy, in a pleased, unconscious tone.

"That really is what I call beautiful," said Mrs. Hilton, after a long and doubtful look. "Our other one was only tin. I never did look so high as a chiny one with flowers, but I can get us another anytime for every day. That's a proper hat, as good as you could have got, John. Where's your new hoe?" she asked as he came toward her from the barn, smiling with satisfaction.

"I declare to Moses if I didn't forget all about it," meekly acknowledged the leader of the great excursion. "That an' my yellow-turnip seed, too; they went clean out o' my head, there was so many other things to think of. But 'tain't no sort o' matter; I can get a hoe just as well to Ira Speed's."

His wife could not help laughing. "You an' the little girls have had a great time. They was full o' wonder to me about everything, and I expect they'll talk about it for a week. I guess we was right about havin' 'em see somethin' more o' the world."

"Yes," answered John Hilton, with humility, "yes, we did have a beautiful day. I didn't expect so much. They looked as nice as anybody, and appeared so modest an' pretty. The little girls will remember it perhaps by an' by. I guess they won't never forget this day they had 'long o' Father."

It was evening again, the frogs were piping in the lower meadows, and in the woods, higher up the great hill, a little owl began to hoot. The sea air, salt and heavy, was blowing in our country at the end of the hot bright day. A lamp was lighted in the house, the happy children were talking together, and supper was waiting. The father and mother lingered for a moment outside and looked down over the shadowy fields; then they went in, without speaking. The great day was over, and they shut the door.

# The Perfect Dinner Table

*Edgar Guest*

This poem is about a time of day families need to spend together. The dinner hour should be more than eating. It should be about teaching, listening, and loving.

A tablecloth that's slightly soiled
Where greasy little hands have toiled;
The napkins kept in silver rings,
And only ordinary things
From which to eat, a simple fare,
And just the wife and kiddies there,
And while I serve, the clatter glad
Of little girl and little lad
Who have so very much to say
About the happenings of the day.

Four big round eyes that dance with glee,
Forever flashing joys at me,
Two little tongues that race and run
To tell of troubles and of fun;
The mother with a patient smile
Who knows that she must wait awhile
Before she'll get a chance to say
What she's discovered through the day.
She steps aside for girl and lad
Who have so much to tell their dad.

Our manners may not be the best;
Perhaps our elbows often rest
Upon the table, and at times
That very worst of dinner crimes,
That very shameful act and rude
Of speaking ere you've downed your food,
Too frequently, I fear, is done,
So fast the little voices run.
Yet why should table manners stay
Those tongues that have so much to say?

At many a table I have been
Where wealth and luxury were seen,
And I have dined in halls of pride
Where all the guests were dignified;
But when it comes to pleasure rare
The perfect dinner table's where
No stranger's face is ever known:
The dinner hour we spend alone,
When little girl and little lad
Run riot telling things to dad.

---

# The Children's Hour

*Henry Wadsworth Longfellow*

Every home should have at least one Children's Hour every evening.

Between the dark and the daylight,
  When the night is beginning to lower,
Comes a pause in the day's occupations,
  That is known as the Children's Hour.

I hear in the chamber above me
  The patter of little feet,
The sound of a door that is opened,
  And voices soft and sweet.

From my study I see in the lamplight,
  Descending the broad hall stair,
Grave Alice, and laughing Allegra,
  And Edith with golden hair.

A whisper, and then a silence:
  Yet I know by their merry eyes
They are plotting and planning together
  To take me by surprise.

A sudden rush from the stairway,
  A sudden raid from the hall!
By three doors left unguarded
  They enter my castle wall!

They climb up into my turret
  O'er the arms and back of my chair;
If I try to escape, they surround me;
  They seem to be everywhere.

They almost devour me with kisses,
  Their arms about me entwine,
Till I think of the Bishop of Bingen
  In his Mouse Tower on the Rhine!

Do you think, O blue-eyed banditti,
  Because you have scaled the wall,
Such an old mustache as I am
  Is not a match for you all!

I have you fast in my fortress,
  And will not let you depart,
But put you down into the dungeon
  In the round-tower of my heart.

And there will I keep you forever,
  Yes, forever and a day,
Till the walls shall crumble to ruin,
  And molder in dust away!

---

# The Funeral Oration of Pericles

*Thucydides*

The late-mid-fifth century B.C. is known as the Age of Pericles in Greek history, for it was during the period of that great statesman's leadership that Athenian democracy flowered and the

Athenian empire reached full development militarily, commercially, and culturally. In his famous funeral oration over Athenians killed in battle, reported by Thucydides, Pericles gave an "exposition of the general principles by virtue of which we came to empire, and of the civic institutions and manners of life in consequence of which our empire became great." The speech reminds participants of democracy two and a half millennia later that the character of the state is determined by the virtues of individual citizens.

We enjoy a form of government which is not in rivalry with the institutions of our neighbors, nay, we ourselves are rather an example to many than imitators of others. By name, since the administration is not in the hands of few but of many, it is called a democracy. And it is true that before the law and in private cases all citizens are on an equality. But in public life every man is advanced to honor according to his reputation for ability—not because of his party, but because of his excellence. And further, provided he is able to do the city good service, not even in poverty does he find any hindrance, since this cannot obscure men's good opinion of him. It is with a free spirit that we engage in public life, and in our scrutiny of one another's private life we are not filled with wrath at our neighbor if he consults his pleasure now and then, nor do we cast sour glances at him. . . .

We cherish beauty in all simplicity, and wisdom without effeminacy. Our wealth supports timely action rather than noisy speech, and as for poverty, the admission of it is no disgrace to a man; not to forge one's way out of it is the real disgrace. The same citizens among us will be found devoted to their homes and to the state, and others who are immersed in business have no mean knowledge of politics. We are the only people to regard the man who takes no interest in politics not as careless, but as useless. In one and the same citizen body we either decide matters, or seek to form correct opinions about them, and we do not regard words as incompatible with deeds, but rather the refusal to learn by discussion before advancing to the necessary action. We are preeminent in this, that we combine in the same citizen body great courage to undertake, and ample discussion of our undertakings; whereas in other men it is ignorance that gives boldness, and discussion that produces hesitation. Surely they will rightly be judged the bravest souls who most clearly distinguish the pains and pleasures of life, and therefore do not avoid danger. In our benevolence also we are the opposite of most men; it is not by receiving, but by conferring favors that we win our friends. . . . To sum up: I declare that our city in general is the school of Hellas, and that each individual man of us will, in my opinion, show himself able to exercise the most varied forms of activity with the greatest ease and grace. That this is no passing boast, but an actual truth, is shown by the power which our city has acquired in virtue of these traits of ours. . . .

It was for such a city, then, that these dead warriors of ours so nobly gave their lives in battle; they deemed it their right not to be robbed of her, and every man who survives them should gladly toil in her behalf.

I have thus dwelt at length on the character of our city both because I would teach the lesson that we have far more at stake than those who are so unlike us, and because I would accompany the words of praise which I now pronounce over these men with manifest proofs. Indeed their highest praise has been already spoken. I have but sung the praises of a city which the virtues of these men and of men like them adorned, and there are few Hellenes like these, whose deeds will be found to balance their praises. I hold that such an end as theirs shows forth a man's real excellence, whether it be a first revelation or a final confirmation. For even those who fall short in other ways may find refuge behind the valor they show in fighting for their country. They make men forget the evil that was in them for the good, and help their country more by their public sacrifice than they injured her by their private failings. Among these men, however, there was no one in wealth who set too high a value on the further enjoyment of it, to his own undoing, nor anyone in poverty who was led, by the hope of escaping it and becoming rich, to postpone the dread ordeal. . . . And in the heat of action, thinking it far better to suffer death than to yield and live, they did indeed fly from the word of disgrace, but they stood firm in deeds of prowess, and so, in a moment, in the twinkling of an eye, at the height of their glory rather than of their fear, they passed away.

Such were these men, and they were worthy of their city. Those who survive them may pray, perhaps, for a less fatal, but should desire no less bold a temper toward their foes. You cannot weigh in words the service they rendered to the state. You know it yourselves fully as well as any speaker who might descant at length upon it, telling you all the good there is in resistance to the foe. You should rather fix your eyes daily upon the city in her power, until you become her fond lovers. And when her greatness becomes manifest to you, reflect that it was by courage, and the recognition of duty, and the shunning of dishonor, that men won that greatness, men who, even if they failed in an undertaking, did not on that account deem it a worthy thing to rob their city of a glorious example, but offered their lives willingly as their fairest contribution to the table of her welfare.

---

# Plato on Responsibility

*From the* Crito

In this famous dialogue by Plato, Crito visits his friend Socrates, who has been legally but unjustly imprisoned and condemned to death for "impiety" and "corrupting the youth." The hour when Socrates must drink the poison hemlock is fast approaching, and Crito tries to persuade his friend to escape. Socrates, however, refuses to break the law of Athens. His argument is one of our finest lessons in the principles that must inform both civil obedience and civil disobedience. His decision to die remains one of history's great examples of an individual who believes his first responsibility to his community, his family, and himself is to follow the dictates of reason-directed conscience.

*Socrates.* Consider the matter in this way: Imagine that I am about to play truant (you may call the proceeding by any name which you like), and the laws and the government come and interrogate me: "Tell us, Socrates," they say; "what are you about? are you not going by an act of yours to overturn us—the laws, and the whole state, as far as in you lies? Do you imagine that a state can subsist and not be overthrown, in which the decisions of law have no power, but are set aside and trampled upon by individuals?" What will be our answer, Crito, to these and the like words? Anyone, and especially a rhetorician, will have a good deal to say on behalf of the law which requires a sentence to be carried out. He will argue that this law should not be set aside; and shall we reply, "Yes; but the state has injured us and given an unjust sentence"? Suppose I say that?

*Crito*. Very good, Socrates.

*Socrates*. "And was that our agreement with you?" the law would answer; "or were you to abide by the sentence of the state?" And if I were to express my astonishment at their words, the law would probably add: "Answer, Socrates, instead of opening your eyes—you are in the habit of asking and answering questions. Tell us—What complaint have you to make against us which justifies you in attempting to destroy us and the state? In the first place did we not bring you into existence? Your father married your mother by our aid and begat you. Say whether you have any objection to urge against those of us who regulate marriage?" None, I should reply. "Or against those of us who after birth regulate the nurture and education of children, in which you also were trained? Were not the laws, which have the charge of education, right in commanding your father to train you in music and gymnastic?" Right, I should reply. "Well then, since you were brought into the world and nurtured and educated by us, can you deny in the first place that you are our child and slave, as your fathers were before you? And if this is true you are not on equal terms with us; nor can you think that you have a right to do to us what we are doing to you. Would you have any right to strike or revile or do any other evil to your father or your master, if you had one, because you have been struck or reviled by him, or received some other evil at his hands?—you would not say this? And because we think right to destroy you, do you think that you have any right to destroy us in return, and your country as far as in you lies? Will you, O professor of true virtue, pretend that you are justified in this? Has a philosopher like you failed to discover that our country is more to be valued and higher and holier far than mother or father or any ancestor, and more to be regarded in the eyes of the gods and of men of understanding? also to be soothed, and gently and reverently entreated when angry, even more than a father, and either to be persuaded, or if not persuaded, to be obeyed? And when we are punished by her, whether with imprisonment or stripes, the punishment is to be endured in silence; and if she leads us to wounds or death in battle, thither we follow as is right; neither may anyone yield or retreat or leave his rank, but whether in battle or in a court of law, or in any other place, he must do what his city and his country order him; or he must change their view of what is just: and if he may do no violence to his father or mother, much less may he do violence to his country." What answer shall we make to this, Crito? Do the laws speak truly, or do they not?

*Crito*. I think that they do.

*Socrates*. Then the laws will say, "Consider, Socrates, if we are speaking truly that in your present attempt you are going to do us an injury. For, having brought you into the world, and nurtured and educated you, and given you and every other citizen a share in every good which we had to give, we further proclaim to any Athenian by the liberty which we allow him, that if he does not like us when he has become of age and has seen the ways of the city, and made our acquaintance, he may go where he pleases and take his goods with him. None of us laws will forbid him or interfere with him. Anyone who does not like us and the city, and who wants to emigrate to a colony or to any other city, may go where he likes, retaining his property. But he who has experience of the manner in which we order justice and administer the state, and still remains, has entered into an implied contract that he will do as we command him. And he who disobeys us is, as we maintain, thrice wrong; first, because in disobeying us he is disobeying his parents; secondly, because we are the authors of his education; thirdly, because he has made an agreement with us that he will duly obey our commands; and he neither obeys them nor convinces us that our commands are unjust; and we do not rudely impose them, but give him the alternative of obeying or convincing us; that is what we offer, and he does neither.

"These are the sort of accusations to which, as we were saying, you, Socrates, will be exposed if you accomplish your intentions; you, above all other Athenians." Suppose now I ask, why I rather than anybody else? They will justly retort upon me that I above all other men have acknowledged the agreement. "There is clear proof," they will say, "Socrates, that we and the city were not displeasing to you. Of all Athenians you have been the most constant resident in the city, which, as you never leave, you may be supposed to love. For you never went out of the city either to see the games, except once when you went to the Isthmus, or to any other place unless when you were on military service; nor did you travel as other men do. Nor had you any curiosity to know other states or their laws: your affections did not go beyond us and our state; we were your special favorites, and you acquiesced in our government of you; and here in this city you begat your children, which is a proof of your satisfaction. Moreover, you might in the course of the trial, if you had liked, have fixed the penalty at banishment; the state which refuses to let you go now would have let you go then. But you pretended that you preferred death to exile, and that you were not unwilling to die. And now you have forgotten these fine sentiments, and pay no respect to us the laws, of whom you are the destroyer; and are doing what only a miserable slave would do, running away and turning your back upon the compacts and agreements which you made as a citizen. And first of all answer this very question: Are we right in saying that you agreed to be governed according to us in deed, and not in word only? Is that true or not?" How shall we answer, Crito? Must we not assent?

*Crito.* We cannot help it, Socrates.

*Socrates.* Then will they not say: "You, Socrates, are breaking the covenants and agreements which you made with us at your leisure, not in any haste or under any compulsion or deception, but after you have had seventy years to think of them, during which time you were at liberty to leave the city, if we were not to your mind, or if our covenants appeared to you to be unfair. You had your choice, and might have gone either to Lacedaemon or Crete, both which states are often praised by you for their good government, or to some other Hellenic or foreign state. Whereas you, above all other Athenians, seemed to be so fond of the state, or, in other words, of us her laws (and who would care about a state which has no laws?), that you never stirred out of her; the halt, the blind, the maimed were not more stationary in her than you were. And now you run away and forsake your agreements. Not so, Socrates, if you will take our advice; do not make yourself ridiculous by escaping out of the city.

"For just consider, if you transgress and err in this sort of way, what good will you do either to yourself or to your friends? That your friends will be driven into exile and deprived of citizenship, or will lose their property, is tolerably certain; and you yourself, if you fly to one of the neighboring cities, as, for example, Thebes or Megara, both of which are well governed, will come to them as an enemy, Socrates, and their government will be against you, and all patriotic citizens will cast an evil eye upon you as a subverter of the laws, and you will confirm in the minds of the judges the justice of their own condemnation of you. For he who is a corrupter of the laws is more than likely to be a corrupter of the young and foolish portion of mankind. Will you then flee from well-ordered cities and virtuous men? and is existence worth having on these terms? Or will you go to them without shame, and talk to them, Socrates? And what will you say to them? What you say here about virtue and justice and institutions and laws being the best things among men? Would that be decent of you? Surely not. But if you go away from well-governed states to Crito's friends in Thessaly, where there is great disorder and license, they will be charmed to hear the tale of your escape from prison, set off with ludicrous particulars of the manner in which you were wrapped in a goatskin or some other disguise, and metamorphosed as the manner is of runaways; but will there be no one to remind you that in your old age you were not ashamed to violate the most sacred laws from a miserable desire of a little more life? Perhaps not, if you keep them in a good temper; but if they are out of temper you will hear many degrading things; you will live, but how?—as the flatterer of all men, and the servant of all men; and doing what?—eating and drinking in Thessaly, having gone abroad in order that you may get a dinner. And where will be your fine sentiments about justice and virtue? Say that you wish to live for the sake of your children—you want to bring them up and educate them—will you take them into Thessaly and deprive them of Athenian citizenship? Is this the benefit which you will confer upon them? Or are you under the impression that they will be better cared for and educated here if you are still alive, although absent from them; for your friends will take care of them? Do you fancy that if you are an inhabitant of Thessaly they will take care of them, and if you are an inhabitant of the other world that they will not take care of them? Nay; but if they who call themselves friends are good for anything, they will—to be sure they will.

"Listen, then, Socrates, to us who have brought you up. Think not of life and children first, and of justice afterward, but of justice first, that you may be justified before the princes of the world below. For neither will you nor any that belong to you be happier or holier or juster in this life, or happier in another, if you do as Crito bids. Now you depart in innocence, a sufferer and not a doer of evil; a victim, not of the laws but of men. But if you go forth, returning evil for evil, and injury for injury, breaking the covenants and agreements which you have made with us, and wronging those whom you ought least of all to wrong, that is to say, yourself, your friends, your country, and us, we shall be angry with you while you live, and our brethren, the laws in the world below, will receive you as an enemy; for they will know that you have done your best to destroy us. Listen, then, to us and not to Crito."

This, dear Crito, is the voice which I seem to hear murmuring in my ears, like the sound of the flute in the ears of the mystic; that voice, I say, is humming in my ears, and prevents me from hearing any other. And I know that anything more which you may say will be vain. Yet speak, if you have anything to say.

*Crito.* I have nothing to say, Socrates.

*Socrates.* Leave me then, Crito, to fulfill the will of God, and to follow whither he leads.

# The Declaration of Independence

*Thomas Jefferson*

The opening lines of the Declaration of Independence provide one of our most important moral anchors. If we truly hold these liberties to be gifts from God, we realize the moral duty to respect, preserve, and defend those rights for others.

When in the Course of human events, it becomes necessary for one people to dissolve the political bands which have connected them with another, and to assume among the Powers of the earth, the separate and equal station to which the Laws of Nature and of Nature's God entitle them, a decent respect to the opinions of mankind requires that they should declare the causes which impel them to the separation.—We hold these truths to be self-evident, that all men are created equal, that they are endowed by their Creator with certain unalienable Rights, that among these are Life, Liberty and the pursuit of Happiness.—That to secure these rights, Governments are instituted among Men, deriving their just powers from the consent of the governed,—That whenever any Form of Government becomes destructive of these ends, it is the Right of the People to alter or to abolish it, and to institute new Government, laying its foundation on such principles and organizing its powers in such form, as to them shall seem most likely to effect their Safety and Happiness.

# Federalist No. 55

*James Madison*

The essays known as the Federalist Papers first appeared in New York City newspapers between the autumn of 1787 and summer of 1788. Written by Alexander Hamilton, James Madison, and John Jay, they were addressed "To the People of the State of New York" and signed with the pseudonym "Publius." Their purpose was to convince the citizens of New York to ratify the Constitution recently drafted by the Philadelphia convention. Although penned in haste, the brilliant set of essays remains one of our most significant political documents and commentaries on American democracy. Here, in Federalist No. 55, James Madison takes up the question of whether a relatively small number of legislators can be trusted to safeguard the public liberty. Such a system can work, Madison argues, as long as the political and moral responsibilities of the people remain intact. Democracy presupposes the virtue of its individual citizens.

The true question to be decided then is, whether the smallness of the number, as a temporary regulation, be dangerous to the public liberty? Whether sixty-five members for a few years, and a hundred or two hundred for a few more, be a safe depositary for a limited and well-guarded power of legislating for the United States? I must own that I could not give a negative answer to this question without first obliterating every impression which I have received with regard to the present genius of the people of America, the spirit which actuates the State legislatures, and the principles which are incorporated with the political character of every class of citizens. I am unable to conceive that the people of America, in their present temper, or under any circumstances which can speedily happen, will choose, and every second year repeat the choice of, sixty-five or a hundred men who would be disposed to form and pursue a scheme of tyranny or treachery. I am unable to conceive that the State legislatures, which must feel so many motives to watch, and which possess so many means of counteracting, the federal legislature, would fail either to detect or to defeat a conspiracy of the latter against the liberties of their common constituents. I am equally unable to conceive that there are at this time, or can be in any short time, in the United States, any sixty-five or a hundred men capable of recommending themselves to the choice of the people at large, who would either desire or dare, within the short space of two years, to betray the solemn trust committed to them. What change of circumstances, time, and a fuller population of our country may produce, requires a prophetic spirit to declare, which makes no part of my pretensions. But judging from the circumstances now before us, and from the probable state of them within a moderate period of time, I must pronounce that the liberties of America cannot be unsafe in the number of hands proposed by the federal Constitution. . . .

As there is a degree of depravity in mankind which requires a certain degree of circumspection and distrust, so there are other qualities in human nature which justify a certain portion of esteem and confidence. Republican government presupposes the existence of these qualities in a higher degree than any other form. Were the pictures which have been drawn by the political jealousy of some among us faithful likenesses of the human character, the inference would be that there is not sufficient virtue among men for self-government; and that nothing less than the chains of despotism can restrain them from destroying and devouring one another.

# The Conscience of the Nation Must Be Roused

*Frederick Douglass*

Frederick Douglass was born a slave in 1817 and raised by his grandmother on a Maryland plantation until sent to work at age eight in Baltimore. There, with the help of his new master's wife, he began to educate himself, an activity forbidden by law. In 1838, he escaped and settled in New Bedford, Massachusetts, and began working for the antislavery cause. It was not long before he was the nation's leading black abolitionist and one of its most brilliant orators.

In 1852, having been invited to deliver an Independence Day address in Rochester, New York, Douglass seized the occasion to hold the "scorching iron" of moral reproach to the nation's conscience. For Douglass and all black Americans, the Fourth of July was not an anniversary on which to rejoice at the rights and freedoms conferred by democracy; it was a day of deepest shame for those betraying the most basic moral obligations toward their fellow men. Here is a brave soul holding America accountable for its sins.

Fellow citizens, pardon me, allow me to ask, why am I called upon to speak here today? What have I, or those I represent, to do with your national independence? Are the great principles of political freedom and of natural justice, embodied in that Declaration of Independence, extended to us? and am I, therefore, called upon to bring our humble offering to the national altar, and to confess the benefits and express devout gratitude for the blessings resulting from your independence to us?

Would to God, both for your sakes and ours, that an affirmative answer could be truthfully returned to these questions! . . .

But such is not the state of the case. I say it with a sad sense of the disparity between us. I am not included within the pale of this glorious anniversary! Your high independence only reveals the immeasurable distance between us. The blessings in which you, this day, rejoice are not enjoyed in common. The rich inheritance of justice, liberty, prosperity, and independence bequeathed by your fathers is shared by you, not by me. The sunlight that brought light and healing to you has brought stripes and death to me. This Fourth of July is yours, not mine. You may rejoice, I must mourn. To drag a man in fetters into the grand illuminated temple of liberty, and call upon him to join you in joyous anthems, were inhuman mockery and sacrilegious irony. . . .

Fellow citizens, above your national, tumultuous joy, I hear the mournful wail of millions! whose chains, heavy and grievous yesterday, are, today, rendered more intolerable by the jubilee shouts that reach them. If I do forget, if I do not faithfully remember those bleeding children of sorrow this day, "may my right hand forget her cunning, and may my tongue cleave to the roof of my mouth!" To forget them, to pass lightly over their wrongs, and to chime in with the popular theme would be treason most scandalous and shocking, and would make me a reproach before God and the world. My subject, then, fellow citizens, is *American slavery*. I shall see this day and its popular characteristics from the slave's point of view. Standing there identified with the American bondman, making his wrongs mine, I do not hesitate to declare with all my soul that the character and conduct of this nation never looked blacker to me than on this Fourth of July! Whether we turn to the declarations of the past or to the professions of the present, the conduct of the nation seems equally hideous and revolting. America is false to the past, false to the present, and solemnly binds herself to be false to the future. Standing with God and the crushed and bleeding slave on this occasion, I will, in the name of humanity which is outraged, in the name of liberty which is fettered, in the name of the Constitution and the Bible which are disregarded and trampled upon, dare to call in question and to denounce, with all the emphasis I can command, everything that serves to perpetuate slavery—the great sin and shame of America! . . .

What, am I to argue that it is wrong to make men brutes, to rob them of their liberty, to work them without wages, to keep them ignorant of their relations to their fellow men, to beat them with sticks, to flay their flesh with the lash, to load their limbs with irons, to hunt them with dogs, to sell them at auction, to sunder their families, to knock out their teeth, to burn their flesh, to starve them into obedience and submission to their masters? Must I argue that a system thus marked with blood, and stained with pollution, is wrong? No! I will not. I have better employment for my time and strength than such arguments would imply.

What, then, remains to be argued? Is it that slavery is not divine; that God did not establish it; that our doctors of divinity are mistaken? There is blasphemy in the thought. That which is inhuman cannot be divine! Who can reason on such a proposition? They that can may; I cannot. The time for such argument is past.

At a time like this, scorching iron, not convincing argument, is needed. O! had I the ability, and could I reach the nation's ear, I would today pour out a fiery stream of biting ridicule, blasting reproach, withering sarcasm, and stern rebuke. For it is not light that is needed, but fire; it is not the gentle shower, but thunder. We need the storm, the whirlwind, and the earthquake. The feeling of the nation must be quickened; the conscience of the nation must be roused; the propriety of the nation must be startled; the hypocrisy of the nation must be exposed; and its crimes against God and man must be proclaimed and denounced.

What, to the American slave, is your Fourth of July? I answer: a day that reveals to him, more than all other days in the year, the gross injustice and cruelty to which he is the constant victim. To him, your celebration is a sham; your boasted liberty, an unholy license; your national greatness, swelling vanity; your sounds of rejoicing are empty and heartless; your denunciation of tyrants, brass-fronted impudence; your shouts of liberty and equality, hollow mockery; your prayers and hymns, your sermons and thanksgivings, with all your religious parade and solemnity, are, to Him, mere bombast, fraud, deception, impiety, and hypocrisy—a thin veil to cover up crimes which would disgrace a nation of savages. There is not a nation of savages, there is not a nation on the earth guilty of practices more shocking and bloody than are the people of the United States at this very hour.

---

## Second Message to Congress

*Abraham Lincoln*

In December 1862, with the Northern war effort seemingly grinding to a halt and public opinion turning against him, Abraham Lincoln resolutely wrote Congress that the federal government now faced two moral and political obligations: preserve the Union, and free the slaves. In Lincoln's mind, the two objectives had, at this point, become inseparable. He made his plea despite the protestations of some advisors who called his emancipation plans reckless and destructive. Here is the voice of a leader asking his fellow countrymen to cast off the prejudices of generations and follow the dictates of right and reason. One month later, Lincoln would sign the Emancipation Proclamation.

A nation may be said to consist of its territory, its people, and its laws. The territory is the only part which is of certain durability.

"One generation passeth away, and another generation cometh, but the earth abideth forever." It is of the first importance to duly consider, and estimate, this ever-enduring part. That portion of the earth's surface which is owned and inhabited by the people of the United States, is well adapted to be the home of one national family; and it is not well adapted for two, or more. Its vast extent, and its variety of climate and productions, are of advantage, in this age, for one people, whatever they might have been in former ages. Steam, telegraphs, and intelligence, have brought these, to be an advantageous combination, for one united people.

In the inaugural address I briefly pointed out the total inadequacy of disunion, as a remedy for the differences between the people of the two sections. I did so in language which I cannot improve, and which, therefore, I beg to repeat:

"One section of our country believes slavery is *right,* and ought to be extended, while the other believes it is *wrong,* and ought not to be extended. This is the only substantial dispute. . . . Physically speaking, we cannot separate. We cannot remove our respective sections from each other, nor build an impassable wall between them. A husband and wife may be divorced, and go out of the presence, and beyond the reach of each other; but the different parts of our country cannot do this. They cannot but remain face-to-face; and intercourse, either amicable or hostile, must continue between them. Is it possible, then, to make that intercourse more advantageous, or more satisfactory, *after* separation than *before?* Can aliens make treaties, easier than friends can make laws? Can treaties be more faithfully enforced between aliens, than laws can among friends? Suppose you go to war, you cannot fight always; and when, after much loss on both sides, and no gain on either, you cease fighting, the identical old questions, as to terms of intercourse, are again upon you. . . ."

If there ever could be a proper time for mere catch arguments, that time surely is not now. In times like the present, men should utter nothing for which they would not willingly be responsible through time and in eternity. . . .

I do not forget the gravity which should characterize a paper addressed to the Congress of the nation by the Chief Magistrate of the nation. Nor do I forget that some of you are my seniors, nor that many of you have more experience than I, in the conduct of public affairs. Yet I trust that in view of the great responsibility resting upon me, you will perceive no want of respect to yourselves, in any undue earnestness I may seem to display. . . .

The dogmas of the quiet past, are inadequate to the stormy present. The occasion is piled high with difficulty, and we must rise with the occasion. As our case is new, so we must think anew, and act anew. We must disenthrall ourselves, and then we shall save our country.

Fellow citizens, *we* cannot escape history. We of this Congress and this administration, will be remembered in spite of ourselves. No personal significance, or insignificance, can spare one or another of us. The fiery trial through which we pass, will light us down, in honor or dishonor, to the latest generation. We *say* we are for the Union. The world will not forget that we say this. We know how to save the Union. The world knows we do know how to save it. We—even *we here*—hold the power, and bear the responsibility. In *giving* freedom to the *slave,* we *assure* freedom to the *free*—honorable alike in what we give, and what we preserve. We shall nobly save, or meanly lose, the last best hope of earth. Other means may succeed; this could not fail. The way is plain, peaceful, generous, just—a way which, if followed, the world will forever applaud, and God must forever bless.

---

# Letter from Birmingham City Jail

*Martin Luther King, Jr.*

Martin Luther King, Jr., wrote "Letter from Birmingham City Jail" on Easter weekend 1963 while in solitary confinement for leading nonviolent protests against racial discrimination. The letter was a response to a published statement by several leading clergymen calling for an end to the demonstrations. King asserted that the demonstrators' course was the morally responsible one, and he predicted that one day the nation would recognize the heroes who acted with "the noble sense of purpose that enables them to face jeering and hostile mobs, and with the agonizing loneliness that characterizes the life of the pioneer." Here are excerpts from one of the nation's most important political and moral documents dealing with the issues of respect for law and the grounds for justified civil disobedience.

I think I should indicate why I am here in Birmingham, since you have been influenced by the view which argues against "outsiders coming in." . . . So I, along with several members of my staff, am here because I was invited here. I am here because I have organizational ties here.

But more basically, I am in Birmingham because injustice is here. Just as the prophets of the eighth century B.C. left their villages and carried their "thus saith the Lord" far beyond the boundaries of their hometowns, and just as the Apostle Paul left his village of Tarsus and carried the gospel of Jesus Christ to the far corners of the Greco-Roman world, so am I compelled to carry the gospel of freedom beyond my own hometown. Like Paul, I must constantly respond to the Macedonian call for aid.

Moreover, I am cognizant of the interrelatedness of all communities and states. I cannot sit idly by in Atlanta and not be concerned about what happens in Birmingham. Injustice anywhere is a threat to justice everywhere. We are caught in an inescapable network of mutuality, tied in a single garment of destiny. Whatever affects one directly, affects all indirectly. Never again can we afford to live with the narrow, provincial "outside agitator" idea. Anyone who lives inside the United States can never be considered an outsider anywhere within its bounds.

You deplore the demonstrations taking place in Birmingham. But your statement, I am sorry to say, fails to express a similar concern for the conditions that brought about the demonstrations. I am sure that none of you would want to rest content with the superficial kind of social analysis that deals merely with effects and does not grapple with underlying causes. It is unfortunate that demonstrations are taking place in Birmingham, but it is even more unfortunate that the city's white power structure left the Negro community with no alternative.

In any nonviolent campaign there are four basic steps: collection of the facts to determine whether injustices exist; negotiation; self-purification; and direct action. We have gone through all these steps in Birmingham. There can be no gainsaying the fact that racial injustice engulfs this community. Birmingham is probably the most thoroughly segregated city in the United States. Its ugly record of brutality is widely known. Negroes have experienced grossly unjust treatment in the courts. There have been more unsolved bombings of Negro homes and churches in Birmingham than in any other city in the nation. These are the hard, brutal facts of the case. . . .

You express a great deal of anxiety over our willingness to break laws. This is certainly a legitimate concern. Since we so diligently urge people to obey the Supreme Court's decision of 1954 outlawing segregation in the public schools, at first glance it may seem rather paradoxical for us consciously to break laws. One may well ask: "How can you advocate breaking some laws and obeying others?" The answer lies in the fact that there are two types of laws: just and unjust. I would be the first to advocate obeying just laws. One has not only a legal but a moral responsibility to obey just laws. Conversely, one has a moral responsibility to disobey unjust laws. I would agree with St. Augustine that "an unjust law is no law at all."

Now, what is the difference between the two? How does one determine whether a law is just or unjust? A just law is a man-made code that squares with the moral law or the law of God. An unjust law is a code that is out of harmony with the moral law. To put it in the terms of St. Thomas Aquinas: an unjust law is a human law that is not rooted in eternal law and natural law. Any law that uplifts human personality is just. Any law that degrades human personality is unjust. All segregation statutes are unjust because segregation distorts the soul and damages the personality. It gives the segregator a false sense of superiority and the segregated a false sense of inferiority. Segregation, to use the terminology of the Jewish philosopher Martin Buber, substitutes an "I–it" relationship for an "I–thou" relationship and ends up relegating persons to the status of things. Hence segregation is not only politically, economically, and sociologically unsound, it is morally wrong and sinful. Paul Tillich has said that sin is separation. Is not segregation an existential expression of man's tragic separation, his awful estrangement, his terrible sinfulness? Thus it is that I can urge men to obey the 1954 decision of the Supreme Court, for it is morally right; and I can urge them to disobey segregation ordinances, for they are morally wrong.

Let us consider a more concrete example of just and unjust laws. An unjust law is a code that a numerical or power majority group compels a minority group to obey but does not make binding on itself. This is *difference* made legal. By the same token, a just law is a code that a majority compels a minority to follow and that it is willing to follow itself. This is *sameness* made legal.

Let me give another explanation. A law is unjust if it is inflicted on a minority that, as a result of being denied the right to vote, had no part in enacting or devising the law. Who can say that the legislature of Alabama which set up the state's segregation laws was democratically elected? Throughout Alabama all sorts of devious methods are used to prevent Negroes from becoming registered voters, and there are some counties in which, even though Negroes constitute a majority of the population, not a single Negro is registered. Can any law enacted under such circumstances be considered democratically structured?

Sometimes a law is just on its face and unjust in its application. For instance, I have been arrested on a charge of parading without a permit. Now, there is nothing wrong in having an ordinance which requires a permit for a parade. But such an ordinance becomes unjust when it is used to maintain segregation and to deny citizens the First Amendment privilege of peaceful assembly and protest.

I hope you are able to see the distinction I am trying to point out. In no sense do I advocate evading or defying the law, as would the rabid segregationist. That would lead to anarchy. One who breaks an unjust law must do so openly, lovingly, and with a willingness to accept the penalty. I submit that an individual who breaks a law that conscience tells him is unjust, and who willingly accepts the penalty of imprisonment in order to arouse the conscience of the community over its injustice, is in reality expressing the highest respect for law. . . .

You speak of our activity in Birmingham as extreme. . . . But though I was initially disappointed at being categorized as an extremist, as I continued to think about the matter I gradually gained a measure of satisfaction from the label. Was not Jesus an extremist for love: "Love your enemies, bless them that curse you, do good to them that hate you, and pray for them which despitefully use you, and persecute you." Was not Amos an extremist for justice: "Let justice roll down like waters and righteousness like an ever-flowing stream." Was not Paul an extremist for the Christian gospel: "I bear in my body the marks of the Lord Jesus." Was not Martin Luther an extremist: "Here I stand; I cannot do otherwise, so help me God." And John Bunyan: "I will stay in jail to the end of my days before I make a butchery of my conscience." And Abraham Lincoln: "This nation cannot survive half slave and half free." And Thomas Jefferson: "We hold these truths to be self-evident, that all men are created equal. . . ." So the question is not whether we will be extremists, but what kind of extremists we will be. Will we be extremists for hate or for love? Will we be extremists for the preservation of injustice or for the extension of justice? . . .

One day the South will recognize its real heroes. They will be the James Merediths, with the noble sense of purpose that enables them to face jeering and hostile mobs, and with the agonizing loneliness that characterizes the life of the pioneer. They will be old, oppressed, battered Negro women, symbolized in a seventy-two-year-old woman in Montgomery, Alabama, who rose up with a sense of dignity and with her people decided not to ride segregated buses, and who responded with ungrammatical profundity to one who inquired about her weariness: "My feets is tired, but my soul is at rest." They will be the young high school and college students, the young ministers of the gospel and a host of their elders, courageously and nonviolently sitting in at lunch counters and willingly going to jail for conscience' sake. One day the South will know that when these disinherited children of God sat down at lunch counters, they were in reality standing up for what is best in the American dream and for the most sacred values in our Judeo-Christian heritage, thereby bringing our nation back to those great wells of democracy which were dug deep by the founding fathers in their formulation of the Constitution and the Declaration of Independence.. . .

I hope this letter finds you strong in the faith. I also hope that circumstances will soon make it possible for me to meet each of you, not as an integrationist or a civil rights leader but as a fellow clergyman and a Christian brother. Let us all hope that the dark clouds of racial prejudice will soon pass away and the deep fog of misunderstanding will be lifted from our fear-drenched communities, and in some not too distant tomorrow the radiant stars of love and brotherhood will shine over our great nation with all their scintillating beauty.

Yours for the cause of Peace and Brotherhood,
MARTIN LUTHER KING, JR.

# Men Without Chests

*C. S. Lewis*

C. S. Lewis (1898–1963) was one of our greatest modern thinkers about the responsibility of adults in educating the young. Here, in *The Abolition of Man,* he makes the case that if we fail to pass along specific standards of right and wrong, of what is worthwhile or worthless, admirable or ignoble, then we must share blame for the consequent failings of character. The closing paragraph of this excerpt is one of my favorite passages in all the literature about education.

Until quite modern times all teachers and even all men believed the universe to be such that certain emotional reactions on our part could be either congruous or incongruous to it—believed, in fact, that objects did not merely receive, but could *merit,* our approval or disapproval, our reverence, or our contempt. . . .

"Can you be righteous," asks Traherne, "unless you be just in rendering to things their due esteem? All things were made to be yours and you were made to prize them according to their value." St. Augustine defines virtue as *ordo amoris,* the ordinate condition of the affections in which every object is accorded that kind and degree of love which is appropriate to it. Aristotle says that the aim of education is to make the pupil like and dislike what he ought. When the age for reflective thought comes, the pupil who has been thus trained in "ordinate affections" or "just sentiments" will easily find the first principles in Ethics: but to the corrupt man they will never be visible at all and he can make no progress in that science. Plato before him had said the same. The little human animal will not at first have the right responses. It must be trained to feel pleasure, liking, disgust, and hatred at those things which really are pleasant, likable, disgusting, and hateful. In the *Republic,* the well-nurtured youth is one "who would see most clearly whatever was amiss in ill-made works of man or ill-grown works of nature, and with a just distaste would blame and hate the ugly even from his earliest years and would give delighted praise to beauty, receiving it into his soul and being nourished by it, so that he becomes a man of gentle heart.

All this before he is of an age to reason; so that when Reason at length comes to him, then, bred as he has been, he will hold out his hands in welcome and recognize her because of the affinity he bears to her." In early Hinduism that conduct in men which can be called good consists in conformity to, or almost participation in, the *Rta*—that great ritual or pattern of nature and supernature which is revealed alike in the cosmic order, the moral virtues, and the ceremonial of the temple. Righteousness, correctness, order, the *Rta,* is constantly identified with *satya* or truth, correspondence to reality. As Plato said that the Good was "beyond existence" and Wordsworth that through virtue the stars were strong, so the Indian masters say that the gods themselves are born of the *Rta* and obey it. The Chinese also speak of a great thing (the greatest thing) called the *Tao.* It is the reality beyond all predicates, the abyss that was before the Creator Himself. It is Nature, it is the Way, the Road. It is the Way in which the universe goes on, the Way in which things everlastingly emerge, stilly and tranquilly, into space and time. It is also the Way which every man should tread in imitation of that cosmic and supercosmic progression, conforming all activities to that great exemplar. "In ritual," say the Analects, "it is harmony with Nature that is prized." The ancient Jews likewise praise the Law as being "true." . . .

But what is common to them all is something we cannot neglect. It is the doctrine of objective value, the belief that certain attitudes are really true, and others really false, to the kind of thing the universe is and the kind of things we are. . . .

Hence the educational problem is wholly different according as you stand within or without the *Tao.* For those within, the task is to train in the pupil those responses which are in themselves appropriate, whether anyone is making them or not, and in making which the very nature of man consists. Those without, if they are logical, must regard all sentiments as equally nonrational, as mere mists between us and the real objects. As a result, they must either decide to remove all sentiments, as far as possible, from the pupil's mind: or else to encourage some sentiments for reasons that have nothing to do with their intrinsic "justness" or "ordinacy." The latter course involves them in the questionable process of creating in others by "suggestion" or incantation a mirage which their own reason has successfully dissipated. . . .

And all the time—such is the tragicomedy of our situation—we continue to clamor for those very qualities we are rendering impossible. You can hardly open a periodical without coming across the statement that what our civilization needs is more "drive," or dynamism, or self-sacrifice, or "creativity." In a sort of ghastly simplicity we remove the organ and demand the function. We make men without chests and expect of them virtue and enterprise. We laugh at honor and are shocked to find traitors in our midst. We castrate and bid the geldings be fruitful.

# 4

# Friendship

Good stories invite us to slip into the shoes of other people, a crucial step in acquiring a moral perspective. Stories about friendship require taking the perspective of friends, taking others seriously for their own sakes. In the best friendships we see in perhaps its purest form a moral paradigm for all human relations.

As the selections in this chapter make plain, friendship is more than acquaintance, and it involves more than affection. Friendship usually rises out of mutual interests and common aims, and these pursuits are strengthened by the benevolent impulses that sooner or later grow. The demands of friendship—for frankness, for self-revelation, for taking friends' criticisms as seriously as their expressions of admiration or praise, for stand-by-me loyalty, and for assistance to the point of self-sacrifice—are all potent encouragements to moral maturation and even ennoblement.

Of course, weaknesses induce companionship just as easily, in fact more easily, than do virtues. There are relationships undeserving of the title friendship that go by that name nonetheless, the kinds of "friendship" English essayist Joseph Addison called "confederacies in vice, or leagues of pleasure." Mutual desires and selfishness can be the foundations of counterfeit friendships. In our age, when casual acquaintance often comes so easily, and when intimacy comes too soon and too cheaply, we need to be reminded that genuine friendships take time. They take effort to make, and work to keep. Friendship is a deep thing. It is, indeed, a form of love. And while it may be, as C. S. Lewis said, the least biological form of love, it is also one of the most important.

Every parent knows how crucial the choice of friends is for every child. Childhood friendships tell parents which ways their children are tending. They are important because good friends bring you up, and bad friends bring you down. So it matters who our children's friends are. And it matters, as examples to our children, who our friends are. Friends should be allies of our better natures.

We must teach children how to recognize counterfeit friendships, to know they are injurious, to realize they reinforce what is less than noble in us.

*Having* friends is only half the relationship, of course, though it is the half that both children and parents tend to be most consciously concerned with. *Being* a friend is often more important to our moral development. The other side of "good friends bring you up" is the side where you are the good friend, the active agent that brings the other up. To *befriend* a friendless or less fortunate schoolmate can be a profoundly maturing activity for a child. Such familiar exhortations as "Friends don't let friends drive drunk" and "To *have* a friend, *be* a friend" help keep us mindful of this more active side of friendship.

Here, then, are some varieties of friendship. Here we find friends who stick together in adversity, friends who give more than they expect to receive, friends who incite each other to higher purposes. We find small deeds done for the sake of friendship, as well as great acts of sacrifice; friends simply going a little out of their way for each other, and friends risking or even offering their lives. We see pleasure found in new friendships, comfort known in old ones, and pain suffered for those lost. From these varieties of friendships, we learn to improve our own.

# The Pasture

*Robert Frost*

This little poem reminds us that a friend is someone we want to be with.

I'm going out to clean the pasture spring;
I'll only stop to rake the leaves away
(And wait to watch the water clear, I may):
I sha'n't be gone long.—You come too.

I'm going out to fetch the little calf
That's standing by the mother. It's so young,
It totters when she licks it with her tongue.
I sha'n't be gone long.—You come too.

---

# The Bear and the Travelers

*Aesop*

Fair-weather friends were around in the days of Aesop, in the sixth century B.C., and they still abound today. Children should learn how to recognize one, and how not to be one.

Two Travelers were on the road together, when a Bear suddenly appeared on the scene. Before he observed them, one made for a tree at the side of the road, and climbed up into the branches and hid there. The other was not so nimble as his companion; and, as he could not escape, he threw himself on the ground and pretended to be dead. The Bear came up and sniffed all round him, but he kept perfectly still and held his breath; for they say that a bear will not touch a dead body. The Bear took him for a corpse, and went away. When the coast was clear, the Traveler in the tree came down, and asked the other what it was the Bear had whispered to him when he put his mouth to his ear. The other replied, "He told me never again to travel with a friend who deserts you at the first sign of danger."

Misfortune tests the sincerity of friendship.

---

# Cat and Mouse in Partnership

*The Brothers Grimm*

As this story shows us, picking the wrong friend can be disappointing or even disastrous.

A cat having made acquaintance with a mouse, professed such great love and friendship for her, that the mouse at last agreed that they should live and keep house together.

"We must make provision for the winter," said the cat, "or we shall suffer hunger, and you, little mouse, must not stir out, or you will be caught in a trap."

So they took counsel together and bought a little pot of honey. And then they could not tell where to put it for safety, but after long consideration the cat said there could not be a better place than the church, for nobody would steal there, and they would put it under the altar and not touch it until they were really in want. So this was done, and the little pot placed in safety.

But before long the cat was seized with a great wish to taste it.

"Listen to me, little mouse," said he, "I have been asked by my cousin to stand godfather to a little son she has brought into the world. He is white with brown spots. And they want to have the christening today, so let me go to it, and you stay at home and keep house."

"Oh yes, certainly," answered the mouse, "pray go by all means. And when you are feasting on all the good things, think of me. I should so like a drop of the sweet red wine."

But there was not a word of truth in all this. The cat had no cousin, and had not been asked to stand godfather. He went to the church, straight up to the little pot, and licked the honey off the top. Then he took a walk over the roofs of the town, saw his acquaintances, stretched himself in the sun, and licked his whiskers as often as he thought of the little pot of honey. And then when it was evening he went home.

"Here you are at last," said the mouse. "I expect you have had a merry time."

"Oh, pretty well," answered the cat.

"And what name did you give the child?" asked the mouse.

"Top-off," answered the cat, dryly.

"Top-off!" cried the mouse. "That is a singular and wonderful name! Is it common in your family?"

"What does it matter?" said the cat. "It's not any worse than Crumb-picker, like your godchild."

A little time after this the cat was again seized with a longing.

"Again I must ask you," said he to the mouse, "to do me a favor, and keep house alone for a day. I have been asked a second time to stand godfather. And as the little one has a white ring around its neck, I cannot well refuse."

So the kind little mouse consented, and the cat crept along by the town wall until he reached the church, and going straight to the little pot of honey, devoured half of it.

"Nothing tastes so well as what one keeps to oneself," said he, feeling quite content with his day's work. When he reached home, the mouse asked what name had been given to the child.

"Half-gone," answered the cat.

"Half-gone!" cried the mouse. "I never heard such a name in my life! I'll bet it's not to be found in the calendar."

Soon after that the cat's mouth began to water again for the honey.

"Good things always come in threes," said he to the mouse. "Again I have been asked to stand godfather, the little one is quite black with white feet, and not any white hair on its body. Such a thing does not happen every day, so you will let me go, won't you?"

"Top-off, Half-gone," murmured the mouse. "They are such curious names, I cannot but wonder at them!"

"That's because you are always sitting at home," said the cat, "in your little gray frock and hairy tail, never seeing the world, and fancying all sorts of things."

So the little mouse cleaned up the house and set it all in order. Meanwhile the greedy cat went and made an end of the little pot of honey.

"Now all is finished one's mind will be easy," said he, and came home in the evening, quite sleek and comfortable. The mouse asked at once what name had been given to the third child.

"It won't please you any better than the others," answered the cat. "It is called All-gone."

"All-gone!" cried the mouse. "What an unheard-of name! I never met with anything like it! All-gone! Whatever can it mean?" And shaking her head, she curled herself round and went to sleep. After that the cat was not again asked to stand godfather.

When the winter had come and there was nothing more to be had out of doors, the mouse began to think of their store.

"Come, cat," said she, "we will fetch our pot of honey, how good it will taste, to be sure!"

"Of course it will," said the cat.

So they set out, and when they reached the place, they found the pot, but it was standing empty.

"Oh, now I know what it all meant," cried the mouse, "now I see what sort of a partner you have been! Instead of standing godfather you have devoured it all, first Top-off, then Half-gone, then—"

"Will you hold your tongue!" screamed the cat. "Another word, and I'll devour you too!"

And the poor little mouse having "All-gone" on her tongue, out it came, and the cat leaped upon her and made an end of her. And that is the way of the world.

# The Velveteen Rabbit

*Margery Williams*

Since the early part of this century, this story of how a toy rabbit becomes real has helped children learn that sometimes what we go through for a friend makes us a little worn and torn, but that's what makes the friendship real. Friendship often contains some trial, but true friendship endures the test and even grows from it.

There was once a Velveteen Rabbit, and in the beginning he was really splendid. He was fat and bunchy, as a rabbit should be; his coat was spotted brown and white, he had real thread whiskers, and his ears were lined with pink sateen. On Christmas morning, when he sat wedged in the top of the Boy's stocking, with a sprig of holly between his paws, the effect was charming.

There were other things in the stocking, nuts and oranges and a toy engine, and chocolate almonds and a clockwork mouse, but the Rabbit was quite the best of all. For at least two hours the Boy loved him, and then Aunts and Uncles came to dinner, and there was a great rustling of tissue paper and unwrapping of parcels, and in the excitement of looking at all the new presents the Velveteen Rabbit was forgotten.

For a long time he lived in the toy cupboard or on the nursery floor, and no one thought very much about him. He was naturally shy, and being only made of velveteen, some of the more expensive toys quite snubbed him. The mechanical toys were very superior, and looked down upon everyone else; they were full of modern ideas, and pretended they were real. The model boat, who had lived through two seasons and lost most of his paint, caught the tone from them and never missed an opportunity of referring to his rigging in technical terms. The Rabbit could not claim to be a model of anything, for he didn't know that real rabbits existed; he thought they were all stuffed with sawdust like himself, and he understood that sawdust was quite out-of-date and should never be mentioned in modern circles. Even Timothy, the jointed wooden lion, who was made by the disabled soldiers, and should have had broader views, put on airs and pretended he was connected with Government. Between them all the poor little Rabbit was made to feel himself very insignificant and commonplace, and the only person who was kind to him at all was the Skin Horse.

The Skin Horse had lived longer in the nursery than any of the others. He was so old that his brown coat was bald in patches and showed the seams underneath, and most of the hairs in his tail had been pulled out to string bead necklaces. He was wise, for he had seen a long succession of mechanical toys arrive to boast and swagger, and by and by break their mainsprings and pass away, and he knew that they were only toys, and would never turn into anything else. For nursery magic is very strange and wonderful, and only those playthings that are old and wise and experienced like the Skin Horse understand all about it.

"What is REAL?" asked the Rabbit one day, when they were lying side by side near the nursery fender, before Nana came to tidy the room. "Does it mean having things that buzz inside you and a stick-out handle?"

"Real isn't how you are made," said the Skin Horse. "It's a thing that happens to you. When a child loves you for a long, long time, not just to play with, but REALLY loves you, then you become Real."

"Does it hurt?" asked the Rabbit.

"Sometimes," said the Skin Horse, for he was always truthful. "When you are Real you don't mind being hurt."

"Does it happen all at once, like being wound up," he asked, "or bit by bit?"

"It doesn't happen all at once," said the Skin Horse. "You become. It takes a long time. That's why it doesn't often happen to people who break easily, or have sharp edges, or who have to be carefully kept. Generally, by the time you are Real, most of your hair has been loved off, and your eyes drop out and you get loose in the joints and very shabby. But these things don't matter at all, because once you are Real you can't be ugly, except to people who don't understand."

"I suppose *you* are Real?" said the Rabbit. And then he wished he had not said it, for he thought the Skin Horse might be sensitive. But the Skin Horse only smiled.

"The Boy's uncle made me Real," he said. "That was a great many years ago; but once you are Real you can't become unreal again. It lasts for always."

The Rabbit sighed. He thought it would be a long time before this magic called Real happened to him. He longed to become Real, to know what it felt like; and yet the idea of growing shabby and losing his eyes and whiskers was rather sad. He wished that he could become it without these uncomfortable things happening to him.

There was a person called Nana who ruled the nursery. Sometimes she took no notice of the playthings lying about, and sometimes, for no reason whatever, she went swooping about like a great wind and hustled them away in cupboards. She called this "tidying up," and the playthings all hated it, especially the tin ones. The Rabbit didn't mind it so much, for wherever he was thrown he came down soft.

One evening, when the Boy was going to bed, he couldn't find the china dog that always slept with him. Nana was in a hurry, and it was too much trouble to hunt for china dogs at bedtime, so she simply looked about her, and seeing that the toy cupboard door stood open, she made a swoop.

"Here," she said, "take your old Bunny! He'll do to sleep with you!" And she dragged the Rabbit out by one ear, and put him into the Boy's arms.

That night, and for many nights after, the Velveteen Rabbit slept in the Boy's bed. At first he found it rather uncomfortable, for the boy hugged him very tight, and sometimes he rolled over on him, and sometimes he pushed him so far under the pillow that the Rabbit could scarcely breathe. And he missed, too, those long moonlight hours in the nursery, when all the house was silent, and his talks with the Skin Horse. But very soon he grew to like it, for the Boy used to talk to him, and made nice tunnels for him under the bedclothes that he said were like the burrows the real rabbits lived in. And they had splendid games together, in whispers, when Nana had gone away to her supper and left the night-light burning on the mantelpiece. And when the Boy dropped off to sleep, the Rabbit would snuggle down close under his little warm chin and dream, with the Boy's hands clasped close round him all night long.

And so time went on, and the little Rabbit was very happy—so happy that he never noticed how his beautiful velveteen fur was getting shabbier and shabbier, and his tail coming unsewn, and all the pink rubbed off his nose where the Boy had kissed him.

Spring came, and they had long days in the garden, for wherever the Boy went the Rabbit went, too. He had rides in the wheelbarrow, and picnics on the grass, and lovely fairy huts built for him under the raspberry canes behind the flower border. And once, when the boy was called away suddenly to go out to tea, the Rabbit was left out on the lawn until long after dusk, and Nana had to come and look for him with the candle because the Boy couldn't go to sleep unless he was there. He was wet through with the dew and quite earthy from diving into the burrows the Boy had made for him in the flower bed, and Nana grumbled as she rubbed him off with a corner of her apron.

"You must have your old Bunny!" she said. "Fancy all that fuss for a toy!"

The boy sat up in bed and stretched out his hands.

"Give me my Bunny!" he said. "You mustn't say that. He isn't a toy. He's REAL!"

When the little Rabbit heard that he was happy, for he knew that what the Skin Horse had said was true at last. The nursery magic had happened to him, and he was a toy no longer. He was Real. The Boy himself had said it.

That night he was almost too happy to sleep, and so much love stirred in his little sawdust heart that it almost burst. And into his boot-button eyes, that had long ago lost their polish, there came a look of wisdom and beauty, so that even Nana noticed it next morning when she picked him up, and said, "I declare if that old Bunny hasn't got quite a knowing expression!"

That was a wonderful summer!

Near the house where they lived there was a wood, and in the long June evenings the Boy liked to go there after tea to play. He took the Velveteen Rabbit with him, and before he wandered off to pick flowers, or play at brigands among the trees, he always made the Rabbit a little nest somewhere among the bracken, where he would be quite cosy, for he was a kindhearted little boy and he liked Bunny to be comfortable. One evening, while the Rabbit was lying there alone, watching the ants that ran to and fro between his velvet paws in the grass, he saw two strange beings creep out of the tall bracken near him.

They were rabbits like himself, but quite furry and brand-new. They must have been very well made, for their seams didn't show at all, and they changed shape in a queer way when they moved; one minute they were long and thin and the next minute fat and bunchy, instead of always staying the same like he did. Their feet padded softly on the ground, and they crept quite close to him, twitching their noses, while the rabbit stared hard to see which side the clockwork stuck out, for he knew that people who jump generally have something to wind them up. But he couldn't see it. They were evidently a new kind of rabbit altogether.

They stared at him, and the little Rabbit stared back. And all the time their noses twitched.

"Why don't you get up and play with us?" one of them asked.

"I don't feel like it," said the Rabbit, for he didn't want to explain that he had no clockwork.

"Ho!" said the furry rabbit. "It's as easy as anything." And he gave a big hop sideways and stood on his hind legs.

"I don't believe you can!" he said.

"I can!" said the little Rabbit. "I can jump higher than anything!" He meant when the Boy threw him, but of course he didn't want to say so.

"Can you hop on your hind legs?" asked the furry rabbit.

That was a dreadful question, for the Velveteen Rabbit had no hind legs at all! The back of him was made all in one piece, like a pincushion. He sat still in the bracken, and hoped that the other rabbits wouldn't notice.

"I don't want to!" he said again.

But the wild rabbits have very sharp eyes. And this one stretched out his neck and looked.

"He hasn't got any hind legs!" he called out. "Fancy a rabbit without any hind legs!" And he began to laugh.

"I have!" cried the little Rabbit. "I have got hind legs! I am sitting on them!"

"Then stretch them out and show me, like this!" said the wild rabbit. And he began to whirl round and dance, till the little Rabbit got quite dizzy.

"I don't like dancing," he said. "I'd rather sit still!"

But all the while he was longing to dance, for a funny new tickly feeling ran through him, and he felt he would give anything in the world to be able to jump about like these rabbits did.

The strange rabbit stopped dancing, and came quite close. He came so close this time that his long whiskers brushed the Velveteen Rabbit's ear, and then he wrinkled his nose suddenly and flattened his ears and jumped backward.

"He doesn't smell right!" he exclaimed. "He isn't a rabbit at all! He isn't real!"

"I *am* Real!" said the little Rabbit. "I am Real! The Boy said so!" And he nearly began to cry.

Just then there was a sound of footsteps, and the Boy ran past near them, and with a stamp of feet and a flash of white tails the two strange rabbits disappeared.

"Come back and play with me!" called the little Rabbit. "Oh, do come back! I *know* I am Real!"

But there was no answer, only the little ants ran to and fro, and the bracken swayed gently where the two strangers had passed. The Velveteen Rabbit was all alone.

"Oh, dear!" he thought. "Why did they run away like that? Why couldn't they stop and talk to me?"

For a long time he lay very still, watching the bracken, and hoping that they would come back. But they never returned, and presently the sun sank lower and the little white moths fluttered out, and the Boy came and carried him home.

Weeks passed, and the little Rabbit grew very old and shabby, but the Boy loved him just as much. He loved him so hard that he loved all his whiskers off, and the pink lining to his ears turned gray, and his brown spots faded. He even began to lose his shape, and he scarcely looked like a rabbit anymore, except to the Boy. To him he was always beautiful, and that was all that the little Rabbit cared about. He didn't mind how he looked to other people, because the nursery magic had made him Real, and when you are Real, shabbiness doesn't matter.

And then, one day, the Boy was ill.

His face grew very flushed, and he talked in his sleep, and his little body was so hot that it burned the Rabbit when he held him close. Strange people came and went in the nursery, and a light burned all night and through it all the little Velveteen Rabbit lay there, hidden from sight under the bedclothes, and he never stirred, for he was afraid that if they found him someone might take him away, and he knew that the Boy needed him.

It was a long weary time, for the Boy was too ill to play, and the little Rabbit found it rather dull with nothing to do all day long. But he snuggled down patiently, and looked forward to the time when the Boy should be well again, and they would go out in the garden amongst the flowers and the butterflies and play splendid games in the raspberry thicket like they used to. All sorts of delightful things he planned, and while the Boy lay half asleep he crept up close to the pillow and whispered them in his ear. And presently the fever turned, and the Boy got better. He was able to sit up in bed and look at picture books, while the little Rabbit cuddled close at his side. And one day, they let him get up and dress.

It was a bright, sunny morning, and the windows stood wide open. They had carried the Boy out onto the balcony, wrapped in a shawl, and the little Rabbit lay tangled up among the bedclothes, thinking.

The Boy was going to the seaside tomorrow. Everything was arranged, and now it only remained to carry out the doctor's orders. They talked about it all, while the little Rabbit lay under the bedclothes, with just his head peeping out, and listened. The room was to be disinfected, and all the books and toys that the Boy had played with in bed must be burned.

"Hurrah!" thought the little Rabbit. "Tomorrow we shall go to the seaside!" For the Boy had often talked of the seaside, and he wanted very much to see the big waves coming in, and the tiny crabs, and the sand castles.

Just then Nana caught sight of him.

"How about his old Bunny?" she asked.

"*That?*" said the doctor. "Why, it's a mass of scarlet fever germs!—Burn it at once. What? Nonsense! Get him a new one. He mustn't have that anymore!"

And so the little Rabbit was put into a sack with the old picture books and a lot of rubbish, and carried out to the end of the garden behind the fowl house. That was a fine place to make a bonfire, only the gardener was too busy just then to attend to it. He had the potatoes to dig and the green peas to gather, but next morning he promised to come quite early and burn the whole lot.

That night the Boy slept in a different bedroom, and he had a new bunny to sleep with him. It was a splendid bunny, all white plush with real glass eyes, but the Boy was too excited to care very much about it. For tomorrow he was going to the seaside, and that in itself was such a wonderful thing that he could think of nothing else.

And while the Boy was asleep, dreaming of the seaside, the little Rabbit lay among the old picture books in the corner behind the fowl house, and he felt very lonely. The sack had been left untied, and so by wriggling a bit he was able to get his head through the opening and look out. He was shivering a little, for he had always been used to sleeping in a proper bed, and by this time his coat had worn so thin and threadbare from hugging that it was no longer any protection to him. Nearby he could see the thicket of raspberry canes, growing tall and close like a tropical jungle, in whose shadow he had played with the Boy on bygone mornings. He thought of those long sunlit hours in the garden—how happy they were—and a great sadness came over him. He seemed to see them all pass before him, each more beautiful than the other, the fairy huts in the flower bed, the quiet evenings in the wood when he lay in the bracken and the little ants ran over his paws; the wonderful day when he first knew that he was Real. He thought of the Skin Horse, so wise and gentle, and all that he had told him. Of what use was it to be loved and lose one's beauty and become Real if it all ended like this? And a tear, a real tear, trickled down his little shabby velvet nose and fell to the ground.

And then a strange thing happened. For where the tear had fallen a flower grew out of the ground, a mysterious flower, not at all like any that grew in the garden. It had slender green leaves the color of emeralds, and in the center of the leaves a blossom like a golden cup. It was so beautiful that the little Rabbit forgot to cry, and just lay there watching it. And presently the blossom opened, and out of it there stepped a Fairy.

She was quite the loveliest Fairy in the whole world. Her dress was of pearl and dewdrops, and there were flowers round her neck and in her hair, and her face was like the most perfect flower of all. And she came close to the little Rabbit and gathered him up in her arms and kissed him on his velveteen nose that was all damp from crying.

"Little Rabbit," she said, "don't you know who I am?"

The Rabbit looked up at her, and it seemed to him that he had seen her face before, but he couldn't think where.

"I am the nursery magic Fairy," she said. "I take care of all the playthings that the children have loved. When they are old and worn out and the children don't need them anymore, then I come and take them away with me and turn them into Real."

"Wasn't I Real before?" asked the little Rabbit.

"You were Real to the Boy," the Fairy said, "because he loved you. Now you shall be Real to everyone."

And she held the little Rabbit close in her arms and flew him into the wood.

It was light now, for the moon had risen. All the forest was beautiful, and the fronds of the bracken shone like frosted silver. In the open glade between the tree trunks the wild rabbits danced with their shadows on the velvet grass, but when they saw the Fairy they all stopped dancing and stood round in a ring to stare at her.

"I've brought you a new playfellow," the Fairy said. "You must be very kind to him and teach him all he needs to know in Rabbitland, for he is going to live with you forever and ever!"

And she kissed the little Rabbit again and put him down on the grass.

"Run and play, little Rabbit!" she said.

But the little Rabbit sat quite still for a moment and never moved. For when he saw all the wild rabbits dancing around him he suddenly remembered about his hind legs, and he didn't want them to see that he was made all in one piece. He did not know that when the Fairy kissed him that last time she had changed him altogether. And he might have sat there a long time, too shy to move, if just then something hadn't tickled his nose, and before he thought what he was doing he lifted his hind toe to scratch it.

And he found that he actually had hind legs! Instead of dingy velveteen he had brown fur, soft and shiny, his ears twitched by themselves, and his whiskers were so long that they brushed the grass. He gave one leap and the joy of using those hind legs was so great that he went springing about the turf on them, jumping sideways and whirling round as the others did, and he grew so excited that when at last he did stop to look for the Fairy she had gone.

He was a Real Rabbit at last, at home with the other rabbits.

Autumn passed and winter, and in the spring, when the days grew warm and sunny, the Boy went out to play in the wood behind the house. And while he was playing, two rabbits crept out from the bracken and peeped at him. One of them was brown all over, but the other had strange markings under his fur, as though long ago he had been spotted, and the spots still showed through. And about his little soft nose and his round black eyes there was something familiar, so that the Boy thought to himself:

"Why, he looks just like my old Bunny that was lost when I had scarlet fever!"

But he never knew that it really was his own Bunny, come back to look at the child who had first helped him to be Real.

# Friendship

This poem reminds us of some of the "rules" of friendship, as well as some of the rewards.

Friendship needs no studied phrases,
  Polished face, or winning wiles;
Friendship deals no lavish praises,
  Friendship dons no surface smiles.

Friendship follows Nature's diction,
  Shuns the blandishments of art,
Boldly severs truth from fiction,
  Speaks the language of the heart.

Friendship favors no condition,
  Scorns a narrow-minded creed,
Lovingly fulfills its mission,
  Be it word or be it deed.

Friendship cheers the faint and weary,
  Makes the timid spirit brave,
Warns the erring, lights the dreary,
  Smooths the passage to the grave.

Friendship—pure, unselfish friendship,
  All through life's allotted span,
Nurtures, strengthens, widens, lengthens,
  Man's relationship with man.

# Why Frog and Snake Never Play Together

This African folktale makes us think about how much companionship the world has missed because people are told they "can't" be friends with each other.

Once upon a time, the child of the Frog was hopping along in the bush when he spied someone new lying across the path before him. This someone was long and slender, and his skin seemed to shine with all the colors of the rainbow.

"Hello there," called Frog-child. "What are you doing lying here in the path?"

"Just warming myself in the sun," answered the someone new, twisting and turning and uncoiling himself. "My name is Snake-child. What's yours?"

"I'm Frog-child. Would you like to play with me?"

So Frog-child and Snake-child played together all morning long in the bush.

"Watch what I can do," said Frog-child, and he hopped high into the air. "I'll teach you how, if you want," he offered.

So he taught Snake-child how to hop, and together they hopped up and down the path through the bush.

"Now watch what I can do," said Snake-child, and he crawled on his belly straight up the trunk of a tall tree. "I'll teach you if you want."

So he taught Frog-child how to slide on his belly and climb into trees.

After a while they both grew hungry and decided to go home for lunch, but they promised each other to meet again the next day.

"Thanks for teaching me how to hop," called Snake-child.

"Thanks for teaching me how to crawl up trees," called Frog-child.

Then they each went home.

"Look what I can do, Mother!" cried Frog-child, crawling on his belly.

"Where did you learn how to do that?" his mother asked.

"Snake-child taught me," he answered. "We played together in the bush this morning. He's my new friend."

"Don't you know the Snake family is a bad family?" his mother asked. "They have poison in their teeth. Don't ever let me catch you playing with one of them again. And don't let me see you crawling on your belly, either. It isn't proper."

Meanwhile, Snake-child went home and hopped up and down for his mother to see.

"'Who taught you to do that?" she asked.

"Frog-child did," he said. "He's my new friend."

"What foolishness," said his mother. "Don't you know we've been on bad terms with the Frog family for longer than anyone can remember? The next time you play with Frog-child, catch him and eat him up. And stop that hopping. It isn't our custom."

So the next morning when Frog-child met Snake-child in the bush, he kept his distance.

"I'm afraid I can't go crawling with you today," he called, hopping back a hop or two.

Snake-child eyed him quietly, remembering what his mother had told him. "If he gets too close, I'll spring at him and eat him," he thought. But then he remembered how much fun they had had together, and how nice Frog-child had been to teach him how to hop. So he sighed sadly to himself and slid away into the bush.

And from that day onward, Frog-child and Snake-child never played together again. But they often sat alone in the sun, each thinking about their one day of friendship.

## Rocking Horse Land

*Laurence Housman*

In this wonderfully imaginative story we see that good friends are always mindful of each other's interests and give each other room to grow.

Prince Fredolin woke up, both eyes at once, and sprang out of bed into the sunshine. He was five years old that morning, by all the clocks and calendars in the kingdom; and the day was going to be beautiful. Every golden minute was precious. He was dressed and out of his room before the attendants knew that he was awake.

In the antechamber stood piles on piles of glittering presents; when he walked among them they came up to the measure of his waist. His fairy godmother had sent him a toy with the most humorous effect. It was labeled, "Break me and I shall turn into something else." So every time he broke it he got a new toy more beautiful than the last. It began by being a hoop, and from that it ran on, while the Prince broke it incessantly for the space of one hour, during which it became by turn—a top, a Noah's ark, a skipping rope, a man-of-war, a box of bricks, a picture puzzle, a pair of stilts, a drum, a trumpet, a kaleidoscope, a steam engine, and nine hundred and fifty other things exactly. Then he began to grow discontented because it would never turn into the same thing again, and after having broken the man-of-war he wanted to get it back again. Also he wanted to see if the steam engine would go inside the Noah's ark, but the toy would never be two things at the same time either. This was very unsatisfactory. He thought his fairy godmother ought to have sent him two toys, out of which he could make combinations.

At last he broke it once more, and it turned into a kite. And while he was flying the kite he broke the string, and the kite went sailing away up into the nasty clear sky, and was never heard of again.

Then Fredolin sat down and howled at his fairy godmother. What a dissembling lot fairy godmothers were, to be sure! They were always setting traps to make their godchildren unhappy. Nevertheless, when told to, he took up his pen and wrote her a nice little note, full of bad spelling and tarradiddles, to say what a happy birthday he was spending in breaking up the beautiful toy she had sent him.

Then he went to look at the rest of the presents, and found it quite refreshing to break a few that did not send him giddy by turning into anything else.

Suddenly his eyes became fixed with delight. Alone, right at the end of the room, stood a great black rocking horse. The saddle and bridle were hung with tiny gold bells and balls of coral, and the horse's tail and mane flowed till they almost touched the ground.

The Prince scampered across the room, and threw his arms around the beautiful creature's neck. All its bells jangled as the head swayed gracefully down, and the prince kissed it between the eyes. Great eyes they were, the color of fire, so wonderfully bright, it semed they must be really alive, only they did not move, but gazed continually with a set stare at the tapestry-hung wall, on which were figures of armed knights riding by to battle.

So Prince Fredolin mounted to the back of his rocking horse, and all day long he rode and shouted to the figures of the armed knights, challenging them to fight, or leading them against the enemy.

At length, when it came to be bedtime, weary of so much glory, he was lifted down from the saddle and carried away to bed.

In his sleep Fredolin still felt his black rocking horse swinging to and fro under him, and heard the melodious chime of its bells, and, in the land of dreams, saw a great country open before him, full of the sound of the battle cry and the hunting horn calling him to strange perils and triumphs.

In the middle of the night he grew softly awake, and his heart was full of love for his black rocking horse. He crept gently out of bed: he would go and look at it where it was standing so grand and still in the next room, to make sure that it was all safe and not afraid of being by itself in the dark night. Parting the door hangings he passed through into the wide hollow chamber beyond, all littered about with toys.

The moon was shining in through the window, making a square cistern of light upon the floor. And then, all at once, he saw that the rocking horse had moved from the place where he had left it! It had crossed the room, and was standing close to the window, with its head toward the night, as though watching the movement of the clouds and the trees swaying in the wind.

The Prince could not understand how it had been moved. He was a little bit afraid, and stealing timidly across, he took hold of the bridle to comfort himself with the jangle of its bells. As he came close, and looked up into the dark solemn face he saw that the eyes were full of tears, and reaching up felt one fall warm against his hand.

"Why do you weep, my Beautiful?" said the Prince.

The rocking horse answered, "I weep because I am a prisoner, and not free. Open the window, Master, and let me go!"

"But if I let you go I shall lose you," said the Prince. "Cannot you be happy here with me?"

And the horse said, "Let me go, for my great brothers call me out of Rocking Horse Land, and I hear my sweet mare whinnying to her foals, and they all cry, seeking me through the ups and hollows of my native fastnesses! Sweet Master, let me go this night, and I will return to you when it is day!"

Then Prince Fredolin said, "How shall I know that you will return to me, and what name shall I call you by?"

And the rocking horse answered, "My name is Rollonde. Search among my mane till you find in it a white hair, draw it out and wind it upon one of your fingers. And so long as you have it wound about your finger, you are my master; and wherever I am I must go or return at your bidding."

So the Prince drew down the rocking horse's head, and searched in the mane, till he had found there the white hair, and he wound it upon his finger and tied it. After that he kissed Rollonde between the eyes, saying, "Go then, Rollonde, since I love you, and would see you happy. Only return to me when it is day!" And so saying he threw open the window to the stir of the night.

Then the rocking horse lifted his dark head and neighed aloud for joy, and swaying forward with a mighty circling motion rose full into the air, and sprang out into the free world before him.

Fredolin watched how with plunge and curve he went over the bowed trees. And again he neighed into the darkness of the night, then swifter than wind disappeared in the distance; and faintly from far away came a sound of the neighing of many horses answering him.

Then the Prince closed the window and crept back to bed, and all night long he dreamed strange dreams of Rocking Horse Land. There he saw smooth hills and valleys that rose and sank without a stone or a tree to disturb the steel-like polish of their surface, slippery as glass, and driven over by a strong wind; and over them, with a sound like the humming of bees, flew the rocking horses. Up and down, up and down, with bright manes streaming like colored fires, and feet motionless behind and before, went the swift pendulum of their flight. Their long bodies bowed and rose; their heads worked to carry impetus to their going; they cried, neighing to each other over hill and valley, "Which of us shall be first? Which of us shall be first?" After them the mares with their tall foals came spinning to watch, crying also among themselves, "Ah! Which shall be first?"

"Rollonde, Rollonde is first!" shouted the Prince, clapping his hands together as they reached the goal. And at that, all at once, he woke and saw it was broad day. Then he ran and threw open the window, and holding out the finger that carried the white hair, cried, "Rollonde, Rollonde, come back, Rollonde!"

Far away he heard an answering sound, and in another moment there came the great rocking horse himself, dipping and dancing over the hills. He crossed the woods and cleared the palace wall at a single bound, and floating in through the window, dropped down onto the floor by Prince Fredolin's side, rocking himself gently to and fro as though panting from the strain of his long flight.

"Now are you happy?" asked the Prince as he caressed him.

"Ah! sweet Prince," said Rollonde, "ah kind Master!" And then he said no more, but became the stock-still staring rocking horse of the day before, with fixed eyes and rigid limbs, which could do nothing but rock up and down with a jangling of sweet bells so long as the Prince rode him.

That night Fredolin came again when all had become still in the palace. And now as before Rollonde had moved from his place and was standing with his head against the window waiting to be let out. "Ah, dear Master," he said, as soon as he saw the Prince coming, "let me go this night also, and I will surely return before day."

"So again the Prince opened the window, and watched him disappear, and heard from far away the neighing of the horses in Rocking Horse Land calling to him. And in the morning with the white hair round his finger he called "Rollonde, Rollonde!" and Rollonde neighed and came back to him, dipping and dancing over the hills.

Now this same thing happened every night. And every morning the horse kissed Fredolin, saying, "Ah! dear Prince and kind Master," and became stock-still once more.

So a year went by, till one morning Fredolin woke up to find it was his sixth birthday. And as six is to five, so were the presents he received on his sixth birthday for magnificence and multitude to the presents he had received the year before. His fairy godmother had sent him a bird, a real live bird. But when he pulled its tail it became a lizard, and when he pulled the lizard's tail it became a mouse, and when he pulled the mouse's tail it became a cat. Then he did very much want to see if the cat would eat the mouse, and not being able to have them both together he got rather vexed with his fairy godmother. However, he pulled the cat's tail and the cat became a dog, and the dog became a goat. And so it went on till he got to a cow. And he pulled the cow's tail and it became a camel, and he pulled the camel's tail and it became an elephant, and still not being contented, he pulled the elephant's tail and it became a guinea pig. Now a guinea pig has got no tail to pull, so it remained a guinea pig, while Prince Fredolin sat down and howled at his fairy godmother.

But the best of all his presents was the one given to him by the King his father. It was a most beautiful horse, for, said the King, "You are now old enough to learn to ride."

So Fredolin was put upon his horse's back, and from having ridden so long upon his rocking horse he learned to ride perfectly in a single day, and was declared by all the courtiers to be the most perfect equestrian that was ever seen.

But these praises and the pleasure of riding about on a real horse so occupied his thoughts that that night he forgot altogether to go and set Rollonde free, but fell fast asleep and dreamed of nothing but real horses and horsemen going to battle. And so it was the next night too.

But the night after that, just as he was falling asleep, he heard something sobbing by his bed, and a voice saying, "Ah! dear Prince and kind Master, let me go, for my heart breaks for a sight of my native land." And there stood his poor rocking horse, Rollonde, with tears falling out of his beautiful eyes onto the white coverlet.

Then the Prince, full of shame at having forgotten his old friend, sprang up and threw his arms around his neck saying, "Be of good cheer, Rollonde, for now surely I will let you go!" and he ran to the window and opened it for the horse to go through. "Ah, dear Prince and kind Master!" said Rollonde. Then he lifted his head and neighed so that the whole palace shook, and swaying forward till his head almost touched the ground he sprang out and away into the night over the hills toward Rocking Horse Land.

Then Prince Fredolin, standing by the window, thoughtfully unloosed the white hair from his finger, and let it float away into the darkness, out of sight of his eye or reach of his hand.

"Goodbye, Rollonde," he murmured softly, "brave Rollonde, my own good Rollonde! Go and be happy in your own land, since I, your Master, was forgetting to be kind to you." And far away he heard the neighing of horses in Rocking Horse Land.

Many years after, when Fredolin had become King in his father's stead, the fifth birthday of the Prince his son came to be celebrated. And there on the morning of the day, among all the presents that covered the floor of the chamber, stood a beautiful foal rocking horse, black, with deep burning eyes.

No one knew how it had come there, or whose present it was, till the King himself came to look at it. And when he saw it so like the old Rollonde he had loved as a boy, he smiled, and stroking its dark mane, said softly in its ear, "Are you, then, the son of Rollonde?" And the foal answered him, "Ah, dear Prince and kind Master!" but never a word more.

Then the King took the little Prince his son, and told him all the story of Rollonde as I have told it to you here. And at the end he went and searched in the foal's mane till he found one white hair, and, drawing it out, he wound it about the little Prince's finger, bidding him guard it well and be ever a kind master to Rollonde's son.

So here is my story of Rollonde come to a good ending.

# The Selfish Giant

*Oscar Wilde*

Like the giant in this tale, we find friendship when we give something of ourselves.

Every afternoon, as they were coming from school, the children used to go and play in the Giant's garden.

It was a large lovely garden, with soft green grass. Here and there over the grass stood beautiful flowers like stars, and there were twelve peach trees that in the springtime broke out into delicate blossoms of pink and pearl, and in the autumn bore rich fruit. The birds sat on the trees and sang so sweetly that the children used to stop their games in order to listen to them. "How happy we are here!" they cried to each other.

One day the Giant came back. He had been to visit his friend the Cornish ogre, and had stayed with him for seven years. After the seven years were over he had said all that he had to say, for his conversation was limited, and he determined to return to his own castle. When he arrived he saw the children playing in the garden.

"What are you doing here?" he cried in a very gruff voice, and the children ran away.

"My own garden is my own garden," said the Giant. "Any one can understand that, and I will allow nobody to play in it but myself." So he built a high wall all around it, and put up a notice board.

**TRESPASSERS**
**WILL BE**
**PROSECUTED**

He was a very selfish Giant.

The poor children had now nowhere to play. They tried to play on the road, but the road was very dusty and full of hard stones, and they did not like it. They used to wander round the high walls when their lessons were over, and talk about the beautiful garden inside. "How happy we were there!" they said to each other.

Then the spring came, and all over the country there were little blossoms and little birds. Only in the garden of the Selfish Giant it was still winter. The birds did not care to sing in it as there were no children, and the trees forgot to blossom. Once a beautiful flower put its head out from the grass, but when it saw the notice board it was so sorry for the children that it slipped back into the ground again, and went off to sleep. The only people who were pleased were the Snow and the Frost. "Spring has forgotten this garden," they cried, "so we will live here all the year round." The Snow covered up the grass with her great white cloak, and the Frost painted all the trees silver. Then they invited the North Wind to stay with them, and he came. He was wrapped in furs, and he roared all day about the garden, and blew the chimney pots down. "This is a delightful spot," he said. "We must ask the Hail on a visit." So the Hail came. Every day for three hours he rattled on the roof of the castle till he broke most of the slates, and then he ran round and round the garden as fast as he could go. He was dressed in gray and his breath was like ice.

"I cannot understand why the Spring is so late in coming," said the Selfish Giant, as he sat at the window and looked out at his cold, white garden. "I hope there will be a change in the weather."

But the Spring never came, nor the Summer. The Autumn gave golden fruit to every garden, but to the Giant's garden she gave none. "He is too selfish," she said. So it was always Winter there, and the North Wind and the Hail, and the Frost, and the Snow danced about through the trees.

One morning the Giant was lying awake in bed when he heard some lovely music. It sounded so sweet to his ears that he thought it must be the King's musicians passing by. It was really only a little linnet singing outside his window, but it was so long since he had heard a bird sing in his garden that it seemed to him to be the most beautiful music in the world. Then the Hail stopped dancing over his head, and the North Wind ceased roaring, and a delicious perfume came to him through the open casement. "I believe the Spring has come at last," said the Giant, and he jumped out of bed and looked out.

What did he see?

He saw a most wonderful sight. Through a little hole in the wall the children had crept in, and they were sitting in the branches of the trees. In every tree that he could see there was a little child. And the trees were so glad to have the children back again that they had covered themselves with blossoms, and were waving their arms gently above the children's heads. The birds were flying about and twittering with delight, and the flowers were looking up through the green grass and laughing. It was a lovely scene, only in one corner it was still winter. It was the farthest corner of the garden, and in it was standing a little boy. He was so small that he could not reach up to the branches of the tree, and he was wandering all around it, crying bitterly. The poor tree was still covered with frost and snow, and the North Wind was blowing and roaring above it. "Climb up! little boy," said the Tree, and it bent its branches down as low as it could; but the boy was too tiny.

And the Giant's heart melted as he looked out. "How selfish I have been!" he said. "Now I know why the Spring would not come here. I will put that poor little boy on the top of the tree, and then I will knock down the wall, and my garden shall be the children's playground for ever and ever." He was really very sorry for what he had done.

So he crept downstairs and opened the front door quite softly, and went out into the garden. But when the children saw him they were so frightened that they all ran away, and the garden became winter again. Only the little boy did not run, for his eyes were so full of tears that he did not see the Giant coming. And the Giant stole up behind him and took him gently in his hand, and put him up into the tree. And the tree broke at once into blossom, and the birds came and sang on it, and the little boy stretched out his two arms and flung them around the Giant's neck, and kissed him. And the other children, when they saw that the Giant was not wicked any longer, came running back, and with them came the Spring. "It is your garden now, little children" said the Giant, and he took a great axe and knocked down the wall. And when the people were going to market at twelve o'clock they found the Giant playing with the children in the most beautiful garden they had ever seen.

All day long they played, and in the evening they came to the Giant to bid him goodbye.

"But where is your little companion?" he said. "The boy I put into the tree." The Giant loved him the best because he had kissed him.

"We don't know," answered the children. "He has gone away."

"You must tell him to be sure and come tomorrow," said the Giant. But the children said that they did not know where he lived and had never seen him before; and the Giant felt very sad.

Every afternoon, when school was over, the children came and played with the Giant. But the little boy whom the Giant loved was never seen again. The Giant was very kind to all the children, yet he longed for his first little friend, and often spoke of him. "How I would like to see him!" he used to say.

Years went over, and the Giant grew very old and feeble. He could not play about anymore, so he sat in a huge armchair, and watched the children at their games, and admired his garden. "I have many beautiful flowers," he said. "But the children are the most beautiful flowers of all."

One winter morning he looked out of his window as he was dressing. He did not hate the Winter now, for he knew that it was merely the Spring asleep, and that the flowers were resting.

Suddenly he rubbed his eyes in wonder and looked and looked. It certainly was a marvelous sight. In the farthest corner of the garden was a tree quite covered with lovely white blossoms. Its branches were golden, and silver fruit hung down from them, and underneath it stood the little boy he had loved.

Downstairs ran the Giant in great joy, and out into the garden. He hastened across the grass, and came near to the child. And when he came quite close his face grew red with anger, and he said, "Who hath dared to wound thee?" For on the palms of the child's hands were the prints of two nails, and the prints of two nails were on the little feet.

"Who hath dared to wound thee?" cried the Giant. "Tell me, that I may take my big sword and slay him."

"Nay," answered the child. "But these are the wounds of Love."

"Who art thou?" said the Giant, and a strange awe fell on him, and he knelt before the little child.

And the child smiled on the Giant, and said to him, "You let me play once in your garden; today you shall come with me to my garden, which is Paradise."

And when the children ran in that afternoon, they found the Giant lying dead under the tree, all covered with white blossoms.

# Ruth and Naomi

*Retold by Jesse Lyman Hurlbut*

The book of Ruth in the Bible is the story of a widow's courageous decision to leave Moab, her homeland, and travel to Judah with her Hebrew mother-in-law, who has lost her own husband and sons. Ruth's words to Naomi are one of the greatest statements of friendship and loyalty in all of literature: "Whither thou goest, I will go; and where thou lodgest, I will lodge: thy people shall be my people, and thy God my God. Where thou diest, will I die, and there will I be buried." In Judah, Ruth's fidelity and kindness were rewarded with the love of Boaz, and through marriage to him she became the great-grandmother of King David.

In the time of the judges in Israel, a man named Elimelech was living in the town of Bethlehem, in the tribe of Judah, about six miles south of Jerusalem. His wife's name was Naomi, and his two sons were Mahlon and Chilion. For some years the crops were poor, and food was scarce in Judah; and Elimelech, with his family, went to live in the land of Moab, which was on the east of the Dead Sea, as Judah was on the west.

There they stayed ten years, and in that time Elimelech died. His two sons married women of the country of Moab, one woman named Orpah, the other named Ruth. But the two young men also died in the land of Moab, so that Naomi and her two daughters-in-law were all left widows.

Naomi heard that God had again given good harvests and bread to the land of Judah, and she rose up to go from Moab back to her own land and her own town of Bethlehem. Her two daughters-in-law loved her and both would have gone with her, though the land of Judah was a strange land to them, for they were of the Moabite people.

Naomi said to them, "Go back, my daughters, to your own mothers' homes. May the Lord deal kindly with you, as you have been kind to your husbands and to me. May the Lord grant that each of you may yet find another husband and a happy home." Then Naomi kissed them in farewell, and the three women all wept together. The two young widows said to her, "You have been a good mother to us, and we will go with you, and live among your people."

"No, no," said Naomi. "You are young and I am old. Go back and be happy among your own people."

Then Orpah kissed Naomi and went back to her people; but Ruth would not leave her. She said, "Do not ask me to leave you, for I never will. Where you go, I will go; where you live, I will live; your people shall be my people; and your God shall be my God. Where you die, I will die, and be buried. Nothing but death itself shall part you and me."

When Naomi saw that Ruth was firm in her purpose, she ceased trying to persuade her; so the two women went on together. They walked around the Dead Sea, and crossed the river Jordan, and climbed the mountains of Judah, and came to Bethlehem.

Naomi had been absent from Bethlehem for ten years, but her friends were all glad to see her again. They said, "Is this Naomi, whom we knew years ago?" Now the name Naomi means "pleasant." And Naomi said:

"Call me not Naomi; call me Mara, for the Lord has made my life bitter. I went out full, with my husband and two sons; now I come home empty, without them. Do not call me 'Pleasant'; call me 'Bitter.' " The name "Mara," by which Naomi wished to be called, means "bitter." But Naomi learned later that "Pleasant" was the right name for her after all.

There was living in Bethlehem at that time a very rich man named Boaz. He owned large fields that were abundant in their harvests; and he was related to the family of Elimelech, Naomi's husband, who had died.

It was the custom in Israel when they reaped the grain not to gather all the stalks, but to leave some for the poor people, who followed after the reapers with their sickles, and gathered what was left. When Naomi and Ruth came to Bethlehem it was the time of the barley harvest; and Ruth went out into the fields to glean the grain which the reapers had left. It so happened that she was gleaning in the field that belonged to Boaz, this rich man.

Boaz came out from the town to see his men reaping, and he said to them, "The Lord be with you"; and they answered him, "The Lord bless you." And Boaz said to his master of the reapers, "Who is this young woman that I see gleaning in the field?"

The man answered, "It is the young woman from the land of

Moab, who came with Naomi. She asked leave to glean after the reapers, and has been here gathering grain since yesterday."

Then Boaz said to Ruth, "Listen to me, my daughter. Do not go to any other field, but stay here with my young women. No one shall harm you; and when you are thirsty, go and drink at our vessels of water."

Then Ruth bowed to Boaz, and thanked him for his kindness, all the more kind because she was a stranger in Israel. Boaz said:

"I have heard how true you have been to your mother-in-law, Naomi, in leaving your own land and coming with her to this land. May the Lord, under whose wings you have come, give you a reward!" And at noon, when they sat down to rest and to eat, Boaz gave her some of the food. And he said to the reapers:

"When you are reaping, leave some of the sheaves for her; and drop out some sheaves from the bundles, where she may gather them."

That evening Ruth showed Naomi how much she had gleaned, and told her of the rich man Boaz, who had been so kind to her. And Naomi said, "This man is a near relation of ours. Stay in his fields as long as the harvest lasts." And so Ruth gleaned in the fields of Boaz until the harvest had been gathered.

At the end of the harvest Boaz held a feast on the threshing floor. And after the feast, by the advice of Naomi, Ruth went to him, and said to him, "You are a near relation of my husband and of his father, Elimelech. Now will you not do good to us for his sake?"

And when Boaz saw Ruth he loved her; and soon after this he took her as his wife. And Naomi and Ruth went to live in his home, so that Naomi's life was no more bitter, but pleasant. And Boaz and Ruth had a son, whom they named Obed; and later Obed had a son named Jesse; and Jesse was the father of David, the shepherd boy who became king. So Ruth, the young woman of Moab, who chose the people and the God of Israel, became the mother of kings.

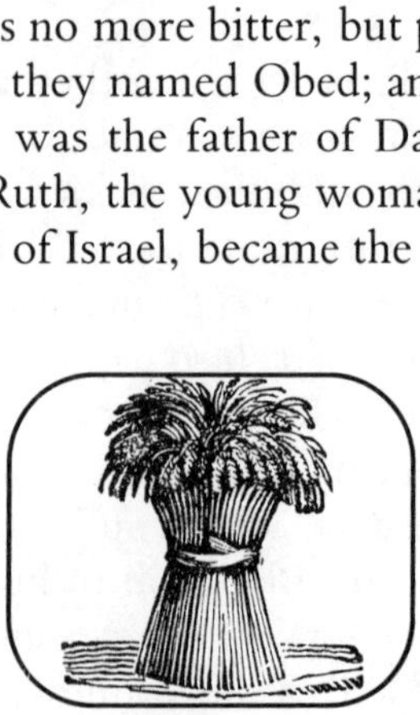

# Jonathan and David

*Retold by Jesse Lyman Hurlbut*

Sometimes the duties of friendship compete with other obligations and affections. The story of Jonathan, told in the first book of Samuel in the Bible, is one such instance. Jonathan was the eldest son and heir of King Saul of Israel. He was also David's sworn friend. After David killed Goliath, Saul grew jealous of his popularity, and fearing that he would eventually become king, sought to murder him. Jonathan's defense of David, made doubly painful because of his filial duties and his own claim to the throne, is one of our greatest examples of loyalty in friendship.

After David had slain the giant he was brought before King Saul, still holding the giant's head. Saul did not remember in this bold fighting man the boy who a few years before had played in his presence. He took him into his own house, and made him an officer among his soldiers. David was as wise and as brave in the army as he had been when facing the giant, and very soon he was in command of a thousand men. All the men loved him, both in Saul's court and in his camp, for David had the spirit that drew all hearts toward him.

When David was returning from his battle with the Philistines, the women of Israel came to meet him out of the cities, with instruments of music, singing and dancing, and they sang:

"Saul has slain his thousands,
And David his ten thousands."

This made Saul very angry, for he was jealous and suspicious in his spirit. He thought constantly of Samuel's words, that God would take the kingdom from him and would give it to one who was more worthy of it. He began to think that perhaps this young man, who had come in a single day to greatness before the people, might try to make himself king.

His former feeling of unhappiness again came over Saul. He

raved in his house, talking as a man talks who is crazed. By this time they all knew that David was a musician, and they called him again to play on his harp and to sing before the troubled king. But now, in his madness, Saul would not listen to David's voice. Twice he threw his spear at him; but each time David leaped aside, and the spear went into the wall of the house.

Saul was afraid of David, for he saw that the Lord was with David, as the Lord was no longer with himself. He would have killed David, but did not dare kill him, because everybody loved David. Saul said to himself, "Though I cannot kill him myself, I will have him killed by the Philistines."

And he sent David out on dangerous errands of war; but David came home in safety, all the greater and the more beloved after each victory. Saul said, "I will give you my daughter Merab for your wife if you will fight the Philistines for me."

David fought the Philistines; but when he came home from the war he found that Merab, who had been promised to him, had been given as wife to another man. Saul had another daughter, named Michal. She loved David, and showed her love for him. Then Saul sent word to David, saying, "You shall have Michal, my daughter, for your wife when you have killed a hundred Philistines."

Then David went out and fought the Philistines, and killed two hundred of them; and they brought the word to Saul. Then Saul gave him his daughter Michal as his wife; but he was all the more afraid of David as he saw him growing in power and drawing nearer to the throne of the kingdom.

But if Saul hated David, Saul's son Jonathan saw David's courage, and the soul of Jonathan was knit to the soul of David, and Jonathan loved him as his own soul. He took off his own royal robe, and his sword, and his bow, and gave them all to David. It grieved Jonathan greatly that his father, Saul, was so jealous of David. He spoke to his father, and said: "Let not the king do harm to David; for David has been faithful to the king, and he has done great things for the kingdom. He took his life in his hand, and killed the Philistine, and won a great victory for the Lord and for the people. Why should you seek to kill an innocent man?"

For the time Saul listened to Jonathan, and said, "As the Lord lives, David shall not be put to death."

And again David sat at the king's table, among the princes; and when Saul was troubled again David played on his harp and sang before him. But once more Saul's jealous anger arose, and he threw his spear at David. David was watchful and quick. He leaped aside, and, as before, the spear fastened into the wall.

Saul sent men to David's house to seize him; but Michal, Saul's daughter, who was David's wife, let David down out of the window, so that he escaped. She placed an image on David's bed and covered it with the bedclothes. When the men came, she said, "David is ill in the bed, and cannot go."

They brought the word to Saul, and he said, "Bring him to me in the bed, just as he is."

When the image was found in David's bed, David was in a safe place, far away. David went to Samuel at Ramah, and stayed with him among the men who were prophets worshipping God and singing and speaking God's word. Saul heard that David was there, and sent men to take him. But when these men came and saw Samuel and the prophets praising God and praying, the same spirit came on them, and they began to praise and to pray. Saul sent other men, but these also, when they came among the prophets, felt the same power, and joined in the worship.

Finally, Saul said, "If no other man will bring David to me, I will go myself and take him."

And Saul went to Ramah; but when he came near to the company of the worshippers, praising God, and praying, and preaching, the same spirit came on Saul. He, too, began to join in the songs and the prayers, and stayed there all that day and that night, worshipping God very earnestly. When the next day he went again to his home in Gibeah, his feeling was changed for the time, and he was again friendly to David.

But David knew that Saul was at heart his bitter enemy and would kill him if he could as soon as his madness came upon him. He met Jonathan out in the field away from the place. Jonathan said to David:

"Stay away from the king's table for a few days, and I will find out how he feels toward you, and will tell you. Perhaps even now my father may become your friend. But if he is to be your enemy, I know that the Lord is with you, and that Saul will not succeed against you. Promise me that as long as you live you will be kind to me, and not only to me while I live, but to my children after me."

Jonathan believed, as many others believed, that David would yet become the king of Israel, and he was willing to give up to David his right to be king, such was his great love for him. That day a promise was made between Jonathan and David, that they and their children, and those who should come after them, should be friends forever.

Jonathan said to David, "I will find how my father feels toward you, and will bring you word. After three days I will be here with my bow and arrows, and I will send a little boy out near your place of hiding, and I will shoot three arrows. If I say to the boy, 'Run, find the arrows, they are on this side of you,' then you can come safely, for the king will not harm you. But if I call out to the boy, 'The arrows are away beyond you,' that will mean that there is danger, and you must hide from the king."

So David stayed away from Saul's table for two days. At first Saul said nothing of his absence, but at last he said:

"Why has not the son of Jesse come to meals yesterday and today?"

And Jonathan said, "David asked leave of me to go to his home at Bethlehem and visit his oldest brother."

Then Saul was very angry. He cried out, "You are a disobedient son! Why have you chosen this enemy of mine as your best friend? Do you not know that as long as he is alive you can never be king? Send after him, and let him be brought to me, for he shall surely die!"

Saul was so fierce in his anger that he threw his spear at his own son Jonathan. Jonathan rose up from the table, so anxious for his friend David that he could eat nothing. The next day, at the hour agreed upon, Jonathan went out into the field with a little boy. He said to the boy, "Run out yonder, and be ready to find the arrows that I shoot."

And as the boy was running Jonathan shot arrows beyond him, and he called out, "The arrows are away beyond you; run quickly and find them."

The boy ran and found the arrows, and brought them to Jonathan. He gave the bow and arrows to the boy, saying to him, "Take them back to the city. I will stay here awhile."

And as soon as the boy was out of sight David came from his hiding place and ran to Jonathan. They fell into each other's arms and kissed each other again and again, and wept together. For David knew now that he must no longer hope to be safe in Saul's hands. He must leave home, and wife, and friends, and his father's house, and hide wherever he could from the hate of King Saul.

Jonathan said to him, "Go in peace; for we have sworn together saying, 'The Lord shall be between you and me, and between your children and my children forever.' "

Then Jonathan went again to his father's palace, and David went out to find a hiding place.

---

# Baucis and Philemon

*Retold by Thomas Bulfinch*

The ancient Greeks understood that the health of the community depended on how well its individual citizens treated one another. To them, Zeus, the king of the gods, was both the guardian of the state and the protector of human relations among civilized men. All social institutions, including the family, lay in his care. Travelers in particular honored him, for he rewarded those who remembered the rules of hospitality and duties of friendship, as we see in this story in which Zeus and Hermes (Jupiter and Mercury to the Romans) seek shelter among the mortals.

Once upon a time Jupiter, in human shape, visited the land of Phrygia, and with him Mercury, without his wings. They presented themselves as weary travelers at many a door, seeking rest and shelter, but found all closed; for it was late, and the inhospitable inhabitants would not rouse themselves to open for their reception. At last a small thatched cottage received them, where Baucis, a pious old dame, and her husband, Philemon, had grown old together. Not ashamed of their poverty, they made it endurable by moderate desires and kind dispositions. When the two guests crossed the humble threshold and bowed their heads to pass under the low door, the old man placed a seat, on which Baucis, bustling and attentive, spread a cloth, and begged them to sit down. Then she raked out the coals from the ashes, kindled a fire, and prepared some pot-herbs and bacon for them. A beechen bowl was filled with warm water, that their guests might wash. While all was doing, they beguiled the time with conversation.

The old woman with trembling hand set the table. One leg was shorter than the rest, but a piece of slate put under restored the level. When it was steady she rubbed the table down with sweet-smelling herbs. Upon it she set some of chaste Minerva's olives, some cornel berries preserved in vinegar, and added radishes and cheese, with eggs lightly cooked in the ashes. The meal was served in earthen dishes; and an earthenware pitcher, with wooden cups, stood beside them. When all was ready the stew, smoking hot, was set on the table. Some wine, not of the oldest, was added, and for dessert, apples and wild honey.

Now while the repast proceeded, the old folks were astonished to see that the wine, as fast as it was poured out, renewed itself in the pitcher of its own accord. Struck with terror, Baucis and Philemon recognized their heavenly guests, fell on their knees, and with clasped hands implored forgiveness for their poor entertainment. There was an old goose, which they kept as the guardian of their humble cottage, and they bethought them to make this a sacrifice in honor of their guests. But the goose, too nimble for the old folk, with the aid of feet and wings eluded their pursuit and at last took shelter between the gods themselves. They forbade it to be slain, and spoke in these words: "We are gods. This inhospitable village shall pay the penalty of its impiety; you alone shall go free from the chastisement. Quit your house and come with us to the top of yonder hill." They hastened to obey. The country behind them was speedily sunk in a lake, only their own house left standing. While they gazed with wonder at the sight, that old house of theirs was changed. Columns took the place of the corner posts, the thatch grew yellow and appeared a gilded roof, the floors became marble, the doors were enriched with carving and ornaments of gold. Then spoke Jupiter in benign accents: "Excellent old man, and woman worthy of such a husband, speak, tell us your wishes. What favor have you to ask of us?" Philemon took counsel with Baucis a few moments, then declared to the gods their common wish. "We ask to be priests and guardians of this thy temple, and that one and the same hour may take us both from life." Their prayer was granted. When they had attained a great age, as they stood one day before the steps of the sacred edifice and were telling the story of the place, Baucis saw Philemon begin to put forth leaves, and Philemon saw Baucis changing in like manner. While still they exchanged parting words, a leafy crown grew over their heads. "Farewell, dear spouse," they said together, and at the same moment the bark closed over their mouths. The Tyanean shepherd still shows the two trees —an oak and a linden, standing side by side.

# The House by the Side of the Road

*Sam Walter Foss*

New England poet Sam Walter Foss (1858–1911) evokes the age-old image of a humble house where the weary traveler finds a welcome—a house such as Baucis and Philemon's—to remind us that we are here to help one another along life's journey. Friends are "help-mates" to each other.

There are hermit souls that live withdrawn
In the peace of their self-content;
There are souls, like stars, that swell apart,
In a fellowless firmament;
There are pioneer souls that blaze their paths
Where highways never ran;
But let me live by the side of the road
And be a friend to man.

Let me live in a house by the side of the road,
Where the race of men go by—
The men who are good and the men who are bad,
As good and as bad as I.
I would not sit in the scorner's seat,
Or hurl the cynic's ban;
Let me live in a house by the side of the road
And be a friend to man.

I see from my house by the side of the road,
By the side of the highway of life,
The men who press with the ardor of hope,
The men who are faint with the strife.
But I turn not away from their smiles nor their tears—
Both parts of an infinite plan;
Let me live in my house by the side of the road
And be a friend to man.

Let me live in my house by the side of the road
  Where the race of men go by—
They are good, they are bad, they are weak,
    they are strong.
  Wise, foolish—so am I.
Then why should I sit in the scorner's seat
  Or hurl the cynic's ban?—
Let me live in my house by the side of the road
  And be a friend to man.

---

## Damon and Pythias

This story takes place in the Sicilian city-state of Syracuse in the fourth century B.C. The Roman orator Cicero tells us that Damon and Pythias (also called Phintias) were followers of the philosopher Pythagoras. Even today, their story sets the standard for absolute friendship, which gives every reason for confidence and leaves no room for doubts.

Damon and Pythias had been the best of friends since childhood. Each trusted the other like a brother, and each knew in his heart there was nothing he would not do for his friend. Eventually the time came for them to prove the depth of their devotion. It happened this way.

Dionysius, the ruler of Syracuse, grew annoyed when he heard about the kind of speeches Pythias was giving. The young scholar was telling the public that no man should have unlimited power over another, and that absolute tyrants were unjust kings. In a fit of rage, Dionysius summoned Pythias and his friend.

"Who do you think you are, spreading unrest among the people?" he demanded.

"I spread only the truth," Pythias answered. "There can be nothing wrong with that."

"And does your truth hold that kings have too much power and that their laws are not good for their subjects?"

"If a king has seized power without permission of the people, then that is what I say."

"This kind of talk is treason," Dionysius shouted. "You are conspiring to overthrow me. Retract what you've said, or face the consequences."

"I will retract nothing," Pythias answered.

"Then you will die. Do you have any last requests?"

"Yes. Let me go home just long enough to say goodbye to my wife and children and to put my household in order."

"I see you not only think I'm unjust, you think I'm stupid as well," Dionysius laughed scornfully. "If I let you leave Syracuse, I have no doubt I will never see you again."

"I will give you a pledge," Pythias said.

"What kind of pledge could you possibly give to make me think you will ever return?" Dionysius demanded.

At that instant Damon, who had stood quietly beside his friend, stepped forward.

"I will be his pledge," he said. "Keep me here in Syracuse, as your prisoner, until Pythias returns. Our friendship is well known to you. You can be sure Pythias will return so long as you hold me."

Dionysius studied the two friends silently. "Very well," he said at last. "But if you are willing to take the place of your friend, you must be willing to accept his sentence if he breaks his promise. If Pythias does not return to Syracuse, you will die in his place."

"He will keep his word," Damon replied. "I have no doubt of that."

Pythias was allowed to go free for a time, and Damon was thrown into prison. After several days, when Pythias failed to reappear, Dionysius's curiosity got the better of him, and he went to the prison to see if Damon was yet sorry he had made such a bargain.

"Your time is almost up," the ruler of Syracuse sneered. "It will be useless to beg for mercy. You were a fool to rely on your friend's promise. Did you really think he would sacrifice his life for you or anyone else?"

"He has merely been delayed," Damon answered steadily. "The winds have kept him from sailing, or perhaps he has met with some accident on the road. But if it is humanly possible, he will be here on time. I am as confident of his virtue as I am of my own existence."

Dionysius was startled at the prisoner's confidence. "We shall soon see," he said, and left Damon in his cell.

The fatal day arrived. Damon was brought from prison and led before the executioner. Dionysius greeted him with a smug smile.

"It seems your friend has not turned up," he laughed. "What do you think of him now?"

"He is my friend," Damon answered. "I trust him."

Even as he spoke, the doors flew open, and Pythias staggered into the room. He was pale and bruised and half speechless from exhaustion. He rushed to the arms of his friend.

"You are safe, praise the gods," he gasped. "It seemed as though the fates were conspiring against us. My ship was wrecked in a storm, and then bandits attacked me on the road. But I refused to give up hope, and at last I've made it back in time. I am ready to receive my sentence of death."

Dionysius heard his words with astonishment. His eyes and his heart were opened. It was impossible for him to resist the power of such constancy.

"The sentence is revoked," he declared. "I never believed that such faith and loyalty could exist in friendship. You have shown me how wrong I was, and it is only right that you be rewarded with your freedom. But I ask that in return you do me one great service."

"What service do you mean?" the friends asked.

"Teach me how to be part of so worthy a friendship."

# How Robin Hood Met Little John

*Adapted from Henry Gilbert*

Every once in a while, it takes a legendary outlaw to teach lessons about fairness, generosity, chivalry, and comradeship. Robin Hood and his band of merry men ranged the forests of Sherwood, in Nottinghamshire, and Barnsdale, in Yorkshire, during the days when King Richard the Lionhearted was far away fighting in the Crusades, and the cunning, greedy Prince John ruled in his absence. In this story, good sportsmanship—grace in victory, humor in defeat—makes good friendship.

Once Robin Hood was journeying through the forest of Barnsdale when he came to a broad stream crossed by a narrow beam of oak. It was wide enough for only one man to cross at a time, and, of course, had no railing. Robin walked some two or three feet along it, when on the other bank a tall man appeared and, jumping onto the bridge, also began to cross it.

They stopped and frowned at each other when they were but some ten feet apart.

"Where are your manners, fellow?" Robin called. "Couldn't you see I was already on the bridge before you placed your great big feet on it? Go back!"

"Go back yourself, acorn-head," retorted the other. "The small jack should always give way to the big pot."

"You're a stranger in these parts, you chucklehead," said Robin. "Your currish tongue betrays you. But I'll give you a good Barnsdale lesson, if you don't retreat and let me pass." Saying which, he took up his bow and drew an arrow. The tall man, with a half-angry, half-humorous twinkle in his eyes, glanced at it.

"If this is your Barnsdale teaching," he rejoined, "it is the teaching of cowards. Here you are, with a bow in your hands, ready to shoot a man who has only his walking staff for a weapon."

Robin paused. He was downright angry with the stranger, but there was something honest and good-natured about the giant which he liked.

"Have it your way, then," he said. "Wait here." He turned and went back to the bank, where he cut a stout staff of his own, and trimmed it to the weight and length he desired. Then he jumped back onto the bridge.

"Now," said Robin, "we will play a little game together. Whoever is knocked from the bridge into the stream shall lose the battle. Ready? Go!"

With the first twirl of Robin's staff, the huge stranger could see he had no novice to deal with, and he soon found that Robin's arm had strength equal to his own. For a long time their staffs whirled like the arms of two windmills, and when they clashed, the crack of wood was tossed to and fro between the trees on either side of the stream. The stranger lunged, and his stick came down with a sharp rap on Robin's skull.

"First hit goes to you!" cried Robin.

"Second hit to you!" said the giant with a good-natured laugh, rubbing a new bruise on his left forearm.

Quick as lightning the blows descended now, and the very bones of both men rattled. Keeping their footing on the narrow bridge was almost impossible. Every step made forward or backward had to be taken with great care, and the power of every blow they gave or received almost threw them over the side.

Suddenly, Robin landed a blow on the big man's crown, but the next instant, with a furious stroke, the stranger struck Robin off his balance. With a mighty splash the outlaw landed in the water.

For a moment the giant man seemed surprised to find no enemy before him. Wiping the sweat from his eyes, he cried,

"Hello, good laddie, where have you gone?"

He bent down anxiously, and peered into the water flowing rapidly beneath the bridge. "By Saint Peter," he said, "I hope the bold man is not hurt!"

"Faith!" came a voice from the bank a little farther down. "Here I am, big fellow, as right as rain. You have the day, and I shall not need to cross the bridge."

Robin pulled himself up the bank and, kneeling down, washed his face in the water. When he rose, he found the big stranger at his side, dashing water over his own head.

"What?" cried Robin. "Have you not gone forward on your journey? You were in such a hurry to cross that bridge, and now you've come back!"

"Scorn me not, good fellow," said the big man. "I have nowhere to go that I know of. I am but a serf who has run away from his manor, and tonight, instead of my warm hut, I shall have only a bush to sleep under. But I would like to shake hands with you before I go, for you are as true and good a fighter as I've ever met."

Robin's hand was on the other's at once, and they gave a shake of mutual respect and liking.

"Stay awhile," said Robin. "Perhaps you would like supper before you go wandering."

With these words, Robin placed his horn to his lips and blew a blast that woke the echoes, made the blackbirds fly shrieking away, and every animal in the forest dive for the nearest cover. Then came sounds as if deer were hurrying through the bushes, and in a moment the forms of men emerged from the dark wall of trees.

"Why, good Robin," one called, "what happened to you? You're soaked to the skin!"

" 'Tis no matter at all," laughed Robin. "You see that tall lad there. We fought on the bridge with our staffs, and he tumbled me in."

"Seize him, lads!" Robin's men cried, springing toward the stranger. "Toss him in and duck him well!"

"Nay, nay," shouted Robin, laughing. "Hold back, lads. I have no ill will, for he's a good fellow and bold. Listen here, my man," he said to the stranger. "We are outlaws, brave lads who hide here in the forest from the evil lords, and we make it our business to take from the rich what they've stolen from the poor. Join us if you will. I can promise both hard knocks and good cheer."

"By earth and water, I'll be your man," cried the stranger, seizing Robin's hand. "Never heard I sweeter words than those you've said, and with all my heart will I serve you and your fellowship."

"What is your name, good man?" asked Robin.

"John o' the Stubbs," replied the other, and then with a great laugh, "but men call me John the Little."

The others laughed too, and pressed forward to shake hands with him. Then they raced back to camp, where a great iron pot waited for them over a fire, from which rose most appetizing odors for men grown hungry in greenwood air. Standing around John the Little, who overtopped them all, the outlaws held their mugs to a great wooden cask to be filled to the brim with brown ale.

"Now, lads," cried Robin, "we will baptize our new comrade into our good free company of forest lads. He has until now been called John the Little, and a sweet pretty babe he is. But from now on, he shall be called Little John. Three cheers, lads, for Little John!"

How they made the twilight ring! The leaves overhead quivered with their shouts! Then they tossed off their mugs of ale, and gathering around the caldron, they dipped their bowls into the rich stew and fell to feasting.

## A Wayfaring Song

*Henry van Dyke*

O who will walk a mile with me
  Along life's merry way?
A comrade blithe and full of glee,
Who dares to laugh out loud and free
And let his frolic fancy play,
Like a happy child, through the flowers gay
That fill the field and fringe the way
  Where he walks a mile with me.

And who will walk a mile with me
  Along life's weary way?
A friend whose heart has eyes to see
The stars shine out o'er the darkening lea,
And the quiet rest at the end o' the day—
A friend who knows, and dares to say,
The brave, sweet words that cheer the way
  Where he walks a mile with me.

With such a comrade, such a friend,
I fain would walk till journey's end,
Through summer sunshine, winter rain,
And then?—Farewell, we shall meet again!

---

## Helen Keller and Anne Sullivan

There is no friendship more sacred than that between student and teacher, and one of the greatest of these was the friendship of Helen Keller (1880–1968) and Anne Mansfield Sullivan (1866–1936).

Illness destroyed Helen Keller's sight and hearing when she was not yet two years old, leaving her cut off from the world. For nearly five years she grew up, as she later described it, "wild and unruly, giggling and chuckling to express pleasure; kicking, scratching, uttering the choked screams of the deaf-mute to indicate the opposite."

Anne Sullivan's arrival at the Kellers' Alabama home from the Perkins Institution for the Blind in Boston changed Helen's life. Sullivan herself had been half-blind from an eye infection from which she never fully recovered, and she came to Helen with experience, unbending dedication, and love. Through the sense of touch she was able to make contact with the young girl's mind, and within three years she had taught Helen to read and write in braille. By sixteen, Helen could speak well enough to go to preparatory school and college. She graduated *cum laude* from Radcliffe in 1904, and devoted the rest of her life to helping the blind and deaf-blind, as her teacher had done. The two women continued their remarkable friendship until Anne's death.

Helen wrote about Anne Mansfield's arrival in her autobiography, *The Story of My Life*.

The most important day I remember in all my life is the one on which my teacher, Anne Mansfield Sullivan, came to me. I am filled with wonder when I consider the immeasurable contrasts between the two lives which it connects. It was the third of March, 1887, three months before I was seven years old.

On the afternoon of that eventful day, I stood on the porch, dumb, expectant. I guessed vaguely from my mother's signs and from the hurrying to and fro in the house that something unusual was about to happen, so I went to the door and waited on the steps. The afternoon sun penetrated the mass of honeysuckle that covered the porch, and fell on my upturned face. My fingers lingered almost unconsciously on the familiar leaves and blossoms which had just come forth to greet the sweet Southern spring. I did not know what the future held of marvel or surprise for me. Anger and bitterness had preyed upon me continually for weeks and a deep languor had succeeded this passionate struggle.

Have you ever been at sea in a dense fog, when it seemed as if a tangible white darkness shut you in, and the great ship, tense and anxious, groped her way toward the shore with plummet and sounding-line, and you waited with beating heart for something to happen? I was like that ship before my education began, only I was without compass or sounding-line, and had no way of knowing how near the harbor was. "Light! give me light!" was the wordless cry of my soul, and the light of love shone on me in that very hour.

I felt approaching footsteps. I stretched out my hand as I supposed to my mother. Someone took it, and I was caught up and held close in the arms of her who had come to reveal all things to me, and, more than all things else, to love me.

The morning after my teacher came she led me into her room and gave me a doll. The little blind children at the Perkins Institution had sent it and Laura Bridgman had dressed it; but I did not know this until afterward. When I had played with it a little while, Miss Sullivan slowly spelled into my hand the word "d-o-l-l." I was at once interested in this finger play and tried to imitate it. When I finally succeeded in making the letters correctly I was flushed with childish pleasure and pride. Running downstairs to my mother I held up my hand and made the letters for doll. I did not know that I was spelling a word or even that words existed; I was simply making my fingers go in monkey-like imitation. In the days that followed I learned to spell in this uncomprehending way a great many words, among them *pin, hat, cup,* and a few verbs like *sit, stand,* and *walk.* But my teacher had been with me several weeks before I understood that everything has a name.

One day, while I was playing with my new doll, Miss Sullivan put my big rag doll into my lap also, spelled "d-o-l-l" and tried to make me understand that "d-o-l-l" applied to both. Earlier in the day we had had a tussle over the words "m-u-g" and "w-a-t-e-r." Miss Sullivan had tried to impress it upon me that "m-u-g" is *mug* and that "w-a-t-e-r" is *water,* but I persisted in confounding the two. In despair she had dropped the subject for the time, only to renew it at the first opportunity. I became impatient at her repeated attempts and, seizing the new doll, I dashed it upon the floor. I was keenly delighted when I felt the fragments of the broken doll at my feet. Neither sorrow nor regret followed my passionate outburst. I had not loved the doll. In the still, dark world in which I lived there was no strong sentiment or tenderness. I felt my teacher sweep the fragments to one side of the hearth, and I had a sense of satisfaction that the cause of my discomfort was removed. She brought me my hat, and I knew I was going out into the warm sunshine. This thought, if a wordless sensation may be called a thought, made me hop and skip with pleasure.

We walked down the path to the well-house, attracted by the fragrance of the honeysuckle with which it was covered. Someone was drawing water and my teacher placed my hand under the spout. As the cool stream gushed over one hand she spelled into the other the word water, first slowly, then rapidly. I stood still, my whole attention fixed upon the motions of her fingers. Suddenly I felt a misty consciousness as of something forgotten—a thrill of returning thought; and somehow the mystery of language was revealed to me. I knew then that "w-a-t-e-r" meant the wonderful cool something that was flowing over my hand. That living word awakened my soul, gave it light, hope, joy, set it free! There were barriers still, it is true, but barriers that could in time be swept away.

I left the well-house eager to learn. Everything had a name, and each name gave birth to a new thought. As we returned to the house every object which I touched seemed to quiver with life. That was because I saw everything with the strange, new sight that had come to me. On entering the door I remembered the doll I had broken. I felt my way to the hearth and picked up the pieces. I tried vainly to put them together. Then my eyes filled with tears; for I realized what I had done, and for the first time I felt repentance and sorrow.

I learned a great many new words that day. I do not remember what they all were; but I do know that *mother, father, sister, teacher* were among them—words that were to make the world blossom for me, "like Aaron's rod, with flowers." It would have been difficult to find a happier child than I was as I lay in my crib at the close of that eventful day and lived over the joys it had brought me, and for the first time longed for a new day to come.

Anne Mansfield, in her letters, described the "miracle" she saw taking place in Helen.

*March 20, 1887.*

My heart is singing for joy this morning. A miracle has happened! The light of understanding has shone upon my little pupil's mind, and behold, all things are changed!

The wild little creature of two weeks ago has been transformed into a gentle child. She is sitting by me as I write, her face serene and happy, crocheting a long red chain of Scotch wool. She learned the stitch this week, and is very proud of the achievement. When she succeeded in making a chain that would reach across the room, she patted herself on the arm and put the first work of her hands lovingly against her cheek. She lets me kiss her now, and when she is in a particularly gentle mood, she will sit in my lap for a minute or two; but she does not return my caresses. The great step—the step that counts—has been taken. The little savage has learned her first lesson in obedience, and finds the yoke easy. It now remains my pleasant task to direct and mold the beautiful intelligence that is beginning to stir in the child-soul. Already people remark the change in Helen. Her father looks in at us morning and evening as he goes to and from his office, and sees her contentedly stringing her beads or making horizontal lines on her sewing card, and exclaims, "How quiet she is!" When I came, her movements were so insistent that one always felt there was something unnatural and almost weird about her. I have noticed also that she eats much less, a fact which troubles her father so much that he is anxious to get her home. He says she is homesick. I don't agree with him; but I suppose we shall have to leave our little bower very soon.

Helen has learned several nouns this week. "M-u-g" and "m-i-l-k," have given her more trouble than other words. When she spells "milk," she points to the mug, and when she spells "mug," she makes the sign for pouring or drinking, which shows that she has confused the words. She has no idea yet that everything has a name.

*April 5, 1887.*

I must write you a line this morning because something very important has happened. Helen has taken the second great step in her education. She has learned that *everything has a name, and that the manual alphabet is the key to everything she wants to know.*

In a previous letter I think I wrote you that "mug" and "milk" had given Helen more trouble than all the rest. She confused the nouns with the verb "drink." She didn't know the word for "drink," but went through the pantomime of drinking whenever she spelled "mug" or "milk." This morning, while she was washing, she wanted to know the name for "water." When she wants to know the name of anything, she points to it and pats my hand. I spelled "w-a-t-e-r" and thought no more about it until after breakfast. Then it occurred to me that with the help of this new word I might succeed in straightening out the "mug-milk" difficulty. We went out to the pump-house, and I made Helen hold her mug under the spout while I pumped. As the cold water gushed forth, filling the mug, I spelled "w-a-t-e-r" in Helen's free hand. The word coming so close upon the sensation of cold water rushing over her hand seemed to startle her. She dropped the mug and stood as one transfixed. A new light came into her face. She spelled "water" several times. Then she dropped on the ground and asked for its name and pointed to the pump and the trellis, and suddenly turning round she asked for my name. I spelled "Teacher." Just then the nurse brought Helen's little sister into the pump-house, and Helen spelled "baby" and pointed to the nurse. All the way back to the house she was highly excited, and learned the name of every object she touched, so that in a few hours she had added thirty new words to her vocabulary. Here are some of them: *Door, open, shut, give, go, come,* and a great many more.

P.S.—I didn't finish my letter in time to get it posted last night; so I shall add a line. Helen got up this morning like a radiant fairy. She has flitted from object to object, asking the name of everything and kissing me for very gladness. Last night when I got in bed, she stole into my arms of her own accord and kissed me for the first time, and I thought my heart would burst, so full was it of joy.

---

## The Human Touch

*Spencer Michael Free*

This simple poem reminds us that genuine friendship is about the closeness of hands, hearts, and souls. It also, incidentally, captures the profundity of "touch" between Helen Keller and Anne Mansfield Sullivan.

'Tis the human touch in this world that counts,
  The touch of your hand and mine,
Which means far more to the fainting heart
  Than shelter and bread and wine;
For shelter is gone when the night is o'er,
  And bread lasts only a day,
But the touch of the hand and the sound of the voice
  Sing on in the soul alway.

# Little Girls Wiser Than Men

*Leo Tolstoy*

All friendships have their ups and downs. Learning to put aside disagreements makes companionship long-lasting.

It was an early Easter. Sledging was only just over; snow still lay in the yards, and water ran in streams down the village street.

Two little girls from different houses happened to meet in a lane between two homesteads, where the dirty water after running through the farmyards had formed a large puddle. One girl was very small, the other a little bigger. Their mothers had dressed them both in new frocks. The little one wore a blue frock, the other a yellow print, and both had red kerchiefs on their heads. They had just come from church when they met, and first they showed each other their finery, and then they began to play. Soon the fancy took them to splash about in the water, and the smaller one was going to step into the puddle, shoes and all, when the elder checked her.

"Don't go in so, Malásha," said she. "Your mother will scold you. I will take off my shoes and stockings, and you take off yours."

They did so, and then, picking up their skirts, began walking toward each other through the puddle. The water came up to Malásha's ankles, and she said:

"It is deep, Akoúlya. I'm afraid!"

"Come on," replied the other. "Don't be frightened. It won't get any deeper."

When they got near one another, Akoúlya said:

"Mind, Malásha, don't splash. Walk carefully!"

She had hardly said this, when Malásha plumped down her foot so that the water splashed right on to Akoúlya's frock. The frock was splashed, and so were Akoúlya's eyes and nose. When she saw the stains on her frock, she was angry and ran after Malásha to strike her. Malásha was frightened, and seeing that she had got herself into trouble, she scrambled out of the puddle, and prepared to run home. Just then Akoúlya's mother happened to be passing, and seeing that her daughter's skirt was splashed, and her sleeves dirty, she said:

"You naughty, dirty girl, what have you been doing!"

"Malásha did it on purpose," replied the girl.

At this Akoúlya's mother seized Malásha, and struck her on the back of her neck. Malásha began to howl so that she could be heard all down the street. Her mother came out.

"What are you beating my girl for?" said she, and began scolding her neighbor. One word led to another and they had an angry quarrel. The men came out, and a crowd collected in the street, every one shouting and no one listening. They all went on quarreling, till one gave another a push, and the affair had very nearly come to blows, when Akoúlya's old grandmother, stepping in among them, tried to calm them.

"What are you thinking of, friends? Is it right to behave so? On a day like this, too! It is a time for rejoicing, and not for such folly as this."

They would not listen to the old woman, and nearly knocked her off her feet. And she would not have been able to quiet the crowd, if it had not been for Akoúlya and Malásha themselves. While the women were abusing each other, Akoúlya had wiped the mud off her frock, and gone back to the puddle. She took a stone and began scraping away the earth in front of the puddle to make a channel through which the water could run out into the street. Presently Malásha joined her, and with a chip of wood helped her dig the channel. Just as the men were beginning to fight, the water from the little girls' channel ran streaming into the street toward the very place where the old woman was trying to pacify the men. The girls followed it, one running on each side of the little stream.

"Catch it, Malásha! Catch it!" shouted Akoúlya, while Malásha could not speak for laughing.

Highly delighted, and watching the chip float along on their stream, the little girls ran straight into the group of men; and the old woman, seeing them, said to the men:

"Are you not ashamed of yourselves? To go fighting on account of these lassies, when they themselves have forgotten all about it, and are playing happily together. Dear little souls! They are wiser than you!"

The men looked at the little girls, and were ashamed, and, laughing at themselves, went back each to his own home.

"Except ye turn, and become as little children, ye shall in no wise enter into the kingdom of heaven."

# The Enchanted Bluff

*Willa Cather*

This is a story about the kind of commonplace dreams and adventures friends share in youth. Memories of such times spent together make friendships span the years and miles that later separate us.

We had our swim before sundown, and while we were cooking our supper the oblique rays of light made a dazzling glare on the white sand about us. The translucent red ball itself sank behind the brown stretches of corn field as we sat down to eat, and the warm layer of air that had rested over the water and our clean sand bar grew fresher and smelled of the rank ironweed and sunflowers growing on the flatter shore. The river was brown and sluggish, like any other of the half-dozen streams that water the Nebraska corn lands. On one shore was an irregular line of bald clay bluffs where a few scrub oaks with thick trunks and flat, twisted tops threw light shadows on the long grass. The western shore was low and level, with corn fields that stretched to the skyline, and all along the water's edge were little sandy coves and beaches where slim cottonwoods and willow saplings flickered.

The turbulence of the river in springtime discouraged milling, and, beyond keeping the old red bridge in repair, the busy farmers did not concern themselves with the stream; so the Sandtown boys were left in undisputed possession. In the autumn we hunted quail through the miles of stubble and fodder land along the flat shore, and, after the winter skating season was over and the ice had gone out, the spring freshets and flooded bottoms gave us our great excitement of the year. The channel was never the same for two successive seasons. Every spring the swollen stream undermined a bluff to the east, or bit out a few acres of corn field to the west and whirled the soil away to deposit it in spumy mud banks somewhere else. When the water fell low in midsummer, new sand bars were thus exposed to dry and whiten in the August sun. Sometimes these were banked so firmly that the fury of the next freshet failed to unseat them; the little willow seedlings emerged triumphantly from the yellow froth, broke into spring leaf, shot up into summer growth, and with their mesh of roots bound together the moist sand beneath them against the batterings of another April. Here and there a cottonwood soon glittered among them, quivering in the low current of air that, even on breathless days when the dust hung like smoke above the wagon road, trembled along the face of the water.

It was on such an island, in the third summer of its yellow green, that we built our watch fire; not in the thicket of dancing willow wands, but on the level terrace of fine sand which had been added that spring; a little new bit of world, beautifully ridged with ripple marks, and strewn with the tiny skeletons of turtles and fish, all as white and dry as if they had been expertly cured. We had been careful not to mar the freshness of the place, although we often swam to it on summer evenings and lay on the sand to rest.

This was our last watch fire of the year, and there were reasons why I should remember it better than any of the others. Next week the other boys were to file back to their old places in the Sandtown High School, but I was to go up to the Divide to teach my first country school in the Norwegian district. I was already homesick at the thought of quitting the boys with whom I had always played; of leaving the river, and going up into a windy plain that was all windmills and corn fields and big pastures; where there was nothing willful or unmanageable in the landscape, no new islands, and no chance of unfamiliar birds—such as often followed the water-courses.

Other boys came and went and used the river for fishing or skating, but we six were sworn to the spirit of the stream, and we were friends mainly because of the river. There were the two Hassler boys, Fritz and Otto, sons of the little German tailor. They were the youngest of us; ragged boys of ten and twelve, with sunburned hair, weather-stained faces, and pale blue eyes. Otto, the elder, was the best mathematician in school, and clever at his books, but he always dropped out in the spring term as if the river could not get on without him. He and Fritz caught the fat, horned catfish and sold them about the town, and they lived so much in the water that they were as brown and sandy as the river itself.

There was Percy Pound, a fat, freckled boy with chubby cheeks, who took half a dozen boys' story-papers and was always being kept in for reading detective stories behind his desk. There was Tip Smith, destined by his freckles and red hair to be the buffoon in all our games, though he walked like a timid little old man and had a funny, cracked laugh. Tip worked hard in his father's grocery store every afternoon and swept it out before school in the morning. Even his recreations were laborious. He collected cigarette cards and tin tobacco-tags indefatigably, and would sit for hours humped up over a snarling little scroll-saw which he kept in his attic. His dearest possessions were some little pill bottles that purported to contain grains of wheat from the Holy Land, water from the Jordan and the Dead Sea, and earth from the Mount of Olives. His father had bought these dull things from a Baptist missionary who peddled them, and Tip seemed to derive great satisfaction from their remote origin.

The tall boy was Arthur Adams. He had fine hazel eyes that were almost too reflective and sympathetic for a boy, and such a pleasant voice that we all loved to hear him read aloud. Even when he had to read poetry aloud at school, no one ever thought of laughing. To be sure, he was not at school very much of the time. He was seventeen and should have finished the High School the year before, but he was always off somewhere with his gun. Arthur's mother was dead, and his father, who was feverishly absorbed in promoting schemes, wanted to send the boy away to school and get him off his hands; but Arthur always begged off for another year and promised to study. I remember him as a tall, brown boy with an intelligent face, always lounging among a lot of us little fellows, laughing at us oftener than with us, but such a soft, satisfied laugh that we felt rather flattered when we provoked it. In after-years people said that Arthur had been given to evil ways even as a lad, and it is true that we often saw him with the gambler's sons and with old Spanish Fanny's boy, but if he learned anything ugly in their company he never betrayed it to us. We would have followed Arthur anywhere, and I am bound to say that he led us into no worse places than the cattail marshes and the stubble fields. These, then, were the boys who camped with me that summer night upon the sand bar.

After we finished our supper we beat the willow thicket for driftwood. By the time we had collected enough, night had fallen, and the pungent, weedy smell from the shore increased with the coolness. We threw ourselves down about the fire and made another futile effort to show Percy Pound the Little Dipper. We had tried it often before, but he could never be got past the big one.

"You see those three big stars just below the handle, with the bright one in the middle?" said Otto Hassler; "That's Orion's belt, and the bright one is the clasp." I crawled behind Otto's shoulder and sighted up his arm to the star that seemed perched upon the tip of his steady forefinger. The Hassler boys did seine-fishing at night, and they knew a good many stars.

Percy gave up the Little Dipper and lay back on the sand, his hands clasped under his head. "I can see the North Star," he announced, contentedly, pointing toward it with his big toe. "Anyone might get lost and need to know that."

We all looked up at it.

"How do you suppose Columbus felt when his compass didn't point north anymore?" Tip asked.

Otto shook his head. "My father says that there was another North Star once, and that maybe this one won't last always. I wonder what would happen to us down here if anything went wrong with it?"

Arthur chuckled. "I wouldn't worry, Ott. Nothing's apt to happen to it in your time. Look at the Milky Way! There must be lots of good dead Indians."

We lay back and looked, meditating, at the dark cover of the world. The gurgle of the water had become heavier. We had often noticed a mutinous, complaining note in it at night, quite different from its cheerful daytime chuckle, and seeming like the voice of a much deeper and more powerful stream. Our water had always these two moods: the one of sunny complaisance, the other of inconsolable, passionate regret.

"Queer how the stars are all in sort of diagrams," remarked Otto. "You could do most any proposition in geometry with 'em. They always look as if they meant something. Some folks say everybody's fortune is all written out in the stars, don't they?"

"They believe so in the old country," Fritz affirmed.

But Arthur only laughed at him. "You're thinking of Napoleon, Fritzey. He had a star that went out when he began to lose battles. I guess the stars don't keep any close tally on Sandtown folks."

We were speculating on how many times we could count a hundred before the evening star went down behind the corn fields, when someone cried, "There comes the moon, and it's as big as a cart wheel!"

We all jumped up to greet it as it swam over the bluffs behind us. It came up like a galleon in full sail; an enormous, barbaric thing, red as an angry heathen god.

"When the moon came up red like that, the Aztecs used to sacrifice their prisoners on the temple top," Percy announced.

"Go on, Perce. You got that out of *Golden Days*. Do you believe that, Arthur?" I appealed.

Arthur answered, quite seriously: "Like as not. The moon was one of their gods. When my father was in Mexico City he saw the stone where they used to sacrifice their prisoners."

As we dropped down by the fire again someone asked whether the Mound-Builders were older than the Aztecs. When we once got upon the Mound-Builders we never willingly got away from them, and we were still conjecturing when we heard a loud splash in the water.

"Must have been a big cat jumping," said Fritz. "They do sometimes. They must see bugs in the dark. Look what a track the moon makes!"

There was a long, silvery streak on the water, and where the current fretted over a big log it boiled up like gold pieces.

"Suppose there ever *was* any gold hid away in this old river?" Fritz asked. He lay like a little brown Indian, close to the fire, his chin on his hand and his bare feet in the air. His brother laughed at him, but Arthur took his suggestion seriously.

"Some of the Spaniards thought there was gold up here somewhere. Seven cities chuck full of gold, they had it, and Coronado and his men came up to hunt it. The Spaniards were all over this country once."

Percy looked interested. "Was that before the Mormons went through?"

We all laughed at this.

"Long enough before. Before the Pilgrim Fathers, Perce. Maybe they came along this very river. They always followed the watercourses."

"I wonder where this river really does begin?" Tip mused. That was an old and a favorite mystery which the map did not clearly explain. On the map the little black line stopped somewhere in western Kansas; but since rivers generally rose in mountains, it was only reasonable to suppose that ours came from the Rockies. Its destination, we knew, was the Missouri, and the Hassler boys always maintained that we could embark at Sandtown in floodtime, follow our noses, and eventually arrive at New Orleans. Now they took up their old argument. "If us boys had grit enough to try it, it wouldn't take no time to get to Kansas City and St. Joe."

We began to talk about the places we wanted to go to. The Hassler boys wanted to see the stockyards in Kansas City, and Percy wanted to see a big store in Chicago. Arthur was interlocutor and did not betray himself.

"Now it's your turn, Tip."

Tip rolled over on his elbow and poked the fire, and his eyes looked shyly out of his queer, tight little face. "My place is awful far away. My Uncle Bill told me about it."

Tip's Uncle Bill was a wanderer, bitten with mining fever, who had drifted into Sandtown with a broken arm, and when it was well had drifted out again.

"Where is it?"

"Aw, it's down in New Mexico somewheres. There aren't no railroads or anything. You have to go on mules, and you run out of water before you get there and have to drink canned tomatoes."

"Well, go on, kid. What's it like when you do get there?"

Tip sat up and excitedly began his story.

"There's a big red rock there that goes right up out of the sand for about nine hundred feet. The country's flat all around it, and this here rock goes up all by itself, like a monument. They call it the Enchanted Bluff down there, because no white man has ever been on top of it. The sides are smooth rock, and straight up, like a wall. The Indians say that hundreds of years ago, before the Spaniards came, there was a village away up there in the air. The tribe that lived there had some sort of steps, made out of wood and bark, hung down over the face of the bluff, and the braves went down to hunt and carried water up in big jars swung on their backs. They kept a big supply of water and dried meat up there, and never went down except to hunt. They were a peaceful tribe that made cloth and pottery, and they went up there to get out of the wars. You see, they could pick off any war party that tried to get up their steps. The Indians say they were a handsome people, and they had some sort of queer religion. Uncle Bill thinks they were Cliff-Dwellers who had got into trouble and left home. They weren't fighters, anyhow.

"One time the braves were down hunting and an awful storm came up—a kind of waterspout—and when they got back to their rock they found their little staircase had been all broken to pieces, and only a few steps were left hanging away up in the air. While they were camped at the foot of the rock, wondering what to do, a war party from the north came along and massacred 'em to a man, with all the old folks and women looking on from the rock. Then the war party went on south and left the village to get down the best way they could. Of course they never got down. They starved to death up there, and when the war party came back on their way north, they could hear the children crying from the edge of the bluff where they had crawled out, but they didn't see a sign of a grown Indian, and nobody has ever been up there since."

We exclaimed at this dolorous legend and sat up.

"There couldn't have been many people up there," Percy demurred. "How big is the top, Tip?"

"Oh, pretty big. Big enough so that the rock doesn't look nearly as tall as it is. The top's bigger than the base. The bluff is sort of worn away for several hundred feet up. That's one reason it's so hard to climb.'"

I asked how the Indians got up, in the first place.

"Nobody knows how they got up or when. A hunting party came along once and saw that there was a town up there, and that was all."

Otto rubbed his chin and looked thoughtful. "Of course there must be some way to get up there. Couldn't people get a rope over someway and pull a ladder up?"

Tip's little eyes were shining with excitement. "I know a way. Me and Uncle Bill talked it all over. There's a kind of rocket that would take a rope over—life-savers use 'em—and then you could hoist a rope ladder and peg it down at the bottom and make it tight with guy ropes on the other side. I'm going to climb that there bluff, and I've got it all planned out."

Fritz asked what he expected to find when he got up there.

"Bones, maybe, or the ruins of their town, or pottery, or some of their idols. There might be 'most anything up there. Anyhow, I want to see."

"Sure nobody else has been up there, Tip?" Arthur asked.

"Dead sure. Hardly anybody ever goes down there. Some hunters tried to cut steps in the rock once, but they didn't get higher than a man can reach. The Bluff's all red granite, and Uncle Bill thinks it's a boulder the glaciers left. It's a queer place, anyhow. Nothing but cactus and desert for hundreds of miles, and yet right under the Bluff there's good water and plenty of grass. That's why the bison used to go down there."

Suddenly we heard a scream above our fire, and jumped up to see a dark, slim bird floating southward far above us—a whooping crane, we knew by her cry and her long neck. We ran to the edge of the island, hoping we might see her alight, but she wavered southward along the river course until we lost her. The Hassler boys declared that by the look of the heavens it must be after midnight, so we threw more wood on our fire, put on our jackets, and curled down in the warm sand. Several of us pretended to doze, but I fancy we were really thinking about Tip's Bluff and the extinct people. Over in the wood the ring doves were calling mournfully to one another, and once we heard a dog bark, far away. "Somebody getting into old Tommy's melon patch," Fritz murmured sleepily, but nobody answered him. By and by Percy spoke out of the shadows.

"Say, Tip, when you go down there will you take me with you?"

"Maybe."

"Suppose one of us beats you down there, Tip?"

"Whoever gets to the Bluff first has got to promise to tell the rest of us exactly what he finds," remarked one of the Hassler boys, and to this we all readily assented.

Somewhat reassured, I dropped off to sleep. I must have dreamed about a race for the Bluff, for I awoke in a kind of fear that other people were getting ahead of me and that I was losing my chance. I sat up in my damp clothes and looked at the other boys, who lay tumbled in uneasy attitudes about the dead fire. It was still dark, but the sky was blue with the last wonderful azure of night. The stars glistened like crystal globes, and trembled as if they shone through a depth of clear water. Even as I watched, they began to pale and the sky brightened. Day came suddenly, almost instantaneously. I turned for another look at the blue night, and it was gone. Everywhere the birds began to call, and all manner of little insects began to chirp and hop about in the willows. A breeze sprang up from the west and brought the heavy smell of ripened corn. The boys rolled over and shook themselves. We stripped and plunged into the river just as the sun came up over the windy bluffs.

When I came home to Sandtown at Christmas time, we skated out to our island and talked over the whole project of the Enchanted Bluff, renewing our resolution to find it.

Although that was twenty years ago, none of us have ever climbed the Enchanted Bluff. Percy Pound is a stockbroker in Kansas City and will go nowhere that his red touring car cannot carry him. Otto Hassler went on the railroad and lost his foot braking; after which he and Fritz succeeded their father as the town tailors.

Arthur sat about the sleepy little town all his life—he died before he was twenty-five. The last time I saw him, when I was home on one of my college vacations, he was sitting in a steamer chair under a cottonwood tree in the little yard behind one of the two Sandtown saloons. He was very untidy and his hand was not steady, but when he rose, unabashed, to greet me, his eyes were as clear and warm as ever. When I had talked with him for an hour and heard him laugh again, I wondered how it was that when Nature had taken such pains with a man, from his hands to the arch of his long foot, she had ever lost him in Sandtown. He joked about Tip Smith's Bluff, and declared he was going down there just as soon as the weather got cooler; he thought the Grand Canyon might be worthwhile, too.

I was perfectly sure when I left him that he would never get beyond the high plank fence and the comfortable shade of the cottonwood. And, indeed, it was under that very tree that he died one summer morning.

Tip Smith still talks about going to New Mexico. He married a slatternly, unthrifty country girl, has been much tied to a perambulator, and has grown stooped and gray from irregular meals and broken sleep. But the worst of his difficulties are now over, and he has, as he says, come into easy water. When I was last in Sandtown I walked home with him late one moonlight night, after he had balanced his cash and shut up his store. We took the long way around and sat down on the schoolhouse steps, and between us we quite revived the romance of the lone red rock and the extinct people. Tip insists that he still means to go down there, but he thinks now he will wait until his boy Bert is old enough to go with him. Bert has been let into the story, and thinks of nothing but the Enchanted Bluff.

# Keep Friendships in Constant Repair

## *From* The Life of Samuel Johnson

James Boswell (1740–1795), the Scottish lawyer best known for his biography of Samuel Johnson, once wrote that "we cannot tell the precise moment when friendship is formed. As in filling a vessel drop by drop, there is at last a drop which makes it run over; so in a series of kindnesses there is at last one which makes the heart run over." Here, in his *Life of Samuel Johnson,* he advises that we should fill our lives with friendships both old and new. Once formed, friendship must be replenished from time to time so it remains in "constant repair."

I have often thought, that as longevity is generally desired, and, I believe, generally expected, it would be wise to be continually adding to the number of our friends, that the loss of some may be supplied by others. Friendship, "the wine of life," should, like a well-stocked cellar, be thus continually renewed; and it is consolatory to think, that although we can seldom add what will equal the generous *first-growths* of our youth, yet friendship becomes insensibly old in much less time than is commonly imagined, and not many years are required to make it very mellow and pleasant. *Warmth* will, no doubt, make a considerable difference. Men of affectionate temper and bright fancy will coalesce a great deal sooner than those who are cold and dull.

The proposition which I have now endeavored to illustrate was, at a subsequent period of his life, the opinion of Johnson himself. He said to Sir Joshua Reynolds, "If a man does not make new acquaintances as he advances through life, he will soon find himself left alone. A man, Sir, should keep his friendship *in constant repair.*"

## New Friends and Old Friends

What is real endures; it is as true of friendship as of other kinds of love.

Make new friends, but keep the old;
Those are silver, these are gold.
New-made friendships, like new wine,
Age will mellow and refine.
Friendships that have stood the test—
Time and change—are surely best;
Brow may wrinkle, hair grow gray;
Friendship never knows decay.
For 'mid old friends, tried and true,
Once more we our youth renew.
But old friends, alas! may die;
New friends must their place supply.
Cherish friendship in your breast—
New is good, but old is best;
Make new friends, but keep the old;
Those are silver, these are gold.

---

## The Lover Pleads with his Friend for Old Friends

*William Butler Yeats*

We cannot afford to make new friends at the expense of our old ones.

Though you are in your shining days,
Voices among the crowd
And new friends busy with your praise,
Be not unkind or proud,

But think about old friends the most:
Time's bitter flood will rise,
Your beauty perish and be lost
For all eyes but these eyes.

---

## A Time to Talk

*Robert Frost*

Work always calls us. But we make time for friends when they call too.

When a friend calls to me from the road
And slows his horse to a meaning walk,
I don't stand still and look around
On all the hills I haven't hoed,
And shout from where I am, What is it?
No, not as there is a time to talk.
I thrust my hoe in the mellow ground,
Blade-end up and five feet tall,
And plod: I go up to the stone wall
For a friendly visit.

---

## Aristotle on Friendship

*From the* Nicomachean Ethics

The ancients listed friendship among the highest of virtues. It was an essential element in the happy or fully flourishing life. "For without friends," Aristotle says, "no one would choose to live, though he had all other goods." Words worth remembering in a world of perishable "goods."

According to Aristotle, friendship either is, or it involves, a state of character, a virtue. There are three kinds of friendship. These are based on pleasure in another's company (friendship of pleasure), or on usefulness in association (friendships of utility), or on mutual admiration (friendships in virtue). All are essential to the good life, and the best sorts of friends will not only admire each other's excellence, but take pleasure in each other's company and find their association of mutual advantage. Here is a portion of Aristotle's classic discussion.

As the motives to Friendship differ in kind, so do the respective feelings and Friendships. The species then of Friendship are three, in number equal to the objects of it, since in the line of each there may be "mutual affection mutually known."

Now they who have Friendship for one another desire one another's good according to the motive of their Friendship; accordingly they whose motive is utility have no Friendship for one another really, but only insofar as some good arises to them from one another.

And they whose motive is pleasure are in like case: I mean, they have Friendship for men of easy pleasantry, not because they are of a given character but because they are pleasant to themselves. So then they whose motive to Friendship is utility love their friends for what is good to themselves; they whose motive is pleasure do so for what is pleasurable to themselves; that is to say, not insofar as the friend beloved *is* but insofar as he is useful or pleasurable. These Friendships then are a matter of result: since the object is not beloved in that he is the man he is but in that he furnishes advantage or pleasure as the case may be.

Such Friendships are of course very liable to dissolution if the parties do not continue alike: I mean, that the others cease to have any Friendship for them when they are no longer pleasurable or useful. Now it is the nature of utility not to be permanent but constantly varying: so, of course, when the motive which made them friends is vanished, the Friendship likewise dissolves; since it existed only relatively to those circumstances. . . .

That then is perfect Friendship which subsists between those who are good and whose similarity consists in their goodness: for these men wish one another's good in similar ways; insofar as they are good (and good they are in themselves); and those are specially friends who wish good to their friends for their sakes, because they feel thus toward them on their own account and not as a mere matter of result; so the Friendship between these men continues to subsist so long as they are good; and goodness, we know, has in it a principle of permanence. . . .

Rare it is probable Friendships of this kind will be, because men of this kind are rare. Besides, all requisite qualifications being presupposed, there is further required time and intimacy: for, as the proverb says, men cannot know one another "till they have eaten the requisite quantity of salt together"; nor can they in fact admit one another to intimacy, much less be friends, till each has appeared to the other and been proved to be a fit object of Friendship. They who speedily commence an interchange of friendly actions may be said to wish to be friends, but they are not so unless they are also proper objects of Friendship and mutually known to be such: that is to say, a desire for Friendship may arise quickly but not Friendship itself.

# Cicero on Friendship

## *From* Laelius

It has been said that through Cicero (106–43 B.C.) Greek philosophy passed to Western Europe. The Roman statesman's writings have proved to be an inexhaustible fountain, one that has watered the thought and expression of succeeding ages. His examination of the question of what friendship really means is still a cogent prescription for good conduct in modern life. Laelius, the chief speaker in the dialogue, defines friendship as "a complete identity of feeling about all things in heaven and earth: an identity which is strengthened by mutual goodwill and affection." Moral goodness, or "goodness of character," is the quality that makes friendship possible: "All harmony, and permanence, and fidelity, come from that."

I desire it may be understood that I am now speaking, not of that inferior species of amity which occurs in the common intercourse of the world (although this, too, is not without its pleasures and advantages), but of that genuine and perfect friendship, examples of which are so extremely rare as to be rendered memorable by their singularity. It is this sort alone that can truly be said to heighten the joys of prosperity, and mitigate the sorrows of adversity, by a generous participation of both; indeed, one of the chief among the many important offices of this connection is exerted in the day of affliction, by dispelling the gloom that overcasts the mind, encouraging the hope of happier times, and preventing the depressed spirits from sinking into a state of weak and unmanly despondence. Whoever is in possession of a true friend sees the exact counterpart of his own soul. In consequence of this moral resemblance between them, they are so intimately one that no advantage can attend either which does not equally communicate itself to both; they are strong in the strength, rich in the opulence, and powerful in the power of each other. They can scarcely, indeed, be considered in any respect as separate individuals, and wherever the one appears the other is virtually present. I will venture even a bolder assertion, and affirm that in despite of death they must both continue to exist so long as either of them shall remain alive; for the deceased may, in a certain sense, be said still to live whose memory is preserved with the highest veneration and the most tender regret in the bosom of the survivor, a circumstance which renders the former happy in death, and the latter honored in life.

If that benevolent principle which thus intimately unites two persons in the bands of amity were to be struck out of the human heart, it would be impossible that either private families or public communities should subsist—even the land itself would lie waste, and desolation overspread the earth. Should this assertion stand in need of a proof, it will appear evident by considering the ruinous consequences which ensue from discord and dissension; for what family is so securely established, or what government fixed upon so firm a basis, that it would not be overturned and utterly destroyed were a general spirit of enmity and malevolence to break forth amongst its members?—a sufficient argument, surely, of the inestimable benefits which flow from the kind and friendly affections.

# Thinking on Friendship

*William Shakespeare*

Thinking of friends and their worth is often enough to drive away an army of fears, regrets, and envies.

SONNET XXIX

When, in disgrace with fortune and men's eyes,
I all alone beweep my outcast state,
And trouble deaf heaven with my bootless cries,
And look upon myself, and curse my fate,
Wishing me like to one more rich in hope,
Featured like him, like him with friends possess'd,
Desiring this man's art and that man's scope,
With what I most enjoy contented least;
Yet in these thoughts myself almost despising,
Haply I think on thee, and then my state,
Like to the lark at break of day arising
From sullen earth, sings hymns at heaven's gate;
For thy sweet love remember'd such wealth brings
That then I scorn to change my state with kings.

SONNET XXX

When to the sessions of sweet silent thought
I summon up remembrance of things past,
I sigh the lack of many a thing I sought,
And with old woes new wail my dear time's waste:
Then can I drown an eye, unused to flow,
For precious friends hid in death's dateless night,
And weep afresh love's long since cancel'd woe,
And moan the expense of many a vanish'd sight:
Then can I grieve at grievances foregone,
And heavily from woe to woe tell o'er
The sad account of fore-bemoaned moan,
Which I new pay as if not paid before.
But if the while I think on thee, dear friend,
All losses are restored and sorrows end.

# Emerson on Friendship

*From "Friendship"*

Emerson writes that friendships are gifts and expressions of God; they form when the divine spirit in one individual finds the divine spirit in another, and "both deride and cancel the thick walls of individual character, relation, age, sex, and circumstance." The essay "Friendship" was first published in 1841.

I do not wish to treat friendships daintily, but with roughest courage. When they are real, they are not glass threads or frost-work, but the solidest thing we know. For now, after so many ages of experience, what do we know of nature, or of ourselves? Not one step has man taken toward the solution of the problem of his destiny. In one condemnation of folly stand the whole universe of men. But the sweet sincerity of joy and peace, which I draw from this alliance with my brother's soul, is the nut itself whereof all nature and all thought is but the husk and shell. Happy is the house that shelters a friend! It might well be built, like a festal bower or arch, to entertain him a single day. Happier, if he know the solemnity of that relation, and honor its law! He who offers himself a candidate for that covenant comes up like an Olympian to the great games where the first born of the world are the competitors. He proposes himself for contests where Time, Want, Danger are in the lists, and he alone is victor who has truth enough in his constitution to preserve the delicacy of his beauty from the wear and tear of all these. The gifts of fortune may be present or absent, but all the hap in that contest depends on intrinsic nobleness and the contempt of trifles. . . . A friend is a person with whom I may be sincere. Before him, I may think aloud. I am arrived at last in the presence of a man so real and equal that I may drop even those undermost garments of dissimulation, courtesy, and second thought, which men never put off, and may deal with him with the simplicity and wholeness with which one chemical atom meets another. Sincerity is the luxury allowed, like diadems and authority, only to the highest rank, that being permitted to speak truth as having none above it to court or conform unto. Every man alone is sincere. At the entrance of a second person hypocrisy begins. We parry and fend the approach of our fellow man by compliments, by gossip, by amusements, by affairs. We cover up our thought from him under a hundred folds. I knew a man who, under a certain religious frenzy, cast off this drapery, and, omitting all compliments and commonplace, spoke to the conscience of every person he encountered, and that with great insight and beauty. At first he was resisted, and all men agreed he was mad. By persisting, as indeed he could not help doing, for some time in this course, he attained to the advantage of bringing every man of his acquaintance into true relations with him. No man would think of speaking falsely with him, or of putting him off with any chat of markets or reading rooms. But every man was constrained by so much sincerity to the like plain dealing, and what love of nature, what poetry, what symbol of truth he had, he did certainly show him. But to most of us society shows not its face and eye, but its side and its back. To stand in true relations with men in a false age is worth a fit of insanity, is it not? We can seldom go erect. Almost every man we meet requires some civility, requires to be humored; he has some fame, some talent, some whim of religion or philanthropy in his head that is not to be questioned, and which spoils all conversation with him. But a friend is a sane man who exercises not my ingenuity, but me. My friend gives me entertainment without requiring any stipulation on my part. A friend, therefore, is a sort of paradox in nature. I who alone am, I who see nothing in nature whose existence I can affirm with equal evidence to my own, behold now the semblance of my being in all its height, variety, and curiosity reiterated in a foreign form; so that a friend may well be reckoned the masterpiece of nature.

# Mending Wall

*Robert Frost*

We want to make sure we don't fall into the habit of walling friendships in or out.

Something there is that doesn't love a wall,
That sends the frozen-ground-swell under it,
And spills the upper boulders in the sun;
And makes gaps even two can pass abreast.
The work of hunters is another thing:
I have come after them and made repair
Where they have left not one stone on a stone,
But they would have the rabbit out of hiding,
To please the yelping dogs. The gaps I mean,
No one has seen them made or heard them made,
But at spring mending-time we find them there.
I let my neighbor know beyond the hill;
And on a day we meet to walk the line
And set the wall between us once again.
We keep the wall between us as we go.
To each the boulders that have fallen to each.
And some are loaves and some so nearly balls
We have to use a spell to make them balance:
"Stay where you are until our backs are turned!"
We wear our fingers rough with handling them.
Oh, just another kind of outdoor game,
One on a side. It comes to little more:
There where it is we do not need the wall:
He is all pine and I am apple orchard.
My apple trees will never get across
And eat the cones under his pines, I tell him.
He only says, "Good fences make good neighbors."
Spring is the mischief in me, and I wonder
If I could put a notion in his head:
"*Why* do they make good neighbors? Isn't it
Where there are cows? But here there are no cows.
Before I built a wall I'd ask to know

What I was walling in or walling out,
And to whom I was like to give offense.
Something there is that doesn't love a wall,
That wants it down." I could say "Elves" to him,
But it's not elves exactly, and I'd rather
He said it for himself. I see him there
Bringing a stone grasped firmly by the top
In each hand, like an old-stone savage armed.
He moves in darkness as it seems to me,
Not of woods only and the shade of trees.
He will not go behind his father's saying,
And he likes having thought of it so well
He says again, "Good fences make good neighbors."

---

# Childhood and Poetry

*Pablo Neruda*

Chilean poet Pablo Neruda (1904–1973) once linked his creation of verse to a simple exchange of gifts in his childhood. As in Robert Frost's poem, "something there is that doesn't love a wall," or in this case a backyard fence, in the exchange. The curious story suggests that every time we offer friendship to someone we do not know, we strengthen the bond of brotherhood for all of humanity.

One time, investigating in the backyard of our house in Temuco the tiny objects and minuscule beings of my world, I came upon a hole in one of the boards of the fence. I looked through the hole and saw a landscape like that behind our house, uncared for, and wild. I moved back a few steps, because I sensed vaguely that something was about to happen. All of a sudden a hand appeared—a tiny hand of a boy about my own age. By the time I came close again, the hand was gone, and in its place there was a marvelous white sheep.

The sheep's wool was faded. Its wheels had escaped. All of this only made it more authentic. I had never seen such a wonderful sheep. I looked back through the hole but the boy had disappeared. I went into the house and brought out a treasure of my own: a pinecone, opened, full of odor and resin, which I adored. I set it down in the same spot and went off with the sheep.

I never saw either the hand or the boy again. And I have never again seen a sheep like that either. The toy I lost finally in a fire. But even now, in 1954, almost fifty years old, whenever I pass a toy shop, I look furtively into the window, but it's no use. They don't make sheep like that anymore.

I have been a lucky man. To feel the intimacy of brothers is a marvelous thing in life. To feel the love of people whom we love is a fire that feeds our life. But to feel the affection that comes from those whom we do not know, from those unknown to us, who are watching over our sleep and solitude, over our dangers and our weaknesses—that is something still greater and more beautiful because it widens out the boundaries of our being, and unites all living things.

That exchange brought home to me for the first time a precious idea: that all of humanity is somehow together. That experience came to me again much later; this time it stood out strikingly against a background of trouble and persecution.

It won't surprise you then that I attempted to give something resiny, earthlike, and fragrant in exchange for human brotherhood. Just as I once left the pinecone by the fence, I have since left my words on the door of so many people who were unknown to me, people in prison, or hunted, or alone.

That is the great lesson I learned in my childhood, in the backyard of a lonely house. Maybe it was nothing but a game two boys played who didn't know each other and wanted to pass to the other some good things of life. Yet maybe this small and mysterious exchange of gifts remained inside me also, deep and indestructible, giving my poetry light.

# The Arrow and the Song

*Henry Wadsworth Longfellow*

In this poem, Longfellow suggests that if we offer something of ourselves to the world—a good deed, a kind word, our love—eventually we will discover its effects. It may come back to us in the form of a friend.

I shot an arrow into the air,
It fell to earth, I knew not where;
For, so swiftly it flew, the sight
Could not follow it in its flight.

I breathed a song into the air,
It fell to earth, I knew not where;
For who has sight so keen and strong,
That it can follow the flight of song?

Long, long afterward, in an oak
I found the arrow, still unbroke;
And the song, from beginning to end,
I found again in the heart of a friend.

---

# Thomas Jefferson and James Madison

Thomas Jefferson and James Madison met in 1776—could it have been any other year?—and worked together, starting then, to further the American Revolution and later to shape the new scheme of government. From that work sprang a friendship perhaps incomparable in intimacy, in the trustfulness of collaboration, and in duration: it lasted fifty years. It was the embodiment of that kind of perfect friendship Aristotle describes. It included pleasure and utility, but over and above them there was shared purpose, a common end, and an enduring goodness on both sides.

Four and a half months before he died, when he was ailing, debt-ridden, and worried about his impoverished family, Jefferson wrote to his longtime friend. His words, and Madison's reply, remind us that friends are friends until death. They also remind us that sometimes a friendship has a bearing on things larger than the friendship itself. For has there ever been a friendship of greater public consequence than this one?

The friendship which has subsisted between us now half a century and the harmony of our political principles and pursuits have been sources of constant happiness to me through that long period. It has also been a great solace to me to believe that you are engaged in vindicating to posterity the course we have pursued for preserving to them in all their purity the blessings of self-government which we had assisted in acquiring for them. If ever the earth has beheld a system of administration conducted with a single and steadfast eye to the general interest and happiness of those committed to it, one which protected by truth can never know reproach, it is that to which our lives have been devoted. To myself you have been a pillar of support through life. Take care of me when dead, and be assured that I shall leave you with my last affections.

A week later Madison replied:

You cannot look back to the long period of our private friendship and political harmony with more affecting recollections than I do. If they are a source of pleasure to you, what ought they not to be to me? We cannot be deprived of the happy consciousness of the pure devotion to the public good with which we discharged the trust committed to us. And I indulge a confidence that sufficient evidence will find its way to another generation to insure, after we are gone, whatever of justice may be withheld whilst we are here.

# A Legacy

*John Greenleaf Whittier*

Friend of my many years!
When the great silence falls, at last, on me,
Let me not leave, to pain and sadden thee,
A memory of tears,

But pleasant thoughts alone
Of one who was thy friendship's honored guest
And drank the wine of consolation pressed
From sorrows of thy own.

I leave with thee a sense
Of hands upheld and trials rendered less—
The unselfish joy which is to helpfulness
Its own great recompense;

The knowledge that from thine,
As from the garments of the Master, stole
Calmness and strength, the virtue which makes whole
And heals without a sign;

Yea more, the assurance strong
That love, which fails of perfect utterance here,
Lives on to fill the heavenly atmosphere
With its immortal song.

# 5

# Work

What are you going to be when you grow up?" is a question about work. What is your work in the world going to be? What will be your works? These are not fundamentally questions about jobs and pay, but questions about life. Work is applied effort; it is whatever we put ourselves into, whatever we expend our energy on for the sake of accomplishing or achieving something. Work in this fundamental sense is not what we do *for* a living but what we do *with* our living.

Parents and teachers both *work* at the upbringing of children, but only teachers receive paychecks for it. The housework of parents is real work, though it brings in no revenue. The schoolwork, homework, and teamwork of children are all real work, though the payoff is not in dollars. A child's household chores may be accompanied *by* an allowance, but they are not done *for* an allowance. They are done because they need to be done.

The opposite of work is not leisure or play or having fun but idleness—not *investing* ourselves in anything. Even sleeping can be a form of investment if it is done for the sake of future activity. But sleep, like amusement, can also be a form of escape—oblivion sought for its own sake rather than for the sake of renewal. It can be a waste of time. Leisure activity or play or having fun, on the other hand, can involve genuine investment of the self and not be a waste of time at all.

We want our children to flourish, to live well and fare well—to be happy. Happiness, as Aristotle long ago pointed out, resides in activity, both physical and mental. It resides in doing things that one can take pride in doing well, and hence that one can *enjoy* doing. It is a great mistake to identify enjoyment with mere amusement or relaxing or being entertained. Life's greatest joys are not what one does *apart from* the work of one's life, but *with* the work of one's life. Those who have missed the joy of work, of a job well done, have missed something very important. This applies to our children, too.

When we want our children to be happy, we want them to enjoy *life*. We want them to find and enjoy their work in the world.

How do we help prepare our children for lives like that? Once again, the keys are practice and example: practice in *doing* various things that require a level of effort and engagement compatible with some personal investment in the activity, and the examples of our own lives.

The first step in doing things is *learning how* to do them. (And learning how to turn on the television doesn't count—though learning how to turn it *off* might.) Good habits of personal hygiene, and helping with meals or bed-making or laundry or caring for pets or any other such household chores all require learning. All can be done well or poorly. All can be done cheerfully and with pride, or grudgingly and with distaste. And which way we do them is really up to us. It is a matter of choice. That is perhaps the greatest insight that the ancient Roman Stoics championed for humanity. There are no menial jobs, only menial attitudes. And our attitudes are up to us.

Parents show their children how to enjoy doing the things that have to be done by working with them, by encouraging and appreciating their efforts, and by the witness of their own cheerful and conscientious example. And since the possibilities for happy and productive lives are largely opened up for youth by the quality and extent of their education, parents who work most effectively at providing their offspring with what it takes to lead flourishing lives take education very seriously.

Work is effort applied toward some end. The most satisfying work involves directing our efforts toward achieving ends that we ourselves endorse as worthy expressions of our talent and character. Volunteer service work, if it is genuinely voluntary and exercises our talents in providing needed service, is typically satisfying in this way. Youth needs experience of this kind of work. It is a good model for our working lives.

# The Song of the Bee

*Marian Douglas*

If you look in old American schoolbooks, you'll find that this poem and others like it were among the first reading lessons offered to young students. They set the tone for work in school and life. God seems to have created bees to inspire us toward industry.

Buzz! buzz! buzz!
   This is the song of the bee.
His legs are of yellow;
A jolly, good fellow,
   And yet a great worker is he.

In days that are sunny
He's getting his honey;
In days that are cloudy
   He's making his wax:
On pinks and on lilies,
And gay daffodillies,
And columbine blossoms,
   He levies a tax!

Buzz! buzz! buzz!
The sweet-smelling clover,
He, humming, hangs over;
The scent of the roses
  Makes fragrant his wings:
He never gets lazy;
From thistle and daisy,
And weeds of the meadow,
  Some treasure he brings.

Buzz! buzz! buzz!
From morning's first light
Till the coming of night,
He's singing and toiling
  The summer day through.
Oh! we may get weary,
And think work is dreary;
'Tis harder by far
  To have nothing to do.

---

## Wynken, Blynken, and Nod

*Eugene Field*

"In dreams begins responsibility," William Butler Yeats wrote. We can begin to teach our youngest children about the responsibility as well as the joy of work by sending them off to their dreams with this wonderful Eugene Field (1850–1895) poem.

Wynken, Blynken, and Nod one night
  Sailed off in a wooden shoe—
Sailed on a river of crystal light
  Into a sea of dew.
"Where are you going, and what do you wish?"
  The old moon asked the three.
"We have come to fish for the herring fish
  That live in this beautiful sea;
  Nets of silver and gold have we!"
    Said Wynken,
    Blynken,
    And Nod.

The old moon laughed and sang a song,
  As they rocked in the wooden shoe;
And the wind that sped them all night long
  Ruffled the waves of dew.
The little stars were the herring fish
  That lived in that beautiful sea—
"Now cast your nets wherever you wish—
  Never afeared are we!"
  So cried the stars to the fishermen three
    Wynken,
    Blynken,
    And Nod.

All night long their nets they threw
  To the stars in the twinkling foam—
Then down from the skies came the wooden shoe,
  Bringing the fishermen home;
'Twas all so pretty a sail it seemed
  As if it could not be,
And some folk thought 'twas a dream they'd dreamed
  Of sailing that beautiful sea—
  But I shall name you the fishermen three:
    Wynken,
    Blynken,
    And Nod.

Wynken and Blynken are two little eyes,
  And Nod is a little head,
And the wooden shoe that sailed the skies
  Is a wee one's trundle-bed;
So shut your eyes while Mother sings
  Of wonderful sights that be,
And you shall see the beautiful things
  As you rock in the misty sea
  Where the old shoe rocked the fishermen three—
    Wynken,
    Blynken,
    And Nod.

---

# The Little Red Hen

*Retold by Penryhn W. Coussens*

From this longtime favorite we learn, as it says in the third chapter of Genesis, "In the sweat of thy face shalt thou eat bread."

A little red hen once found a grain of wheat. "Who will plant this wheat?" she said.

"I won't," says the dog.

"I won't," says the cat.

"I won't," says the pig.

"I won't," says the turkey.

"Then I will," says the little red hen. "Cluck! cluck!"

So she planted the grain of wheat. Very soon the wheat began to grow and the green leaves came out of the ground. The sun shone and the rain fell and the wheat kept on growing until it was tall, strong, and ripe.

"Who will reap this wheat?" says the little red hen.

"I won't," says the dog.

"I won't," says the cat.

"I won't," says the pig.

"I won't," says the turkey.

"I will, then," says the little red hen. "Cluck! cluck!"

So she reaped the wheat.

"Who will thresh this wheat?" says the little red hen.

"I won't," says the dog.

"I won't," says the cat.

"I won't," says the pig.

"I won't," says the turkey.

"I will, then," says the little red hen. "Cluck! cluck!"

So she threshed the wheat.

"Who will take this wheat to mill to have it ground?" says the little red hen.

"I won't," says the dog.

"I won't," says the cat.

"I won't," says the pig.

"I won't," says the turkey.

"I will, then," says the little red hen. "Cluck! cluck!"

So she took the wheat to mill, and by and by she came back with the flour.

"Who will bake this flour?" says the little red hen.

"I won't," says the dog.

"I won't," says the cat.

"I won't," says the pig.

"I won't," says the turkey.

"I will, then," says the little red hen. "Cluck! cluck!"

So she baked the flour and made a loaf of bread.

"Who will eat this bread?" says the little red hen.

"I will," says the dog.

"I will," says the cat.

"I will," says the pig.

"I will," says the turkey.

"No, *I* will," says the little red hen. "Cluck! cluck!"

And she ate up the loaf of bread.

---

## Five Little Chickens

Said the first little chicken,
With a queer little squirm,
"Oh, I wish I could find
A fat little worm!"

Said the next little chicken,
With an odd little shrug,
"Oh, I wish I could find
A fat little bug!"

Said the third little chicken,
With a sharp little squeal,
"Oh, I wish I could find
Some nice yellow meal!"

Said the fourth little chicken,
With a small sigh of grief,
"Oh, I wish I could find
A green little leaf!"

Said the fifth little chicken,
With a faint little moan,
"Oh, I wish I could find
A wee gravel-stone!"

"Now, see here," said the mother,
From the green garden-patch,
"If you want any breakfast,
You must come and scratch."

---

# The Ants and the Grasshopper

*Aesop*

The ant, like the bee, has long been held up as a paradigm of industriousness. As Proverbs 6:6–8 in the Bible says, "Go to the ant, thou sluggard; consider her ways and be wise: which having no guide, overseer, or ruler, provideth her meat in the summer, and gathereth her food in the harvest."

One fine day in winter some ants were busy drying their store of corn, which had got rather damp during a long spell of rain. Presently up came a grasshopper and begged them to spare her a few grains. "For," she said, "I'm simply starving." The ants stopped work for a moment, though this was against their principles. "May we ask," said they, "what you were doing with yourself all last summer? Why didn't you collect a store of food for the winter?" "The fact is," replied the grasshopper, "I was so busy singing that I hadn't the time." "If you spent the summer singing," replied the ants, "you can't do better than spend the winter dancing." And they chuckled and went on with their work.

## Work While You Work

This poem, which children memorized from *McGuffey's Primer* in the nineteenth and early twentieth centuries, is a good one for those modern souls who turn on the TV while they're doing their homework, or spend more time at the coffee machine than at their desk. On the other hand, it's also a good one for those who can't bring themselves to venture onto a beach or into a movie theater without taking their beepers with them.

Work while you work,
   Play while you play;
One thing each time,
   That is the way.
All that you do,
   Do with your might;
Things done by halves
   Are not done right.

# The Sheep and the Pig Who Built a House

*Retold by Carolyn Sherwin Bailey*

This Scandinavian tale is a good companion for "The Little Red Hen." In this story, there's no shortage of animals willing to pitch in and help.

One morning, bright and early, a sheep and a curly-tailed pig started out through the world to find a home.

"We will build us a house," said the sheep and the curly-tailed pig, "and there we will live together."

So they went a long, long way, until they came to a rabbit.

"Where are you going?" asked the rabbit of the two.

"We are going to build us a house," said the sheep and the pig.

"May I live with you?" asked the rabbit.

"What can you do to help?" asked the sheep and the pig.

The rabbit said: "I can gnaw pegs with my sharp teeth; I can put them in with my paws."

"Good!" said the sheep and the pig. "You may come with us."

So the three went on, a long, long way farther, until they came to a gray goose.

"Where are you going?" asked the gray goose of the three.

"We are going to build us a house," said the sheep, the pig, and the rabbit.

"May I live with you?" asked the gray goose.

"What can you do to help?" asked the sheep, the pig, and the rabbit.

The gray goose said: "I can pull moss, and stuff it in the cracks with my broad bill."

"Good!" said the sheep, the pig, and the rabbit. "You may come with us."

So the four went on, a long, long way, until they came to a barnyard cock.

"Where are you going?" asked the cock of the four.

"We are going to build us a house," said the sheep, the pig, the rabbit, and the goose.

"May I live with you?" asked the barnyard cock.

"What can you do to help?" asked the sheep, the pig, the rabbit, and the goose.

The cock said: "I can crow very early in the morning; I can awaken you all."

"Good!" said the sheep, the pig, the rabbit, and the goose. "You may come with us."

So the five went on, a long, long way until they found a good place for a house.

Then the sheep hewed logs and drew them.

The pig made bricks for the cellar.

The rabbit gnawed pegs with his sharp teeth, and hammered them in with his paws.

The goose pulled moss, and stuffed it in the cracks with her bill.

The cock crowed early every morning to tell them that it was time to rise.

And they all lived happily together in their little house.

---

# The Three Little Pigs

*Retold by Clifton Johnson*

Here is a story about working smart. It reminds us that you need the right tools and the right materials to do a job right.

Once upon a time there was an old mother pig and three little pigs and they lived in the middle of an oak forest. While the children were still quite small the acorn crop failed. That made it difficult for Mrs. Piggy-wiggy to find enough for her children to eat, and the little pigs had to go hungry. So at last the mother pig sent the little pigs off to seek their fortunes.

The first little pig to go walked on and on until he met a man carrying a bundle of straw, and the little pig said, "Please, man, give me that straw to build a house."

So the man gave the little pig the straw, and the little pig built a house of it. In this house of straw the little pig lived very comfortably; but one day a wolf came along and rapped at the door. "Little pig, little pig, let me come in," said the wolf.

"No, no, not by the hair of my chinny, chin, chin," said the little pig.

"Then I'll huff and I'll puff and I'll blow your house down," said the wolf.

So he huffed and he puffed and he blew the house down and carried the little pig off to his den.

The second little pig that left the mother pig walked on and on until he met a man carrying a bundle of sticks, and the little pig said, "Please, man, give me those sticks to build a house."

So the man gave the little pig the sticks, and the little pig built a house of them. In this house of sticks the little pig lived very comfortably; but one day the wolf came along and rapped at the door. "Little pig, little pig, let me come in," said the wolf.

"No, no, not by the hair of my chinny, chin, chin," said the little pig.

"Then I'll huff and I'll puff and I'll blow your house down," said the wolf.

So he huffed and he puffed, and he puffed and he huffed, and at last he blew the house down and carried off the little pig.

The third little pig, after he left the mother pig, walked on and on until he met a man with a load of bricks, and the little pig said, "Please, man, give me those bricks to build a house."

So the man gave the little pig the bricks and the little pig built a house of them. In this house of bricks the little pig lived very comfortably; but one day the wolf came along and rapped at the door. "Little pig, little pig, let me come in," said the wolf.

"No, no, not by the hair of my chinny, chin, chin," said the little pig.

"Then I'll huff and I'll puff and I'll blow your house down," said the wolf.

So he huffed and he puffed, and he huffed and he puffed, and he puffed and he huffed. But the house was built of bricks and he could not blow it down. At last he had no breath left to huff and puff with, so he gave up and went on his way. And the third, wise little pig lives in his brick house to this very day.

# Hercules and the Wagoner

*Aesop*

Some people exhibit an almost miraculous resolve in waiting for someone else to come along and do their work for them. This old fable may help us learn early that the only certain labor is your own.

A wagoner was driving his team along a muddy lane with a full load behind them, when the wheels of his wagon sank so deep in the mire that no efforts of his horses could move them. As he stood there, looking helplessly on, and calling loudly at intervals upon Hercules for assistance, the god himself appeared, and said to him, "Put your shoulder to the wheel, man, and goad on your horses, and then you may call on Hercules to assist you. If you won't lift a finger to help yourself, you can't expect Hercules or any one else to come to your aid."

Heaven helps those who help themselves.

---

# Alice's Supper

*Laura E. Richards*

We should remember that everything which comes to our table is the harvest of labor.

Far down in the meadow the wheat grows green,
And the reapers are whetting their sickles so keen;
And this is the song that I hear them sing,
While cheery and loud their voices ring:
" 'Tis the finest wheat that ever did grow!
And it is for Alice's supper, ho! ho!"

Far down in the valley the old mill stands,
And the miller is rubbing his dusty white hands;
And these are the words of the miller's lay,
As he watches the millstones a-grinding away:
" 'Tis the finest flour that money can buy,
And it is for Alice's supper, hi! hi!"

Downstairs in the kitchen the fire doth glow,
And Maggie is kneading the soft white dough;
And this is the song that she's singing today,
While merry and busy she's working away:
" 'Tis the finest dough, by near or by far,
And it is for Alice's supper, ha! ha!"

And now to the nursery comes Nanny at last,
And what in her hand is she bringing so fast?
'Tis a plate full of something all yellow and white,
And she sings as she comes with her smile so bright:
" 'Tis the best bread and butter I ever did see!
And it is for Alice's supper, hee! hee!"

# The Darning Needle

*Hans Christian Andersen*

In which we see what happens to those who believe they are above hard work.

There was once a Darning Needle who thought herself so fine that she came at last to believe that she was fit for embroidery.

"Mind now that you hold me fast," she said to the Fingers that took her up. "Pray don't lose me. If I should fall on the ground I should certainly be lost, I am so fine."

"That's more than you can tell," said the Fingers, as they grasped her tightly by the waist.

"I come with a train, you see," said the Darning Needle, as she drew her long thread after her; but there was no knot in the thread.

The Fingers pressed the point of the Needle upon an old pair of slippers, in which the upper leather had burst and must be sewed together. The slippers belonged to the cook.

"This is very coarse work!" said the Darning Needle. "I shall never get through alive. There, I'm breaking! I'm breaking!" and break she did. "Did I not say so?" said the Darning Needle. "I'm too delicate for such work as that."

"Now it's quite useless for sewing," said the Fingers. But they still held her all the same, for the cook presently dropped some melted sealing wax upon the needle and then pinned her neckerchief in front with it.

"See, now I'm a breastpin," said the Darning Needle. "I well knew that I should come to honor; when one is something, one always comes to something. Merit is sure to rise." And at this she laughed, only inwardly, of course, for one can never see when a Darning Needle laughs. There she sat now, quite at her ease, and as proud as if she sat in a state carriage and gazed upon all about her.

"May I take the liberty to ask if you are made of gold?" she asked of the pin, her neighbor. "You have a splendid appearance and quite a remarkable head, though it is so little. You should do what you can to grow—of course it is not everyone that can have sealing wax dropped upon her."

And the Darning Needle drew herself up so proudly that she fell out of the neckerchief into the sink, which the cook was at that moment rinsing.

"Now I'm going to travel," said the Darning Needle, "if only I don't get lost."

But that was just what happened to her.

"I'm too delicate for this world," she said, as she found herself in the gutter. "But I know who I am, and there is always some little pleasure in that!" It was thus that the Darning Needle kept up her proud bearing and lost none of her good humor. And now all sorts of things swam over her—chips and straws and scraps of old newspapers.

"Only see how they sail along," said the Darning Needle to herself. "They little know what is under them, though it is I, and I sit firmly here. See! there goes a chip! It thinks of nothing in the world but itself—of nothing in the world but a chip! There floats a straw; see how it turns and twirls about. Do think of something besides yourself or you may easily run against a stone. There swims a bit of a newspaper. What's written upon it is forgotten long ago, yet how it spreads itself out and gives itself airs! I sit patiently and quietly here! I know what I am, and I shall remain the same—always."

One day there lay something beside her that glittered splendidly. She thought it must be a diamond, but it was really only a bit of broken glass from a bottle. As it shone so brightly the Darning Needle spoke to it, introducing herself as a breastpin.

"You are a diamond, I suppose," she said.

"Why, yes, something of the sort."

So each believed the other to be some rare and costly trinket; and they began to converse together upon the world, saying how very conceited it was.

"Yes," said the Darning Needle, "I have lived in a young lady's box; and the young lady happened to be a cook. She had five fingers upon each of her hands, and anything more conceited and arrogant than those five fingers, I never saw. And yet they were only there that they might take me out of the box or put me back again."

"Were they of high descent?" asked the Bit of Bottle. "Did they shine?"

"No, indeed," replied the Darning Needle. "But they were nonetheless haughty. There were five brothers of them—all of the Finger family. And they held themselves so proudly side by side, though they were of quite different heights. The outermost, Thumbling he was called, was short and thick set. He generally stood out of the rank, a little in front of the others; he had only one joint in his back, and could only bow once. But he used to say that if he were cut off from a man, that man would be cut off from military service. Foreman, the second, put himself forward on all occasions, meddled with sweet and sour, pointed to sun and moon, and when the fingers wrote, it was he who pressed the pen. Middleman, the third of the brothers, could look over the others' heads, and gave himself airs for that. Ringman, the fourth, went about with a gold belt about his waist. And little Playman, whom they called Peter Spielman, did nothing at all and was proud of that, I suppose. There was nothing to be heard but boasting, and that is why I took myself away."

"And now we sit here together and shine," said the Bit of Bottle.

At that very moment some water came rushing along the gutter, so that it overflowed and carried the glass diamond along with it.

"So he is off," said the Darning Needle, "and I still remain. I am left here because I am too slender and genteel. But that's my pride, and pride is honorable." And proudly she sat, thinking many thoughts.

"I could almost believe I had been born of a sunbeam, I'm so fine. It seems as if the sunbeams were always trying to seek me under the water. Alas, I'm so delicate that even my own mother cannot find me. If I had my old eye still, which broke off, I think I should cry—but no, I would not; it's not genteel to weep."

One day a couple of street boys were paddling about in the gutter, hunting for old nails, pennies, and such like. It was dirty work, but they seemed to find great pleasure in it.

"Hullo!" cried one of them, as he pricked himself with the Darning Needle. "Here's a fellow for you!"

"I'm not a fellow! I'm a young lady!" said the Darning Needle, but no one heard it.

The sealing wax had worn off, and she had become quite black. "But black makes one look slender, and is always becoming." She thought herself finer even than before.

"There goes an eggshell sailing along," said the boys; and they stuck the Darning Needle into the shell.

"A lady in black, and within white walls!" said the Darning Needle. "That is very striking. Now everyone can see me. I hope I shall not be seasick, for then I shall break."

But the fear was needless; she was not seasick, neither did she break.

"Nothing is so good to prevent seasickness as to have a steel stomach and to bear in mind that one is something a little more than an ordinary person. My seasickness is all over now. The more genteel and honorable one is, the more one can endure."

Crash went the eggshell, as a wagon rolled over both of them. It was a wonder that she did not break.

"Mercy, what a crushing weight!" said the Darning Needle. "I'm growing seasick, after all. I'm going to break!"

But she was not sick, and she did not break, though the wagon wheels rolled over her. She lay at full length in the road, and there let her lie.

# Mr. Meant-To

Hear the famous words of Benjamin Franklin: "Work while it is called today, for you know not how much you may be hindered tomorrow. One today is worth two tomorrows; never leave that till tomorrow which you can do today."

Mr. Meant-To has a comrade,
  And his name is Didn't-Do;
Have you ever chanced to meet them?
  Did they ever call on you?

These two fellows live together
  In the house of Never-Win,
And I'm told that it is haunted
  By the ghost of Might-Have-Been.

# The Husband Who Was to Mind the House

This old Scandinavian tale teaches us to respect others' hard work.

Once upon a time there was a man so surly and cross, he never thought his wife did anything right around the house. One evening, during hay-making time, he came home complaining that dinner wasn't on the table, the baby was crying, and the cow had not been put in the barn.

"I work and I work all day," he growled, "and you get to stay home and mind the house. I wish I had it so easy. I could get dinner ready on time, I'll tell you that."

"Dear love, don't be so angry," said his wife. "Tomorrow let's change our work. I'll go out with the mowers and cut the hay, and you stay home and mind the house."

The husband thought that would do very well. "I could use a

day off," he said. "I'll do all your chores in an hour or two, and sleep the afternoon away."

So early the next morning the wife put a scythe over her shoulder and trudged out to the hayfield with the mowers. The husband stayed behind to do all the work at home.

First of all, he washed some clothes, and then he began to churn the butter. But after he had churned a while, he remembered he needed to hang the clothes up to dry. He went out to the yard, and had just finished hanging his shirts on the line when he saw the pig run into the kitchen.

So off he dashed to the kitchen to look after the pig, lest it should upset the churn. But as soon as he got through the door, he saw the pig had already knocked the churn over. There it was, grunting and rooting in the cream, which was running all over the floor. The man became so wild with rage, he quite forgot about his shirts on the line, and ran at the pig as hard as he could.

He caught it, too, but it was so slippery from all the butter, it shot out of his arms and right through the door. The man raced into the yard, bound to catch that pig no matter what, but he stopped dead in his tracks when he saw his goat. It was standing right beneath the clothesline, chewing and chomping at every last shirt. So the man ran off the goat, and locked up the pig, and took what was left of his shirts off the line.

Then he went into the dairy and found enough cream to fill the churn again, and so he began to churn, for butter they must have at dinner. When he had churned a bit, he remembered that their cow was still shut up in the barn, and had not had a mouthful to eat or a drop to drink all morning, though the sun was high.

He thought it was too far to take her down to the meadow, so he decided to put her on top of the house, for the roof, you must know, was thatched with grass. The house lay next to a steep hill, and he thought if he lay a wide plank from the side of the hill to the roof, he'd easily get the cow up.

But still he couldn't leave the churn, for here was the little baby crawling about on the floor. "If I leave it," he thought, "the child is sure to upset it."

So he put the churn on his back and went out with it. Then he thought he'd better water the cow before he put her on the roof, and he got a bucket to draw water out of the well. But as he stooped down at the brink of the well, the cream ran out of the churn, over his shoulders, down his back, and into the well!

Now it was near dinnertime, and he didn't even have any butter yet. So as soon as he put the cow on the roof, he thought he'd best boil the porridge. He filled the pot with water, and hung it over the fire.

When he had done that, he thought the cow might fall off the roof and break her neck. So he climbed onto the house to tie her up. He tied one end of the rope around the cow's neck, and the other he slipped down the chimney. Then he went back inside and tied it around his own waist. He had to make haste, for the water now began to boil in the pot, and he still had to grind the oatmeal.

So he began to grind away. But while he was hard at it, down fell the cow off the housetop after all, and as she fell she dragged the poor man up the chimeny by the rope! There he stuck fast. And as for the cow, she hung halfway down the wall, swinging between heaven and earth, for she could neither get down nor up.

Meanwhile the wife, who was out in the field, waited and waited for her husband to call her home to dinner. At last she thought she'd waited enough and went home.

When she got there and saw the cow hanging in such an ugly place, she ran up and cut the rope with her scythe. But as soon as she did, down came her husband out of the chimney! So when she went inside the kitchen, she found him standing on his head in the porridge pot.

"Welcome back," he said, after she had fished him out. "I have something to say to you."

So he said he was sorry, and gave her a kiss, and never complained again.

---

# Mother Holly

*Retold by Etta Austin Blaisdell and Mary Frances Blaisdell*

The Brothers Grimm, who collected this story, tell us that in Germany people say "Mother Holly is making her bed" whenever it snows. In this tale, idleness and industry get their just rewards when helping Mother Holly with her chores becomes a test of character for two sisters.

A widow, who lived in a cottage at a little distance from the village, had two daughters. One of them was beautiful and industrious, the other idle and ugly.

The mother loved the ugly one best, because she was her own child. She cared so little for the other that she made her do all the work and be like a Cinderella in the house.

Poor maiden, she was obliged to go every day and seat herself beside a well which stood near the broad highway. Here she had to sit and spin until she thought her poor, tired fingers would fall off.

One day when the spindle was so covered with dust that she could not use it, she rose and dipped it in the water of the well to wash it. While she was doing so, it slipped from her hand and fell to the bottom.

In terror and tears, she ran and told her stepmother what had happened.

The woman scolded her. "As you have let the spindle fall into the water," she said, "you may go and get it, for I will not buy another."

The maiden went back to the well, and, hardly knowing what she was about, threw herself into the water to get the spindle.

At first she knew nothing, but as her senses returned, she found herself in a beautiful meadow, where the sun was shining brightly and thousands of flowers were growing.

She walked a long way across the meadow, until she came to a baker's oven which was full of new bread. The loaves cried, "Ah, pull us out! pull us out, or we shall burn; we have been so long baking!"

Then she stepped near to the oven and with the long bread-shovel took out the loaves.

She walked on after this, and presently came to a tree full of apples. The tree cried, "Shake me, shake me! My apples are ripe!"

She shook the tree till the fruit fell around her like rain, and at last there was not one apple left upon it.

After this she gathered the apples into one large heap, and went on farther.

Soon she came to a small house, and looking at it she saw an old woman peeping out. The woman had such large teeth that the girl was frightened and turned to run away.

The old woman cried after her, "What dost thou fear, dear child? Come and live here with me, and do all the work in the house, and I will make you happy. You must, however, take care to make my bed well, and to shake it with energy, for then the feathers fly about, and in the world they will say it snows, for I am Mother Holly."

As the old woman talked in this kind manner, she won the maiden's heart, so that she agreed to enter her service.

She took care to shake the bed well, so that the feathers might fly down like snowflakes. Therefore she had a very happy life with Mother Holly. She had plenty to eat and drink, and never heard an angry word.

After she had stayed a long time with the kind old woman, she began to feel sad. She could not explain to herself why, till at last she discovered that she was homesick. It seemed to her a thousand times better to go home than to stay with Mother Holly, though the old woman made her so happy.

The longing to go home grew so strong that at last she was obliged to speak.

"Dear Mother Holly," she said, "you have been very kind to me, but I have such sorrow in my heart that I cannot stay here any longer. I must return to my own people."

"Good," said Mother Holly. "I am pleased to hear that you are longing to go home. As you have served me so well and truly, I will show you the way myself."

So she took her by the hand and led her to a broad gateway. The gate was open, and as the young girl passed through there fell upon her a shower of gold. It clung to her dress and remained hanging to it, so that she was covered with gold from head to foot.

"This is your reward for having been so industrious," said the old woman. As she spoke she placed in her hand the spindle which had fallen into the well.

The great gate closed softly and the maiden found herself once more in the world, and not far from her stepmother's house. As she entered the farmyard a cock perched on the wall crowed loudly, and cried, "Our golden lady has come home, I see!"

She went in to her stepmother, and because she was so covered with gold both the mother and sister welcomed her kindly. The maiden told all that had happened to her. And when the mother heard how her wealth had been gained, she was anxious that her own ugly and idle daughter should try her fortune in the same way.

So she made her sit at the well and spin. But the girl, who wished to have all the riches without working for them, did not spin very long at all, for she was daydreaming of all she would buy with her gold.

As soon as she thought enough time had passed, she tossed the spindle into the well. It sank to the bottom, and she sprang in after it, just as her sister had done. And just as her sister had said, she found herself in a beautiful meadow.

She walked for some distance along the same path till she came to the baker's oven. She heard the loaves cry, "Pull us out, pull us out! or we shall burn; we have been so long baking!"

But the idle girl answered, "No, indeed, I have no wish to soil my hands with your dirty oven." And so she walked on till she came to the apple tree.

"Shake me, shake me!" it cried, "for my apples are ripe."

"I do not agree to that at all," she replied, "for some of the apples might fall on my head." And as she spoke she walked lazily on farther.

When at last she stood before the door of Mother Holly's house, she had no fear of her great teeth, for she had heard all about them from her sister. She walked up to the old woman and offered to be her servant.

Mother Holly accepted the offer of her help. For a whole day the girl was very industrious, as she thought of the gold that was to be showered upon her.

On the second day, however, she gave way to her laziness, and on the third it was worse. Several days passed, and she would not get up early in the morning. The bed was never shaken so that the feathers could fly about.

At last Mother Holly was tired of her, and said she must go away, that her help was not needed.

The lazy girl was quite overjoyed at going, for she thought the golden rain was sure to come when Mother Holly led her to the gate. But as she passed under it, a large kettle full of soot was upset over her.

"That is the reward of your service," said the old woman as she shut the gate.

The idle girl walked home with the soot sticking all over her. As she entered the yard the cock on the wall cried out, "Our sooty young lady has come home, I see."

The soot stuck closely and hung all about her hair and her clothes, and do what she would as long as she lived, it never would come off again.

# The Farmer and His Sons

*Aesop*

A farmer, being at death's door, and desiring to impart to his sons a secret of much moment, called them round him and said, "My sons, I am shortly about to die. I would have you know, therefore, that in my vineyard there lies a hidden treasure. Dig, and you will find it." As soon as their father was dead, the sons took spade and fork and turned up the soil of the vineyard over and over again, in their search for the treasure which they supposed to lie buried there. They found none, however: but the vines, after so thorough a digging, produced a crop such as had never before been seen.

There is no treasure without toil.

---

# The Shoemaker and the Elves

*Retold by J. Berg Esenwein and Marietta Stockard*

This tale, adapted from the Brothers Grimm, reminds us that service given is owed service in return.

There once lived a Shoemaker and his Wife who were very poor, and had to work hard to get money enough for food and clothes. The Shoemaker sat all day at his bench, sewing and hammering, making the shoes, while his Wife worked just as hard in her house. They tried to save a little money, but it was very little that they could save.

By and by the Shoemaker fell ill, and all of the money they had saved was spent for medicine and food—at least, nearly all, for when the Shoemaker was able to creep about the house again he had just money enough left to buy the leather for one little pair of shoes. He took the money and went down into the town, bought the leather, and carried it home. Then he cut out the little shoes, but he felt so weak and tired that he could not work anymore.

"I must go to bed now and rest," he said to the good Wife. "Tomorrow morning early I will come down and finish the shoes."

It was scarcely light the next morning when the Shoemaker came down to his work. He stared in surprise, for there on the table stood a little pair of shoes.

"Why, Wife!" he said. "Did you make these shoes?"

"Of course I did not," said the Wife. "I could not make a pair of shoes to save my life." And she was just as surprised as he.

They looked at the neat little stitches and wondered much who could have made them. At last the man set them in the window, hoping someone might come to buy them. Sure enough, they were scarcely in the window when a man came down the street and saw them. "Those are just the shoes I want for my little girl," he said.

So he bought them and gave the Shoemaker more money than he had ever had for a pair of shoes before. It was enough to buy leather for two pairs of shoes. So that day he went down into the town again and bought more leather. When he came back he cut out his work, just as he had done before, then again he felt so weary that he went up to bed, saying that he would finish the work early the next morning. When he came down he found, to his surprise, that the two pairs of shoes, all neatly finished, stood on the table.

"Who can be helping us?" he said.

"Tonight we will hide behind the curtains there, and watch," said his Wife.

So that night when he had cut out his work, and placed it on the table, the Shoemaker and his Wife hid behind the curtains instead of going up to bed. They waited, and waited. Ten o'clock came, but nothing happened; eleven o'clock, and still nothing happened.

"I am so tired," whispered the Shoemaker, "I cannot wait any longer."

"Oh, do wait just a little!" said his Wife.

And so they waited until the clock went dong, dong, twelve times. At the last stroke of twelve, the door flew open and in came a troop of little brownies. They scampered across the floor to the table where the Shoemaker had left his work. Then they began hammering and sewing, making the little shoes. Soon they were all finished and stood in a neat little row on the table. Then the brownies gathered up the scraps of leather, for they were neat little elves, and they scampered off again.

"Well," said the Shoemaker, "I had often heard that brownies came to help those who needed it, but I never dreamed it was they who were working for us."

"Nor I," said his Wife. "But did you notice that the poor little things didn't have any clothes? I should think they would be cold, these frosty nights. They have worked so hard for us that I think we should make them some clothes to keep them warm. I'll make them some little trousers, jackets, and coats."

"And I'll make them some shoes," said the Shoemaker.

"Of course they must have some stockings too, and some little stocking caps," said his Wife.

So they set to work. They stitched and sewed and stitched and sewed. It took a long time and hard work to make so many little brownie suits, but the very day before Christmas the last little suit was finished.

On Christmas Eve the Shoemaker and his Wife put the clothes and shoes on the table, instead of the work. Then they hid behind the curtains again, to see what would happen.

Just as before, they waited until the clock struck twelve. Then the door flew open, and in came the brownies. They ran over to the table and began looking for their work, but of course they did not find it. Presently one brownie picked up a little pair of trousers. He held them up and looked at them. Then he popped one leg down into them, and then another. The other brownies capered and laughed and struggled into pairs of trousers too. They put on the jackets and coats, the shoes and stockings. Then they pulled the funny little stocking caps down over their ears. You should have seen their big, round eyes, and heard their giggles.

Then they began dancing. It was such fun to hear their little shoes clatter that they danced and danced and danced. Finally they put their hands on each other's shoulders and danced round and round the room, out through the door, and off.

When after a great many nights the brownies did not come back again, the Shoemaker and his Wife began wondering where they had gone.

"Perhaps the elves are helping someone else who needs them," said the Shoemaker. "Of course I am well now, so we can work for ourselves."

Perhaps he was right, for, at any rate, the brownies never came back to the Shoemaker's house.

# How the Camel Got His Hump

*Rudyard Kipling*

Rudyard Kipling's *Just So Stories,* from which this tale is taken, have enchanted generations since their first publication in 1902. Kipling created the whimsical stories for his daughter Josephine while he was living in America.

In the beginning of years, when the world was so new and all, and the Animals were just beginning to work for Man, there was a Camel, and he lived in the middle of a Howling Desert because he did not want to work; and besides, he was a Howler himself. So he ate sticks and thorns and tamarisks and milkweed and prickles, most 'scruciating idle; and when anybody spoke to him he said "Humph!" Just "Humph!" and no more.

Presently the Horse came to him on Monday morning, with a saddle on his back and a bit in his mouth, and said, "Camel, O Camel, come out and trot like the rest of us."

"Humph!" said the Camel and the Horse went away and told the Man.

Presently the Dog came to him, with a stick in his mouth, and said, "Camel, O Camel, come and fetch and carry like the rest of us."

"Humph!" said the Camel; and the Dog went away and told the Man.

Presently the Ox came to him, with the yoke on his neck and said, "Camel, O Camel, come and plow like the rest of us."

"Humph!" said the Camel; and the Ox went away and told the Man.

At the end of the day the Man called the Horse and the Dog and the Ox together, and said, "Three, O Three, I'm very sorry for you (with the world so new-and-all); but that Humph-thing in the Desert can't work, or he would have been here by now, so I am going to leave him alone, and you must work double time to make up for it."

That made the Three very angry (with the world so new-and-all), and they held a palaver, and an *indaba,* and a *punchayet,* and a pow-wow on the edge of the Desert; and the Camel came chewing milkweed *most* 'scruciating idle, and laughed at them. Then he said "Humph!" and went away again.

Presently there came along the Djinn in charge of All Deserts, rolling in a cloud of dust (Djinns always travel that way because it is Magic), and he stopped to palaver and pow-wow with the Three.

"Djinn of All Deserts," said the Horse, "*is* it right for anyone to be idle, with the world so new-and-all?"

"Certainly not," said the Djinn.

"Well," said the Horse, "there's a thing in the middle of your Howling Desert (and he's a Howler himself) with a long neck and long legs, and he hasn't done a stroke of work since Monday morning. He won't trot."

"Whew!" said the Djinn, whistling. "That's my Camel, for all the gold in Arabia! What does he say about it?"

"He says 'Humph!' " said the Dog. "And he won't fetch and carry."

"Does he say anything else?"

"Only 'Humph!' and he won't plow," said the Ox.

"Very good," said the Djinn. "I'll humph him if you will kindly wait a minute."

The Djinn rolled himself up in his dustcloak, and took a bearing across the desert, and found the Camel most 'scruciatingly idle, looking at his own reflection in a pool of water.

"My long and bubbling friend," said the Djinn, "what's this I hear of your doing no work, with the world so new-and-all?"

"Humph!" said the Camel.

The Djinn sat down, with his chin in his hand, and began to think a Great Magic, while the Camel looked at his own reflection in the pool of water.

"You've given the Three extra work ever since Monday morning, all on account of your 'scruciating idleness," said the Djinn; and he went on thinking Magics, with his chin in his hand.

"Humph!" said the Camel.

"I shouldn't say that again if I were you," said the Djinn; "you might say it once too often. Bubbles, I want you to work."

And the Camel said "Humph!" again; but no sooner had he said it than he saw his back, that he was so proud of, puffing up and puffing up into a great big lolloping humph.

"Do you see that?" said the Djinn. "That's your very own humph that you've brought upon your very own self by not working. Today is Thursday, and you've done no work since Monday, when the work began. Now you are going to work."

"How can I," said the Camel, "with this humph on my back?"

"That's made a-purpose," said the Djinn, "all because you missed those three days. You will be able to work now for three days without eating, because you can live on your humph; and don't you ever say I never did anything for you. Come out of the Desert and go to the Three, and behave. Humph yourself!"

And the Camel humphed himself, humph and all, and went away to join the Three. And from that day to this the Camel always wears a humph (we call it "hump" now, not to hurt his feelings); but he has never yet caught up with the three days that he missed at the beginning of the world, and he has never yet learned how to behave.

The Camel's hump is an ugly lump
  Which well you may see at the Zoo;
But uglier yet is the hump we get
  From having too little to do.

Kiddies and grown-ups too-oo-oo,
If we haven't enough to do-oo-oo,
  We get the hump—
  Cameelious hump—
The hump that is black and blue!

We climb out of bed with a frouzly head
  And a snarly-yarly voice.
We shiver and scowl and we grunt and we growl
  At our bath and our boots and our toys;

And there ought to be a corner for me
(And I know there is one for you)
  When we get the hump—
  Cameelious hump—
The hump that is black and blue!

The cure for this ill is not to sit still,
  Or frowst with a book by the fire;
But to take a large hoe and a shovel also,
  And dig till you gently perspire.

And then you will find that the sun and the wind
And the Djinn of the Garden too,
  Have lifted the hump—
  The horrible hump—
The hump that is black and blue!

I get it as well as you-oo-oo—
If I haven't enough to do-oo-oo—
  We all get hump—
  Cameelious hump—
Kiddies and grown-ups too!

---

## Dust Under the Rug

*Maud Lindsay*

This story reminds us that we are rewarded well—both in coin and in character—only when our work unseen is just as good as our work seen.

There was once a mother who had two little daughters; and, as her husband was dead and she was very poor, she worked diligently all the time that they might be well fed and clothed. She was a skilled worker, and found work to do away from home, but her two little girls were so good and so helpful that they kept her house as neat and as bright as a new pin.

One of the little girls was lame, and could not run about the house; so she sat still in her chair, and sewed, while Minnie, the sister, washed the dishes, swept the floor, and made the home beautiful.

Their home was on the edge of a great forest; and after their tasks were finished the little girls would sit at the window and watch the tall trees as they bent in the wind, until it would seem as though the trees were real persons, nodding and bending and bowing to each other.

In the spring there were birds, in the summer the wild flowers, in autumn the bright leaves, and in winter the great drifts of white snow; so that the whole year was a round of delight to the two happy children. But one day the dear mother came home sick; and then they were very sad. It was winter, and there were many things to buy. Minnie and her little sister sat by the fireside and talked it over, and at last Minnie said:

"Dear sister, I must go out to find work, before the food gives out." So she kissed her mother, and, wrapping herself up, started from home. There was a narrow path leading through the forest, and she determined to follow it until she reached someplace where she might find the work she wanted.

As she hurried on, the shadows grew deeper. The night was coming fast when she saw before her a very small house, which was a welcome sight. She made haste to reach it, and to knock at the door.

Nobody came in answer to her knock. When she had tried again and again, she thought that nobody lived there; and she opened the door and walked in, thinking that she would stay all night.

As soon as she stepped into the house, she started back in surprise; for there before her she saw twelve little beds with the bedclothes all tumbled, twelve little dirty plates on a very dusty table, and the floor of the room so dusty that I am sure you could have drawn a picture on it.

"Dear me!" said the little girl. "This will never do!" And as soon as she had warmed her hands, she set to work to make the room tidy.

She washed the plates, she made up the beds, she swept the floor, she straightened the great rug in front of the fireplace, and set the twelve little chairs in a half circle around the fire; and, just as she finished, the door opened and in walked twelve of the queerest little people she had ever seen. They were just about as tall as a carpenter's rule, and all wore yellow clothes; and when Minnie saw this, she knew that they must be the dwarfs who kept the gold in the heart of the mountain.

"Well!" said the dwarfs, all together, for they always spoke together and in rhyme,

"Now isn't this a sweet surprise?
We really can't believe our eyes!"

Then they spied Minnie, and cried in great astonishment:

"Who can this be, so fair and mild?
Our helper is a stranger child."

Now when Minnie saw the dwarfs, she came to meet them. "If you please," she said, "I'm little Minnie Grey; and I'm looking for work because my dear mother is sick. I came in here when the night drew near, and—"

Here all the dwarfs laughed, and called out merrily:

"You found our room a sorry sight,
But you have made it clean and bright."

They were such dear funny little dwarfs! After they had thanked Minnie for her trouble, they took white bread and honey from the closet and asked her to sup with them.

While they sat at supper, they told her that their fairy housekeeper had taken a holiday, and their house was not well kept because she was away.

They sighed when they said this; and after supper, when Minnie washed the dishes and set them carefully away, they looked at her often and talked among themselves. When the last plate was in its place they called Minnie to them and said:

"Dear mortal maiden, will you stay
All through our fairy's holiday?
And if you faithful prove, and good,
We will reward you as we should."

Now Minnie was much pleased, for she liked the kind dwarfs, and wanted to help them, so she thanked them, and went to bed to dream happy dreams.

Next morning she was awake with the chickens, and cooked a nice breakfast; and after the dwarfs left, she cleaned up the rooms and mended the dwarfs' clothes. In the evening when the dwarfs came home, they found a bright fire and a warm supper waiting for them. And every day Minnie worked faithfully until the last day of the fairy housekeeper's holiday.

That morning, as Minnie looked out of the window to watch the dwarfs go to their work, she saw on one of the windowpanes the most beautiful picture she had ever seen.

A picture of fairy palaces with towers of silver and frosted pinnacles, so wonderful and beautiful that as she looked at it she forgot that there was work to be done, until the cuckoo clock on the mantel struck twelve.

Then she ran in haste to make up the beds, and wash the dishes. But because she was in a hurry she could not work quickly, and when she took the broom to sweep the floor it was almost time for the dwarfs to come home.

"I believe," said Minnie, aloud, "that I will not sweep under the rug today. After all, it is nothing for dust to be where it can't be seen." So she hurried to her supper and left the rug unturned.

Before long the dwarfs came home. As the rooms looked just as usual, nothing was said; and Minnie thought no more of the dust until she went to bed and the stars peeped through the window.

Then she thought of it, for it seemed to her that she could hear the stars saying:

"There is the little girl who is so faithful and good." And Minnie turned her face to the wall, for a little voice, right in her own heart, said:

"Dust under the rug! Dust under the rug!"

"There is the little girl," cried the stars, "who keeps home as bright as starshine."

"Dust under the rug! Dust under the rug!" said the little voice in Minnie's heart.

"We see her! We see her!" called all the stars joyfully.

"Dust under the rug! Dust under the rug!" said the little voice in Minnie's heart, and she could bear it no longer. So she sprang out of bed, and, taking her broom in her hand, she swept the dust away. And lo! under the rug lay twelve shining gold-pieces, as round and as bright as the moon.

"Oh! oh! oh!" cried Minnie, in great surprise. And all the little dwarfs came running to see what was the matter.

Minnie told them all about it; and when she had ended her story, the dwarfs gathered lovingly around her and said:

"Dear child, the gold is all for you,
For faithful you have proved and true;
But had you left the rug unturned,
A groat was all you would have earned.
Our love goes with the gold we give,
And oh! forget not while you live,
That in the smallest duty done
Lies wealth of joy for everyone."

Minnie thanked the dwarfs for their kindness to her, and early next morning she hastened home with her golden treasure, which bought many things for the dear mother and little sister.

She never saw the little dwarfs again. But she never forgot their lesson, to do her work faithfully, and she always swept under the rug.

## The Week of Sundays

In this old tale we see the difference between idle time, which we steal, and leisure time, which we earn. The truth is that people who never have anything to do are usually the most dissatisfied because they are the most bored. Our leisure time, on the other hand, we enjoy largely because we've put plenty of work behind us to get it.

Once upon a time there was a man named Bobby O'Brien who never did a stitch of work in his life unless he absolutely had to.

"Come now, Bobby," his friends used to say, "what's so wrong with a little hard work? You'd think it was the black plague itself, the way you guard yourself against it."

"My friends, I have no more against work than the next man," Bobby would reply. "In fact, nothing fascinates me more than work. I can sit here and watch it all day, if you'll only give me the chance."

And of course, he was perfectly useless around the house.

"Aren't you ashamed of yourself, now?" his wife, Katie, moaned one afternoon. "A fine example you're setting for the children! Do you want them to grow up to be lazy slugs too?"

"It's Sunday, my dear, the day of rest," Bobby pointed out. "Now why would you want to be disturbing it? If you want my opinion, it's the only day out of the whole week worth getting out of bed for. The only problem with Sunday is that as soon as it's over, the rest of the week starts up again." Bobby was a great philosopher, having so much time on his hands.

That very night the whole family was sitting around the fire, waiting for their soup to boil, when what should they hear but a tap-tap-tap at the window. Bobby strolled over and raised the sash, and into the room hopped a little man no bigger than a strutting rooster.

"I was just passing by," the wee man said, "and smelled something good and strong, and thought I might have a bite to eat."

"You're welcome to as much as you want," Bobby said, thinking that such a little man couldn't possibly hold more than a spoonful or two. So the tiny fellow sat down at the fireside, but no sooner had Katie given him a steaming bowl than he slurped it down and asked for another. Katie gave him seconds, and he swallowed that one faster than the first. She gave him thirds, and he drained the bowl almost before she had filled it up.

"What a little pig," Bobby thought to himself. "He'll have all of our suppers, before he's through. Still, I asked him in, and he is our guest, so we must hold our tongues."

After five or six bowls the little man smacked his lips and jumped off his stool.

"It's most kind you've been," he laughed. "A more hospitable family I've never met. Now I must be on my way, but as way of thanks I'll be more than happy to grant the next wish uttered aloud beneath this roof." And with that he hopped through the window and vanished into the night.

Well, everyone wanted to wish for something different. One child wanted a bag of sweets, and the other child wanted a box of toys. Katie thought a new bed would be nice, as the old one was showing signs of collapse. Bobby could name a dozen or so things he'd like to have, right off the top of his head, perhaps a new fishing pole, or maybe a chocolate cake.

"We need more time to think it over," he declared. "The trouble is, tomorrow's Monday morning, and there'll be work and chores to get in the way of our thinking. I wish we had a week of Sundays, and then we could take our time and figure it out."

"Now you've done it!" Katie cried. "You've gone and wasted our only wish on a week of Sundays! You might have wished for a few more brains in that thick head of yours before you opened your mouth for a wish like that!"

"Well, well, it's not such a bad wish, you know," said Bobby, who was just now realizing what he had done. "A week of Sundays will be a fine thing, after all. I've been needing a little rest, and this will give me the chance."

"Rest is the last thing you need, you lazy bag of bones," Katie moaned, hustling the children off to bed.

But the next morning when Bobby woke up to hear the churchbells pealing, and he remembered he had seven whole days before him of not having a thing in the world to do, he decided he'd made the wisest of all possible wishes. He lolled around bed all morning, while Katie took the children to church, and didn't bother to rouse himself until he finally smelled a nice plump chicken coming out of the oven for Sunday dinner.

"What a remarkable event!" he yawned and stretched as he sat down at the table. "King Solomon himself could never have wished for such a wonderful thing as a week of Sundays." And after he stuffed himself, he wandered outside and took a nap beneath his favorite tree.

The next day he lay in bed all morning again, and got up only when church was safely over. But the only thing Katie put on the table was a few chicken bones left from the day before, when Bobby had eaten the whole Sunday dinner. The next day was even worse. Bobby sat down with roaring appetite, only to find porridge and potatoes gracing the table.

"Now what kind of dinner is this?" he asked. "Have you forgotten what day of the week it is? Porridge and potatoes aren't fit for Sunday, my dear."

"And what else did you expect?" Katie cried. "How am I supposed to buy a new chicken with every shop in the village closed for seven straight days? It's all that we have in the cupboard, so you'd better get used to it, my good man."

Well, the next morning Bobby's stomach was growling so fiercely he couldn't help but getting out of bed a little earlier than his usual Sunday custom. He wandered around the kitchen a bit, checking here and there for a bite to eat, but he found only a loaf of stale bread in the pantry.

"You know, my dear," he said, "I've been thinking I need a bit of exercise. I believe I'll go out to the garden and dig a few potatoes for dinner."

"You'll do nothing of the sort," Katie snapped. "I won't have you digging potatoes on Sunday morning, with the neighbors passing by on their way to church. That won't do at all."

"But there's nothing in the house but bits of stale bread," Bobby cried.

"And who do you have to blame but yourself and your week of Sundays for that?" Katie asked.

The next day Bobby was up at the crack of dawn, pacing back and forth across the house and drumming his fingers on every windowsill. The children followed him everywhere he went until the churchbells began to peal, and then they bawled and whimpered to no end.

"What's wrong with these young ones?" Bobby whined. "Have all their manners gone and left them?"

"And what do you expect, after all?" Katie cried. "The poor little things have sat through more sermons in a week now than you've snored through all year. Their backs are sore from living in pews, and they've tossed every last penny they've been saving into that collection plate."

"They should be in school, that's where," Bobby declared.

"And who, may I ask, is to blame for that?" Katie inquired.

On the sixth Sunday, Bobby was so fidgety and bored, he decided to go to church with the rest of the family. Every head in the congregation swung around when he came through the door and crept up the aisle.

"There's the man!" the preacher cried from the pulpit. "Here's the rascal who's kept me up every night this week, wracking my poor brain for another new sermon! Here's the troublemaker who's ruined every last throat in the choir, and almost worn the fingers off the poor organist! I guess you've come to survey your dirty work now, have you?"

And when the service was over, Bobby found his neighbors lined up to greet him.

"Well, now," asked one, "did you stop to think of how we're to bring in the harvest with so many Sundays getting in the way?"

"And how are the rest of us to make a living, having to keep our doors closed all week?" asked the butcher and the baker.

"And what about the washing and ironing and mending?" someone called. "Do you know how much is piled up for next Monday, should it ever come again?"

"And by the way," said the schoolmaster, "have you been taking care of your children's lessons, or have they forgotten how to read and write by now?"

Bobby made his way home as fast as he could.

"Thank goodness there's only one Sunday left!" he sighed as soon as he was safe behind his own door. "Any more would be dangerous to a man's health."

That last Sunday was the longest day of Bobby O'Brien's life. The minutes passed like hours, and the hours stretched into eternities. Bobby twiddled his thumbs, and stood on one foot, and walked in circles, and watched the clock.

"Is this thing broken?" he cried, grabbing it from the mantel and shaking it till its insides rattled. "You can't tell me the time has ever dragged by so slow!"

"When have you ever wanted a Sunday to end?" Katie asked. "Aren't you forgetting that tomorrow is Monday?"

"Forgetting it? It's all I can think about," Bobby exclaimed. "I've never in my life looked forward to any day as much as this Monday morning."

The shadows slowly crept across the lawn, the sun finally went down, and just as the first star popped into the sky, who should come rapping at the window but the same little man who visited one week ago.

"And how did you enjoy your wish?" he asked Bobby.

"Not very much, I'm afraid," said Bobby.

"Really?" exclaimed the little man. "Then you wouldn't want to trade another bite to eat for another week of Sundays?"

"For goodness' sake, no!" cried Bobby. "The only days of rest I want are the ones I've worked six days to earn. It took me all week to learn that lesson, and I won't be forgetting it anytime soon. So I'll thank you to be gone with your wishes, my friend."

And at that the little man disappeared, and was never seen again.

## What Have We Done Today?

*Nixon Waterman*

Work is not a plan for work. Putting off work can be the same as just plain not working.

We shall do much in the years to come,
  But what have we done today?
We shall give our gold in a princely sum,
  But what did we give today?
We shall lift the heart and dry the tear,
We shall plant a hope in the place of fear,
We shall speak the words of love and cheer,
  But what did we speak today?

We shall be so kind in the after while,
  But have we been today?
We shall bring to each lonely life a smile,
  But what have we brought today?
We shall give to truth a grander birth,
And to steadfast faith a deeper worth,
We shall feed the hungering souls of earth,
  But whom have we fed today?

We shall reap such joys in the by and by,
  But what have we sown today?
We shall build us mansions in the sky,
  But what have we built today?
'Tis sweet in the idle dreams to bask;
But here and now, do we our task?
Yet, this is the thing our souls must ask,
  What have we done today?

---

# I Meant to Do My Work Today

*Richard Le Gallienne*

I include this little poem as a reminder that, as the saying goes, "All work and no play makes Jack a dull boy." But we should also remember that we enjoy play the most when it crowns good, hard work.

I meant to do my work today,
But a brown bird sang in the apple tree,
And a butterfly flitted across the field,
And all the leaves were calling me.

And the wind went sighing over the land,
Tossing the grasses to and fro,
And a rainbow held out its shining hand—
So what could I do but laugh and go?

# The Rebellion Against the Stomach

Variations on this story about cooperation and communal effort were common in classical antiquity. Paul employs one such variation in I Corinthians 12:14–26. The version below reminds us of the responsibilities involved in the division of labor. It also reminds us that industry keeps the whole body healthy, and that those who live on nothing but complaints may well die fasting.

Once a man had a dream in which his hands and feet and mouth and brain all began to rebel against his stomach.

"You good-for-nothing sluggard!" the hands said. "We work all day long, sawing and hammering and lifting and carrying. By evening we're covered with blisters and scratches, and our joints ache, and we're covered with dirt. And meanwhile you just sit there, hogging all the food."

"We agree!" cried the feet. "Think how sore we get, walking back and forth all day long. And you just stuff yourself full, you greedy pig, so that you're that much heavier to carry about."

"That's right!" whined the mouth. "Where do you think all that food you love comes from? I'm the one who has to chew it all up, and as soon as I'm finished you suck it all down for yourself. Do you call that fair?"

"And what about me?" called the brain. "Do you think it's easy being up here, having to think about where your next meal is going to come from? And yet I get nothing at all for my pains."

And one by one the parts of the body joined the complaint against the stomach, which didn't say anything at all.

"I have an idea," the brain finally announced. "Let's all rebel against this lazy belly, and stop working for it."

"Superb idea!" all the other members and organs agreed. "We'll teach you how important we are, you pig. Then maybe you'll do a little work of your own."

So they all stopped working. The hands refused to do any lifting or carrying. The feet refused to walk. The mouth promised not to chew or swallow a single bite. And the brain swore it wouldn't come up with any more bright ideas. At first the stomach growled a bit, as it always did when it was hungry. But after a while it was quiet.

Then, to the dreaming man's surprise, he found he could not walk. He could not grasp anything in his hands. He could not even open his mouth. And he suddenly began to feel rather ill.

The dream seemed to go on for several days. As each day passed, the man felt worse and worse. "This rebellion had better not last much longer," he thought to himself, "or I'll starve."

Meanwhile, the hands and feet and mouth and brain just lay there, getting weaker and weaker. At first they roused themselves just enough to taunt the stomach every once in a while, but before long they didn't even have the energy for that.

Finally the man heard a faint voice coming from the direction of his feet.

"It could be that we were wrong," they were saying. "We suppose the stomach might have been working in his own way all along."

"I was just thinking the same thing," murmured the brain. "It's true he's been getting all the food. But it seems he's been sending most of it right back to us."

"We might as well admit our error," the mouth said. "The stomach has just as much work to do as the hands and feet and brain and teeth."

"Then let's all get back to work," they cried together. And at that the man woke up.

To his relief, he discovered his feet could walk again. His hands could grasp, his mouth could chew, and his brain could now think clearly. He began to feel much better.

"Well, there's a lesson for me," he thought as he filled his stomach at breakfast. "Either we all work together, or nothing works at all."

---

# The Kingdom of the Bees

*William Shakespeare*

William Shakespeare used the story of the Rebellion against the Stomach in his *Coriolanus* to illustrate a state fallen into anarchy when its citizens refuse to work together. Here in *Henry the Fifth,* by contrast, he returned to the beehive to illustrate the well-ordered, working state.

So work the honeybees;
Creatures, that, by a rule in nature, teach
The act of order to a peopled kingdom.
They have a king, and officers of sorts:
Where some like magistrates, correct at home;
Others, like merchants, venture trade abroad;
Others, like soldiers, armed in their stings,
Make boot upon the summer's velvet buds;
Which pillage they with merry march bring home
To the tent-royal of their emperor:
Who, busied in his majesties, surveys
The singing masons building roofs of gold;
The civil citizens kneading up the honey;
The poor mechanic porters crowding in
Their heavy burthens at his narrow gate;
The sad-ey'd justice, with his surly hum,
Delivering o'er to executors pale
The lazy yawning drone.

---

# The Bundle of Sticks

*Aesop*

A certain man had several sons who were always quarreling with one another, and, try as he might, he could not get them to live together in harmony. So he determined to convince them of their folly by the following means. Bidding them fetch a bundle of sticks, he invited each in turn to break it across his knee. All tried and all failed: and then he undid the bundle, and handed them the sticks one by one, when they had no difficulty at all in breaking them. "There, my boys," said he, "united you will be more than a match for your enemies: but if you quarrel and separate, your weakness will put you at the mercy of those who attack you."

Union is strength.

# Results and Roses

*Edgar Guest*

The man who wants a garden fair,
  Or small or very big,
With flowers growing here and there,
  Must bend his back and dig.

The things are mighty few on earth
  That wishes can attain.
Whate'er we want of any worth
  We've got to work to gain.

It matters not what goal you seek
  Its secret here reposes:
You've got to dig from week to week
  To get Results or Roses.

---

# Hercules Cleans the Augean Stables

The cleaning of the Augean stables was the fifth of the famous Twelve Labors of Hercules, which the great Greek hero performed by order of his cousin, King Eurystheus of Mycenae. We usually think of Hercules as embodying strength more than intelligence, but here we admire his ingenuity as much as his brute force in tackling a nearly impossible job.

The fifth labor of Hercules was the famous cleaning of the Augean stables. Augeas, the king of Elis, had a herd of three thousand cattle, and he had built a stable miles long for them. Year after year his herd kept growing, and he could not get enough men to take care of the barns. The cows could hardly get into them because of the filth, or if they did get in, they were never quite sure of getting out again because the dirt was piled so high. It was said the stables had not been cleaned in thirty years.

Hercules told Augeas he would clean the barns in one day if the king would give him one tenth of all his cows. Augeas thought the great hero could never do it in so short a time, so he made the agreement in the presence of his young son.

The king's stables were near the two rivers Alpheus and Peneus. Hercules cut a great channel to bring the two streams together and then run into the stables. They rushed along and carried the dirt out so quickly the king could not believe it. He did not intend to pay the reward, so he pretended he had never made a promise.

The dispute was taken before a court for the judges to decide. Hercules called the little prince as a witness, and the boy told the truth about it, which caused the king to fall into such a rage he sent both his son and Hercules out of the country. So Hercules left the land of Elis and continued his twelve labors, but his heart was filled with contempt for the faithless king.

---

# The Choice of Hercules

*Retold by James Baldwin*

In his famous choice of labor over pleasure, Hercules sees a distinction far too many fail to discern. He sees that to choose labor is to choose virtue, and thereby happiness. It is important to note, however, that happiness is not his goal; it is rather a result of his dedication to labor. It's a crucial point. Many people pursue pleasure as an end because they believe, as the personification of pleasure says in this story, that ease is the state in which "you shall not want for anything that makes life joyous." But even if you attain that kind of pleasure, something fundamental is missing—the satisfaction of the soul that comes only through human striving. We know true happiness will come to Hercules as we see him set off down the road of Virtue and Labor.

When Hercules was a fair-faced youth, and life was all before him, he went out one morning to do an errand for his stepfather. But as he walked his heart was full of bitter thoughts; and he murmured because others no better than himself were living in ease and pleasure, while for him there was naught but a life of labor and pain.

As he thought upon these things, he came to a place where two roads met; and he stopped, not certain which one to take.

The road on his right was hilly and rough. There was no beauty in it or about it, but he saw that it led straight toward the blue mountains in the far distance.

The road on his left was broad and smooth, with shade trees on either side, where sang an innumerable choir of birds; and it went winding among green meadows, where bloomed countless flowers. But it ended in fog and mist long before it reached the wonderful blue mountains in the distance.

While the lad stood in doubt as to these roads, he saw two fair women coming toward him, each on a different road. The one who came by the flowery way reached him first, and Hercules saw that she was as beautiful as a summer day.

Her cheeks were red, her eyes sparkled; she spoke warm, persuasive words. "O noble youth," she said, "be no longer bowed down with labor and sore trials, but come and follow me. I will lead you into pleasant paths, where there are no storms to disturb and no troubles to annoy. You shall live in ease, with one unending round of music and mirth; and you shall not want for anything that makes life joyous—sparkling wine, or soft couches, or rich robes, or the loving eyes of beautiful maidens. Come with me, and life shall be to you a daydream of gladness."

By this time the other fair woman had drawn near, and she now spoke to the lad. "I have nothing to promise you," said she, "save that which you shall win with your own strength. The road upon which I would lead you is uneven and hard, and climbs many a hill, and descends into many a valley and quagmire. The views which you will sometimes get from the hilltops are grand and glorious, but the deep valleys are dark, and the ascent from them is toilsome. Nevertheless, the road leads to the blue mountains of endless fame, which you see far away on the horizon. They cannot be reached without labor; in fact, there is nothing worth having that must not be won by toil. If you would have fruits and flowers, you must plant them and care for them; if you would gain the love of your fellow men, you must love them and suffer for them; if you would enjoy the favor of heaven, you must make yourself worthy of that favor; if you would have eternal fame, you must not scorn the hard road that leads to it."

Then Hercules saw that this lady, although she was as beautiful as the other, had a countenance pure and gentle, like the sky on a balmy morning in May.

"What is your name?" he asked.

"Some call me Labor," she answered, "but others know me as Virtue."

Then he turned to the first lady. "And what is your name?" he asked.

"Some call me Pleasure," she said, with bewitching smile, "but I choose to be known as the Joyous and Happy One."

"Virtue," said Hercules, "I will take thee as my guide! The road of labor and honest effort shall be mine, and my heart shall no longer cherish bitterness or discontent."

And he put his hand into that of Virtue, and entered with her upon the straight and forbidding road which leads to the fair blue mountains on the pale and distant horizon.

---

# True Nobility

*Edgar Guest*

Who does his task from day to day
And meets whatever comes his way,
Believing God has willed it so,
Has found real greatness here below.

Who guards his post, no matter where,
Believing God must need him there,
Although but lowly toil it be,
Has risen to nobility.

For great and low there's but one test:
'Tis that each man shall do his best.
Who works with all the strength he can
Shall never die in debt to man.

# The Ballad of John Henry

The John Henry of American folklore was a black railroad worker celebrated for his feats of great strength and skill. His most famous exploit was his classic man-versus-machine battle against the new steam drill, which threatened to take the place of the "steel-drivin' " men who hammered long steel bits into solid rock to make holes for dynamite. The story is said to be based on the digging of the Big Bend Tunnel for the Chesapeake and Ohio Railroad in West Virginia's Allegheny Mountains in the 1870s. It is a great American tale of pride and dignity in work.

John Henry was a little baby boy
You could hold him in the palm of your hand.
He gave a long and lonesome cry,
"Gonna be a steel-drivin' man, Lawd, Lawd,
Gonna be a steel-drivin' man."

They took John Henry to the tunnel,
Put him in the lead to drive,
The rock was so tall, John Henry so small,
That he laid down his hammer and he cried, "Lawd, Lawd,"
Laid down his hammer and he cried.

John Henry started on the right hand,
The steam drill started on the left,
"Fo' I'd let that steam drill beat me down,
I'd hammer my fool self to death, Lawd, Lawd,
Hammer my fool self to death."

John Henry told his captain,
"A man ain't nothin' but a man,
Fo' I let your steam drill beat me down
I'll die with this hammer in my hand, Lawd, Lawd,
Die with this hammer in my hand."

Now the captain told John Henry,
"I believe my tunnel's sinkin' in."
"Stand back, Captain, and doncha be afraid,
That's nothin' but my hammer catchin' wind, Lawd, Lawd,
That's nothin' but my hammer catchin' wind."

John Henry told his cap'n,
"Look yonder, boy, what do I see?
Your drill's done broke and your hole's done choke,
And you can't drive steel like me, Lawd, Lawd,
You can't drive steel like me."

John Henry hammerin' in the mountain,
Til the handle of his hammer caught on fire,
He drove so hard till he broke his po' heart,
Then he laid down his hammer and he died, Lawd, Lawd,
He laid down his hammer and he died.

They took John Henry to the tunnel,
And they buried him in the sand,
An' every locomotive come rollin' by
Say, "There lies a steel-drivin' man, Lawd, Lawd,
There lies a steel-drivin' man."

---

# Robinson Crusoe Builds a Boat

*Daniel Defoe*

Daniel Defoe's *The Life and Strange Surprising Adventures of Robinson Crusoe,* published in 1719, was the first major novel in English literature, and few storytellers since have been able to surpass the tale's adventure and romance. In this scene Crusoe, who spends twenty-eight years on an uninhabited island off the coast of Venezuela, tries to build a boat. The episode teaches us all something about organizing and planning *before* we start a job.

This at length put me upon thinking, whether it was not possible to make myself a *canoe,* or *periagua,* such as the natives of those climates make, even without tools, or, as I might say, without hands, *viz.* of the trunk of a great tree. This I not only thought possible, but easy, and pleased myself extremely with the thoughts of making it, and with my having much more convenience for it than any of the Negroes or Indians; but not at all considering the particular inconveniences which I lay under, more than the Indians did, *viz.* want of hands to move it, when it was made, into the water, a difficulty much harder for me to surmount, than all the consequences of want of tools could be to them; for what was it to me, that when I had chosen a vast tree in the woods, I might with much trouble cut it down, if after I might be able with my tools to hew and dub the outside into the proper shape of a boat, and burn or cut out the inside to make it hollow, so to make a boat of it—if after all this, I must leave it just there where I found it, and was not able to launch it into the water?

One would have thought, I could not have had the least reflection upon my mind of my circumstance, while I was making this boat; but I should have immediately thought how I should get it into the sea; but my thoughts were so intent upon my voyage over the sea in it, that I never once considered how I should get it off of the land; and it was really in its own nature more easy for me to guide it over forty-five miles of sea, than about forty-five fathom of land, where it lay, to set it afloat in the water.

I went to work upon this boat the most like a fool that ever man did, who had any of his senses awake. I pleased myself with the design, without determining whether I was ever able to undertake it; not but that the difficulty of launching my boat came often into my head; but I put a stop to my own inquiries into it, by this foolish answer which I gave myself, "Let's first make it, I'll warrant I'll find some way or other to get it along, when 't is done."

This was a most preposterous method; but the eagerness of my fancy prevailed, and to work I went. I felled a cedar tree. I question much whether Solomon ever had such a one for the building of the Temple at Jerusalem. It was five foot ten inches diameter at the lower part next the stump, and four foot eleven inches diameter at the end of twenty-two foot, after which it lessened for a while, and then parted into branches. It was not without infinite labor that I felled this tree. I was twenty days hacking and hewing at it at the bottom. I was fourteen more getting the branches and limbs, and the vast spreading head of it cut off, which I hacked and hewed through with axe and hatchet, and inexpressible labor. After this, it cost me a month to shape it, and dub it to a proportion, and to something like the bottom of a boat, that it might swim upright as it ought to do. It cost me near three months more to clear the inside, and work it out so as to make an exact boat of it. This I did indeed without fire, by mere mallet and chisel, and by the dint of hard labor, till I had brought it to be a very handsome *periagua,* and big enough to have carried six and twenty men, and consequently big enough to have carried me and all my cargo.

When I had gone through this work, I was extremely delighted with it. The boat was really much bigger than I ever saw a *canoe,* or *periagua,* that was made of one tree, in my life. Many a weary stroke it had cost, you may be sure; and there remained nothing but to get it into the water; and had I gotten it into the water, I make no question but I should have began the maddest voyage, and the most unlikely to be performed, that ever was undertaken.

But all my devices to get it into the water failed me; tho' they cost me infinite labor too. It lay about one hundred yards from the water, and not more. But the first inconvenience was, it was uphill toward the creek; well, to take away this discouragement, I resolved to dig into the surface of the earth, and so make a declivity. This I begun, and it cost me a prodigious deal of pains; but who grutches pains, that have their deliverance in view? But when this was worked through, and this difficulty managed, it was still much at one; for I could no more stir the *canoe,* than I could the other boat.

Then I measured the distance of ground, and resolved to cut a dock, or canal, to bring the water up to the *canoe,* seeing I could not bring the *canoe* down to the water. Well, I began this work, and when I began to enter into it, and calculate how deep it was to be dug, how broad, how the stuff to be thrown out, I found, that by the number of hands I had, being none but my own, it must have been ten or twelve years before I should have gone through with it; for the shore lay high, so that at the upper end, it must have been at least twenty foot deep; so at length, tho' with great reluctancy, I gave this attempt over also.

This grieved me heartily, and now I saw, tho' too late, the folly of beginning a work before we count the cost; and before we judge rightly of our own strength to go through with it.

# The Village Blacksmith

*Henry Wadsworth Longfellow*

Longfellow said that he wrote this poem in praise of an ancestor, and that it was suggested to him by a smithy beneath a horse chestnut tree near his house in Cambridge, Massachusetts. Here is the character of true, honest, willing labor. It is surely one of the most appealing images in American verse.

Under a spreading chestnut tree
  The village smithy stands;
The smith, a mighty man is he,
  With large and sinewy hands;
And the muscles of his brawny arms
  Are strong as iron bands.

His hair is crisp, and black, and long,
  His face is like the tan;
His brow is wet with honest sweat,
  He earns whate'er he can,
And looks the whole world in the face,
  For he owes not any man.

Week in, week out, from morn till night,
  You can hear his bellows blow;
You can hear him swing his heavy sledge,
  With measured beat and slow,
Like a sexton ringing the village bell,
  When the evening sun is low.

And children coming home from school
  Look in at the open door;
They love to see the flaming forge,
  And hear the bellows roar,
And catch the burning sparks that fly
  Like chaff from a threshing floor.

He goes on Sunday to the church,
And sits among his boys;
He hears the parson pray and preach,
He hears his daughter's voice,
Singing in the village choir,
And it makes his heart rejoice.

It sounds to him like her mother's voice,
Singing in Paradise!
He needs must think of her once more,
How in the grave she lies;
And with his hard, rough hand he wipes
A tear out of his eyes.

Toiling—rejoicing—sorrowing
Onward through life he goes;
Each morning sees some task begin,
Each evening sees it close;
Something attempted, something done,
Has earned a night's repose.

Thanks, thanks to thee, my worthy friend,
For the lesson thou hast taught!
Thus at the flaming forge of life
Our fortunes must be wrought;
Thus on its sounding anvil shaped
Each burning deed and thought!

---

# Tom Sawyer Gives Up the Brush

*Mark Twain*

Here is one of the most famous scenes in American literature, in which we learn a thing or two about how *not* to apply ourselves to a job. Fortunately, we also learn here a good bit about the right attitude toward work. As Tom's friends show us (without realizing it themselves), whether or not a task constitutes "work" in the unpleasant sense of the word can depend largely on how we choose to view it. As Milton said, "The mind is its own place, and in itself can make a Heaven of Hell, a Hell of Heaven."

Mark Twain's *Tom Sawyer,* published in 1876, is set in a Mississippi River town before the Civil War. It and its even greater companion work, *Huckleberry Finn,* deserve to be read by every American child.

Saturday morning was come, and all the summer world was bright and fresh, and brimming with life. There was a song in every heart; and if the heart was young the music issued at the lips. There was cheer in every face and a spring in every step. The locust trees were in bloom and the fragrance of the blossoms filled the air. Cardiff Hill, beyond the village and above it, was green with vegetation, and it lay just far enough away to seem a Delectable Land, dreamy, reposeful, and inviting.

Tom appeared on the sidewalk with a bucket of whitewash and a long-handled brush. He surveyed the fence, and all gladness left him and a deep melancholy settled down upon his spirit. Thirty yards of board fence nine feet high. Life to him seemed hollow, and existence but a burden. Sighing he dipped his brush and passed it along the topmost plank; repeated the operation; did it again; compared the insignificant whitewashed streak with the far-reaching continent of unwhitewashed fence, and sat down on a tree-box discouraged. . . .

Soon the free boys would come tripping along on all sorts of delicious expeditions, and they would make a world of fun of him for having to work—the very thought of it burnt him like fire. He got out his worldly wealth and examined it—bits of toys, marbles, and trash; enough to buy an exchange of *work,* maybe, but not half enough to buy so much as half an hour of pure freedom. So he returned his straitened means to his pocket, and gave up the idea of trying to buy the boys. At this dark and hopeless moment an inspiration burst upon him! Nothing less than a great, magnificent inspiration.

He took up his brush and went tranquilly to work. Ben Rogers hove in sight presently—the very boy, of all boys, whose ridicule he had been dreading. Ben's gait was the hop-skip-and-jump—proof enough that his heart was light and his anticipations high. He was eating an apple, and giving a long, melodious whoop, at intervals, followed by a deep-toned ding-dong-dong, ding-dong-dong, for he was personating a steamboat. As he drew near, he slackened speed, took the middle of the street, leaned far over to starboard and rounded to ponderously and with laborious pomp and circumstance—for he was personating the *Big Missouri,* and considered himself to be drawing nine feet of water. He was boat and captain and engine bells combined, so he had to imagine himself standing on his own hurricane deck giving the orders and executing them:

"Stop her, sir! Ting-a-ling-ling!" The headway ran almost out and he drew up slowly toward the sidewalk.

"Ship up to back! Ting-a-ling-ling!" His arms straightened and stiffened down his sides.

"Set her back on the stabboard! Ting-a-ling-ling! Chow! ch-chow-wow! Chow!" His right hand, meantime, describing stately circles—for it was representing a forty-foot wheel.

"Let her go back on the labboard! Ting-a-ling-ling! Chow-ch-chow-chow!" The left hand began to describe circles.

"Stop the stabboard! Ting-a-ling-ling! Stop the labboard! Come ahead on the stabboard! Stop her! Let your outside turn over slow! Ting-a-ling-ling! Chow-ow-ow! Get out that head-line! *Lively* now! Come—out with your spring-line—what're you about there! Take a turn round that stump with the bight of it! Stand by that stage, now—let her go! Done with the engines, sir! Ting-a-ling-ling! *Sh't! s'h't! sh't!"* (trying the gaugecocks).

Tom went on whitewashing—paid no attention to the steamboat. Ben stared a moment and then said:

"Hi-*yi! You're* up a stump, ain't you!"

No answer. Tom surveyed his last touch with the eye of an artist, then he gave his brush another gentle sweep and surveyed the result, as before. Ben ranged up alongside of him. Tom's mouth watered for the apple, but he stuck to his work. Ben said:

"Hello, old chap, you got to work, hey?"

Tom wheeled suddenly and said:

"Why, it's you, Ben! I warn't noticing."

"Say—*I*'m going in a-swimming, *I* am. Don't you wish you could? But of course you'd druther *work*—wouldn't you? Course you would!"

Tom contemplated the boy a bit, and said:

"What do you call work?"

"Why, ain't *that* work?"

Tom resumed his whitewashing, and answered carelessly:

"Well, maybe it is, and maybe it ain't. All I know is, it suits Tom Sawyer."

"Oh come, now, you don't mean to let on that you *like* it?"

The brush continued to move.

"Like it? Well, I don't see why I oughtn't to like it. Does a boy get a chance to whitewash a fence every day?"

That put the thing in a new light. Ben stopped nibbling his apple. Tom swept his brush daintily back and forth—stepped back to note the effect—added a touch here and there—criticized the effect again—Ben watching every move and getting more and more interested, more and more absorbed. Presently he said:

"Say, Tom, let *me* whitewash a little."

Tom considered, was about to consent; but he altered his mind:

"No—no—I reckon it wouldn't hardly do, Ben. You see, Aunt Polly's awful particular about this fence—right here on the street, you know—but if it was the back fence I wouldn't mind and *she* wouldn't. Yes, she's awful particular about this fence; it's got to be done very careful; I reckon there ain't one boy in a thousand, maybe two thousand, that can do it the way it's got to be done."

"No—is that so? Oh come, now—lemme just try. Only just a little—I'd let *you,* if you was me, Tom."

"Ben, I'd like to, honest Injun; but Aunt Polly—well, Jim wanted to do it, but she wouldn't let him; Sid wanted to do it, and she wouldn't let Sid. Now don't you see how I'm fixed? If you was to tackle this fence and anything was to happen to it—"

"Oh, shucks, I'll be just as careful. Now lemme try. Say—I'll give you the core of my apple"

"Well, here— No, Ben, now don't. I'm afeard—"

"I'll give you *all* of it!"

Tom gave up the brush with reluctance in his face, but alacrity in his heart. And while the late steamer *Big Missouri* worked and sweated in the sun, the retired artist sat on a barrel in the shade close by, dangled his legs, munched his apple, and planned the slaughter of more innocents. There was no lack of material; boys happened along every little while; they came to jeer, but remained to whitewash. By the time Ben was fagged out, Tom had traded the next chance to Billy Fisher for a kite, in good repair; and when *he* played out, Johnny Miller bought in for a dead rat and a string to swing it with—and so on, and so on, hour after hour. And when the middle of the afternoon came, from being a poor poverty-stricken boy in the morning, Tom was literally rolling in wealth. He had beside the things before mentioned, twelve marbles, part of a Jew's-harp, a piece of blue bottle glass to look through, a spool cannon, a key that wouldn't unlock anything, a fragment of chalk, a glass stopper of a decanter, a tin soldier, a couple of tadpoles, six firecrackers, a kitten with only one eye, a brass doorknob, a dog collar—but no dog—the handle of a knife, four pieces of orange peel, and a dilapidated old window sash.

He had had a nice, good, idle time all the while—plenty of company—and the fence had three coats of whitewash on it! If he hadn't run out of whitewash, he would have bankrupted every boy in the village.

Tom said to himself that it was not such a hollow world, after all. He had discovered a great law of human action, without knowing it—namely, that in order to make a man or a boy covet a thing, it is only necessary to make the thing difficult to attain. If he had been a great and wise philosopher, like the writer of this book, he would now have comprehended that Work consists of whatever a body is *obliged* to do, and that Play consists of whatever a body is not obliged to do. And this would help him to understand why constructing artificial flowers or performing on a treadmill is work, while rolling tenpins or climbing Mont Blanc is only amusement. There are wealthy gentlemen in England who drive four-horse passenger coaches twenty or thirty miles on a daily line, in the summer, because the privilege costs them considerable money; but if they were offered wages for the service, that would turn it into work and then they would resign.

The boy mused awhile over the substantial change which had taken place in his worldly circumstances, and then wended toward headquarters to report.

---

# Abraham Lincoln Denies a Loan

Abraham Lincoln wrote this letter to his stepbrother, John D. Johnston, who had written Lincoln that he was "broke" and "hard-pressed" on the family farm in Coles County, Illinois, and needed a loan. Lincoln's offer of a matching grant, as we call it today, was a recognition that "this habit of uselessly wasting time, is the whole difficulty," and that getting into the habit of working was far more important to Johnston than getting a loan.

[*Dec. 24, 1848*]

*Dear Johnston:*

Your request for eighty dollars, I do not think it best to comply with now. At the various times when I have helped you a little, you have said to me, "We can get along very well now," but in a very short time I find you in the same difficulty again. Now this can only happen by some defect in your conduct. What that defect is, I think I know. You are not *lazy,* and still you are an *idler.* I doubt whether since I saw you, you have done a good whole day's work, in any one day. You do not very much dislike to work, and still you do not work much, merely because it does not seem to you that you could get much for it.

This habit of uselessly wasting time, is the whole difficulty; it is vastly important to you, and still more so to your children, that you should break this habit. It is more important to them, because they have longer to live, and can keep out of an idle habit before they are in it, easier than they can get out after they are in.

You are now in need of some ready money; and what I propose is, that you shall go to work, "tooth and nail," for somebody who will give you money for it.

Let father and your boys take charge of your things at home—prepare for a crop, and make the crop, and you go to work for the best money wages, or in discharge of any debt you owe, that you can get. And to secure you a fair reward for your labor, I now promise you that for every dollar you will, between this and the first of May, get for your own labor either in money or in your own indebtedness, I will then give you one other dollar.

By this, if you hire yourself at ten dollars a month, from me you will get ten more, making twenty dollars a month for your work. In this, I do not mean you shall go off to St. Louis, or the lead mines, or the gold mines, in California, but I mean for you to go at it for the best wages you can get close to home—in Coles County.

Now if you will do this, you will soon be out of debt, and what is better, you will have a habit that will keep you from getting in debt again. But if I should now clear you out, next year you will be just as deep in as ever. You say you would almost give your place in

Heaven for $70 or $80. Then you value your place in Heaven very cheaply, for I am sure you can with the offer I make you get the seventy or eighty dollars for four or five months' work. You say if I furnish you the money you will deed me the land, and if you don't pay the money back, you will deliver possession—

Nonsense! If you can't now live *with* the land, how will you then live without it? You have always been kind to me, and I do not now mean to be unkind to you. On the contrary, if you will but follow my advice, you will find it worth more than eight times eighty dollars to you.

Affectionately

*Your brother*
*A. Lincoln*

---

# Up from Slavery

*Booker T. Washington*

*Up from Slavery* is Booker T. Washington's account of his life, which began in 1856 on a Virginia plantation where his mother was a cook, and ended in 1915 at Tuskegee, Alabama, where he had built one of the world's leading centers of black education. In this excerpt, Washington tells of his determination to "secure an education at any cost," a resolve that led him to Hampton Institute in Hampton, Virginia. This is a passage every college-bound student should read. Here is the soul who is willing to work—and work, and work—to earn an education.

One day, while at work in the coal mine, I happened to overhear two miners talking about a great school for colored people somewhere in Virginia. This was the first time that I had ever heard anything about any kind of school or college that was more pretentious than the little colored school in our town.

In the darkness of the mine I noiselessly crept as close as I could to the two men who were talking. I heard one tell the other that not only was the school established for the members of my race, but that opportunities were provided by which poor but worthy students could work out all or part of the cost of board, and at the same time he taught some trade or industry.

As they went on describing the school, it seemed to me that it must be the greatest place on earth, and not even Heaven presented more attractions for me at that time than did the Hampton Normal and Agricultural Institute in Virginia, about which these men were talking. I resolved at once to go to that school, although I had no idea where it was, or how many miles away, or how I was going to reach it; I remembered only that I was on fire constantly with one ambition, and that was to go to Hampton. This thought was with me day and night.

After hearing of the Hampton Institute, I continued to work for a few months longer in the coal mine. While at work there, I heard of a vacant position in the household of General Lewis Ruffner, the owner of the salt furnace and coalmine. Mrs. Viola Ruffner, the wife of General Ruffner, was a "Yankee" woman from Vermont. Mrs. Ruffner had a reputation all through the vicinity for being very strict with her servants, and especially with the boys who tried to serve her. Few of them had remained with her more than two or three weeks. They all left with the same excuse: she was too strict. I decided, however, that I would rather try Mrs. Ruffner's house than remain in the coal mine, and so my mother applied to her for the vacant position. I was hired at a salary of $5 per month.

I had heard so much about Mrs. Ruffner's severity that I was almost afraid to see her, and trembled when I went into her presence. I had not lived with her many weeks, however, before I began to understand her. I soon began to learn that, first of all, she wanted everything kept clean about her, that she wanted things done promptly and systematically, and that at the bottom of everything she wanted absolute honesty and frankness. Nothing must be sloven or slipshod; every door, every fence, must be kept in repair.

I cannot now recall how long I lived with Mrs. Ruffner before going to Hampton, but I think it must have been a year and a half. At any rate, I here repeat what I have said more than once before, that the lessons that I learned in the home of Mrs. Ruffner were as valuable to me as any education I have ever gotten anywhere since. Even to this day I never see bits of paper scattered around a house or in the street that I do not want to pick them up at once. I never see a filthy yard that I do not want to clean it, a paling off of a fence that

I do not want to put it on, an unpainted or unwhitewashed house that I do want to paint or whitewash it, or a button off one's clothes, or a grease spot on them or on a floor, that I do not want to call attention to it.

From fearing Mrs. Ruffner I soon learned to look upon her as one of my best friends. When she found that she could trust me she did so implicitly. During the one or two winters that I was with her she gave me an opportunity to go to school for an hour in the day during a portion of the winter months, but most of my studying was done at night, sometimes alone, sometimes under someone whom I could hire to teach me. Mrs. Ruffner always encouraged and sympathized with me in all my efforts to get an education. It was while living with her that I began to get together my first library. I secured a dry goods box, knocked out one side of it, put some shelves in it, and began putting into it every kind of book that I could get my hands upon, and called it my "library."

Notwithstanding my success at Mrs. Ruffner's I did not give up the idea of going to the Hampton Institute. In the fall of 1872 I determined to make an effort to get there, although, as I have stated, I had no idea of the direction in which Hampton was, or what it would cost to go there. I do not think that anyone thoroughly sympathized with me in my ambition to go to Hampton unless it was my mother, and she was troubled with a grave fear that I was starting out on a "wild-goose chase." At any rate, I got only a halfhearted consent from her that I might start. The small amount of money that I had earned had been consumed by my stepfather and the remainder of the family, with the exception of a very few dollars, and so I had very little with which to buy clothes and pay traveling expenses. My brother John helped me all that he could, but of course that was not a great deal, for his work was in the coal mine, where he did not earn much, and most of what he did earn went in the direction of paying the household expenses.

Perhaps the thing that touched and pleased me most in connection with my starting for Hampton was the interest that many of the older colored people took in the matter. They had spent the best days of their lives in slavery, and hardly expected to live to see the time when they would see a member of their race leave home to attend a boarding school. Some of these older people would give me a nickel, others a quarter, or a handkerchief.

Finally the great day came, and I started for Hampton. I had only a small, cheap satchel that contained what few articles of clothing I could get. My mother at the time was rather weak and broken in health. I hardly expected to see her again, and thus our parting was all the more sad. She, however, was very brave through it all. At that time there were no through trains connecting that part of West Virginia with eastern Virginia. Trains ran only a portion of the way, and the remainder of the distance was traveled by stage-coaches. . . .

By walking, begging rides both in wagons and in the cars, in some way, after a number of days, I reached the city of Richmond, Virginia, about eighty-two miles from Hampton. When I reached there, tired, hungry, and dirty, it was late in the night. I had never been in a large city, and this rather added to my misery. When I reached Richmond, I was completely out of money. I had not a single acquaintance in the place, and, being unused to city ways, I did not know where to go. I applied at several places for lodging, but they all wanted money, and that was what I did not have. Knowing nothing else better to do, I walked the streets. In doing this I passed by many foodstands where fried chicken and half-moon apple pies were piled high and made to present a most tempting appearance. At that time it seemed to me that I would have promised all that I expected to possess in the future to have gotten hold of one of those chicken legs or one of those pies. But I could not get either of these, nor anything else to eat.

I must have walked the streets till after midnight. At last I became so exhausted that I could walk no longer. I was tired, I was hungry, I was everything but discouraged. Just about the time when I reached extreme physical exhaustion, I came upon a portion of a street where the board sidewalk was considerably elevated. I waited for a few minutes, till I was sure that no passersby could see me, and then crept under the sidewalk and lay for the night upon the ground, with my satchel of clothing for a pillow. Nearly all night I could hear the tramp of feet over my head. The next morning I found myself refreshed, but I was extremely hungry, because it had been a long time since I had had sufficient food. As soon as it became light enough for me to see my surroundings I noticed that I was near a large ship, and that this ship seemed to be unloading a cargo of pig iron. I went at once to the vessel and asked the captain to permit me to help unload the vessel in order to get money for food. The captain, a white man, who seemed to be kindhearted, consented. I worked long enough to earn money for my breakfast, and it seems to me, as I remember it now, to have been about the best breakfast that I have ever eaten.

My work pleased the captain so well that he told me if I desired

I could continue working for a small amount per day. This I was very glad to do. I continued working on this vessel for a number of days. After buying food with the small wages I received there was not much left to add to the amount I must get to pay my way to Hampton. In order to economize in every way possible, so as to be sure to reach Hampton in a reasonable time, I continued to sleep under the same sidewalk that gave me shelter the first night I was in Richmond. Many years after that the colored citizens of Richmond very kindly tendered me a reception at which there must have been two thousand people present. This reception was held not far from the spot where I slept the first night I spent in that city, and I must confess that my mind was more upon the sidewalk that first gave me shelter than upon the reception, agreeable and cordial as it was.

When I had saved what I considered enough money with which to reach Hampton, I thanked the captain of the vessel for his kindness, and started again. Without any unusual occurrence I reached Hampton, with a surplus of exactly fifty cents with which to begin my education. To me it had been a long, eventful journey; but the first sight of the large, three-story, brick school building seemed to have rewarded me for all that I had undergone in order to reach the place.

---

# Opportunity

*John James Ingalls*

"There is a tide in the affairs of men," William Shakespeare wrote, "which, taken at the flood, leads on to fortune." The catch is that opportunity almost always involves some breasting of the tide—i.e., hard work. Many people would rather simply wait for their ship to come in.

Master of human destinies am I!
Fame, love, and fortune on my footsteps wait.
Cities and fields I walk; I penetrate
Deserts and seas remote, and passing by
Hovel and mart and palace—soon or late
I knock unbidden once at every gate!

If sleeping, wake—if feasting, rise before
I turn away. It is the hour of fate,
And they who follow me reach every state
Mortals desire, and conquer every foe
Save death; but those who doubt or hesitate,
Condemned to failure, penury and woe,
Seek me in vain and uselessly implore.
I answer not, and I return no more!

---

# "It's Plain Hard Work That Does It"

*Charles Edison*

The story of Thomas Alva Edison's life (1847–1931) is the stuff the American Dream is made of. The inquisitive youngster dropped out of school in Port Huron, Michigan, just a few months after beginning when his teacher called him "addled." His mother continued teaching him at home, however, and he set up a chemical laboratory in his cellar.

At age twelve, Edison took a job as a sandwich and peanut salesman on the Grand Trunk Railway to earn money for chemicals and equipment. He moved his laboratory into a baggage car and, after buying a small printing press, started putting out the first newspaper ever published on a moving train. He was thrown off the train when his chemicals burst into flames and set the baggage car on fire.

In 1869, Edison arrived in New York penniless but determined to make a living as an inventor. Several months later he received $40,000 for improvements he had made on the stock ticker, and with this windfall he launched his long inventing career. He worked practically nonstop to patent more than one thousand inventions over the years. This wonderful portrait by his son Charles lets us glimpse the character of one of America's greatest minds.

Shuffling about his laboratory at Menlo Park, New Jersey, a shock of hair over one side of his forehead, sharp blue eyes sparkling, stains and chemical burns on his wrinkled clothing, Thomas Alva Edison never looked like a man whose inventions had revolutionized the world in less than his lifetime. Certainly he never acted like it. Once when a visiting dignitary asked him whether he had received many medals and awards, he said, "Oh yes, Mom's got a couple of quarts of them up at the house." "Mom" was his wife, my mother.

Yet every day, to those of us who were close to him, he demonstrated what a giant among men he was. Great as were his contributions to mankind—he patented a record 1,093 inventions in his lifetime—it is not for these I remember him, but for his matchless courage, his imagination and determination, his humility and wit. At times, he was just plain mischievous.

Because of his prodigious work schedule, his home life was relatively restricted. But he did find time to go fishing, motoring, and the like with the family, and when we children were young to play parchisi and romp on the floor with us. One thing I remember well is Independence Day at Glenmont, our three-story gabled home in West Orange, New Jersey, which is now a national monument. This was Father's favorite holiday. He might start by throwing a firecracker into a barrel at dawn, awakening us and the neighbors as well. Then we would shoot off fireworks in varying combinations all day.

"Mom's not going to like it," he would say mischievously, "but let's put twenty together and see what happens."

Always Father encouraged our experimentation and exploration. He provided clocks and other gadgets to tinker with, and kidded, challenged and questioned us into doing things. He had me washing beakers in his chemical laboratory when I was six, and when I was ten he helped me get started building a full-sized car. It never had a body, but it did have a little two-cycle marine engine and a belt drive. It worked. We kids had a lot of fun with it. Several times my brother Theodore and I played "polo" on the lawn with croquet mallets and autos—and nobody but Mother and the gardener objected.

At home or at work, Father seemed to have a knack for motivating others. He could and often did give orders but he preferred to inspire people by his own example. This was one of the secrets of his success. For he was not, as many believe, a scientist who worked in solitude in a laboratory. Once he had marketed his first successful invention—a stock ticker and printer—for $40,000, he began employing chemists, mathematicians, machinists, anyone whose talents he thought might help him solve a knotty problem. Thus he married science to industry with the "team" research concept, which is standard today.

Sometimes, during his recurrent financial crises, Father couldn't pay his men. But, as one recalled: "It didn't matter. We all came to work just the same. We wouldn't stay away."

Father himself usually worked eighteen or more hours a day. "Accomplishing something provides the only real satisfaction in life," he told us. His widely reported ability to get by with no more than four hours' sleep—plus an occasional catnap—was no exaggeration. "Sleep," he maintained, "is like a drug. Take too much at a time and it makes you dopey. You lose time, vitality, and opportunities."

His successes are well known. In the phonograph, which he invented when he was thirty, he captured sound on records; his incandescent bulb lighted the world. He invented the microphone, mimeograph, medical fluoroscope, the nickel-iron-alkaline storage battery, and the movies. He made the inventions of others—the telephone, telegraph, typewriter—commercially practical. He conceived our entire electrical distribution system.

It is sometimes asked, "Didn't he ever fail?" The answer is yes. Thomas Edison knew failure frequently. His first patent, when he was all but penniless, was for an electric vote-recorder, but maneuver-minded legislators refused to buy it. Once he had his entire fortune tied up in machinery for a magnetic separation process for low-grade iron ore—only to have it made obsolete and uneconomical by the opening of the rich Mesabi Range. But he never hesitated out of fear of failure.

"Shucks," he told a discouraged co-worker during one trying series of experiments, "we haven't failed. We now know a thousand things that won't work, so we're that much closer to finding what will."

His attitude toward money (or lack of it) was similar. He considered it as a raw material, like metal, to be used rather than amassed, and so he kept plowing his funds into new projects. Several times he was all but bankrupt. But he refused to let dollar signs govern his actions.

One day at his ore-crushing mill, Father became dissatisfied with the way a rock-crusher machine was working. "Give her another turn of speed," he ordered the operator.

"I dassn't," came the reply. "She'll break."

Father turned to the foreman. "How much did she cost, Ed?"

"Twenty-five thousand dollars."

"Have we got that much money in the bank? All right, go ahead and give her another notch."

The operator increased the power. And then once more. "She's pounding somethin' awful," he warned. "She'll break our heads!"

"Damn our heads," Father shouted. "Let her out!"

As the pounding became louder, they began to retreat. Suddenly there was a crash and pieces flew in all directions. The crusher was broken.

"Well," the foreman asked Father, "what did you learn from that?"

"Why," said Father with a smile, "that I can put on 40 percent more power than the builder said she could stand—all but that last notch. Now I can build one just as good, and get more production out of it."

I especially recall a freezing December night in 1914, at a time when still-unfruitful experiments on the nickel-iron-alkaline storage battery, to which Father had devoted much of ten years, had put him on a financial tightrope. Only profits from movie and record production were supporting the laboratory. On that December evening the cry of "Fire!" echoed through the plant. Spontaneous combustion had occurred in the film room. Within moments all the packing compounds, celluloid for records, film, and other flammable goods had gone up with a whoosh. Fire companies from eight towns arrived, but the heat was so intense, and the water pressure so low, that the fire hoses had no effect.

When I couldn't find Father, I became concerned. Was he safe? With all his assets going up in smoke, would his will be broken? He was sixty-seven, no age to begin anew. Then I saw him in the plant yard, running toward me.

"Where's Mom?" he shouted. "Go get her! Tell her to get her friends! They'll never see a fire like this again!"

At 5:30 the next morning, with the fire barely under control, he called his employees together and announced, "We're rebuilding." One man was told to lease all the machine shops in the area. Another, to obtain a wrecking crane from the Erie Railroad. Then, almost as an afterthought he added, "Oh, by the way. Anybody know where we can get some money?"

"You can always make capital out of disaster," he said. "We've just cleared out a bunch of old rubbish. We'll build bigger and better on the ruins." With that he rolled up his coat, curled up on a table, and immediately fell asleep.

His remarkable succession of inventions made him appear to possess almost magical powers, so that he was called "The Wizard of Menlo Park." The notion alternately amused and angered him.

"Wizard?" he would say. "Pshaw. It's plain hard work that does it." Or, his much quoted statement: "Genius is one percent inspiration and 99 percent perspiration." Laziness, mental laziness in particular, tried his patience. He kept a statement attributed to Sir Joshua Reynolds hanging prominently in his laboratory and factories: "There is no expedient to which a man will not resort to avoid the real labor of thinking."

Father never changed his sense of values or his hat size. In Boston, when the power failed at the opening of the first American theater to use incandescent lights, he doffed his tie and tails (which he detested) and unhesitatingly headed for the basement to help find the trouble. In Paris, shortly after receiving the Legion of Honor, he quietly removed the tiny red rosette from his lapel, lest friends "think I'm a dude."

After the death of his first wife, Father married the woman who became my mother, Mina Miller. In her he found a perfect complement. She was poised, gracious, self-sufficient; she willingly adjusted to Father's busy schedule. Theirs was a marriage that warmed all whom it touched. Father's diary, the only one he kept (covering nine days in 1885, before they were married), indicated how smitten he was by her. "Got to thinking of Mina and came near being run over by a streetcar," he confessed.

When he proposed, it was in Morse code, which she had learned during their courtship. In later life, when he worked at a desk at home, she was at hers beside him, usually busy with civic projects, in which she was extremely active.

Thomas Edison has sometimes been represented as uneducated. Actually he had only six months of formal schooling, but under his mother's tutelage in Port Huron, Michigan, he had read such classics as *Decline and Fall of the Roman Empire* at the age of eight or nine. After becoming a vendor and newsboy on the Grand Trunk Railroad, he spent whole days in the Detroit Free Library—which he read "from top to bottom." In our home he always had books and magazines, as well as half a dozen daily newspapers.

From childhood, this man who was to accomplish so much was almost totally deaf. He could hear only the loudest noises and shouts, but this did not bother him. "I haven't heard a bird sing since I was twelve," he once said. "But rather than a handicap my deafness probably has been beneficial." He believed it drove him early to reading, enabled him to concentrate, and shut him off from small talk.

People asked him why he didn't invent a hearing aid. Father always replied, "How much have you heard in the last twenty-four hours that you couldn't do without?" He followed this up with: "A man who has to shout can never tell a lie."

He enjoyed music, and if the arrangement emphasized the melody, he could "listen" by biting a pencil and placing the other end of it against a phonograph cabinet. The vibrations and rhythm came through perfectly. The phonograph, incidentally, was his favorite of all his inventions.

Although his deafness required shouted conversation or written questions and answers, reporters enjoyed interviewing him for his pithy, penetrating comments. Once, asked what advice he had for youth, he replied, "Youth doesn't take advice." He never accepted happiness or contentment as worthwhile goals. "Show me a thoroughly satisfied man," he said, "and I will show you a failure." Asked if technological progress could lend to overproduction, he replied, "There cannot be overproduction of anything which men and women want. And their wants are unlimited, except by the size of their stomachs!"

Many tributes were paid Father but two pleased him especially. One came on October 21, 1929, the golden anniversary of the incandescent lamp, when Henry Ford re-created Father's Menlo Park, New Jersey, laboratory in Dearborn, Michigan, to be a permanent shrine in Ford's vast exhibit of Americana at Greenfield Village. This was Ford's expression of gratitude to Father for his words of encouragement when doubt and despair almost turned Ford from the development of his first auto. We could see by his smile that Father was deeply touched.

The other outstanding salute came in 1928, in his own library-laboratory-office in West Orange. He had received honors and medals from many nations. But it was particularly gratifying when, on this occasion, Father was awarded a special gold "Medal of the Congress of the United States" in recognition of his achievements.

He never retired. Nor did he have qualms about the onset of old age. At the age of eighty, he entered a science completely new to him, botany. His goal: to find a native source of rubber. After testing and classifying seventeen thousand varieties of plants, he and his assistants succeeded in devising a method of extracting latex from goldenrod in substantial quantities.

At eighty-three, hearing that Newark Airport was the busiest in the East, he dragged Mother down there to "see how a real airport works." When he saw his first helicopter, he beamed, "That's the way I always thought it should be done." And he started sketching improvements for the little-known whirlybird.

Finally, at eighty-four, ill with uremic poisoning, he started to fail. Scores of reporters arrived to keep vigil. Hourly the news was relayed to them: "The light still burns." But at 3:24 A.M. on October 18, 1931, word came: "The light is out."

The final salute, on the day of his funeral, was to be the cutoff of all electric current in the nation for one minute. But this was deemed too costly and dangerous. Instead, only certain lights were dimmed. The wheels of progress were not stilled, even for an instant.

Thomas Edison, I am sure, would have wanted it that way.

---

# Heaven Is Not Reached in a Single Bound

*J. G. Holland*

Heaven is not reached at a single bound,
  But we build the ladder by which we rise
  From the lowly earth to the vaulted skies,
And we mount to its summit round by round.

I count this thing to be grandly true:
  That a noble deed is a step toward God—
  Lifting the soul from the common clod
To a purer air and a broader view.

# In Praise of the Strenuous Life

*Theodore Roosevelt*

As a sickly, weak child of a wealthy New York family, Theodore Roosevelt (1858–1919) could certainly have found plenty of excuses to fall into a life of rich, idle ease. But that was not his way. With unyielding determination, he committed himself to rigorous physical exercise, turned himself into a devoted outdoorsman, and threw himself into a life of public service. Roosevelt gave this speech in Chicago in 1899, a few months after becoming governor of New York, and it has remained one of his most popular. Here he speaks to a nation just beginning to feel tremendous wealth and power, and he cautions against the temptation of the life of "ignoble ease" that prosperity and security can bring. He reminds us that the character of a nation—like that of an individual—appears through its work.

In speaking to you, men of the greatest city of the West, men of the state which gave to the country Lincoln and Grant, men who preeminently and distinctly embody all that is most American in the American character, I wish to preach not the doctrine of ignoble ease but the doctrine of the strenuous life; the life of toil and effort; of labor and strife; to preach that highest form of success which comes not to the man who desires mere easy peace but to the man who does not shrink from danger, from hardship, or from bitter toil, and who out of these wins the splendid ultimate triumph.

A life of ignoble ease, a life of that peace which springs merely from lack either of desire or of power to strive after great things, is as little worthy of a nation as of an individual. I ask only that what every self-respecting American demands from himself, and from his sons, shall be demanded of the American nation as a whole. Who among you would teach your boys that ease, that peace is to be the first consideration in your eyes—to be the ultimate goal after which they strive? You men of Chicago have made this city great, you men of Illinois have done your share, and more than your share, in making America great, because you neither preach nor practice such a doctrine. You work yourselves, and you bring up your sons to work. If you are rich, and are worth your salt, you will teach your sons that though they may have leisure it is not to be spent in idleness; for wisely used leisure merely means that those who possess it, being free from the necessity of working for their livelihood, are all the more bound to carry on some kind of nonremunerative work in science, in letters, in art, in exploration, in historical research—work of the type we most need in this country, the successful carrying out of which reflects most honor upon the nation.

We do not admire the man of timid peace. We admire the man who embodies victorious effort; the man who never wrongs his neighbor; who is prompt to help a friend; but who has those virile qualities necessary to win in the stern strife of actual life. It is hard to fail; but it is worse never to have tried to succeed. In this life we get nothing save by effort. Freedom from effort in the present, merely means that there has been stored-up effort in the past. A man can be freed from the necessity of work only by the fact that he or his fathers before him have worked to good purpose. If the freedom thus purchased is used aright, and the man still does actual work, though of a different kind, whether as a writer or a general, whether in the field of politics or in the field of exploration and adventure, he shows he deserves his good fortune. But if he treats this period of freedom from the need of actual labor as a period not of preparation but of mere enjoyment, he shows that he is simply a cumberer on the earth's surface; and he surely unfits himself to hold his own with his fellows if the need to do so should again arise. A mere life of ease is not in the end a satisfactory life, and above all it is a life which ultimately unfits those who follow it for serious work in the world. . . .

I preach to you, then, my countrymen, that our country calls not for the life of ease, but for the life of strenuous endeavor. The twentieth century looms before us big with the fate of many nations. If we stand idly by, if we seek merely swollen, slothful ease, and ignoble peace, if we shrink from the hard contests where men must win at hazard of their lives and at the risk of all they hold dear, then the bolder and stronger peoples will pass us by and will win for themselves the domination of the world. Let us therefore boldly face the life of strife, resolute to do our duty well and manfully; resolute to uphold righteousness by deed and by word; resolute to be both honest and brave, to serve high ideals, yet to use practical methods. Above all, let us shrink from no strife, moral or physical, within or without the nation, provided we are certain that the strife is justified; for it is only through strife, through hard and dangerous endeavor, that we shall ultimately win the goal of true national greatness.

---

# Great Men

*Ralph Waldo Emerson*

Not gold, but only man can make
  A people great and strong;
Men who, for truth and honor's sake,
  Stand fast and suffer long.

Brave men who work while others sleep,
  Who dare while others fly—
They build a nation's pillars deep
  And lift them to the sky.

---

# Kill Devil Hill

*Harry Combs*

Here is one of the all-time great American success stories. A childhood fascination with a toy helicopter powered by rubber bands ultimately led Wilbur (1867–1912) and Orville (1871–1948) Wright to what can only be described as one of mankind's most spectacular achievements. In 1900, the Wright brothers began taking their gliders to Kitty Hawk, on North Carolina's Outer Banks, because the ocean breezes and lofty dunes made it an ideal environment for testing their odd-looking flying contraptions. On December 17, 1903, numerous experiments and several "failures" later, Orville made the first powered flight of 120 feet. Wilbur, in the fourth and longest flight of the day, described below, made 852 feet in fifty-nine seconds. If ever we need inspiration as we toil toward some distant, elusive goal, surely we find it here. Here is great work begun by genius, but finished by labor.

The people of Kitty Hawk had always been generous and kind to Wilbur and Orville—friendly and warm, sharing their food and worldly goods, sparing no effort to assist in any way they could to provide physical comfort, and open in their respect for the brothers. Most of them, however, felt less than convinced about the Wrights' being able to fly; Kitty Hawk was an area where the reaction to flight was often expressed in such familiar bits of folk wisdom as "If God had wanted man to fly, He would have given him wings."

Bill Tate, who from the beginning had been a close friend to the Wrights, was not present at the camp on December 17, 1903. This was not a sign of lack of faith; he had assumed that "no one but a crazy man would attempt to fly in such a wind."

The brothers had different ideas. Shortly before twelve o'clock, for the fourth attempt of the day, Wilbur took his position on the flying machine, the engine sputtering and clattering in its strange thunder. His peaked cap was pulled snug across his head, and the wind blowing across the flats reached him with a sandpapery touch. As he had felt it do before, the machine trembled in the gusts, rocking from side to side on the sixty-foot launching track. He settled himself in the hip cradle, feet snug behind him, hands on the controls, studying the three instrument gauges. He looked to each side to be certain no one was near the wings. There were no assistants to hold the wings as they had done with the gliders, for Wilbur believed that unless a man was skilled in what he was doing he ought not to touch anything, and he had insisted on a free launch, for he knew the craft would require only forty feet in the stiff wind to lift itself into the air.

Wilbur shifted his head to study the beach area. Today was different. The wintry gale had greatly reduced the bird population, as far as he could see. It had been that way since they awoke. Very few of the familiar seagulls were about beneath the leaden skies.

Wilbur turned to each side again, looked at his brother, and nodded. Everything was set, and Wilbur reached to the restraining control and pulled the wire free. Instantly, the machine rushed forward and, as he expected, was forty feet down the track when he eased into the air. He had prepared himself for almost every act of the wind, but the gusts were too strong, and he was constantly correcting and overcorrecting. The hundred-foot mark fell behind as the aircraft lunged up and down like a winged bull. Then he was two hundred feet from the start of his run, and the pitch motions were even more violent. The aircraft seemed to stagger as it struck a sudden down draft and darted toward the sands. Only a foot above the ground Wilbur regained control, and eased it back up.

Three hundred feet—and the bucking motions were easing off.

And then the five witnesses and Orville were shouting and gesturing wildly, for it was clear that Wilbur had passed some invisible wall in the sky and had regained control. Four hundred feet out, he was still holding the safety altitude of about fifteen feet above the ground, and the airplane was flying smoother now, no longer darting and lunging about, just easing with the gusts between an estimated eight and fifteen feet.

The seconds ticked away and it was a quarter of a minute since Wilbur had started, and there was no question, now: the machine was under control and was sustaining itself by its own power.

*It was flying.*

The moment had come. It was here, now.

Five hundred feet.

Six hundred.

Seven hundred!

My God, he's trying to reach Kitty Hawk itself, nearly four miles away!

And, indeed, this is just what Wilbur was trying to do, for he kept heading toward the houses and trees still well before him.

*Eight hundred feet . . .*

Still going; still flying. Ahead of him, a rise in the ground, a sprawling hump, a hummock of sand. Wilbur brought the elevator into position to raise the nose, to gain altitude to clear the hummock; for beyond this point lay clear sailing, good flying, and he was lifting, the machine rising slowly. But hummocks do strange things to winds blowing at such high speeds. The wind soared up from the sands, rolling and tumbling, and reached out invisibly to push the flying machine downward. The nose dropped too sharply; Wilbur brought it up; and instantly the oscillations began again, a rapid jerking up and down of the nose. The winds were simply too much, the ground-induced roll too severe, and the *Flyer* "suddenly darted into the ground," as Orville later described it.

They knew as they ran that the impact was greater than that of an intentional landing. The skids dug in, and all the weight of the aircraft struck hard, and above the wind they heard the wood splinter and crack. The aircraft bounced once, borne as much by the wind as by its own momentum, and settled back to the sands, the forward elevator braces askew, broken so that the surfaces hung at an angle. Unhurt, aware that he had been flying a marvelously long time, mildly disappointed at not having continued his flight, stuck in the sand with the wind blowing into his face and the engine grinding out its now familiar clattering, banging roar, Wilbur reached out to shut off power. The propellers whistled and whirred as they slowed, the sounds of the chains came to him more clearly, and then only the wind could be heard. The wind, the sand hissing against fabric and his own clothes and across the ground, and perhaps a gull or two, and certainly the beating of his own heart.

It had happened.

He had flown for fifty-nine seconds.

The distance across the surface from his start to his finish was 852 feet.

The air distance, computing airspeed and wind and all the other factors—more than half a mile.

He—they—had done it.

The air age was *now*.

Just fifty-six days before, Simon Newcomb, the only American scientist since Benjamin Franklin to be an associate of the Institute of France, in an article in *The Independent* had shown by "unassailable logic" that human flight was impossible.

They ran up to the machine, where Wilbur stood waiting for them. No one ever recorded what Wilbur's words were at that moment, and no amount of research has been able to unearth them. It is unfortunate, but they are lost forever. . . .

Orville and Wilbur, stiff with cold, went to their living quarters, where they prepared and ate lunch. They rested for several minutes, washed their dishes, and, ready at last to send word of their achievement, at about two o'clock in the afternoon began the walk to the weather station four miles distant in Kitty Hawk. From the station, still run by Joseph J. Dosher, they could dispatch a wire via government facilities to Norfolk, where the message would be continued by telephone to a commercial telegraph office near Dayton. The message, as it was received in Dayton, read:

176 C KA CS 33 PAID. VIA NORFOLK VA
KITTY HAWK N C DEC 17
BISHOP M WRIGHT
7 HAWTHORNE ST
SUCCESS FOUR FLIGHTS THURSDAY MORNING ALL AGAINST TWENTY ONE MILE WIND STARTED FROM LEVEL WITH ENGINE POWER ALONE AVERAGE SPEED THROUGH AIR THIRTY ONE MILES LONGEST 57 SECONDS INFORM PRESS HOME ##### CHRISTMAS.
OREVELLE WRIGHT 525P

While this slightly garbled message was being transmitted, including the error of flight time of fifty-seven seconds rather than fifty-nine, the brothers went to the life-saving station nearby, to talk with the crew on duty. Captain S. J. Payne, who skippered the facility, told the Wrights he had watched through binoculars as they soared over the ground.

Orville and Wilbur went on to the post office, where they visited Captain and Mrs. Hobbs, who had hauled materials and done other work for them, spent some time with a Dr. Cogswell, and then started their trek back to their camp. It would take them several days to dismantle and pack their *Flyer* into a barrel and two boxes, along with personal gear, and they went to work with their usual thoroughness. It was a strange and a quiet aftermath, and several times they went back outside to stand and look at the ground over which they had flown.

---

# Success

### Henry Wadsworth Longfellow

These lines are from Longfellow's "The Ladder of Saint Augustine."

We have not wings, we cannot soar;
  But we have feet to scale and climb
By slow degrees, by more and more,
  The cloudy summits of our time.

The mighty pyramids of stone
  That wedge-like cleave the desert airs,
When nearer seen, and better known,
  Are but gigantic flights of stairs.

The distant mountains, that uprear
  Their solid bastions to the skies,
Are crossed by pathways, that appear
  As we to higher levels rise.

The heights by great men reached and kept
  Were not attained by sudden flight,
But they, while their companions slept,
  Were toiling upward in the night.

---

# Of Studies

*Francis Bacon*

Francis Bacon made this case for working hard at studies in 1597. All of us who are students should consult it when we find ourselves asking that age-old question: "How is learning this going to do me any good?" This essay may prove a good yardstick in deciding whether an assignment is indeed worth the hard work of true study.

Studies serve for delight, for ornament, and for ability. Their chief use for delight is in privateness and retiring; for ornament, is in discourse; and for ability, is in the judgment and disposition of business. For expert men can execute, and perhaps judge of particulars, one by one; but the general counsels, and the plots and marshaling of affairs, come best from those that are learned. To spend too much time in studies is sloth; to use them too much for ornament, is affectation; to make judgment wholly by their rules, is the humor of a scholar. They perfect nature, and are perfected by experience: for natural abilities are like natural plants, that need pruning, by study;

and studies themselves do give forth directions too much at large, except they be bounded in by experience. Crafty men contemn studies, simple men admire them, and wise men use them; for they teach not their own use; but that is a wisdom without them, and above them, won by observation. Read not to contradict and confute; nor to believe and take for granted; nor to find talk and discourse; but to weigh and consider. Some books are to be tasted, others to be swallowed, and some few to be chewed and digested; that is, some books are to be read only in parts; others to be read, but not curiously; and some few to be read wholly, and with diligence and attention. Some books also may be read by deputy, and extracts made of them by others; but that would be only in the less important arguments, and the meaner sort of books, else distilled books are like common distilled waters, flashy [insipid] things. Reading maketh a full man; conference a ready man; and writing an exact man. And therefore, if a man write little, he had need have a great memory; if he confer little, he had need have a present wit: and if he read little, he had need have much cunning, to seem to know that he doth not. Histories make men wise; poets witty; the mathematics subtile; natural philosophy deep; moral grave; logic and rhetoric able to contend. *Abeunt studia in mores* [Studies pass into and influence manners]. Nay, there is no stond or impediment in the wit but may be wrought out by fit studies; like as diseases of the body may have appropriate exercises. Bowling is good for the stone and reins [kidneys]; shooting for the lungs and breast; gentle walking for the stomach; riding for the head; and the like. So if a man's wit be wandering, let him study the mathematics; for in demonstrations, if his wit be called away never so little, he must begin again. If his wit be not apt to distinguish or find differences, let him study the Schoolmen; for they are *cymini sectores* [splitters of hairs]. If he be not apt to beat over matters, and to call up one thing to prove and illustrate another, let him study the lawyers' cases. So every defect of the mind may have a special receipt.

# Quality

*John Galsworthy*

This is a story about real workmanship, the kind in which the character of the work and the character of the workman have become inseparably good. It reminds us that nothing endures but quality.

I knew him from the days of my extreme youth, because he made my father's boots; inhabiting with his elder brother two little shops let into one; in a small bystreet—now no more, but then most fashionably placed in the West End.

That tenement had a certain quiet distinction; there was no sign upon its face that he made for any of the Royal Family—merely his own German name of Gessler Brothers; and in the window a few pairs of boots. I remember that it always troubled me to account for those unvarying boots in the window, for he made only what was ordered, reaching nothing down, and it seemed so inconceivable that what he made could ever have failed to fit. Had he bought them to put there? That, too, seemed inconceivable. He would never have tolerated in his house leather on which he had not worked himself. Besides, they were too beautiful—the pair of pumps, so inexpressibly slim, the patent leathers with cloth tops, making water come into one's mouth, the tall brown riding boots with marvelous sooty glow, as if, though new, they had been worn a hundred years. Those pairs could only have been made by one who saw before him the Soul of Boot—so truly were they prototypes incarnating the very spirit of all footgear. These thoughts, of course, came to me later, though even when I was promoted to him, at the age of perhaps fourteen, some inkling haunted me of the dignity of himself and brother. For to make boots—such boots as he made—seemed to me then, and still seems to me, mysterious and wonderful.

I remember well my shy remark, one day, while stretching out to him my youthful foot:

"Isn't it awfully hard to do, Mr. Gessler?"

And his answer, given with a sudden smile from out of the sardonic redness of his beard: "Id is an Ardt!"

Himself, he was a little as if made from leather, with his yellow crinkly face, and crinkly reddish hair and beard, and neat folds slanting down his cheeks to the corners of his mouth, and his guttural and one-toned voice; for leather is a sardonic substance, and stiff and slow of purpose. And that was the character of his face, save that his eyes, which were gray-blue, had in them the simple gravity of one secretly possessed by the Ideal. His elder brother was so very like him—though watery, paler in every way, with a great industry—that sometimes in early days I was not quite sure of him until the interview was over. Then I knew that it was he, if the words, "I will ask my brudder," had not been spoken; and that, if they had, it was his elder brother.

When one grew old and wild and ran up bills, one somehow never ran them up with Gessler Brothers. It would not have seemed becoming to go in there and stretch out one's foot to that blue iron-spectacled glance, owing him for more than—say—two pairs, just the comfortable reassurance that one was still his client.

For it was not possible to go to him very often—his boots lasted terribly, having something beyond the temporary—some, as it were, essence of boot stitched into them.

One went in, not as into most shops, in the mood of: "Please serve me, and let me go!" but restfully, as one enters a church; and, sitting on the single wooden chair, waited—for there was never anybody there. Soon, over the top edge of that sort of well—rather dark, and smelling soothingly of leather—which formed the shop, there would be seen his face, or that of his elder brother, peering down. A guttural sound, and the tip-tap of bast slippers beating the narrow wooden stairs, and he would stand before one without coat, a little bent, in leather apron, with sleeves turned back, blinking—as if awakened from some dream of boots, or like an owl surprised in daylight and annoyed at this interruption.

And I would say: "How do you do, Mr. Gessler? Could you make me a pair of Russia leather boots?"

Without a word he would leave me, retiring whence he came, or into the other portion of the shop, and I would continue to rest in the wooden chair, inhaling the incense of his trade. Soon he would come back, holding in his thin, veined hand a piece of gold-brown leather. With eyes fixed on it, he would remark: "What a beaudiful biece!" When I, too, had admired it, he would speak again. "When do you wand dem?" And I would answer: "Oh! As soon as you conveniently can." And he would say: "Tomorrow fordnighd?" Or if he were his elder brother: "I will ask my brudder!"

Then I would murmur: "Thank you! Good morning, Mr. Gessler." "Goot morning!" he would reply, still looking at the leather in his hand. And as I moved to the door, I would hear the tip-tap of his bast slippers restoring him, up the stairs, to his dream of boots. But if it were some new kind of footgear that he had not yet made me, then indeed he would observe ceremony—divesting me of my boot and holding it long in his hand, looking at it with eyes at once critical and loving, as if recalling the glow with which he had created it, and rebuking the way in which one had disorganized this masterpiece. Then, placing my foot on a piece of paper, he would two or three times tickle the outer edges with a pencil and pass his nervous fingers over my toes, feeling himself into the heart of my requirements.

I cannot forget that day on which I had occasion to say to him: "Mr. Gessler, that last pair of town walking boots creaked, you know."

He looked at me for a time without replying, as if expecting me to withdraw or qualify the statement, then said:

"Id shouldn'd 'ave greaked."

"It did, I'm afraid."

"You goddem wed before dey found demselves?"

"I don't think so."

At that he lowered his eyes, as if hunting for memory of those boots, and I felt sorry I had mentioned this grave thing.

"Zend dem back!" he said; "I will look at dem."

A feeling of compassion for my creaking boots surged up in me, so well could I imagine the sorrowful long curiosity of regard which he would bend on them.

"Zome boods," he said slowly, "are bad from birdt. If I can do noding wid dem, I dake dem off your bill."

Once (once only) I went absentmindedly into his shop in a pair of boots bought in an emergency at some large firm's. He took my order without showing me any leather, and I could feel his eyes penetrating the inferior integument of my foot. At last he said:

"Dose are nod my boods."

The tone was not one of anger, nor of sorrow, not even of contempt, but there was in it something quite that froze the blood. He put his hand down and pressed a finger on the place where the left boot, endeavoring to be fashionable, was not quite comfortable.

"Id 'urds you dere," he said. "Dose big virms 'ave no self-respect. Drash!" And then, as if something had given way within him, he spoke long and bitterly. It was the only time I ever heard him discuss the conditions and hardships of his trade.

"Dey get id all," he said, "dey get id by adverdisement, nod by work. Dey dake it away from us, who lofe our boods. Id gomes to this—bresently I haf no work. Every year id gets less—you will see." And looking at his lined face I saw things I had never noticed before, bitter things and bitter struggle—and what a lot of gray hairs there seemed suddenly in his red beard!

As best I could, I explained the circumstances of the purchase of those ill-omened boots. But his face and voice made so deep an impression that during the next few minutes I ordered many pairs. Nemesis fell! They lasted more terribly than ever. And I was not able conscientiously to go to him for nearly two years.

When at last I went I was surprised to find that outside one of the two little windows of his shop another name was painted, also that of a bootmaker—making, of course, for the Royal Family. The old familiar boots, no longer in dignified isolation, were huddled in the single window. Inside, the now contracted well of the one little shop was more scented and darker than ever. And it was longer than usual, too, before a face peered down, and the tip-tap of the bast slippers began. At last he stood before me, and, gazing through those rusty iron spectacles, said:

"Mr.——, isn'd it?"

"Ah! Mr. Gessler," I stammered, "but your boots are really *too* good, you know! See, these are quite decent still!" And I stretched out to him my foot. He looked at it.

"Yes," he said, "beople do nod wand good boods, id seems."

To get away from his reproachful eyes and voice I hastily remarked: "What have you done to your shop?"

He answered quietly: "Id was too exbensif. Do you wand some boods?"

I ordered three pairs, though I had only wanted two, and quickly left. I had, I do not know quite what feeling of being part, in his mind, of a conspiracy against him; or not perhaps so much against him as against his idea of boot. One does not, I suppose, care to feel like that; for it was again many months before my next visit to his shop, paid, I remember, with the feeling: "Oh! well, I can't leave the old boy—so here goes! Perhaps it'll be his elder brother!"

For his elder brother, I knew, had not character enough to reproach me, even dumbly.

And, to my relief, in the shop there did appear to be his elder brother, handling a piece of leather.

"Well, Mr. Gessler," I said, "how are you?"

He came close, and peered at me.

"I am breddy well," he said slowly, "but my elder brudder is dead."

And I saw that it was indeed himself—but how aged and wan! And never before had I heard him mention his brother. Much shocked, I murmured: "Oh! I am sorry!"

"Yes," he answered, "he was a good man, he made a good bood; but he is dead." And he touched the top of his head, where the hair had suddenly gone as thin as it had been on that of his poor brother, to indicate, I suppose, the cause of death. "He could nod ged over losing de oder shop. Do you wand any boods?" And he held up the leather in his hand: "Id's a beaudiful biece."

I ordered several pairs. It was very long before they came—but they were better than ever. One simply could not wear them out. And soon after that I went abroad.

It was over a year before I was again in London. And the first shop I went to was my old friend's. I had left a man of sixty, I came back to one of seventy-five, pinched and worn and tremulous, who genuinely, this time, did not at first know me.

"Oh! Mr. Gessler," I said, sick at heart; "how splendid your boots are! See, I've been wearing this pair nearly all the time I've been abroad; and they're not half worn out, are they?"

He looked long at my boots—a pair of Russia leather, and his face seemed to regain steadiness. Putting his hand on my instep, he said:

"Do dey vid you here? I 'ad drouble wid dat bair, I remember."

I assured him that they had fitted beautifully.

"Do you wand any boods?" he said. "I can make dem quickly; id is a slack dime."

I answered: "Please, please! I want boots all round—every kind!"

"I will make a vresh model. Your food must be bigger." And with utter slowness, he traced round my foot, and felt my toes, only once looking up to say:

"Did I dell you my brudder was dead?"

To watch him was painful, so feeble had he grown; I was glad to get away.

I had given those boots up, when one evening they came. Opening the parcel, I set the four pairs out in a row. Then one by one I tried them on. There was no doubt about it. In shape and fit, in finish and quality of leather, they were the best he had ever made me. And in the mouth of one of the Town walking boots I found his bill. The amount was the same as usual, but it gave me quite a shock. He had never before sent it in till quarter day. I flew downstairs, and wrote a check, and posted it at once with my own hand.

A week later, passing the little street, I thought I would go in and tell him how splendidly the new boots fitted. But when I came to where his shop had been, his name was gone. Still there, in the window, were the slim pumps, the patent leathers with cloth tops, the sooty riding boots.

I went in, very much disturbed. In the two little shops—again made into one—was a young man with an English face.

"Mr. Gessler in?" I said.

He gave me a strange, ingratiating look.

"No, sir," he said, "no. But we can attend to anything with pleasure. We've taken the shop over. You've seen our name, no doubt, next door. We make for some very good people."

"Yes, yes," I said; "but Mr. Gessler?"

"Oh!" he answered; "dead."

"Dead! But I only received these boots from him last Wednesday week."

"Ah!" he said; "a shockin' go. Poor old man starved 'imself."

"Good God!"

"Slow starvation, the doctor called it! You see he went to work in such a way! Would keep the shop on; wouldn't have a soul touch his boots except himself. When he got an order, it took him such a time. People won't wait. He lost everybody. And there he'd sit, goin' on and on—I will say that for him—not a man in London made a better boot! But look at the competition! He never advertised! Would 'ave the best leather, too, and do it all 'imself. Well, there it is. What could you expect with his ideas?"

"But starvation—!"

"That may be a bit flowery, as the sayin' is—but I know myself he was sittin' over his boots day and night, to the very last. You see I used to watch him. Never gave 'imself time to eat; never had a penny in the house. All went in rent and leather. How he lived so long I don't know. He regular let his fire go out. He was a character. But he made good boots."

"Yes," I said, "he made good boots."

And I turned and went out quickly, for I did not want that youth to know that I could hardly see.

# The Noble Nature

*Ben Jonson*

If we devote care to details, our work will shine in small bits and pieces—and our characters will improve degree by degree.

It is not growing like a tree
In bulk, doth make man better be;
Or standing long an oak, three hundred year,
To fall a log at last, dry, bald, and sear:
A lily of a day
Is fairer far in May,
Although it fall and die that night—
It was the plant and flower of Light.
In small proportions we just beauties see,
And in short measures life may perfect be.

# Elias

*Leo Tolstoy*

"For half a century we sought happiness," Elias's wife says in this story, "and as long as we were rich we never found it. Now that we have nothing left, and have taken service as laborers, we have found such happiness that we want nothing better." This simple yet profound story is a good one for anybody choosing a career, job, or task. There's certainly nothing wrong with working to get money, but there may be something very wrong if you think getting the money gets you happiness.

There once lived, in the Government of Ufa, a Bashkir named Elias. His father, who died a year after he had found his son a wife, did not leave him much property. Elias then had only seven mares, two cows, and about a score of sheep. He was a good manager, however, and soon began to acquire more. He and his wife worked from morn till night; rising earlier than others and going later to bed; and his possessions increased year by year. Living in this way, Elias little by little acquired great wealth. At the end of thirty-five years he had 200 horses, 150 head of cattle, and 1,200 sheep. Hired laborers tended his flocks and herds, and hired women milked his mares and cows, and made kumiss, butter, and cheese. Elias had abundance of everything, and everyone in the district envied him. They said of him:

"Elias is a fortunate man: he has plenty of everything. This world must be a pleasant place for him."

People of position heard of Elias and sought his acquaintance. Visitors came to him from afar; and he welcomed every one, and gave them food and drink. Whoever might come, there was always kumiss, tea, sherbet, and mutton to set before them. Whenever visitors arrived a sheep would be killed, or sometimes two; and if many guests came he would even slaughter a mare for them.

Elias had three children: two sons and a daughter; and he married them all off. While he was poor, his sons worked with him and looked after the flocks and herds themselves; but when he grew rich they got spoiled, and one of them took to drink. The elder was killed in a brawl; and the younger, who had married a self-willed woman, ceased to obey his father, and they could not live together anymore.

So they parted, and Elias gave his son a house and some of the cattle, and this diminished his wealth. Soon after that, a disease broke out among Elias's sheep, and many died. Then followed a bad harvest, and the hay crop failed; and many cattle died that winter. Then the Kirghiz captured his best herd of horses; and Elias's property dwindled away. It became smaller and smaller, while at the same time his strength grew less; till, by the time he was seventy years old, he had begun to sell his furs, carpets, saddles, and tents. At last he had to part with his remaining cattle, and found himself face-to-face with want. Before he knew how it had happened, he had lost everything, and in their old age he and his wife had to go into service. Elias had nothing left, except the clothes on his back, a fur cloak, a cup, his indoor shoes and overshoes, and his wife, Sham-Shemagi, who also by this time was old. The son who had parted from him had gone into a far country, and his daughter was dead, so that there was no one to help the old couple.

Their neighbor, Muhammad-Shah, took pity on them. Muhammad-Shah was neither rich nor poor, but lived comfortably, and was a good man. He remembered Elias's hospitality, and, pitying him, said:

"Come and live with me, Elias, you and your old woman. In summer you can work in my melon garden as much as your strength allows, and in winter feed my cattle; and Sham-Shemagi shall milk my mares and make kumiss. I will feed and clothe you both. When you need anything, tell me, and you shall have it."

Elias thanked his neighbor, and he and his wife took service with Muhammad-Shah as laborers. At first the position seemed hard to them, but they got used to it, and lived on, working as much as their strength allowed.

Muhammad-Shah found it was to his advantage to keep such people, because, having been masters themselves, they knew how to manage and were not lazy, but did all the work they could. Yet it grieved Muhammad-Shah to see people brought so low who had been of such high standing.

It happened once that some of Muhammad-Shah's relatives came from a great distance to visit him, and a Mullah came too. Muhammad-Shah told Elias to catch a sheep and kill it. Elias skinned the sheep and boiled it, and sent it in to the guests. The guests ate the mutton, had some tea, and then began drinking kumiss. As they were sitting with their host on down cushions on a carpet, conversing and sipping kumiss from their cups, Elias, having finished his work, passed by the open door. Muhammad-Shah, seeing him pass, said to one of the guests:

"Did you notice that old man who passed just now?"

"Yes," said the visitor, "what is there remarkable about him?"

"Only this—that he was once the richest man among us," replied the host. "His name is Elias. You may have heard of him."

"Of course I have heard of him," the guest answered. "I never saw him before, but his fame has spread far and wide."

"Yes, and now he has nothing left," said Muhammad-Shah, "and he lives with me as my laborer, and his old woman is here too—she milks the mares."

The guest was astonished: he clicked with his tongue, shook his head, and said:

"Fortune turns like a wheel. One man it lifts, another it sets down! Does not the old man grieve over all he has lost?"

"Who can tell? He lives quietly and peacefully, and works well."

"May I speak to him?" asked the guest. "I should like to ask him about his life."

"Why not?" replied the master, and he called from the kibitka in which they were sitting:

"Babay" (which in the Bashkir tongue means "Grandfather"), "come in and have a cup of kumiss with us, and call your wife here also."

Elias entered with his wife; and after exchanging greetings with his master and the guests, he repeated a prayer and seated himself near the door. His wife passed in behind the curtain and sat down with her mistress.

A cup of kumiss was handed to Elias; he wished the guests and his master good health, bowed, drank a little, and put down the cup.

"Well, Daddy," said the guest who had wished to speak to him, "I suppose you feel rather sad at the sight of us. It must remind you of your former prosperity and of your present sorrows."

Elias smiled, and said:

"If I were to tell you what is happiness and what is misfortune, you would not believe me. You had better ask my wife. She is a woman, and what is in her heart is on her tongue. She will tell you the whole truth."

The guest turned toward the curtain.

"Well, Granny," he cried, "tell me how your former happiness compares with your present misfortune."

And Sham-Shemagi answered from behind the curtain:

"This is what I think about it: My old man and I lived for fifty years seeking happiness and not finding it; and it is only now, these last two years, since we had nothing left and have lived as laborers, that we have found real happiness, and we wish for nothing better than our present lot."

The guests were astonished, and so was the master; he even rose and drew the curtain back, so as to see the old woman's face. There she stood with her arms folded, looking at her old husband, and smiling; and he smiled back at her. The old woman went on:

"I speak the truth and do not jest. For half a century we sought for happiness, and as long as we were rich we never found it. Now that we have nothing left and have taken service as laborers, we have found such happiness that we want nothing better."

"But in what does your happiness consist?" asked the guest.

"Why, in this," she replied, "when we were rich, my husband and I had so many cares that we had no time to talk to one another, or to think of our souls, or to pray to God. Now we had visitors, and had to consider what food to set before them, and what presents to give them, lest they should speak ill of us. When they left we had to look after our laborers, who were always trying to shirk work and get the best food, while we wanted to get all we could out of them. So we sinned. Then we were in fear lest a wolf should kill a foal or a calf, or thieves steal our horses. We lay awake at night worrying lest the ewes should overlie their lambs, and we got up again and again to see that all was well. One thing attended to, another care would spring up: how, for instance, to get enough fodder for the winter. And besides that, my old man and I used to disagree. He would say we must do so and so, and I would differ from him; and then we disputed—sinning again. So we passed from one trouble to another, from one sin to another, and found no happiness."

"Well, and now?"

"Now, when my husband and I wake in the morning we always have a loving word for one another, and we live peacefully having nothing to quarrel about. We have no care but how best to serve our master. We work as much as our strength allows, and do it with a will, that our master may not lose, but profit by us. When we come in, dinner or supper is ready and there is kumiss to drink. We have fuel to burn when it is cold, and we have our fur cloak. And we have time to talk, time to think of our souls, and time to pray. For fifty years we sought happiness, but only now at last have we found it."

The guests laughed.

But Elias said:

"Do not laugh, friends. It is not a matter for jesting—it is the truth of life. We also were foolish at first and wept at the loss of our wealth; but now God has shown us the truth, and we tell it, not for our own consolation, but for your good."

And the Mullah said:

"That is a wise speech. Elias has spoken the exact truth. The same is said in Holy Writ."

And the guests ceased laughing and became thoughtful.

# A Psalm of Life

*Henry Wadsworth Longfellow*

Henry Wadsworth Longfellow said of this poem: "I kept it some time in manuscript, unwilling to show it to anyone, it being a voice from my inmost heart, at a time when I was rallying from depression." The verse reminds us that work is often the best cure for unhappiness. Another great American writer and contemporary of Longfellow, Nathaniel Hawthorne, gives the same prescription in *The Scarlet Letter:* "Preach! Write! Act! Do anything, save to lie down and die!"

Tell me not, in mournful numbers,
Life is but an empty dream!—
For the soul is dead that slumbers,
And things are not what they seem.

Life is real! Life is earnest!
And the grave is not its goal;
Dust thou art, to dust returnest,
Was not spoken of the soul.

Not enjoyment, and not sorrow,
Is our destined end or way;
But to act, that each tomorrow
Find us farther than today.

Art is long, and Time is fleeting,
And our hearts, though stout and brave,
Still, like muffled drums, are beating
Funeral marches to the grave.

In the world's broad field of battle,
In the bivouac of Life,
Be not like dumb, driven cattle!
Be a hero in the strife!

Trust no Future, howe'er pleasant!
  Let the dead Past bury its dead!
Act—act in the living Present!
  Heart within, and God o'erhead!

Lives of great men all remind us
  We can make our lives sublime,
And, departing, leave behind us
  Footprints on the sands of time;

Footprints, that perhaps another,
  Sailing o'er life's solemn main,
A forlorn and shipwrecked brother,
  Seeing, shall take heart again.

Let us, then, be up and doing,
  With a heart for any fate;
Still achieving, still pursuing,
  Learn to labor and to wait.

# 6

# Courage

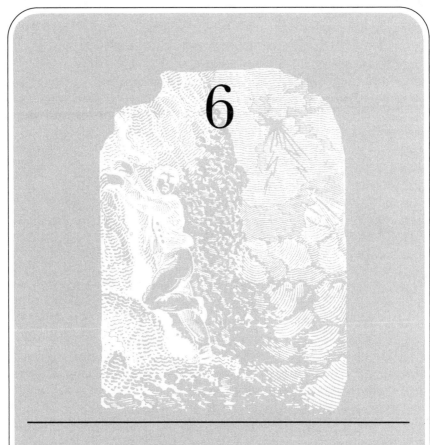

"We become brave by doing brave acts," observed Aristotle in the *Nicomachean Ethics*. Dispositions of character, virtues and vices, are progressively fixed in us through practice. Thus "by being habituated to despise things that are terrible and to stand our ground against them we become brave, and it is when we have become so that we shall be most able to stand our ground against them."

Standing ground against threatening things is not to be confused with fearlessness, however. Being afraid is a perfectly appropriate emotion when confronted with fearful things. The great American novelist Herman Melville makes the Aristotelian point beautifully in a telling passage in *Moby-Dick,* where Starbuck, the chief mate of the *Pequod,* first addresses the crew. " 'I will have no man in my boat,' said Starbuck, 'who is not afraid of a whale.' By this, he seemed to mean, not only that the most reliable and useful courage was that which arises from the fair estimation of the encountered peril, but that an utterly fearless man is a far more dangerous comrade than a coward."

The brave person is not one who is never afraid. That is rather the description of a rash or reckless person, someone who may be more harm than help in an emergency. It is hard to "educate" such a person on the spot. The coward, on the other hand, the one who characteristically lacks confidence and is disposed to be overly fearful, may yet be susceptible to the *encouragement* of example.

The infectious nature of strikingly courageous behavior on the part of one person can inspire—and also in part can shame—a whole group. That was one key to the kind of courage inspired by Horatius at the bridge in ancient Rome and by Henry V at Agincourt. It was one key to the kind of courage displayed by those who silently suffered abuse when they joined ranks with Gandhi and Martin Luther King, Jr., in acts of nonviolent protest directed at rousing the public conscience against injustice.

Another key to their success, of course, was reason: practical reason delivered with the kind of eloquence that is informed by a real command of one's cultural heritage and that steels the will to take intelligent action. The mere inclination to do the right thing is not in itself enough. We have to know what the right thing to do is. We need wisdom—often the wisdom of a wise leader—to give our courage determinate form, to give it intelligent direction. And we need the will, the motivating power that inspiring leaders can sometimes help us discover within ourselves even when we are unable to find it readily on our own.

If Aristotle is right—and I think that he is—then courage is a settled disposition to feel appropriate degrees of fear and confidence in challenging situations (what is "appropriate" varying a good deal with the particular circumstances). It is also a settled disposition to stand one's ground, to advance or to retreat as wisdom dictates. Before such dispositions become settled, however, they need to be established in the first place. And that means practice, which in turn means facing fears and taking stands in advance of any settled disposition to do so: *acting* bravely when we don't really *feel* brave.

Fear of the dark is almost universal among young children, and it provides relatively safe opportunities for first lessons in courage. In families, older siblings are greatly assisted in cultivating their own dispositions in this respect by putting up a brave front before their younger brothers or sisters. "You see? There's really nothing to be afraid of." This is excellent practice, and a fine place to begin. Occasions for being brave on behalf of others—for standing by them in challenging circumstances—are occasions for becoming brave ourselves; that is, for learning how to handle our own confidence and fear, for figuring out the right thing to do, and for mustering the will to do it.

# Chicken Little

Mark Twain once said he had known a lot of troubles in his life, and most of them never happened. We imagine many of our fears into existence. To avoid foolish cowardice, refrain from too much mountain-making out of molehills. Courage, said Plato, is *knowing* what to fear.

Chicken Little was in the woods one day when an acorn fell on her head. It scared her so much she trembled all over. She shook so hard, half her feathers fell out.

"Help! Help!" she cried. "The sky is falling! I must go tell the king!" So she ran in great fright to tell the king.

Along the way she met Henny Penny. "Where are you going, Chicken Little?" Henny Penny asked.

"Oh, help!" Chicken Little cried. "The sky is falling!"

"How do you know?" asked Henny Penny.

"Oh! I saw it with my own eyes, and heard it with my own ears, and part of it fell on my head!"

"This is terrible, just terrible!" Henny Penny clucked. "We'd better run." So they both ran away as fast as they could.

Soon they met Ducky Lucky. "Where are you going, Chicken Little and Henny Penny?" he asked.

"The sky is falling! The sky is falling! We're going to tell the king!" they cried.

"How do you know?" asked Ducky Lucky.

"I saw it with my own eyes, and heard it with my own ears, and part of it fell on my head," Chicken Little said.

"Oh dear, oh dear!" Ducky Lucky quacked. "We'd better run!" So they all ran down the road as fast as they could.

Soon they met Goosey Loosey waddling along the roadside.

"Hello there," Chicken Little, Henny Penny, and Ducky Lucky," called Goosey Loosey. "Where are you all going in such a hurry?"

"We're running for our lives!" cried Chicken Little.

"The sky is falling!" clucked Henny Penny.

"And we're running to tell the king!" quacked Ducky Lucky.

"How do you know the sky is falling?" asked Goosey Loosey.

"I saw it with my own eyes, and heard it with my own ears, and part of it fell on my head," Chicken Little said.

"Goodness!" squawked Goosey Loosey. "Then I'd better run with you." And they all ran in great fright across a meadow.

Before long they met Turkey Lurkey strutting back and forth.

"Hello there, Chicken Little, Henny Penny, Ducky Lucky, and Goosey Loosey," he called. "Where are you all going in such a hurry?"

"Help! Help!" cried Chicken Little.

"We're running for our lives!" clucked Henny Penny.

"The sky is falling!" quacked Ducky Lucky.

"And we're running to tell the king!" squawked Goosey Loosey.

"How do you know the sky is falling?" asked Turkey Lurkey.

"I saw it with my own eyes, and heard it with my own ears, and part of it fell on my head," Chicken Little said.

"Oh dear! I always suspected the sky would fall someday," Turkey Lurkey gobbled. "I'd better run with you."

So they all ran with all their might, until they met Foxy Loxy.

"Well, well," said Foxy Loxy. "Where are you rushing on such a fine day?"

"Help! Help!" cried Chicken Little, Henny Penny, Ducky Lucky, Goosey Loosey, and Turkey Lurkey. "It's not a fine day at all. The sky is falling, and we're running to tell the king!"

"How do you know the sky is falling?" said Foxy Loxy.

"I saw it with my own eyes, and heard it with my own ears, and part of it fell on my head," Chicken Little said.

"I see," said Foxy Loxy. "Well then, follow me, and I'll show you the way to the king."

So Foxy Loxy led Chicken Little, Henny Penny, Ducky Lucky, Goosey Loosey, and Turkey Lurkey across a field and through the woods. He led them straight to his den, and they never saw the king to tell him the sky was falling.

# The Wee Wee Woman

*Retold by James H. Van Sickle and Wilhelmina Seegmiller*

This isn't exactly a spine-tingling tale, but it is designed to make the listener jump a little, and should be read (or better yet, told) to children only when they are old enough to enjoy the suspense. It's an old tale parents have been telling a long time, not just because it's fun, but because it teaches children that things that go bump in the night are usually just bumping around inside our own heads. It also reminds children that fear of "noise in the night" is a very old and natural thing. It's how you react to it that matters.

Once upon a time there was a wee wee woman, who lived in a wee wee house.

One night, when she was in her wee wee bed, she heard a noise!

So she crept out of bed and lighted her wee wee candle.

She looked under her wee wee bed. She looked under her wee wee table. She looked under her wee wee chair.

There was nothing there.

So she blew out her wee wee candle and crept back into her wee wee bed.

The wee wee woman closed her eyes. She was just going to sleep, when—she heard a noise!

So she crept out of her wee wee bed and lighted her wee wee candle and crept down her wee wee stairs.

She went into her wee wee sitting room. She looked under her wee wee table. She looked under her wee wee chairs.

There was nothing there.

So she crept up her wee wee stairs. She blew out her wee wee candle. She crept into her wee wee bed.

The wee wee woman closed her eyes. She was just going to sleep, when—she heard a noise!

She crept out of bed. She lighted her candle. She crept down stairs. She went into her wee wee dining room. She crept to the table. She lifted the cloth. She peeped under. And out popped—BOO!

"Well, well," said the wee wee woman, "think of that! To be frightened by nothing but boo!"

---

## How the Little Kite Learned to Fly

It's amazing how much of the world's virtue comes from one little word: "Try." Trying something for the first time often calls for bravery. "Try, try again," on the other hand, requires that sibling virtue: perseverance (see "The Little Steam Engine").

"I never can do it," the little kite said,
As he looked around at the others high over his
head.
"I know I should fall if I tried to fly."
"Try," said the big kite, "only try!
Or I fear you never will learn at all."
But the little kite said, "I'm afraid I'll fall."

The big kite nodded: "Ah well, goodbye;
I'm off," and he rose toward the tranquil sky.
Then the little kite's paper stirred at the sight,
And trembling he shook himself free for flight.
First whirling and frightened, then braver grown,
Up, up he rose through the air alone,
Till the big kite looking down could see
The little one rising steadily.

Then how the little kite thrilled with pride,
As he sailed with the big kite side by side!
While far below he could see the ground,
And the boys like small spots moving round.
They rested high in the quiet air,
And only the birds and the clouds were there.
"Oh, how happy I am!" the little kite cried,
"And all because I was brave, and tried."

# David and Goliath

## *Retold by J. Berg Esenwein and Marietta Stockard*

This story has it all: the dauntless courage of youth, the thrill of a terrible giant, the overthrowing of a seemingly invincible warrior by means of a mere child's weapon, and a hero who wins through the strength of his faith.

Long ago, in the land of Bethlehem, there lived a man named Jesse, who had eight stalwart sons. The youngest of these sons was David.

Even as a little lad, David was ruddy, beautiful of countenance, and strong of body. When his older brothers drove the flocks to the fields, he ran with them. Each day as he leaped over the hillsides, listened to the gurgling water in the brooks, and the songs of birds in the trees, he grew stronger of limb, and more filled with joy and courage. Sometimes he made songs of the beautiful things he saw and heard. His eye was keen, his hands strong, and his aim sure. When he fitted a stone into his sling, he never missed the mark at which he threw it.

As he grew older, he was given the care of a part of the flocks. One day as he lay on the hillside keeping watch over his sheep, a lion rushed out of the woods and seized a lamb. David leaped to his feet and ran forward. He had no fear in his heart, no thought but to save the lamb. He sprang upon the lion, seized him by his hairy head, and with no weapon but the staff in his strong young hands, he slew him. Another day, a bear came down upon them. Him also, David slew.

Now, soon after this, the Philistines marshaled their armies and came across the hills to drive the children of Israel away from their homes. King Saul gathered his armies and went out to meet them. David's three oldest brothers went with the king, but David was left at home to tend the sheep. "Thou art too young; stay in the fields and keep the flocks safe," they said to David.

Forty days went by, and no news of the battle came; so Jesse called David to him and said: "Take this food for thy brethren, and go up to the camp to see how they fare."

David set out early in the morning, and journeyed up to the

hill on which the army was encamped. There was great shouting and the armies were drawn up in battle array when David arrived. He made his way through the ranks and found his brethren. As he stood talking with them, silence fell upon King Saul's army; and there on the hillside opposite stood a great giant. He strode up and down, his armor glittering in the sun. His shield was so heavy that the strongest man in King Saul's army could not have lifted it, and the sword at his side was so great that the strongest arm could not have wielded it.

"It is the great giant, Goliath," David's brethren told him. "Each day he strides over the hill and calls out his challenge to the men of Israel, but no man amongst us dares to stand before him."

"What! Are the men of Israel afraid?" asked David. "Will they let this Philistine defy the armies of the living God? Will no one go forth to meet him?" He turned from one to another, questioning them.

Eliab, David's oldest brother, heard him and was angry. "Thou art naughty and proud of heart," he said. "Thou hast stolen away from home thinking to see a great battle. With whom hast thou left the sheep?"

"The keeper hath charge of them; and our father, Jesse, sent me hither; and my heart is glad that I am come," answered David. "I myself will go forth to meet this giant. The God of Israel will go with me, for I have no fear of Goliath nor of all his hosts!"

The men standing near hastened to the tent of King Saul and told him of David's words.

"Let him stand before me," commanded the king.

When David was brought into his presence, and Saul saw that he was but a youth, he attempted to dissuade him. But David told him how he had slain the lion and the bear with his naked hands. "The Lord who delivered me from them will deliver me out of the hand of this Philistine," he said.

Then King Saul said: "Go, and the Lord go with thee!"

He had his own armor fetched for David, his helmet of brass, his coat of mail, and his own sword. But David said: "I cannot fight with these. I am not skilled in their use." He put them down, for he knew that each man must win his battles with his own weapons.

Then he took his staff in his hand, his shepherd's bag and sling he hung at his side, and he set out from the camp of Israel. He ran lightly down the hillside, and when he came to the brook which ran at the foot of the hill, he stooped, and choosing five smooth stones from the brook, dropped them into his bag.

The army of King Saul upon one hill, and the host of the Philistines upon the other, looked on in silent wonder. The great giant strode toward David, and when Goliath saw that he was but a youth, ruddy and fair of countenance, his anger knew no bounds.

"Am I a dog, that thou comest to me with sticks?" he shouted. "Do the men of Israel make mock of me to send a child against me? Turn back, or I will give thy flesh to the birds of the air and to the beasts of the field!" Then Goliath cursed David in the name of all his gods.

But no fear came to David's heart. He called out bravely: "Thou comest to me with a sword, and with a spear, and with a shield: but I come to thee in the name of the Lord of hosts, the God of the armies of Israel, whom thou hast defied. This day will the Lord deliver thee into mine hands; and I will smite thee, that all the earth may know that there is a God in Israel!"

Then Goliath rushed forward to meet David, and David ran still more swiftly to meet the giant. He put his hand into his bag, and took one of the stones from it. He fitted it into his sling, and his keen eye found the place in the giant's forehead where the helmet joined. He drew his sling, and with all the force of his strong right arm, he hurled the stone.

It whizzed through the air, and struck deep into Goliath's forehead. His huge body tottered—then fell crashing to the ground. As he lay with his face upon the earth, David ran swiftly to his side, drew forth the giant's own sword, and severed his huge head from his body.

When the army of Israel saw this, they rose up with a great shout, and rushed down the hillside to throw themselves upon the frightened Philistines who were fleeing in terror. When they saw their greatest warrior slain by this lad, they fled toward their own land, leaving their tents and all their riches to be spoiled by the men of Israel.

When the battle was ended, King Saul caused David to be brought before him, and he said: "Thou shalt go no more to the house of thy father but thou shalt be as mine own son."

So David stayed in the tents of the king, and at length he was given command over the king's armies. All Israel honored him, and long years after, he was made the king in King Saul's stead.

# Jack and the Beanstalk

*Adapted from Andrew Lang*

After David, Jack is probably our most famous and beloved giant-slayer. He begins his adventure as a thoughtless boy, but redeems himself through a bravery that rises from a sense of duty to his mother. Courage leads upward, and sooner or later we must all climb our own beanstalks.

Once upon a time there was a poor widow who lived in a little cottage with her only son, Jack. Jack was a silly, thoughtless boy, but very kind-hearted.

One morning the old woman told her son to go to the market and sell their cow. So Jack started out, but on the way he met a butcher with some beautiful beans in his hand. The butcher told the boy they were of great value and persuaded the silly lad to swap the cow for the beans.

Well, of course, when Jack came home with nothing but a handful of beans to show for their cow, his mother shed many a tear. At that Jack realized his foolishness and felt terrible. "At least," he thought, "I may as well sow the beans." So he planted them in the garden and went sadly to bed.

The next day he got up at daybreak and went into the garden. To his amazement he found that the beans had grown up in the night, and their stalks climbed up and up like a ladder disappearing into the clouds!

"It would be easy to climb it," Jack thought.

So he began to climb, and went up and up the stalk until he had left everything behind—cottage, village, even the church tower. At last he reached the top and found himself in a beautiful country, finely wooded, with lush meadows covered with sheep. A crystal stream ran through the pastures, and nearby stood a fine, strong castle. While he was standing looking at it, an ancient lady came walking along.

"If you please, ma'am," said Jack, "is this your house?"

"No," said the old lady. "That is the castle of a wicked giant who keeps wonderful treasures inside. It is said that someday a young lad will come from the valley below to challenge the giant and win the treasures for his poor mother. Perhaps you are the one. But the task is very difficult and full of peril. Have you the courage to undertake it?"

"I fear nothing when I am doing right," said Jack.

"Then," said the old lady, "you are one of those who slay giants. If you can get into the castle, you may find a hen that lays golden eggs, and a harp that talks, as well as two bags full of gold. If you can get them, they will be a great comfort to your poor mother."

So Jack marched forward and knocked at the castle gate. The door was opened in a minute or two by a frightful giantess, with one great eye in the middle of her forehead. At once she grabbed Jack and dragged him inside.

"Ho, ho!" she laughed terribly. "I've been needing somebody to clean the knives, and shine the boots, and make the fires. You will be my servant. But I must hide you whenever the giant is home, for he has eaten up all my other servants, and you would be a dainty morsel too, my lad."

Well, Jack was very much frightened, as you can imagine, but he struggled to be brave and make the best of things.

"I am quite ready to serve you," he said, "only I beg you to hide me from your husband, for I should not like to be eaten at all."

"That's a good boy," said the giantess. "It is lucky you did not scream when you saw me, or he would have heard you and eaten you for supper, as he has done with so many others. Come here, child. Go into my closet. He never looks in there, and you will be safe."

She opened a huge door that stood in the great hall, and shut him in. But the keyhole was so large that it admitted plenty of air, and he could see everything that took place through it. By and by he heard a heavy tramp on the stairs, like the lumbering along of a great cannon, and then a voice like thunder cried out:

Fe, fi, fo, fum,
I smell the blood of an Englishman.
Be he alive or be he dead,
I'll grind his bones to make my bread.

"Wife," cried the giant, "there is a man in the castle. Let me have him for supper."

"You have grown old and stupid," said the lady in her loud tones. "You smell only the dinner I have cooked for you. There, sit down and have a good supper."

So the giant sat down at his table. Jack watched him through the keyhole and was amazed to see him swallow a whole roast pig in one bite. Then he drank a whole barrel of ale in one gulp.

When the supper was ended he asked his wife to bring him his hen that laid the golden eggs. The giantess went away, and soon returned with a little brown hen, which she placed on the table before her husband.

"Lay!" said the giant, and instantly the hen laid a golden egg.

"Lay!" said the giant, and she laid another.

"Lay!" he repeated, and again a golden egg appeared on the table.

After a while he put the hen down on the floor, and called on his wife to bring him his moneybags. The giantess went and soon returned with two large bags over her shoulders, which she set down by her husband. The giant took out heaps and heaps of golden pieces, and counted them, and put them in piles, till he was tired of the amusement. Then he swept them all back into their bags.

"I think I will take a nap," he said to his wife. "But first, bring me my harp, for I will have a little music."

So the giantess went away and returned with a beautiful harp. The framework sparkled with diamonds and rubies, and the strings were all of gold.

"Play!" said the giant, and the harp played a very soft, sad song.

"Play something merrier!" said the giant, and the harp played a merry tune.

"Now play me a lullaby," roared the giant. The harp played a sweet lullaby, and its master fell asleep.

Jack stole softly out of the closet and peeped into the huge kitchen to make sure the giantess was not looking. Then he crept up to the giant's chair and quietly gathered the bags of money, and the wonderful hen, and finally the magic harp. Then he ran as fast as he could—but just as he got to the door, the harp called out, "Master! Master!"

And the giant woke up!

With a tremendous roar he sprang from his seat, and in two strides he reached the door.

Jack was very nimble and fled like lightning. The giant came on fast and stretched out his great hand to catch the boy. But Jack darted away, and ran for the top of the beanstalk, and climbed down through the clouds as fast as his feet would move.

He gave a great sigh of relief when he reached his own garden, only to look up and behold the giant climbing down after him!

"Mother! Mother!" cried Jack. "Make haste and bring me the ax!"

His mother ran to him with a hatchet, and Jack began to chop away. But the giant was getting closer and closer.

"Mother, stand out of the way!" Jack yelled. With one last blow he cut the tree stem through and jumped back from the spot.

Down came the giant with a terrible crash, and broke his neck, and stretched dead from one end of the garden to the other.

Well, of course, Jack's poor old mother was scared out of her wits, for it wasn't every day that a giant came crashing down in her garden. But Jack told her all about his adventure, and showed her the bags of money, and how the wonderful hen could lay golden eggs, and how the magic harp could play and sing.

Jack's mother was glad to have such treasures. But she was even more grateful to have her son back safe and sound, and proud of him for his courage.

"Yesterday I worried that you were only a foolish and thoughtless boy," she said. "But today you've shown how brave you can be. Now I know you are destined to climb the ladder of fortune, just as you climbed the beanstalk."

So together they buried the wicked giant and then went inside to count their blessings.

---

## Hansel and Gretel

*Adapted from the Brothers Grimm*

This universally loved tale reminds us that brothers and sisters must rely on each other for the courage and strength to find their way out of danger's woods.

Near a forest there lived a woodcutter and his wife and two children, a little boy named Hansel and a little girl named Gretel. They were so poor they had very little to eat, and the woodcutter could not stop worrying about how to feed his children.

"What will become of them?" he asked his wife one night. "We have barely enough food to last the week."

"I will tell you," answered the wife, who was the children's stepmother, and a wicked woman. "Early in the morning we will give them each a loaf of bread, and we will lead them into the forest where it is thickest, and leave them alone. They will never find their way home again, and will have to learn to fend for themselves."

"I cannot do that," cried the woodcutter. "It would break my heart to leave them alone in the wilderness."

"Oh, you fool," said the wife, "then they will starve, for we have no food to give them. They stand a better chance in the woods, where perhaps a stranger will find them and take pity on them. If you cannot do it, I will."

So at last the husband consented, and the wife decided to set out at sunrise. But the two little children had not been able to sleep for hunger, and they overheard what their stepmother said.

"Don't be afraid," Hansel told his sister. "I have an idea to help us find our way home again."

Early the next morning the wife came and pulled the children out of bed, saying, "Get up, you lazybones; we are going into the forest to cut wood." She gave them each a loaf of bread, and they set off together into the forest.

They walked all morning, twisting and turning through the old trees, deeper and deeper into the woods. But Hansel was careful to walk behind, and every few steps he tore a small piece of bread from his loaf and dropped it on the ground.

At last the stepmother stopped and told the two children to sit on a log and wait for her. Then she disappeared into the forest.

Gretel shared her bread with Hansel, who had dropped all of his to mark their path, and they went to sleep. When they woke it was getting dark, and no one had come to take them home.

"Wait a bit, Gretel, until the moon gets up," Hansel said, "and then we will be able to find our way back by following the crumbs."

So when the moon rose they got up, but all the bread crumbs were gone! The birds of the woods and fields had picked them up, and now the children were truly lost.

They tried to find their way home but only went round and

round in circles. They walked through the night and into the next morning, finding berries to eat now and then. At last, just when they were ready to give up, they came upon a little cottage in the woods. When they came nearer they saw it was built of gingerbread, and its roof was made of cakes, and its window of sugar!

"We will have some of this!" Hansel cried. "I will eat a piece of the roof, Gretel, and you can have some of the window."

So Hansel reached up and broke off a bit of the roof, just to see how it tasted, and Gretel stood by the window and gnawed at it. Then they heard a thin voice call out from inside:

Nibble, nibble, like a mouse,
Who is nibbling at my house?

The door opened and an old woman came out, leaning on a crutch. Hansel and Gretel were very frightened and dropped what they had in their hands.

The old woman, however, nodded her head and said, "Ah, my dear children, how came you here? You must come indoors and stay with me, and you will be safe."

So she took them each by the hand, and led them into her little cottage, and fed them milk and pancakes with sugar, apples, and nuts. After that she showed them two little white beds, and Hansel and Gretel went to sleep and thought they were in heaven.

But the old woman was really a wicked witch who had built the gingerbread house in the woods to trap little children, and then she would eat them!

Early in the morning, before Hansel and Gretel were awake, she got up to look at them, and as they lay sleeping so peacefully with round rosy cheeks, she said to herself, "What a fine feast I shall have!"

Then she grasped Hansel with her withered hand, led him to the stable, and shut him in; call and scream as he might, it was no use. Then she went back to Gretel and shook her, crying, "Get up, lazybones! Fetch water and cook something nice for your brother. He is outside in the stable and must be fattened up. And when he is fat enough, I will eat him!"

Gretel wept bitterly, but it was no use. She had to do what the wicked witch told her. And so the best foods were cooked for poor Hansel, while Gretel got nothing but crab shells.

Each morning the old woman visited the stable and cried, "Stick out your finger, little boy, so I can feel it and tell if you are fat enough to eat."

Hansel, however, would hold out a little chicken bone, and the old woman, who had weak eyes, could not see what it was. She felt it and wondered why he was not getting fatter. When four weeks had passed and he seemed to remain so thin, she lost patience.

"Now then, Gretel," she cried, "be quick and draw some water. Be Hansel fat or be he lean, I must kill and cook him."

Poor little Gretel trembled with grief, but she knew that now was the time to find her courage.

"I must be brave," she told herself. "The only way I can save Hansel is to keep my wits about me and watch for my chance."

The old lady, meanwhile, had built a fire, and flames were leaping out of the oven.

"Creep in," she said, "and see if it is hot enough."

But Gretel saw that the witch meant to shut the oven door upon her, and let her be baked. So she said, "I don't know how to do it. How shall I get in?"

"Stupid goose," said the old woman, "the opening is big enough, do you see? I could get in myself!" She stooped to put her head in the oven's mouth, and Gretel suddenly gave her a push, so that she went in all the way, and shut the iron door upon her! Then Gretel ran outside and opened the stable door.

"Hansel, we are free!" she cried. "The wicked old witch is dead!"

Out flew Hansel like a bird from its cage, and they danced about and kissed each other! Then they searched the old witch's house, and in every corner found pearls and precious stones.

"Now, away we go," said Hansel, filling his pockets, "if only we can get out of the witch's woods."

When they had journeyed a few hours they came to a lake.

"We can never get across this," said Hansel.

"Here comes a white duck," said Gretel. "Perhaps she will help us over." So she cried:

Duck, duck, here we stand,
Hansel and Gretel, on the land,
Stepping-stones and bridge we lack,
Carry us over on your nice white back.

So the duck carried them over, and after that they went on happily, until they finally saw their father's house. They ran till they reached it, rushed through the door, and fell on their father's neck.

The poor man had not spent a happy hour since he had lost his children. His wicked wife had died, and he had wandered for days through the woods, trying to find his little boy and precious girl.

Then Hansel emptied his pockets, and the pearls and precious stones were scattered all over the floor. So all their cares were at an end, and they lived happily ever after.

# The Brave Mice

*Aesop*

Saying you'll do something may take one kind of courage, but actually doing it requires a different type. Real bravery lies in deeds, not words.

An old cat was in the habit of catching all the mice in the barn.

One day the mice met to talk about the great harm that she was doing them. Each one told of some plan by which to keep out of her way.

"Do as I say," said an old gray mouse that was thought to be very wise. "Do as I say. Hang a bell to the cat's neck. Then, when we hear it ring, we shall know that she is coming, and can scamper out of her way."

"Good! good!" said all the other mice, and one ran to get the bell.

"Now which of you will hang this bell on the cat's neck?" said the old gray mouse.

"Not I! Not I!" said all the mice together. And they scampered away to their holes.

# Chanticleer and Partlet

*Retold by J. Berg Esenwein and Marietta Stockard*

This story comes from the "Nun's Priest's Tale," one of Chaucer's *Canterbury Tales*. It reminds us that there is such a thing as false courage, which may rise from our own vanity. There are some dangers we should rightly fear, and we shouldn't be embarrassed about a proper wariness of them.

Once there was a barnyard close to a wood, in a little valley. Here dwelt a cock, Chanticleer by name. His comb was redder than coral, his feathers were like burnished gold, and his voice was wonderful to hear. Long before dawn each morning his crowing sounded over the valley, and his seven wives listened in admiration.

One night as he sat on the perch by the side of Dame Partlet, his most loved mate, he began to make a curious noise in his throat.

"What is it, my dear?" said Dame Partlet. "You sound frightened."

"Oh!" said Chanticleer, "I had the most horrible dream. I thought that as I roamed down by the wood a beast like a dog sprang out and seized me. His color was red, his nose was small, and his eyes were like coals of fire. Ugh! It was fearful!"

"Tut, tut! Are you a coward to be frightened by a dream? You've been eating more than was good for you. I wish my husband to be wise and brave if he would keep my love!" Dame Partlet clucked, as she smoothed her feathers, and slowly closed her scarlet eyes. She felt disgusted at having her sleep disturbed.

"Of course you are right, my love, yet I have heard of many dreams which came true. I am sure I shall meet with some misfortune, but we will not talk of it now. I am quite happy to be here by your side. You are very beautiful, my dear!"

Dame Partlet unclosed one eye slowly and made a pleased sound, deep in her throat.

The next morning, Chanticleer flew down from the perch and called his hens about him for their breakfast. He walked about boldly, calling, "Chuck! chuck!" at each grain of corn which he found. He felt very proud as they all looked at him so admiringly. He strutted about in the sunlight, flapping his wings to show off his feathers, and now and then throwing back his head and crowing exultantly. His dream was forgotten; there was no fear in his heart.

Now all this time, Reynard, the fox, was lying hidden in the bushes on the edge of the wood bordering the barnyard. Chanticleer walked nearer and nearer his hiding place. Suddenly he saw a butterfly in the grass, and as he stooped toward it, he spied the fox.

"Cok! cok!" he cried in terror, and turned to flee.

"Dear friend, why do you go?" said Reynard in his gentlest voice. "I only crept down here to hear you sing. Your voice is like an angel's. Your father and mother once visited my house. I should so love to see you there too. I wonder if you remember your father's singing? I can see him now as he stood on tiptoe, stretching out his long slender neck, sending out his glorious voice. He always flapped his wings and closed his eyes before he sang. Do you do it in the same way? Won't you sing just once and let me hear you? I am so anxious to know if you really sing better than your father."

Chanticleer was so pleased with this flattery that he flapped his wings, stood up on tiptoe, shut his eyes and crowed as loudly as he could.

No sooner had he begun then Reynard sprang forward, caught him by the throat, threw him over his shoulder, and made off toward his den in the woods.

The hens made a loud outcry when they saw Chanticleer being carried off, so that the people in the cottage nearby heard and ran out after the fox. The dog heard and ran yelping after him. The cow ran, the calf ran, the pigs began to squeal and run too. The ducks and geese quacked in terror and flew up into the treetops. Never was there heard such an uproar. Reynard began to feel a bit frightened himself.

"How swiftly you do run!" said Chanticleer from his back. "If I were you I should have some sport out of those slow fellows who are trying to catch you. Call out to them and say, 'Why do you creep along like snails? Look! I am far ahead of you and shall soon be feasting on this cock in spite of all of you!' "

Reynard was pleased at this and opened his mouth to call to his pursuers; but as soon as he did so, the cock flew away from him and perched up in a tree safely out of reach.

The fox saw he had lost his prey and began his old tricks again. "I was only proving to you how important you are in the barnyard.

See what a commotion we caused! I did not mean to frighten you. Come down now and we will go along together to my home. I have something very interesting to show you there."

"No, no," said Chanticleer. "You will not catch me again. A man who shuts his eyes when he ought to be looking deserves to lose his sight entirely."

By this time, Chanticleer's friends were drawing near, so Reynard turned to flee. "The man who talks when he should be silent deserves to lose what he has gained," he said as he sped away through the wood.

# The Leopard's Revenge

Courage involves knowing what to fear, but that in itself is not enough, as this African folktale reminds us. The father leopard of this story may be circumspect, but his taking revenge on a weaker, innocent party is hardly courageous.

Once a leopard cub strayed from his home and ventured into the midst of a great herd of elephants. His mother and father had warned him to stay out of the way of the giant beasts, but he did not listen. Suddenly, the elephants began to stampede, and one of them stepped on the cub without even knowing it. Soon afterward, a hyena found his body and went to tell his parents.

"I have terrible news," he said. "I've found your son lying dead in the field."

The mother and father leopard gave great cries of grief and rage.

"How did it happen?" the father demanded. "Tell me who did this to our son! I will never rest until I have my revenge!"

"The elephants did it," answered the hyena.

"The elephants?" asked the father leopard, quite startled. "You say it was the elephants?"

"Yes," said the hyena, "I saw their tracks."

The leopard paced back and forth for a few minutes, growling and shaking his head.

"No, you are wrong," he said at last. "It was not the elephants. It was the goats. The goats have murdered my boy!"

And at once he bounded down the hill and sprang upon a herd of goats grazing in the valley below, and in a violent rage killed as many as he could in revenge.

---

# Our Heroes

*Phoebe Cary*

Seeing what is right and doing it with firm resolve, despite the opinions of the crowd, is the mark of moral courage.

Here's a hand to the boy who has courage
To do what he knows to be right;
When he falls in the way of temptation,
He has a hard battle to fight.
Who strives against self and his comrades
Will find a most powerful foe.
All honor to him if he conquers.
A cheer for the boy who says "NO!"

There's many a battle fought daily
The world knows nothing about;
There's many a brave little soldier
Whose strength puts a legion to rout.
And he who fights sin singlehanded
Is more of a hero, I say,
Than he who leads soldiers to battle
And conquers by arms in the fray.

Be steadfast, my boy, when you're tempted,
To do what you know to be right.
Stand firm by the colors of manhood,
And you will o'ercome in the fight.
"The right," be your battle cry ever
In waging the warfare of life,
And God, who knows who are the heroes,
Will give you the strength for the strife.

# The Minotaur

*Adapted from Andrew Lang*

The Greek myth of the thread leading Theseus through King Minos's labyrinth is a story of compassion guiding courage. There are two heroes here: Theseus, who ventures into the maze to save his fellow Athenians, and Ariadne, who searches her heart and realizes she must defy her own father in order to save the doomed Athenians from a cruel fate. Conscience is the root of real courage.

This story begins in Athens, one of the greatest and most noble cities of ancient Greece. At the time it takes place, however, Athens was only a little town, perched on the top of a cliff rising out of the plain, two or three miles from the sea. King Aegeus, who ruled Athens in those days, had just welcomed home a son he had not seen since the child's birth, a youth name Theseus, who was destined to become one of Greece's greatest heroes.

Aegeus was overjoyed at having his son home at last, but Theseus could not help but notice moments when the king seemed distracted and sad. Gradually, Theseus began to sense the same melancholy among the people of Athens. Mothers were silent, fathers shook their heads, and young people watched the sea all day, as if they expected something fearful to come from it. Many of the Athenian youth seemed to be missing, and were said to have gone to visit friends in faraway parts of Greece. At last Theseus decided to ask his father what troubled the land.

"I'm afraid you've come home at an unhappy time," Aegeus sighed. "There is a curse upon Athens, a curse so terrible and strange that not even you, Prince Theseus, can deal with it."

"Tell me all," said Theseus, "for though I am but one man, yet the ever-living gods protect me and help me."

"The trouble is an old one," Aegeus said. "It dates to a time when young men came to Athens from all over Greece and other lands to take part in contests in running, boxing, wrestling, and foot races. The son of the great Minos, king of Crete, was among the contestants, and he died while he was here. His death is still a puzzle to me. Some say it was an accident; others say he was murdered by jealous rivals. At any rate, his comrades fled in the night, bearing the news to Crete.

"The sea was black with King Midas's ships when he arrived seeking vengeance. His army was far too powerful for us. We went humbly out of the city to meet him and ask for mercy. 'This is the mercy I will show you,' he said. 'I will not burn your city, I will not take your treasures, and I will not make your people my captives. But every seven years, you must pay a tribute. You must swear to choose by lot seven youths and seven maidens, and send them to me.' We had no choice but to agree. Every seven years, a ship with black sails arrives from Crete and bears away the captives. This is the seventh year, and the coming of the ship is at hand."

"And what happens to them once they reach Crete?" Theseus asked.

"We do not know, because they never return. But the sailors of Minos say he places them in a strange prison, a kind of maze, called the Labyrinth. It is full of dark winding ways, cut in the solid rock, and therein lives a horrible monster called the Minotaur. This monster has the body of a man, but his head is the head of a bull, and his teeth are the teeth of a lion, and he devours everyone he meets. That, I fear, is the fate of our Athenian youth."

"We could burn the black-sailed ship when it arrives, and slay its sailors," Theseus said.

"Yes, we could," answered Aegeus, "but then Minos would return with his fleet and his army, and destroy all of Athens."

"Then let me go as one of the captives," said Theseus, rising to his feet, "and I will slay the Minotaur. I am your son and heir, and it is only right that I try to free Athens of this awful curse."

Aegeus tried to persuade his son that such a plan was useless, but Theseus was determined, and when the ship with black sails touched the shore, he joined the doomed group. His father came to tell him goodbye for the last time, weeping bitterly.

"If you do manage to come back alive," he said to Theseus, "lower the black sails as you approach, and hoist white sails in their place, so that I may know you did not die in the Labyrinth."

"Do not worry," Theseus told him. "Look for white sails. I will return in triumph." As he spoke, the dark ship put to sea, and soon sailed past the horizon.

After many days' sailing, the ship reached Crete. The Athenian prisoners were marched to the palace, where King Minos sat on his gilded throne, surrounded by his chiefs and princes, all gloriously clothed in silken robes and jewels of gold. Minos, a dark-faced man, with touches of white in his hair and long beard, sat with his elbow on his knee, and his chin in his hand, and he fixed his eyes on the eyes of Theseus. Theseus bowed and then stood erect, with his eyes on the eyes of Minos.

"You are fifteen in number," Minos said at last, "and my law claims only fourteen."

"I came of my own will," answered Theseus.

"Why?" asked Minos.

"The people of Athens have a mind to be free, O King."

"There is a way," said Minos. "Slay the Minotaur, and you are free of my tribute."

"I am minded to slay him," said Theseus, and as he spoke, there was a stir in the throng of chiefs and princes, and a beautiful young woman glided through them, and stood a little behind the throne. This was Ariadne, the daughter of Minos, a wise and tender-hearted maiden. Theseus bowed low, and again stood erect, with his eyes on the face of Ariadne.

"You speak like a king's son," Minos said with a smile. "Perhaps one who has never known hardship."

"I have known hardship, and my name is Theseus, Aegeus's son. I have come to ask you to let me face the Minotaur alone. If I cannot slay it, my companions will follow me into the Labyrinth."

"I see," Minos said. "Very well. The king's son wishes to die alone. Let him do so."

The Athenians were led upstairs and along galleries, each to a chamber more rich and beautiful than they had seen before in their dreams. Each was taken to a bath, and washed and clothed in new garments, and then treated to a lavish feast. None had the appetite to eat, though, except Theseus, who knew he would need his strength.

That night, as he was preparing for bed, Theseus heard a soft knock at his door, and suddenly Ariadne, the king's daughter, was standing in his room. Once again Theseus gazed into her eyes, and saw there a kind of strength and compassion he had never known before.

"Too many of your countrymen have disappeared into my father's Labyrinth," she said quietly. "I have brought you a dagger, and I can show you and your friends the way to flee."

"I thank you for the dagger," Theseus answered, "but I cannot flee. If you wish to show me a way, show me the way to the Minotaur."

"Even if you are strong enough to kill the monster," Ariadne whispered, "you will need to find your way out of the Labyrinth. It is made of so many dark twists and turns, so many dead ends and false passages, not even my father knows the secrets of its windings. If you are determined to go forward with your plan, you must take this with you." She took from her gown a spool of gold thread, and pressed it into Theseus's hand.

"As soon as you get inside the Labyrinth," she said, "tie the end of the thread to a stone, and hold tight to the spool as you wander through the maze. When you are ready to come back, the thread will be your guide."

Theseus gazed at her, hardly knowing what to say. "Why are you doing this?" he finally asked. "If your father finds out, you'll be in great danger."

"Yes," Ariadne answered slowly, "but if I had not acted, you and your friends would be in far greater danger."

And Theseus knew then that he loved her.

The next morning Theseus was led to the Labyrinth. As soon as the guards shut him inside, he fastened one end of the thread to a pointed rock, and began to walk slowly, keeping firm hold of the precious string. He made his way down the broadest corridor, from which others turned off to the right and left, until he came to a wall. He retraced his steps, and tried another hallway, and then another, always stopping every few feet to listen for the monster. He passed through many dark, winding passages, sometimes coming to places he had already been before, but gradually descending further and further into the Labyrinth. Finally he reached a room heaped high with bones, and he knew now he was very near the beast.

He sat still, and from far away he heard a faint sound, like the end of the echo of a roar. He stood up and listened keenly. The sound came nearer and louder, not deep like the roar of a bull, but more shrill and thin. Theseus stooped quickly and scooped up a handful of dirt from the floor of the Labyrinth, and with his other hand drew his dagger.

The roars of the Minotaur came nearer and nearer. Now his feet could be heard thudding along the echoing floor. There was a heavy rustling, then sniffing, then silence. Theseus moved to the shadowy corner of the narrow path and crouched there. His heart was beating quickly. On came the Minotaur—it caught sight of the crouching figure, gave a great roar, and rushed straight for it. Theseus leaped up and, dodging to one side, dashed his handful of dirt into the beast's eyes.

The Minotaur bellowed in pain. It rubbed its eyes with its monstrous hands, shrieking and confused. It tossed its great head up and down, and it turned around and around, feeling with its hands for the wall. It was quite blind. Theseus drew his dagger, crept up behind the monster, and quickly slashed at its legs. Down fell the Minotaur, with a crash and a roar, biting at the rocky floor with its lion's teeth, waving its hands, and clawing at the empty air. Theseus waited for his chance, when the clutching hands rested, and then three times he drove the sharp blade through the heart of the Minotaur. The body leaped, and lay still.

Theseus kneeled and thanked all the gods, and when he had finished his prayer, he took his dagger and hacked off the head of the Minotaur. With the head in his hand, he began following the string out of the Labyrinth. It seemed he would never come out of those dark, gloomy passages. Had the thread snapped somewhere, and had he, after all, lost his way? But still he followed it anxiously, until at last he came to the entrance, and he sank to the ground, worn out with his struggle and his wanderings.

"I don't know what miracle caused you to come out of the Labyrinth alive," Minos said when he saw the monster's head, "but I will keep my word. I promised you freedom if you slew the Minotaur. You and your comrades may go. Now let there be peace between your people and mine. Farewell."

Theseus knew he owed his life and his country's freedom to Ariadne's courage, and he knew he could not leave without her. Some say he asked Minos for her hand in marriage, and that the king gladly consented. Others say she stole onto the departing ship at the last minute without her father's knowledge. Either way, the two lovers were together when the anchor lifted and the dark ship sailed away from Crete.

But this happy ending is mixed with tragedy, as stories sometimes are. For the Cretan captain of the vessel did not know he was to hoist white sails if Theseus came home in triumph, and King Aegeus, as he anxiously watched the waters from a high cliff, spied the black sails coming over the horizon. His heart broke at once, and he fell from the towering cliff into the sea, which is now called the Aegean.

# Ulysses and the Cyclops

*Retold by Andrew Lang*

This story is from the *Odyssey,* Homer's great epic of the Greek king Odysseus's long journey home after the Trojan War. Of all the Greek heroes, Odysseus was the one whose courage was the most rooted in cleverness. Time after time, when others sank into despair, Odysseus instead summoned his own powers of ingenuity. In this retelling of his famous encounter with the Cyclops Polyphemus, he is called by his Roman name, Ulysses.

Ulysses and his ships reached the coast of the land of the Cyclopes, which means the round-eyed men, men with only one eye apiece, set in the middle of their foreheads. They lived not in houses, but in caves among the hills, and they had no king and no laws, and did not plow or sow, but wheat and vines grew wild, and they kept great flocks of sheep.

There was a beautiful wild desert island lying across the opening of a bay; the isle was full of wild goats, and made a bar against the waves, so that ships could lie behind it safely, run up on the beach, for there was no tide in that sea. There Ulysses ran up his ships, and the men passed the time in hunting wild goats, and feasting on fresh meat and wine. Next day, Ulysses left all the ships and men there, except his own ship, and his own crew, and went out to see what kind of people lived on the mainland, for as yet none had been seen. He found a large cave close to the sea, with laurels growing on the rocky roof, and a wall of rough stones built around a court in front. Ulysses left all his men but twelve with the ship; filled a goat skin with strong wine, put some corn flour in a sack, and went up to the cave. Nobody was there, but there were all the things that are usually in a dairy, baskets full of cheese, pails and bowls full of milk and whey, and kids and lambs were playing in their folds.

All seemed very quiet and pleasant. The men wanted to take as much cheese as they could carry back to the ship, but Ulysses wished to see the owner of the cave. His men, making themselves at home, lit a fire, and toasted and ate the cheeses, far within the cave. Then a shadow thrown by the setting sun fell across the opening of the cave, and a monstrous man entered, and threw down a dry trunk of a tree that he carried for firewood. Next he drove in the ewes of his flock, leaving the rams in the yard, and he picked up a huge flat stone, and set it so as to make a shut door to the cave, for twenty-four yoke of horses could not have dragged away that stone. Lastly the man milked his ewes, and put the milk in pails to drink at supper. All this while Ulysses and his men sat quiet and in great fear, for they were shut up in a cave with a one-eyed giant, whose cheese they had been eating.

Then the giant, when he had lit the fire, happened to see the men, and asked them who they were. Ulysses said that they were Greeks, who had taken Troy, and were wandering lost on the seas, and he asked the man to be kind to them in the name of their chief god, Zeus.

"We Cyclopes," said the giant, "do not care for Zeus or the gods, for we think that we are better men than they. Where is your ship?" Ulysses answered that it had been wrecked on the coast, to which the man made no answer, but snatched up two of the twelve, knocked out their brains on the floor, tore the bodies limb from limb, roasted them at his fire, ate them, and, after drinking many pailfuls of milk, lay down and fell asleep. Now Ulysses had a mind to drive his sword-point into the giant's liver, and he felt for the place with his hand. But he remembered that, even if he killed the giant, he could not move the huge stone that was the door of the cave, so he and his men would die of hunger, when they had eaten all the cheeses.

In the morning the giant ate two more men for breakfast, drove out his ewes, and set the great stone in the doorway again, as lightly as a man would put a quiverlid on a quiver of arrows. Then away he went, driving his flock to graze on the green hills.

Ulysses did not give way to despair. The giant had left his stick in the cave: it was as large as the mast of a great ship. From this Ulysses cut a portion six feet long, and his men cut and rubbed as if they were making a spear shaft. Ulysses then sharpened it to a point, and hardened the point in the fire. It was a thick, rounded bar of wood, and the men cast lots to choose four, who should twist the bar in the giant's eye when he feel asleep at night. Back he came at sunset, and drove his flocks in the cave, rams and all. Then he put up his stone door, milked his ewes, and killed two men and cooked them.

Ulysses meanwhile had filled one of the wooden ivy bowls full of strong wine, without putting a drop of water into it. This bowl he offered to the giant, who had never heard of wine. He drank one bowl after another, and when he was merry he said that he would make Ulysses a present. "What is your name?" he asked. "My name is *Nobody,"* said Ulysses. "Then I shall eat the others first and Nobody last," said the giant. "That shall be your gift." Then he fell asleep.

Ulysses took his bar of wood, and made the point red-hot in the fire. Next his four men rammed it into the giant's one eye, and held it down, while Ulysses twirled it round, and the eye hissed like red-hot iron when men dip it into cold water, which is the strength of iron. The Cyclops roared and leaped to his feet and shouted for help to the other giants who lived in the neighboring caves. "Who is troubling you, Polyphemus," they answered. "Why do you wake us out of our sleep?" The giant answered, "Nobody is killing me by his cunning, not at all in fair fight." "Then if nobody is harming you nobody can help you," shouted a giant. "If you are ill, pray to your father, Poseidon, who is the god of the sea." So the giants all went back to bed, and Ulysses laughed low to see how his cunning had deceived them. Then the giant went and took down his door and sat in the doorway, stretching out his arms, so as to catch his prisoners as they went out.

But Ulysses had a plan. He fastened sets of three rams together with twisted vines, and bound a man to each ram in the middle, so that the blind giant's hands would only feel the two outside rams. The biggest and strongest ram Ulysses seized, and held on by his hands and feet to its fleece, under its belly, and then all the sheep went out through the doorway, and the giant felt them, but did not know that they were carrying out the men. "Dear ram," he said to the biggest, which carried Ulysses, "you do not come out first, as usual, but last, as if you were slow with sorrow for your master, whose eye Nobody has blinded!"

Then all the rams went out into the open country, and Ulysses unfastened his men, and drove the sheep down to his ship and so on board. His crew wept when they heard of the death of six of their friends, but Ulysses made them row out to sea. When he was just so far away from the cave as to be within hearing distance he shouted at the Cyclops and mocked him. Then that giant broke off the rocky peak of a great hill and threw it in the direction of the sound. The rock fell in front of the ship, and raised a wave that drove it back to shore, but Ulysses punted it off with a long pole, and his men rowed out again, far out. Ulysses again shouted to the giant, "If any one asks who blinded you, say that it was Ulysses, Laertes' son, of Ithaca, the stormer of cities."

Then the giant prayed to the Sea God, his father, that Ulysses might never come home, or if he did, that he might come late and lonely, with loss of all his men, and find sorrow in his house. Then the giant heaved and threw another rock, but it fell at the stern of the ship, and the wave drove the ship farther out to sea.

---

# Horatius at the Bridge

*Retold by James Baldwin*

The events surrounding the legend of Horatius are said to have taken place at the end of the sixth century B.C., during Rome's struggle against the Etruscans. The English poet and historian Thomas Macaulay retold the story in his *Lays of Ancient Rome,* from which the verses below are taken.

Once there was a war between the Roman people and the Etruscans who lived in the towns on the other side of the Tiber River. Porsena, the King of the Etruscans, raised a great army, and marched toward Rome. The city had never been in so great danger.

The Romans did not have very many fighting men at that time, and they knew that they were not strong enough to meet the Etruscans in open battle. So they kept themselves inside of their walls, and set guards to watch the roads.

One morning the army of Porsena was seen coming over the hills from the north. There were thousands of horsemen and footmen, and they were marching straight toward the wooden bridge which spanned the river at Rome.

"What shall we do?" said the white-haired Fathers who made the laws for the Roman people. "If they gain the bridge, we cannot hinder them from crossing; and then what hope will there be for the town?"

Now, among the guards at the bridge, there was a brave man

named Horatius. He was on the farther side of the river, and when he saw that the Etruscans were so near, he called out to the Romans who were behind him.

Then out spake brave Horatius,
 The captain of the gate:
"To every man upon this earth
 Death cometh soon or late.
And how can man die better
 Than facing fearful odds,
For the ashes of his fathers
 And the temple of his gods?

"Hew down the bridge with all the speed that you can!" he cried. "I, with the two men who stand by me, will keep the foe at bay."

Then, with their shields before them, and their long spears in their hands, the three brave men stood in the road, and kept back the horsemen whom Porsena had sent to take the bridge.

On the bridge the Romans hewed away at the beams and posts. Their axes rang, the chips flew fast; and soon it trembled, and was ready to fall.

"Come back! Come back, and save your lives!" they cried to Horatius and the two of who were with him.

But just then Porsena's horsemen dashed toward them again.

"Run for your lives!" said Horatius to his friends. "I will keep the road."

They turned, and ran back across the bridge. They had hardly reached the other side when there was a crashing of beams and timbers. The bridge toppled over to one side, and then fell with a great splash into the water.

When Horatius heard the sound, he knew that the city was safe. With his face still toward Porsena's men, he moved slowly backward till he stood on the river's bank. A dart thrown by one of Porsena's soldiers put out his left eye; but he did not falter. He cast his spear at the foremost horseman, and then he turned quickly around. He saw the white porch of his own home among the trees on the other side of the stream.

And he spake to the noble river
  That rolls by the walls of Rome:
"Oh Tiber! Father Tiber!
  To whom the Romans pray,
A Roman's life, a Roman's arms,
  Take thou in charge today."

He leaped into the deep, swift stream. He still had his heavy armor on; and when he sank out of sight, no one thought that he would ever be seen again. But he was a strong man, and the best swimmer in Rome. The next minute he rose. He was halfway across the river, and safe from the spears and darts which Porsena's soldiers hurled after him.

Soon he reached the farther side, where his friends stood ready to help him. Shout after shout greeted him as he climbed upon the bank. Then Porsena's men shouted also, for they had never seen a man so brave and strong as Horatius. He had kept them out of Rome, but he had done a deed which they could not help but praise.

As for the Romans, they were very grateful to Horatius for having saved their city. They called him Horatius Cocles, which meant the "one-eyed Horatius," because he had lost an eye in defending the bridge; they caused a fine statue of brass to be made in his honor; and they gave him as much land as he could plow around in a day. And for hundreds of years afterward—

With weeping and with laughter,
  Still was the story told,
How well Horatius kept the bridge
  In the brave days of old.

---

# The Brave Three Hundred

*Adapted from James Baldwin*

The famous battle at the narrow Pass of Thermopylae took place in 480 B.C., when Xerxes led a Persian army into Greece. Even though they were defeated at Thermopylae, the Spartans' heroic stand against overwhelming odds inspired the Greeks in later resistance and forever made Sparta's name synonymous with courage.

All of Greece was in danger. A mighty army, led by Xerxes, the great king of Persia, had come from the east. It was marching along the seashore, and in a few days would be in Greece. Xerxes had sent messengers into every city and state, demanding that they send him water and earth as symbols that the land and the sea were his. The Greeks refused, and resolved to defend their freedom against the invaders.

And so there was a great stir throughout all the land. The Greeks armed themselves and hurried to go out and drive back their foe.

There was only one way by which the Persian army could go into Greece on that side, and that was through a narrow pass between the mountains and the sea. It was called the pass at Thermopylae, a word which meant "hot gates" because of the hot springs nearby.

This pass was guarded by Leonidas, the king of the Spartans, with only a few thousand troops. They were greatly outnumbered by the Persian army, but they felt confident. They had positioned themselves in the narrowest part of the pass, where a few men armed with long spears could hold back an entire company.

The first Persian wave of attack started toward the pass at dawn. The Spartan scouts reported that there were so many troops, their arrows would darken the sun like a cloud.

"So much the better," Leonidas said. "We can fight better in the shade."

The arrows came down, but the Greeks' shields deflected them, and their long spears held back the Persians who pressed into the pass. The invaders attacked again and again, but each time they were repulsed with terrible losses. At last Xerxes sent forward his best troops, known as the Ten Thousand Immortals, but even they fared no better against the determined Greeks.

After two days of attacks, Leonidas still held the pass. But that night a man was brought to Xerxes' camp. He was a Greek who knew the local terrain well, and he was ready to sell a secret: the pass was not the only way through. A hunters' footpath wound the long way around, to a trail along the spine of the mountain. It was held by only a handful of Greeks. They could be easily routed, and then Xerxes could attack the Spartan army from the rear.

The treacherous plan worked. The men guarding the secret trail were surprised and beaten. A few managed to escape in time to warn Leonidas.

The Greeks knew that if they did not abandon the pass at once, they would be trapped. But Leonidas also knew he must delay Xerxes longer while the Greek cities prepared their defenses. He made his decision. He ordered almost all of his troops to slip through the mountains and back to their cities, where they would be needed. He kept his royal guard of three hundred Spartans as well as a few other troops, and prepared to defend the pass to the end.

Xerxes and his army came forward. The Spartans stood fast, but one by one they fell. When their spears broke, they stood side by side, fighting with swords or daggers or only their fists.

All day long they kept the Persian army at bay. But when the sun went down, there was not one Spartan left alive. Where they had stood was only a heap of the slain, all bristled over with spears and arrows.

Xerxes had taken the pass, but at a cost of thousands of men and a delay of several days. The time cost him dearly. The Greek navy was able to gather its forces, and soon afterward it managed to drive Xerxes back to Asia.

Many years later a monument was erected at the pass of Thermopylae, inscribed in memory of the courageous stand of a few in defense of their homeland:

> Pause, traveler, ere you go your way. Then tell
> How, Spartan to the last, we fought and fell.

---

# Compensation

*Theodosia Garrison*

Teddy Roosevelt said that "far better it is to dare mighty things, to win glorious triumphs, even though checkered by failure, than to take rank with those poor spirits who neither enjoy much nor suffer much, because they live in the gray twilight that knows neither victory nor defeat." This poem reminds us as well that a mighty heart reaches high.

Because I craved a gift too great
For any prayer of mine to bring,
Today with empty hands I go;
Yet must my heart rejoice to know
I did not ask a lesser thing.

Because the goal I sought lay far
In cloud-hid heights, today my soul
Goes unaccompanied of its own;
Yet this shall comfort me alone,
I did not seek a nearer goal.

O gift ungained, O goal unwon!
Still am I glad, remembering this,
For all I go unsatisfied,
I have kept faith with joy denied,
Nor cheated life with cheaper bliss.

---

# A Laconic Answer

This story, another famous anecdote about the Spartans' bravery, is from the time of Philip of Macedon (382–336 B.C.), who forcibly unified most of Greece's cities.

Long ago the people of Greece were not united, as they are today. Instead there were several cities and states, each with its own leader. King Philip of Macedon, a land in the northern part of Greece, wanted to bring all of Greece together under his rule. So he raised a great army and made war upon the other states, until nearly all were forced to call him their king. Sparta, however, resisted.

The Spartans lived in the southern part of Greece, an area called Laconia, and so they were sometimes called Lacons. They were noted for their simple habits and their bravery. They were also known as a people who used few words and chose them carefully; even today a short answer is often described as being "laconic."

Philip knew he must subdue the Spartans if all of Greece was to be his. So he brought his great army to the borders of Laconia, and sent a message to the Spartans.

"If you do not submit at once," he threatened them, "I will invade your country. And if I invade, I will pillage and burn everything you hold dear. If I march into Laconia, I will level your great city to the ground."

In a few days, Philip received an answer. When he opened the letter, he found only one word written there.

That word was "IF."

---

# If—

*Rudyard Kipling*

Brave men and women (as well as cowardly men and women) are not born that way; they become that way through their acts. Here are the acts that make us not just grow up, but grow up well.

If you can keep your head when all about you
Are losing theirs and blaming it on you;
If you can trust yourself when all men doubt you,
But make allowance for their doubting too;
If you can wait and not be tired by waiting,
Or, being lied about, don't deal in lies,
Or, being hated, don't give way to hating,
And yet don't look too good, nor talk too wise;

If you can dream—and not make dreams your master;
If you can think—and not make thoughts your aim;
If you can meet with triumph and disaster
And treat those two impostors just the same;
If you can bear to hear the truth you've spoken
Twisted by knaves to make a trap for fools,
Or watch the things you gave your life to broken,
And stoop and build 'em up with worn-out tools;

If you can make one heap of all your winnings
  And risk it on one turn of pitch-and-toss,
And lose, and start again at your beginnings
  And never breathe a word about your loss;
If you can force your heart and nerve and sinew
  To serve your turn long after they are gone,
And so hold on when there is nothing in you
  Except the Will which says to them: "Hold on!"

If you can talk with crowds and keep your virtue,
  Or walk with kings—nor lose the common touch;
If neither foes nor loving friends can hurt you;
  If all men count with you, but none too much;
If you can fill the unforgiving minute
  With sixty seconds' worth of distance run—
Yours is the Earth and everything that's in it,
  And—which is more—you'll be a Man, my son!

---

# Crossing the Rubicon

*Adapted from James Baldwin*

In Roman days the Rubicon, a stream in north-central Italy, marked the boundary between Italy and Gaul. By law, Roman magistrates could bring armies into Italy only by permission of the Senate. By marching his legions across the Rubicon in 49 B.C., Julius Caesar committed himself to a showdown with Rome itself.

Rome was the most powerful city in the world. The Romans had conquered all the countries on the north side of the Mediterranean Sea and most of those on the south side. They also occupied the islands of the sea and all that part of Asia that now belongs to Turkey.

Julius Caesar had become the hero of Rome. He had led a large army into Gaul, that part of Europe which today includes France,

Belgium, and Switzerland, and turned it into a Roman province. He had crossed the Rhine and subdued a part of Germany. Caesar's army even went into Britain, a wild and remote country to the Romans, and established colonies there.

For nine years Caesar and his army had served Rome loyally and well. But Caesar had many enemies at home, people who feared his ambitions and envied his accomplishments, people who cringed every time they heard Caesar called a great hero.

One of these persons was Pompey, who had long been the most powerful man in Rome. Like Caesar, he was the commander of a great army, but his troops had done very little to win the applause of the people. Pompey saw that, unless something occurred to prevent it, Caesar would in time be his master. He therefore began to lay plans to destroy him.

In another year the time of Caesar's service in Gaul would end. It was understood that he would then return home and be elected consul, or ruler, of the mighty Roman republic. He would then be the most powerful man in the world.

Pompey and other enemies of Caesar were determined to prevent this. They induced the Roman Senate to send a command to Caesar to leave his army in Gaul and come at once to Rome. "If you do not obey this command," said the Senate, "you shall be considered an enemy to the republic."

Caesar knew what that meant. If he went to Rome alone, his enemies would make false accusations against him. They would try him for treason, and keep him from being elected consul.

He called the soldiers of his favorite legion together and told them about the plot that had been made for his ruin. The veterans who had followed him through so many perils, and had helped him win so many victories, declared they would not leave him. They would go with him to Rome and see that he received his due rewards. They would serve without pay, and even share the expenses of the long march.

The troops started toward Italy with flags flying. The soldiers were even more enthusiastic than Caesar himself. They climbed mountains, waded rivers, endured fatigue, faced all kinds of dangers for the sake of their leader.

At last they came to a little river called the Rubicon. It was the boundary line of Caesar's province of Gaul; on the other side lay Italy. Caesar paused a moment on the bank.

He knew that to cross the stream would be to declare war

against Pompey and the Roman Senate. It might involve all Rome in a fearful strife, the end of which no man could foresee.

"We could still go back," he told himself. "Behind us lies safety. But once we cross the Rubicon into Italy, turning around is impossible. I must make the choice here."

He did not hesitate long. He gave the word, and rode boldly across the shallow stream.

"We have crossed the Rubicon!" he cried as he reached the far shore. "There is no turning back."

The news was shouted along the roads and byways leading to Rome: Caesar had crossed the Rubicon! People from every town and village turned out to welcome the returning hero as he marched through the countryside. The closer he drew to Rome, the wilder people celebrated his arrival. Finally Caesar and his army reached the gates of the city. No troops came out to challenge them, and there was no resistance when Caesar marched into the city itself. Pompey and his allies had fled.

For more than two thousand years, men and women facing daring decisions have thought of Caesar at the edge of the stream before they too crossed their Rubicons.

---

# Doors of Daring

*Henry van Dyke*

Barriers are invitations to courage.

The mountains that inclose the vale
    With walls of granite, steep and high,
Invite the fearless foot to scale
    Their stairway toward the sky.

The restless, deep, dividing sea
    That flows and foams from shore to shore,
Calls to its sunburned chivalry,
    "Push out, set sail, explore!"

The bars of life at which we fret,
    That seem to prison and control,
Are but the doors of daring, set
    Ajar before the soul.

Say not, "Too poor," but freely give;
    Sigh not, "Too weak," but boldly try;
You never can begin to live
    Until you dare to die.

---

# William Tell

*Retold by James Baldwin*

This famous story of the legendary Swiss hero William Tell takes place in the early part of the fourteenth century, during the Swiss people's struggle for independence from Austrian rule. It is one of our greatest tales of cool and calm bravery in the face of bullying tyranny.

The people of Switzerland were not always free and happy as they are today. Many years ago a proud tyrant, whose name was Gessler, ruled over them, and made their lot a bitter one indeed.

One day this tyrant set up a tall pole in the public square, and put his own cap on the top of it; and then he gave orders that every man who came into the town should bow down before it. But there was one man, named William Tell, who would not do this. He stood up straight with folded arms, and laughed at the swinging cap. He would not bow down to Gessler himself.

When Gessler heard of this, he was very angry. He was afraid that other men would disobey, and that soon the whole country would rebel against him. So he made up his mind to punish the bold man.

William Tell's home was among the mountains, and he was a famous hunter. No one in all the land could shoot with bow and arrow so well as he. Gessler knew this, and so he thought of a cruel plan to make the hunter's own skill bring him to grief. He ordered that Tell's little boy should be made to stand up in the public square with an apple on his head; and then he bade Tell shoot the apple with one of his arrows.

Tell begged the tyrant not to have him make this test of his skill. What if the boy should move? What if the bowman's hand should tremble? What if the arrow should not carry true?

"Will you make me kill my boy?" he said.

"Say no more," said Gessler. "You must hit the apple with your one arrow. If you fail, my soldiers shall kill the boy before your eyes."

Then, without another word, Tell fitted the arrow to his bow. He took aim, and let it fly. The boy stood firm and still. He was not afraid, for he had all faith in his father's skill.

The arrow whistled through the air. It struck the apple fairly in the center, and carried it away. The people who saw it shouted with joy.

As Tell was turning away from the place, an arrow which he had hidden under his coat dropped to the ground.

"Fellow!" cried Gessler, "what mean you with this second arrow?"

"Tyrant!" was Tell's proud answer, "this arrow was for your heart if I had hurt my child."

And there is an old story, that not long after this, Tell did shoot the tyrant with one of his arrows, and thus he set his country free.

---

# Dolley Madison Saves the National Pride

*Dorothea Payne Madison*

In August 1814, a British army marched on Washington, D.C., thinking that by burning the American capital it could bring an end to the War of 1812. Panic reigned in the city as the red-coated columns approached. Many public records, including the Declaration of Independence, had already been stuffed into linen bags and carted off to Virginia, where they were piled up in a vacant house. Now the roads leading out of town began to fill with fleeing American soldiers and statesmen as well as wagons loaded with families and their valuables.

Dolley Madison, wife of the fourth president, calmly directed evacuation details at the White House. A large portrait of George Washington by Gilbert Stuart hung in the dining room. It would be an unbearable disgrace if it fell into British hands. Mrs. Madison ordered the doorkeeper and gardener to bring it along, but the huge frame was screwed so tightly to the wall that no one could get it down. Minutes ticked by as they tugged and pulled. At last someone found an ax. They chopped the frame apart, removed the canvas, and sent it off for safekeeping. Soon afterward the British entered the District of Columbia, setting fire to the Capitol and the White House.

The rescue of Washington's portrait quickly took its place as one of Americans' most cherished acts of heroism. This letter, written by Dolley to her sister, Anna, even as the city fell, speaks to us of unflinching courage and levelheadedness amid chaos and retreat.

Tuesday, August 23, 1814

Dear Sister:

My husband left me yesterday morning to join General Winder. He inquired anxiously whether I had courage or firmness to remain in the President's house until his return on the morrow, or succeeding day, and on my assurance that I had no fear but for him, and the success of our army, he left, beseeching me to take care of myself, and of the Cabinet papers, public and private. I have since received two dispatches from him, written with a pencil. The last is alarming, because he desires I should be ready at a moment's warning to enter my carriage, and leave the city; that the enemy seemed stronger than had at first been reported, and it might happen that they would reach the city with the intention of destroying it. I am accordingly ready; I have pressed as many Cabinet papers into trunks as to fill one carriage; our private property must be sacrificed, as it is impossible to procure wagons for its transportation.

I am determined not to go myself until I see Mr. Madison safe, so that he can accompany me, as I hear of much hostility toward him. Disaffection stalks around us. My friends and acquaintances are all gone, even Colonel C. with his hundred, who were stationed as a guard in this enclosure. French John [a faithful servant], with his usual activity and resolution, offers to spike the cannon at the gate, and lay a train of powder, which would blow up the British, should they enter the house. To this last proposition I positively object, without being able to make him understand why all advantages in war may not be taken.

Wednesday morning, twelve o'clock. Since sunrise I have been turning my spy-glass in every direction, and watching with unwearied anxiety, hoping to discover the approach of my dear husband and his friends; but, alas! I can descry only groups of military, wandering in all directions, as if there was a lack of arms, or of spirit to fight for their own fireside.

Three o'clock. Will you believe it, my sister? we have had a battle, or skirmish, near Bladensburg, and here I am still, within sound of the cannon! Mr. Madison comes not. May God protect us! Two messengers, covered with dust, come to bid me fly; but here I mean to wait for him. . . . At this late hour a wagon has been procured, and I have had it filled with plate and the most valuable portable articles, belonging to the house. Whether it will reach its destination, the "Bank of Maryland," or fall into the hands of British soldiery, events must determine. Our kind friend, Mr. Carroll, has come to hasten my departure, and in a very bad humor with me, because I insist on waiting until the large picture of General Washington is secured, and it requires to be unscrewed from the wall. This process was found too tedious for these perilous moments; I have ordered the frame to be broken, and the canvas taken out. It is done! and the precious portrait placed in the hands of two gentlemen of New York, for safekeeping. And now, dear sister, I must leave this house, or the retreating army will make me a prisoner of it by filling up the road I am directed to take. When I shall again write to you, or where I shall be tomorrow, I cannot tell!

Dolley

# An Appeal from the Alamo

*William Barret Travis*

The Alamo in San Antonio, Texas, has become an American symbol of unyielding courage and self-sacrifice. A force of Texans captured the mission fort in late 1835 after the outbreak of revolution against the dictatorship of Mexican General Antonio López de Santa Anna. By early 1836, Lieutenant Colonel William Barret Travis and the fort's garrison found themselves hemmed in by a Mexican army swelling to six thousand troops. On February 24, Travis dispatched couriers to nearby Texas towns, carrying frantic appeals for aid. Fewer than three dozen men picked their way through enemy lines to join the Alamo's defenders. The siege continued until March 6, when Santa Anna's forces overwhelmed the fort. The entire garrison was killed, some 180 men, including Colonel Travis, James Bowie, and Davy Crockett.

COMMANDANCY OF THE ALAMO, TEXAS
*February 24, 1836*

*To the People of Texas and All Americans in the World.*
FELLOW CITIZENS AND COMPATRIOTS:

I am besieged by a thousand or more of the Mexicans under Santa Anna. I have sustained a continual bombardment and cannonade for twenty-four hours and have not lost a man. The enemy has demanded a surrender at discretion; otherwise the garrison are to be put to the sword if the fort is taken. I have answered the demand with a cannon shot, and our flag still waves proudly from the walls. *I shall never surrender nor retreat.* Then, I call on you in the name of Liberty, of patriotism, and of everything dear to the American character, to come to our aid with all dispatch. The enemy is receiving reinforcements daily and will no doubt increase to three or four thousand in four or five days. If this call is neglected, I am determined to sustain myself as long as possible and die like a soldier who never forgets what is due to his own honor and that of his country.

VICTORY OR DEATH.

WILLIAM BARRET TRAVIS
*Lieutenant Colonel, Commandant*

---

# Susan B. Anthony

*Joanna Strong and Tom B. Leonard*

The Nineteenth Amendment to the Constitution, which provides for full woman suffrage, was not ratified until fourteen years after Susan B. Anthony's death in 1906. Nevertheless, her name more than any other is associated with American women's long struggle to vote. Her firm resolve made her one of our greatest examples of political courage.

"What the blazes are you doing here?" shouted the man at the big desk. "You women go home about your business. Go home and wash the dishes. And if you don't clear out of here fast, I'll get the cops to put you out!"

Everybody in the store stopped and listened. Some of the men just turned around and sneered. Others looked at the fifteen women mockingly and guffawed. One man piped, "Beat it, youse dames. Your kids are dirty." And at that, every man in the place bellowed with laughter.

But this banter didn't faze the tall, dignified woman who stood with a piece of paper in her hand at the head of the fourteen other ladies. She didn't budge an inch.

"I've come here to vote for the President of the United States," she said. "He will be my President as well as yours. We are the women who bear the children who will defend this country. We are the women who make your homes, who bake your bread, who rear your sons and give you daughters. We women are citizens of this country just as much as you are, and we insist on voting for the man who is to be the leader of this government."

Her words rang out with the clearness of a bell, and they struck to the heart. No man in the place dared move now. The big man at the desk who had threatened her was turned to stone. And then, in silence and dignity, Susan B. Anthony strode up to the ballot box and dropped into it the paper bearing her vote. Each of the other fourteen women did the same, while every man in the room stood silent and watched.

It was the year 1872. Too long now had women been denied the rights that should naturally be theirs. Too long now had they endured the injustice of an unfair law—a law that made them mere possessions of men.

Women could earn money, but they might not own it. If a woman was married and went to work, every penny she earned became the property of her husband. In 1872, a man was considered complete master of the household. His wife was taken to be incapable of managing her own affairs. She was supposed to be a nitwit unable to think clearly, and therefore the law mercifully protected her by appointing a guardian—a male guardian, of course—over any property that she was lucky enough to possess.

Women like Susan Anthony writhed at this injustice. Susan saw no reason why her sex should be discriminated against. "Why should only men make the laws?" she cried. "Why should men forge the chains that bind us down? No!" she exclaimed. "It is up to us women to fight for our rights." And then she vowed that she would carry on an everlasting battle, as long as the Lord gave her strength to see that women were made equal in the sight of the law.

And fight she did. Susan B. Anthony was America's greatest champion of women's rights. She traveled unceasingly, from one end of the country to the other. She made thousands of speeches, pleading with men, and trying to arouse women to fight for their rights. She wrote hundreds of pamphlets and letters of protest. It was a bitter and difficult struggle that she entered upon, for the people who opposed her did not hesitate to say all kinds of ugly and untrue things about her and her followers. "No decent woman would talk like that. No refined lady would force her way before judges and men's associations and insist on talking. She is vulgar!"

Many women who knew that Susan Anthony was a refined, intelligent, and courageous woman were afraid to say so. They were afraid that *they* would be looked down on. But in time, they grew to love her for trying to help them.

After a while, many housewives gained courage from her example. Then, in great meetings, they joined her by the thousands. Many a man began to change his notions when his wife, inspired by Susan B. Anthony, made him feel ashamed at the unfair treatment accorded women. Slowly the great Susan B. Anthony was undermining the fierce stubbornness of men.

On that important day in 1872, she and her faithful followers cast their first ballots for President. But though the men in the polling place were momentarily moved, their minds were not yet opened. In a few days, Susan was arrested and brought before a judge, accused of having illegally entered a voting booth.

"How do you plead?" asked the judge.

"Guilty!" cried Susan. "Guilty of trying to uproot the slavery in which you men have placed us women. Guilty of trying to make you see that we mothers are as important to this country as are the men. Guilty of trying to lift the standard of womanhood, so that men may look with pride upon their wives' awareness of public affairs."

And then, before the judge could recover from this onslaught, she added, "But, Your Honor, *not* guilty of acting against the Constitution of the United States, which says that no person is to be deprived of equal rights under the law. Equal rights!" she thundered. "How can it be said that we women have equal rights, when it is you and you alone who take upon yourselves the right to make the laws, the right to choose your representatives, the right to send only sons to higher education. You, you blind men, have become slaveholders of your own mothers and wives."

The judge was taken aback. Never before had he heard these ideas expressed to him in such a forceful manner. However, the law was the law! The judge spoke quietly, and without much conviction. "I am forced to fine you one hundred dollars," he said.

"I will not pay it!" said Susan Anthony. "Mark my words, the law will be changed!" And with that, she strode from the court.

"Shall I follow her and bring her back?" said the court clerk to the judge.

"No, let her go," answered the elderly judge. "I fear that she is right, and that the law will soon be changed."

And Susan did go on, on to further crusades, on across the vast stretches of the United States, proclaiming in every hamlet where her feet trod, her plea for womanhood.

Today, voting by women is an established fact. Women may keep what they earn; and whether married or single, own their own property. It is taken for granted that a woman may go to college and work in any business or profession she may choose. But these rights, enjoyed by the women of today, were secured through the valiant effort of many fighters for women's freedom, such as the great Susan B. Anthony.

# The Things That Haven't Been Done Before

*Edgar Guest*

The ones who dared to do what we now take for granted are the ones we remember.

The things that haven't been done before,
Those are the things to try;
Columbus dreamed of an unknown shore
At the rim of the far-flung sky,
And his heart was bold and his faith was strong
As he ventured in dangers new,
And he paid no heed to the jeering throng
Or the fears of the doubting crew.

The many will follow the beaten track
With guideposts on the way.
They live and have lived for ages back
With a chart for every day.
Someone has told them it's safe to go
On the road he has traveled o'er,
And all that they ever strive to know
Are the things that were known before.

A few strike out, without map or chart,
  Where never a man has been,
From the beaten paths they draw apart
  To see what no man has seen.
There are deeds they hunger alone to do;
  Though battered and bruised and sore,
They blaze the path for the many, who
  Do nothing not done before.

The things that haven't been done before
  Are the tasks worthwhile today;
Are you one of the flock that follows, or
  Are you one that shall lead the way?
Are you one of the timid souls that quail
  At the jeers of a doubting crew,
Or dare you, whether you win or fail,
  Strike out for a goal that's new?

---

# Rosa Parks

*Kai Friese*

Rosa Parks's refusal to "move to the back" of the bus on the evening of December 1, 1955, marked a historic moment: the start of a movement that would bring an end to a tradition of legal segregation across the South and entire nation. Parks certainly never suspected her gesture would turn a new page in the history of American race relations. She didn't move, she later explained, because she was just suddenly fed up with being pushed around. But the courage of the moment sparked the fires of change.

It was Thursday, December 1, 1955. The workday was over, and crowds of people boarded the green-and-white buses that trundled through the streets of Montgomery. Rosa Parks was tired after a full day of stitching and ironing shirts at the Montgomery Fair department store. She thought she was lucky to have gotten one of the last seats in the rear section of the Cleveland Avenue bus that would take her home.

Soon the back of the bus was full, and several people were standing in the rear. The bus rolled on through Court Square, where African-Americans had been auctioned off during the days of the Confederacy, and came to a stop in front of the Empire Theater. The next passenger aboard stood in the front of an aisle. He was a white man.

When he noticed that a white person had to stand, the bus driver, James F. Blake, called out to the four black people who were sitting just behind the white section. He said they would have to give up their seats for the new passenger. No one stood up. "You'd better make it light on yourself and let me have those seats," the driver said threateningly. Three men got up and went to stand at the back of the bus. But Rosa Parks wasn't about to move. She had been in this situation before, and she had always given up her seat. She had always felt insulted by the experience. "It meant that I didn't have a right to do anything but get on the bus, give them my fare and then be pushed around wherever they wanted me," she said.

By a quirk of fate, the driver of the bus on this December evening was the same James F. Blake who had once before removed the troublesome Rosa Parks from his bus for refusing to enter by the back door. That was a long time ago, in 1943. Rosa Parks didn't feel like being pushed around again. She told the driver that she wasn't in the white section and she wasn't going to move.

Blake knew the rules, though. He knew that the white section was wherever the driver said it was. If more white passengers got on the bus, he could stretch the white section to the back of the bus and make all the blacks stand. He shouted to Rosa Parks to move to the back of the bus. She wasn't impressed. She told him again that she wasn't moving. Everyone in the bus was silent, wondering what would happen next. Finally Blake told Rosa Parks that he would have her arrested for violating the racial segregation codes. In a firm but quiet voice, she told him that he could do what he wanted to do because she wasn't moving.

Blake got off the bus and came back with an officer of the Montgomery Police Department. As the officer placed Rosa Parks under arrest, she asked him plainly, "Why do you people push us around?"

With the eyes of all the passengers on him, the officer could only answer in confusion. "I don't know. I'm just obeying the law," he said.

Rosa Parks was taken to the police station, where she was booked and fingerprinted. While the policemen were filling out forms, she asked if she could have a drink of water. She was told that the drinking fountain in the station was for whites only. Then a policewoman marched her into a long corridor facing a wall of iron bars. A barred door slid open. She went inside. The door clanged shut, and she was locked in. She was in jail.

Rosa Parks's decision to challenge her arrest in court led Montgomery's black community to organize a bus boycott as a show of support.

Rosa Parks woke up on the morning of Monday, December 5, thinking about her trial. As she and her husband got out of bed, they heard the familiar sound of a City Lines bus pulling up to a stop across the road. There was usually a crowd of people waiting for the bus at this time. The Parkses rushed to the window and looked out. Except for the driver, the bus was empty and there was no one getting on either. The bus stood at the stop for more than a minute, puffing exhaust smoke into the cold December air as the puzzled driver waited for passengers. But no one appeared, and the empty bus chugged away.

Rosa Parks was filled with happiness. Her neighbors were actually boycotting the buses. She couldn't wait to drive to the courthouse so that she could see how the boycott was going in the rest of Montgomery. When Fred Gray arrived to drive her to the trial, she wasn't disappointed. Rosa Parks had expected some people to stay off the buses. She thought that with luck, maybe even half the usual passengers would stay off. But these buses were just plain empty.

All over the city, empty buses bounced around for everyone to see. There was never more than the usual small group of white passengers in front and sometimes a lonely black passenger in back, wondering what was going on. The streets were filled with black people walking to work.

As Rosa Parks and her lawyer drove up to the courthouse, there was another surprise waiting for them. A crowd of about five hundred blacks had gathered to show their support for her. Mrs. Parks and the lawyer made their way slowly through the cheering crowd into the courtroom. Once they were inside, the trial didn't take long. Rosa Parks was quickly convicted of breaking the bus segregation laws and fined ten dollars, as well as four dollars for the cost of her trial. This was the stage at which Claudette Colvin's trial had ended seven months earlier. Colvin had had little choice but to accept the guilty verdict and pay the fine.

This time, however, Fred Gray rose to file an appeal on Rosa Parks's case. This meant that her case would be taken to a higher court at a later date. Meanwhile, Mrs. Parks was free to go.

Outside the courthouse, the crowd was getting restless. Some of them were carrying sawed-off shotguns, and the policemen were beginning to look worried. E. D. Nixon went out to calm them, but nobody could hear him in the din. Voices from the crowd shouted out that they would storm the courthouse if Rosa Parks didn't come out safely within a few minutes. When she did appear, a great cheer went up again.

After seeing the empty buses that morning, and this large and fearless crowd around her now, Rosa Parks knew that she had made the right decision. Black people were uniting to show the city administration that they were tired of the insults of segregation. Together, they could change Montgomery. They could do some good.

---

# It Can Be Done

True courage is mixed with circumspection, the kind of healthy skepticism that asks, "Is this the best way to do this?" True cowardice is marked by chronic skepticism, which always says, "It can't be done."

The man who misses all the fun  
Is he who says, "It can't be done."  
In solemn pride he stands aloof  
And greets each venture with reproof.  
Had he the power he'd efface  
The history of the human race;  
We'd have no radio or motor cars,  
No streets lit by electric stars;

No telegraph nor telephone,
We'd linger in the age of stone.
The world would sleep if things were run
By men who say, "It can't be done."

---

# Men Wanted for Hazardous Journey

*Ernest Shackleton*

British Antarctic explorer Sir Ernest Shackleton (1874–1922) placed this advertisement in London newspapers in 1900 in preparation for the National Antarctic Expedition (which subsequently failed to reach the South Pole). Shackleton later said of the call for volunteers that "it seemed as though all the men in Great Britain were determined to accompany me, the response was so overwhelming."

MEN WANTED FOR HAZARDOUS JOURNEY. Small wages, bitter cold, long months of complete darkness, constant danger, safe return doubtful. Honor and recognition in case of success. —Ernest Shackleton.

---

# The End of the Scott Expedition

*Robert Falcon Scott*

In 1910, Captain Robert Falcon Scott, of the British Navy, set sail on a second attempt to reach the South Pole. Two years later, on January 18, 1912, after a treacherous journey across vast stretches of ice-covered Antarctica, Scott and four companions reached their destination, only to find that a rival expedition led by Norwegian explorer Roald Amundsen had beaten them by thirty-five days. They found Amundsen's tent still uncovered by snow.

Disheartened and exhausted, Scott and his party began their seven-hundred mile homeward trek, a journey that would end in tragedy. Food and fuel ran low, temperatures plummeted, and frostbite worsened daily. On March 3, Scott wrote in his diary: "God help us, we can't keep up this pulling, that is certain. Amongst ourselves we are unendingly cheerful, but what each man feels in his heart I can only guess." On March 16, he wrote: ". . . assuredly the end is not far." And finally, on March 29: "It seems a pity, but I do not think I can write more. R. Scott. . . . For God's sake, look after our people."

Scott and two companions made it to within fifteen miles of a supply camp. Months later, a search party found the bodies in their sleeping bags, half buried in snow. Among the records of the trip, they found this last message by Scott to the public, a farewell letter showing, as Scott wrote in an accompanying note, that "Englishmen can still die with a bold spirit, fighting it out to the end."

The causes of the disaster are due not to faulty organisation, but to the misfortune in all risks which had to be undertaken.

1. The loss of pony transport in March 1911 obliged me to start later than I had intended, and obliged the limits of stuff transported to be narrowed.

2. The weather throughout the outward journey, and especially the long gale in 83° S., stopped us.

3. The soft snow in lower reaches of glacier again reduced pace.

We fought these untoward events with a will and conquered, but it cut into our provision reserve.

Every detail of our food supplies, clothing and depots made on the interior ice-sheet and over that long stretch of 700 miles to the Pole and back, worked out to perfection. The advance party would have returned to the glacier in fine form and with surplus of food, but for the astonishing failure of the man whom we had least expected to fail. Edgar Evans was thought the strongest man of the party.

The Beardmore Glacier is not difficult in fine weather, but on our return we did not get a single completely fine day; this with a sick companion enormously increased our anxieties.

As I have said elsewhere we got into frightfully rough ice and Edgar Evans received a concussion of the brain—he died a natural death, but left us a shaken party with the season unduly advanced.

But all the facts above enumerated were as nothing to the surprise which awaited us on the Barrier. I maintain that our arrangements for returning were quite adequate, and that no one in the world would have expected the temperatures and surfaces which we encountered at this time of the year. On the summit in lat. 85° 86° we had −20°, −30°. On the Barrier in lat. 80°, 10,000 feet lower, we had −30° in the day, −47° at night pretty regularly, with continuous head wind during our day marches. It is clear that these circumstances come on very suddenly, and our wreck is certainly due to this sudden advent of severe weather, which does not seem to have any satisfactory cause. I do not think human beings ever came through such a month as we have come through, and we should have got through in spite of the weather but for the sickening of a second companion, Captain Oates, and a shortage of fuel in our depots for which I cannot account, and finally, but for the storm which has fallen on us within 11 miles of the depot at which we hoped to secure our final supplies.

Surely misfortune could scarcely have exceeded this last blow. We arrived within 11 miles of our old One Ton Camp with fuel for one last meal and food for two days.

For four days we have been unable to leave the tent—the gale howling about us. We are weak, writing is difficult, but for my own sake I do not regret this journey, which has shown that Englishmen can endure hardships, help one another, and meet death with as great a fortitude as ever in the past. We took risks, we knew we took them; things have come out against us, and therefore we have no cause for complaint, but bow to the will of Providence, determined still to do our best to the last. But if we have been willing to give our lives to this enterprise, which is for the honour of our country, I appeal to our countrymen to see that those who depend upon us are properly cared for.

Had we lived, I should have had a tale to tell of the hardihood, endurance, and courage of my companions which would have stirred the heart of every Englishman. These rough notes and our dead bodies must tell the tale, but surely, surely, a great rich country like ours will see that those who are dependent on us are properly provided for.

R. Scott

---

# The Iron Horse

*Bob Considine*

Lou Gehrig (1903–1941) played a record 2,130 consecutive ballgames for the New York Yankees from June 1, 1925, to May 2, 1939, earning the nickname "the Iron Horse." The power-hitting first baseman hit .300 or better for twelve straight seasons, batted in 100 or more runs for thirteen consecutive years, and hit 493 home runs. The form of spine paralysis that ended his career and eventually his life has come to be known as Lou Gehrig's disease, not just because of the publicity surrounding his sickness, but because of the remarkable courage with which he faced the end.

The Yanks won easily in 1938, Lou's fifteenth year with the ball team. They went on to demolish the Chicago Cubs in the World Series. But Lou's contribution was modest. During the regular season he hit .295, a highly acceptable figure in today's baseball, but a source of great embarrassment for Gehrig in 1938. It was the first time he had hit under .300 since joining the team. DiMag had beat him in home run production the year before. Lou played through the Series against the Cubs, but the four hits he got in fourteen times at bat were all singles.

The first hint I had that Lou's problem was more sinister than a routine slump that year was provided by a wild-and-woolly Washington pitcher named Joe Krakauskas. After a game at Yankee Stadium he told Shirley Povich of the *Washington Post* and me that a frightening thing had happened to him while pitching against Gehrig. Joe had uncorked his high inside fast ball with the expectation that Lou would move back and take it, as a ball. Instead, Krakauskas said, Lou—a renowned judge of balls and strikes—moved closer to the plate.

"My pitch went between his wrists," Joe said, still shaken. "Scared the hell outta me. Something's wrong with Gehrig. . . ."

Lou's salary was cut three thousand dollars a year before he went south with the Yankees in 1939. There was no beef from him. He had had a bum year, for him, so the cut was deserved. He'd come back. After all, the Babe played twenty-two years without ever taking good care of himself. . . .

Joe McCarthy started Gehrig at first base on opening day of the 1939 season, contemptuous of a fan who, a few days before in an exhibition game at Ebbets Field, had bawled, in earshot of both of them, "Hey, Lou, why don't you give yourself up? What do you want McCarthy to do, burn that uniform off you?"

Lou hobbled as far into the 1939 season as May 2. Then, on the morning of the first game of a series against Detroit, he called McCarthy on the hotel's house phone and asked to see him.

"I'm benching myself, Joe," he said, once in the manager's suite. McCarthy did not speak.

"For the good of the team," Lou went on. "I can't tell you how grateful I am to you for the kindness you've shown me, and your patience . . . I just can't seem to get going. The time has come for me to quit."

McCarthy snorted and told him to forget the consecutive-games-played record, take a week or two off, and he'd come back strong.

Gehrig shook his head. "I can't go on, Joe," he said. "Johnny Murphy told me so."

McCarthy cursed the relief pitcher.

"I didn't mean it that way, Joe," Gehrig said. "All the boys have been swell to me. Nobody's said a word that would hurt my feelings. But Johnny said something the other day that made me know it was time for me to get out of the lineup . . . and all he meant to do was to be encouraging."

McCarthy, still angry, asked for details.

"You remember the last play in that last game we played at the Stadium?" Lou asked. "A ball was hit between the box and first base. Johnny fielded it, and I got back to first just in time to take the throw from him."

"So?"

"So, well, I had a hard time getting back there, Joe," Lou said. "I should have been there in plenty of time. I made the put-out, but when Johnny and I were trotting to the bench he said, 'Nice play,

Lou.' I knew then it was time to quit. The boys were beginning to feel sorry for me."

At the urging of his devoted wife, Eleanor, Lou checked into the Mayo Clinic in Rochester, Minnesota. In due time he emerged with a bleak "To Whom It May Concern" document signed by the eminent Dr. Harold C. Harbeing:

"This is to certify that Mr. Lou Gehrig has been under examination at the Mayo Clinic from June 13 to June 19, 1939, inclusive. After a careful and complete examination, it was found that he is suffering from amyotrophic lateral sclerosis. This type of illness involves the motor pathways and cells of the central nervous system and, in lay terms, is known as a form of chronic poliomyelitis—infantile paralysis.

"The nature of this trouble makes it such that Mr. Gehrig will be unable to continue his active participation as a baseball player, inasmuch as it is advisable that he conserve his muscular energy. He could, however, continue in some executive capacity."

Lou returned to the team for the remainder of the 1939 season, slowly suiting up each day, taking McCarthy's lineups to home plate to deliver to the umpires before each game. It was his only duty as captain. It was another winning season for the Yankees, but hardly for Lou. The short walk from the dugout to home plate and back exhausted him. But more exhausting was a cruel (but mostly true) story in the *New York Daily News* to the effect that some of his teammates had become afraid of drinking out of the Yankee dugout's drinking fountain after Lou used it.

"Gehrig Appreciation Day" (July 4, 1939) was one of those emotional salutes which only baseball seems able to produce: packed stands, the prospect of a doubleheader win over the Washington Senators, a peppery speech from Mayor Fiorello La Guardia, the presence of Yankee fan and Gehrig buff Postmaster General Jim Farley, and the array of rheumatic and fattening old teammates of yesteryear. And The Family in a sidelines box. Presents and trophies filled a table.

For Lou, now beginning to hollow out from his disease, one basic ingredient was missing. Babe Ruth wasn't there. Babe, the one he wanted to be there more than he wanted any of his old buddies, had not answered the invitations or the management's phone calls.

Then, with little warning, a great commotion and rustle and rattle in the stadium. The Babe was entering. He magnetized every eye, activated every tongue. Lou wheezed a prayer of thanksgiving.

The ceremony between games of the doubleheader was not calculated to be anything requiring a stiff upper lip. Joe McCarthy's voice cracked as he began his prepared tribute. He promptly abandoned his script and blurted, "Don't let's cry about this . . ." which had just the opposite effect among the fans.

When Lou's turn came, he, too, pocketed the small speech he had worked on the night before. He swallowed a few times to make his voice stronger, then haltingly said:

"They say I've had a bad break. But when the office force and the groundkeepers and even the Giants from across the river, whom we'd give our right arm to beat in the World Series—when *they* remember you, that's something . . . and when you have a wonderful father and mother who worked hard to give you an education . . . and a wonderful wife . . ."

His words began to slither when he tried to say something about Jake Ruppert and Miller Huggins, dead, and McCarthy, Barrow and Bill Dickey, alive.

But nobody missed his ending.

"I may have been given a bad break," he concluded, briefly touching his nose as if to discourage a sniff, "but I have an awful lot to live for. With all this, I consider myself the luckiest man on the face of the earth."

Babe, the irrepressible, stepped forward, embraced him and blubbered, an act that turned out to be epidemic.

Gehrig made the trip to Cincinnati that fall to watch his old club clobber the Reds in the World Series. He had a good time, but some of his friends found it a troubling experience being around him. Going out to dinner one night, with Dickey at his side, Lou staggered and was on the brink of plunging down the long flight of marble steps that led from the lobby of the Netherlands Plaza hotel to the street level. Dicky made one of the better catches of his life and saved Lou from a possibly fatal fall.

Then there was a scene on the train that brought the victorious Yanks back to New York. Lou spotted his friend Henry McLemore of the United Press and invited him into his drawing room for a drink. A table had been set up. Lou slowly but surely put ice in the glasses, then reached for the partly filled fifth of Johnnie Walker Black Label. He wrapped a bony hand around the cork and tried to pull it loose. It was not in tightly, but he did not have the strength to loosen it. Henry stopped listening to what Lou was saying about the Series. He was mesmerized by Lou's struggle, and too reverent of the man to offer to help. Finally, Lou raised the bottle to his lips, closed his teeth on the cork, and let his elbows drop to the table. The cork stayed in his teeth. He removed it, poured the drinks, and went on with what he had been saying.

Henry got very drunk that night.

Just before he died on June 2, 1941, Lou called me from his office. Mayor La Guardia had appointed him to the New York City Parole Board to work with and encourage youthful lawbreakers. Gehrig threw himself into the work with everything he had, or had left. He also kept up a lively interest in research into the disease that had driven him out of baseball.

It was a note about the latter that prompted his phone call.

"I've got some good news for you," he said. "Looks like the boys in the labs might have come up with a real breakthrough. They've got some new serum that they've tried on ten of us who have the same problem. And, you know something? It seems to be working on nine out of the ten. How about that?" He was elated.

I tried not to ask the question, but it came out anyway, after a bit.

"How about *you,* Lou?"

Lou said, "Well, it didn't work on me. But how about that for an average?—nine out of ten! Isn't that great?"

I said yes, it was great.

So was he.

# A Smile

Those who fight the good fight and win need to be brave only once. Those who lose must show courage twice. So we must steel ourselves for harder things than triumph.

Let others cheer the winning man,
There's one I hold worthwhile;
'Tis he who does the best he can,
Then loses with a smile.
Beaten he is, but not to stay
Down with the rank and file;
That man will win some other day,
Who loses with a smile.

---

# The Moses of Her People

*Sarah Bradford*

Harriet Tubman was born into slavery on a Maryland plantation around 1821. Like most slaves, she received no education and could not read or write. In 1844 her owner forced her to marry a fellow slave, John Tubman. One summer night in 1849, she began to walk north toward her freedom. She later returned to help members of her family escape, and eventually made some twenty trips into the South to guide three hundred slaves along the Underground Railroad to Northern havens. With the outbreak of the Civil War, she traveled to South Carolina with the Union army to serve as a nurse, cook, scout, and spy. After the war, she continued to work to improve freed slaves' conditions.

The following account is from the first biography of Harriet Tubman, published in 1869 and in revised form in 1886; it rightly calls her "the Moses of Her People."

One day there were scared faces seen in the Negro quarter, and hurried whispers passed from one to another. No one knew how it had come out, but someone had heard that Harriet and two of her brothers were very soon, perhaps today, perhaps tomorrow, to be sent far south with a gang, bought up for plantation work. Harriet was about twenty or twenty-five years old at this time, and the constantly recurring idea of escape at *sometime,* took sudden form that day, and with her usual promptitude of action she was ready to start at once.

She held a hurried consultation with her brothers, in which she so wrought upon their fears that they expressed themselves as willing to start with her that very night, for that far North, where, could they reach it in safety, freedom awaited them.

The brothers started with her, but the way was strange, the North was far away, and all unknown, the masters would pursue and recapture them, and their fate would be worse than ever before. And so they broke away from her, and bidding her goodbye, they hastened back to the known horrors of slavery, and the dread of that which was worse.

Harriet was now left alone, but after watching the retreating forms of her brothers, she turned her face toward the north, and fixing her eyes on the guiding star, and committing her way unto the Lord, she started again upon her long, lonely journey. Her farewell song was long remembered in the cabins, and the old mother sat and wept for her lost child. No intimation had been given her of Harriet's intention, for the old woman was of a most impulsive disposition, and her cries and lamentations would have made known to all within hearing Harriet's intended escape. With only the North Star for her guide, our heroine started on the way to liberty.

And so without money, and without friends, she started on through unknown regions; walking by night, hiding by day, but always conscious of an invisible pillar of cloud by day, and of fire by night, under the guidance of which she journeyed or rested. Without knowing whom to trust, or how near the pursuers might be, she carefully felt her way, and by her native cunning, or by God-given wisdom, she managed to apply to the right people for food, and sometimes for shelter; though often her bed was only the cold ground, and her watchers the stars of night.

After many long and weary days of travel, she found that she had passed the magic line, which then divided the land of bondage from the land of freedom. But where were the lovely white ladies whom in her visions she had seen, who, with arms outstretched, welcomed her to their hearts and homes? All these visions proved deceitful: she was more alone than ever; but she had crossed the line; no one could take her now, and she would never call any man "Master" more. . . .

It would be impossible here to give a detailed account of the journeys and labors of this intrepid woman for the redemption of her kindred and friends during the years that followed. Those years were spent in work, almost by night and day, with the one object of the rescue of her people from slavery. All her wages were laid away with this sole purpose, and as soon as a sufficient amount was secured, she disappeared from her Northern home, and as suddenly and mysteriously she appeared some dark night at the door of one of the cabins on a plantation, where a trembling band of fugitives, forewarned as to time and place, were anxiously awaiting their deliverer. Then she piloted them north, traveling by night, hiding by day, scaling the mountains, fording the rivers, threading the forests, lying concealed as the pursuers passed them. She, carrying the babies, drugged with paregoric, in a basket on her arm. So she went *nineteen* times, and so she brought away over three hundred pieces of living and breathing "property," with God-given souls. . . .

On one of their journeys to the North, as she was piloting a company of refugees, Harriet came, just as morning broke, to a town where a colored man had lived whose house had been one of her stations of the underground, or unseen railroad. They reached the house, and leaving her party huddled together in the middle of the street, in a pouring rain, Harriet went to the door, and gave the peculiar rap which was her customary signal to her friends. There was not the usual ready response, and she was obliged to repeat the signal several times. At length a window was raised, and the head of a *white man* appeared, with the gruff question, "Who are you?" and "What do you want?" Harriet asked after her friend, and was told that he had been obliged to leave for "harboring niggers."

Here was an unforeseen trouble; day was breaking, and daylight was the enemy of the hunted and flying fugitives. Their faithful leader stood one moment in the street, and in that moment she had flashed a message quicker than that of the telegraph to her unseen Protector, and the answer came as quickly in a suggestion to her of an almost forgotten place of refuge. Outside of the town there was a little island in a swamp, where the grass grew tall and rank, and where no human being could be suspected of seeking a hiding place. To this spot she conducted her party; she waded the swamp, carrying in a basket two well-drugged babies (these were a pair of little twins, whom I have since seen well-grown young women), and the rest of the company following. She ordered them to lie down in the tall, wet grass, and here she prayed again, and waited for deliverance. The poor creatures were all cold, and wet, and hungry, and Harriet did not dare to leave them to get supplies. For no doubt the man at whose house she had knocked, had given the alarm in the town; and officers might be on the watch for them. They were truly in a wretched condition, but Harriet's faith never wavered, her silent prayer still ascended, and she confidently expected help from some quarter or other.

It was after dusk when a man came slowly walking along the solid pathway on the edge of the swamp. He was clad in the garb of a Quaker, and proved to be a "friend" in need and indeed. He seemed to be talking to himself, but ears quickened by sharp practice caught the words he was saying:

"My wagon stands in the barnyard of the next farm across the way. The horse is in the stable; the harness hangs on a nail." And the man was gone. Night fell, and Harriet stole forth to the place designated. Not only a wagon, but a wagon well provisioned stood in the yard; and before many minutes the party were rescued from their wretched position, and were on their way rejoicing to the next town. Here dwelt a Quaker whom Harriet knew, and he readily took charge of the horse and wagon, and no doubt returned them to their owner. How the good man who thus came to their rescue had received any intimation of their being in the neighborhood Harriet never knew. But these sudden deliverances never seemed to strike her as at all strange or mysterious; her prayer was the prayer of faith, and she *expected* an answer.

# Instant Hero

*Blaine Harden*
*from the* Washington Post

On January 13, 1982, Air Florida Flight 90 struck the 14th Street Bridge after taking off from Washington, D.C.'s National Airport and plunged into the icy Potomac River, killing seventy-eight people. Hundreds of commuters, heading home early because of a rare Washington blizzard, stood on the river's banks and watched the torturous rescue attempts. Lenny Skutnik was one who suddenly stopped being a bystander and went into the river to save a life. "Nobody else was doing anything," he later said. "It was the only way."

Lenny Skutnik, who dove into the ice-choked Potomac River Wednesday to save the life of a drowning woman following the jetliner crash in the Potomac, has had little experience in the hero business.

Skutnik, twenty-eight, whose full name is Martin Leonard Skutnik III, is experienced in less exalted matters. He's been a meat-packer, house painter, furniture-plant worker, hamburger cook, and strip-and-wax man at Ralph's supermarket in Simi Valley, California.

Skutnik now works for the Congressional Budget Office, where he runs errands, delivers mail, and makes $14,000 a year. A big night out, Skutnik says, is taking his wife, Linda, and their two sons to Brothers Pizza near their $325-a-month rented town house in Lorton, Virginia. "Every once in a while we'll close our eyes and blow a couple of bucks," he says.

The only other time in his life that he had a chance to be a hero, Skutnik says, he flubbed it. He was anchoring a relay team in a high school race and he could have won the race, but he pooped out and stopped. The coach yelled at him: "You quit, Skutnik. You quit."

Late Wednesday afternoon, as one of hundreds of homeward-bound commuters drawn to the banks of the Potomac by the crash of Air Florida Flight 90, Skutnik, who's never taken a life-saving course, saved a woman who was too weak to grasp rescue rings lowered from a hovering helicopter. Television spread pictures of his valor to the nation.

President Reagan, in a speech yesterday in New York, spoke of Skutnik's bravery: "Nothing had picked him out particularly to be a hero, but without hesitation there he was and he saved her life."

Interviewed yesterday at his home twenty miles south of the 14th Street bridge, Skutnik could offer no fancy explanations for risking his life. "Nobody else was doing anything," he said. "It was the only way."

The woman Skutnik rescued apparently was Priscilla Tirado, whose husband and infant son perished in the crash. Skutnik was sure yesterday he had rescued Kelly Duncan, an Air Florida stewardess, because a woman who identified herself as Duncan's roommate called from Florida to thank him. However, an Air Florida official said last night she had talked to Duncan, who remembers being pulled to shore by a helicopter. Tirado's father said family members recognized his daughter on television as the one Skutnik pulled to safety.

After the rescue, as he waited in an ambulance that had run out of blankets, Skutnik gave his coat to Joseph Stiley, a survivor of the crash who had two broken legs and was shivering. Shirtless and shivering himself, Skutnik, who lost his watch and a cap in the river, was taken to National Hospital for Orthopaedics and Rehabilitation in Arlington for treatment of hypothermnia. He didn't want to go.

"I'd heard all these horror stories about hospitals and all the forms. The first thing I said when I got there was, 'Is this going to cost me anything?' " said Skutnik, who's described by his colleagues at CBO as an exemplary worker.

He was dispatched, free of charge, to a hot tub in the hospital to soak for forty minutes and warm up. When Skutnik got out of the tub, he faced reporters—scores of them, frenzied and facing deadlines. They pushed and shoved to ask him what "it felt like." He had never met a reporter before. He told his story again and again.

Skutnik's instant celebrity began Wednesday afternoon near the 14th Street bridge when traffic in the express lane he was car-pooling home in came to an abrupt stop. Skutnik followed scores of stalled commuters down to the river, where there was a rumor that someone had been hurt. He said he didn't hear the metallic crash of the plane.

From the shore, Skutnik said he saw the partially submerged

plane with a half dozen passengers clinging to it. He saw one spectator tie a rope around his waist and attempt a rescue.

The man who tried to swim out to the wreckage was Roger Olian, thirty-four, a sheet metal worker from Arlington, who was drawn to the accident after getting caught in traffic near the bridge on his way home from work.

"I went in with a makeshift rope that kept getting stuck on the ice," Olian said yesterday. "I was about five feet from the plane when the helicopters arrived. But by then [he'd been in the water more than fifteen minutes] I'd just about had it. I nearly sank, but they pulled me in," said Olian.

Later, when it became obvious that a helicopter could not save the drowning woman, Skutnik said he didn't have any profound thoughts. "I just did it," he said. "When I got out of the water, I was satisfied. I did what I set out to do."

---

# Courage

*John Galsworthy*

Here is the kind of bravery that shoulders another's misfortunes. John Galsworthy (1867–1933) has depicted a particularly dramatic example, but if we look around we'll see the same strong-hearted courage in teachers, ministers, policemen, and others who spend whole lives coming to the rescue.

At that time (said Ferrand) I was in poverty. Not the kind of poverty that goes without dinner, but the sort that goes without breakfast, lunch, and dinner, and exists as it can on bread and tobacco. I lived in one of those fourpenny lodging houses, Westminster way. Three, five, seven beds in a room; if you pay regularly, you keep your own bed; if not, they put someone else there who will certainly leave you a memento of himself. It's not the foreigners' quarter; they are nearly all English, and drunkards. Three quarters of them don't eat—can't; they have no capacity for solid food. They drink and drink. They're not worth wasting your money on—cab runners, newspaper boys, sellers of laces, and what you call sandwich men; three fourths of them brutalized beyond the power of recovery. What can you expect? They just live to scrape enough together to keep their souls in their bodies; they have no time or strength to think of anything but that. They come back at night and fall asleep—and how dead that sleep is! No, they never eat—just a bit of bread; the rest is drink!

There used to come to that house a little Frenchman, with a yellow crow's-footed face; not old either, about thirty. But his life had been hard—no one comes to these houses if life is soft, especially no Frenchman; a Frenchman hates to leave his country. He came to shave us—charged a penny; most of us forgot to pay him, so that in all he shaved about three for a penny. He went to others of these houses—this gave him his income—he kept the little shop next door, too, but he never sold anything. How he worked! He also went to one of your Public Institutions; this was not so profitable, for there he was paid a penny for ten shaves. He used to say to me, moving his tired fingers like little yellow sticks: "Pff! I slave! To gain a penny, friend, I'm spending fourpence. What would you have? One must nourish oneself to have the strength to shave ten people for a penny." He was like an ant, running round and round in his little hole, without any chance but just to live; and always in hopes of saving enough to take him back to France, and set him up there. We had a liking for each other. He was the only one, in fact—except a sandwichman who had been an actor, and was very intelligent, when he wasn't drunk—the only one in all that warren who had ideas. He was fond of pleasure and loved his music hall—must have gone at least twice a year, and was always talking of it. He had little knowledge of its joys, it's true—hadn't the money for that—but his intentions were good. He used to keep me till the last, and shave me slowly.

"This rests me," he would say. It was amusement for me, too, for I had got into the habit of going for days without opening my lips. It's only a man here and there one can talk with; the rest only laugh. You seem to them a fool, a freak—something that should be put into a cage or tied by the leg.

"Yes," the little man would say, "when I came here first I thought I should soon go back, but now I'm not so sure. I'm losing my illusions. Money has wings, but it's not to *me* it flies. Believe me, friend, I am shaving my soul into these specimens. And how unhappy they are, poor creatures; how they must suffer! Drink! you say. Yes, that saves them—they get a little happiness from that. Unfortunately, I haven't the constitution for it—here." And he would show me where he had no constitution. "You, too, comrade, you don't seem to be in luck; but then, you're young. Ah, well, *faut être philosophe*—but imagine what kind of a game it is in this climate, especially if you come from the South!"

When I went away, which was as soon as I had nothing left to pawn, he gave me money—there's no question of lending in those houses: if a man parts with money he *gives* it, and lucky if he's not robbed into the bargain. There are fellows there who watch for a new pair of shoes, or a good overcoat, profit by their wakefulness as soon as the other is asleep, and promptly disappear. There's no morality in the face of destitution—it needs a man of iron, and these are men of straw. But one thing I will say of the low English—they are not bloodthirsty, like the low French and Italians.

Well, I got a job as fireman on a steamer, made a tour tramping, and six months later I was back again. The first morning I saw the Frenchman. It was shaving day. He was more like an ant than ever, working away with all his legs and arms; a little yellower, and perhaps more wrinkled.

"Ah!" he called out to me in French, "there you are—back again. I knew you'd come. Wait till I've finished with this specimen —I've a lot to talk about."

We went into the kitchen—a big stone-floored room, with tables for eating—and sat down by the fire. It was January, but, summer or winter, there's always a fire burning in that kitchen.

"So," he said, "you have come back? No luck? Eh! Patience! A few more days won't kill you at your age. What fogs, though! You see, I'm still here, but my comrade, Pigon, is dead. You remember him—the big man with black hair who had the shop down the street. Amiable fellow, good friend to me, and married. Fine woman his wife—a little ripe, seeing she has had children, but of good family. He died suddenly of heart disease. Wait a bit; I'll tell you about that. . . .

"It was not long after you went away, one fine day in October, when I had just finished with these specimens here, and was taking my coffee in the shop, and thinking of that poor Pigon—dead then just three days—when *pom!* comes a knock, and there is Madame Pigon! Very calm—a woman of good family, well brought up, well made—fine woman. But the cheeks pale, and the eyes so red, poor soul.

" 'Well, Madame,' I asked her, 'what can I do for you?'

"It seems this poor Pigon died bankrupt; there was not a cent in the shop. He was two days in his grave, and the bailiffs in already.

" 'Ah, Monsieur!' she says to me, 'what am I to do?'

" 'Wait a bit, Madame!' I get my hat and go back to the shop with her.

"What a scene! Two bailiffs, who would have been the better for a shave, sitting in a shop before the basins; and everywhere, *ma foi,* everywhere, children! Tk! Tk! A little girl of ten, very like her mother; two little boys with little trousers, and one with nothing but a chemise; and others—two, quite small, all rolling on the floor. And what a horrible noise!—all crying, all but the little girl, fit to break themselves in two. The bailiffs seemed perplexed. It was enough to make one weep! Seven! And some quite small! That poor Pigon, I had no idea!

"The bailiffs behaved very well.

" 'Well,' said the biggest, 'you can have four-and-twenty hours to find this money; my mate can camp out here in the shop—we don't want to be hard on you!'

"I helped Madame to soothe the children.

" 'If I had the money,' I said, 'it should be at your service, Madame—in each well-born heart there should exist humanity; but I have no money. Try and think whether you have no friends to help you.'

" 'Monsieur,' she answered, 'I have none. Have I had time to make friends—I, with seven children?'

" 'But in France, Madame?'

" 'None, Monsieur. I have quarreled with my family; and reflect—it is now seven years since we came to England, and then only because no one would help us.'

"That seemed to me bad, but what could I do? I could only say, 'Hope always, Madame—trust in me!'

"I went away. All day long I thought how calm she was—magnificent! And I kept saying to myself: 'Come, tap your head! Tap your head! Something must be done!' But nothing came.

"The next morning it was my day to go to that sacred Institution, and I started off still thinking what on earth could be done for the poor woman. It was as if the little ones had got hold of my legs and were dragging at me. I arrived late, and, to make up time, I shaved them as I have never shaved them; a hot morning—I perspired! Ten for a penny! Ten for a penny! I thought of that, and of the poor woman. At last I finished and sat down. I thought to myself: 'It's too strong! Why do you do it? It's stupid! You are wasting yourself!' And then, my idea came to me! I asked for the manager.

" 'Monsieur,' I said, 'it is impossible for me to come here again.'

" 'What do you mean?' says he.

" 'I have had enough of your—"ten for a penny"—I am going to get married. I can't afford to come here any longer. I lose too much flesh for the money.'

" 'What!' he says, 'you're a lucky man if you can afford to throw away your money like this!'

" 'Throw away my money! Pardon, Monsieur, but look at me' —I was still very hot—'for every penny I make I lose threepence, not counting the boot leather to and fro. While I was still a bachelor, Monsieur, it was my own affair—I could afford these extravagances. But now—it must finish—I have the honor, Monsieur!'

"I left him, and walked away. I went to the Pigons' shop. The bailiff was still there—Pfui! He must have been smoking all the time.

" 'I can't give them much longer,' he said to me.

" 'It is of no importance,' I replied, and I knocked, and went into the back room.

"The children were playing in the corner, that little girl, a heart of gold, watching them like a mother; and Madame at the table with a pair of old black gloves on her hands. My friend, I have never seen such a face—calm, but so pale, so frightfully discouraged, so overwhelmed. One would say she was waiting for her death. It was bad, it was bad—with the winter coming on!

" 'Good morning, Madame,' I said. 'What news? Have you been able to arrange anything?'

" 'No, Monsieur. And you?'

" 'No!' And I looked at her again—a fine woman; ah! a fine woman.

" 'But,' I said, 'an idea has come to me this morning. Now, what would you say if I asked you to marry me? It might possibly be better than nothing.'

"She regarded me with her black eyes, and answered, 'But willingly, Monsieur!' And then, comrade, but not till then, she cried."

The little Frenchman stopped, and stared at me hard.

"H'm!" I said at last, "you have courage!"

He looked at me again; his eyes were troubled, as if I had paid him a bad compliment.

"You think so?" he said at last, and I saw that the thought was gnawing at him, as if I had turned the light on some desperate, dark feeling in his heart.

"Yes!" he said, taking his time, while his good yellow face wrinkled and wrinkled, and each wrinkle seemed to darken. "I was afraid of it even when I did it. Seven children!" Once more he looked at me. "And since!—sometimes—sometimes—I could—" He broke off, then burst out again.

"Life is hard! What would you have? I knew her husband. Could I leave her to the streets?"

---

# Plato on Fear

*From the* Gorgias

What should we fear?

Socrates spoke of courage as involving a knowledge of what really is to be feared, and he viewed it as an integral part of all virtue, which consists in knowing which things are really good or evil. Furthermore, if moral evil is the only real evil, then the so-called evils that fortune and men inflict upon us, such as poverty, sickness, suffering, and even death, are not to be feared; if they are faced in the proper spirit, they cannot make us morally worse creatures.

Here, near the conclusion of Plato's dialogue *Gorgias,* Socrates calmly and confidently predicts his own unjust death. The sinister trial he envisions (which actually came to pass in 399 B.C.) is not something he fears, because the evil actions of other men cannot harm him morally. There is only one thing Socrates truly fears, and that is to do injustice to others.

*Socrates.* Do not repeat the old story—that he who likes will kill me and get my money; for then I shall have to repeat the old answer, that he will be a bad man and will kill the good, and that the money will be of no use to him, but that he will wrongly use that which he wrongly took, and if wrongly, basely, and if basely, hurtfully.

*Callicles.* How confident you are, Socrates, that you will never come to harm! You seem to think that you are living in another country, and can never be brought into a court of justice, as you very likely may be brought by some miserable and mean person.

Then I must indeed be a fool, Callicles, if I do not know that in the Athenian state any man may suffer anything. And if I am brought to trial and incur the dangers of which you speak, he will be a villain who brings me to trial—of that I am very sure, for no good man would accuse the innocent. Nor shall I be surprised if I am put to death. Shall I tell you why I anticipate this?

By all means.

I think that I am the only or almost the only Athenian living who practices the true art of politics; I am the only politician of my time. Now, seeing that when I speak my words are not uttered with any view of gaining favor, and that I look to what is best and not to what is most pleasant, having no mind to use those arts and graces which you recommend, I shall have nothing to say in the justice court. And you might argue with me, as I was arguing with Polus: I shall be tried just as a physician would be tried in a court of little boys at the indictment of the cook. What would he reply under such circumstances, if someone were to accuse him, saying, "Oh my boys, many evil things has this man done to you: he is the death of you, especially of the younger ones among you, cutting and burning and starving and suffocating you, until you know not what to do; he gives you the bitterest potions, and compels you to hunger and thirst. How unlike the variety of meats and sweets on which I feasted you!" What do you suppose that the physician would be able to reply when he found himself in such a predicament? If he told the truth he could only say, "All these evil things, my boys, I did for your health," and then would there not just be a clamor among a jury like that? How they would cry out!

I dare say.

Would he not be utterly at a loss for a reply?

He certainly would.

And I too shall be treated in the same way, as I well know, if I am brought before the court. For I shall not be able to rehearse to the people the pleasures which I have procured for them, and which, although I am not disposed to envy either the procurers or enjoyers of them, are deemed by them to be benefits and advantages. And if anyone says that I corrupt young men, and perplex their minds, or that I speak evil of old men, and use bitter words toward them, whether in private or public, it is useless for me to reply, as I truly might: "All this I do for the sake of justice, and with a view to your interest, my judges, and to nothing else." And therefore there is no saying what may happen to me.

And do you think, Socrates, that a man who is thus defenseless is in a good position?

Yes, Callicles, if he have that defense, which as you have often acknowledged he should have—if he be his own defense, and have never said or done anything wrong, either in respect of gods or men; and this has been repeatedly acknowledged by us to be the best sort of defense. And if anyone could convict me of inability to defend myself or others after this sort, I should blush for shame, whether I was convicted before many, or before a few, or by myself alone; and if I died from want of ability to do so, that would indeed grieve me. But if I died because I have no powers of flattery or rhetoric, I am very sure that you would not find me repining at death. For no man who is not an utter fool and coward is afraid of death itself, but he is afraid of doing wrong. For to go to the world below having one's soul full of injustice is the last and worst of all evils.

---

# Henry's Speech at Agincourt

*William Shakespeare*

It would be hard to read Henry's address at Agincourt and escape a brief twinge of regret for not having been one of the "happy few" to fight on St. Crispin's day. The scene (from Shakespeare's *King Henry the Fifth*) is the English camp the moment before the battle. The year is 1415. Young King Henry of England has landed a well-equipped army in Normandy and begun a campaign to conquer France. Reaching Agincourt, the English forces found themselves facing a much larger French army. I believe, from my experience, that this speech is the model for all half-time talks given by all football coaches every autumn in America.

*Westmoreland:* O that we now had here
But one ten thousand of those men in England
That do no work today!
*King Henry:* What's he that wishes so?
My cousin Westmoreland? No, my fair cousin.
If we are mark'd to die, we are enow
To do our country loss; and if to live,
The fewer men, the greater share of honour.
God's will! I pray thee, wish not one man more.
By Jove, I am not covetous for gold,
Nor care I who doth feed upon my cost;
It yearns me not if men my garments wear;
Such outward things dwell not in my desires;
But if it be a sin to covet honour,
I am the most offending soul alive.
No, faith, my coz, wish not a man from England.
God's peace! I would not lose so great an honour
As one man more, methinks, would share from me
For the best hope I have. O, do not wish one more!
Rather proclaim it, Westmoreland, through my host,
That he which hath no stomach to this fight,
Let him depart; his passport shall be made
And crowns for convoy put into his purse.
We would not die in that man's company
That fears his fellowship to die with us.
This day is call'd the feast of Crispian.
He that outlives this day, and comes safe home,
Will stand a tip-toe when this day is named,
And rouse him at the name of Crispian.
He that shall live this day, and see old age,
Will yearly on the vigil feast his neighbours,
And say, "To-morrow is Saint Crispian."
Then will he strip his sleeve and show his scars,
And say "These wounds I had on Crispin's day."
Old men forget; yet all shall be forgot,
But he'll remember with advantages
What feats he did that day. Then shall our names,
Familiar in his mouth as household words,
Harry the king, Bedford and Exeter,
Warwick and Talbot, Salisbury and Gloucester,
Be in their flowing cups freshly remember'd.

This story shall the good man teach his son;
And Crispin Crispian shall ne'er go by,
From this day to the ending of the world,
But we in it shall be remembered,
We few, we happy few, we band of brothers.
For he to-day that sheds his blood with me
Shall be my brother; be he ne'er so vile,
This day shall gentle his condition;
And gentlemen in England now a-bed
Shall think themselves accursed they were not here,
And hold their manhoods cheap whiles any speaks
That fought with us upon Saint Crispin's day.

---

## Prisoner of War

*James Bond Stockdale*

Vice Admiral James Bond Stockdale was a prisoner of war for seven and one-half years during the Vietnam war, four of them in solitary confinement. Despite repeated torture, he maintained secret communication with other American POWs and was a leader in setting the policy and standards for the prisoners' resistance to their captors. Stockdale was awarded the Congressional Medal of Honor in 1976 and was a candidate for Vice President of the United States in 1992.

As my last tutorial session came to an end, Dr. Rhinelander reached up to one of his many packed bookshelves and picked out a little, heavily used volume and handed it to me. "As I remember, you are a military man. Frederick the Great carried a copy of this book on all his campaigns. Its author, the Stoic philosopher Epictetus, referred to it as a 'field manual for soldiers,' but you will see that it's a good deal more than that. It is a philosophy for a soldier."

Back home in Los Altos Hills that night, I eagerly opened it.

The essence of good and evil lies in an attitude of the will.

That made sense to me, and then I read on.

> There are things which are within your power, and there are things which are beyond your power. Within your power are opinion, aim, desire, aversion; in a word, whatever affairs are your own. Beyond your power are body, property, reputation, office; in a word, affairs not properly your own. Concern yourself only with what is within your power.
>
> The essence of good consists of things within your own power; with them there is no room for envy or emulation. For your part, do not desire to be a general, or a senator or a consul, but to be free; and the only way to do this is a disregard of things which do not lie within your own power.

"Is Rhinelander crazy?" I thought. . . .

The full message really never struck home until one day on my second combat cruise in Vietnam (a mere three years since I had left Stanford) as I was tooling along at treetop level over familiar territory, dropping snakeye bombs on a railroad yard at about 500 knots. I began hearing, even above the cockpit noise, a "boom" "boom" "boom" and looked up to stare down the barrels of what had to be the biggest anti-aircraft gun in the world. All my red cockpit lights came on, the aircraft caught on fire, and I lost the control system and nosed over abruptly. I pulled the handle and ejected in the nick of time. Almost instantly I was suspended in my parachute just above those trees, drifting along in a silence interrupted only by the rifle shots from the ground below and the whizz of bullets that luckily passed me by only to tear holes in the parachute canopy above me. In the following seconds, so help me, two meaningful thoughts came to my mind before I settled into the village below. The first was: "Five years to wait before I get out of here" (I had just studied enough modern Southeast Asian history to realize that we had programmed ourselves into a quagmire over there—I turned out to be an optimist and underestimated my stay by three years). My second thought was: "You are leaving the world of technology and entering the world of Epictetus."

Well, my "world of Epictetus," I soon learned, was a world in which chivalry, if it ever existed, was dead. I entered a physical world, and I got the hell knocked out of me from the moment my feet hit the ground. The world of Epictetus was also a hard-nosed political world. I had my leg broken in the street by a mob just after

I landed. My leg was either going to get medical aid or remain rigid and deformed for the rest of my life. Some weeks later the man in charge of the prison camps took note of my refusal to make a statement critical of the United States and set me straight on priorities. "You have a medical problem and a political problem. Politics come before medicine in the DRV [Democratic Republic of Vietnam]. You fix the political problem in your head first, and then we'll see the doctors." The leg was never fixed.

I'll never forget my Christmas Day conversation with that same senior Vietnamese officer three months after I had been shot down in September 1965. He said, "You are my age, you and I share the military profession, and we have sons the same age, but there is a wall beween us. The wall is there because we come from different social and political systems. But you and I must try to see through that wall and together bring this imperialist war of American aggression to an end. We know how to do this, but you must help me, you must influence the other American prisoners. Through propaganda [not a "bad word" in Communist circles], we will win the war on the streets of New York. All I ask is that you be reasonable. You will help me. You don't know it yet, but you will."

A week later I heard the church bells of Hanoi ring in the New Year 1966 at midnight. I was shivering without a blanket, legs in stocks, hands in cuffs, lying in three days of my own excrement. That was only the beginning. I became immersed in a system of isolation, of extortion, of torture, of silence. Any American who from his solitary cell was caught communicating with another American, by wall tap, by whisper, you name it, was put back in the meat grinder to go from torture to submission to confession to apology to atonement. That was a hard life, but I'm proud to say that became about the only route to propaganda for them, because we met the challenge by communicating and taking the lumps, by organizing, by resisting in unison, by giving them nothing free, making them hurt us before we gave an inch, by fighting "City Hall."

# Liberty or Death

*Patrick Henry*

A member of Virginia's House of Burgesses and the first Virginia Committee of Correspondence, fierce opponent of the Stamp Act, and delegate to the Continental Congress in 1774–1775, Patrick Henry (1736–1799) was one of the colonies' foremost patriots in the growing revolutionary cause. His oratory gave him lasting fame, and today he is remembered mainly for the fiery speech he gave to the Second Virginia Convention on March 23, 1775, at St. John's Church in Richmond. The question before the Convention was whether to arm the Virginia militia to fight the British. Patrick Henry knew the moment had come for the colonies to gather their strength and commit themselves to action.

Mr. President, it is natural to man to indulge in the illusions of hope. We are apt to shut our eyes against a painful truth—and listen to the song of that siren, till she transforms us into beasts. Is this the part of wise men, engaged in a great and arduous struggle for liberty? Are we disposed to be of the number of those who, having eyes, see not, and having ears, hear not, the things which so nearly concern their temporal salvation? For my part, whatever anguish of spirit it might cost, I am willing to know the whole truth; to know the worst, and to provide for it. . . .

*There is no longer any room for hope.* If we wish to be free—if we mean to preserve inviolate those inestimable privileges for which we have been so long contending—if we mean not basely to abandon the noble struggle in which we have been so long engaged, and which we have pledged ourselves never to abandon until the glorious object of our contest shall be obtained—we must fight!—I repeat it, sir, we must fight! An appeal to arms, and to the God of Hosts, is all that is left us!

They tell us, sir, that we are weak—unable to cope with so formidable an adversary. But when shall we be stronger? Will it be the next week, or the next year? Will it be when we are totally disarmed, and when a British guard shall be stationed in every house? Shall we gather strength by irresolution and inaction? Shall we acquire the means of effectual resistance by lying supinely on our backs, and hugging the delusive phantom of Hope, until our enemies shall have bound us hand and foot? Sir, we are not weak, if we make a proper use of those means which the God of nature hath placed in our power. Three millions of people, armed in the holy cause of liberty, and in such a country as that which we possess, are invincible by any force which our enemy can send against us. Besides, sir, we shall not fight our battles alone. There is a just God who presides over the destinies of nations; and who will raise up friends to fight our battles for us. The battle, sir, is not to the strong alone; it is to the vigilant, the active, the brave. Besides, sir, we have no election. If we were base enough to desire it, it is now too late to retire from the contest. There is no retreat, but in submission and slavery! Our chains are forged, their clanking may be heard on the plains of Boston! The war is inevitable—and let it come! I repeat it, sir, let it come!

It is in vain, sir, to extenuate the matter. Gentlemen may cry, peace, peace—but there is no peace. The war is actually begun! The next gale that sweeps from the north will bring to our ears the clash of resounding arms! Our brethren are already in the field! Why stand we here idle? What is it that gentlemen wish? What would they have? Is life so dear, or peace so sweet, as to be purchased at the price of chains and slavery? Forbid it, Almighty God! I know not what course others may take; but as for me, give me liberty, or give me death!

---

# The Rainy Day

*Henry Wadsworth Longfellow*

Life calls for a variety of everyday fortitudes. They may be less spectacular than the valor of a hazardous climax, but they nevertheless determine what kind of students, spouses, parents, workers, and citizens we are. Facing life's realities, its downs as well as its ups, is one kind of daily courage we all must learn.

The day is cold, and dark, and dreary;
It rains, and the wind is never weary;
The vine still clings to the moldering wall,
But at every gust the dead leaves fall,
   And the day is dark and dreary.

My life is cold, and dark, and dreary;
It rains, and the wind is never weary;
My thoughts still cling to the moldering Past,
But the hopes of youth fall thick in the blast,
   And the days are dark and dreary.

Be still, sad heart! and cease repining;
Behind the clouds is the sun still shining;
Thy fate is the common fate of all,
Into each life some rain must fall,
   Some days must be dark and dreary.

---

# Self-Reliance

*Ralph Waldo Emerson*

"Self-Reliance" may be Ralph Waldo Emerson's best-known work. Published in 1841, when the United States was still a young nation, the essay challenged Americans to know themselves, trust their instincts, and recognize their own genius. The divine sufficiency of the individual was Emerson's crusade; he called for the courage of self-trust.

Man is his own star, and the soul that can
Render an honest and a perfect man,
Command all light, all influence, all fate,
Nothing to him falls early or too late.
Our acts our angels are, or good or ill,
Our fatal shadows that walk by us still.
   —Epilogue to Beaumont and Fletcher's
*Honest Man's Fortune.*

I read the other day some verses written by an eminent painter which were original and not conventional. The soul always hears an admonition in such lines, let the subject be what it may. The sentiment they instill is of more value than any thought they may contain. To believe your own thought, to believe that what is true for you in your private heart is true for all men—that is genius. Speak your latent conviction, and it shall be the universal sense; for the inmost in due time becomes the outmost, and our first thought is rendered back to us by the trumpets of the Last Judgment. Familiar as the voice of the mind is to each, the highest merit we ascribe to Moses, Plato, and Milton is that they set at naught books and traditions and spoke not what men, but what they thought. A man should learn to detect and watch that gleam of light which flashes across his mind from within more than the luster of the firmament of bards and sages. Yet he dismisses without notice his thought, because it is his. In every work of genius we recognize our rejected thoughts; they come back to us with a certain alienated majesty. Great works of art have no more affecting lesson for us than this. They teach us to abide by our spontaneous impression with good-humored inflexibility then most when the whole cry of voices is on the other side. Else, tomorrow a stranger will say with masterly good sense precisely what we have thought and felt all the time, and we shall be forced to take with shame our own opinion from another.

There is a time in every man's education when he arrives at the conviction that envy is ignorance; that imitation is suicide; that he must take himself for better, for worse, as his portion; that, though the wide universe is full of good, no kernel of nourishing corn can come to him but through his toil bestowed on that plot of ground which is given to him to till. The power which resides in him is new in nature, and none but he knows what that is which he can do, nor does he know until he has tried. Not for nothing one face, one character, one fact makes much impression on him, and another none. This sculpture in the memory is not without preestablished harmony. The eye was placed where one ray should fall that it might testify of that particular ray. We but half express ourselves, and are ashamed of that divine idea which each of us represents. It may be safely trusted as proportionate and of good issues, so it be faithfully imparted, but God will not have his work made manifest by cowards. A man is relieved and gay when he has put his heart into his work and done his best; but what he has said or done otherwise shall give him no peace. It is a deliverance which does not deliver. In the attempt his genius deserts him; no muse befriends; no invention, no hope.

Trust thyself; every heart vibrates to that iron string. Accept the place the divine providence has found for you, the society of your contemporaries, the connection of events. Great men have always done so, and confided themselves childlike to the genius of their age, betraying their perception that the absolutely trustworthy was seated at their heart, working through their hands, predominating in all their being. And we are now men and must accept in the highest mind the same transcendent destiny; and not minors and invalids in a protected corner, not cowards fleeing before a revolution, but guides, redeemers, and benefactors, obeying the Almighty effort, and advancing on Chaos and the Dark.

# The Road Not Taken

*Robert Frost*

Courage does not follow rutted pathways.

Two roads diverged in a yellow wood,
And sorry I could not travel both
And be one traveler, long I stood
And looked down one as far as I could
To where it bent in the undergrowth;

Then took the other, as just as fair,
And having perhaps the better claim,
Because it was grassy and wanted wear;
Though as for that the passing there
Had worn them really about the same,

And both that morning equally lay
In leaves no step had trodden black.
Oh, I kept the first for another day!
Yet knowing how way leads on to way,
I doubted if I should ever come back.

I shall be telling this with a sigh
Somewhere ages and ages hence:
Two roads diverged in a wood, and I—
I took the one less traveled by,
And that has made all the difference.

# 7

# Perseverance

"The noblest question in the world," observed Benjamin Franklin in *Poor Richard,* "is What good may I do in it?" "Hang in there!" is more than an expression of encouragement to someone experiencing hardship or difficulty; it is sound advice for anyone intent on doing good in the world. Whether by leading or prodding others, or improving oneself, or contributing in the thick of things to some larger cause, perseverance is often crucial to success.

Drawing on an ancient Chinese proverb, Harry Truman recounted in his *Memoirs* that being president "is like riding a tiger. A man has to keep on riding or be swallowed." He went on to explain that "a President either is constantly on top of events or, if he hesitates, events will soon be on top of him. I never felt that I could let up for a single moment." Perseverance is an essential quality of character in high-level leadership. Much good that might have been achieved in the world is lost through hesitation, faltering, wavering, vacillating, or just not sticking with it.

Perseverance is also essential to the watchdog's and gadfly's approaches to working for good in the world. Socrates, self-acknowledged gadfly of ancient Athens, was absolutely serious in proclaiming at his trial (as recounted in Plato's *Apology*) that "as long as I draw breath and am able, I shall not cease to practice philosophy, to exhort you and in my usual way to point out to any one of you whom I happen to meet: Good Sir, you are an Athenian, a citizen of the greatest city with the greatest reputation for both wisdom and power; are you not ashamed of your eagerness to possess as much wealth, reputation, and honors as possible, while you do not care for or give thought to wisdom or truth, or the best possible state of your soul?" Socrates' persistent exhortations proved too much for many Athenians, however, and he was condemned. But there are worse fates, as Socrates himself pointed out: while he had merely been condemned to *death,* his accusers had by that same act been condemned to *wickedness!*

"Slow and steady wins the race," runs the moral of Aesop's familiar fable of the tortoise and the hare. Plutarch in his *Life of Sertorius* recounts how this great Roman soldier, while serving as praetor in Spain in the first century B.C., contrived a demonstration for his troops to the same effect, following which he addressed them in this manner: "You see, fellow soldiers, that perseverance is more prevailing than violence, and that many things which cannot be overcome when they are together, yield themselves up when taken little by little. Assiduity and persistence are irresistible, and in time overthrow and destroy the greatest powers whatever, time being the favorable friend and assistant of those who use their judgment to await his occasions, and the destructive enemy of those who are unreasonably urging and pressing forward."

Like most other virtues, persistence and perseverance cannot operate for good in the world in isolation from practical intelligence. A person who is *merely* persistent may be a carping, pestering, irksome annoyance, having no salutary effect whatsoever. But given the right context, occurring in the right combination with other virtues, perseverance is an essential ingredient in human progress. Sam Adams saw it thus in the gestation period prior to our birth as a nation. "The necessity of the times," he proclaimed in 1771, "more than ever, calls for our utmost circumspection, deliberation, fortitude, and perseverance." And the same holds true today.

How do we encourage our children to persevere, to persist in their efforts to improve themselves, their own lot, and the lot of others? By standing by them, and with them and behind them; by being coaches and cheerleaders, and by the witness of our own example. Modern technology has made some of this much easier for us. Video and tape recordings are convincing evidence of the long-term progress that is sometimes hard to see in the short term.

## Persevere

Stick-to-it-iveness has a lot to do with getting the right answers in math, English, history, and life, as young Americans of the turn of the twentieth century learned when they memorized this little verse from their *McGuffey's Reader.*

The fisher who draws in his net too soon,
  Won't have any fish to sell;
The child who shuts up his book too soon,
  Won't learn any lessons well.

If you would have your learning stay,
  Be patient—don't learn too fast;
The man who travels a mile each day,
  May get round the world at last.

---

## The Tortoise and the Hare

*Aesop*

As Aesop knew, perseverance makes up for all sorts of disadvantages. Here is a case of virtue outdistancing undisciplined ability.

A hare once made fun of a tortoise. "What a slow way you have!" he said. "How you creep along!"

"Do I?" said the tortoise. "Try a race with me and I'll beat you."

"What a boaster you are," said the hare. "But come! I will race with you. Whom shall we ask to mark off the finish line and see that the race is fair?"

"Let us ask the fox," said the tortoise.

The fox was very wise and fair. He showed them where they were to start, and how far they were to run.

The tortoise lost no time. He started out at once and jogged straight on.

The hare leaped along swiftly for a few minutes till he had left the tortoise far behind. He knew he could reach the mark very quickly, so he lay down by the road under a shady tree and took a nap.

By and by he awoke and remembered the race. He sprang up and ran as fast as he could. But when he reached the mark the tortoise was already there!

"Slow and steady wins the race," said the fox.

---

## The Little Steam Engine

The story of the little engine that said "I think I can!" has been entertaining children for generations. This version, which comes from an early-twentieth-century reader, offers a portrait of self-resolve as well as cooperation. It reminds us that we get through the hardest times and tasks by pushing and pulling together.

A little steam engine had a long train of cars to pull.

She went along very well till she came to a steep hill. But then, no matter how hard she tried, she could not move the long train of cars.

She pulled, and she pulled. She puffed, and she puffed. She backed and started off again. Choo! Choo! Choo! Choo!

But no! The cars would not go up the hill.

At last she left the train and started up the track alone. Do you think she had stopped working? No, indeed! She was going for help.

"Surely I can find someone to help me," she thought.

Over the hill and up the track went the little steam engine. Choo, choo! Choo, choo! Choo, choo! Choo, choo!

Pretty soon she saw a big steam engine standing on a side track. He looked very big and strong. Running alongside, she looked up and said,

"Will you help me over the hill with my train of cars? It is so long and so heavy that I can't get it over."

The big steam engine looked down at the little steam engine. Then he said,

"Don't you see that I am through my day's work? I have been all rubbed and scoured ready for my next run. No, I cannot help you."

The little steam engine was sorry, but she went on. Choo, choo! Choo, choo! Choo, choo! Choo, choo!

Soon she came to a second big steam engine standing on a side track. He was puffing and puffing, as if he were tired.

"He may help me," thought the little steam engine. She ran alongside and asked,

"Will you help me bring my train of cars over the hill? It is so long and so heavy that I can't get it over."

The second big steam engine answered,

"I have just come in from a long, long run. Don't you see how tired I am? Can't you get some other engine to help you this time?"

"I'll try," said the little steam engine, and off she went. Choo, choo! Choo, choo! Choo, choo! Choo, choo!

After a while she came to a little steam engine just like herself. She ran alongside and said,

"Will you help me over the hill with my train of cars? It is so long and so heavy that I can't get it over."

"Yes, indeed!" said the second little steam engine. "I'll be glad to help you, if I can."

So the little steam engines started back to where the train of cars had been standing all this time. One little steam engine went to the head of the train, and the other to the end of it.

Puff, puff! Chug, chug! Choo, choo! Off they started!

Slowly the cars began to move. Slowly they climbed the steep hill. As they climbed, each little steam engine began to sing,

"I—think—I—can! I—think—I—can! I—think—I—can! I—think—I—can! I—think—I—can! I—think—I—can! I—think—I—can! I think I can—I think I can—I think I can I think I can—"

And they did! Very soon, they were over the hill and going down the other side.

Now they were on the plain again, and the little steam engine could pull her train herself. So she thanked the little engine who had come to help her, and said goodbye.

And as she went merrily on her way, she sang to herself,

"I—thought—I—could! I—thought—I—could! I—thought—I—could! I—thought—I—could! I thought I could—I thought I could—I thought I could—I thought I could—I thought I could I thought I could—"

---

# Try, Try Again

'Tis a lesson you should heed,
    Try, try again;
If at first you don't succeed,
    Try, try again;
Then your courage should appear,
For, if you will persevere,
You will conquer, never fear;
    Try, try again.

---

# The Crow and the Pitcher

*Aesop*

This is the famous fable from Aesop which tells us that where there's a will accompanied by practical intelligence, there's a way.

Once there was a thirsty crow. She had flown a long way looking for water to drink.

Suddenly she saw a pitcher. She flew down and saw it held a little water, but it was so low in the pitcher that she could not reach it.

"But I must have that water," she cried. "I am too weary to fly farther. What shall I do? I know! I'll tip the pitcher over."

She beat it with her wings, but it was too heavy. She could not move it.

Then she thought awhile. "I know now! I will break it! Then I will drink the water as it pours out. How good it will taste!"

With beak and claws and wings she threw herself against the pitcher. But it was too strong.

The poor crow stopped to rest. "What shall I do now? I cannot die of thirst with water close by. There must be a way, if I only had wit enough to find it out."

After a while the crow had a bright idea. There were many small stones lying about. She picked them up one by one and dropped them into the pitcher. Slowly the water rose, till at last she could drink it. How good it tasted!

"There is always a way out of hard places," said the crow, "if only you have the wit to find it."

# The Little Hero of Holland

*Adapted from Etta Austin Blaisdell*
*and Mary Frances Blaisdell*

Here is true fortitude: someone doing his duty despite pain and loneliness and danger, someone willing to hold on, hold fast, and hold out as long as it takes, someone whose resolution outweighs even the weight of the sea.

Holland is a country where much of the land lies below sea level. Only great walls called dikes keep the North Sea from rushing in and flooding the land. For centuries the people of Holland have worked to keep the walls strong so that their country will be safe and dry. Even the little children know the dikes must be watched every moment, and that a hole no larger than your finger can be a very dangerous thing.

Many years ago there lived in Holland a boy named Peter. Peter's father was one of the men who tended the gates in the dikes, called sluices. He opened and closed the sluices so that ships could pass out of Holland's canals into the great sea.

One afternoon in the early fall, when Peter was eight years old, his mother called him from his play. "Come, Peter," she said. "I want you to go across the dike and take these cakes to your friend, the blind man. If you go quickly, and do not stop to play, you will be home again before dark."

The little boy was glad to go on such an errand, and started off with a light heart. He stayed with the poor blind man a little while to tell him about his walk along the dike and about the sun and the flowers and the ships far out at sea. Then he remembered his mother's wish that he should return before dark, and bidding his friend goodbye, he set out for home.

As he walked beside the canal, he noticed how the rains had swollen the waters, and how they beat against the side of the dike, and he thought of his father's gates.

"I am glad they are so strong," he said to himself. "If they gave way what would become of us? These pretty fields would be covered with water. Father always calls them the 'angry waters.' I suppose he thinks they are angry at him for keeping them out so long."

As he walked along he sometimes stopped to pick the pretty blue flowers that grew beside the road, or to listen to the rabbits' soft tread as they rustled through the grass. But oftener he smiled as he thought of his visit to the poor blind man who had so few pleasures and was always so glad to see him.

Suddenly he noticed that the sun was setting, and that it was growing dark. "Mother will be watching for me," he thought, and he began to run toward home.

Just then he heard a noise. It was the sound of trickling water! He stopped and looked down. There was a small hole in the dike, through which a tiny stream was flowing.

Any child in Holland is frightened at the thought of a leak in the dike.

Peter understood the danger at once. If the water ran through a little hole it would soon make a larger one, and the whole country would be flooded. In a moment he saw what he must do. Throwing away his flowers, he climbed down the side of the dike and thrust his finger into the tiny hole.

The flowing of the water was stopped!

"Oho!" he said to himself. "The angry waters must stay back now. I can keep them back with my finger. Holland shall not be drowned while I am here."

This was all very well at first, but it soon grew dark and cold. The little fellow shouted and screamed. "Come here; come here," he called. But no one heard him; no one came to help him.

It grew still colder, and his arm ached, and began to grow stiff and numb. He shouted again, "Will no one come? Mother! Mother!"

But his mother had looked anxiously along the dike road many times since sunset for her little boy, and now she had closed and locked the cottage door, thinking that Peter was spending the night with his blind friend, and that she would scold him in the morning for staying away from home without her permission.

Peter tried to whistle, but his teeth chattered with the cold. He thought of his brother and sister in their warm beds, and of his dear father and mother. "I must not let them be drowned," he thought. "I must stay here until someone comes, if I have to stay all night."

The moon and stars looked down on the child crouching on a stone on the side of the dike. His head was bent, and his eyes were closed, but he was not asleep, for every now and then he rubbed the hand that was holding back the angry sea.

"I'll stand it somehow," he thought. So he stayed there all night keeping the water out.

Early the next morning a man going to work thought he heard a groan as he walked along the top of the dike. Looking over the edge, he saw a child clinging to the side of the great wall.

"What's the matter?" he called. "Are you hurt?"

"I'm keeping the water back!" Peter yelled. "Tell them to come quickly!"

The alarm was spread. People came running with shovels, and the hole was soon mended.

They carried Peter home to his parents, and before long the whole town knew how he had saved their lives that night. To this day, they have never forgotten the brave little hero of Holland.

# You Mustn't Quit

When things go wrong, as they sometimes will,
When the road you're trudging seems all uphill,
When the funds are low and the debts are high
And you want to smile, but you have to sigh,
When care is pressing you down a bit,
Rest! if you must—but never quit.

Life is queer, with its twists and turns,
As every one of us sometimes learns,
And many a failure turns about
When he might have won if he'd stuck it out;
Stick to your task, though the pace seems slow—
You may succeed with one more blow.

Success is failure turned inside out—
The silver tint of the clouds of doubt—
And you never can tell how close you are,
It may be near when it seems afar;
So stick to the fight when you're hardest hit—
It's when things seem worst that YOU MUSTN'T QUIT.

---

# The Steadfast Tin Soldier

*Hans Christian Andersen*

This is not a "happily ever after" story, but a tale with a bitter-sweet ending. And therein lies its magic and charm. It teaches us that we prevail by enduring until the very end, whatever that end may be. We do not know what to expect from fortune. We only know what to expect of ourselves. This is a favorite story of the Bennett family.

There were once five and twenty tin soldiers. They were brothers, for they had all been made out of the same old tin spoon. They all shouldered their bayonets, held themselves upright, and looked straight before them. Their uniforms were very smart-looking—red and blue—and very splendid. The first thing they heard in the world, when the lid was taken off the box in which they lay, was the words "Tin soldiers!" These words were spoken by a little boy, who clapped his hands for joy. The soldiers had been given him because it was his birthday, and now he was putting them out upon the table.

Each was exactly like the rest to a hair, except one who had but one leg. He had been cast last of all, and there had not been quite enough tin to finish him. But he stood as firmly upon his one leg as the others upon their two, and it was he whose fortunes became so remarkable.

On the table where the tin soldiers had been set up were several other toys, but the one that attracted most attention was a pretty little paper castle. Through its tiny windows one could see straight into the hall. In front of the castle stood little trees, clustering round a small mirror which was meant to represent a transparent lake. Swans of wax swam upon its surface, and it reflected back their images.

All this was very pretty, but prettiest of all was a little lady who stood at the castle's open door. She too was cut out of paper, but she wore a frock of the clearest gauze and a narrow blue ribbon over her shoulders, like a scarf, and in the middle of the ribbon was placed a shining tinsel rose. The little lady stretched out both her arms, for she was a dancer, and then she lifted one leg so high that the Soldier quite lost sight of it. He thought that, like himself, she had but one leg.

"That would be just the wife for me," thought he, "if she were not too grand. But she lives in a castle, while I have only a box, and there are five and twenty of us in that. It would be no place for a lady. Still, I must try to make her acquaintance." A snuffbox happened to be upon the table and he lay down at full length behind it, and here he could easily watch the dainty little lady, who still remained standing on one leg without losing her balance.

When the evening came all the other tin soldiers were put away in their box, and the people in the house went to bed. Now the playthings began to play in their turn. They visited, fought battles, and gave balls. The tin soldiers rattled in the box, for they wished to join the rest, but they could not lift the lid. The nutcrackers turned somersaults, and the pencil jumped about in a most amusing way. There was such a din that the canary woke and began to speak—and in verse, too. The only ones who did not move from their places were the Tin Soldier and the Lady Dancer. She stood on tiptoe with outstretched arms, and he was just as persevering on his one leg. He never once turned away his eyes from her.

Twelve o'clock struck—crash! up sprang the lid of the snuffbox. There was no snuff in it, but a little black goblin. You see it was not a real snuffbox, but a jack-in-the-box.

"Tin Soldier," said the Goblin, "keep thine eyes to thyself. Gaze not at what does not concern thee!"

But the Tin Soldier pretended not to hear.

"Only wait, then, till tomorrow," remarked the Goblin.

Next morning, when the children got up, the Tin Soldier was placed on the windowsill, and, whether it was the Goblin or the wind that did it, all at once the window flew open and the Tin Soldier fell head foremost from the third story to the street below. It was a tremendous fall! Over and over he turned in the air, till at last he rested, his cap and bayonet sticking fast between the paving stones, while his one leg stood upright in the air.

The maidservant and the little boy came down at once to look for him, but, though they nearly trod upon him, they could not manage to find him. If the Soldier had but once called "Here am I!" they might easily enough have heard him, but he did not think it becoming to cry out for help, being in uniform.

It now began to rain; faster and faster fell the drops, until there was a heavy shower; and when it was over, two street boys came by.

"Look you," said one, "there lies a tin soldier. He must come out and sail in a boat."

So they made a boat out of an old newspaper and put the Tin Soldier in the middle of it, and away he sailed down the gutter, while the boys ran along by his side, clapping their hands.

Goodness! how the waves rocked that paper boat, and how fast the stream ran! The Tin Soldier became quite giddy, the boat veered round so quickly. Still he moved not a muscle, but looked straight before him and held his bayonet tightly.

All at once the boat passed into a drain, and it became as dark as his own old home in the box. "Where am I going now?" thought he. "Yes, to be sure, it is all that Goblin's doing. Ah! if the little lady were but sailing with me in the boat, I would not care if it were twice as dark."

Just then a great water rat, that lived under the drain, darted suddenly out.

"Have you a passport?" asked the rat. "Where is your passport?"

But the Tin Soldier kept silence and only held his bayonet with a firmer grasp.

The boat sailed on, but the rat followed. Whew! how he gnashed his teeth and cried to the sticks and straws: "Stop him! stop him! He hasn't paid his toll! He hasn't shown his passport!"

But the stream grew stronger and stronger. Already the Tin Soldier could see daylight at the point where the tunnel ended; but at the same time he heard a rushing, roaring noise, at which a bolder man might have trembled. Think! just where the tunnel ended, the drain widened into a great sheet that fell into the mouth of a sewer. It was as perilous a situation for the Soldier as sailing down a mighty waterfall would be for us.

He was now so near it that he could not stop. The boat dashed on, and the Tin Soldier held himself so well that no one might say of him that he so much as winked an eye. Three or four times the boat whirled round and round; it was full of water to the brim and must certainly sink.

The Tin Soldier stood up to his neck in water; deeper and deeper sank the boat, softer and softer grew the paper; and now the water closed over the Soldier's head. He thought of the pretty little dancer whom he should never see again, and in his ears rang the words of the song:

Wild adventure, mortal danger,
Be thy portion, valiant stranger.

The paper boat parted in the middle, and the Soldier was about to sink, when he was swallowed by a great fish.

Oh, how dark it was! darker even than in the drain, and so narrow. But the Tin Soldier retained his courage; there he lay at full length, shouldering his bayonet as before.

To and fro swam the fish, turning and twisting and making the strangest movements, till at last he became perfectly still.

Something like a flash of daylight passed through him, and a voice said, "Tin Soldier!" The fish had been caught, taken to market, sold and bought, and taken to the kitchen, where the cook had cut him with a large knife. She seized the Tin Soldier between her finger and thumb and took him to the room where the family sat, and where all were eager to see the celebrated man who had traveled in the maw of a fish. But the Tin Soldier remained unmoved. He was not at all proud.

They set him upon the table there. But how could so curious a thing happen? The Soldier was in the very same room in which he had been before. He saw the same children, the same toys stood upon the table, and among them the pretty dancing maiden, who still stood upon one leg. She too was steadfast. That touched the Tin Soldier's heart. He could have wept tin tears, but that would not have been proper. He looked at her and she looked at him, but neither spoke a word.

And now one of the little boys took the Tin Soldier and threw him into the stove. He gave no reason for doing so, but no doubt the Goblin in the snuffbox had something to do with it.

The Tin Soldier stood now in a blaze of red light. The heat he felt was terrible, but whether it proceeded from the fire or from the love in his heart, he did not know. He saw that the colors were quite gone from his uniform, but whether that had happened on the journey or had been caused by grief, no one could say. He looked at the little lady, she looked at him, and he felt himself melting; still he stood firm as ever, with his bayonet on his shoulder. Then suddenly the door flew open; the wind caught the Dancer, and she flew straight into the stove to the Tin Soldier, flashed up in a flame, and was gone! The Tin Soldier melted into a lump. And in the ashes the maid found him the next day, in the shape of a little tin heart, while of the Dancer nothing remained save the tinsel rose, and that was burned as black as a coal.

# Carry On!

*Robert Service*

Here's another one best read out loud.

It's easy to fight when everything's right,
And you're mad with the thrill and the glory;
It's easy to cheer when victory's near,
And wallow in fields that are gory.
It's a different song when everything's wrong,
When you're feeling infernally mortal;
When it's ten against one, and hope there is none,
Buck up, little soldier, and chortle:

Carry on! Carry on!
There isn't much punch in your blow.
You're glaring and staring and hitting out blind;
You're muddy and bloody, but never you mind.
Carry on! Carry on!
You haven't the ghost of a show.
It's looking like death, but while you've a breath,
Carry on, my son! Carry on!

And so in the strife of the battle of life
It's easy to fight when you're winning;
It's easy to slave, and starve and be brave,
When the dawn of success is beginning.
But the man who can meet despair and defeat
With a cheer, there's the man of God's choosing;
The man who can fight to Heaven's own height
Is the man who can fight when he's losing.

Carry on! Carry on!
Things never were looming so black.
But show that you haven't a cowardly streak,
And though you're unlucky you never are weak.
Carry on! Carry on!
Brace up for another attack.
It's looking like hell, but—you never can tell:
Carry on, old man! Carry on!

There are some who drift out in the deserts of doubt,
And some who in brutishness wallow;
There are others, I know, who in piety go
Because of a Heaven to follow.
But to labor with zest, and to give of your best,
For the sweetness and joy of the giving;
To help folks along with a hand and a song;
Why, there's the real sunshine of living.

Carry on! Carry on!
Fight the good fight and true;
Believe in your mission, greet life with a cheer;
There's big work to do, and that's why you are here.
Carry on! Carry on!
Let the world be the better for you;
And at last when you die, let this be your cry:
*Carry on, my soul! Carry on!*

---

# The Stars in the Sky

*Adapted from Carolyn Sherwin Bailey, Kate Douglas Wiggin, and Nora Archibald Smith*

This old English tale reminds us that the higher we reach, the longer and harder we have to try.

Once upon a time there was a little lass who wanted nothing more than to touch the stars in the sky. On clear, moonless nights she would lean out her bedroom window, gazing up at the thousand tiny lights scattered across the heavens, wondering what it would be like to hold one in her hand.

One warm summer evening, a night when the Milky Way shined more brightly than ever before, she decided she couldn't stand it any longer—she just had to touch a star or two, no matter what. So she slipped out the window and started off by herself to see if she could reach them.

She walked a far, far way, and then farther still, until she came to a mill wheel, creaking and grinding away.

"Good evening," she said to the mill wheel. "I would like to play with the stars in the sky. Have you seen any near here?"

"Ah, yes," groaned the old mill wheel. "Every night they shine in my face from the surface of this pond until I cannot sleep. Jump in, my lass, and you will find them."

The little girl jumped into the pond and swam around until her arms were so tired she could swim no longer, but she could not find any stars.

"Excuse me," she called to the old mill wheel, "but I don't believe there are any stars here after all!"

"Well, there certainly were before you jumped in and stirred the water up," the mill wheel called back. So she climbed out and dried herself off as best she could, and set out again across the fields.

After a while she came to a little brook, murmuring over its mossy stones.

"Good evening, brooklet," she said politely. "I'm trying to reach the stars in the sky so I may play with them. Have you seen any near here?"

"Ah, yes," whispered the brooklet. "They glint on my banks at night until I cannot sleep. Wade in, my lassie, and you will find them."

So the little girl waded in and paddled around for a while, and climbed all over the mossy rocks, but never once did she find a star.

"Excuse me," she said as politely as she could, "but I just don't think there are any stars here."

"What do you mean, no stars here?" the little brook babbled. "There are lots of stars here. I see them all the time. On some nights, they cover me from the edge of the woods all the way down to the old mill pond. I have more stars here than I know what to do with." And the brooklet babbled on and on until it even forgot the little girl was there, so she tiptoed away across the fields.

After a while she sat down to rest in a meadow, and it must have been a fairy meadow, because before she knew it a hundred little fairies came scampering out to dance on the grass. They were no taller than toadstools, but they were dressed in silver and gold.

"Good evening, Little Folk," said the girl. "I'm trying to reach the stars in the sky. Have you seen any near here?"

"Ah, yes," sang the fairies. "They glisten every night among the blades of the grass. Come and dance with us, little lass, and you will find as many stars as you like."

So the child danced and danced, she whirled round and round in a ring with the Little Folk, but though the grass gleamed beneath her feet, she never spied a single star. Finally she could dance no longer, and she plopped down inside the ring of fairies.

"I've tried and I've tried, but I can't seem to reach the stars down here," she cried. "If you don't help me, I'll never find any to play with."

The fairies all whispered together. Finally one of them crept up and took her by the hand, and said: "If you're really determined, you must go forward. Keep going forward, and mind you take the right road. Ask Four Feet to carry you to No Feet At All, and then tell No Feet At All to carry you to the Stairs Without Steps, and if you climb that—"

"Then I'll be among the stars in the sky?" cried the lassie.

"If you'll not be there, then you'll be somewhere else, won't you?" laughed the fairy, and he vanished with all the rest.

So the little girl set out again with a light heart, and by and by she came to a saddled horse, tied to a tree.

"Good evening," she said. "I'm trying to reach the stars in the sky, and I've come so far my bones are aching. Will you give me a ride?"

"I don't know anything about stars in the sky," the horse replied. "I'm here only to do the bidding of the Little Folk."

"But I come from the Little Folk," she cried, "and they said to tell Four Feet to carry me to No Feet At All."

"Four Feet? That's me!" the horse whinnied. "Jump up and ride with me."

They rode and they rode and they rode, till they rode out of the forest and found themselves at the edge of the sea.

"I've brought you to the end of the land, and that's as much as Four Feet can do," said the horse. "Now I must get home to my own folk."

So the little girl slid down and walked along the sea, wondering what in the world she would do next, until suddenly the biggest fish she'd ever seen came swimming up to her feet.

"Good evening," she said to the fish. "I'm trying to reach the stars in the sky. Can you help me?"

"I'm afraid I can't," gurgled the fish, "unless, of course, you bring me word from the Little Folk."

"But I do," she cried. "They said Four Feet would bring me to

No Feet At All, and then No Feet At All would carry me to the Stairs Without Steps."

"Ah, well," said the fish, "that's all right then. Get on my back and hold on tight."

And off he went—kerplash!—into the water, swimming along a silver path that glistened on the surface and seemed to stretch toward the end of the sea, where the water met the sky. There, in the distance, the little girl saw a beautiful rainbow rising out of the ocean and into the heavens, shining with all the colors in the world, blues and reds and greens, and wonderful to look at. The nearer they drew, the brighter it gleamed, until she had to shade her eyes from its light.

At last they came to the foot of it, and she saw the rainbow was really a broad bright road, sloping up and away into the sky, and at the far, far end of it she could see wee shining things dancing about.

"I can go no further," said the fish. "Here are the Stairs Without Steps. Climb up, if you can, but hold on tight. These stairs were never meant for little lassies' feet, you know." So the little girl jumped off No Feet's back, and off he splashed through the water.

She climbed and she climbed and she climbed up the rainbow. It wasn't easy. Every time she took one step, she seemed to slide back two. And even though she climbed until the sea was far below, the stars in the sky looked farther away than ever.

"But I won't give up," she told herself. "I've come so far, I can't go back."

Up and up she went. The air grew colder and colder, but the sky turned brighter and brighter, and finally she could tell she was nearing the stars.

"I'm almost there!" she cried.

And sure enough, suddenly she reached the very tip-top of the rainbow. Everywhere she looked, the stars were turning and dancing. They raced up and down, and back and forth, and spun in a thousand colors around her.

"I'm finally here," she whispered to herself. She had never seen anything so beautiful before, and she stood gazing and wondering at the heavens.

But after a while she realized she was shivering with cold, and when she looked down into the darkness, she could no longer see the earth. She wondered where her own home was, so far away, but no streetlamps or window lights marked the blackness below. She began to feel a little dizzy.

"I won't go until I touch one star," she told herself, and she stood on her toes and stretched her arms as high as she could. She reached further and further—and suddenly a shooting star zipped by and surprised her so much she lost her balance.

Down she slid—down—down—down the rainbow. The further she slid, the warmer it grew, and the warmer it grew, the sleepier she felt. She gave a great yawn, and a small sigh, and before she knew it, she was fast asleep.

When she woke up, she found herself in her very own bed. The sun was peeking through her window, and the morning birds sang in the bushes and trees.

"Did I really touch the stars?" she asked herself. "Or was it only a dream?"

Then she felt something in her hand. When she opened her fist, a tiny light flashed in her palm, and at once was gone, and she smiled because she knew it was a speck of stardust.

---

# The Story of Scarface

*Retold by Amy Cruse*

Webster defines fortitude as "strength or firmness of mind that enables a person to encounter danger with coolness and courage or to bear pain or adversity without murmuring, depression, or despondency." John Locke called it the essential virtue, the "guard to every other virtue." In this Blackfoot Indian tale, we find honesty, loyalty, friendship, courage, self-discipline, and more in a young brave's fortitude.

There lived once among a tribe of Indians a poor boy whose father and mother were dead, and who had no friends to take care of him. The kindly Indian women helped him as well as they could, giving him what they could spare of food and clothing, and shelter in the hard days of winter; and the men let him go with them on hunting expeditions, and taught him the Indian woodcraft, just as they taught their own sons. The boy grew up strong and brave, and the men of the tribe said that he would one day make a mighty hunter. While he was quite young he met on one of the hunting parties a great grizzly bear, and fought a desperate fight with him, and at last killed him. But during the struggle the bear set its claws in the boy's face and tore it cruelly; and when the wound healed there was left a red, unsightly mark, so that he thereafter was called Scarface.

The boy thought little of the disfigurement until he fell in love with the beautiful daughter of the chief of his tribe, and then when he saw all the handsome young braves dressing themselves in the splendid dress of the Indian warrior and going to pay court to this maiden at her father's wigwam, his heart ached very sorely because he was poor and friendless, and above all because he bore upon his face the terrible disfiguring scar.

But the maiden did not care for the finery and boastful talk of the young Indians who crowded round her, and each in turn, when he ventured to ask her hand in marriage, found himself refused. Scarface scarcely dared to approach her, but the girl often saw him as he went about the forest, and she felt that he was braver and truer than the other lovers who boldly sought her favor.

One day, as she sat outside her father's lodge, Scarface passed by, and as he passed he looked at her, and his eyes showed the love and admiration that possessed him. A young Indian whose suit the girl had refused noticed the look, and said with a sneer, "Scarface has become a suitor for our chief's daughter. She will have nothing to do with men unblemished; perhaps she desires a man marked and marred. Try then, Scarface, and see if she will take you."

Scarface felt anger rise hot within him against the man who thus mocked him. He stood proudly, as though he were a chief's son instead of a poor, common, disfigured warrior, and, looking very steadily at the young brave, he said, "My brother speaks true words, though he speaks them with an ill tongue. I go indeed to ask the daughter of our great chief to be my wife."

The young brave laughed loudly in mockery. Some other young men of the tribe came up, and he told them what Scarface had said, and they also laughed, calling him the great chief, speaking of his vast wealth and of his marvelous beauty, and pretending to bow down before him. Scarface took no notice, but walked away quietly and with an unmoved face, though in his heart he yearned to spring at them, as the great grizzly had sprung at him in the forest. But when he came down to the river, following the chief's daughter, who had gone there to gather rushes for the baskets she was weaving, his anger died away. He drew near to her, knowing that if he did not speak at once his courage would leave him, for though she was so gentle and so kind, he trembled in her presence as the fiercest warrior or the most terrible bear could not make him tremble.

"Maiden," he said, "I am poor and little thought of, because I have no store of furs or pemmican, as the great warriors of the tribe have. I must gain day by day with my bow and my spear and with hard toil the means by which I live. And my face is marred and unsightly to look upon. But my heart is full of love for you, and I greatly desire you for my wife. Will you marry Scarface and live with him in his poor lodge?"

The maiden looked at him, and in her face he saw the love for which he asked.

"That you are poor," she said, "matters little. My father would give me great store of all needful things for a wedding portion. But I may not be your bride, nor the bride of any man of the tribe. The great Lord of the Sun has laid his commands on me, forbidding me to marry."

The heart of poor Scarface sank at these terrible words, yet he would not give up hope. "Will he not release you?" he asked. "He is kind and gives us many good gifts. He would not wish to make us both miserable."

"Go to him, then," said the girl, "and make your prayer to him that he will set me free from my promise. And ask him, that I may know that he has done so, to take the scar from off your face as a sign."

"I will go," said Scarface, "I will seek out the bright god in his own land, and beseech him to pity us." So he turned and left the maiden by the riverside.

Scarface started at once on his journey, and traveled for many, many miles. Sometimes he went cheerfully, saying to himself, "The sun god is kind; he will give me my bride." Sometimes his heart was sad, and he went heavily, for he thought, "Maybe the sun god desires to marry her himself, and who could expect him to give up a maiden so beautiful?" Through forests and over mountains he went, searching ever for the golden gates which marked the entrance to the country of the great god. The wild animals he met knew that this time he had not come out as a hunter to take them, so they drew near to him and willingly answered his questions. But not one of them could tell him where lay the sun god's land. "We have not traveled beyond the forest," they said. "Perhaps the birds, who fly swiftly and very far, can tell you what you want to know."

Scarface called to the birds who were flying overhead, and they came down and listened. But they answered, "We fly far and see many things, but we have never seen two gleaming gates of gold, nor looked on the face of the bright god of the sun."

Scarface was disappointed, but he went bravely on. One day, when he was very weary, he met a wolverine and asked him the question he had asked so many times before. To his great joy the wolverine answered, "I have seen the gleaming gates, and have entered the bright country of the Lord of the Sun. But the way to it is long and hard, and you will be tired indeed when you reach the end of your journey. I will put you on your way, and if your heart does not fail you, someday you will see what I have seen."

With fresh courage Scarface went on. Day after day he journeyed, walking until he was weary, and taking but short rest. Each morning when he started he had hope that evening would bring him to the golden gates, and then one day he came to a great water, very broad and deep, so that he could not cross it.

Now it seemed that his labor and weariness had been all for nothing, and he sat down on the shore of the great water and felt hope dying out of his heart. But very soon he saw drawing near to him from the other side two beautiful swans. "We will take you across," they said. "Step on our backs and we will swim with you to the farther shore." Up started Scarface, joyful once again, and poised himself carefully on the backs of the two swans; and they glided across and landed him safely on the opposite shore.

"You seek the kingdom of the sun god?" they said. "Go then along the road that lies before you, and you will soon come to it." Scarface thanked them with all his heart. He felt happier than he had done since he had started on his journey, and he walked along with quick, light steps. He had not gone far when he saw lying on the ground a very beautiful bow and arrows. He stopped for a moment to look at them. "These belong to some mighty hunter," he thought, "they are finer than those of a common warrior." But he left them lying where he found them, for though his hunter's heart coveted them, Scarface was honest, and would not take what was not his own. He went on, even lighter of heart than before, and soon he saw a beautiful youth coming gaily along the road toward him. It seemed to Scarface that a soft, bright light shone around as the youth stopped and said, "I have lost a bow and arrows somewhere along the road. Have you seen them?"

"They lie but a little distance behind me," said Scarface, "I have but just passed them."

"Thank you many times," said the youth. "It is well for me that it was an honest man who passed, or I should never have seen my bow and arrows again." He smiled at Scarface, and the Indian felt great joy in his heart, and all the air seemed flecked with golden points of light. "Where are you going?" inquired the stranger.

And Scarface answered, "I seek the land of the great Lord of the Sun, and I believe it is very near."

"It is near indeed," replied the youth. "I am Apisirahts, the Morning Star, and the Sun is my father. Come and I will take you to him."

So the two went down the broad, bright road and passed through the golden gates. Inside they saw a great lodge, shining and glorious, gaily bedecked with such beautiful pictures and carvings as Scarface had never in his life seen before. At the door stood a woman with a fair face and bright clear eyes that looked kindly at the way-worn stranger. "Come in," she said. "I am Kokomikis, the moon goddess, and this youth is my son. Come, for you are tired and footsore and need food and rest."

Scarface, almost bewildered by the beauty of everything around him, went in, and Kokomikis cared for him tenderly, so that he soon felt refreshed and strong. After a time the great Lord of the Sun came home to the lodge, and he, too, was very kind to Scarface. "Stay with us," he said, "you have traveled a weary way to find me, now be my guest for a season. You are a great hunter, and here you will find good game. My son who loves the chase will go with you, and you will live with us and be happy."

Very gladly Scarface replied, "I will stay, great lord." So for many days he lived with the sun god and Kokomikis and Apisirahts, and every morning he and Morning Star went hunting and returned at night to the shining lodge. "Do not go near the Great Water," the Lord of the Sun warned them, "for savage birds dwell there, who will seek to slay the Morning Star."

But Apisirahts secretly longed to meet these savage birds and kill them, so one day he stole away from Scarface and hastened toward the Great Water. For a little while Scarface did not miss him, but believed him to be near by; but after a time he looked round and could not find his companion. He searched anxiously, and then a terrible fear came into his heart, and he set off as fast as he could toward the haunt of the dread birds. Horrid cries came to his ears as he hastened on, and soon he saw a crowd of the monstrous creatures surrounding Morning Star, and pressing on him so closely that he could use his weapons to little purpose to defend himself. Scarface feared to loose an arrow, but he dashed in among the hideous creatures, taking them by surprise, so that they flew off in alarm. Then he seized Morning Star, and hurried him back through the forest to safety.

When they returned to the lodge that night Apisirahts told his father of his own disobedience and the courage of Scarface. The great Lord of the Sun turned to the poor stranger. "You have saved my son from a dreadful death," he said. "Ask of me some boon, that I may repay you. Why was it that you sought me here? Surely you had some desire in your heart or you would not have traveled so far and fared so hardly."

Now all the while he had been at the Shining Lodge the thing he had come to ask had been ever in Scarface's mind. Many times he had thought, "The hour is come when I may speak." But because it was so great a boon he craved his heart failed him, and he thought again, "I will have patience just a little longer. It is too soon to beg so great a favor of the god who has already been so kind to me." But when he heard the words of the sun god, so graciously spoken, he took courage and replied, "In my own land, O mighty Lord, I love a maiden who is the daughter of the chief of my tribe. I am only a poor warrior, and as you see, I am disfigured and hideous to look upon. Yet she of her goodness loves me, and would marry me, but for the reverence in which she holds your commands laid upon her. For she has promised you, O great Lord, that she will marry no man. So I came to seek you in hope that you would free her from her promise that she might come to my lodge, and we might live in happiness together."

Then the sun god smiled, and looked kindly upon the Indian, who spoke bravely, though in his heart he trembled. "Go back," he said, "and take this maiden for your wife. Tell her that it is my will she marry you, and for a token"—he passed his hand before the Indian's face, and immediately the disfiguring scar vanished—"tell her to look upon you and see how the Lord of the Sun has wrought upon your face."

They loaded the Indian—Scarface no longer—with gifts and changed his poor clothes for the rich dress of an Indian chief. Then they led him out from the country of the Sun, through the golden gates, and showed him a short and easy path by which he could return to his own land.

He traveled quickly, and soon was at home once more. All his tribe came out to look at the richly clad young brave, who walked with such a quick, light step, and looked so eager and happy; but none knew him for Scarface, at whom they had mocked and jeered. Even the chief's daughter did not recognize him when she first looked upon him, but a second look told her who he was, and she called his name; then, realizing that the scar was gone, and remembering what its disappearance meant, she sprang toward him with a cry of joy. The story of his wonderful journey was told, and the chief gladly gave his daughter to this warrior on whom the great sun god had looked with favor. That same day they were married, and the chief gave his daughter a splendid wigwam for her marriage portion. There the two lived happily for many years; and Scarface lost his old name and was known to all the tribe as Smoothface.

---

# Solitude

*Ella Wheeler Wilcox*

Sometimes we persevere with the help and compassion of friends and loved ones. Sometimes we have to do it alone. This poem speaks a hard truth, but one we might as well accept nonetheless: pain is harder to share than joy. But if we can bring ourselves to endure cheerfully, we'll find more company along the way.

Laugh, and the world laughs with you;
　Weep, and you weep alone;
For the sad old earth must borrow its mirth,
　But has trouble enough of its own.
Sing, and the hills will answer;
　Sigh, it is lost on the air;
The echoes bound to a joyful sound,
　But shrink from voicing care.

Rejoice, and men will seek you;
  Grieve, and they turn and go;
They want full measure of all your pleasure,
  But they do not need your woe.
Be glad, and your friends are many;
  Be sad, and you lose them all—
There are none to decline your nectared wine,
  But alone you must drink life's gall.

Feast, and your halls are crowded;
  Fast, and the world goes by.
Succeed and give, and it helps you live,
  But no man can help you die.
There is room in the halls of pleasure
  For a large and lordly train,
But one by one we must all file on
  Through the narrow aisles of pain.

---

## Bruce and the Spider

*Bernard Barton*

Robert Bruce (1274–1329) was the king of Scotland who freed his land from English rule by winning the Battle of Bannockburn (1314) and ultimately confirming Scottish independence in the Treaty of Northampton (1328). But the fight was long and hard, as this famous story, set to verse, tells.

For Scotland's and for freedom's right
    The Bruce his part had played,
In five successive fields of fight
    Been conquered and dismayed;
Once more against the English host
His band he led, and once more lost
    The meed for which he fought;
And now from battle, faint and worn,
The homeless fugitive forlorn
    A hut's lone shelter sought.

And cheerless was that resting place
For him who claimed a throne:
His canopy, devoid of grace,
The rude, rough beams alone;
The heather couch his only bed—
Yet well I ween had slumber fled
From couch of eiderdown!
Through darksome night till dawn of day,
Absorbed in wakeful thoughts he lay
Of Scotland and her crown.

The sun rose brightly, and its gleam
Fell on that hapless bed,
And tinged with light each shapeless beam
Which roofed the lowly shed;
When, looking up with wistful eye,
The Bruce beheld a spider try
His filmy thread to fling
From beam to beam of that rude cot;
And well the insect's toilsome lot
Taught Scotland's future king.

Six times his gossamery thread
The wary spider threw;
In vain the filmy line was sped,
For powerless or untrue
Each aim appeared, and back recoiled
The patient insect, six times foiled,
And yet unconquered still;
And soon the Bruce, with eager eye,
Saw him prepare once more to try
His courage, strength, and skill.

One effort more, his seventh and last—
    The hero hailed the sign!—
And on the wished-for beam hung fast
    That slender, silken line!
Slight as it was, his spirit caught
The more than omen, for his thought
    The lesson well could trace,
Which even "he who runs may read,"
That Perseverance gains its meed,
    And Patience wins the race.

---

# The Long, Hard Way Through the Wilderness

*Retold by Walter Russell Bowie*

The story of the Hebrews' flight from Egypt and their forty years of wandering in the wilderness is told primarily in the Biblical book of Exodus. It is one of our greatest accounts of endurance, not only by a people but by a people's leader. As God's agent, Moses led the Hebrews through trial after trial, helping them find their way past starvation, sickness, impatience, and despair. After so long a journey to the border of Canaan, God does not allow Moses himself to enter the Promised Land. It is a final irony that somehow makes him an even more compelling figure of patience and perseverance.

Moses had brought the people out of Egypt. They had come safely across the water, in spite of the chariots of Pharaoh. Now they thought there would be no danger or trouble anymore. But soon they found that they had a long, hard way ahead of them. The country to which they had come was a strip of land, not very wide, between the sea on the one side and great mountains of rock on the other side. The ground between the sea and the mountains was flat sand and gravel. In the daytime the sun beat down with blistering heat, and there were no trees to give shade.

Mile after mile the people traveled without finding water. When at last they came to a pool in the sands, the water tasted so bad that they could not drink it. They named the place Marah, which means bitterness, and they demanded of Moses, "What shall we drink?"

Moses prayed to God to show him what to do. He found some shrubs growing in the sand, and he put these into the pool. Their leaves changed the taste of the water so that it became fit to drink.

After that Moses led the people to a place called Elim. There they found twelve springs of water with seventy palm trees growing near by. To the people who had been dragging their feet through the hot desert, Elim seemed like heaven, and they made camp there at the oasis.

But they could not stay long at Elim, for they had used up all the food they had brought with them out of Egypt. They had to go on farther in the hope of finding something they could eat. But when they had left the oasis, all that they saw around them was the desert again, and they seemed to be worse off than ever. Most of the Israelites were not as brave as Moses, and some of them began to complain aloud. They said to Moses, "Would to God that we had been let alone to die in the land of Egypt. There we had meat to cook, and plenty of bread. And here you have brought us out into this wilderness to kill us all with hunger."

But Moses kept his temper, and he kept his courage. He said that God would send them help.

That evening as the people looked at the sky they saw what seemed like a cloud. As it came near, they saw that it was not a cloud but hundreds and hundreds of quail, blown to land by a strong wind from islands out in the sea. When the tired birds came to earth, the people caught and ate them.

That night there was a heavy dew. In the morning when the people woke up, there on the ground were small white patches like frost. Moses said, "This is the bread that the Lord has given you to eat." The people of Israel called it manna. It was a kind of gum that fell from the desert bushes, and it had to be picked up before the sun rose, for after that it melted and disappeared.

From the place where they were fed with the quail and the manna, the people of Israel went on farther along the sea. Then Moses told them to turn and head for the mountains. Terrible-looking mountains they were, high and bare and grim. Again the people grew so thirsty that their tongues were dry. "Give us water!" they cried to Moses. "Is this what you brought us out of Egypt for—to kill us all with thirst?"

But Moses had been in these mountains before, and there was much that God had helped him learn. He led the people to a great rock cliff in a mountain called Horeb. There he struck the cliff with his staff and showed them water flowing. For a while the Hebrews were satisfied. They liked it still better when Moses brought them after that to another oasis. This was the greenest spot in all that bleak and barren land. Row after row of palm trees were there and springs bubbled up and overflowed, so that the waters made a murmuring stream. Centuries later this oasis was still known as the Pearl of Sinai because of its beauty.

The people of Israel might have liked to pitch their tents here and stay always, but it was a dangerous place in which to linger. An oasis was the one place most wanted, and so most fought for, by all the wild desert tribes. Moses chose a young man named Joshua to be the commander of the fighting men if there was danger.

The people had not been at the oasis long when a band of Amalekites appeared. They were mounted on camels and carried spears. They rode in fiercely to attack the Israelites. But Moses stood on a hill and held up his staff. He prayed to God. As he went on praying, Aaron and a man named Hur held up Moses' hands. While he prayed, Joshua and his fighting men drove the Amalekites away.

All the same, they could not stay at the oasis. Moses knew that other tribes, stronger than the Amalekites, might come there any day. Besides, the country to which Moses hoped to bring them, so that they might settle there, was a long way off on the other side of the mountain.

So on over rocky paths and up deep ravines Moses led the people of Israel. Great mountain peaks frowned over them. Some of these mountains had been volcanoes, and now and then there were rumblings among them, and sometimes even an earthquake. But it was in country like this that Moses, when he had first fled from Pharaoh, had seen the burning bush and heard the voice of God telling him to bring his people out of Egypt. In these same mountains Moses was to hear something else from God—something even more important.

While the people were camped in a valley, Moses climbed high on the greatest of the mountains—Mount Sinai. The people watched him until he disappeared in the distance. Hours and hours went by and he did not come back.

Up there, all alone, with only the rocks around him and the sky above, Moses thought and prayed. What did God want him to teach the people? How did God want them to behave?

Then it was as though Moses saw what he wanted to know. He saw the glory of God passing by, and heard God's voice telling him what he needed to understand. God would give him the Commandments which from this time on all people must obey.

After Moses had taught the people the Ten Commandments, he taught them a great deal more about how they were to live together. He taught them how to arrange the camps on the march, how to keep clean, how to be healthy, and what to do when anyone was sick. He told them what to do to remember God and worship him. They were to make a beautiful little chest, called the ark, and in it they were to carry the stone tablets on which were written the Ten Commandments. They were also to make a tabernacle, which was a tent made of the skins of animals. They were to put this tent up wherever they camped and have it for the place where they would pray to God.

Before long the Israelites left the valley at the foot of Mount Sinai and started on their way again. The ark was carried before them. Moses was still their leader. Often he had a hard time, just as he had had when they first came out of Egypt, because some of the people were forever grumbling. They said they were tired of eating manna all the time. They were tired of going thirsty on long journeys when there was not even so much as a water hole in the barren ground. They kept thinking of Egypt and telling one another that they wished they were back there. When they were there, they had wanted more than anything to be out of the country; but they forgot that now. What they remembered was the good things they had had to eat.

"We remember the fish," they said, "the cucumbers, and the melons." In Egypt there was the Nile with fish for anybody's taking, and there were fresh vegetables and fruits. But here there was nothing but sand and blistering sun and emptiness. Once or twice the people nearly rebelled.

Whenever Moses went by the tents and heard the people in them complaining, he was sad. But he would not let them think he was discouraged. He went off by himself and told everything to God in prayer. It seemed to him that God had given him more to do than any one man could manage. "I am not able to take care of all these people alone," he said. "It is too much for me." But when he prayed, God gave him new strength, and he went on.

All this time, by slow marches, the people were traveling farther north, beyond the mountains, toward the country where Moses believed God meant them to be. It was the same country to which

Abraham had come long before, and it was called the Promised Land. They were near enough to its borders now for Moses to plan how they should enter it. But first he had to learn exactly what the land was like, and what sort of people were living there. He chose twelve scouts, one of whom was Joshua and one a young man named Caleb, and he sent them out secretly in advance.

"Go see the land," he told them, "and the people who live there. Notice whether they are strong or weak, few or many. Is the land good or bad, and is it wooded or not? What sort of homes do the people have? Do they live in tents, or in towns with walls around them? Be of good courage, and bring back with you some of the fruits of the land."

So on ahead the scouts went. From the region around Mount Sinai it was a hundred miles or more to the shores of the Dead Sea. Beyond that they went, up over the high rock country of Moab, and along the valley of the Jordan River. Across the Jordan lay the Promised Land.

After forty days the scouts came back and made their report to Moses. They all said that the country they had looked at was a good land. Compared with the mountains and deserts they had been through, it seemed like a paradise. There were fields of grain in it and olive trees and vineyards, and springs of water in the hills. They brought back a great bunch of grapes which they had taken from a valley they called Eshcol, and they also brought figs and other fruit.

But after that, the scouts began to disagree. Ten of them said that the people in the land were so strong and so warlike they would never let the Israelites in. They said that the people living there looked like giants. Measured against them, the ten scouts said they felt like grasshoppers. But Caleb and Joshua, the other two, said all that was nonsense. The people living in the country were no different from any other people. The thing for the Israelites to do was to march straight ahead and go in.

Most of the Israelites who crowded around and listened believed the ten men instead of the two. They were afraid to trust the ones who were courageous. Then, because it made them uncomfortable to feel cowardly, they pretended that Caleb and Joshua were trying to lead them into trouble. If they had dared, they would have stoned the two brave men to death. They started again to say that they wished they were back in Egypt. They even talked of choosing a captain of their own who would take them there. But they could not find any real leader, so their angry muttering came to nothing.

Yet all this was enough to make Moses know that such fainthearted people could not win the Promised Land. There was no use trying to lead them into it now. He would have to wait a long time, until some of the older ones who had been slaves in Egypt died, and younger and braver men grew up.

Many years went by, and now at last Moses did have a different sort of people under him—people who had been born and had grown up in the wilderness. They moved to the borders of the land of Edom, which lies at the south of the Dead Sea. They asked the Edomites to let them pass through their country peacefully. When the Edomites would not do this, the Israelites circled around that country and came to the land of the Amorites, to the west of the Jordan River.

Moses sent a message to Sihon, the chief of the Amorites, saying: "Let us pass through your land. We will not turn into the fields, nor into the vineyards. We will not drink from your wells. But we will go along the high roads until we have passed your borders."

The Amorites were fierce fighters. Instead of letting the Israelites through, they rode into the camp to attack them. But the younger men who followed Moses and Joshua now were no cowards. They beat off Sihon and his Amorites. And afterward, when Og, the chief of another one of the desert tribes, tried to stop them, they defeated him too.

They were coming close to the Promised Land. But Moses was not to go in with them. He was an old man now. He went up one day to the top of Mount Nebo, four thousand feet above the waters of the Dead Sea. Across the Jordan River he could see the walled city of Jericho. The springs there were fed by the streams that flowed from the hills above. Moses could see mile after mile of the Promised Land which his people would surely enter. There on the mountaintop he died, and it is written that he was buried "in a valley in the land of Moab; but no man knoweth of his grave unto this day."

---

## Go Down, Moses

The spirituals composed by unknown slaves rank among the most beautiful and poignant American songs. Combining elements of African music with Old Testament themes, songs such as "Go Down, Moses" express an entire population's dignified faith despite the worst of conditions. No songs convey more nobility of the soul. After the Civil War, groups such as the Fisk University Jubilee Singers, who sang this particular rendition, introduced the spirituals to the nation at large.

When Israel was in Egypt's land:
  Let my people go;
Oppress'd so hard they could not stand,
  Let my people go.
    Go down, Moses,
      Way down in Egypt land,
    Tell ole Pharaoh,
      Let my people go.

Thus saith the Lord, bold Moses said,
  Let my people go;
If not I'll smite your firstborn dead,
  Let my people go.
    Go down, Moses, *etc.*

The Lord told Moses what to do,
  Let my people go;
To lead the children of Israel through,
  Let my people go.
    Go down, Moses, *etc.*

O come along, Moses, you'll not get lost,
  Let my people go;
Stretch out your rod and come across,
  Let my people go.
    Go down, Moses, *etc.*

As Israel stood by the waterside,
  Let my people go;
At the command of God it did divide,
  Let my people go.
    Go down, Moses, *etc.*

When they had reached the other shore,
Let my people go;
They sang a song of triumph o'er.
Let my people go.
Go down, Moses, *etc.*

We need not always weep and moan,
Let my people go;
And wear these slavery chains forlorn,
Let my people go.
Go down, Moses, *etc.*

This world's a wilderness of woe,
Let my people go;
O, let us on to Canaan go,
Let my people go.
Go down, Moses, *etc.*

What a beautiful morning that will be,
Let my people go;
When time breaks up in eternity,
Let my people go.
Go down, Moses, *etc.*

---

# Eureka!

*Retold by James Baldwin*

Celebrated inventor and mathematician of ancient Greece, Archimedes was born around the year 290 B.C. in Syracuse, Sicily, a Greek colony. This story about one of his most famous discoveries is an invaluable lesson in intellectual perseverance. As the American Archimedes, Thomas Edison, said, genius is one percent inspiration and ninety-nine percent perspiration.

There was once a king of Syracuse whose name was Hiero. The country over which he ruled was quite small, but for that reason he wanted to wear the biggest crown in the world. So he called in a famous goldsmith, who was skillful in all kinds of fine work, and gave him ten pounds of pure gold.

"Take this," he said, "and fashion it into a crown that shall make every other king want it for his own. Be sure that you put into it every grain of the gold I give you, and do not mix any other metal with it."

"It shall be as you wish," said the goldsmith. "Here I receive from you ten pounds of pure gold. Within ninety days I will return to you the finished crown which shall be of exactly the same weight."

Ninety days later, true to his word, the goldsmith brought the crown. It was a beautiful piece of work, and all who saw it said that it had not its equal in the world. When King Hiero put it on his head it felt very uncomfortable, but he did not mind that—he was sure that no other king had so fine a headpiece. After he had admired it from this side and from that, he weighed it on his own scales. It was exactly as heavy as he had ordered.

"You deserve great praise," he said to the goldsmith. "You have wrought very skillfully and you have not lost a grain of my gold."

There was in the king's court a very wise man whose name was Archimedes. When he was called in to admire the king's crown he turned it over many times and examined it very closely.

"Well, what do you think of it?" asked Hiero.

"The workmanship is indeed very beautiful," answered Archimedes, "but—but the gold—"

"The gold is all there," cried the king, "I weighed it on my own scales."

"True," said Archimedes, "but it does not appear to have the same rich red color that it had in the lump. It is not red at all, but a brilliant yellow, as you can plainly see."

"Most gold is yellow," said Hiero. "But now that you speak of it I do remember that when this was in the lump it had a much richer color."

"What if the goldsmith has kept out a pound or two of the gold and made up the weight by adding brass or silver?" asked Archimedes.

"Oh, he could not do that," said Hiero. "The gold has merely changed its color in the working."

But the more he thought of the matter the less pleased he was with the crown. At last he said to Archimedes, "Is there any way to find out whether that goldsmith really cheated me, or whether he honestly gave me back my gold?"

"I know of no way," was the answer.

But Archimedes was not the man to say that anything was impossible. He took great delight in working out hard problems, and when any question puzzled him he would keep studying until he found some sort of answer to it. And so, day after day, he thought about the gold and tried to find some way by which it could be tested without doing harm to the crown.

One morning he was thinking of this question while he was getting ready for a bath. The great bowl or tub was full to the very edge, and as he stepped into it a quantity of water flowed out upon the stone floor. A similar thing had happened a hundred times before, but this was the first time that Archimedes had thought about it.

"How much water did I displace by getting into the tub?" he asked himself. "Anybody can see that I displaced a bulk of water equal to the bulk of my body. A man half my size would displace half as much.

"Now suppose, instead of putting myself into the tub, I had put Hiero's crown into it, it would have displaced a bulk of water equal to its own bulk. Ah, let me see! Gold is much heavier than silver. Ten pounds of pure gold will not make so great a bulk as say seven pounds of gold mixed with three pounds of silver. If Hiero's crown is pure gold it will displace the same bulk of water as any other ten pounds of pure gold. But if it is part gold and part silver it will displace a larger bulk. I have it at last! Eureka! Eureka!"

Forgetful of everything else he leaped from the bath. Without stopping to dress himself, he ran through the streets to the king's palace shouting, "Eureka! Eureka! Eureka!" which in English means, "I have found it! I have found it! I have found it!"

The crown was tested. It was found to displace much more water than ten pounds of pure gold displaced. The guilt of the goldsmith was proved beyond a doubt. But whether he was punished or not, I do not know, neither does it matter.

The simple discovery which Archimedes made in his bathtub was worth far more to the world than Hiero's crown.

# Perseverance

*Johann Wolfgang von Goethe*

We must not hope to be mowers,
And to gather the ripe gold ears,
Unless we have first been sowers
And watered the furrows with tears.

It is not just as we take it,
This mystical world of ours,
Life's field will yield as we make it
A harvest of thorns or of flowers.

---

# Sail on! Sail on!

*Joaquin Miller*

This is the Christopher Columbus whose imagination we admire, whose daring we celebrate, and whose determination we should emulate.

Behind him lay the gray Azores,
Behind the gates of Hercules;
Before him not the ghost of shores,
Before him only shoreless seas.
The good mate said: "Now must we pray,
For lo! the very stars are gone;
Speak, Admiral, what shall I say?"
"Why say, sail on! and on!"

"My men grow mut'nous day by day;
  My men grow ghastly wan and weak."
The stout mate thought of home; a spray
  Of salt wave wash'd his swarthy cheek.
"What shall I say, brave Admiral,
  If we sight naught but seas at dawn?"
"Why, you shall say, at break of day:
  'Sail on! sail on! and on!' "

They sailed and sailed, as winds might blow,
  Until at last the blanch'd mate said:
"Why, now, not even God would know
  Should I and all my men fall dead.
These very winds forget their way,
  For God from these dread seas is gone.
Now speak, brave Admiral, and say—"
  He said: "Sail on! and on!"

They sailed, they sailed, then spoke his mate:
  "This mad sea shows his teeth tonight,
He curls his lip, he lies in wait,
  With lifted teeth as if to bite!
Brave Admiral, say but one word;
  What shall we do when hope is gone?"
The words leaped as a leaping sword:
  "Sail on! sail on! and on!"

Then, pale and worn, he kept his deck,
  And thro' the darkness peered that night.
Ah, darkest night! and then a speck—
  A light! a light! a light! a light!
It grew—a star-lit flag unfurled!
  It grew to be Time's burst of dawn;
He gained a world! he gave that world
  Its watchword: "On! and on!"

# Can't

*Edgar Guest*

"Can't" is a favorite word of some children. Here is the case against it.

*Can't* is the worst word that's written or spoken;
Doing more harm here than slander and lies;
On it is many a strong spirit broken,
And with it many a good purpose dies.
It springs from the lips of the thoughtless each morning
And robs us of courage we need through the day:
It rings in our ears like a timely sent warning
And laughs when we falter and fall by the way.

*Can't* is the father of feeble endeavor,
The parent of terror and halfhearted work;
It weakens the efforts of artisans clever,
And makes of the toiler an indolent shirk.
It poisons the soul of the man with a vision,
It stifles in infancy many a plan;
It greets honest toiling with open derision
And mocks at the hopes and the dreams of a man.

*Can't* is a word none should speak without blushing;
To utter it should be a symbol of shame;
Ambition and courage it daily is crushing;
It blights a man's purpose and shortens his aim.
Despise it with all of your hatred of error;
Refuse it the lodgment it seeks in your brain;
Arm against it as a creature of terror,
And all that you dream of you someday shall gain.

*Can't* is the word that is foe to ambition,
  An enemy ambushed to shatter your will;
Its prey is forever the man with a mission
  And bows but to courage and patience and skill.
Hate it, with hatred that's deep and undying,
  For once it is welcomed 'twill break any man;
Whatever the goal you are seeking, keep trying
  And answer this demon by saying: "I *can.*"

---

# The Gettysburg Address

*Abraham Lincoln*

When Abraham Lincoln rose on November 19, 1863, to dedicate the Soldier's National Cemetery at Gettysburg, Pennsylvania, where four months earlier thousands of Northern and Southern soldiers had fallen, he wanted to tell the country that if it could sustain the will to fight, the Union ultimately would triumph. In two minutes he said as much, and more. He told the world the United States would fight on, not just for its own sake, but for all nations conceived in liberty and dedicated to equality. Here it is, the greatest and most famous speech ever delivered on American soil.

Four score and seven years ago, our fathers brought forth on this continent a new nation, conceived in liberty, and dedicated to the proposition that all men are created equal.

Now we are engaged in a great civil war, testing whether that nation, or any nation so conceived and so dedicated, can long endure. We are met on a great battlefield of that war. We have come to dedicate a portion of that field as a final resting place for those who here gave their lives that that nation might live. It is altogether fitting and proper that we should do this.

But in a larger sense we cannot dedicate, we cannot consecrate, we cannot hallow this ground. The brave men, living and dead, who struggled here, have consecrated it far above our poor power to add or detract. The world will little note, nor long remember, what we say here, but it can never forget what they did here. It is for us the living, rather, to be dedicated here to the unfinished work which they who fought here have thus far so nobly advanced. It is rather for us to be here dedicated to the great task remaining before us—that from these honored dead we take increased devotion to that cause for which they gave the last full measure of devotion, that we here highly resolve that these dead shall not have died in vain, that this nation, under God, shall have a new birth of freedom, and that government of the people, by the people, for the people, shall not perish from the earth.

---

# We Shall Fight in the Fields and in the Streets

*Winston Churchill*

In May 1940, German forces skirted the Maginot line, broke through French defensive positions, and in a matter of days swept westward to the British Channel. The British Expeditionary Force in France, threatened with annihilation, fell back to the beaches of Dunkirk, where an epic evacuation of more than three hundred thousand British and French troops was staged. With the protection of the Royal Air Force, all kinds and sizes of British boats, some manned by civilian volunteers, crossed and recrossed the Channel to ferry the shattered army to England.

On June 4, Winston Churchill reported to Parliament on the success of the evacuation. His description of the heroic effort and his call for courage, unity, determination, and sacrifice buoyed the spirits of the British people. It also helped bolster resolution in the New World; one week later, when Italy entered the war on the side of the Axis powers, President Roosevelt publicly committed American material resources to the Allied cause.

From the moment that the French defenses at Sedan and on the Meuse were broken at the end of the second week of May, only a rapid retreat to Amiens and the south could have saved the British and French armies who had entered Belgium at the appeal of the Belgian King; but this strategic fact was not immediately realized. . . .

The German eruption swept like a sharp scythe around the right and rear of the armies of the north. Eight or nine armored divisions, each of about four hundred armored vehicles of different kinds, but carefully assorted to be complementary and divisible into small self-contained units, cut off all communications between us and the main French armies. It severed our own communications for food and ammunition, which ran first to Amiens and afterward through Abbeville, and it shored its way up the coast to Boulogne and Calais, and almost to Dunkirk. Behind this armored and mechanized onslaught came a number of German divisions in lorries, and behind them again there plodded comparatively slowly the dull brute mass of the ordinary German Army and German people, always so ready to be led to the trampling down in other lands of liberties and comforts which they have never known in their own. . . .

Meanwhile, the Royal Air Force, which had already been intervening in the battle, so far as its range would allow, from home bases, now used part of its main metropolitan fighter strength, and struck at the German bombers and at the fighters which in large numbers protected them. This struggle was protracted and fierce. Suddenly the scene has cleared, the crash and thunder has for the moment—but only for the moment—died away. A miracle of deliverance, achieved by valor, by perseverance, by perfect discipline, by faultless service, by resource, by skill, by unconquerable fidelity, is manifest to us all. The enemy was hurled back by the retreating British and French troops. He was so roughly handled that he did not hurry their departure seriously. The Royal Air Force engaged the main strength of the German Air Force, and inflicted upon them losses of at least four to one; and the navy, using nearly one thousand ships of all kinds, carried over 335,000 men, French and British, out of the jaws of death and shame, to their native land and to the tasks which lie immediately ahead. We must be very careful not to assign to this deliverance the attributes of a victory. Wars are not won by evacuations. But there was a victory inside this deliverance, which should be noted. . . .

This was a great trial of strength between the British and German air forces. Can you conceive a greater objective for the Germans in the air than to make evacuation from these beaches impossible, and to sink all these ships which were displayed, almost to the extent of thousands? Could there have been an objective of greater military importance and significance for the whole purpose of the war than this? They tried hard, and they were beaten back; they were frustrated in their task. We got the army away; and they have paid fourfold for any losses which they have inflicted. Very large formations of German airplanes—and we know that they are a very brave race—have turned on several occasions from the attack of one quarter of their number of the Royal Air Force, and have dispersed in different directions. . . .

I will pay my tribute to these young airmen. The great French Army was very largely, for the time being, cast back and disturbed by the onrush of a few thousands of armored vehicles. May it not also be that the cause of civilization itself will be defended by the skill and devotion of a few thousand airmen? There never has been, I suppose, in all the world, in all the history of war, such an opportunity for youth. The Knights of the Round Table, the Crusaders, all fall back into the past—not only distant but prosaic; these young men, going forth every morn to guard their native land and all that we stand for, holding in their hands these instruments of colossal and shattering power, of whom it may be said that

*Every morn brought forth a noble chance,*
*And every chance brought forth a noble knight,*

deserve our gratitude, as do all of the brave men who, in so many ways and on so many occasions, are ready, and continue ready, to give life and all for their native land. . . .

I have, myself, full confidence that if all do their duty, if nothing is neglected, and if the best arrangements are made, as they are being made, we shall prove ourselves once again able to defend our island home, to ride out the storm of war, and to outlive the menace of tyranny, if necessary for years, if necessary alone. At any rate, that is what we are going to try to do. That is the resolve of His Majesty's Government—every man of them. That is the will of Parliament and the nation. The British Empire and the French Republic, linked together in their cause and in their need, will defend to the death their native soil, aiding each other like good comrades to the utmost of their strength. Even though large tracts of Europe and many old and famous states have fallen or may fall into the grip of the Gestapo and all the odious apparatus of Nazi rule, we shall not flag or fail. We shall go on to the end, we shall fight in France, we shall fight on the seas and oceans, we shall fight with growing confidence and growing strength in the air, we shall defend our island, whatever the cost may be, we shall fight on the beaches, we shall fight on the landing grounds, we shall fight in the fields and in the streets, we shall fight in the hills; we shall never surrender, and even if, which I do not for a moment believe, this island or a large part of it were subjugated and starving, then our Empire beyond the seas, armed and guarded by the British fleet, would carry on the struggle, until, in God's good time, the New World, with all its power and might, steps forth to the rescue and the liberation of the old.

---

# I Have a Dream

*Reverend Martin Luther King, Jr.*

On August 28, 1963, between 200,000 and 250,000 people gathered between the Washington Monument and the Lincoln Memorial in the nation's capital to demonstrate peacefully on behalf of the civil rights struggle. The high point of the day was the Reverend Martin Luther King, Jr.'s, now-famous speech in which he called upon Americans to work with faith that change would come and that someday all would be judged not by the color of their skin, but by the content of their character. His soaring refrain of "I have a dream" still inspires the American conscience. His perseverance and eloquence were rewarded.

Five score years ago, a great American, in whose symbolic shadow we stand, signed the Emancipation Proclamation. This momentous decree came as a great beacon light of hope to millions of Negro slaves who had been seared in the flames of withering injustice. It came as a joyous daybreak to end the long night of captivity.

But one hundred years later, we must face the tragic fact that the Negro is still not free. One hundred years later, the life of the

Negro is still sadly crippled by the manacles of segregation and the chains of discrimination. One hundred years later, the Negro lives on a lonely island of poverty in the midst of a vast ocean of material prosperity. One hundred years later, the Negro still languishes in the corners of American society and finds himself an exile in his own land. So we have come here today to dramatize an appalling condition.

In a sense we have come to our nation's capital to cash a check. When the architects of our republic wrote the magnificent words of the Constitution and the Declaration of Independence, they were signing a promissory note to which every American was to fall heir. This note was a promise that all men would be guaranteed the unalienable rights of life, liberty, and the pursuit of happiness.

It is obvious today that America has defaulted on this promissory note insofar as her citizens of color are concerned. Instead of honoring this sacred obligation, America has given the Negro people a bad check: a check which has come back marked "insufficient funds." But we refuse to believe that the bank of justice is bankrupt. We refuse to believe that there are insufficient funds in the great vaults of opportunity of this nation. So we have come to cash this check—a check that will give us upon demand the riches of freedom and the security of justice.

We have also come to this hallowed spot to remind America of the fierce urgency of *now*. This is not time to engage in the luxury of cooling off or to take the tranquilizing drug of gradualism. *Now* is the time to make real the promises of democracy. *Now* is the time to rise from the dark and desolate valley of segregation to the sunlit path of racial justice. *Now* is the time to open the doors of opportunity to all of God's children. *Now* is the time to lift our nation from the quicksands of racial injustice to the solid rock of brotherhood.

It would be fatal for the nation to overlook the urgency of the moment and to underestimate the determination of the Negro. This sweltering summer of the Negro's legitimate discontent will not pass until there is an invigorating autumn of freedom and equality. Nineteen sixty-three is not an end, but a beginning. Those who hope that the Negro needed to blow off steam and will now be content will have a rude awakening if the nation returns to business as usual. There will be neither rest nor tranquility in America until the Negro is granted his citizenship rights. The whirlwinds of revolt will continue to shake the foundations of our nation until the bright day of justice emerges.

But there is something that I must say to my people who stand on the warm threshold which leads into the palace of justice. In the process of gaining our rightful place we must not be guilty of wrongful deeds. Let us not seek to satisfy our thirst for freedom by drinking from the cup of bitterness and hatred. We must forever conduct our struggle on the high plane of dignity and discipline. We must not allow our creative protest to degenerate into physical violence. Again and again we must rise to the majestic heights of meeting physical force with soul force.

The marvelous new militancy which has engulfed the Negro community must not lead us to a distrust of all white people, for many of our white brothers, as evidenced by their presence here today, have come to realize that their freedom is inextricably bound to our freedom. We cannot walk alone.

And as we walk, we must make the pledge that we shall march ahead. We cannot turn back. There are those who are asking the devotees of civil rights, "When will you be satisfied?"

We can never be satisfied as long as the Negro is the victim of the unspeakable horrors of police brutality.

We can never be satisfied as long as our bodies, heavy with fatigue of travel, cannot gain lodging in the motels of the highways and the cities.

We cannot be satisfied as long as the Negro's basic mobility is from a smaller ghetto to a larger one.

We can never be satisfied as long as a Negro in Mississippi cannot vote and a Negro in New York believes he has nothing for which to vote.

No, no, we are not satisfied, and we will not be satisfied until justice rolls down like waters and righteousness like a mighty stream.

I am not unmindful that some of you have come here out of great trials and tribulations. Some of you have come fresh from narrow jail cells. Some of you have come from areas where your quest for freedom left you battered by the storms of persecution and staggered by the winds of police brutality. You have been the veterans of creative suffering. Continue to work with the faith that unearned suffering is redemptive.

Go back to Mississippi, go back to Alabama, go back to South Carolina, go back to Georgia, go back to Louisiana, go back to the slums and ghettos of our Northern cities, knowing that somehow this situation can and will be changed. Let us not wallow in the valley of despair.

I say to you today, my friends, that in spite of the difficulties and frustrations of the moment I still have a dream. It is a dream deeply rooted in the American dream.

I have a dream that one day this nation will rise up and live out the true meaning of its creed: "We hold these truths to be self-evident; that all men are created equal."

I have a dream that one day on the red hills of Georgia the sons of former slaves and the sons of former slaveowners will be able to sit down together at the table of brotherhood.

I have a dream that one day even the state of Mississippi, a desert state sweltering with the heat of injustice and oppression, will be transformed into an oasis of freedom and justice.

I have a dream that my four little children will one day live in a nation where they will not be judged by the color of their skin but by the content of their character.

I have a dream today.

I have a dream that one day the state of Alabama, whose governor's lips are presently dripping with the words of interposition and nullification, will be transformed into a situation where little black boys and black girls will be able to join hands with little white boys and girls and walk together as sisters and brothers.

I have a dream today.

I have a dream that one day every valley shall be exalted, every hill and mountain shall be made low, the rough places will be made plain, and the crooked places will be made straight, and the glory of the Lord shall be revealed, and all flesh shall see it together.

This is our hope. This is the faith with which I return to the South. With this faith we will be able to hew out of the mountain of despair a stone of hope. With this faith we will be able to transform the jangling discords of our nation into a beautiful symphony of brotherhood.

With this faith we will be able to work together, to pray together, to struggle together, to go to jail together, to stand up for freedom together, knowing that we will be free one day.

This will be the day when all of God's children will be able to sing with new meaning, "My country 'tis of thee, sweet land of liberty, of thee I sing. Land where my father died, land of the Pilgrims' pride, from every mountainside, let freedom ring."

And if America is to be a great nation, this must become true. So let freedom ring from the prodigious hilltops of New Hampshire. Let freedom ring from the mighty mountains of New York. Let freedom ring from the heightening Alleghenies of Pennsylvania!

Let freedom ring from the snowcapped Rockies of Colorado! Let freedom ring from the curvaceous peaks of California. But not only that: let freedom ring from Stone Mountain of Georgia! Let freedom ring from Lookout Mountain of Tennessee!

Let freedom ring from every hill and molehill of Mississippi. From every mountainside, let freedom ring.

When we let freedom ring, when we let it ring from every village and every hamlet, from every state and every city, we will be able to speed up that day when all of God's children, black men and white men, Jews and Gentiles, Protestants and Catholics, will be able to join hands and sing in the words of the old Negro spiritual, "Free at last! Free at last! Thank God Almighty, we are free at last!"

---

# The Donner Party

*Eliza P. Donner Houghton*

In April 1846, a group of pioneers led by brothers George and Jacob Donner and their friend James Reed set out from Illinois to join the growing wave of emigrants heading for Oregon and California. As they crossed the Midwest they were joined by other families with names like Eddy, Pike, and McCutchen, all hoping to buy cheap Western land and begin life anew. By the time the Donner Party was complete, it totaled eighty-seven men, women, and children with twenty-three wagons and numerous head of livestock. The group was headed toward the most spectacular and famous catastrophe of the overland pioneer crossings.

On July 20, the Donners and their companions turned off the main trail onto a cutoff that, according to a promoter named Lansford W. Hastings, was the most direct route to California. But neither Hastings nor anyone else had tried the new route—it existed only in his unscrupulous imagination. By the time the Donner Party found its way through the Wasatch Range and made a torturous crossing of the Great Salt Lake Desert, it had lost too many days of precious time. When they reached the

Sierra Nevada in late October, five feet of snow already lay in the mountain passes.

They waited on the shore of Truckee (now Donner) Lake to gather their strength for the climb, but the snows fell for eight straight days. Winter had come early, and the Donner Party was trapped. They went into winter camp. One group built cabins at the lake, while others, including the Donners, settled in at Alder Creek five miles down the trail. Every day the weather grew colder and the snow deeper. Before long they were faced with starvation.

During the next five months, four relief parties managed to reach the Donner Party. It was the end of April before the last survivor was brought out of the mountains. Only forty of the eighty-seven emigrants lived through the winter of agony, and some of those managed to survive only by eating the remains of their dead companions.

The following excerpts are from *The Expedition of the Donner Party and Its Tragic Fate* by Eliza P. Donner Houghton, daughter of George and Tamsen Donner, who was four years old that winter. Her words and the accounts of other survivors describe the range of human reactions, from magnificent to ignominious, in the face of an almost unimaginable ordeal. The story of the Donner Party is a taproot for me. I go back to it often to puzzle over what it is in people's characters that makes some great and others grotesque.

After the departure of the first relief we who were left in the mountains began to watch and pray for the coming of the second relief, as we had before watched and prayed for the coming of the first. . . .

As father grew weaker, we children spent more time upon the snow above camp. Often, after his wound was dressed and he fell into a quiet slumber, our ever-busy, thoughtful mother would come to us and sit on the tree trunk. Sometimes she brought paper and wrote; sometimes she sketched the mountains and the tall treetops, which now looked like small trees growing up through the snow. And often, while knitting or sewing, she held us spellbound with wondrous tales of "Joseph in Egypt," of "Daniel in the den of lions," of "Elijah healing the widow's son," of dear little Samuel, who said, "Speak Lord, for Thy servant heareth," and of the tender, loving Master, who took young children in his arms and blessed them.

With me sitting on her lap, and Frances and Georgia at either side, she referred to father's illness and lonely condition, and said that when the next "relief" came, we little ones might be taken to the settlement, without either parent, but, God willing, both would follow later. Who could be braver or tenderer than she, as she prepared us to go forth with strangers and live without her? While she, without medicine, without lights, would remain and care for our suffering father, in hunger and in cold, and without her little girls to kiss good morning and good night. She taught us how to gain friends among those whom we should meet, and what to answer when asked whose children we were.

Often her eyes gazed wistfully to westward, where sky and mountains seemed to meet, and she told us that beyond those snowy peaks lay California, our land of food and safety, our promised land of happiness, where God would care for us. Oh, it was painfully quiet some days in those great mountains, and lonesome upon the snow. The pines had a whispering homesick murmur, and we children had lost all inclination to play.

The last food which I remember seeing in our camp before the arrival of the second relief was a thin mold of tallow, which mother had tried out of the trimmings of the jerked beef brought us by the first relief. She had let it harden in a pan, and after all other rations had given out, she cut daily from it three small white squares for each of us, and we nibbled off the four corners very slowly, and then around and around the edges of the precious pieces until they became too small for us to hold between our fingers. . . .

Thirty-one of the company were still in the camps when the second relief party arrived, nearly all of them children, unable to travel without assistance, and the adults were too feeble to give much aid to the little ones upon the snow. Consequently, when my father learned that the second relief comprised only ten men, he felt that he himself would never reach the settlement. He was willing to be left alone, and entreated mother to leave him and try to save herself and us children. He reminded her that his life was almost spent, that she could do little for him were she to remain, and that in caring for us children she would be carrying on his work.

She who had to choose between the sacred duties of wife and mother, thought not of self. She looked first at her helpless little children, then into the face of her suffering and helpless husband, and tenderly, unhesitatingly, announced her determination to remain and care for him until both should be rescued, or death should part them. . . .

Mother, fearing that we children might not survive another storm in camp, begged Messrs. Cady and Stone to take us with them, offering them five hundred dollars in coin, to deliver us to Elitha and Leanna at Sutter's Fort. The agreement was made, and she collected a few keepsakes and other light articles, which she wished us to have, and which the men seemed more than willing to carry out of the mountains. Then, lovingly, she combed our hair and helped us to dress quickly for the journey. When we were ready, except cloak and hood, she led us to the bedside, and we took leave of father. The men helped us up the steps and stood us up on the snow. She came, put on our cloaks and hoods, saying, as if talking to herself, "I may never see you again, but God will take care of you."

Frances was six years and eight months old and could trudge along quite bravely, but Georgia, who was little more than five, and I, lacking a week of four years, could not do well on the heavy trail, and we were soon taken up and carried. After traveling some distance, the men left us sitting on a blanket upon the snow, and went ahead a short distance where they stopped and talked earnestly with many gesticulations. We watched them, trembling lest they leave us there to freeze. Then Frances said,

"Don't feel afraid. If they go off and leave us, I can lead you back to mother by our foot tracks on the snow."

After a seemingly long time, they returned, picked us up and took us on to one of the lake cabins, where without a parting word, they left us.

The second relief party, of which these men were members, left camp on the third of March. They took with them seventeen refugees—the Breen and Graves families, Solomon Hook, Isaac and Mary Donner, and Martha and Thomas, Mr. Reed's two youngest children.

How can I describe that fateful cabin, which was dark as night to us who had come in from the glare of day? We heard no word of greeting and met no sign of welcome, but were given a dreary resting place near the foot of the steps, just inside the open doorway, with a bed of branches to lie upon, and a blanket to cover us. After we had been there a short time, we could distinguish persons on other beds of branches, and a man with bushy hair reclining beside a smouldering fire.

Soon a child began to cry, "Give me some bread. Oh, give me some meat!"

Then another took up the same pitiful wail. It continued so long that I wept in sympathy, and fastened my arms tightly around my sister Frances's neck and hid my eyes against her shoulder. Still I heard that hungry cry, until a husky voice shouted,

"Be quiet, you crying children, or I'll shoot you."

But the silence was again and again broken by that heartrending plea, and again and again were the voices hushed by the same terrifying threat. And we three, fresh from our loving mother's embrace, believed the awful menace no vain threat.

We were cold, and too frightened to feel hungry, nor were we offered food that night, but next morning Mr. Reed's little daughter Mattie appeared carrying in her apron a number of newly baked biscuits which her father had just taken from the hot ashes of his camp fire. Joyfully she handed one to each inmate of the cabin, then departed to join those ready to set forth on the journey to the settlement. Few can know how delicious those biscuits tasted, and how carefully we caught each dropping crumb. The place seemed drearier after their giver left us, yet we were glad that her father was taking her to her mother in California.

Soon the great storm which had been lowering broke upon us. We were not exposed to its fury as were those who had just gone from us, but we knew when it came, for snow drifted down upon our bed and had to be scraped off before we could rise. We were not allowed near the fire and spent most of our time on our bed of branches. . . .

How long the storm had lasted, we did not know, nor how many days we had been there. We were forlorn as children can possibly be, when Simon Murphy, who was older than Frances, climbed to his usual lookout on the snow above the cabin to see if any help were coming. He returned to us, stammering in his eagerness:

"I seen—a woman—on snowshoes—coming from the other camp! She's a little woman—like Mrs. Donner. She is not looking this way—and may pass!"

Hardly had he spoken her name, before we had gathered around him and were imploring him to hurry back and call our mother. We were too excited to follow him up the steps.

She came to us quickly, with all the tenderness and courage needed to lessen our troubles and soften our fears. Oh, how glad we were to see her, and how thankful she appeared to be with us once more! We heard it in her voice and saw it in her face; and when we begged her not to leave us, she could not answer, but clasped us closer to her bosom, kissed us anew for father's sake, then told how the storm had distressed them. Often had they hoped that we had reached the cabins too late to join the relief—then in grieving anguish felt that we had, and might not live to cross the summit.

She had watched the fall of snow, and measured its depth; had seen it drift between the two camps making the way so treacherous that no one had dared to cross it until the day before her own coming; then she induced Mr. Clark to try to ascertain if Messrs. Cady and Stone had really got us to the cabins in time to go with the second relief.

We did not see Mr. Clark, but he had peered in, taken observations, and returned by nightfall and described to her our condition.

John Baptiste had promised to care for father in her absence. She left our tent in the morning as early as she could see the way. She must have stayed with us overnight, for I went to sleep in her arms, and they were still around me when I awoke; and it seemed like a new day, for we had time for many cherished talks. She veiled from us the ghastliness of death, telling us Aunt Betsy and both our little cousins had gone to heaven. She said Lewis had been first to go, and his mother had soon followed; that she herself had carried little Sammie from his sick mother's tent to ours the very day we three were taken away; and in order to keep him warm while the storm raged, she had laid him close to father's side, and that he had stayed with them until "day before yesterday."

I asked her if Sammie had cried for bread. She replied, "No, he was not hungry, for your mother saved two of those little biscuits which the relief party brought, and every day she soaked a tiny piece in water and fed him all he would eat, and there is still half a biscuit left."

How big that half biscuit seemed to me! I wondered why she had not brought at least a part of it to us. While she was talking with Mrs. Murphy, I could not get it out of my mind. I could see that broken half biscuit, with its ragged edges, and knew that if I had a piece, I would nibble off the rough points first. The longer I waited, the more I wanted it. Finally, I slipped my arm around mother's neck, drew her face close to mine and whispered,

"What are you going to do with the half biscuit you saved?"

"I am keeping it for your sick father," she answered, drawing me closer to her side, laying her comforting cheek against mine, letting my arm keep its place, and my fingers stroke her hair.

---

# In Memory of L. H. W.

*Dorothy Canfield Fisher*

This is a story of a lifetime of struggle made noble by compassion, responsibility, work, and a host of other virtues. It reminds us that in helping others persevere, we find the strength and courage and purpose to persevere ourselves. Vermont writer Dorothy Canfield Fisher (1879–1958) said that as a child she knew the protagonist of this story, a New England farmer born to a hard life, and one day she realized he was a saint.

He began life characteristically, depreciated and disparaged. When he was a white, thin, big-headed baby, his mother, stripping the suds from her lean arms, used to inveigh to her neighbors against his existence. "Wa'n't it just like that *do*-less Lem Warren, not even to leave me foot-free when he died, but a baby coming!"

"*Do*-less," in the language of our valley, means a combination of shiftless and impractical, particularly to be scorned.

Later, as he began to have some resemblance to the appearance he was to wear throughout life, her resentment at her marriage, which she considered the one mistake of her life, kept pace with his growth. "Look at him!" she cried to anyone who would listen. "Ain't that Warren, all over? Did any of *my* folks ever look so like a born fool? Shut your mouth, for the Lord's sake, Lem, and maybe you won't scare folks quite so much."

Lem had a foolish, apologetic grin with which he always used to respond to these personalities, hanging his head to one side and opening and shutting his big hands nervously.

The tumbledown, two-roomed house in which the Warrens lived was across the road from the schoolhouse, and Mrs. Warren's voice was penetrating. Lem was accepted throughout his school life at the home estimate. The ugly, overgrown boy, clad in cast-off, misfit clothing, was allowed to play with the other children only on condition that he perform all the hard, uninteresting parts of any game. Inside the schoolroom it was the same. He never learned to shut his mouth, and his speech was always halting and indistinct, so that he not only did not recite well in class, but was never in one of the school entertainments. He chopped the wood and brought it in, swept the floor and made the fires, and then listened in grinning, silent admiration while the others, arrayed in their best, spoke pieces and sang songs.

He was not "smart at his books" and indeed did not learn even to read very fluently. This may have been partly because the only books he ever saw were old schoolbooks, the use of which was given him free on account of his mother's poverty. He was not allowed, of course, to take them from the schoolroom. But if he was not good at book-learning he was not without accomplishments. He early grew large for his age, and strong from much chopping of wood and drawing of water for his mother's washings, and he was the best swimmer of all those who bathed in the cold, swift mountain stream which rushes near the schoolhouse. The chief consequence of this expertness was that in the summer he was forced to teach each succeeding generation of little boys to swim and dive. They tyrannized over him unmercifully—as, in fact, everyone did.

Nothing made his mother more furious than such an exhibition of what she called "Lem's meachin'ness." "Ain't you got no stand-up *in* ye?" she was wont to exhort him angrily. "If you don't look out for yourself in this world, you needn't think anybody else is gunto!"

The instructions in ethics he received at her hands were the only ones he ever knew, for, up to his fourteenth year, he never had clothes respectable enough to wear to church, and after that he had other things to think of. Fourteen years is what we call in our state "over school age." It was a date to which Mrs. Warren had looked forward with eagerness. After that, the long, unprofitable months of enforced schooling would be over, Lem would be earning steady wages, and she could sit back and "live decent."

It seemed to her more than she could bear, that, almost upon her son's birthday, she was stricken down with paralysis. It was the first calamity for which she could not hold her marriage responsible, and her bitterness thereupon extended itself to fate in general. She cannot have been a cheerful housemate during the next ten years, when Lem was growing silently to manhood.

He was in demand as "help" on the farms about him, on account of his great strength and faithfulness, although the farmers found him exasperatingly slow and, when it was a question of animals, not always sure to obey orders. He could be trusted to be kind to horses, unlike most hired men we get nowadays, but he never learned "how to get the work out of their hide." It was his way, on a steep hill with a heavy load, to lay down the whip, get out, and put his own powerful shoulder to the wheel. If this failed, he unloaded part of the logs and made two trips of it. The uncertainty of his progress can be imagined. The busy and impatient farmer and sawyer at the opposite ends of his route were driven to exhaust their entire vocabulary of objurgation on him. He was, they used to inform him in conclusion, "the most *do*-less critter the Lord ever made!"

He was better with cows and sheep—"feller-feelin'," his mother said scornfully, watching him feed a sick ewe—and he had here, even in comparison with his fellow men, a fair degree of success. It was indeed the foundation of what material prosperity he ever enjoyed. A farmer, short of cash, paid him one year with three or four ewes and a ram. He worked for another farmer to pay for the rent of a pasture and had, that first year, as everybody admitted, almighty good luck with them. There were several twin lambs born that spring and everyone lived. Lem used to make frequent night visits during lambing-time to the pasture to make sure that all was well.

I remember as a little girl starting back from some village festivity late one spring night and seeing a lantern twinkle far up on the mountainside. "Lem Warren out fussin' with his sheep," some one of my elders remarked. Later, as we were almost home, we saw the lantern on the road ahead of us and stopped the horses, country-fashion, for an interchange of salutation. Looking out from under the shawl in which I was wrapped, I saw his tall figure stooping over something held under his coat. The lantern lighted his weather-beaten face and the expression of his eyes as he looked down at the little white head against his breast.

"You're foolish, Lem," said my uncle. "The ewe won't own it if you take it away so long the first night."

"I—I—know," stuttered Lem, bringing out the words with his usual difficulty; "but it's mortal cold up on the mounting for little fellers! I'll bring him up as a cosset."

The incident reminded me vaguely of something I had read about, and it has remained in my memory.

After we drove on I remember that there were laughing speculations about what language old Ma'am Warren would use at having another cosset brought to the house. Not that it could make any more work for her, since Lem did all that was done about the housekeeping. Chained to her chair by her paralyzed legs, as she was, she could accomplish nothing more than to sit and cavil at the management of the universe all day, until Lem came home, gave her her supper, and put her to bed.

Badly run as she thought the world, for a time it was more favorable to her material prosperity than she had ever known it. Lem's flock of sheep grew and thrived. For years nobody in our valley has tried to do much with sheep because of dogs, and all Lem's neighbors told him that some fine morning he would find his flock torn and dismembered. They even pointed out the particular big collie dog who would most likely go "sheep-mad." Lem's heavy face drew into anxious, grotesque wrinkles at this kind of talk, and he visited the uplying pasture more and more frequently.

One morning, just before dawn, he came, pale and shamefaced, to the house of the owner of the collie. The family, roused from bed by his knocking, made out from his speech, more incoherent than usual, that he was begging their pardon for having killed their dog. "I saw wh-where he'd bit th-the throats out of two ewes that w-was due to lamb in a few days and I guess I—I—I must ha' gone kind o' crazy. They was ones I liked special. I'd brought 'em up myself. They—they was all over blood, you know."

They peered at him in the gray light, half afraid of the tall apparition. "How *could* you kill a great big dog like Jack?" they asked wonderingly.

In answer he held out his great hands and his huge corded arms, red with blood up to the elbow. "I heard him worrying another sheep and I—I just—killed him."

One of the children now cried out: "But I shut Jackie up in the woodshed last night!"

Someone ran to open the door and the collie bounded out. Lem turned white in thankfulness. "I'm *mortal* glad," he stammered. "I felt awful bad—afterward. I knew your young ones thought a sight of Jack."

"But what dog did you kill?" they asked.

Some of the men went back up on the mountain with him and found, torn in pieces and scattered wide in bloody fragments, as if destroyed by some great revenging beast of prey, the body of a big gray wolf. Once in a while one wanders over the line from the Canada forests and comes down into our woods, following the deer.

The hard-headed farmers who looked on that savage scene drew back from the shambling man beside them in the only impulse of respect they ever felt for him. It was the one act of his life to secure the admiration of his fellowmen; it was an action of which he himself always spoke in horror and shame.

Certainly his marriage aroused no admiration. It was universally regarded as a most addle-pated, imbecile affair from beginning to end. One of the girls who worked at the hotel in the village "got into trouble," as our vernacular runs, and as she came originally from our district and had gone to school there, everyone knew her and was talking about the scandal. Old Ma'am Warren was of the opinion, spiritedly expressed, that "Lottie was a fool not to make that drummer marry her. She could have, if she'd gone the right way to work." But the drummer remained persistently absent.

One evening Lem, starting for his sheep pasture for his last look for the night, heard someone crying down by the river and then, as he paused to listen, heard it no more. He jumped from the bridge without stopping to set down his lantern, knowing well the swiftness of the water, and caught the poor cowardly thing as she came, struggling and gasping, down with the current. He took her home and gave her dry clothes of his mother's. Then leaving the scared and repentant child by his hearth, he set out on foot for the minister's house and dragged him back over the rough country roads.

When Ma'am Warren awoke the next morning, Lem did not instantly answer her imperious call, as he had done for so many years. Instead, a red-eyed girl in one of Mrs. Warren's own nightgowns came to the door and said shrinkingly: "Lem slept in the barn last night. He give his bed to me; but he'll be in soon. I see him fussin' around with the cow."

Ma'am Warren stared, transfixed with a premonition of irremediable evil. "What you doin' here?" she demanded, her voice devoid of expression through stupefaction.

The girl held down her head. "Lem and I were married last night," she said.

Then Mrs. Warren found her voice.

When Lem came in it was to a scene of the furious wrangling which was henceforth to fill his house.

". . . to saddle himself with such trash as you!" his mother was saying ragingly.

His wife answered in kind, her vanity stung beyond endurance. "Well, you can be sure he'd never have got him a wife any other way! Nobody but a girl hard put to it would take up with a drivel-headed fool like Lem Warren!"

And then the bridegroom appeared at the door and both women turned their attention to him.

When the baby was born, Lottie was very sick. Lem took care of his mother, his wife, and the new baby for weeks and weeks. It was at lambing-time, and his flock suffered from lack of attention, although as much as he dared he left his sick women and tended his ewes. He ran in debt, too, to the grocery stores, for he could work very little and earned almost nothing. Of course the neighbors helped out, but it was no cheerful morning's work to care for the vitriolic old woman, and Lottie was too sick for anyone but Lem to handle. We did pass the baby around from house to house during the worst of his siege, to keep her off Lem's hands; but when Lottie began to get better it was haying-time; everybody was more than busy, and the baby was sent back.

Lottie lingered in semi-invalidism for about a year and then died, Lem holding her hand in his. She tried to say something to him that last night, so the neighbors who were there reported, but her breath failed her and she could only lie staring at him from eyes that seemed already to look from the other side of the grave.

He was heavily in debt when he was thus left with a year-old child not his own, but he gave Lottie a decent funeral and put up over her grave a stone stating that she was "Charlotte, loved wife of Lemuel Warren," and that she died in the eighteenth year of her life. He used to take the little girl and put flowers on the grave, I remember.

Then he went to work again. His sandy hair was already streaked with gray, though he was but thirty. The doctor said the reason for this phenomenon was the great strain of his year of nursing; and indeed throughout that period of his life no one knew when he slept, if ever. He was always up and dressed when anyone else was, and late at night we could look across and see his light still burning and know that he was rubbing Lottie's back or feeding little Susie.

All that was changed now, of course. Susie was a strong, healthy child who slept all through the night in her little crib by her stepfather's corded bed, and in the daytime went everywhere he did. Wherever he "worked out" he used to give her her nap wrapped in a horse blanket on the hay in the barn; and he carried her in a sling of his own contrivance up to his sheep pasture. Old Ma'am Warren disliked the pretty, laughing child so bitterly that he was loath to leave her at home; but when he was there with her, for the first time he asserted himself against his mother, bidding her, when she began to berate the child's parentage, to "be still!" with so strange and unexpected an accent of authority that she was quite frightened.

Susie was very fond of her stepfather at first, but when she came of school age, mixed more with the older children, and heard laughing, contemptuous remarks about him, the frank and devouring egotism of childhood made her ashamed of her affection, ashamed of him with his uncouth gait, his mouth always sagging open, his stammering, ignorant speech, which the other children amused themselves by mocking. Though he was prospering again with his sheep, owned the pasture and his house now, and had even built on another room as well as repairing the older part, he spent little on his own adornment. It all went for pretty clothes for Susie, for better food, for books and pictures, for tickets for Susie to go to the circus and the county fair. Susie knew this and loved him by stealth for it, but the intolerably sensitive vanity of her twelve years made her wretched to be seen in public with him.

Divining this, he ceased going with her to school picnics and Sunday school parties, where he had been a most useful pack animal, and, dressing her in her best with his big calloused hands, watched her from the window join a group of the other children. His mother predicted savagely that his "spoilin' on that bad-blooded young one would bring her to no good end," and when, at fifteen, Susie began to grow very pretty and saucy and willful and to have beaux come to see her, the old woman exulted openly over Lem's helpless anxiety.

He was quite gray now, although not yet forty-five, and so stooped that he passed for an old man. He owned a little farm, his flock of sheep was the largest in the township, and Susie was expected to make a good marriage in spite of her antecedents.

And then Frank Gridley's oldest son, Ed, came back from business college with store clothes and city hats and polished tan shoes, and began idling about, calling on the girls. From the first, he and Susie ran together like two drops of water. Bronson Perkins, a cousin of mine, a big, silent, ruminative lad who had long hung about Susie, stood no show at all. One night in county-fair week, Susie, who had gone to the fair with a crowd of girlfriends, was not at home at ten o'clock. Lem, sitting in his doorway and watching the clock, heard the approach of the laughing, singing straw ride in which she had gone, with a long breath of relief; but the big hay wagon did not stop at his gate.

He called after it in a harsh voice and was told that "Ed Gridley and she went off to the hotel to get supper. He said he'd bring her home later."

Lem went out to the barn, hitched up the faster of his two heavy plow horses and drove from his house to Woodville, eight miles and uphill, in forty-five minutes. When he went into the hotel, the clerk told him that the two he sought had had supper served in a private room. Lem ascertained which room and broke the door in with one heave of his shoulders. Susie sprang up from the disordered supper table and ran to him like a frightened child, clinging to him desperately and crying out that Ed scared her so!

"It's all right now, Susie," he said gently, not looking at the man. "Poppa's come to take you home."

The man felt his dignity wounded. He began to protest boisterously and to declare that he was ready to marry the girl—*"now,* this instant, if you choose!"

Lem put one arm about Susie. "I didn't come to make you marry her. I come to keep you from doin' it," he said, speaking clearly for once in his life. "Susie shan't marry a hound that'd do this." And as the other advanced threateningly on him, he struck him a great blow across the mouth that sent him unconscious to the ground.

Then Lem went out, paid for the broken lock, and drove home with Susie behind the foundered plow horse.

The next spring her engagement to Bronson Perkins was announced, though everybody said they didn't see what use it was for folks to get engaged that couldn't ever get married. Mr. Perkins, Bronson's father, was daft, not enough to send him to the asylum, but so that he had to be watched all the time to keep him from doing himself a hurt. He had a horrid way, I remember, of lighting matches and holding them up to his bared arm until the smell of burning flesh went sickeningly through the house and sent someone in a rush to him. Of course it was out of the question to bring a young bride to such a home. Apparently there were years of waiting before them, and Susie was made of no stuff to endure a long engagement.

As a matter of fact, they were married that fall, as soon as Susie could get her things ready. Lem took old Mr. Perkins into the room

Susie left vacant. " 'Twon't be much more trouble taking care of two old people than one," he explained briefly.

Ma'am Warren's comments on this action have been embalmed forever in the delighted memories of our people. We have a taste for picturesque and forceful speech.

From that time we always saw the lunatic and the bent shepherd together. The older man grew quieter under Lem's care than he had been for years, and if he felt one of his insane impulses overtaking him, ran totteringly to grasp his protector's arm until, quaking and shivering, he was himself again. Lem used to take him up to the sheep pasture for the day sometimes. He liked it up there himself, he said, and maybe 'twould be good for Uncle Hi. He often reported with pride that the old man talked as sensible as anybody, "get him off where it's quiet." Indeed, when Mr. Perkins died, six years later, we had forgotten that he was anything but a little queer, and he had known many happy, lucid hours with his grandchildren.

Susie and Bronson had two boys—sturdy, hearty children, in whom Lem took the deepest, shyest pride. He loved to take them off into the woods with him and exulted in their quick intelligence and strong little bodies. Susie got into the way of letting him take a good deal of the care of them.

It was Lem who first took alarm about the fall that little Frank had, down the cellar stairs. He hurt his spine somehow—our local doctor could not tell exactly how—and as the injury only made him limp a little, nobody thought much about it, until he began to have difficulty in walking. Then Lem sent for a doctor from Rutland who, as soon as he examined the child, stuck out his lower lip and rubbed his chin ominously. He pronounced the trouble something with a long name which none of us had ever heard, and said that Frank would be a hopeless cripple if it were not cured soon. There was, he said, a celebrated doctor from Europe now traveling in this country who had a wonderful new treatment for this condition. But under the circumstances—he looked about the plain farm sitting room—he supposed that was out of the question.

"What did the doctor from foreign parts ask?" queried Bronson, and, being informed of some of the customary prices for major operations, fell back hopeless. Susie, her pretty, childish face drawn and blanched into a wan beauty, put her arms about her sick little son and looked at her stepfather. He had never failed her.

He did not fail her now. He sold the land he had accumulated field by field; he sold the great flock of sheep, every one of which he could call by name; he mortgaged the house over the protesting head of his now bedridden mother; he sold the horse and cow, and the very sticks of furniture from the room where Susie had grown up and where the crazy grandfather of Susie's children had known a peaceful old age and death. Little Frank was taken to New York to the hospital to have the great surgeon operate on him—he is there yet, almost completely recovered and nearly ready to come home.

Back in Hillsboro, Lem now began life all over again, hiring out humbly to his neighbors and only stipulating that he should have enough free time to take care of his mother. Three weeks ago she had her last stroke of paralysis and, after lying speechless for a few days, passed away, grim to the last, by the expression in her fierce old eyes.

The day after her funeral Lem did not come to work as he was expected. We went over to his house and found, to our consternation, that he was not out of bed.

"Be ye sick, Lem?" asked my uncle.

He looked at us over the bedclothes with his old foolish, apologetic smile. "Kind o' lazy, I guess," he whispered, closing his eyes.

The doctor was put out by the irregularity of the case. "I can't make out anything *really* the trouble!" he said. "Only the wheels don't go round as fast as they ought. Call it failing heart action if you want a label."

The wheels ran more and more slowly until it was apparent to all of us that before long they would stop altogether. Susie and Bronson were in New York with little Frank, so that Lem's care during the last days devolved on the haphazard services of the neighbors. He was out of his head most of the time, though never violent, and all through the long nights lay flat on his back, looking at the ceiling with bright, blank eyes, driving his ox team, skidding logs, plowing in stony ground and remembering to favor the off-horse whose wind wasn't good, planting, hoeing, tending his sheep, and teaching obstinate lambs to drink. He used quaint, coaxing names for these, such as a mother uses for her baby. He was up in the mountain pasture a good deal, we gathered, and at night, from his constant mention of how bright the stars shone. And sometimes, when he was in evident pain, his delusion took the form that Susie, or the little boys, had gone up with him, and got lost in the woods.

I was on duty the night he died. We thought a change was near, because he had lain silent all day, and we hoped he would come to himself when he awoke from this stupor. Near midnight he began to talk again, and I could not make out at first whether he was still wandering or not. "Hold on hard, Uncle Hi," I heard him whisper.

A spoon fell out of my hand and clattered against a plate. He gave a great start and tried to sit up. "Yes, mother—coming!" he called hoarsely, and then looked at me with his own eyes. "I must ha' forgot about mother's bein' gone," he apologized sheepishly.

I took advantage of this lucid interval to try to give him some medicine the doctor had left. "Take a swallow of this," I said, holding the glass to his lips.

"What's it for?" he asked.

"It's a heart stimulant," I explained. "The doctor said if we could get you through tonight you have a good chance."

His face drew together in grotesque lines of anxiety. "Little Frank worse?"

"Oh, no, he's doing finely."

"Susie all right?"

"Why, yes," I said wonderingly.

"Nothing the matter with her other boy?"

"Why, no, no," I told him. "Everybody's all right. Here, just take this down."

He turned away his head on the pillow and murmured something I did not catch. When I asked him what he said, he smiled feebly as in deprecation of his well-known ridiculous ways. "I'm just as much obliged to you," he said, "but if everybody's all right, I guess I won't have any medicine." He looked at me earnestly. "I'm —I'm real tired," he said.

It came out in one great breath—apparently his last, for he did not move after that, and his ugly, slack-mouthed face was at once quite still. Its expression made me think of the time I had seen it as a child, by lantern light, as he looked down at the newborn lamb on his breast.

# Will

*Ella Wheeler Wilcox*

There is no chance, no destiny, no fate,
Can circumvent or hinder or control
The firm resolve of a determined soul.
Gifts count for nothing; will alone is great;
All things give way before it, soon or late.
What obstacle can stay the mighty force
Of the sea-seeking river in its course,
Or cause the ascending orb of day to wait?

Each well-born soul must win what it deserves.
Let the fool prate of luck. The fortunate
Is he whose earnest purpose never swerves,
Whose slightest action or inaction serves
The one great aim. Why, even Death stands still,
And waits an hour sometimes for such a will.

---

# I Decline to Accept the End of Man

*William Faulkner*

William Faulkner (1897–1962) gave this short but spectacular address on the evening of December 10, 1950, at a state dinner in Stockholm, Sweden, where he had traveled to accept the Nobel Prize for literature. It is foremost an exhortation to young writers, a reminder that artistic creation does have duties, and that forgetting those duties relegates one's work to the ranks of mediocrity. But his words speak to every reader of literature as well. Faulkner reminds us that *what* we study in school and *what* we read in our precious spare time matters. Great literature—the kind we cannot afford to miss—speaks to problems of the spirit, the "human heart in conflict with itself," and nothing less. It lifts our eyes to the virtues we possess and the nobility we would acquire, and helps us to prevail.

I feel that this award was not made to me as a man, but to my work—a life's work in the agony and sweat of the human spirit, not for glory and least of all for profit, but to create out of the materials of the human spirit something which did not exist before. So this award is only mine in trust. It will not be difficult to find a dedication for the money part of it commensurate with the purpose and significance of its origin. But I would like to do the same with the acclaim too, by using this moment as a pinnacle from which I might be listened to by the young men and women already dedicated to the same anguish and travail, among whom is already that one who will someday stand here where I am standing.

Our tragedy today is a general and universal physical fear so long sustained by now that we can even bear it. There are no longer problems of the spirit. There is only the question: When will I be blown up? Because of this, the young man or woman writing today has forgotten the problems of the human heart in conflict with itself which alone can make good writing because only that is worth writing about, worth the agony and the sweat.

He must learn them again. He must teach himself that the basest of all things is to be afraid; and, teaching himself that, forget it forever, leaving no room in his workshop for anything but the old verities and truths of the heart, the old universal truths lacking which any story is ephemeral and doomed—love and honor and pity and pride and compassion and sacrifice. Until he does so, he labors under a curse. He writes not of love but of lust, of defeats in which nobody loses anything of value, of victories without hope and, worst of all, without pity or compassion. His griefs grieve on no universal bones, leaving no scars. He writes not of the heart but of the glands.

Until he relearns these things, he will write as though he stood among and watched the end of man. I decline to accept the end of man. It is easy enough to say that man is immortal simply because he will endure: that when the last ding-dong of doom has clanged and faded from the last worthless rock hanging tideless in the last red and dying evening, that even then there will still be one more sound: that of his puny inexhaustible voice, still talking. I refuse to accept this. I believe that man will not merely endure: he will prevail. He is immortal, not because he alone among creatures has an inexhaustible voice, but because he has a soul, a spirit capable of compassion and sacrifice and endurance. The poet's, the writer's, duty is to write about these things. It is his privilege to help man endure by lifting his heart, by reminding him of the courage and honor and hope and pride and compassion and pity and sacrifice which have been the glory of his past. The poet's voice need not merely be the record of man, it can be one of the props, the pillars to help him endure and prevail.

# 8

# Honesty

TO be honest is to be real, genuine, authentic, and bona fide. To be dishonest is to be partly feigned, forged, fake, or fictitious. Honesty expresses both self-respect and respect for others. Dishonesty fully respects neither oneself nor others. Honesty imbues lives with openness, reliability, and candor; it expresses a disposition to live in the light. Dishonesty seeks shade, cover, or concealment. It is a disposition to live partly in the dark.

Why would anyone want to be dishonest? That is a question with which the Irish satirist Jonathan Swift poignantly confronts his readers in "A Voyage to the Houyhnhnms" in *Gulliver's Travels.* The Houyhnhnms were such rational creatures that they found dishonesty almost unintelligible. As one of them explains to Gulliver, "the use of speech was to make us understand one another, and to receive information of facts; now if anyone *said the thing which was not* [the Houyhnhnms' awkward locution for referring to the curious practice of telling lies], these ends were defeated."

Dishonesty would have no role to play in a world that revered reality and was inhabited by fully rational creatures. Human beings are not fully rational, however, as Swift delighted in pointing out. Humans, unlike Houyhnhnms, harbor a disparate array of tendencies and impulses that do not spontaneously harmonize with reason. Human beings need both practice and study over time to become persons of integrity and effective goodwill. And until they have achieved such a state, they may do all sorts of things that prudence tells them had better be concealed. Lying is an "easy" tool of concealment, and when often employed, all too easily hardens into a malignant vice.

Honesty is of pervasive human importance. "I hate that man like the very Gates of Death who says one thing but hides another in his heart," cries the anguished Achilles in Homer's *Iliad.* Every social activity, every human enterprise requiring people to act in concert, is impeded when people aren't honest with one another. Honesty here is not just veracity—truth-telling—but the honesty of "an honest day's work for an honest day's pay." It is the honesty that the prophet Jeremiah sought. "Run to and fro through the streets of Jerusalem, look around and take note! Search its squares and see if you can find one person who acts justly and seeks truth." It is the honesty that the Cynic philosopher Diogenes sought later in Athens and Corinth, an image that has proved remarkably durable. "With Candle and Lanthorn, when the Sun shin'd I sought Honest Men, but none could I find," as a seventeenth-century chapbook put it. Pinocchio's lie-lengthened nose is an image scarcely a hundred years old now, but it, too, has happily found a place among our enduring popular stories.

How is honesty best cultivated? Like most virtues, it is best developed and exercised in harmony with others. The more it is exercised, the more it becomes a settled disposition. But there is a quick answer that may be given in three words: *take it seriously*. Take recognition of the fact that honesty is a fundamental condition for human intercourse and exchange, for friendship, for all genuine community. But be sure to take it seriously *for itself,* not just as "the best policy."

"Honesty is better than all policy," as the philosopher Immanuel Kant perceptively put it. There is all the moral difference in the world between taking the condition of one's *self* seriously and taking pains not to get caught. Parents often say, "Don't let me catch you doing that again!" and that is all right, but a good, honest life is more than that. Moral development is not a game of "Catch me if you can." It is better to focus clearly on what really matters: *the kind of person one is.*

# The Boy Who Never Told a Lie

An honest heart will always find friends.

Once there was a little boy,
  With curly hair and pleasant eye—
A boy who always told the truth,
  And never, never told a lie.

And when he trotted off to school,
  The children all about would cry,
"There goes the curly-headed boy—
  The boy that never tells a lie."

And everybody loved him so,
  Because he always told the truth,
That every day, as he grew up,
  'Twas said, "There goes the honest youth."

And when the people that stood near
  Would turn to ask the reason why,
The answer would be always this:
  "Because he never tells a lie."

# The Boy Who Cried "Wolf"

*Aesop*

This may be Aesop's most famous fable, and for good reason. The fastest way to lose what we call our "good character" is to lose our honesty.

There was once a shepherd boy who kept his flock at a little distance from the village. Once he thought he would play a trick on the villagers and have some fun at their expense. So he ran toward the village crying out, with all his might:

"Wolf! Wolf! Come and help! The wolves are at my lambs!"

The kind villagers left their work and ran to the field to help him. But when they got there the boy laughed at them for their pains; there was no wolf there.

Still another day the boy tried the same trick, and the villagers came running to help and were laughed at again.

Then one day a wolf did break into the fold and began killing the lambs. In great fright, the boy ran back for help. "Wolf! Wolf!" he screamed. "There is a wolf in the flock! Help!"

The villagers heard him, but they thought it was another mean trick; no one paid the least attention, or went near him. And the shepherd boy lost all his sheep.

That is the kind of thing that happens to people who lie: even when they do tell the truth they will not be believed.

---

# The Honest Woodman

*Adapted from Emilie Poulsson*

This story is retold from a poem by Jean de La Fontaine (1621–1695), who, like Aesop, was a master of the fable.

Once upon a time, out in the green, silent woods near a rushing river that foamed and sparkled as it hurried along, there lived a poor woodcutter who worked hard to make a living for his family. Every day he would trudge into the forest with his strong, sharp axe over his shoulder. He always whistled happily as he went, because he was thinking that as long as he had his health and his axe, he could earn enough to buy all the bread his family needed.

One day he was cutting a large oak tree near the riverside. The chips flew fast at every stroke, and the sound of the ringing axe echoed through the forest so clearly you might have thought a dozen wood choppers were at work that day.

By and by the woodman thought he would rest awhile. He leaned his axe against the tree and turned to sit down, but he tripped over an old, gnarled root, and before he could catch it, his axe slid down the bank and into the river!

The poor woodman gazed into the stream, trying to see the bottom, but it was far too deep there. The river flowed over the lost treasure just as merrily as before.

"What will I do?" the woodman cried. "I've lost my axe! How will I feed my children now?"

Just as he finished speaking, up from the lake rose a beautiful lady. She was the water fairy of the river, and came to the surface when she heard his sad voice.

"What is your sorrow?" she asked kindly. The woodman told her about his trouble, and at once she sank beneath the surface, and reappeared in a moment with an axe made of silver.

"Is this the axe you lost?" she asked.

The woodman thought of all the fine things he could buy for his children with that silver! But the axe wasn't his, so he shook his head, and answered, "My axe was only made of steel."

The water fairy lay the silver axe on the bank, and sank into the river again. In a moment she rose and showed the woodman another axe. "Perhaps this one is yours?" she asked.

The woodman looked. "Oh, no!" he replied. "This one is made of gold! It's worth many times more than mine."

The water fairy lay the golden axe on the bank. Once again she sank. Up she rose. This time she held the missing axe.

"That is mine!" the woodman cried. "That is surely my old axe!"

"It is yours," said the water fairy, "and so are these other two now. They are gifts from the river, because you have told the truth."

And that evening the woodman trudged home with all three axes on his shoulder, whistling happily as he thought of all the good things they would bring for his family.

# Someone Sees You

This folktale reminds us that an act of dishonesty is never truly hidden.

Once upon a time a man decided to sneak into his neighbor's fields and steal some wheat. "If I take just a little from each field, no one will notice," he told himself, "but it will all add up to a nice pile of wheat for me." So he waited for the darkest night, when thick clouds lay over the moon, and he crept out of his house. He took his youngest daughter with him.

"Daughter," he whispered, "you must stand guard, and call out if anyone sees me."

The man stole into the first field to begin reaping, and before long the child called out, "Father, someone sees you!"

The man looked all around, but he saw no one, so he gathered his stolen wheat and moved on to a second field.

"Father, someone sees you!" the child cried again.

The man stopped and looked all around, but once again he saw no one. He gathered more wheat, and moved to a third field.

A little while passed, and the daughter cried out, "Father, someone sees you!"

Once more the man stopped his work and looked in every direction, but he saw no one at all, so he bundled his wheat and crept into the last field.

"Father, someone sees you!" the child called again.

The man stopped his reaping, looked all around, and once again saw no one. "Why in the world do you keep saying someone sees me?" he angrily asked his daughter. "I've looked everywhere, and I don't see anyone."

"Father," murmured the child, "Someone sees you from above."

# George Washington and the Cherry Tree

*Adapted from J. Berg Esenwein and Marietta Stockard*

The chopping down of the cherry tree is surely the most famous truth-telling tale in America. It first appeared in 1806 in the fifth edition of Mason Lock Weems's imaginative biography of Washington, entitled *The Life of George Washington with Curious Anecdotes, Equally Honourable to Himself and Exemplary to His Young Countrymen*. Here is an early twentieth-century rendition.

When George Washington was a little boy he lived on a farm in Virginia. His father taught him to ride, and he used to take young George about the farm with him so that his son might learn how to take care of the fields and horses and cattle when he grew older.

Mr. Washington had planted an orchard of fine fruit trees. There were apple trees, peach trees, pear trees, plum trees, and cherry trees. Once, a particularly fine cherry tree was sent to him from across the ocean. Mr. Washington planted it on the edge of the orchard. He told everyone on the farm to watch it carefully to see that it was not broken or hurt in any way.

It grew well and one spring it was covered with white blossoms. Mr. Washington was pleased to think he would soon have cherries from the little tree.

Just about this time, George was given a shiny new hatchet. George took it and went about chopping sticks, hacking into the rails of fences, and cutting whatever else he passed. At last he came to the edge of the orchard, and thinking only of how well his hatchet could cut, he chopped into the little cherry tree. The bark was soft, and it cut so easily that George chopped the tree right down, and then went on with his play.

That evening when Mr. Washington came from inspecting the farm, he sent his horse to the stable and walked down to the orchard to look at his cherry tree. He stood in amazement when he saw how it was cut. Who would have dared do such a thing? He asked everyone, but no one could tell him anything about it.

Just then George passed by.

"George," his father called in an angry voice, "do you know who killed my cherry tree?

This was a tough question, and George staggered under it for a moment, but quickly recovered.

"I cannot tell a lie, father," he said. "I did it with my hatchet."

Mr. Washington looked at George. The boy's face was white, but he looked straight into his father's eyes.

"Go into the house, son," said Mr. Washington sternly.

George went into the library and waited for his father. He was very unhappy and very much ashamed. He knew he had been foolish and thoughtless and that his father was right to be displeased.

Soon, Mr. Washington came into the room. "Come here, my boy," he said.

George went over to his father. Mr. Washington looked at him long and steadily.

"Tell me, son, why did you cut the tree?"

"I was playing and I did not think—" George stammered.

"And now the tree will die. We shall never have any cherries from it. But worse than that, you have failed to take care of the tree when I asked you to do so."

George's head was bent and his cheeks were red from shame.

"I am sorry, father," he said.

Mr. Washington put his hand on the boy's shoulder. "Look at me," he said. "I am sorry to have lost my cherry tree, but I am glad that you were brave enough to tell me the truth. I would rather have you truthful and brave than to have a whole orchard full of the finest cherry trees. Never forget that, my son."

George Washington never did forget. To the end of his life he was just as brave and honorable as he was that day as a little boy.

# Matilda, Who Told Lies, and Was Burned to Death

*Hilaire Belloc*

In which we learn the fate of a little girl who apparently never took to heart the story of the Boy Who Cried Wolf. This tale takes place in England, the home of its author, Hilaire Belloc (1870–1953).

Matilda told such Dreadful Lies,
It made one gasp and stretch one's eyes;
Her aunt, who, from her earliest youth,
Had kept a strict regard for truth,
Attempted to believe Matilda:
The effort very nearly killed her,
And would have done so, had not she
Discovered this infirmity.
For once, toward the close of day,
Matilda, growing tired of play,
And finding she was left alone,
Went tiptoe
to
the telephone
And summoned the immediate aid
Of London's noble fire brigade.
Within an hour the gallant band
Were pouring in on every hand,
From Putney, Hackney Downs and Bow,
With courage high and hearts aglow
They galloped, roaring through the town,
"Matilda's house is burning down!"
Inspired by British cheers and loud
Proceeding from the frenzied crowd,
They ran their ladders through a score
Of windows on the ballroom floor;
And took peculiar pains to souse

The pictures up and down the house,
Until Matilda's aunt succeeded
In showing them they were not needed
And even then she had to pay
To get the men to go away!

• • • • •

It happened that a few weeks later
Her aunt was off to the theater
To see that interesting play
*The Second Mrs. Tanqueray.*
She had refused to take her niece
To hear this entertaining piece:
A deprivation just and wise
To punish her for telling lies.
That night a fire *did* break out—
You should have heard Matilda shout!
You should have heard her scream and bawl,
And throw the window up and call
To people passing in the street—
(The rapidly increasing heat
Encouraging her to obtain
Their confidence)—but all in vain!
For every time she shouted "Fire!"
They only answered "Little liar!"
And therefore when her aunt returned,
Matilda, and the house, were burned.

---

## Rebecca's Afterthought

*Elizabeth Turner*

In which we learn (with relief) of a much happier ending for a little girl who decided to remain steadfastly honest.

Yesterday, Rebecca Mason,
In the parlor by herself,
Broke a handsome china basin,
Placed upon the mantel shelf.

Quite alarmed, she thought of going
  Very quietly away,
Not a single person knowing,
  Of her being there that day.

But Rebecca recollected
  She was taught deceit to shun;
And the moment she reflected,
  Told her mother what was done;

Who commended her behavior,
Loved her better, and forgave her.

---

# Pinocchio

*Carlo Lorenzini*

The lengthening nose has become one of our instantly recognizable symbols of dishonesty, thanks to this famous scene from Carlo Lorenzini's classic nineteenth-century Italian tale, *Pinocchio*. Here the wooden puppet, with the aid of the Fairy with the Blue Hair, is recovering from the effects of having fallen in with the wrong crowd.

When the three doctors had gone, the Fairy came to Pinocchio and, upon touching his forehead, perceived that he had a high fever. So she put a white powder in a glass of water and gave it to him, saying gently:

"Drink this and after a while you will be well."

Pinocchio gazed at the glass, made a wry face, and asked whiningly:

"Is it sweet or bitter?"

"It is bitter but will do you good."

"If it is bitter, I don't want it."

"Listen to me. Drink it."

"But I don't like bitter things."

"Drink it, and then I will give you a lump of sugar to take the taste out of your mouth."

"Where is the lump of sugar?"

"Here it is."

"Give it to me first, and then I will take the medicine."

"You promise?"

"Yes."

The Fairy gave him the sugar, and Pinocchio soon finished it. Then he said, licking his lips, "How nice it would be if sugar were medicine! I'd take it every day."

"Now keep your promise and take the medicine," said the Fairy. "It will make you well."

Pinocchio held the glass in his hand and sniffed at its contents; then put it to his mouth; then smelled it again; and finally said:

"It's too bitter—too bitter! I can't possibly gulp it down."

"How can you say that when you haven't tasted it?"

"Oh, I can imagine—I can tell by the smell! Give me another lump of sugar and then I will drink it."

So the Fairy, with all the patience of an indulgent mamma, put another lump of sugar in his mouth and then handed him the medicine again.

"Truly I can't drink it!" wailed the marionette with a thousand grimaces.

"Why?"

"Because that pillow is too close to my feet."

The Fairy moved the pillow.

"It's no use—I can't drink it."

"What else annoys you?"

"That door is ajar."

The Fairy shut the door.

"Honestly, I can't drink that bitter stuff," howled Pinocchio. "No, no, no!"

"My boy, you will be sorry."

"I don't care."

"You'll die of the fever."

"I don't care. I'd rather die than take that bitter medicine."

"All right, then," said the Fairy.

At this the door opened and in walked four Rabbits, black as ink, and carrying a coffin on their shoulders.

"What do you want?" cried Pinocchio sitting up.

"We have come to take you away," said the largest Rabbit.

"To take me away? Why, I'm not dead yet!"

"No, not yet, but you will be in a few moments since you have refused the medicine that would make you well."

"O my Fairy, my Fairy!" yelled Pinocchio. "Give me that medicine—quickly! Send them away—I don't want to die—I don't want to die!"

And he seized the glass with both hands and drank the dose down at one gulp.

"Pshaw!" said the Rabbits. "We have come on a fool's errand." And taking the coffin up on their shoulders they went away grumbling.

Not long afterward Pinocchio jumped out of bed entirely well. For, you must know, that wooden boys are rarely ill and then get well quickly. When the Fairy saw him capering around the room happy as a chicken that has just burst its shell, she said:

"So my medicine has really cured you?"

"Yes, indeed. I had a close call."

"Then why did you make such a fuss about taking it?"

"Oh, boys are all alike. We are more afraid of the medicine than of the illness."

"For shame! Boys ought to know that a good remedy taken in time often keeps off a dangerous sickness—perhaps death."

"The next time I shan't be so bad. I shall remember those black Rabbits and the coffin—then I'll take the medicine right away."

"That's right. Now come and tell me how you happened to fall into the hands of thieves."

Pinocchio told faithfully all that had happened to him. When he had ended, the Fairy asked:

"What did you do with the four gold pieces?"

"I lost them," replied Pinocchio. But he told a lie, because he had them in his pocket.

The moment he said this, his nose, which was already long enough, grew four inches longer.

"Where did you lose them?" asked the Fairy.

"In the forest near here."

At this second lie, the nose grew still longer.

"If you have lost them in the forest near here," said the Fairy, "we shall soon find them. For everything here is always found."

"Ah, now I recollect," said the marionette. "I did not lose the coins, but I swallowed them when I took the medicine."

At the third lie, Pinocchio's nose grew so long that he couldn't turn around. If he turned one way he struck it against the bedpost or the window. If he turned the other, he hit the wall or the door.

The Fairy looked at him and began to laugh.

"Why are you laughing?" asked the marionette sheepishly.

"I laugh at the foolish lies you have told."

"How did you know they were lies?"

"Lies, my boy, are recognized at once, because they are of only two kinds. Some have short legs, and others have long noses. Yours are the kind that have long noses."

Pinocchio was so crestfallen that he tried to run away and hide himself, but he couldn't. His nose had grown so long that he couldn't get it through the door.

The Fairy let the marionette cry and howl for a good half hour on account of his long nose. She did this in order to teach him a lesson upon the folly of telling falsehoods. But when she saw his eyes swollen and his face red with weeping, she was moved by pity for him. She clapped her hands together, and at the signal a large flock of woodpeckers flew into the window and, alighting one by one upon Pinocchio's nose, they pecked so hard that in a few moments it was reduced to its usual size.

---

## The Indian Cinderella

*Retold by Cyrus Macmillan*

This North American Indian tale, one of honesty rewarded and dishonesty punished, was recorded in Canada in the early part of the twentieth century. Glooskap, mentioned in the opening paragraph, was a god of the Eastern woodlands Indians.

On the shores of a wide bay on the Atlantic coast there dwelt in old times a great Indian warrior. It was said that he had been one of Glooskap's best helpers and friends, and that he had done for him many wonderful deeds. But that, no man knows. He had, however, a very wonderful and strange power: he could make himself invisible. He could thus mingle unseen with his enemies and listen to their plots. He was known among the people as Strong Wind, the Invisible. He dwelt with his sister in a tent near the sea, and his sister helped him greatly in his work. Many maidens would have been glad to marry him, and he was much sought after because of his mighty deeds; and it was known that Strong Wind would marry the first maiden who could see him as he came home at night. Many made the trial, but it was a long time before one succeeded.

Strong Wind used a clever trick to test the truthfulness of all who sought to win him. Each evening as the day went down, his sister walked on the beach with any girl who wished to make the trial. His sister could always see him, but no one else could see him. And as he came home from work in the twilight, his sister as she saw him drawing near would ask the girl who sought him, "Do you see him?" And each girl would falsely answer "Yes." And his sister would ask, "With what does he draw his sled?" And each girl would answer, "With the hide of a moose," or "With a pole," or "With a great cord." And then his sister would know that they all had lied, for their answers were mere guesses. And many tried and lied and failed, for Strong Wind would not marry any who were untruthful.

There lived in the village a great chief who had three daughters. Their mother had long been dead. One of these was much younger than the others. She was very beautiful and gentle and well beloved by all, and for that reason her older sisters were very jealous of her charms and treated her very cruelly. They clothed her in rags that she might be ugly; and they cut off her long black hair; and they burned her face with coals from the fire that she might be scarred and disfigured. And they lied to their father, telling him that she had done these things herself. But the young girl was patient and kept her gentle heart and went gladly about her work.

Like other girls, the chief's two eldest daughters tried to win Strong Wind. One evening, as the day went down, they walked on the shore with Strong Wind's sister and waited for his coming. Soon he came home from his day's work, drawing his sled. And his sister asked as usual, "Do you see him?" And each one, lying, answered "Yes." And she asked, "Of what is his shoulder strap made?" And each, guessing, said "Of rawhide." Then they entered the tent where they hoped to see Strong Wind eating his supper; and when he took off his coat and his moccasins they could see them, but more than these they saw nothing. And Strong Wind knew that they had lied, and he kept himself from their sight, and they went home dismayed.

One day the chief's youngest daughter with her rags and her

burned face resolved to seek Strong Wind. She patched her clothes with bits of birch bark from the trees, and put on the few little ornaments she possessed, and went forth to try to see the Invisible One as all the other girls of the village had done before. And her sisters laughed at her and called her "fool." And as she passed along the road all the people laughed at her because of her tattered frock and her burned face, but silently she went her way.

Strong Wind's sister received the little girl kindly, and at twilight she took her to the beach. Soon Strong Wind came home drawing his sled. And his sister asked, "Do you see him?" And the girl answered "No," and his sister wondered greatly because she spoke the truth. And again she asked, "Do you see him now?" And the girl answered, "Yes, and he is very wonderful." And she asked, "With what does he draw his sled?" And the girl answered, "With the Rainbow," and she was much afraid. And she asked further, "Of what is his bowstring?" And the girl answered, "His bowstring is the Milky Way."

Then Strong Wind's sister knew that because the girl had spoken the truth at first her brother had made himself visible to her. And she said, "Truly, you have seen him." And she took her home and bathed her, and all the scars disappeared from her face and body; and her hair grew long and black again like the raven's wing; and she gave her fine clothes to wear and many rich ornaments. Then she bade her take the wife's seat in the tent. Soon Strong Wind entered and sat beside her, and called her his bride. The very next day she became his wife, and ever afterward she helped him to do great deeds. The girl's two elder sisters were very cross and they wondered greatly at what had taken place. But Strong Wind, who knew of their cruelty, resolved to punish them. Using his great power, he changed them both into aspen trees and rooted them in the earth. And since that day the leaves of the aspen have always trembled, and they shiver in fear at the approach of Strong Wind, it matters not how softly he comes, for they are still mindful of his great power and anger because of their lies and their cruelty to their sister long ago.

# Truth Is Mighty and Will Prevail

*Retold by Ella Lyman Cabot*

This story is based on events described in the book of Ezra in the Bible. Zorobabel (more frequently spelled "Zerubbabel") was a leader of the Jewish people at the time of their return home from the Babylonian exile, around 520 B.C.

When Darius was crowned king of Persia, he made a great feast to all his subjects throughout one hundred and twenty-seven provinces.

When the celebration was over, Darius went to his palace and fell asleep, but was soon awakened by the conversation of three young men who were standing guard over his bedchamber.

They were disputing as to what was the strongest thing in the world; and, as they became excited, they talked so loud that they awakened their king. But he, instead of telling them to be quiet, listened to their argument. They were saying: "Let each of us write a sentence telling what we think is strongest, and put it under the king's pillow. Then on the morrow he with the three princes of Persia will decide which is wisest. The winner then shall be given great gifts for his victory."

They did as they had agreed. The first wrote: "Wine is strongest."

The second wrote: "The king is strongest."

The third wrote: "Above all, truth beareth the victory."

These writings they placed under the king's pillow. The next day the king sat in his judgment hall with all the princes and governors of provinces around him, and ordered that the three young men should be called to justify their opinions.

The one who thought wine the strongest thing in the world arose, and said: "O men, how strong is wine! It makes fools of even the greatest men. The mightiest king and the most ignorant child are equal when under its power. The sad become gay because of it. It maketh all, even the poorest, feel rich. Their talk becomes inflated, their memories dulled, so that, whether they love or quarrel over their cups, it amounts to the same thing, because afterward they forget all about it. If wine can do this, is it not the strongest thing in the world?"

Then the second defended his belief that the king was the strongest with these words:

"The king is mighty above all else. If he bids men go to war, they do it. They cross countries and mountains, tear down city walls and attack the towers, and, when they have conquered the country, they bring all the spoil to the king. In the same way, when the farmer tills his land and reaps again after his sowing, he pays a large share of it to the king as taxes. He is but a single man, but, when he orders a person put to death, it is done. When he commands others to be spared, they are saved. So all his people obey him, and he does as he pleases. O judges, does not this prove that the king is mightiest?"

Then spake the third young man. Zorobabel was his name.

"O king, great is truth, and stronger than all things. Wine is wicked, the king is wicked, all the children of men are wicked, and they shall perish. But truth lasts forever. She is always strong, she never dies and is never defeated. With truth there is no respect of persons, and she cannot be bribed. She doeth the things that are just. She is the strength, kingdom, power, and majesty of all ages. Blessed be the God of truth."

With these words he finished, and the people burst out in a great shout: "Great is truth, and mighty above all things."

Then the king said: "Ask of me whatever thou wilt. Thou art the wisest."

And the young man said: "Remember thy promise to build Jerusalem in the day when thou comest to thy kingdom. Behold thou hast vowed to rebuild our temple, and now, O king, I desire thee to keep close to truth, and fulfill the promise which thou hast made before the King of heaven."

Then the king kissed him, and sent him to Jerusalem, rejoicing. And the young man turned his face toward heaven, and prayed to Jehovah, saying: "From thee cometh victory, from thee cometh wisdom. Thine is the glory, and I am thy servant."

Thus by the wisdom of the young man Zorobabel, the king of Persia was persuaded to rebuild Jerusalem.

# The Story of Regulus

*Retold by James Baldwin*

This ancient story about the Roman general and statesman Marcus Atilius Regulus takes place in the third century B.C. during the First Punic War between Rome and Carthage. The legend of how Regulus kept his word immortalized him in Roman history.

On the other side of the sea from Rome there was once a great city named Carthage. The Roman people were never very friendly to the people of Carthage, and at last a war began between them. For a long time it was hard to tell which would prove the stronger. First the Romans would gain a battle, and then the men of Carthage would gain a battle; and so the war went on for many years.

Among the Romans there was a brave general named Regulus —a man of whom it was said that he never broke his word. It so happened after a while that Regulus was taken prisoner and carried to Carthage. Ill and very lonely, he dreamed of his wife and little children so far away beyond the sea; and he had but little hope of ever seeing them again. He loved his home dearly, but he believed that his first duty was to his country; and so he had left all, to fight in this cruel war.

He had lost a battle, it is true, and had been taken prisoner. Yet he knew that the Romans were gaining ground, and the people of Carthage were afraid of being beaten in the end. They had sent into other countries to hire soldiers to help them. But even with these they would not be able to fight much longer against Rome.

One day some of the rulers of Carthage came to the prison to talk with Regulus.

"We should like to make peace with the Roman people," they said, "and we are sure that, if your rulers at home knew how the war is going, they would be glad to make peace with us. We will set you free and let you go home, if you will agree to do as we say."

"What is that?" asked Regulus.

"In the first place," they said, "you must tell the Romans about the battles which you have lost, and you must make it plain to them that they have not gained anything by the war. In the second place, you must promise us that, if they will not make peace, you will come back to your prison."

"Very well," said Regulus. "I promise you that if they will not make peace, I will come back to prison."

And so they let him go, for they knew that a great Roman would keep his word.

When he came to Rome, all the people greeted him gladly. His wife and children were very happy, for they thought that now they would not be parted again. The white-haired Fathers who made the laws for the city came to see him. They asked him about the war.

"I was sent from Carthage to ask you to make peace," he said. "But it will not be wise to make peace. True, we have been beaten in a few battles, but our army is gaining ground every day. The people of Carthage are afraid, and well they may be. Keep on with the war a little while longer, and Carthage shall be yours. As for me, I have come to bid my wife and children and Rome farewell. Tomorrow I will start back to Carthage and to prison, for I have promised."

Then the Fathers tried to persuade him to stay.

"Let us send another man in your place," they said.

"Shall a Roman not keep his word?" answered Regulus. "I am ill, and at the best have not long to live. I will go back as I promised."

His wife and little children wept, and his sons begged him not to leave them again.

"I have given my word," said Regulus. "The rest will be taken care of."

Then he bade them goodbye, and went bravely back to the prison and the cruel death which he expected.

This was the kind of courage that made Rome the greatest city in the world.

# The Character of a Happy Life

*Henry Wotton*

How happy is he born and taught,
That serveth not another's will;
Whose armor is his honest thought,
And simple truth his utmost skill!

Whose passions not his masters are,
Whose soul is still prepared for death,
Untied unto the worldly care
Of public fame, or private breath;

Who envies none that chance doth raise,
Or vice; who never understood
How deepest wounds are given by praise;
Nor rules of state, but rules of good:

Who hath his life from rumors freed,
Whose conscience is his strong retreat;
Whose state can neither flatterers feed,
Nor ruin make oppressors great;

Who God doth late and early pray,
More of his grace than gifts to lend;
And entertains the harmless day
With a religious book or friend

This man is freed from servile bands,
Of hope to rise, or fear to fall;
Lord of himself, though not of lands;
And having nothing, yet hath all.

# Honest Abe

*Retold by Horatio Alger*

It is surely no accident that the two most beloved American presidents, Washington and Lincoln, possessed a proverbial honesty. The following stories come from Horatio Alger's *Abraham Lincoln, The Backwoods Boy,* published in 1883. (Alger, in turn, is drawing from earlier works.) The tales remind us that honesty in private life makes honesty in public office. More important, they show us that habits of a truthful heart begin early in life.

## *The Young Storekeeper*

As a clerk he proved honest and efficient, and my readers will be interested in some illustrations of the former trait which I find in Dr. Holland's interesting volume.

One day a woman came into the store and purchased sundry articles. They footed up two dollars and six and a quarter cents, or the young clerk thought they did. We do not hear nowadays of six and a quarter cents, but this was a coin borrowed from the Spanish currency, and was well known in my own boyhood.

The bill was paid, and the woman was entirely satisfied. But the young storekeeper, not feeling quite sure as to the accuracy of his calculation, added up the items once more. To his dismay he found that the sum total should have been but two dollars.

"I've made her pay six and a quarter cents too much," said Abe, disturbed.

It was a trifle, and many clerks would have dismissed it as such. But Abe was too conscientious for that.

"The money must be paid back," he decided.

This would have been easy enough had the woman lived "just round the corner," but, as the young man knew, she lived between two and three miles away. This, however, did not alter the matter. It was night, but he closed and locked the store, and walked to the residence of his customer. Arrived there, he explained the matter, paid over the six and a quarter cents, and returned satisfied. If I were a capitalist, I would be willing to lend money to such a young man without security.

Here is another illustration of young Lincoln's strict honesty:

A woman entered the store and asked for half a pound of tea.

The young clerk weighed it out, and handed it to her in a parcel. This was the last sale of the day.

The next morning, when commencing his duties, Abe discovered a four-ounce weight on the scales. It flashed upon him at once that he had used this in the sale of the night previous, and so, of course, given his customer short weight. I am afraid that there are many country merchants who would not have been much worried by this discovery. Not so the young clerk in whom we are interested. He weighed out the balance of the half pound, shut up the store, and carried it to the defrauded customer. I think my young readers will begin to see that the name so often given, in later times to President Lincoln, of "Honest Old Abe," was well deserved. A man who begins by strict honesty in his youth is not likely to change as he grows older, and mercantile honesty is some guarantee of political honesty.

## *Working Out a Book*

All the information we can obtain about this early time is interesting for it was then that Abe was laying the foundation of his future eminence. His mind and character were slowly developing, and shaping themselves for the future.

From Mr. Lamon's *Life* I quote a paragraph which will throw light upon his habits and tastes at the age of seventeen:

"Abe loved to lie under a shade tree, or up in the loft of the cabin, and read, cipher, and scribble. At night he sat by the chimney jamb, and ciphered by the light of the fire, on the wooden fire shovel. When the shovel was fairly covered, he would shave it off with Tom Lincoln's drawing knife, and begin again. In the daytime he used boards for the same purpose, out of doors, and went through the shaving process everlastingly. His stepmother repeats often that 'he read every book he could lay his hands on.' She says, 'Abe read diligently. He read every book he could lay his hands on, and when he came across a passage that struck him, he would write it down on boards if he had no paper, and keep it there until he did get paper. Then he would rewrite it, look at it, repeat it. He had a copybook, a kind of scrapbook, in which he put down all things, and thus preserved them.' "

I am tempted also to quote a reminiscence of John Hanks, who lived with the Lincolns from the time Abe was fourteen to the time he became eighteen years of age: "When Lincoln—Abe—and I returned to the house from work, he would go to the cupboard, snatch a piece of cornbread, take down a book, sit down on a chair, cock his legs up as high as his head, and read. He and I worked barefooted, grubbed it, plowed, mowed, and cradled together; plowed corn, gathered it, and shucked corn. Abraham read constantly when he had opportunity."

It may well be supposed, however, that the books upon which Abe could lay hands were few in number. There were no libraries, either public or private, in the neighborhood, and he was obliged to read what he could get rather than those which he would have chosen, had he been able to select from a large collection. Still, it is a matter of interest to know what books he actually did read at this formative period. Some of them certainly were worth reading, such as *Aesop's Fables, Robinson Crusoe, Pilgrim's Progress,* a *History of the United States,* and Weems's *Life of Washington.* The last book Abe borrowed from a neighbor, old Josiah Crawford (I follow the statement of Mr. Lamon, rather than of Dr. Holland, who says it was Master Crawford, his teacher). When not reading it, he laid it away in a part of the cabin where he thought it would be free from harm, but it so happened that just behind the shelf on which he placed it was a great crack between the logs of the wall. One night a storm came up suddenly, the rain beat in through the crevice, and soaked the borrowed book through and through. The book was almost utterly spoiled. Abe felt very uneasy, for a book was valuable in his eyes, as well as in the eyes of its owner.

He took the damaged volume and trudged over to Mr. Crawford's in some perplexity and mortification.

"Well, Abe, what brings you over so early?" said Mr. Crawford.

"I've got some bad news for you," answered Abe, with lengthened face.

"Bad news! What is it?"

"You know the book you lent me—the *Life of Washington?*"

"Yes, yes."

"Well, the rain last night spoiled it." And Abe showed the book, wet to a pulp inside, at the same time explaining how it had been injured.

"It's too bad, I vum! You'd ought to pay for it, Abe. You must have been dreadful careless!"

"I'd pay for it if I had any money, Mr. Crawford."

"If you've got no money, you can work it out," said Crawford.

"I'll do whatever you think right."

So it was arranged that Abe should work three days for Crawford, "pulling fodder," the value of his labor being rated at twenty-five cents a day. As the book had cost seventy-five cents this would be regarded as satisfactory. So Abe worked his three days, and discharged the debt. Mr. Lamon is disposed to find fault with Crawford for exacting this penalty, but it appears to me only equitable, and I am glad to think that Abe was willing to act honorably in the matter.

---

# The Frog Prince

*Adapted from the Brothers Grimm*

We catch the moral of this story in the king's conscience: "That which thou hast promised must thou perform."

In the old times, when it was still of some use to wish for the thing one wanted, there lived a King whose daughters were all handsome, but the youngest was so beautiful that the sun himself, who has seen so much, wondered each time he shone over her because of her beauty. Near the royal castle there was a great dark wood, and in the wood under an old linden tree was a well. When the day was hot, the King's daughter used to go forth into the wood and sit by the brink of the cool well, and if the time seemed long, she would take out a golden ball, and throw it up and catch it again, and this was her favorite pastime.

Now it happened one day that the golden ball, instead of falling back into the maiden's little hand which had sent it aloft, dropped to the ground near the edge of the well and rolled in. The king's daughter followed it with her eyes as it sank, but the well was deep, so deep that the bottom could not be seen. Then she began to weep, and she wept and wept as if she could never be comforted. And in the midst of her weeping she heard a voice saying to her,

"What ails thee, king's daughter? Thy tears would melt a heart of stone."

And when she looked to see where the voice came from, there was nothing but a frog stretching his thick ugly head out of the water.

"Oh, is it you, old waddler?" said she. "I weep because my golden ball has fallen into the well."

"Never mind, do not weep," answered the frog. "I can help you. But what will you give me if I fetch up your ball again?"

"Whatever you like, dear frog," said she. "Any of my clothes, my pearls and jewels, or even the golden crown that I wear."

"Thy clothes, thy pearls and jewels, and thy golden crown are not for me," answered the frog. "But if thou wouldst love me, and have me for thy companion and playfellow, and let me sit by thee at table, and eat from thy plate, and drink from thy cup, and sleep in thy little bed—if thou wouldst promise all this, then would I dive below the water and fetch thee thy golden ball again."

"Oh yes," she answered. "I will promise it all, whatever you want, if you will only get me my ball again."

But she thought to herself, "What nonsense he talks! As if he could do anything but sit in the water and croak with the other frogs, or could possibly be anyone's companion."

But the frog, as soon as he heard her promise, drew his head under the water and sank down out of sight, but after a while he came to the surface again with the ball in his mouth, and he threw it on the grass.

The King's daughter was overjoyed to see her pretty plaything again, and she caught it up and ran off with it.

"Stop, stop!" cried the frog. "Take me up too! I cannot run as fast as you!"

But it was of no use, for croak, croak after her as he might, she would not listen to him, but made haste home, and very soon forgot all about the poor frog, who had to betake himself to his well again.

The next day, when the King's daughter was sitting at the table with the King and all the court, and eating from her golden plate, there came something pitter patter up the marble stairs, and then there came a knocking at the door, and a voice crying, "King's youngest daughter, let me in!"

And she got up and ran to see who it could be, but when she opened the door, there was the frog sitting outside. Then she shut the door hastily and went back to her seat, feeling very uneasy. The King noticed how quickly her heart was beating, and said, "My child, what are you afraid of? Is there a giant standing at the door ready to carry you away?"

"Oh no," answered she, "no giant, but a horrid frog."

"And what does the frog want?" asked the King.

"O dear father," answered she, "when I was sitting by the well yesterday, and playing with my golden ball, it fell into the water, and while I was crying for the loss of it, the frog came and got it again for me on condition I would let him be my companion, but I never thought that he could leave the water and come after me; and now there he is outside the door, and he wants to come in to me."

And then they all heard him knocking the second time and crying,

"King's youngest daughter,
Open to me!
By the well water
What promised you me?
King's youngest daughter
Now open to me!"

"That which thou hast promised must thou perform," said the King. "So go now and let him in."

So she went and opened the door, and the frog hopped in, following at her heels, till she reached her chair. Then he stopped and cried, "Lift me up to sit by you."

But she delayed doing so until the King ordered her. When once the frog was on the chair, he wanted to get on the table, and there he sat and said, "Now push your golden plate a little nearer, so that we may eat together."

And so she did, but everybody might see how unwilling she was, and the frog feasted heartily, but every morsel seemed to stick in her throat.

"I have had enough now," said the frog at last, "and as I am tired, you must carry me to your room, and make ready your silken bed, and we will lie down and go to sleep."

Then the King's daughter began to weep, and was afraid of the cold frog, that nothing would satisfy him but he must sleep in her pretty clean bed. Now the King grew angry with her, saying, "That which thou hast promised in thy time of necessity, must thou now perform."

So she picked up the frog with her finger and thumb, carried him upstairs and put him in a corner, and when she had lain down to sleep, he came creeping up, saying, "I am tired and want sleep as much as you. Take me up, so I can rest."

He looked so sad, she suddenly felt ashamed. "Father is right," she thought. "I must keep my promises." She lifted him and gently dropped him onto a pillow.

But as he fell, he ceased to be a frog, and became all at once a prince with beautiful kind eyes. And it came to pass that, with her father's consent, they became bride and bridegroom. And he told her how a wicked witch had bound him by her spells, and how no one but she alone could have released him, and that they two would go together to his father's kingdom. And there came to the door a carriage drawn by eight white horses, with white plumes on their heads, and with golden harness, and behind the carriage was standing faithful Henry, the servant of the young prince. Now, faithful Henry had suffered such care and pain when his master was turned into a frog, that he had been obliged to wear three iron bands over his heart, to keep it from breaking with trouble and anxiety. When the carriage started to take the prince to his kingdom, and faithful Henry had helped them both in, he got up behind, and was full of joy at his master's deliverance. And when they had gone a part of the way, the prince heard a sound at the back of the carriage, as if something had broken, and he turned around and cried,

"Henry, the wheel must be breaking!" But Henry answered:

"The wheel does not break,
'Tis the band round my heart
That, to lessen its ache,
When I grieved for your sake,
I bound round my heart."

Again, and yet once again there was the same sound, and the prince thought it must be the wheel breaking, but it was the breaking of the other bands from faithful Henry's heart, because it was now so relieved and happy.

# The Pied Piper of Hamelin

*Adapted from Joseph Jacobs*

This famous German legend of a broken bargain seems to be based at least in part on an actual occurrence. Old writings on the walls of some of Hamelin's houses indicate that one day in July of 1284, a piper did indeed lead some 130 children out of town, and that they were lost somehow in nearby Koppen Hill. Some believe that outlaws kidnapped the children, while others speculate that the mysterious piper was actually recruiting youths to emigrate to eastern Europe.

A very long time ago the sleepy little town of Hamelin was invaded by rats, the likes of which had never been seen before. The awful creatures ran through the streets and swarmed over the houses. They fought the dogs, and chased the cats, and nibbled at babies in their cradles, and hid inside pockets, and made nests out of hats. It got so bad, you couldn't set your foot down anywhere without hearing a squeak from beneath your heel.

Well, needless to say, the mayor and the town council were at their wits' end. As they were sitting one day in the town hall racking their poor brains, and bewailing their hard fate, who should run in but the chief of police.

"Please, your honor," he said, "there is a very strange fellow who demands to see you. He just came to town, and I don't know quite what to make of him."

"Show him in," said the mayor, and in he stepped. He was an odd-looking stranger, without a doubt. He was tall and gawky, dried and bronzed, with a crooked nose, a long rat-tail mustache, and keen piercing eyes. And if you looked hard enough, you could find every single color of the rainbow in his jacket and breeches.

"I'm called the Pied Piper," he began. "And what might you be willing to pay me, if I rid Hamelin of every last rat?"

Well, as much as the town government feared the rats, it feared even more spending the good taxpayers' money (for those were very different times, you know), so they haggled and haggled. But the

Pied Piper was not a man to stand for any nonsense, and the upshot was that fifty dollars were promised (which was a lot of money in those days, even to elected officials) as soon as not a rat was left to squeak or scurry in Hamelin.

Out of the hall stepped the Pied Piper, and as he stepped he laid his pipe to his lips, and a shrill, keen tune sounded through every street and house. And as each note pierced the air, you would have seen a strange sight if you'd been in Hamelin that day. For out of every hole the rats came tumbling. There were none too old and none too young, none too big and none too little, to crowd at the Pied Piper's heels. With eager feet and upturned noses they pattered after him as he paced the streets. Nor was the Pied Piper unmindful of the little toddling ones, for every fifty yards he'd stop and give an extra flourish on his pipe just to give them time to keep up with the older and stronger of the band.

Up Silver Street he went, and down Gold Street, and the end of Gold Street was the river. As he paced along, slowly and gravely, the townspeople flocked to their doors and windows, and many a blessing they called down upon his head.

When he reached the river's edge, he stepped into a boat, and as he shoved off into the water, piping shrilly all the time, every single rat followed him, splashing, paddling, and wagging their tails with delight. On and on he played until he was way downstream, where the current gets quick, and every last rat was swept away, never to be seen again.

Then the Pied Piper landed his boat and walked back upstream to Hamelin. You may fancy the townspeople had been throwing up their caps and hurrahing and stopping up rat holes and setting the church bells ringing. But when the Pied Piper stepped ashore and not so much as a single squeak was to be heard, the mayor and the council, and the townspeople generally, began to hah and to hum and to shake their heads.

For the town chest had been sadly emptied of late (which goes to show that governments then weren't really much different than they are today, after all) and where was the fifty dollars to come from? And besides, the Pied Piper's job had been so easy. Just getting into a boat and playing a pipe! Why, the mayor himself could have done that if only he'd thought of it.

So the mayor hahed and hummed and at last said, "Come, my good man, you see what poor folk we are. How can we manage to pay you fifty dollars? Will you not take twenty? When all is said and done, it will be good pay for the trouble you've taken."

"Fifty dollars is what I bargained for," said the Pied Piper shortly, "and if I were you, I'd live up to my word. For I can pipe many kinds of tunes, as folks sometimes find to their cost."

"Would you threaten us, you strolling vagabond?" shrieked the mayor, and at the same time he winked to the council. "The rats are dead and drowned, so you may do your worst, good man." And with that he turned upon his heel.

"'Very well," said the Pied Piper, and he smiled a quiet smile. "It's not the first time I've met a broken promise, and it won't be the last, I'm sure."

He laid his pipe to his lips afresh, but now there came forth no shrill notes, as it were, of scraping and gnawing, and squeaking and scurrying. This time the tune was joyous and resonant, full of happy laughter and merry play. And as he paced down the streets the elders mocked, but from schoolroom and playroom, from nursery and backyard, the children came running with eager glee at the Pied Piper's call. Dancing, laughing, and joining hands, the bright throng moved up Gold Street and down Silver Street, and beyond Silver Street lay the cool green forest full of old oaks and wide-spreading beeches. Beyond the forest lay the rising hills, and when the merry parade reached the tallest of them all, a door in the earth opened, and the Pied Piper went inside, still playing his tune. All the children followed, and then the door closed.

Only one little boy, who was lame and could not march as fast as the other children, did not make it to the hillside before the door shut fast. When the mayor and the town council came running, they found him wailing.

"What has happened?" they cried.

"I wanted to go with the other children," the child sobbed. "When the man played his pipe, it told of a beautiful land where the sun always shines and the birds always sing and the children are never ill or lame. I ran as fast as I could, but I couldn't keep up, and now they're all gone."

And they were, indeed. The townspeople searched high and low, and the mayor sent his deputies north, south, east, and west to find the Pied Piper. "Tell him I will give him all the gold in the town if he will only bring back the children," the mayor said, but of course who would believe him by then?

The mothers and fathers of Hamelin waited and waited, but their little ones never came back. And it's said that to this day, the people of Hamelin are careful to keep their promises, especially to strange pipers.

# The Emperor's New Clothes

*Hans Christian Andersen*

In this classic, we see that it is often harder to be honest than it is to be silent, and that trusting ourselves is the best road to the truth. We see the pestilence of false flattery, and we find that honesty, unlike new clothes, never goes out of fashion.

Many years ago there was an emperor who was so fond of new clothes that he spent all his money on them. He did not give himself any concern about his army; he cared nothing about the theater or for driving about in the woods, except for the sake of showing himself off in new clothes. He had a costume for every hour in the day, and just as they say of a king or emperor, "He is in his council chamber," they said of him, "The emperor is in his dressing room."

Life was merry and gay in the town where the emperor lived, and numbers of strangers came to it every day. Among them there came one day two rascals, who gave themselves out as weavers and said that they knew how to weave the most exquisite stuff imaginable. Not only were the colors and patterns uncommonly beautiful, but the clothes that were made of the stuff had the peculiar property of becoming invisible to every person who was unfit for the office he held or who was exceptionally stupid.

"Those must be valuable clothes," thought the emperor. "By wearing them I should be able to discover which of the men in my empire are not fit for their posts. I should distinguish wise men from fools. Yes, I must order some of the stuff to be woven for me directly." And he paid the swindlers a handsome sum of money in advance, as they required.

As for them, they put up two looms and pretended to be weaving, though there was nothing whatever on their shuttles. They called for a quantity of the finest silks and of the purest gold thread, all of which went into their own bags, while they worked at their empty looms till late into the night.

"I should like to know how those weavers are getting on with the stuff," thought the emperor. But he felt a little queer when he reflected that those who were stupid or unfit for their office would not be able to see the material. He believed, indeed, that he had nothing to fear for himself, but still he thought it better to send someone else first, to see how the work was coming on. All the people in the town had heard of the peculiar property of the stuff, and everyone was curious to see how stupid his neighbor might be.

"I will send my faithful old prime minister to the weavers," thought the emperor. "He will be best capable of judging this stuff, for he is a man of sense and nobody is more fit for his office than he."

So the worthy old minister went into the room where the two swindlers sat working the empty looms. "Heaven save us!" thought the old man, opening his eyes wide. "Why, I can't see anything at all!" But he took care not to say so aloud.

Both the rogues begged him to step a little nearer and asked him if he did not think the patterns very pretty and the coloring fine. They pointed to the empty loom as they did so, and the poor old minister kept staring as hard as he could—without being able to see anything on it, for of course there was nothing there to see.

"Heaven save us!" thought the old man. "Is it possible that I am a fool! I have never thought it, and nobody must know it. Is it true that I am not fit for my office? It will never do for me to say that I cannot see the stuff."

"Well, sir, do you say nothing about the cloth?" asked the one who was pretending to go on with his work.

"Oh, it is most elegant, most beautiful!" said the dazed old man, as he peered again through his spectacles. "What a fine pattern, and what fine colors! I will certainly tell the emperor how pleased I am with the stuff."

"We are glad of that," said both the weavers; and then they named the colors and pointed out the special features of the pattern. To all of this the minister paid great attention, so that he might be able to repeat it to the emperor when he went back to him.

And now the cheats called for more money, more silk, and more gold thread, to be able to proceed with the weaving, but they put it all into their own pockets, and not a thread went into the stuff, though they went on as before, weaving at the empty looms.

After a little time the emperor sent another honest statesman to see how the weaving was progressing, and if the stuff would soon be ready. The same thing happened with him as with the minister. He gazed and gazed, but as there was nothing but empty looms, he could see nothing else.

"Is not this an exquisite piece of stuff?" asked the weavers, pointing to one of the looms and explaining the beautiful pattern and the colors which were not there to be seen.

"I am not stupid, I know I am not!" thought the man, "so it must be that I am not fit for my good office. It is very strange, but I must not let it be noticed." So he praised the cloth he did not see and assured the weavers of his delight in the lovely colors and the exquisite pattern. "It is perfectly charming," he reported to the emperor.

Everybody in the town was talking of the splendid cloth. The emperor thought he should like to see it himself while it was still on the loom. With a company of carefully selected men, among whom were the two worthy officials who had been there before, he went to visit the crafty impostors, who were working as hard as ever at the empty looms.

"Is it not magnificent?" said both the honest statesmen. "See, Your Majesty, what splendid colors, and what a pattern!" And they pointed to the looms, for they believed that others, no doubt, could see what they did not.

"What!" thought the emperor. "I see nothing at all. This is terrible! Am I a fool? Am I not fit to be emperor? Why nothing more dreadful could happen to me!"

"Oh, it is very pretty! It has my highest approval," the emperor said aloud. He nodded with satisfaction as he gazed at the empty looms, for he would not betray that he could see nothing.

His whole court gazed and gazed, each seeing no more than the others, but, like the emperor, they all exclaimed, "Oh, it is beautiful!" They even suggested to the emperor that he wear the splendid new clothes for the first time on the occasion of a great procession which was soon to take place.

"Splendid! Gorgeous! Magnificent!" went from mouth to mouth. All were equally delighted with the weavers' workmanship. The emperor gave each of the impostors an order of knighthood to be worn in their buttonholes, and the title Gentleman Weaver of the Imperial Court.

Before the day on which the procession was to take place, the weavers sat up the whole night, burning sixteen candles, so that people might see how anxious they were to get the emperor's new clothes ready. They pretended to take the stuff from the loom, they cut it out in the air with huge scissors, and they stitched away with needles that had no thread in them. At last they said, "Now the clothes are finished."

The emperor came to them himself with his grandest courtiers, and each of the rogues lifted his arm as if he held something, saying, "See! here are the trousers! Here is the coat! Here is the cloak," and so on. "It is as light as a spider's web. One would almost feel as if one had nothing on, but that is the beauty of it!"

"Yes," said all the courtiers, but they saw nothing, for there was nothing to see.

"Will Your Majesty be graciously pleased to take off your clothes so that we may put on the new clothes here, before the great mirror?"

The emperor took off his clothes, and the rogues pretended to put on first one garment and then another of the new ones they had pretended to make. They pretended to fasten something round his waist and to tie on something. This they said was the train, and the emperor turned around and around before the mirror.

"How well his Majesty looks in the new clothes! How becoming they are!" cried all the courtiers in turn. "That is a splendid costume!"

"The canopy that is to be carried over Your Majesty in the procession is waiting outside," said the master of ceremonies.

"Well, I am ready," replied the emperor. "Don't the clothes look well?" and he turned around and around again before the mirror, to appear as if he were admiring his new costume.

The chamberlains, who were to carry the train, stooped and put their hands near the floor as if they were lifting it. Then they pretended to be holding something in the air. They would not let it be noticed that they could see and feel nothing.

So the emperor went along in the procession, under the splendid canopy, and everyone in the streets said: "How beautiful the emperor's new clothes are! What a splendid train! And how well they fit!"

No one wanted to let it appear that he could see nothing, for that would prove him not fit for his post. None of the emperor's clothes had been so great a success before.

"But he has nothing on!" said a little child.

"Just listen to the innocent," said its father. And one person whispered to another what the child had said. "He has nothing on. A child says he has nothing on!"

"But he has nothing on," cried all the people. The emperor was startled by this, for he had a suspicion that they were right. But he thought, "I must face this out to the end and go on with the procession." So he held himself more stiffly than ever, and the chamberlains held up the train that was not there at all.

---

## The Boy Who Went to the Sky

*Retold by Carolyn Sherwin Bailey*

This Cherokee Indian tale about fair play takes place in the Blue Ridge country of what is now western North Carolina. Playing by the rules is a big part of "how you play the game," both on and off the field.

There was once upon a time a boy who was a fine ball player of his village of the Cherokee nation. He could catch well, run swiftly to the goal, and almost never did he lose a game for his side. And one season it was decided that his village should play a ball game with the village of the Cherokees on the other side of the Ridge. So the two teams met not far from Pilot Knob, and the game began.

This boy was very anxious, just as a boy of today would be, to help win the game for his village, and for a while the game seemed to be going against him. Time and time again the players from the Indian village on the other side of the Ridge ran and made goal. This made the boy discouraged, and it also made him forget his honor.

His village must make the goal, he thought, so he did a thing which was forbidden in the rules of ball playing. He picked up the ball in his hand and tried to throw it to the goal. The Indians kicked the ball. It was not considered fair to touch it with their hands.

He thought that no one had seen him, and he was successful. The ball went straight to goal, but it did not stop there. The boys and girls and the braves who sat in a wide circle on the grassy field to watch the game saw a strange thing. Bounding away from the goal, the ball went up into the air. Following the ball went the boy who had forgotten the rules of the game. His feet left the ball field. He seemed to be leaping up toward the sky to try and bring back the ball, but neither he nor the ball stopped. Up, up, higher and farther through the blue air they went until the ball was out of sight, and then the boy could no longer be seen.

It was magic which had happened, and the people rubbed their eyes with their wonder, and then they silently went home to their villages. It seemed to them to have been a lesson, for the boy's wrong play had been seen, not only by the Great Spirit of the Cherokee People, but by some of the ball players. They knew why the boy had been taken away from his friends.

That was in the ancient days before the Moon had appeared in the sky, but that night a strange thing happened. Sitting late beside their campfires the braves of all the villages of the Cherokee country saw a huge, round ball of silver rise in the sky and then hang there, lighting the forest trees with its wonderful, pale light. And on the surface of this ball of silver could be seen the face of the boy who had not played fair in the ball game.

It was the ball which had been taken from the ball field up to the sky, and fastened there. In its light could be seen the boy who had been taken from the earth with it. The Moon had come to the heavens, a ball taken from the game field.

Sometimes it was seen that the Moon was smaller. It was sometimes eclipsed. Everybody was amazed at an eclipse of the Moon, for the night would suddenly darken and the tribes would gather and fire guns and beat a drum. This eclipse came about because of a great Frog, who tried to swallow the Moon, and the drum frightened him away.

But the oddest thing about the Moon was its way of waxing and waning. From night to night it would be so large that the Indians could see the face of the Boy-in-the-Moon, and then it would be nothing but a silver thread in the sky above the pine trees.

This happened, the Boy-in-the-Moon told them, to remind ball players never to cheat. When the Moon looked small and pale it was because someone had handled a ball unfairly. So it came about in the Cherokee country that they played ball after that only in the full of the moon.

# Truth and Falsehood

As this folktale from Greece points out, the virtuous soul not only loves truth for its own sake, it loathes the actions of falsehood. Deceit is far more painful for that soul than bearing the hardships that sometimes accompany honesty.

Once upon a time Truth and Falsehood met each other on the road.

"Good afternoon," said Truth.

"Good afternoon," returned Falsehood. "And how are you doing these days?"

"Not very well at all, I'm afraid," sighed Truth. "The times are tough for a fellow like me, you know."

"Yes, I can see that," said Falsehood, glancing up and down at Truth's ragged clothes. "You look like you haven't had a bite to eat in quite some time."

"To be honest, I haven't," admitted Truth. "No one seems to want to employ me nowadays. Wherever I go, most people ignore me or mock me. It's getting discouraging, I can tell you. I'm beginning to ask myself why I put up with it."

"And why the devil do you? Come with me, and I'll show you how to get along. There's no reason in the world why you can't stuff yourself with as much as you want to eat, like me, and dress in the finest clothes, like me. But you must promise not to say a word against me while we're together."

So Truth promised and agreed to go along with Falsehood for a while, not because he liked his company so much, but because he was so hungry he thought he'd faint soon if he didn't get something into his stomach. They walked down the road until they came to a city, and Falsehood at once led the way to the very best table at the very best restaurant.

"Waiter, bring us your choicest meats, your sweetest sweets, your finest wine!" he called, and they ate and drank all afternoon. At last, when they could hold no more, Falsehood began banging his fist on the table and calling for the manager, who came running at once.

"What the devil kind of place is this?" Falsehood snapped. "I gave that waiter a gold piece nearly an hour ago, and he still hasn't brought our change."

The manager summoned the waiter, who said he'd never even seen a penny out of the gentleman.

"What?" Falsehood shouted, so that everyone in the place turned and looked. "I can't believe this place! Innocent, law-abiding citizens come in to eat, and you rob them of their hard-earned money! You're a pack of thieves and liars! You may have fooled me once, but you'll never see me again! Here!" He threw a gold piece at the manager. "Now this time bring me my change!"

But the manager, fearing his restaurant's reputation would suffer, refused to take the gold piece, and instead brought Falsehood change for the first gold piece he claimed to have spent. Then he took the waiter aside and called him a scoundrel, and said he had a mind to fire him. And as much as the waiter protested that he'd never collected a cent from the man, the manager refused to believe him.

"Oh Truth, where have you hidden yourself?" the waiter sighed. "Have you now deserted even us hard-working souls?"

"No, I'm here," Truth groaned to himself, "but my judgment gave way to my hunger, and now I can't speak up without breaking my promise to Falsehood."

As soon as they were on the street, Falsehood gave a hearty laugh and slapped Truth on the back. "You see how the world works?" he cried. "I managed it all quite well, don't you think?"

But Truth slipped from his side.

"I'd rather starve than live as you do," he said.

And so Truth and Falsehood went their separate ways, and never traveled together again.

## Truth, Falsehood, Fire, and Water

This tale about the eternal struggle between truth and falsehood is told in Ethiopia and other eastern African nations.

Long ago Truth, Falsehood, Fire, and Water were journeying together and came upon a herd of cattle. They talked it over and decided it would be fairest to divide the herd into four parts, so each could take home an equal share.

But Falsehood was greedy and schemed to get more for himself.

"Listen to my warning," he whispered, pulling Water to one side. "Fire plans to burn all the grass and trees along your banks and drive your cattle away across the plains so he can have them for himself. If I were you, I'd extinguish him now, and then we can have his share of the cattle for ourselves."

Water was foolish enough to listen to Falsehood, and he dashed himself upon Fire and put him out.

Next Falsehood crept toward Truth.

"Look what Water has done," he whispered. "He has murdered Fire and taken his cattle. We should not consort with the likes of him. We should take all the cattle and go to the mountains."

Truth believed Falsehood and agreed to his plan. Together they drove the cattle into the mountains.

"Wait for me!" Water called, and he hurried after them, but of course he could not run uphill. So he was left all alone in the valley below.

When they reached the top of the highest mountain, Falsehood turned to Truth and laughed.

"I've tricked you, stupid fool," he shrieked. "Now you must give me all the cattle and be my servant, or I'll destroy you."

"Yes, you have tricked me," Truth admitted, "but I will never be your servant."

And so they fought, and when they clashed the thunder rolled back and forth across the mountaintops. Again and again they threw themselves together, but neither could destroy the other.

Finally they decided to call upon the Wind to declare a winner of the contest. So Wind came rushing up the mountain slopes, and he listened to what they had to say.

"It is not for me to declare a winner in this fight," he told them. "Truth and Falsehood are destined to struggle. Sometimes Truth will win, but other times Falsehood will prevail, and then Truth must rise up and fight again. Until the end of the world, Truth must battle Falsehood, and must never rest or let down his guard, or he will be finished once and for all."

And so Truth and Falsehood are fighting to this day.

# Lady Clare

*Alfred Tennyson*

Tennyson (1809–1892) offers us a very old, very valuable lesson that modern ministers and counselors continue to confirm: honesty is one of the most crucial elements of a successful relationship between a man and a woman. Love loves honesty.

It was the time when lilies blow
  And clouds are highest up in air;
Lord Ronald brought a lily-white doe
  To give his cousin, Lady Clare.

I trow they did not part in scorn:
  Lovers long-betroth'd were they:
They too will wed the morrow morn:
  God's blessing on the day!

"He does not love me for my birth,
  Nor for my lands so broad and fair;
He loves me for my own true worth,
  And that is well," said Lady Clare.

In there came old Alice the nurse;
  Said: "Who was this that went from thee?"
"It was my cousin," said Lady Clare;
  "Tomorrow he weds with me."

"O God be thank'd!" said Alice the nurse,
  "That all comes round so just and fair:
Lord Ronald is heir of all your lands,
  And you are not the Lady Clare."

"Are ye out of your mind, my nurse, my nurse,"
  Said Lady Clare, "that ye speak so wild?"
"As God's above," said Alice the nurse,
  "I speak the truth: you are my child.

"The old Earl's daughter died at my breast;
I speak the truth, as I live by bread!
I buried her like my own sweet child,
And put my child in her stead."

"Falsely, falsely have ye done,
O mother," she said, "if this be true,
To keep the best man under the sun
So many years from his due."

"Nay now, my child," said Alice the nurse,
"But keep the secret for your life,
And all you have will be Lord Ronald's
When you are a man and wife."

"If I'm a beggar born," she said,
"I will speak out, for I dare not lie.
Pull off, pull off the brooch of gold,
And fling the diamond necklace by."

"Nay now, my child," said Alice the nurse,
"But keep the secret all ye can."
She said: "Not so: but I will know
If there be any faith in man."

"Nay now, what faith?" said Alice the nurse;
"The man will cleave unto his right."
"And he shall have it," the lady replied,
"Tho' I should die tonight."

"Yet give one kiss to your mother dear!
Alas! my child, I sinn'd for thee."
"O mother, mother, mother," she said,
"So strange it seems to me.

"Yet here's a kiss for my mother dear,
My mother dear, if this be so,
And lay your hand upon my head,
And bless me, mother, ere I go."

She clad herself in a russet gown,
  She was no longer Lady Clare:
She went by dale, and she went by down,
  With a single rose in her hair.

The lily-white doe Lord Ronald had brought
  Leapt up from where she lay,
Dropt her head in the maiden's hand,
  And follow'd her all the way.

Down stept Lord Ronald from his tower:
  "O Lady Clare, you shame your worth!
Why come you drest like a village maid.
  That are the flower of the earth?"

"If I come drest like a village maid,
  I am but as my fortunes are:
I am a beggar born," she said,
  "And not the Lady Clare."

"Play me no tricks," said Lord Ronald,
  "For I am yours in word and in deed.
Play me no tricks," said Lord Ronald,
  "Your riddle is hard to read."

O and proudly stood she up!
  Her heart within her did not fail:
She look'd into Lord Ronald's eyes,
  And told him all her nurse's tale.

He laugh'd a laugh of merry scorn:
  He turn'd and kiss'd her where she stood.
"If you are not the heiress born,
  And I," said he, "the next in blood—

"If you are not the heiress born,
  And I," said he, "the lawful heir,
We two will wed tomorrow morn,
  And you shall still be Lady Clare."

# Truth

*Ben Jonson*

Ben Jonson (1572–1637) reminds us that faith and love depend on truth.

Truth is the trial of itself,
And needs no other touch;
And purer than the purest gold,
Refine it ne'er so much.

It is the life and light of love,
The sun that ever shineth,
And spirit of that special grace,
That faith and love defineth.

It is the warrant of the word,
That yields a scent so sweet,
As gives a power to faith to tread
All falsehood under feet.

---

# The Woman Caught in Adultery

This story from the Gospel according to John in the New Testament, which depicts Jesus' compassion for the sinner, is a powerful reminder that the hypocrisy of the crowd is one of the most common varieties of dishonesty.

Jesus went unto the mount of Olives. And early in the morning he came again into the temple, and all the people came unto him, and he sat down, and taught them.

And the Scribes and Pharisees brought unto him a woman taken in adultery. And when they had set her in the midst, they say unto him, Master, this woman was taken in adultery, in the very act.

Now Moses in the law commanded us that such should be stoned. But what sayest thou?

This they said, tempting him, that they might have to accuse him. But Jesus stooped down, and with *his* finger wrote on the ground, *as though he heard them not.*

So when they continued asking him, he lifted up himself, and said unto them: he that is without sin among you, let him first cast a stone at her.

And again he stooped down, and wrote on the ground.

And they which heard *it,* being convicted by *their own* conscience, went out one by one, beginning at the eldest, *even* unto the last. And Jesus was left alone, and the woman standing in the midst.

When Jesus had lifted up himself and saw none but the woman, he said unto her, Woman, where are those thine accusers? Hath no man condemned thee?

She said, No man, Lord. And Jesus said unto her, Neither do I condemn thee: go, and sin no more.

---

## The Question

Seek honesty in yourself before you seek it in your neighbors.

Were the whole world good as you—not an atom better—
  Were it just as pure and true,
  Just as pure and true as you;
  Just as strong in faith and works;
  Just as free from crafty quirks;
  All extortion, all deceit;
  Schemes its neighbors to defeat;
  Schemes its neighbors to defraud;
  Schemes some culprit to applaud—
Would this world be better?

If the whole world followed you—followed to the letter—
Would it be a nobler world,
All deceit and falsehood hurled
From it altogether;
Malice, selfishness, and lust,
Banished from beneath the crust,
Covering human hearts from view—
Tell me, if it followed you,
Would the world be better?

---

# The Good Bishop

*Adapted from Victor Hugo*

Truth can be so complicated a thing as to call for certain noble dishonesties on some rare occasions. In this scene adapted from Victor Hugo's *Les Misérables,* we witness a lie told not merely for the sake of compassion, but in order to secure virtue in another man's soul. As James Russell Lowell put it, "As one lamp lights another nor grows less, So nobleness enkindleth nobleness."

Jean Valjean was a wood-chopper's son, who, while very young, was left an orphan. His older sister brought him up, but when he was seventeen years of age, his sister's husband died, and upon Jean came the labor of supporting her seven little children. Although a man of great strength, he found it very difficult to provide food for them at the poor trade he followed.

One winter day he was without work, and the children were crying for bread. They were nearly starved. And, when he could withstand their entreaties no longer, he went out in the night, and, breaking a baker's window with his fist, carried home a loaf of bread for the famished children. The next morning he was arrested for stealing, his bleeding hand convicting him.

For this crime he was sent to the galleys with an iron collar riveted around his neck, with a chain attached, which bound him to his galley seat. Here he remained four years, then he tried to escape, but was caught, and three years were added to his sentence. Then he

made a second attempt, and also failed, the result of which was that he remained nineteen years as a galley slave for stealing a single loaf of bread.

When Jean left the prison, his heart was hardened. He felt like a wolf. His wrongs had embittered him, and he was more like an animal than a man. He came with every man's hand raised against him to the town where the good bishop lived.

At the inn they would not receive him because they knew him to be an ex-convict and a dangerous man. Wherever he went, the knowledge of him went before, and everyone drove him away. They would not even allow him to sleep in a dog kennel or give him the food they had saved for the dog. Everywhere he went they cried: "Be off! Go away, or you will get a charge of shot." Finally, he wandered to the house of the good bishop, and a good man he was.

For his duties as a bishop, he received from the state 3,000 francs a year; but he gave away to the poor 2,800 francs of it. He was a simple, loving man, with a great heart, who thought nothing of himself, but loved everybody. And everybody loved him.

Jean, when he entered the bishop's house, was a most forbidding and dangerous character. He shouted in a harsh loud voice: "Look here, I am a galley slave. Here is my yellow passport. It says: 'Five years for robbery and fourteen years for trying to escape. The man is very dangerous.' Now that you know who I am, will you give me a little food, and let me sleep in the stable?"

The good bishop said: "Sit down and warm yourself. You will take supper with me, and after that sleep here."

Jean could hardly believe his senses. He was dumb with joy. He told the bishop that he had money, and would pay for his supper and lodging.

But the priest said: "You are welcome. This is not my house, but the house of Christ. Your name was known to me before you showed me your passport. You are my brother."

After supper the bishop took one of the silver candlesticks that he had received as a Christmas present, and, giving Jean the other, led him to his room, where a good bed was provided. In the middle of the night Jean awoke with a hardened heart. He felt that the time had come to get revenge for all his wrongs. He remembered the silver knives and forks that had been used for supper, and made up his mind to steal them, and go away in the night. So he took what he could find, sprang into the garden, and disappeared.

When the bishop awoke, and saw his silver gone, he said: "I have been thinking for a long time that I ought not to keep the silver. I should have given it to the poor, and certainly this man was poor."

At breakfast time five soldiers brought Jean back to the bishop's house. When they entered, the bishop, looking at him, said: "Oh, you are back again! I am glad to see you. I gave you the candlesticks, too, which are silver also, and will bring forty francs. Why did you not take them?"

Jean was stunned indeed by these words. So were the soldiers. "This man told us the truth, did he?" they cried. "We thought he had stolen the silver and was running away. So we quickly arrested him."

But the good bishop only said: "It was a mistake to have him brought back. Let him go. The silver is his. I gave it to him."

So the officers went away.

"Is it true," Jean whispered to the bishop, "that I am free? I may go?"

"Yes," he replied, "but before you go take your candlesticks."

Jean trembled in every limb, and took the candlesticks like one in a dream.

"Now," said the bishop, "depart in peace, but do not go through the garden, for the front door is always open to you day and night."

Jean looked as though he would faint.

Then the bishop took his hand, and said: "Never forget you have promised me you would use the money to become an honest man."

He did not remember having promised anything, but stood silent while the bishop continued solemnly:

"Jean Valjean, my brother, you no longer belong to evil, but to good. I have bought your soul for you. I withdrew it from black thoughts and the spirit of hate, and gave it to God."

# Insincere Honesty

*Retold by Warren Horton Stuart*

We should love truth for its own sake, but not for *our* own sake. Glorifying our own devotion to an abstract truth is something less than a noble pursuit, as this Chinese folktale illustrates.

In the kingdom of Ts'u was a young man named Honest. His father stole a sheep, so he went and informed the magistrate, who had the guilty one arrested, and was on the point of punishing him. Young Honest then asked to be allowed to bear the penalty in his father's stead. Just as it was about to be inflicted, he said to the officer: "When my father stole a sheep and I reported the theft, was I not honest? When my father was about to be punished, and I offered to bear the penalty, was I not as a son honoring my father? If you punish even the honest and the filial, who is there in all the kingdom that would not be punished?" When the magistrate heard this, he released the young man. When Confucius heard the story, he said: "Strange! That a fellow could sell his father's good name to make a reputation for his own honesty. If that be honesty, 'twere better to be dishonest."

# The Injustice of Mere Suspicion

*Retold by Warren Horton Stuart*

This Chinese folktale helps us appreciate the policy of "innocent until proven guilty." We must guard against projecting our suspicions onto others' characters and actions.

A certain man lost an axe. He at once suspected the son of his neighbor had stolen it. When he saw the boy walking by, the boy looked like a fellow who had stolen an axe; when he listened to the boy's words, they sounded like those of a boy who had stolen an axe. All his actions and manners were those of a boy who had stolen an axe. Later, when digging a ditch, the man found the lost axe. The next day he saw again his neighbor's son, but in all the boy's manners and actions, there was nothing like a boy who had stolen an axe. The boy had not changed, but the man himself had changed! And the only reason for this change lay in his suspicion.

---

# The Piece of String

*Guy de Maupassant*

This story of slander, set among the French peasantry, reminds us of the devastating consequences that one person's dishonesty can have on another's life.

Along all the roads around Goderville peasants and their wives were coming in toward the town, for it was market day.

There was a crowd in Goderville marketplace, a confusion of men and beasts. Horns of oxen, long-napped tall hats of the richer peasants, and the women's headdresses rose above the surface of the throng. Voices, bawling, sharp, and squeaky, were mingled in barbarous never-ending clamor, dominated at times by the mighty guffaw of some broad-chested countryman having his joke, or by the long-drawn lowing of a cow tied up to the wall of a house.

It all smelled of stables, milk and manure, of hay and sweat, gave off, in fact, that terribly sour savor, human, yet bestial, characteristic of workers in the fields.

Master Hauchecorne, of Breauté, coming in to Goderville, was making his way toward the marketplace, when he perceived on the ground a short piece of string. Master Hauchecorne, thrifty like every true Norman, thought that anything was worth picking up that could be put to any use; so, stooping painfully, for he suffered from rheumatism, he picked up the bit of thin cord, and was carefully rolling it up when he observed Master Malandain, the saddler, standing in his doorway, looking at him. They had once had a difference about a halter, and owed each other a grudge, for both were by nature inclined to bear malice. Master Hauchecorne was seized with a sort of shame at being thus seen by his enemy, grubbing in the mud for a bit of string. He abruptly hid his spoil under his blouse, then put it in his trouser pocket, and pretended to be still looking on the ground for something he could not find. Finally he went off toward the market, with his head poked forward, bent nearly double by his rheumatism.

He was swallowed up at once in the slow-moving, noisy crowd, disputing over its interminable bargainings. Peasants were punching the cows, moving hither and thither, in perpetual fear of being taken in, and not daring to make up their minds; scrutinizing the seller's eye, to try and discover the deceit in the man, and the blemish in his beast.

The women, placing their great baskets at their feet, had taken out their fowls, which lay on the ground with legs tied together, eyes wild with fright, and crests all scarlet.

They listened to the offers made, and held out for their prices with wooden, impassive faces; then, suddenly deciding to take the bid, would scream after the customer as he slowly walked away:

"Done with you, Master Anthime. You shall have it."

Then, little by little, the marketplace emptied, and, the Angelus ringing midday, those who lived too far away straggled into the inns.

At Jourdain's, the big dining room was crowded with guests, just as the huge courtyard was crowded with vehicles of every breed, carts, cabriolets, wagonettes, tilburys, covered carts innumerable, yellow with mud, out of trim and patched, some raising their two shafts, like arms, to the sky, some with nose on the ground and tail in the air.

Right up against the diners the immense fireplace, flaming brightly, threw a mighty heat onto the backs of the right-hand row seated at table. Three jacks were turning, garnished with chickens, pigeons, and legs of mutton, and a delectable odor of roast meat, and of gravy streaming over the well-browned crackling, rose from the hearth, bringing joy to the heart, and water to the mouth.

All the aristocracy of the plow dined at M. Jourdain's, innkeeper and horse-dealer, a shrewd fellow, and a "warm man."

The dishes were passed, and emptied, together with mugs of golden cider. Everyone told the story of his bargains, and asked his neighbor about the crops. The weather was good for green stuff, but a little damp for corn.

Suddenly, from the courtyard in front of the house, came the roll of a drum.

All but a few, too lazy to move, jumped up at once, and flew to the doors and windows, their mouths still full and their napkins in their hands.

Finishing off the roll of his drum, the town crier shouted in staccato tones, with a scansion of phrase peculiarly out of rhythm:

"This is to inform the inhabitants of Goderville, and all others —present at the market, that there was lost this morning on the Beuzeville road between nine and ten o'clock, a black leather pocket-book, containing five hundred francs and some business papers. It should be returned—to the Town Hall immediately, or to Master Fortuné Houlbrèque at Manneville. A reward of twenty francs is offered."

The man went by, and presently the dull rumble of the drum was heard again, and then the crier's voice, fainter in the distance.

Everyone began discussing the event, calculating the chances of Master Houlbrèque's recovering or not recovering his pocket-book.

And so the meal came to an end.

They were finishing their coffee when the brigadier of gendarmes appeared at the door, and asked:

"Is Master Hauchecorne, of Breauté, here?"

Master Hauchecorne, seated at the far end of the table, answered:

"Here!"

"Master Hauchecorne," proceeded the officer, "will you be so good as to come with me to the Town Hall? The mayor would like to speak to you."

Surprised and uneasy, the peasant gulped down his cognac, rose, and stooping even more than in the morning, for the first steps after resting were always particularly painful, got himself started, repeating:

"All right! I'm coming!" and followed the sergeant.

The mayor was awaiting him, seated in an armchair. He was the notary of the district, a stout, serious man, full of pompous phrases.

"Master Hauchecorne," said he, "you were seen this morning to pick up, on the Beuzeville road, the pocket-book lost by Master Houlbrèque, of Manneville."

The peasant, in stupefaction, gazed at the mayor, intimidated at once by this suspicion which lay heavy upon him without his comprehending it.

"Me? Me—me pick up that pocket-book?"

"Yes, you."

"On my word of honor, I didn't! Why, I didn't even know about it!"

"You were seen."

"Seen? I? Who saw me?"

"M. Malandain, the saddler."

Then the old man remembered, and understood. Reddening with anger, he said:

"Ah! He saw me, that animal! Well, what he saw me pick up was this string, look here, M. le Maire!"

And rummaging in his pocket, he pulled out the little piece of string.

But the mayor shook his head incredulously.

"You won't make me believe, Master Hauchecorne, that M. Malandain, a trustworthy man, took that piece of string for a pocket-book."

The enraged peasant raised his hand, spat solemnly to show his good faith, and repeated:

"It's God's truth, all the same, the sacred truth, M. le Maire. There, on my soul and honor, I say it again."

The mayor proceeded.

"After having picked up the article in question, you even went on searching in the mud, to make sure a coin or two mightn't have fallen out."

The poor old fellow choked with indignation and fear.

"To say such things! . . . How can anyone . . . telling lies like that, to undo an honest man! How can anyone?"

Protest as he would, he was not believed.

They confronted him with M. Malandain, who repeated and substantiated his story. The two abused each other for a whole hour. By his own request, Master Hauchecorne was searched. Nothing was found on him.

At last the mayor, thoroughly puzzled, dismissed him, warning him that he was going to give notice to the public prosecutor and take his instructions.

The news had spread. As he went out of the Town Hall the old man was surrounded, and all sorts of serious or mocking questions were put to him, but no one showed the slightest indignation. He began to tell the story of the piece of string. They did not believe him. Everybody laughed.

He went on, stopped by everyone, stopping everyone he knew, to tell his story over and over again, protesting, showing his pockets turned inside out, to prove that he had nothing on him. The only answer he got was:

"Get along, you sly old dog!"

He began to feel angry, worrying himself into a fever of irritation, miserable at not being believed, at a loss what to do, and continually repeating his story.

Night came on. It was time to go home. He set out with three neighbors, to whom he showed the spot where he had picked up the piece of string; and the whole way home he kept talking of his misadventure.

In the evening he made a round of the village of Breauté, to tell everybody all about it. He came across unbelievers only.

He was ill all night.

The next day, about one o'clock, Marius Paumelle, a laborer at Master Breton's, a farmer at Ymauville, restored the pocket-book and its contents to Master Houlbrèque, of Manneville.

This man declared that he had found the object on the road; but not being able to read, he had taken it home and given it to his master.

The news spread through the neighborhood. Master Hauchecorne was informed of it, and started off at once on a round, to tell his story all over again, with its proper ending. It was a triumph.

"What knocked me over," he said, "was not so much the thing itself, you know, but that charge of lying. There's nothing hurts a man so much as being thought a liar."

The whole day long he talked of his adventure, telling it to people he met on the roads, to people drinking at the inns, and even at the church door on the following Sunday. He stopped perfect strangers to tell him about it. He was easy in his mind now, and yet—there was something that bothered him, though he could not exactly arrive at what it was. People had an amused look while they were listening to him. They did not seem convinced. He felt as if a lot of tattle was going on behind his back.

On the Tuesday of the following week he went off to Goderville market, urged thereto solely by the desire to tell his story. Malandain, standing at his door, began to laugh as he went past. Why?

He began his story to a farmer of Criquetot, who did not let him finish, but, giving him a dig in the pit of the stomach, shouted in his face: "Get along, you old rogue!" and turned his back.

Master Hauchecorne stopped short, confused, and more and more uneasy. Why was he being called an "old rogue"?

When he was seated at the table at Jourdain's inn he began again to explain the whole affair.

A horse-dealer from Montvillier called out:

"Come, come, that's an old trick; I know all about your piece of string!"

Hauchecorne stammered:

"But it's been found, that pocket-book!"

But the other went on:

"Oh! Shut up, old boy,there's one who finds, and another who brings back. All on the strict QT."

The peasant was thunderstruck. He understood at last. It was insinuated that he had caused the pocket-book to be taken by someone else, an accomplice.

He tried to protest, but the whole table began laughing.

He could not finish his dinner, and went away, with every one jeering at him.

He returned home, ashamed and indignant, choking with anger and bewilderment, and all the more overwhelmed because, in his artful Norman brain, he knew himself capable of having done what they accused him of, and of even boasting about it afterward, as though it were a feat. He realized confusedly that it would be impossible to prove his innocence, his tricky nature being known to all. And he felt wounded to the heart by the injustice of this suspicion.

Then he began again to tell his story, making the tale a little longer every day, adding new reasons every time, more energetic protestations, most solemn oaths which he thought out and prepared in his solitary moments, for his mind was solely occupied by the story of the piece of string. They believed him less and less as his defense became more and more elaborate, his arguments more subtle.

"H'm! That's only to cover up his tracks," the hearers would say behind his back.

He was conscious of all this, but went on eating his heart out, exhausting himself in fruitless efforts.

Before the very eyes of people, he wasted away.

Jokers now would make him tell them the "piece of string" to amuse them, as one makes old soldiers tell about their battles. His spirit, undetermined, grew feebler and feebler.

Toward the end of December he took to his bed.

He died at the beginning of January, and in his last delirium still protested his innocence, repeating:

"A little piece of string . . . a little piece of string . . . look, here it is, M. le Maire!"

---

# Nobility

*Alice Cary*

This poem brings to mind the words of Alexander Pope: "An honest man's the noblest work of God."

True worth is in *being*, not *seeming*—
  In doing, each day that goes by,
Some little good—not in dreaming
  Of great things to do by and by.
For whatever men say in their blindness,
  And spite of the fancies of youth,
There's nothing so kingly as kindness,
  And nothing so royal as truth.

We get back our mete as we measure—
  We cannot do wrong and feel right,
Nor can we give pain and gain pleasure,
  For justice avenges each slight.
The air for the wing of the sparrow,
  The bush for the robin and wren,
But always the path that is narrow
  And straight, for the children of men.

'Tis not in the pages of story
The heart of its ills to beguile,
Though he who makes courtship to glory
Gives all that he hath for her smile.
For when from her heights he has won her,
Alas! it is only to prove
That nothing's so sacred as honor,
And nothing so loyal as love!

We cannot make bargains for blisses,
Nor catch them like fishes in nets;
And sometimes the thing our life misses
Helps more than the thing which it gets.
For good lieth not in pursuing,
Nor gaining of great nor of small,
But just in the doing, and doing
As we would be done by, is all.

Through envy, through malice, through hating,
Against the world, early and late,
No jot of our courage abating—
Our part is to work and to wait.
And slight is the sting of his trouble
Whose winnings are less than his worth;
For he who is honest is noble,
Whatever his fortunes or birth.

# Truth in Advertising

*P. T. Barnum*

Often erroneously associated with the slogan "There's a sucker born every minute," showman P. T. Barnum (1810–1891) was one of the first American businessmen to fully appreciate the value of publicity. Since we live in an age of ever-growing media influence and ever-present concern about truth in advertising, it is instructive to read this excerpt from Barnum's 1866 *Humbugs of the World,* in which he draws a line between cheating the public and attracting its attention. (Barnum's environmental and cultural sensitivities apparently had not caught up with his concern for the truth.)

Upon a careful consideration of my undertaking to give an account of the "Humbugs of the World," I find myself somewhat puzzled in regard to the true definition of the word. To be sure, Webster says that "humbug," as a noun, is an "imposition under fair pretenses"; and as a verb, it is "to deceive; to impose on." With all due deference to Dr. Webster, I submit that, according to present usage, this is not the only, nor even the generally accepted definition of that term. . . . As generally understood, "humbug" consists in putting on glittering appearances—outside show—novel expedients, by which to suddenly arrest public attention, and attract the public eye and ear.

Clergymen, lawyers, or physicians, who should resort to such methods of attracting the public, would not, for obvious reasons, be apt to succeed. Bankers, insurance agents, and others, who aspire to become custodians of the money of their fellow men, would require a different species of advertising from this; but there are various trades and occupations which need only notoriety to insure success, always provided that when customers are once attracted, they never fail to get their money's worth. An honest man who thus arrests public attention will be called a "humbug," but he is not a swindler or an impostor. . . .

When the great blacking-maker of London dispatched his agent to Egypt to write on the pyramids of Ghiza, in huge letters:

"Buy Warren's Blacking, 30 Strand, London."

he was not "cheating" travelers upon the Nile. His blacking was really a superior article, and well worth the price charged for it, but he was "humbugging" the public by this queer way of arresting attention. It turned out just as he anticipated, that English travelers in that part of Egypt were indignant at this desecration, and they wrote back to the London *Times* (every Englishman writes or threatens to "write to the *Times*" if anything goes wrong) denouncing the "Goth" who had thus disfigured these ancient pyramids by writing on them in monstrous letters: "Buy Warren's Blacking, 30 Strand, London." The *Times* published these letters, and backed them up by several of those awful, grand, and dictatorial editorials peculiar to the greater "Thunderer," in which the blacking-maker, "Warren, 30

Strand," was stigmatized as a man who had no respect for the ancient patriarchs, and it was hinted that he would probably not hesitate to sell his blacking on the sarcophagus of Pharaoh, "or any other" mummy, if he could only make money by it. In fact, to cap the climax, Warren was denounced as a "humbug." These indignant articles were copied into all the provincial journals, and very soon, in this manner, the columns of every newspaper in Great Britain were teeming with this advice: "Try Warren's Blacking, 30 Strand, London." The curiosity of the public was thus aroused, and they did "try" it, and finding it a superior article, they continued to purchase it and recommend it to their friends, and Warren made a fortune by it. He always attributed his success to his having "humbugged" the public by this unique method of advertising his blacking in Egypt! But Warren did not cheat his customers, nor practice "an imposition under fair pretenses." He was a humbug, but he was an honest upright man, and no one called him an impostor or a cheat.

---

# Plato on Justice

## *From* The Republic

The main questions asked in *The Republic* are: what is justice, how can we humans achieve it in society, and why should we? But the ancient Greek word for "just" is a slippery one for modern translators. Depending on the context, it can mean honest, pious, fair, legally correct, lawful, or obligated, to name a few possibilities. In the end, it may be that the meaning of Plato's "justice" comes closer to our modern notion of "integrity." Plato's answer to the question "Why should I be a person of integrity?" is, to put it briefly, "Because it is healthier." Integrity—having one's psychological parts *integrated,* "having it all together," as we say—is the psychological counterpart of physical fitness. It is the sort of condition in which any really rational human being would choose to be, if one really saw it for what it was. Acquiring integrity is getting one's person in shape.

The dialogue here is between Socrates and Glaucon.

*Socrates.* Then our dream has been realized; and the suspicion, which we entertained at the beginning of our work of construction, that some divine power must have conducted us to a primary form of justice, has now been verified?

*Glaucon.* Yes. Certainly.

And the division of labor which required the carpenter and the shoemaker and the rest of the citizens to be doing each his own business, and not another's, was a shadow of justice, and for that reason it was of use?

Clearly.

But in reality justice was such as we were describing, being concerned however, not with the outward man, but with the inward, which is the true self and concernment of man: for the just man does not permit the several elements within him to interfere with one another, or any of them to do the work of others—he sets in order his own inner life, and is his own master and his own law, and at peace with himself; and when he has bound together the three principles within him, which may be compared to the higher, lower, and middle notes of the scale, and the intermediate intervals—when he has bound all these together, and is no longer many, but has become one entirely temperate and perfectly adjusted nature, then he proceeds to act, if he has to act, whether in a matter of property, or in the treatment of the body, or in some affair of politics or private business; always thinking and calling that which preserves and cooperates with this harmonious condition, just and good action, and the knowledge which presides over it, wisdom, and that which at any time impairs this condition, he will call unjust action, and the opinion which presides over it ignorance.

You have said the exact truth, Socrates.

Very good; and if we were to affirm that we had discovered the just man and the just state, and the nature of justice in each of them, we should not be telling a falsehood?

Most certainly not.

May we say so, then?

Let us say so.

And now, I said, injustice has to be considered.

Clearly.

Must not injustice be a strife which arises among the three principles—a meddlesomeness, and interference, and rising up of a part of the soul against the whole, an assertion of unlawful authority, which is made by a rebellious subject against a true prince, of whom he is the natural vassal—what is all this confusion and delusion but injustice, and intemperance and cowardice and ignorance, and every form of vice?

Exactly so.

And if the nature of justice and injustice be known, then the meaning of acting unjustly and being unjust, or, again, of acting justly, will also be perfectly clear?

What do you mean? he said.

Why, I said, they are like disease and health; being in the soul just what disease and health are in the body.

How so? he said.

Why, I said, that which is healthy causes health, and that which is unhealthy causes disease.

Yes.

And just actions cause justice, and unjust actions cause injustice?

That is certain.

And the creation of health is the institution of a natural order and government of one by another in the parts of the body; and the creation of disease is the production of a state of things at variance with this natural order?

True.

And is not the creation of justice the institution of a natural order and government of one by another in the parts of the soul, and the creation of injustice the production of a state of things at variance with the natural order.

Exactly so, he said.

Then virtue is the health and beauty and well-being of the soul, and vice the disease and weakness and deformity of the same?

True.

And do not good practices lead to virtue, and evil practices to vice?

Assuredly.

Still our old question of the comparative advantage of justice and injustice has not been answered: which is the more profitable, to be just and act justly and practice virtue, whether seen or unseen of gods and men, or to be unjust and act unjustly, if only unpunished and unreformed?

In my judgment, Socrates, the question has now become ridiculous. We know that, when the bodily constitution is gone, life is no longer endurable, though pampered with all kinds of meats and drinks, and having all wealth and all power; and shall we be told that when the very essence of the vital principle is undermined and corrupted, life is still worth having to a man, if only he be allowed to do whatever he likes with the single exception that he is not to acquire justice and virtue, or to escape from injustice and vice; assuming them both to be such as we have described?

Yes, I said, the question is, as you say, ridiculous.

---

## Francis Bacon on Truth

*From "Of Truth"*

In this famous essay, first published in 1625, Francis Bacon (1561–1626) declares that truth in the philosophical and theological sense, as well as honesty in the civil business sense, are the "sovereign good of human nature."

Truth, which only doth judge itself, teacheth that the inquiry of truth, which is the love-making or wooing of it, the knowledge of truth, which is the presence of it, and the belief of truth, which is the enjoying of it, is the sovereign good of human nature. The first creature of God, in the works of the days, was the light of the sense; the last was the light of reason; and his sabbath work ever since is the illumination of his Spirit. First he breathed light upon the face of the matter or chaos; then he breathed light into the face of man; and still he breatheth and inspireth light into the face of his chosen. The poet that beautified the sect that was otherwise inferior to the rest saith yet excellently well: *It is a pleasure to stand upon the shore and to see ships tossed upon the sea; a pleasure to stand in the window of a castle and to see a battle and the adventures thereof below; but no pleasure is comparable to the standing upon the vantage ground of truth* (a hill not to be commanded, and where the air is always clear and serene), *and to see the errors and wanderings and mists and tempests in the vale below;* so always that this prospect be with pity, and not with swelling or pride. Certainly, it is heaven upon earth to have a man's mind move in charity, rest in providence, and turn upon the poles of truth.

To pass from theological and philosophical truth to the truth of civil business: it will be acknowledged even by those that practice it not that clear and round dealing is the honor of man's nature; and that mixture of falsehood is like alloy in coin of gold and silver, which may make the metal work the better, but it embaseth it. For these winding and crooked courses are the goings of the serpent, which goeth basely upon the belly, and not upon the feet. There is no vice that doth so cover a man with shame as to be found false and perfidious. And therefore Montaigne said prettily, when he inquired the reason why the word of the lie should be such a disgrace and such an odious charge. Saith he, *If it be well weighed, to say that a man lieth is as much to say as that he is brave toward God and a coward toward men.* For a lie faces God, and shrinks from man. Surely the wickedness of falsehood and breach of faith cannot possibly be so highly expressed as in that it shall be the last peal to call the judgments of God upon the generations of men; it being foretold that when Christ cometh, *he shall not find faith upon the earth.*

---

## Truth Never Dies

This poem is inspiring in its assertion that truth is eternal, but perhaps more valuable is its reminder that truth must be "caught and handed onward by the wise." Truth must be passed from friend to friend, from teacher to student, from parent to child.

Truth never dies. The ages come and go.
The mountains wear away, the stars retire.
Destruction lays earth's mighty cities low;
  And empires, states and dynasties expire;
But caught and handed onward by the wise,
  Truth never dies.

Though unreceived and scoffed at through the years;
  Though made the butt of ridicule and jest;
Though held aloft for mockery and jeers,
  Denied by those of transient power possessed,
Insulted by the insolence of lies,
  Truth never dies.

It answers not. It does not take offense,
  But with a mighty silence bides its time;
As some great cliff that braves the elements
  And lifts through all the storms its head sublime,
It ever stands, uplifted by the wise;
  And never dies.

As rests the Sphinx amid Egyptian sands;
  As looms on high the snowy peak and crest;
As firm and patient as Gibraltar stands,
  So truth, unwearied, waits the era blessed
When men shall turn to it with great surprise.
  Truth never dies.

# 9

# Loyalty

Our loyalties are important signs of the kinds of persons we have chosen to become. They mark a kind of constancy or steadfastness in our attachments to those other persons, groups, institutions, or ideals with which we have deliberately decided to associate ourselves. To be a loyal citizen or friend means to operate within a certain framework of caring seriously about the well-being of one's country or comrade. This is very different from being a rubber stamp. Loyalty operates on a higher level than that. For example, the president takes an oath of loyalty to the Constitution of the United States, and so do other federal employees, law enforcement personnel, and members of the armed services. Citizens across the nation pledge allegiance to the flag. These expressions leave plenty of room for disagreement apart from the fundamentals they emphasize.

Ceremonial expressions aside, loyalty is like courage in that it shows itself most clearly when we are operating under stress. Real loyalty endures inconvenience, withstands temptation, and does not cringe under assault. Yet the trust that genuine loyalty tends to generate can pervade our whole lives.

The Bible provides many illuminating examples. Potiphar placed Joseph in charge of his entire household. "He has put everything that he has in my hand," Joseph explains to Potiphar's wife in rejecting her advances (Genesis 39:8). He is a loyal steward, and will not betray Potiphar's trust.

Potiphar is a loyal husband, too, however. He acts on his wife's trumped-up complaint and has Joseph jailed (Genesis 39:19–20). Virtue by itself is no guarantee of right action, which requires more than good intentions. We need in addition both the wisdom to know what the right thing to do is, and the will to do it.

In another illuminating case David remains loyal to his king—Saul, the Lord's anointed, and the father of his best friend, Jonathan—even as Saul is trying to kill him (see the story of Jonathan and David in the chapter on Friendship). On two occasions David has clear opportunity to destroy Saul, but refrains from doing so out of loyalty (1 Samuel 24 and 26). And after Saul and Jonathan die in battle, David's famous lament—"How the mighty have fallen"—is equally for both (2 Samuel 1:17–27). We don't have to *like* those to whom we are loyal, and they don't have to like us. Loyalty is thus quite different from friendship, although the two often go hand in hand.

The loyalties associated with our family connections, friendships, religious or political affiliations, professional lives, and so on, can all change as these associations themselves develop. Sometimes the changes in loyalties can be quite dramatic, as in the case of Paul's conversion on the road to Damascus (Acts 9:1–22). Others may be more measured and deliberate, though no less radical, as when Ruth the Moabite commits herself to accompany Naomi back to her homeland of Judah (see the story of Ruth and Naomi in the Friendship chapter).

Conflicting loyalties may sometimes force one to make disagreeable decisions. But here it is important to keep in mind that there is a real difference between a decision that is unpleasant and one that is difficult. Daniel faced no dilemma when he had to choose between loyalty to his king, Darius, and loyalty to his God. The latter clearly took precedence. *Choosing* was easy enough, but it was certainly disagreeable, and he ended up in the lions' den (Daniel 6).

Conflicting loyalties may on occasion prove to be *only* apparent. A sufficiently astute intelligence can sometimes see ways of dissolving difficulties that appear insuperable to others. Thus Jesus met one of his loyalty tests by formulating the memorable dilemma-dissolving rule, "Render therefore unto Caesar the things which are Caesar's; and unto God the things that are God's" (Matthew 22:21). Most cases are *not* like Daniel's singular exception. The times when one cannot stand both "for God *and* for country" are rare indeed.

# Little Boy Blue

*Eugene Field*

Some of our earliest, most faithful friends are our childhood toys. May we all learn to be as steadfast in our loyalties as the companions of Little Boy Blue.

The little toy dog is covered with dust,
  But sturdy and stanch he stands;
And the little toy soldier is red with rust,
  And his musket molds in his hands.
Time was when the little toy dog was new
  And the soldier was passing fair;
And that was the time when our Little Boy Blue
  Kissed them and put them there.

"Now, don't you go till I come," he said,
  "And don't you make any noise!"
So, toddling off to his trundle-bed,
  He dreamed of the pretty toys;
And as he was dreaming, an angel song
  Awakened our Little Boy Blue—
Oh! the years are many, the years are long,
  But the little toy friends are true!

Aye, faithful to Little Boy Blue they stand,
  Each in the same old place—
Awaiting the touch of a little hand,
  And the smile of a little face;
And they wonder, as waiting these long years through
  In the dust of that little chair,
What has become of our Little Boy Blue,
  Since he kissed them and put them there.

---

# The Cap That Mother Made

*Adapted from Carolyn Sherwin Bailey*

As this Swedish tale reminds us, the loyalties expressed in our attachments—even to such humble things as the cap that Mother made—are important elements in the kinds of persons that we have chosen to make of ourselves.

Once upon a time there was a little boy named Anders who had a new cap. A more handsome cap you never have seen, for Anders's mother herself had knit it, and nobody can make anything quite so nice as a mother! It was red except for a small part in the middle, which was green (that was because Anders's mother had run out of red yarn), and the tassel was blue.

Anders walked around his house for a while, letting his brothers and sisters admire him in his new cap. Then he put his hands in his pockets and went out for a walk, because he wanted everybody to see how fine a cap his mother had made.

The first person he met was a farmer walking down the road alongside a wagon loaded with wood. The farmer bowed so deeply, Anders thought he might fall over.

"Well, if it isn't Anders," cried the cheerful farmer. "At first I thought you were a duke, or maybe even prince, with such a fine cap as that. Would you like to ride in my wagon?"

But Anders smiled politely and shook his head, and walked proudly by, holding his head high.

At the turn in the road he met Lars, the tanner's son. He was such a big boy that he wore high boots and carried a pocket knife. When he saw Anders's cap, he couldn't help but stop and gape at it, and he couldn't keep himself from coming up close and fingering the blue tassel.

"Let's trade caps," he suggested. "I'll even give you my pocket-knife too."

Now this knife was a very good one, though half the blade was gone and the handle was a little cracked. Anders had often admired that knife, but still it did not measure up to the new cap his mother had made.

"No, I don't think I could make a trade like that," he told Lars, and he nodded and went on his way.

Soon he met a very old woman who curtsied until her skirts looked like a balloon.

"My, my, you look like such a little gentleman," she said. "I dare say you're dressed up to go to the royal ball."

"Yes, why not?" thought Anders. "Seeing that I look so fine, I may as well go and visit the king."

And so he did.

In the palace yard stood two soldiers with shining helmets, and with muskets over their shoulders. When Anders reached the gate, both the muskets were leveled at him.

"Where may you be going?" demanded one of the soldiers.

"I am going to the royal ball," answered Anders.

"No, you are not," said the other soldier, stepping forward. "Nobody can go to the royal ball without a uniform."

But at that very instant, the princess came tripping across the yard. She was dressed in white silk, with bows of gold ribbon.

"This lad has no uniform, it's true," she told the soldiers, "but he has a very fine cap on his head, and that will do just as well."

And she took Anders's hand and walked him up the broad marble stairs where soldiers were posted at every third step, and through the beautiful halls where courtiers in silk and velvet stood bowing wherever he went. For no doubt they thought him a prince when they saw his fine cap.

At the far end of the largest hall, a table was set with golden cups and golden plates in long rows. On huge silver dishes were piles of tarts and cakes, and red wine sparkled in shining glasses.

The princess sat down at the head of the long table. She let Anders sit in a golden chair by her side.

"But you must not eat with your cap on your head," she said, putting out her hand to take it off.

"Oh, yes, I can eat just as well with it on," said Anders, holding tight to his cap. For he thought that if they took it away from him, they would no longer believe he was a prince. Besides, he did not feel sure he would get it back again.

"Well, well, give it to me," said the princess, "and I will give you a kiss."

The princess was certainly beautiful, and Anders would have liked to be kissed by her, but not for anything in the world could he give up the cap Mother had made. He only shook his head.

The princess filled his pockets with cakes, and even put her own gold chain around his neck, and bent down and kissed him.

"Now will you give me the cap?" she asked.

But Anders only moved farther back in his chair and did not take his hands away from his head.

Suddenly the doors flew open, and in marched the king with all his gentlemen in glittering uniforms and plumed hats. The king himself wore a purple mantle which trailed behind him, and he had a large gold crown on his white curly hair.

He smiled when he saw Anders in the golden chair.

"That is a very fine cap you have," he said.

"So it is," replied Anders. "Mother knit it of her very best yarn, and everyone who sees it tries to get it from me."

"But surely you would like to change caps with me," said the king, raising his heavy crown from his head.

Anders stayed as quiet as a mouse. He sat as still as he could, and held on to his red cap. But when the king came nearer to him, with his gold crown between his hands, Anders grew frightened as never before. If he didn't watch out, the king might grab his cap! For a king can do whatever he likes, of course.

With one jump, Anders was out of his chair. He darted like an arrow through all the beautiful halls, down all the marble stairs, and across the yard.

He twisted himself like an eel between the outstretched arms of the courtiers, and jumped like a little rabbit over the soldiers' muskets.

He ran so fast, the princess's necklace fell off his neck, and all the cakes jumped out of his pockets. But he still had his cap! No matter what else, he still had his cap! He clutched it with both hands as he rushed into his cottage.

"Well, Anders, where have you been?" his mother asked. So he climbed into her lap and told her all his adventures, and how everybody wanted his cap. His brothers and sisters stood around and listened with their mouths open.

When his big brother heard that Anders had refused to trade his cap for the king's golden crown, he whistled and whooped.

"Now weren't you foolish!" he exclaimed. "You could have sold that crown for a whole fortune in gold, and bought a castle, and a carriage with horses, and a boat to sail on the river. And you still would have had enough money left over to buy a brand-new hat with a purple plume sticking out!"

Anders had not thought of that, and his face turned three shades of red. He put his arms around his mother's neck. "Mother," he asked, "was I foolish?"

His mother hugged him close and kissed him.

"No, my little son," she said. "If you were dressed in silver and gold from top to toe, you could not look any nicer than you do in your little red cap."

Then Anders felt fine again. He knew well enough that mother's cap was the best cap in the whole world.

---

# The Story of Cincinnatus

*Retold by James Baldwin*

This story of Roman statesman and general Lucius Quinctius Cincinnatus takes place in 458 B.C., when Rome was besieged by an Italic tribe called the Aequi. It is one of our most famous reminders that the loyal citizen expects no great reward for coming to his country's aid. Whenever I visit Cincinnati, I try to stop by the statue of Cincinnatus there, one of my favorites.

There was a man named Cincinnatus who lived on a little farm not far from the city of Rome. He had once been rich, and had held the highest office in the land, but in one way or another he had lost all his wealth. He was now so poor that he had to do all the work on his farm with his own hands. But in those days it was thought to be a noble thing to till the soil.

Cincinnatus was so wise and just that everybody trusted him, and asked his advice. When anyone was in trouble, and did not know what to do, his neighbors would say,

"Go and tell Cincinnatus. He will help you."

Now there lived among the mountains, not far away, a tribe of fierce, half-wild men, who were at war with the Roman people. They persuaded another tribe of bold warriors to help them, and then marched toward the city, plundering and robbing as they came. They boasted that they would tear down the walls of Rome, and burn the houses, and kill all the men, and make slaves of the women and children.

At first the Romans, who were very proud and brave, did not think there was much danger. Every man in Rome was a soldier, and the army which went out to fight the robbers was the finest in the world. No one stayed at home but the white-haired "Fathers," as they were called, who made the laws for the city, and a small company of men who guarded the walls. Everybody thought that it would be an easy thing to drive the men of the mountains back to the place where they belonged.

But one morning five horsemen came riding down the road from the mountains. They rode with great speed, and both men and horses were covered with dust and blood. The watchman at the gate knew them, And shouted to them as they galloped in. Why did they ride thus? And what had happened to the Roman army?

They did not answer him, but rode into the city and along the quiet streets. Everybody ran after them, eager to find out what was the matter. Rome was not a large city at that time, and soon they reached the marketplace where the white-haired Fathers were sitting. Then they leaped from their horses, and told their story.

"Only yesterday," they said, "our army was marching through a narrow valley between two steep mountains. All at once a thousand savage men sprang out from among the rocks before us and above us. They had blocked up the way, and the pass was so narrow that we could not fight. We tried to come back, but they had blocked up the way on this side of us too. The fierce men of the mountains were before us and behind us, and they were throwing rocks down upon us from above. We had been caught in a trap. Then ten of us set spurs to our horses, and five of us forced our way through, but the other five fell before the spears of the mountain men. And now,

O Roman Fathers! Send help to our army at once, or every man will be slain, and our city will be taken."

"What shall we do?" said the white-haired Fathers. "Whom can we send but the guards and the boys? And who is wise enough to lead them, and thus save Rome?"

All shook their heads and were very grave, for it seemed as if there was no hope. Then one said, "Send for Cincinnatus. He will help us."

Cincinnatus was in the field plowing when the men who had been sent to him came in great haste. He stopped and greeted them kindly, and waited for them to speak.

"Put on your cloak, Cincinnatus," they said, "and hear the words of the Roman people."

Then Cincinnatus wondered what they could mean. "Is all well with Rome?" he asked. And he called to his wife to bring him his cloak.

She brought the cloak; and Cincinnatus wiped the dust from his hands and arms, and threw it over his shoulders. Then the men told their errand.

They told him how the army with all the noblest men of Rome had been entrapped in the mountain pass. They told him about the great danger the city was in. Then they said, "The people of Rome make you their ruler and the ruler of their city, to do with everything as you choose. And the Fathers bid you come at once and go out against our enemies, the fierce men of the mountains."

So Cincinnatus left his plow standing where it was, and hurried to the city. When he passed through the streets, and gave orders as to what should be done, some of the people were afraid, for they knew that he had all power in Rome to do what he pleased. But he armed the guards and the boys, and went out at their head to fight the fierce mountain men, and free the Roman army from the trap into which it had fallen.

A few days afterward there was great joy in Rome. There was good news from Cincinnatus. The men of the mountains had been beaten with great loss. They had been driven back into their own place.

And now the Roman army, with the boys and the guards, was coming home with banners flying, and shouts of victory. And at their head rode Cincinnatus. He had saved Rome.

Cincinnatus might then have made himself king, for his word was law, and no man dared lift a finger against him. But, before the people could thank him enough for what he had done, he gave back the power to the white-haired Roman Fathers, and went again to his little farm and his plow.

He had been the ruler of Rome for sixteen days.

---

# The Devoted Friend

*Oscar Wilde*

Devotion is a two-way street between friends, as this Oscar Wilde story reminds us.

One morning the old Water Rat put his head out of his hole. He had bright beady eyes and stiff gray whiskers, and his tail was like a long bit of black india rubber. The little ducks were swimming about in the pond, looking just like a lot of yellow canaries, and their mother, who was pure white with real red legs, was trying to teach them how to stand on their heads in the water.

"You will never be in the best society unless you can stand on your heads," she kept saying to them, and every now and then she showed them how it was done. But the little ducks paid no attention to her. They were so young that they did not know what an advantage it is to be in society at all.

"What disobedient children!" cried the old Water Rat. "They really deserve to be drowned."

"Nothing of the kind," answered the Duck. "Everyone must make a beginning, and parents cannot be too patient."

"Ah! I know nothing about the feelings of parents," said the Water Rat. "I am not a family man. In fact, I have never been married, and I never intend to be. Love is all very well in its way, but friendship is much higher. Indeed, I know of nothing in the world that is either nobler or rarer than a devoted friendship."

"And what, pray, is your idea of the duties of a devoted friend?" asked a green Linnet, who was sitting in a willow tree hard by, and had overheard the conversation.

"Yes, that is just what I want to know," said the Duck, and she swam away to the end of the pond, and stood upon her head, in order to give her children a good example.

"What a silly question!" cried the Water Rat. "I should expect my devoted friend to be devoted to me, of course."

"And what would you do in return?" said the little bird, swinging upon a silver spray, and flapping his tiny wings.

"I don't understand you," answered the Water Rat.

"Let me tell you a story on the subject," said the Linnet.

"Is the story about me?" asked the Water Rat. "If so, I will listen to it, for I am extremely fond of fiction."

"It is applicable to you," answered the Linnet. And he flew down, and alighting upon the bank, he told the story of The Devoted Friend.

"Once upon a time," said the Linnet, "there was an honest little fellow named Hans."

"Was he very distinguished?" asked the Water Rat.

"No," answered the Linnet. "I don't think he was distinguished at all, except for his kind heart, and his funny round good-humored face. He lived in a tiny cottage all by himself, and every day he worked in his garden. In all the countryside there was no garden so lovely as his. Sweet William grew there, and gillyflowers, and shepherds' purses, and fair maids of France. There were damask roses, and yellow roses, lilac crocuses, and gold, purple violets and white. Columbine and ladysmock, marjoram and wild basil, the cowslip and the fleur-de-lis, the daffodil and the clove pink bloomed or blossomed in their proper order as the months went by, one flower taking another flower's place, so that there were always beautiful things to look at, and pleasant odors to smell.

"Little Hans had a great many friends, but the most devoted friend of all was big Hugh the Miller. Indeed, so devoted was the rich Miller to little Hans, that he would never go by his garden without leaning over the wall and plucking a large nosegay, or a handful of sweet herbs, or filling his pockets with plums and cherries if it was the fruit season.

" 'Real friends should have everything in common,' the Miller used to say, and little Hans nodded and smiled, and felt very proud of having a friend with such noble ideas.

"Sometimes, indeed, the neighbors thought it strange that the rich Miller never gave little Hans anything in return, though he had a hundred sacks of flour stored away in his mill, and six milch cows, and a large flock of woolly sheep; but Hans never troubled his head about these things, and nothing gave him greater pleasure than to listen to all the wonderful things the Miller used to say about the unselfishness of true friendship.

"So little Hans worked away in his garden. During the spring, the summer, and the autumn he was very happy, but when the winter came, and he had no fruit or flowers to bring to the market, he suffered a good deal from cold and hunger, and often had to go to bed without any supper but a few dried pears or some hard nuts. In the winter, also, he was extremely lonely, as the Miller never came to see him then.

" 'There is no good in my going to see little Hans as long as the snow lasts,' the Miller used to say to his Wife, 'for when people are in trouble they should be left alone, and not be bothered by visitors. That at least is my idea about friendship, and I am sure I am right. So I shall wait till the spring comes, and then I shall pay him a visit, and he will be able to give me a large basket of primroses, and that will make him so happy.'

" 'You are certainly very thoughtful about others,' answered the Wife, as she sat in her comfortable armchair by the big pinewood fire. 'Very thoughtful indeed. It is quite a treat to hear you talk about friendship. I am sure the clergyman himself could not say such beautiful things as you do, though he does live in a three-storied house, and wear a gold ring on his little finger.'

" 'But could we not ask little Hans up here?' said the Miller's youngest son. 'If poor Hans is in trouble I will give him half my porridge, and show him my white rabbits.'

" 'What a silly boy you are!' cried the Miller. 'I really don't know what is the use of sending you to school. You seem not to learn anything. Why, if little Hans came up here, and saw our warm fire, and our good supper, and our great cask of red wine, he might get envious, and envy is a most terrible thing, and would spoil anybody's nature. I certainly will not allow Hans's nature to be spoiled. I am his best friend, and I will always watch over him, and see that he is not led into any temptations. Besides, if Hans came here, he might ask me to let him have some flour on credit, and that I could not do. Flour is one thing, and friendship is another, and they should not be confused. Why, the words are spelt differently, and mean quite different things. Everybody can see that.'

" 'How well you talk!' said the Miller's Wife, pouring herself out a large glass of warm ale. 'Really I feel quite drowsy. It is just like being in church.'

" 'Lots of people act well,' answered the Miller, 'but very few people talk well, which shows that talking is much the more difficult thing of the two, and much the finer thing also.' And he looked sternly across the table at his little son, who felt so ashamed of himself that he hung his head down, and grew quite scarlet, and began to cry into his tea. However, he was so young that you must excuse him."

"Is that the end of the story?" asked the Water Rat.

"Certainly not," answered the Linnet. "That is the beginning."

"Then you are quite behind the age," said the Water Rat. "Every good storyteller nowadays starts with the end, and then goes on to the beginning, and concludes with the middle. That is the new method. I heard all about it the other day from a critic who was walking round the pond with a young man. He spoke of the matter at great length, and I am sure he must have been right, for he had blue spectacles and a bald head, and whenever the young man made any remark, he always answered 'Pooh!' But pray go on with your story. I like the Miller immensely. I have all kinds of beautiful sentiments myself, so there is a great sympathy between us."

"Well," said the Linnet, hopping now on one leg and now on the other, "as soon as the winter was over, and the primroses began to open their pale yellow stars, the Miller said to his Wife that he would go down and see little Hans.

" 'Why, what a good heart you have!' cried his Wife. 'You are always thinking of others. And mind you take the big basket with you for the flowers.'

"So the Miller tied the sails of the windmill together with a strong iron chain, and went down the hill with the basket on his arm.

" 'Good morning, little Hans,' said the Miller.

" 'Good morning,' said Hans, leaning on his spade, and smiling from ear to ear.

" 'And how have you been all the winter?' said the Miller.

" 'Well, really,' cried Hans, 'it is very good of you to ask, very good indeed. I am afraid I had rather a hard time of it, but now the spring has come, and I am quite happy, and all my flowers are doing well.'

" 'We often talked of you during the winter, Hans,' said the Miller, 'and wondered how you were getting on.'

" 'That was kind of you,' said Hans. 'I was half afraid you had forgotten me.'

" 'Hans, I am surprised at you,' said the Miller. 'Friendship never forgets. That is the wonderful thing about it, but I am afraid you don't understand the poetry of life. How lovely your primroses are looking, by the by!'

" 'They are certainly very lovely,' said Hans, 'and it is a most lucky thing for me that I have so many. I am going to bring them into the market and sell them to the Burgomaster's daughter, and buy back my wheelbarrow with the money.'

" 'Buy back your wheelbarrow? You don't mean to say you have sold it? What a very stupid thing to do!'

" 'Well, the fact is,' said Hans, 'that I was obliged to. You see the winter was a very bad time for me, and I really had no money at all to buy bread with. So I first sold the silver buttons off my Sunday coat, and then I sold my silver chain, and then I sold my big pipe, and at last I sold my wheelbarrow. But I am going to buy them all back again now.'

" 'Hans,' said the Miller, 'I will give you my wheelbarrow. It is not in very good repair. Indeed, one side is gone, and there is something wrong with the wheel spokes. But in spite of that I will give it to you. I know it is very generous of me, and a great many people would think me extremely foolish for parting with it, but I am not like the rest of the world. I think that generosity is the essence of friendship, and, besides, I have got a new wheelbarrow for myself. Yes, you may set your mind at ease. I will give you my wheelbarrow.'

" 'Well, really, that is generous of you,' said little Hans, and his funny round face glowed all over with pleasure. 'I can easily put it in repair, as I have a plank of wood in the house.'

" 'A plank of wood!' said the Miller. 'Why, that is just what I want for the roof of my barn. There is a very large hole in it, and the corn will all get damp if I don't stop it up. How lucky you mentioned it! It is quite remarkable how one good action always breeds another. I have given you my wheelbarrow, and now you are going to give me your plank. Of course, the wheelbarrow is worth far more than the plank, but true friendship never notices things like that. Pray get it at once, and I will set to work at my barn this very day.'

" 'Certainly,' cried little Hans, and he ran into the shed and dragged the plank out.

" 'It is not a very big plank,' said the Miller, looking at it, 'and I am afraid that after I have mended my barn roof there won't be any left for you to mend the wheelbarrow with. But, of course, that is not my fault. And now, as I have given you my wheelbarrow, I am sure you would like to give me some flowers in return. Here is the basket, and mind you fill it quite full.'

" 'Quite full?' said little Hans, rather sorrowfully, for it was really a very big basket, and he knew that if he filled it he would have no flowers left for the market, and he was very anxious to get his silver buttons back.

" 'Well, really,' answered the Miller, 'as I have given you my wheelbarrow, I don't think that it is much to ask you for a few flowers. I may be wrong, but I should have thought that friendship, true friendship, was quite free from selfishness of any kind.'

" 'My dear friend, my best friend,' cried little Hans, 'you are welcome to all the flowers in my garden. I would much sooner have your good opinion than my silver buttons, any day.' And he ran and plucked all his pretty primroses, and filled the Miller's basket.

" 'Goodbye, little Hans,' said the Miller, as he went up the hill with the plank on his shoulder, and the big basket in his hand.

" 'Goodbye,' said little Hans, and he began to dig away quite merrily, he was so pleased about the wheelbarrow.

"The next day he was nailing up some honeysuckle against the porch, when he heard the Miller's voice calling to him from the road. So he jumped off the ladder, and ran down the garden, and looked over the wall.

"There was the Miller with a large sack of flour on his back.

" 'Dear little Hans,' said the Miller, 'would you mind carrying this sack of flour for me to market?'

" 'Oh, I am so sorry,' said Hans, 'but I am really very busy today. I have got all my creepers to nail up, and all my flowers to water, and all my grass to roll.'

" 'Well, really,' said the Miller. 'I think that, considering that I am going to give you my wheelbarrow, it is rather unfriendly of you to refuse.'

" 'Oh, don't say that,' cried little Hans. 'I wouldn't be unfriendly for the whole world.' And he ran in for his cap, and trudged off with the big sack on his shoulders.

"It was a very hot day, and the road was terribly dusty, and before Hans had reached the sixth milestone he was so tired that he had to sit down and rest. However, he went on bravely, and at last he reached the market. After he had waited there some time, he sold the sack of flour for a very good price, and then he returned home at once, for he was afraid that if he stopped too late he might meet some robbers on the way.

" 'It has certainly been a hard day,' said little Hans to himself as he was going to bed, 'but I am glad I did not refuse the Miller, for he is my best friend, and, besides, he is going to give me his wheelbarrow.'

"Early the next morning the Miller came down to get the money for his sack of flour, but little Hans was so tired that he was still in bed.

" 'Upon my word,' said the Miller, 'you are very lazy. Really, considering that I am going to give you my wheelbarrow, I think you might work harder. Idleness is a great sin, and I certainly don't like any of my friends to be idle or sluggish. You must not mind my speaking quite plainly to you. Of course I should not dream of doing so if I were not your friend. But what is the good of friendship if one cannot say exactly what one means? Anybody can say charming things and try to please and to flatter, but a true friend always says unpleasant things, and does not mind giving pain. Indeed, if he is a really true friend he prefers it, for he knows that then he is doing good.'

" 'I am very sorry,' said little Hans, rubbing his eyes and pulling off his nightcap. 'But I was so tired that I thought I would lie in bed for a little time, and listen to the birds singing. Do you know that I always work better after hearing the birds sing?'

" 'Well, I am glad of that,' said the Miller, clapping little Hans on the back, 'for I want you to come up to the mill as soon as you are dressed, and mend my barn roof for me.'

"Poor little Hans was very anxious to go and work in his garden, for his flowers had not been watered for two days, but he did not like to refuse the Miller, as he was such a good friend to him.

" 'Do you think it would be unfriendly of me if I said I was busy?' he inquired in a shy and timid voice.

" 'Well, really,' answered the Miller, 'I do not think it is much to ask of you, considering that I am going to give you my wheelbarrow. But of course if you refuse I will go and do it myself.'

" 'Oh! on no account,' cried little Hans. And he jumped out of bed, and dressed himself, and went up to the barn.

"He worked there all day long, till sunset, and at sunset the Miller came to see how he was getting on.

" 'Have you mended the hole in the roof yet, little Hans?' cried the Miller in a cheery voice.

" 'It is quite mended,' answered little Hans, coming down the ladder.

" 'Ah!' said the Miller, 'there is no work so delightful as the work one does for others.'

" 'It is certainly a great privilege to hear you talk,' answered little Hans, sitting down and wiping his forehead. 'A very great privilege. But I am afraid I shall never have such beautiful ideas as you have.'

" 'Oh! they will come to you,' said the Miller. 'But you must take more pains. At present you have only the practice of friendship. Someday you will have the theory also.'

" 'Do you really think I shall?' asked little Hans.

" 'I have no doubt of it,' answered the Miller, 'but now that you have mended the roof, you had better go home and rest, for I want you to drive my sheep to the mountain tomorrow.'

"Poor little Hans was afraid to say anything to this, and early the next morning the Miller brought his sheep round to the cottage, and Hans started off with them to the mountain. It took him the whole day to get there and back, and when he returned he was so tired that he went off to sleep in his chair, and did not wake up till it was broad daylight.

" 'What a delightful time I shall have in my garden,' he said, and he went to work at once.

"But somehow he was never able to look after his flowers at all, for his friend the Miller was always coming round and sending him off on long errands, or getting him to help at the mill. Little Hans was very much distressed at times, as he was afraid his flowers would think he had forgotten them, but he consoled himself by the reflection that the Miller was his best friend. 'Besides,' he used to say, 'he is going to give me his wheelbarrow, and that is an act of pure generosity.'

"So little Hans worked away for the Miller, and the Miller said all kinds of beautiful things about friendship, which Hans took down in a notebook, and used to read over at night, for he was a very good scholar.

"Now it happened that one evening little Hans was sitting by his fireside when a loud rap came at the door. It was a very wild night, and the wind was blowing and roaring round the house so terribly that at first he thought it was merely the storm. But a second rap came, and then a third, louder than either of the others.

" 'It is some poor traveler,' said little Hans to himself, and he ran to the door.

"There stood the Miller with a lantern in one hand and a big stick in the other.

" 'Dear little Hans,' cried the Miller. 'I am in great trouble. My little boy has fallen off a ladder and hurt himself, and I am going for the Doctor. But he lives so far away, and it is such a bad night, that it has just occurred to me that it would be much better if you went instead of me. You know I am going to give you my wheelbarrow, and so it is only fair that you should do something for me in return.'

" 'Certainly,' cried little Hans. 'I take it quite as a compliment your coming to me, and I will start off at once. But you must lend me your lantern, as the night is so dark that I am afraid I might fall into the ditch.'

" 'I am very sorry,' answered the Miller. 'But it is my new lantern, and it would be a great loss to me if anything happened to it.'

" 'Well, never mind, I will do without it,' cried little Hans, and he took down his great fur coat, and his warm scarlet cap, and tied a muffler round his throat, and started off.

"What a dreadful storm it was! The night was so black that little Hans could hardly see, and the wind was so strong that he could scarcely stand. However, he was very courageous, and after he had been walking about three hours, he arrived at the Doctor's house, and knocked at the door.

" 'Who is there?' cried the Doctor, putting his head out of his bedroom window.

" 'Little Hans, Doctor.'

" 'What do you want, little Hans?'

" 'The Miller's son has fallen from a ladder, and has hurt himself, and the Miller wants you to come at once.'

" 'All right!' said the Doctor. And he ordered his horse, and his big boots, and his lantern, and came downstairs, and rode off in the direction of the Miller's house, little Hans trudging behind him.

"But the storm grew worse and worse, and the rain fell in torrents, and little Hans could not see where he was going, or keep up with the horse. At last he lost his way, and wandered off on the moor, which was a very dangerous place, as it was full of deep holes, and there poor little Hans was drowned. His body was found the next day by some goatherds, floating in a great pool of water, and was brought back by them to the cottage.

"Everybody went to little Hans's funeral, as he was so popular, and the Miller was the chief mourner.

" 'As I was his best friend,' said the Miller, 'it is only fair that I should have the best place. So he walked at the head of the procession in a long black cloak, and every now and then he wiped his eyes with a big pocket-handkerchief.

" 'Little Hans is certainly a great loss to everyone,' said the Blacksmith, when the funeral was over, and they were all seated comfortably in the inn, drinking spiced wine and eating sweet cakes.

" 'A great loss to me at any rate,' answered the Miller. 'Why, I had as good as given him my wheelbarrow, and now I really don't know what to do with it. It is very much in my way at home, and it is in such bad repair that I could not get anything for it if I sold it. I will certainly take care not to give away anything again. One always suffers for being generous.' "

"Well?" said the Water Rat, after a long pause.

"Well, that is the end," said the Linnet.

"But what became of the Miller?" asked the Water Rat.

"Oh! I really don't know," replied the Linnet. "And I am sure that I don't care."

"It is quite evident then that you have no sympathy in your nature," said the Water Rat.

"I am afraid you don't quite see the moral of the story," remarked the Linnet.

"The what?" screamed the Water Rat.

"The moral."

"Do you mean to say that the story has a moral?"

"Certainly," said the Linnet.

"Well, really," said the Water Rat, in a very angry manner, "I think you should have told me that before you began. If you had done so, I certainly would not have listened to you. In fact, I should have said 'Pooh,' like the critic. However, I can say it now." So he shouted out "Pooh" at the top of his voice, gave a whisk with his tail, and went back into his hole.

"And how do you like the Water Rat?" asked the Duck, who came paddling up some minutes afterward. "He has a great many good points, but for my own part I have a mother's feelings, and I can never look at a confirmed bachelor without the tears coming into my eyes."

"I am rather afraid that I have annoyed him," answered the Linnet. "The fact is, that I told him a story with a moral."

"Ah! that is always a very dangerous thing to do," said the Duck.

And I quite agree with her.

# Yudisthira at Heaven's Gate

This story is from the *Mahabharata,* which with the *Ramayana* is one of the two great epic poems of India. Here loyalty is literally the test to gain entrance to heaven.

Good King Yudisthira had ruled over the Pandava people for many years and had led them in a successful, but very long war against giant forces of evil. At the end of his labors, Yudisthira felt that he had had enough years on earth and it was time to go on to the kingdom of the Immortals. When all his plans were made, he set out for the high Mount Meru to go from there to the Celestial City. His beautiful wife, Drapaudi, went with him and also his four brothers. Very soon, they were joined by a dog which followed quietly behind him.

But the journey to the mountain was a long and sorrowful one. Yudisthira's four brothers died one by one along the way, and after that his wife, the beautiful Drapaudi. The King was all alone then, except for the dog, which continued to follow him faithfully up and up the steep, long road to the Celestial City.

At last the two, weak and exhausted, stopped before the gates of Heaven. Yudisthira bowed humbly there as he asked to be admitted.

Sky and earth were filled with a loud noise as the God Indra, God of a Thousand Eyes, arrived to meet and welcome the King to Paradise. But Yudisthira was not quite ready.

"Without my brothers and my beloved wife, my innocent Drapaudi, I do not wish to enter Heaven, O Lord of all the deities," he said.

"Have no fear," Indra answered. "You shall meet them all in Heaven. They came before you and are already there!"

But Yudisthira had yet another request to make.

"This dog has come all the way with me. He is devoted to me. Surely for his faithfulness I cannot leave him outside! And besides, my heart is full of love for him!"

Indra shook his great head and the earth quaked.

"You yourself may have immortality," he said, "and riches and success and all the joys of Heaven. You have won these by making this hard journey. But you cannot bring a dog into Heaven. Cast off the dog, Yudisthira! It is no sin!"

"But where would he go?" demanded the king. "And who would go with him? He has given up all the pleasures of earth to be my companion. I cannot desert him now."

The God was irritated at this.

"You must be pure to enter Paradise," he said firmly. "Just to *touch* a dog will take away all the merits of prayer. Consider what you are doing, Yudisthira. Let the dog go!"

But Yudisthira insisted. "O God of a Thousand Eyes, it is difficult for a person who has always tried to be righteous to do something that he knows is *un*righteous—even in order to get into Heaven. I do not wish immortality if it means casting off one that is devoted to me."

Indra urged him once more.

"You left on the road behind you your four brothers and your wife. Why can't you also leave the dog?"

But Yudisthira said, "I abandoned those only because they had died already and I could no longer help them nor bring them back to life. As long as they lived I did not leave them."

"You are willing to abandon Heaven, then, for this dog's sake?" the God asked him.

"Great God of all Gods," Yudisthira replied, "I have steadily kept this vow—that I will never desert one that is frightened and seeks my protection, one that is afflicted and destitute, or one that is too weak to protect himself and desires to live. Now I add a fourth. I have promised never to forsake one that is devoted to me. I will not abandon my friend."

Yudisthira reached down to touch the dog and was about to turn sadly away from Heaven when suddenly before his very eyes a wonder happened. The faithful dog was changed into Dharma, the God of Righteousness and Justice.

Indra said, "You are a good man, King Yudisthira. You have shown faithfulness to the faithful and compassion for all creatures. You have done this by renouncing the very Gods themselves instead of renouncing this humble dog that was your companion. You shall be honored in heaven, O King Yudisthira, for there is no act which is valued more highly and rewarded more richly than compassion for the humble."

So Yudisthira entered the Celestial City with the God of Righteousness beside him. He was reunited there with his brothers and his beloved wife to enjoy eternal happiness.

# Thunder Falls

*Retold by Allan Macfarlan*

This story comes from the Kickapoo Indians, a Midwestern tribe once noted for their frequent wanderings; their name comes from a word meaning "he who moves about, standing now here, now there."

The blanket of night had wrapped the Kickapoo village in darkness. The people were gathered around the story-fire, awaiting the tale which the storyteller would tell. The listeners knew that the tale would not be of braves on the war trail or warriors who risked their lives on raids into the country of their enemies. And yet, the story which they were about to hear was one of high courage. It was of two brave women who were still honored in song and dance, because of their great courage and their noble sacrifice made for their tribe. This is the story that the people heard.

A band of our men were hunting, when the green earth had come from beneath the snow, and rivers were fat and fast. Women were with the men, to help skin the animals taken in the chase, and to strip and dry the meat. For three suns the party had hunted, and deer had fallen to their hunting arrows.

As they traveled in country distant from our territory, there was always danger of attack by enemies. Braves kept watch always, but they did not watch well enough. One day, the chief said it would be a good thing to return to the tribe, and the party made ready to go back when the sun came. Some of the braves and women did not see the sun again. A big war party of Shawnee surrounded and attacked the camp, when night was leaving to let morning come.

The Kickapoo who were not killed or badly wounded escaped down into the gorges. They had hunted there and found a great cave, beneath the thundering falls of a mighty river. The chief had decided that they would hide there, if they saw a large war party of the enemy, so all of the Kickapoo knew the hiding place.

The savage Shawnee killed the wounded, and took two of our women back to their camp, as prisoners. The women were young and would be made to work. The camp of the Shawnee was far above the place where they had attacked our party. Their lodges were on the banks of the wide, fast-flowing river.

For six suns after the attack, the Shawnee warriors searched for our people who had escaped the raid. Sentries were placed at distant points, so that the Kickapoo could not escape without being seen. The big war party of the Shawnee would be told of their movements. The enemy searched well, but our people hid better and were not discovered. Our chief did not let his party leave the great cavern, nor did they need to, for they had dried meat and water in plenty.

After some suns had passed, the people begged the chief to let them leave the shelter of the big cave beneath the falls. They felt safe there, but the terrible noise of the falls hurt their ears, as it roared like a curtain of thunder before the cavern. Their minds were afraid too, for they feared that spirits of evil dwelt in the dark, rocky gorges which surrounded them.

The chief was brave, but he knew how his band felt. He too would be happy to leave the great roaring and rumbling far behind him, even if, in escaping, more of his band would fall to the arrows of the Shawnee. "Tomorrow, the day of the seventh sun since the attack, will be the last that we remain here," he told his band. "When darkness comes, we will try to escape from the enemy into our own territory. Be ready!"

Our chief knew that the chances of reaching safety were few, as the Shawnee were many and must be angry that any of our people had escaped the raid. "Their anger must be very great," the Kickapoo chief thought, "because though they could follow the trails in the forest, their best trailers could not see footprints on the rocky ground which formed the river gorges."

The medicine man of the Shawnee went to their chief on the morning of the seventh sun, and told him of a dream which he had had. His totem bird, the red-tailed hawk, had come to him in a dream and flown around and around him in circles, giving shrill cries and tempting him to follow it. The medicine man could not refuse to follow his totem bird, so his spirit followed it, as it flew swiftly before him, until the hawk reached a clearing in the forest. Here, in the dream, the medicine man saw a circle of Shadow People.

"Can I follow the Shadow People to where our enemies are hidden?" the medicine man asked the hawk. "Who among them knows where the band is hiding?"

The hawk flew straight to the two women who were the prisoners of the Shawnee and circled the head of each.

"These women must know," declared the medicine man, as he told his chief of the dream. "My hawk totem never leads me on a false trail."

The Shawnee chief had great faith in the medicine man and his totem bird; so he called a council of his warriors. He told them of the dream and had the two captive women brought before him. When questioned, they declared that they did not know where the band to which they belonged was hidden.

"They speak with a crooked tongue," shouted the medicine man, "but torture will make it straight."

The women were tortured, and under the bite of blazing twigs held to their wrists, they cried out that they would reveal the hiding place of their band. For a moment, they spoke softly together in their own dialect and then, by signs, showed that they were ready to lead the Shawnee war party to the hiding place.

When the Shawnee were armed, and about to follow them, the two women pointed to the river, instead of leading the way into the forest. By signs, they showed that our people were far away and could be reached quicker by the Shawnees if they went by canoe. When the chief pointed toward the forest and his braves pushed the women in that direction, they showed by sign talk that they could not lead the Shawnees by land. Only by water did they know the way to the hidden Kickapoo band.

The chief believed the women, and they were taken to the big canoes that lay on the riverbank. With hands and sounds, the women told that close to the falls there was a little branch of the main river, which they must follow to reach the Kickapoo. The chief ordered the women into the leading canoe. He too sat in it, with his medicine man and six of his best warriors. The rest of the party followed close behind, in many canoes. Paddles flashed and the canoes went swift as a fish downstream.

After paddling far, the chief asked the women if they were not yet near the hiding place of his enemies. The women sign-talked that the place was near, and again the paddles rose and fell. The braves did not have to paddle so hard now, because the current was becoming swifter and stronger, as the canoes sped along. Quicker and quicker the canoes traveled. From the distance came the thunder of the falls. Closer and closer came the earth-shaking roar.

The chief was brave, but even he feared the mighty force of the swift-rushing waters. He was directly behind the two captive women, who sat in the bow. He touched them on the shoulders, and they turned to him at once. The chief ceased to fear when he saw that both women were smiling. The elder of the two, with a wave of her arm toward the south bank, showed that in a moment they would reach the fork of the river, where the paddlers could swing the canoes from the rushing current into the calm water of the smaller stream.

Faster, ever faster, the canoes now dashed through the foaming torrent. Narrower grew the rushing river as it roared between solid walls of rock. No time to try to turn the canoes!

Too late, the chief and warriors knew that they had been tricked. The bravest had but time to sing a few notes of their death songs before the raging torrent swept the shattered canoes over the crest of the mighty waterfall. Proudly leading the band of enemy warriors to death on the jagged rocks below were the two brave women of the Kickapoo.

My story is done, but that of the two who saved our band of warriors from death will go on as long as grass grows and water runs.

---

# How Queen Esther Saved Her People

*Retold by Walter Russell Bowie*

The events of the book of Esther in the Bible are reported to have occurred during the reign of the Persian king Ahasuerus, whom biblical scholars usually identify with Xerxes (c. 519–465 B.C.). Esther and her kinsman Mordecai were members of the Jewish population remaining in the East after many other Jews had returned to Jerusalem from the Babylonian exile. The story is one of a young queen who must face danger alone to save her people.

The story of the book of Esther begins with one of the kings of Persia, who is called Ahasuerus. According to the story, Ahasuerus decided one day to have a great feast in the garden of his palace. He invited all the chief men of the kingdom to come. The garden court was a beautiful place within the palace walls. It had marble pillars and a pavement of red, blue, white, and black marble. There were hangings of white and green and blue, fastened on silver rings. The goblets in which the wine was served were gold.

The feasting went on for seven days. By that time everyone, including the king, had eaten and drunk a great deal too much. The queen, whose name was Vashti, was very beautiful. Suddenly the king had a notion that he would show her off to his guests. She was in her rooms with her maids. The king sent seven of his servants to tell the queen to come to the feast.

Vashti was ashamed and indignant that the king had sent her such a message. She had no intention of appearing before a large company of half-drunken men. She told the servants to tell the king that she would not come.

When the king heard that, he was furious. He had boasted of the queen's beauty. Now he would seem foolish in the sight of his guests. He asked some of them what they thought he ought to do. These men did not have much respect for women. They began to think that if their wives heard that the queen had disobeyed the king, they would disobey their husbands. The men told the king that he ought to get rid of Vashti and find a new queen.

That was exactly what Ahasuerus decided to do. He sent Vashti away. Then came the question of choosing a new queen. The king's servants looked everywhere in the kingdom, and brought to the palace the most beautiful maidens they could find. Among them was a maiden from a Jewish family, whose name was Esther. She was young and innocent and lovely, and could never have dreamed that she might become the queen of Persia. When the king saw Esther, he preferred her to everyone else, and he made her his wife. But he did not know that she had come from among the Jews.

Now Esther had a cousin named Mordecai. Mordecai, who was older than Esther, had brought her up like a daughter, because her own father was dead. Esther trusted him in everything, and whatever he advised her to do, she did. Mordecai told her not to tell the king that she was a Jew.

Mordecai came often to the palace, to speak with Esther. Often he would sit in the gate where people went in and out and where they stood together talking. One day he saw two men who were plainly very angry. They talked excitedly, and Mordecai overheard what they were saying. They were plotting together to kill the king.

Mordecai sent word of that to Esther, and Esther warned the king. The king had the two men arrested and put to death. By his warning, Mordecai had saved the king's life. The king should have been very grateful, but he was more interested in himself than in anyone else. Although he had been told that it was Mordecai who had brought the warning, he soon forgot it.

Meanwhile there was another man who was becoming the king's favorite. His name was Haman. The king's servants had to bow to Haman whenever he passed by. But Mordecai would not bow to Haman or give any sign that he noticed him at all. Every day Mordecai was warned that he would find himself in trouble if he did not do as the king's servants did, but Mordecai paid no attention. After a while someone asked Haman if he had noticed that Mordecai, the Jew, never bowed to him when he went by. The very idea made Haman angry, for he was proud and jealous. To hear that anybody had dared not show respect to him was more than he would stand. He began to consider what would be the worst thing he would do to Mordecai. He thought about it for some time. Finally he decided that there was something worse than having Mordecai punished alone. Since Mordecai was a Jew, Haman would make all the Jewish people suffer.

So one day Haman went to the king and poured into his ears all the ugly tales he could think of about the Jews. He reminded Ahasuerus that the Jews were scattered all through the kingdom. He said there were entirely too many of them for the kingdom's good. Had the king stopped to remember that the Jews were different from the people of Persia, and had different laws? He suggested getting rid of these Jewish people who might turn out to be enemies of Persia. And Haman said that he would put ten thousand talents of silver, a huge amount of money, into the king's treasury if the king would sign an order that all the Jews should be destroyed.

Ahasuerus not only had a quick temper but he was stupid, too. He believed everything that Haman told him. He flew into a rage against the Jews and told Haman to have them killed.

Haman heard that with wicked pleasure. He lost no time in making sure that what he had planned should happen. He sent out orders, in the king's name and with the king's seal, to the governors of all the parts of the kingdom. These orders commanded that on a certain day every Jewish person—man, woman, and child—should be put to death. Then Haman went in and sat down to drink wine with the king, and to rejoice.

Out in the city the people who had begun to hear the news were shocked and troubled. Before long the news reached Mordecai. He dressed himself in rough sackcloth and poured ashes on his head as a sign of distress. Then he went to the gate of the palace to weep and mourn.

One of the palace maids told Esther of this. Esther was greatly troubled. She sent to Mordecai to beg him to take off his sackcloth, and to let her know quickly what was wrong. Mordecai told the messenger the terrible truth—that all the Jews in the kingdom were in danger of death. Only she might save them by going to the king and begging him to change the order.

Esther seemed to be faced with more than a woman could bear. She was the queen, but she knew only too well the cruel laws of the Persian court. She knew that no one, least of all a woman, might dare to cross the king. Esther sent the messenger back to Mordecai. Did he not know that if anyone went to the king uninvited, he might be put to death? This would certainly happen unless the king was in good humor and held out his golden scepter as a sign of permission to come near. Esther had no reason to think that the king would treat her so kindly. It had been many days since he had sent for her and since she had seen him.

Mordecai sent back word that there was only one hope for the Jews in Persia; only one person could do anything, and that person was Esther. She must not think, Mordecai added, that if the king's order for the killing of Jews was carried out she would escape. It would be found out that she too was a Jew, and she would be treated like the rest. But she alone might be able to do what everyone else put together could not do. Perhaps this was her chance to show a kind of courage that few would dare to show. "Who knows," said Mordecai, "but that you have come to the kingdom for such a time as this?"

When Esther received Mordecai's message, all her heart rose bravely to answer. So much depended on her that she could not be timid anymore. She sent word back to Mordecai that he should gather the Jews together to fast and pray. She and her maids in the palace would do the same. Then she would go to the king and try to persuade him. "And if I perish," she said, "I perish."

The moment came when she must take the great and final risk. Ahasuerus, in all his pomp and power, was sitting on his royal throne. Esther dressed herself in her queenliest robes. She went to the door of the throne room. The door was opened, and she stood there, beautiful and silent, waiting, looking at the king. If he were angry, that would be the end.

But the king stretched out the golden scepter toward her. "Queen Esther!" he said. "What will you have? What is your request? It shall be given you, even if it be half of the kingdom!"

So the king was not angry! He was fond of her, and perhaps he would listen to her more than he had listened to the wicked Haman. But she would not tell him her real wish now. Instead, she said, "If it seems good to the king, will he, and Haman also, come to a banquet which I have made ready today?"

The king said that he would come, and that Haman should come, too.

When they were seated at the table, the king told Esther again that he would give her anything she wanted, no matter what it might be. But she begged him not to have her tell him then what she wanted. Would he wait until tomorrow? And would he and Haman come to another banquet the next day? Yes, the king said, they would come.

Haman went out, proud and pleased. He had been invited to a banquet alone with the king and queen, and he was invited again tomorrow! But as he left the palace, there, sitting at the gate, was Mordecai. Mordecai did not stand up or bow, or even notice him. That spoiled everything. Haman snapped his lips shut and walked by Mordecai without a word. When he reached home he called his wife and some of his friends, and broke into a storm of complaining. He told them all of the honors the king had given him, and that anybody could see how great a man he was, but that this Mordecai still despised him.

Haman's wife and friends were as bad-tempered as Haman. Why did he not go at once and ask the king's permission to hang Mordecai? "Ask the king to make a gallows fifty cubits high," they said. That seemed to Haman a good idea. Without asking the king, he had the gallows built to hang Mordecai on.

Then things began to happen in a way Haman had not expected. That night the king could not sleep. He tossed about impatiently. Finally he decided he would read awhile, and he told one of his servants to bring him a book. The book the servant happened to bring was a history of the events of the king's court during the last few years. The king commanded that the book be read aloud to him. As he listened, he heard about the two men who had plotted to kill him, and how Mordecai had overheard them and had given warning.

Suddenly the king remembered that he had never rewarded Mordecai for this. It annoyed him to think that he had forgotten about it all this time. He asked his servants, "What about this Mordecai? What has been done for him?"

They told him, "Nothing."

"Who is in the court right now?" the king asked.

It happened that at just that moment Haman had come to the palace to tell the king about the gallows he had had built for Mordecai. The servants told the king that Haman was outside.

"Let him come in," said the king.

So Haman came in. The king's mind was full of what he had been hearing. "Haman," he asked, "what ought to be done to a man whom the king wants very much to honor?"

He means me! thought Haman. He tried not to look excited.

"What ought to be done for a man whom the king wants very much to honor?" Haman repeated. "Let royal robes be brought like those which the king wears, and the king's horse, too, and the king's own crown. Let these be put in charge of one of the noblest of the princes. Let the prince put the royal robes on the man the king has chosen to honor. Then the prince shall lead this man, on horseback, through the city and proclaim to the people that he is the man whom the king delights to honor."

"Good!" said the king. "Now hurry and do exactly as you have said. Take one of my royal robes and have the king's horse brought. Find Mordecai the Jew and lead him through the city."

If the king had struck Haman with a hammer between the eyes, Haman could not have been more stunned. But there was no escape from what the king had commanded, and Haman did not dare even to look surprised. In a black and bitter fury he had to go out and give Mordecai the honors he had supposed were meant for him. He held the bridle of the king's horse, with Mordecai riding on it, dressed in a royal robe. And he had to cry to the people who crowded the streets, "This is the man whom the king delights to honor!"

But that was not all. The banquet with the king and queen was still to come.

When the three of them were sitting there together, Ahasuerus asked Esther again what she wanted him to do for her. This time she really told him. She reminded him of the order that had gone out in his name that all the Jews in the kingdom should be killed. Then she told him that she herself belonged to the Jewish people. She pleaded that he would take back that dreadful order and spare them. "If I have found favor in your sight," she said, "grant me this petition!"

When the king looked at Esther, so lovely and so distressed, he was angry to think that he had been tricked by someone, he had almost forgotten who, into giving that order. "Who has done this?" he demanded. "Where is he?"

Then Esther the queen looked straight at Haman. "It is this wicked Haman," she said.

The king was so full of rage that he got up and strode out into the garden. Haman was terrified, and he fell down on the couch where the queen was sitting. In came the king again at that moment, and he thought Haman was trying to hurt the queen. "What!" he cried. "Will he attack the queen here in my own palace?" He called his servants, and they took Haman out.

One of the king's officers came and asked the king if he knew that Haman had built a gallows near his own house, a gallows nearly a hundred feet high. No, the king had not known it, but now that he knew, he knew also what should be done with it. "Take Haman and hang him on it," he commanded. So on the very gallows which he had intended for Mordecai, Haman himself was hanged.

That is the story of the book of Esther. And from that day the Jewish people, who had suffered a great deal, were glad to remember the truthful Mordecai, and the young queen who, all alone, carried through a dangerous duty.

---

# Judas and Peter

Here, from the Gospel according to Matthew, is one of our greatest stories of betrayal. We are horrified most, of course, by what Judas Iscariot did for thirty pieces of silver. At the same time, though, we are stunned in a completely different way by Peter's failure. Despite his vow at the Mount of Olives ("I will not deny thee"), Peter in fear and misery commits a much more forgivable, more human kind of betrayal. Judas Iscariot's treachery seems beyond comprehension, while Peter's denial is on a scale of which we are all capable.

Then one of the twelve, called Judas Iscariot, went unto the chief priests,

And said unto them, What will ye give me, and I will deliver him unto you? And they covenanted with him for thirty pieces of silver.

And from that time he sought opportunity to betray him.

Now the first day of the feast of Unleavened Bread the disciples came to Jesus, saying unto him, Where wilt thou that we prepare for thee to eat the Passover?

And he said, Go into the city to such a man, and say unto him, The Master saith, My time is at hand; I will keep the Passover at thy house with my disciples.

And the disciples did as Jesus had appointed them; and they made ready the Passover.

Now when the even was come, he sat down with the twelve.

And as they did eat, he said, Verily I say unto you, that one of you shall betray me.

And they were exceeding sorrowful, and began every one of them to say unto him, Lord, is it I?

And he answered and said, He that dippeth his hand with me in the dish, the same shall betray me.

The Son of Man goeth as it is written of him: but woe unto that man by whom the Son of Man is betrayed! it had been good for that man if he had not been born.

Then Judas, which betrayed him, answered and said, Master, is it I? He said unto him, Thou hast said.

And as they were eating, Jesus took bread, and blessed it, and brake it, and gave it to the disciples, and said, Take, eat; this is my body.

And he took the cup, and gave thanks, and gave it to them, saying, Drink ye all of it;

For this is my blood of the new testament, which is shed for many for the remission of sins.

But I say unto you, I will not drink henceforth of this fruit of the vine, until that day when I drink it new with you in my Father's kingdom.

And when they had sung a hymn, they went out into the Mount of Olives.

Then saith Jesus unto them, All ye shall be offended because of me this night: for it is written, I will smite the shepherd, and the sheep of the flock shall be scattered abroad.

But after I am risen again, I will go before you into Galilee.

Peter answered and said unto him, Though all men shall be offended because of thee, yet will I never be offended.

Jesus said unto him, Verily I say unto thee, That this night, before the cock crow, thou shalt deny me thrice.

Peter said unto him, Though I should die with thee, yet will I not deny thee. Likewise also said all the disciples.

Then cometh Jesus with them unto a place called Gethsemane, and saith unto the disciples, Sit ye here, while I go and pray yonder.

And he took with him Peter and the two sons of Zebedee, and began to be sorrowful and very heavy.

Then saith he unto them, My soul is exceeding sorrowful, even unto death: tarry ye here, and watch with me.

And he went a little further, and fell on his face, and prayed, saying, O my Father, if it be possible, let this cup pass from me: nevertheless, not as I will, but as thou wilt.

And he cometh unto the disciples, and findeth them asleep, and saith unto Peter, What, could ye not watch with me one hour?

Watch and pray, that ye enter not into temptation: the spirit indeed is willing, but the flesh is weak.

He went away again the second time, and prayed, saying, O my Father, if this cup may not pass away from me, except I drink it, thy will be done.

And he came and found them asleep again: for their eyes were heavy.

And he left them, and went away again, and prayed the third time, saying the same words.

Then cometh he to his disciples, and saith unto them, Sleep on now, and take your rest: behold, the hour is at hand, and the Son of Man is betrayed into the hands of sinners.

Rise, let us be going: behold, he is at hand that doth betray me.

And while he yet spake, lo, Judas, one of the twelve, came, and with him a great multitude with swords and staves, from the chief priests and elders of the people.

Now he that betrayed him gave them a sign, saying, Whomsoever I shall kiss, that same is he; hold him fast.

And forthwith he came to Jesus, and said, Hail, Master; and kissed him.

And Jesus said unto him, Friend, wherefore art thou come? Then came they, and laid hands on Jesus, and took him.

And, behold, one of them which were with Jesus stretched out his hand, and drew his sword, and struck a servant of the high priest, and smote off his ear.

Then said Jesus unto him, Put up again thy sword into his place: for all they that take the sword shall perish with the sword.

Thinkest thou that I cannot now pray to my Father, and he shall presently give me more than twelve legions of angels?

But how then shall the Scriptures be fulfilled, that thus it must be?

In that same hour said Jesus to the multitudes, Are ye come out as against a thief with swords and staves for to take me? I sat daily with you teaching in the temple, and ye laid no hold on me.

But all this was done, that the Scriptures of the prophets might be fulfilled. Then all the disciples forsook him, and fled.

And they that had laid hold on Jesus led him away to Caiaphas the high priest, where the scribes and the elders were assembled.

But Peter followed him afar off unto the high priest's palace, and went in, and sat with the servants, to see the end.

Now the chief priests, and elders, and all the council, sought false witness against Jesus, to put him to death;

But found none: yea, though many false witnesses came, yet found they none. At the last came two false witnesses,

And said, This fellow said, I am able to destroy the temple of God, and to build it in three days.

And the high priest arose, and said unto him, Answerest thou nothing? What is it which these witness against thee?

But Jesus held his peace. And the high priest answered and said unto him, I adjure thee by the living God, that thou tell us whether thou be the Christ, the Son of God.

Jesus saith unto him, Thou hast said: nevertheless I say unto you, Hereafter shall ye see the Son of Man sitting on the right hand of power, and coming in the clouds of heaven.

Then the high priest rent his clothes, saying, He hath spoken blasphemy; what further need have we of witnesses? Behold, now ye have heard his blasphemy.

What think ye? They answered and said, He is guilty of death.

Then did they spit in his face, and buffeted him; and others smote him with the palms of their hands,

Saying, Prophesy unto us, thou Christ, Who is he that smote thee?

Now Peter sat without in the palace: and a damsel came unto him, saying, Thou also wast with Jesus of Galilee.

But he denied before them all, saying, I know not what thou sayest.

And when he was gone out into the porch, another maid saw him, and said unto them that were there, This fellow was also with Jesus of Nazareth.

And again he denied with an oath, I do not know the man.

And after a while came unto him they that stood by, and said to Peter, Surely thou also art one of them; for thy speech bewrayeth thee.

Then began he to curse and to swear, saying, I know not the man. And immediately the cock crew.

And Peter remembered the word of Jesus, which said unto him, Before the cock crow, thou shalt deny me thrice. And he went out, and wept bitterly.

When the morning was come, all the chief priests and elders of the people took counsel against Jesus to put him to death:

And when they had bound him, they led him away, and delivered him to Pontius Pilate the governor.

Then Judas, which had betrayed him, when he saw that he was condemned, repented himself, and brought again the thirty pieces of silver to the chief priests and elders,

Saying, I have sinned in that I have betrayed the innocent blood. And they said, What is that to us? See thou to that.

And he cast down the pieces of silver in the temple, and departed, and went and hanged himself.

---

# Castor and Pollux

The Athenian dramatist Menander said that to live is not to live for one's self alone. The story of Castor and Pollux illuminates this grander meaning of the word brotherhood.

On winter nights the constellation Gemini lies high overhead, and its two principal stars, Castor and Pollux, are among the brightest in the heavens. We know them as the Twins, but old myths from the days of Greek heroes say they were really half-brothers. Leda was the mother of both, while Castor's father was Tyndareus, the king of Sparta, and Pollux's father was Zeus, king of the gods. So the span of Castor's life was fixed, but Pollux was immortal.

By all accounts, the brothers were never apart, so great was their devotion to each other, and they shared many adventures. They sailed with Jason and the Argonauts on the quest for the Golden Fleece, and they rescued their sister Helen when she was kidnapped by Theseus, the same beautiful Helen whose face later "launched a thousand ships" and brought about the Trojan War. They also took part in the famous Calydonian hunt, in which many of Greece's bravest heroes gathered to rid the land of a monstrous boar.

The most famous legend about Castor and Pollux is about how they ended their earthly lives. The Greek poet Pindar tells us that Castor was wounded in battle. His brother rushed to his side, only to find him almost dead, gasping out his life with short-drawn breath. Pollux did everything he could to save him, but there was no hope.

"Oh father Zeus," Pollux cried, "take my life instead of my brother's! Or if not that, let me die also! Without him, I will know nothing but grief for the rest of my days."

As he spoke, Zeus approached and answered:

"You are my son, Pollux, and therefore enjoy eternal life. Your brother was born of mortal seed, and destined like all humans to taste death. But I will give you a choice. You may come to Olympus, as is your right, and dwell with Athena and Ares and the rest of the gods. Or, if you wish to share your immortality with your brother, then half the time you must spend beneath the earth, and the other half in the golden home of heaven."

Pollux did not for an instant waver, but gave up his life in Olympus, and chose to share light and darkness forever with his brother. So Zeus unclosed Castor's eyes and restored his breath. And even now we see them as the constellation Gemini. They spend half their time fixed in the starry heavens, and the other half sunk beneath the horizon.

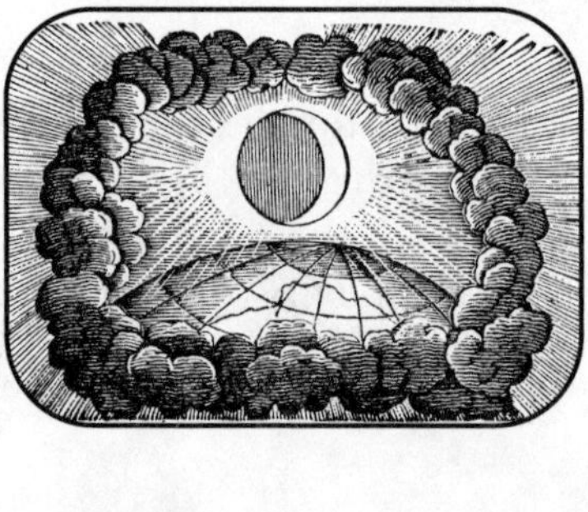

# Penelope's Web

*Adapted from James Baldwin*

Penelope's long wait for her husband's return from the Trojan War may be our ultimate tale of fidelity. The Ithacan queen's patience, resourcefulness, constancy, and love make her one of Greek mythology's most memorable characters. The story comes from Homer's *Odyssey*. In this retelling, Odysseus is called by his Latin name, Ulysses.

Of all the heroes who fought against Troy, the wisest and shrewdest was Ulysses, king of Ithaca. Yet, he went unwillingly to war. He longed to stay at home with his wife, Penelope, and their baby boy, Telemachus. But the princes of Greece demanded that he help them, and at last he consented.

"Go, Ulysses," said Penelope, "and I will keep your home and kingdom safe until you return."

"Do your duty, Ulysses," said his old father, Laertes. "Go, and may wise Athena speed your coming back."

And so, bidding farewell to Ithaca and all he held dear, he sailed away to the Trojan War.

Ten long years passed, and then news reached Ithaca that the weary siege of Troy was ended, the city lay in ashes, and the Greek kings were returning to their native lands. One by one, all the heroes reached their homes, but of Ulysses and his companions there came no word. Every day, Penelope and young Telemachus and feeble old Laertes stood by the shore and gazed with aching eyes far over the waves. But no sign of sail or glinting oars could they discern. Months passed by, and then years, and still no word.

"His ships are wrecked, and he lies at the bottom of the sea," sighed old Laertes, and after that he shut himself up in his narrow room and went no more to the shore.

But Penelope still hoped and hoped. "He is not dead," she said. "And until he comes home, I will hold this fair kingdom for him."

Every day his seat was placed for him at the table. His coat was hung by his chair, his chamber was dusted, and his great bow that hung in the hall was polished.

Ten more years passed with constant watching. Telemachus became a tall, gentle-mannered young man. And throughout all Greece, men began to talk of nothing but Penelope's great nobility and beauty.

"How foolish of her," the Greek princes and chiefs said, "to be forever looking for Ulysses. Everyone knows he is dead. She ought to marry one of us now."

So one after another, the chiefs and princes who were looking for wives sailed to Ithaca, hoping to win Penelope's love. They were haughty and overbearing fellows, glorying in their own importance and wealth. Straight to the palace they went, not waiting for an invitation, for they knew they would be treated as honored guests, whether they were welcome or not.

"Come now, Penelope," they said, "we all know Ulysses is dead. We have come as suitors for your hand, and you dare not turn us away. Choose one of us, and the rest will depart."

But Penelope answered sadly, "Princes and heroes, this cannot be. I am quite sure Ulysses lives, and I must hold his kingdom for him till he returns."

"Return he never will," said the suitors. "Make your choice now."

"Give me a month longer to wait for him," she pleaded. "In my loom I have a half-finished web of soft linen. I am weaving it for the shroud of our father, Laertes, who is very old and cannot live much longer. If Ulysses fails to return by the time this web is finished, then I will choose, though unwillingly."

The suitors agreed, and made themselves at home in the palace. They seized the best of everything. They feasted daily in the great dining hall, wasting much, and helped themselves to all the wine in the cellar. They were rude and uproarious in the once quiet chambers of the palace, and insulting to the people of Ithaca.

Every day Penelope sat at her loom and wove. "See how much I have added to the length of the web?" she would say when evening came. But at night, when the suitors were asleep, she raveled out all the threads she had woven during the day. Thus although she was always at work, the web was never finished.

As the weeks passed, however, the suitors began to grow weary of waiting.

"When will that web be finished?" they impatiently asked.

"I am busy with it every day," Penelope answered, "but it grows very slowly. Such a delicate piece of work cannot be completed so quickly."

But one of the suitors, a man named Agelaus, was not satisfied. That night he crept quietly through the palace and peeped into the weaving room. There he saw Penelope busily unravelling the web by the light of a little lamp, while she whispered to herself the name of Ulysses.

The next morning the secret was known to every one of the unwelcome guests. "Fair queen," they said, "you are very cunning, but we have found you out. That web must be finished before the sun rises again, and then tomorrow you must make your choice. We shall wait no longer."

The following afternoon the unwelcome guests assembled in the great hall. The feast was set, and they ate and drank and sang and shouted as never before. They made such an uproar that the very timbers of the palace shook.

While the turmoil was at its height, Telemachus came in, followed by Eumaeus, his father's oldest and most faithful servant. Together they began to remove all the shields and swords that hung on the walls and rattled from so much commotion.

"What are you doing with those weapons?" shouted the suitors, who finally noticed the old man and the youth.

"They are becoming tarnished with smoke and dust," said Eumaeus, "and will keep much better in the treasure room."

"But we will leave my father's great bow that hangs at the head of the hall," added Telemachus. "My mother polishes it every day, and she would sadly miss it if it were removed."

"She won't be polishing it much longer," the suitors laughed. "Before this day is over, Ithaca will have a new king."

At that moment a strange beggar entered the courtyard. His feet were bare, his head was uncovered, his clothes were in rags. He approached the kitchen door, where an old greyhound, Argos, was lying on a heap of ashes. Twenty years before, Argos had been Ulysses' favorite and most loyal hunting dog. But now, grown toothless and almost blind, he was only abused by the suitors.

When he saw the beggar slowly moving through the yard, he raised his head to look. Then a strange look came suddenly into his old eyes. His tail wagged feebly, and he tried with all his failing strength to rise. He looked up lovingly into the beggar's face, and uttered a long but joyful howl like that which he once uttered in his youth when greeting his master.

The beggar stooped and patted his head. "Argos, old friend," he whispered.

The dog staggered to his feet, then fell, and was dead with the look of joy still in his eyes.

A moment later the beggar stood in the doorway of the great hall, where he was seen whispering a few words to Telemachus and faithful Eumaeus.

"What do you want here, Old Rags?" the suitors called, hurling crusts of bread at his head. "Get out! Be gone!"

But at that moment, down the stairs came Penelope, stately and beautiful, with her servants and maids around her.

"The queen! The queen!" cried the suitors. "She has come to choose one of us!"

"Telemachus, my son," said Penelope, "what poor man is this whom our guests treat so roughly?"

"Mother, he is a wandering beggar whom the waves cast upon our shores last night," answered the prince. "He says that he brings news of my father."

"Then he shall tell me of it," said the queen. "But first he must rest." At this she caused the beggar to be led to a seat at the farther side of the room, and gave orders that he be fed and refreshed.

An old woman, who had been Ulysses' nurse when he was a child, brought a great bowl of water and towels. Kneeling on the stones before the stranger, she began to wash his feet. Suddenly she sprang back, overturning the bowl in her confusion.

"O, master! The scar!" she muttered quietly.

"Dear nurse," whispered the beggar, "you were ever discreet and wise. You know me by the old scar I have carried on my knee since boyhood. Keep well the secret, for I bide my time, and the hour of vengeance is nigh."

This man in rags was indeed Ulysses, the king. Alone in a little boat he had been cast, that very morning, upon the shore of his own island. He had made himself known to Telemachus and old Eumaeus alone, and by his orders they had removed the weapons that hung on the wall of the great hall.

Meanwhile, the suitors had gathered again around the feast table and were more boisterous than before. "Come, fair Penelope!" they shouted. "This beggar can tell his tale tomorrow. It is time for you to choose a new husband! Choose now!"

"Chiefs and princes," said Penelope, in trembling tones, "let us leave this decision to the gods. Behold, there hangs the great bow of Ulysses, which he alone was able to string. Let each of you try his strength in bending it, and I will choose the one who can shoot an arrow from it the most skillfully."

"Well said!" cried all the suitors, and they lined up to try their strength. The first took the bow in his hands, and struggled long to bend it. Then, losing patience, he threw it on the ground and strode away. "None but a giant can string a bow like that," he said.

Then, one by one, the other suitors tried their strength, but all in vain.

"Perhaps the old beggar would like to take part in this contest," one said with a sneer.

Then Ulysses in his beggar's rags rose from his seat and went with halting steps to the head of the hall. He fumbled with the great bow, gazing at its polished back and its long, well-shaped arms, stout as bars of iron. "Methinks," he said, "that in my younger days I once saw a bow like this."

"Enough! Enough!" shouted the suitors. "Get out, you old fool!"

Suddenly, a great change came over the stranger. Almost without effort, he bent the great bow and strung it. Then he rose to his full height, and even in his beggar's rags appeared every inch a king.

"Ulysses! Ulysses!" Penelope cried.

The suitors were speechless. Then, in the wildest alarm, they turned and tried to escape from the hall. But the arrows of Ulysses were swift and sure, and not one missed its mark. "Now I avenge myself upon those who have tried to destroy my home!" he cried. And thus, one after another, the lawless suitors perished.

The next day Ulysses sat in the great hall with Penelope and Telemachus and all the joyful members of the household, and he told the story of his long wanderings over the sea. And Penelope, in turn, related how she had faithfully kept the kingdom, as she had promised, though beset by insolent and wicked suitors. Then she brought from her chamber a roll of soft, white cloth of wonderful delicacy and beauty, and said, "This is the web, Ulysses. I promised that on the day of its completion I would choose a husband, and I choose you."

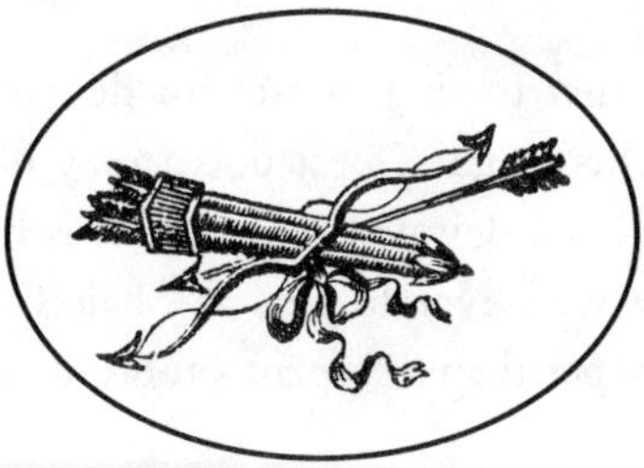

# Loyalty to a Brother

*Walter MacPeek*

Family loyalties involve certain obligations. They are duties we perform out of love, as this simple story from an old Boy Scout book reminds us.

One of two brothers fighting in the same company in France fell by a German bullet. The one who escaped asked permission of his officer to go and bring his brother in.

"He is probably dead," said the officer, "and there is no use in your risking your life to bring in his body."

But after further pleading the officer consented. Just as the soldier reached the lines with his brother on his shoulders, the wounded man died.

"There, you see," said the officer, "you risked your life for nothing."

"No," replied Tom. "I did what he expected of me, and I have my reward. When I crept up to him and took him in my arms, he said, 'Tom, I knew you would come—I just felt you would come.' "

There you have the gist of it all; somebody expects something fine and noble and unselfish of us; someone expects us to be faithful.

---

# Only a Dad

*Edgar Guest*

We should not forget to sing praises for devoted fathers—especially our *own*. This Edgar Guest poem may help us remember that the only reward a devoted father seeks is his family's flourishing. And may we never forget, as Shakespeare's King Lear told us, "how sharper than a serpent's tooth it is to have a thankless child."

Only a dad with a tired face,
Coming home from the daily race,
Bringing little of gold or fame
To show how well he has played the game;
But glad in his heart that his own rejoice
To see him come and to hear his voice.

Only a dad with a brood of four,
One of ten million men or more
Plodding along in the daily strife,
Bearing the whips and the scorns of life,
With never a whimper of pain or hate,
For the sake of those who at home await.

Only a dad, neither rich nor proud,
Merely one of the surging crowd,
Toiling, striving from day to day,
Facing whatever may come his way,
Silent whenever the harsh condemn,
And bearing it all for the love of them.

Only a dad but he gives his all,
To smooth the way for his children small,
Doing with courage stern and grim
The deeds that his father did for him.
This is the line that for him I pen:
Only a dad, but the best of men.

---

## Home Sweet Home

*John Howard Payne*

Home is the place where we find comfort, security, memories, friendship, hospitality, and, above all, family. It is the place that deserves our commitment and loyalty.

'Mid pleasures and palaces though we may roam,
Be it ever so humble, there's no place like home;
A charm from the sky seems to hallow us there,
Which, seek through the world, is ne'er met with elsewhere.
Home, home, sweet, sweet home!
There's no place like home! There's no place like home!

An exile from home, splendor dazzles in vain;
Oh, give me my lowly thatched cottage again!
The birds singing gayly, that came at my call—
Give me them—and the peace of mind, dearer than all!
Home, home, sweet, sweet home!
There's no place like home! There's no place like home!

How sweet 'tis to sit 'neath a fond father's smile,
And the caress of a mother to soothe and beguile!
Let others delight mid new pleasures to roam,
But give me, oh, give me, the pleasures of home!
Home, home, sweet, sweet home!
There's no place like home! There's no place like home!

To thee I'll return, overburdened with care;
The heart's dearest solace will smile on me there;
No more from that cottage again will I roam;
Be it ever so humble, there's no place like home.
Home, home, sweet, sweet home!
There's no place like home! There's no place like home!

---

# Paul Revere's Ride

*Henry Wadsworth Longfellow*

Generations of American schoolchildren have discovered the spirit of the American Revolution by memorizing this poem, which first appeared in 1863. As a historical record it is certainly flawed. (Paul Revere in fact never made it all the way to Concord; he was detained on the road from Lexington by a British patrol, while a companion escaped and carried forward the news that the British were coming.) As a story of high adventure, intrigue, and daring deeds for the sake of American independence, however, it is unsurpassed.

The events of the story take place on the night of April 18, 1775, when seven hundred British troops marched out of occupied Boston to destroy colonial arms caches reportedly hidden in Concord. The British had hoped to move in secret, but American spies were alert, and soon silversmith Paul Revere was galloping ahead of the redcoats to warn John Hancock and Samuel Adams, who were staying at Lexington. That mission accomplished, Revere dashed down the road to Concord to spread the alarm further.

Listen, my children, and you shall hear
Of the midnight ride of Paul Revere,
On the eighteenth of April, in Seventy-five;
Hardly a man is now alive
Who remembers that famous day and year.

He said to his friend, "If the British march
By land or sea from the town tonight,
Hang a lantern aloft in the belfry arch
Of the North Church tower as a signal light—
One, if by land, and two, if by sea;
And I on the opposite shore will be,
Ready to ride and spread the alarm
Through every Middlesex village and farm,
For the country folk to be up and to arm."

Then he said, "Good night!" and with muffled oar
Silently rowed to the Charlestown shore,
Just as the moon rose over the bay,
Where swinging wide at her moorings lay
The *Somerset,* British man-of-war;
A phantom ship, with each mast and spar
Across the moon like a prison bar,
And a huge black hulk, that was magnified
By its own reflection in the tide.

Meanwhile, his friend, through alley and street,
Wanders and watches with eager ears,
Till in the silence around him he hears
The muster of men at the barrack door,
The sound of arms, and the tramp of feet,
And the measured tread of the grenadiers,
Marching down to their boats on the shore.

Then he climbed the tower of the Old North Church,
By the wooden stairs, with stealthy tread,
To the belfry chamber overhead,
And startled the pigeons from their perch
On the somber rafters, that round him made
Masses and moving shapes of shade—
By the trembling ladder, steep and tall,
To the highest window in the wall,
Where he paused to listen and look down
A moment on the roofs of the town,
And the moonlight flowing over all.

Beneath, in the churchyard, lay the dead,
In their night encampment on the hill,
Wrapped in silence so deep and still
That he could hear, like a sentinel's tread,
The watchful night wind, as it went
Creeping along from tent to tent,
And seeming to whisper, "All is well!"
A moment only he feels the spell
Of the place and the hour, and the secret dread
Of the lonely belfry and the dead;
For suddenly all his thoughts are bent
On a shadowy something far away,
Where the river widens to meet the bay—
A line of black that bends and floats
On the rising tide, like a bridge of boats.

Meanwhile, impatient to mount and ride,
Booted and spurred, with a heavy stride
On the opposite shore walked Paul Revere.
Now he patted his horse's side,
Now gazed at the landscape far and near,
Then, impetuous, stamped the earth,

And turned and tightened his saddle girth;
But mostly he watched with eager search
The belfry tower of the Old North Church,
As it rose above the graves on the hill,
Lonely and spectral and somber and still.
And lo! as he looks, on the belfry's height
A glimmer, and then a gleam of light!
He springs to the saddle, the bridle he turns,
But lingers and gazes, till full on his sight
A second lamp in the belfry burns!

A hurry of hoofs in a village street,
A shape in the moonlight, a bulk in the dark,
And beneath, from the pebbles, in passing, a spark
Struck out by a steed flying fearless and fleet;
That was all! And yet, through the gloom and the light
The fate of a nation was riding that night;
And the spark struck out by that steed in his flight,
Kindled the land into flame with its heat.

He has left the village and mounted the steep,
And beneath him, tranquil and broad and deep,
Is the Mystic, meeting the ocean tides;
And under the alders, that skirt its edge,
Now soft on the sand, now loud on the ledge,
Is heard the tramp of his steed as he rides.

It was twelve by the village clock
When he crossed the bridge into Medford town.
He heard the crowing of the cock,
And the barking of the farmer's dog,
And felt the damp of the river fog,
That rises after the sun goes down.

It was one by the village clock,
When he galloped into Lexington.
He saw the gilded weathercock
Swim in the moonlight as he passed,
And the meeting house windows, blank and bare,
Gaze at him with a spectral glare,
As if they already stood aghast
At the bloody work they would look upon.

It was two by the village clock,
When he came to the bridge in Concord town.
He heard the bleating of the flock,
And the twitter of birds among the trees,
And felt the breath of the morning breeze
Blowing over the meadows brown.
And one was safe and asleep in his bed
Who at the bridge would be first to fall,
Who that day would be lying dead,
Pierced by a British musket ball.

You know the rest. In the books you have read,
How the British Regulars fired and fled—
How the farmers gave them ball for ball,
From behind each fence and farmyard wall,
Chasing the redcoats down the lane,
Then crossing the fields to emerge again
Under the trees at the turn of the road,
And only pausing to fire and load.
So through the night rode Paul Revere;
And so through the night went his cry of alarm
To every Middlesex village and farm—
A cry of defiance, and not of fear,
A voice in the darkness, a knock at the door,
And a word that shall echo forevermore!
For, borne on the night wind of the Past,
Through all our history, to the last,
In the hour of darkness and peril and need,
The people will waken and listen to hear
The hurrying hoofbeats of that steed,
And the midnight message of Paul Revere.

# Concord Hymn

*Ralph Waldo Emerson*

Emerson wrote "Concord Hymn" as a tribute to the "embattled farmers" who fought the professional British troops at Concord on April 19, 1775. The minutemen's steadfastness became the "shot heard round the world" that inspired other colonists to shoulder their rifles and march for the Revolutionary cause. The poem was first sung as a hymn on July 4, 1837, at a ceremony marking the completion of a monument that commemorates the battles of Lexington and Concord.

By the rude bridge that arched the flood,
  Their flag to April's breeze unfurled,
Here once the embattled farmers stood
  And fired the shot heard round the world.

The foe long since in silence slept;
  Alike the conqueror silent sleeps;
And Time the ruined bridge has swept
  Down the dark stream which seaward creeps.

On this green bank, by this soft stream,
  We set today a votive stone;
That memory may their deed redeem,
  When, like our sires, our sons are gone.

Spirit, that made those heroes dare
  To die, and leave their children free,
Bid Time and Nature gently spare
  The shaft we raise to them and thee.

# Nathan Hale

### *From* American Heritage *magazine*

Americans look to the Revolutionary War to find the two names that mark the extremes of loyalty to country. On one end of the spectrum we find Benedict Arnold, perhaps the most despised name in the nation's history. At the other end stands Nathan Hale.

Ever since he was executed by the British on the morning of September 22, 1776, the death of Nathan Hale has been recognized as one of the great moments of American patriotism. Some years ago the late George Dudley Seymour gathered all the contemporary descriptions of the young hero's career that he could find, and had them privately printed in a *Documentary Life of Nathan Hale*. In the selections below we can read at first hand, in the words of both his friends and his foes, a story that has inspired generations of Hale's countrymen.

Following his graduation from Yale in 1773 at the age of eighteen, Hale taught school for a time in his native Connecticut. Then, on July 1, 1775—two months after Lexington and Concord—he was commissioned a lieutenant in the Continental Army, and closed his one-room school in New London, a building still proudly preserved by the town. We see him first in the reminiscences of a comrade-in-arms, Lieutenant Elisha Bostwick:

> I can now in imagination see his person and hear his voice—his person, I should say, was a little above the common stature in height, his shoulders of a moderate breadth, his limbs strait and very plump: regular features—very fair skin—blue eyes—flaxen or very light hair which was always kept short—his eyebrows a shade darker than his hair and his voice rather sharp or piercing—his bodily agility was remarkable. I have seen him follow a football and kick it over the tops of the trees in the Bowery at New York (an exercise which he was fond of)—his mental powers seemed to be above the common sort—his mind of a sedate and sober cast, and he was undoubtedly pious; for it was remarked that when any of the soldiers of his

> company were sick he always visited them and usually prayed for and with them in their sickness.

Early in the fall of 1776, after being disastrously defeated on Long Island, Washington needed to know the dispositions and the intentions of the British forces. Hale and other officers of the picked regiment known as Knowlton's Rangers were asked to volunteer for an intelligence mission behind enemy lines. On the first call, none responded; on the second, Nathan Hale alone stepped forward. A little later he told his friend Captain (afterward General) William Hull what he had done:

> [Hale] asked my candid opinion [says Hull's memoir]. I replied, that it was an action which involved serious consequences, and the propriety of it was doubtful. . . . Stratagems are resorted to in war; they are feints and evasions, performed under no disguise . . . and, considered in a military view, lawful and advantageous. . . . But who respects the character of a spy, assuming the garb of friendship but to betray? . . . I ended by saying, that should he undertake the enterprise, his short, bright career would close with an ignominious death.
>
> He replied, "I am fully sensible of the consequences of discovery and capture in such a situation. . . . Yet . . . I wish to be useful, and every kind of service, necessary to the public good, becomes honorable by being necessary. If the exigencies of my country demand a peculiar service, its claims to perform that service are imperious."

Sergeant Stephen Hempstead of New London accompanied him as he set out on his mission from Norwalk, Connecticut:

> Captain Hale had a general order to all armed vessels to take him to anyplace he should designate: he was set across the Sound . . . at Huntington (Long Island). . . . Captain Hale had changed his uniform for a plain suit of citizen's brown clothes, with a round broad-brimmed hat, assuming the character of a Dutch schoolmaster, leaving all his other clothes, commission, public and private papers, with me, and also his silver shoe buckles, saying they would not comport with his character of schoolmaster, and retaining nothing but his college diploma, as an introduction to his assumed calling. Thus equipped, we parted.

Hale's servant, Asher Wright, who had remained behind, told what happened next:

> He passed all their guards on Long Island, went over to New York in a ferryboat and got by all the guards but the last. They stopped him, searched and found drawings of the works, with descriptions in Latin, under the inner sole of the pumps which he wore. Some say his cousin, Samuel Hale, a Tory, betrayed him. I don't know; guess he did.

"Betrayed" is probably too strong; "identified" is closer to the truth. A surviving letter from Samuel, a Harvard man (1766), seems to deny any misdeed, or at least any guilt, as the story was spread in a Newburyport newspaper—but he thereafter fled to England and never returned to America, even after the war, for his wife and son.

The next day a kindhearted British officer, Captain John Montresor, approached the American lines under a flag of truce to report the inevitable denouement. Captain Hull recorded Montresor's words:

> Hale at once declared his name, his rank in the American army, and his object in coming within the British lines.
>
> Sir William Howe, without the form of a trial, gave orders for his execution the following morning. He was placed in the custody of the provost marshal, who was . . . hardened to human suffering and every softening sentiment of the heart. Captain Hale, alone, without sympathy or support, save that from above, on the near approach of death asked for a clergyman to attend him. It was refused. He then requested a Bible; that too was refused by his inhuman jailer.
>
> On the morning of his execution . . . my station was near the fatal spot, and I requested the provost marshal to permit the prisoner to sit in my marquee, while he was making the necessary preparations. Captain Hale entered: he was calm, and bore himself with gentle dignity, in the consciousness of rectitude and high intentions. He asked for writing materials, which I furnished him: he wrote two letters. . . . He was shortly after summoned to the gallows. But a few persons were around him, yet his characteristic dying words were remembered. He said, "I only regret, that I have but one life to lose for my country."

A brief excerpt from a letter written at Coventry, Connecticut, the following spring by Nathan Hale's father, Richard, who had six sons altogether in the Revolution, betrays the deep grief of this unlettered man:

> You desired me to inform you about my son Nathan. . . . He was executed about the twenty-second of September last by the accounts we have had. A child I sot much by but he is gone. . . .

This letter, addressed to Richard Hale's brother, Major Samuel Hale, in Portsmouth, New Hampshire, on March 28, 1777, was put away in a secret drawer of the major's desk. In 1908, the old desk was sold at auction as an antique, and three years later the new owner, the Honorable Frank L. Howe of Barrington, New Hampshire, chanced upon it. Such is the thrill of historical discovery.

---

# Washington Rejects a Crown

Not long after the American victory at Yorktown, an officer of the Revolutionary Army wrote to George Washington suggesting that the newly liberated colonies could "never become a nation under a republican form of government" and proposing "the establishment of a kingdom with Washington at the head." Washington fired off an immediate reply. Like Cincinnatus, who also had turned down dictatorship more than two thousand years before, his loyalties lay with his country's interests, not his own.

Newburgh May 22, 1782

Sir,

With a mixture of great surprise and astonishment I have read with attention the sentiments you have submitted to my perusal. Be assured sir, no occurrence in the course of the war has given me more painful sensations than your information of there being such ideas existing in the army as you have expressed, and I must view with abhorrence, and reprehend with severety—for the present, the communication of them will rest in my own bosom, unless some further agitation of the matter shall make a disclosure necessary.

I am much at a loss to conceive what part of my conduct could have given encouragement to an address which to me seems big with the greatest mischiefs that can befall my country. If I am not deceived in the knowledge of myself, you could not have found a person to whom your schemes are more disagreeable—at the same time in justice to my own feeling I must add, that no man possesses a more sincere wish to see ample justice done to the army than I do, and as far as my powers and influence, in a constitution, may extend, they shall be employed to the utmost of my abilities to effect it, should there be any occasion—Let me conjure you then, if you have any regard for your country—concern for yourself or posterity—or respect for me, to banish these thoughts from your mind, and never communicate, as from yourself, or anyone else, a sentiment of the like nature.

With esteem I am Sir
Your Most Obedient Servant
G. Washington

# America

*Samuel Smith*

The Reverend Samuel Smith wrote the lyrics to "America" in Amherst, Massachusetts, in February 1832, and it was first performed at an Independence Day celebration in Boston later that year. Then, as now, it was sung to the tune of "God Save the King." Most Americans are familiar with the first verse, but all are worth knowing.

My country 'tis of thee
Sweet land of liberty:
  Of thee I sing.
Land where my fathers died
Land of the Pilgrims' pride
From every mountainside
  Let freedom ring.

My native country—thee
Land of the noble free
  Thy name I love:
I love thy rocks and rills
Thy woods and templed hills
My heart with rapture thrills
  Like that above.

Let music swell the breeze
And ring from all the trees
  Sweet freedom's song.
Let all that breathe partake
Let mortal tongues awake
Let rocks their silence break
  The sound prolong.

Our fathers' God to thee
Author of liberty
  To thee we sing.
Long may our land be bright
With freedom's holy light
Protect us by thy might
  Great God, our King.

# Barbara Frietchie

*John Greenleaf Whittier*

Sometimes our sense of loyalty demands that we show the flag even in the enemy's midst. John Greenleaf Whittier (1807–1892) wrote this poem in 1863, during the Civil War, and claimed its story is true.

Up from the meadows rich with corn,
Clear in the cool September morn,
The clustered spires of Frederick stand
Green-walled by the hills of Maryland.
Round about them orchards sweep,
Apple and peach tree fruited deep,
Fair as the garden of the Lord
To the eyes of the famished rebel horde,
On that pleasant morn of the early fall
When Lee marched over the mountain wall;
Over the mountains winding down,
Horse and foot, into Frederick town.

Forty flags with their silver stars,
Forty flags with their crimson bars,
Flapped in the morning wind: the sun
Of noon looked down, and saw not one.
Up rose old Barbara Frietchie then,
Bowed with her fourscore years and ten;
Bravest of all in Frederick town,
She took up the flag the men hauled down;
In her attic window the staff she set,
To show that one heart was loyal yet.

Up the street came the rebel tread,
Stonewall Jackson riding ahead.
Under his slouched hat left and right
He glanced; the old flag met his sight.
"Halt"—the dust-brown ranks stood fast.
"Fire"—out blazed the rifle blast.
It shivered the window, pane and sash;
It rent the banner with seam and gash.
Quick, as it fell, from the broken staff
Dame Barbara snatched the silken scarf.
She leaned far out on the windowsill,
And shook it forth with a royal will.
"Shoot, if you must, this old gray head,
But spare your country's flag," she said.

A shade of sadness, a blush of shame,
Over the face of the leader came;
The nobler nature within him stirred
To life at that woman's deed and word;
"Who touches a hair on yon gray head
Dies like a dog! March on!" he said.
All day long through Frederick street
Sounded the tread of marching feet:
All day long that free flag tost
Over the heads of the rebel host.
Ever its torn folds rose and fell
On the loyal winds that loved it well;
And through the hill gaps sunset light
Shone over it with a warm good night.

Barbara Frietchie's work is o'er,
And the Rebel rides on his raids no more.
Honor to her! and let a tear
Fall, for her sake, on Stonewall's bier.
Over Barbara Frietchie's grave
Flag of Freedom and Union, wave!
Peace and order and beauty draw
Round thy symbol of light and law;
And ever the stars above look down
On thy stars below in Frederick town!

# America the Beautiful

*Katharine Lee Bates*

Massachusetts educator and author Katharine Lee Bates wrote "America the Beautiful" in 1893 after being inspired by the view from Pikes Peak in Colorado. She revised the lyrics to their final form in 1911. They are set to the music of Samuel A. Ward's "Materna."

O beautiful for spacious skies,
For amber waves of grain,
For purple mountain majesties
Above the fruited plain!
America! America!
God shed His grace on thee
And crown thy good with brotherhood
From sea to shining sea!

O beautiful for Pilgrim feet,
Whose stern, impassioned stress
A thoroughfare for freedom beat
Across the wilderness!
America! America!
God mend thine every flaw,
Confirm thy soul in self-control,
Thy liberty in law!

O beautiful for heroes proved
In liberating strife,
Who more than self their country loved,
And mercy more than life!
America! America!
May God thy gold refine,
Till all success be nobleness
And every gain divine!

O beautiful for patriot dream
  That sees beyond the years
Thine alabaster cities gleam
  Undimmed by human tears!
America! America!
  God shed His grace on thee,
And crown thy good with brotherhood
  From sea to shining sea!

---

## In Flanders Fields

*John McCrae*

Canadian physician, soldier, and poet John McCrae (1872–1918) published in 1915 this famous poem about the Allied dead buried in Belgium. It reminds us that others' self-sacrifice is one reason for loyalty to cause.

In Flanders fields the poppies blow
Between the crosses, row on row,
  That mark our place; and in the sky
  The larks, still bravely singing, fly
Scarce heard amid the guns below.

We are the Dead. Short days ago
We lived, felt dawn, saw sunset glow,
  Loved and were loved, and now we lie
  In Flanders fields.

Take up our quarrel with the foe:
To you from failing hands we throw
  The torch; be yours to hold it high.
  If ye break faith with us who die
We shall not sleep, though poppies grow
  In Flanders fields.

# Flag Day

This editorial appeared in *The New York Times* on June 14, 1940, to mark Flag Day, a holiday that seems to have fallen into neglect in more recent years. Flag Day commemorates the day in 1777 when the Continental Congress adopted the Stars and Stripes as the official flag of the United States.

What's a flag? What's the love of country for which it stands? Maybe it begins with love of the land itself. It is the fog rolling in with the tide at Eastport, or through the Golden Gate and among the towers of San Francisco. It is the sun coming up behind the White Mountains, over the Green, throwing a shining glory on Lake Champlain and above the Adirondacks. It is the storied Mississippi rolling swift and muddy past St. Louis, rolling past Cairo, pouring down past the levees of New Orleans. It is lazy noontide in the pines of Carolina, it is a sea of wheat rippling in Western Kansas, it is the San Francisco peaks far north across the glowing nakedness of Arizona, it is the Grand Canyon and a little stream coming down out of a New England ridge, in which are trout.

It is men at work. It is the storm-tossed fishermen coming into Gloucester and Providence and Astoria. It is the farmer riding his great machine in the dust of harvest, the dairyman going to the barn before sunrise, the lineman mending the broken wire, the miner drilling for the blast. It is the servants of fire in the murky splendor of Pittsburgh, between the Allegheny and the Monongahela, the trucks rumbling through the night, the locomotive engineer bringing the train in on time, the pilot in the clouds, the riveter running along the beam a hundred feet in air. It is the clerk in the office, the housewife doing the dishes and sending the children off to school. It is the teacher, doctor, and parson tending and helping, body and soul, for small reward.

It is small things remembered, the little corners of the land, the houses, the people that each one loves. We love our country because there was a little tree on a hill, and grass thereon, and a sweet valley below; because the hurdy-gurdy man came along on a sunny morning in a city street; because a beach or a farm or a lane or a house that might not seem much to others were once, for each of us, made magic. It is voices that are remembered only, no longer heard. It is parents, friends, the lazy chat of street and store and office, and the ease of mind that makes life tranquil. It is summer and winter, rain and sun and storm. These are flesh of our flesh, bone of our bone, blood of our blood, a lasting part of what we are, each of us and all of us together.

It is stories told. It is the Pilgrims dying in their first dreadful winter. It is the minuteman standing his ground at Concord Bridge, and dying there. It is the army in rags, sick, freezing, starving at Valley Forge. It is the wagons and the men on foot going westward over Cumberland Gap, floating down the great rivers, rolling over the great plains. It is the settler hacking fiercely at the primeval forest on his new, his own lands. It is Thoreau at Walden Pond, Lincoln at Cooper Union, and Lee riding home from Appomattox. It is corruption and disgrace, answered always by men who would not let the flag lie in the dust, who have stood up in every generation to fight for the old ideals and the old rights, at risk of ruin or of life itself.

It is a great multitude of people on pilgrimage, common and ordinary people, charged with the usual human failings, yet filled with such a hope as never caught the imaginations and the hearts of any nation on earth before. The hope of liberty. The hope of justice. The hope of a land in which a man can stand straight, without fear, without rancor.

The land and the people and the flag—the land a continent, the people of every race, the flag a symbol of what humanity may aspire to when the wars are over and the barriers are down; to these each generation must be dedicated and consecrated anew, to defend with life itself, if need be, but, above all, in friendliness, in hope, in courage, to live for.

---

# Ethical Loyalty

*Richard A. Gabriel*

In this excerpt from *To Serve with Honor,* his treatise on military ethics, Richard A. Gabriel draws a careful distinction between blind and informed loyalties, and asserts that the latter is the duty of the ethical soldier.

Whether one examines the fifteenth-century doctrine of *respondiat superior* ("let the superior be responsible") or the notion of just war, or even the more recent cases of the My Lai massacre or the execution of General Yamashita, or, finally, the Nuremberg trials, it is clear that Western society has long held that men cannot escape ethical responsibility for their acts by transferring that responsibility to others. The doctrine of accepting ethical responsibility was formally enshrined in the United States military profession as early as 1863 in General Order number 100 of the United States Army Field Manual: "Men who take up arms against another in public war do not cease on this account to be moral beings responsible to one another." Individuals always remain ethically responsible for their actions, for the choices they make among conflicting moral obligations, as well as for the consequences which result from them. To deny that a soldier has ethical responsibility is to negate the very nature of ethics as ethics applies to the military profession. . . .

Members of the profession must set standards of proper military behavior and must observe the standards, being consciously aware of why the obligations bind as they do. When they merely execute the precepts of the code without knowing why, they are engaged only in acts of obedience. Ethical action involving as it does judgment, choice, and responsibility is the antithesis of obedience. Members of the profession of arms must understand that sterile loyalty to a stated code is meaningless unless the precepts are understood and its obligations undertaken willingly. . . .

In short, a soldier's moral obligations transcend and surpass the obligations owed to his immediate superiors and even his civilian superiors in certain conditions. General Marshall, the epitome of the loyal soldier, was echoing General MacArthur's sentiments when he said that "an officer's ultimate commanding loyalty at all times is to his country and not to his service or his superiors." In a crisis, the soldier must exercise his sense of loyalty as *fides* [faith], and it must always take precedence over any sense of *obsequium* [obedience]. Indeed, the problem is even more complex, for in a deep moral crisis the soldier may even have to override his oath to the profession and to the Constitution in order to be loyal to humanity itself.

The Germans, who perhaps have had more direct experience with officers and soldiers being crushed between demands of their oath and the course of immoral events, have developed an interesting distinction in dealing with the question of loyalty to superiors. They distinguish between *hochverrat* and *landesverrat*. *Hochverrat* is disloyalty to a superior, which in Germanic terms meant disloyalty to the monarch or other governmental head of state. *Landesverrat,* by contrast, is disloyalty or betrayal of the nation. Within this distinction there is room for maneuver in making an ethical choice. In order to serve the nation or the Constitution, a soldier may sometimes have to be disloyal to his superiors or refuse to execute their orders. The Germanic distinction between the two notions of loyalty throws into focus what every member of the military profession knows in his heart, and that is that fundamentally a soldier's first loyalty is to behave ethically and humanly, and that in times of severe moral crisis he must be prepared to follow that higher morality. . . .

In essence, to be an ethical soldier is to do one's duty as to what is ethically right and to know why those ethics bind. Duty is not to be blindly tied to following orders.

# The Last Lesson

*Alphonse Daudet*

The Franco-Prussian War of 1870–1871 moved French author Alphonse Daudet (1840–1897) to write this story, but the events could easily concern almost any war. Here is a case of tragedy inspiring a loyalty that, because of its nobility, cannot be said to be futile. The story is also a warning that we should not wait until the customs and heritages we love are gone before we begin to feel devoted to them.

I was very late for school that morning, and I was terribly afraid of being scolded, especially as Monsieur Hamel had told us that he should examine us on participles, and I did not know the first thing about them. For a moment I thought of staying away from school and wandering about the fields. It was such a warm, lovely day. I could hear the blackbirds whistling on the edge of the wood, and in the Rippert field, behind the sawmill, the Prussians going through their drill. All that was much more tempting to me than the rules concerning participles; but I had the strength to resist, and I ran as fast as I could to school.

As I passed the mayor's office, I saw that there were people gathered about the little board on which notices were posted. For two years all our bad news had come from that board—battles lost, conscriptions, orders from headquarters; and I thought without stopping:

"What can it be now?"

Then, as I ran across the square, Wachter the blacksmith, who stood there with his apprentice, reading the placard, called out to me:

"Don't hurry so, my boy; you'll get to your school soon enough!"

I thought that he was making fun of me, and I ran into Monsieur Hamel's little yard all out of breath.

Usually, at the beginning of school, there was a great uproar which could be heard in the street, desks opening and closing, lessons repeated aloud in unison, with our ears stuffed in order to learn quicker, and the teacher's stout ruler beating on the desk:

"A little more quiet!"

I counted on all this noise to reach my bench unnoticed; but as it happened, that day everything was quiet, like a Sunday morning. Through the open window I saw my comrades already in their places, and Monsieur Hamel walking back and forth with the terrible iron ruler under his arm. I had to open the door and enter, in the midst of that perfect silence. You can imagine whether I blushed and whether I was afraid!

But no! Monsieur Hamel looked at me with no sign of anger and said very gently:

"Go at once to your seat, my little Frantz; we were going to begin without you."

I stepped over the bench and sat down at once at my desk. Not until then, when I had partly recovered from my fright, did I notice that our teacher had on his handsome blue coat, his plaited ruff, and the black silk embroidered breeches, which he wore only on days of inspection or of distribution of prizes. Moreover, there was something extraordinary, something solemn about the whole class. But what surprised me most was to see at the back of the room, on the benches which were usually empty, some people from the village sitting, as silent as we were: old Hauser with his three-cornered hat, the ex-mayor, the ex-postman, and others besides. They all seemed depressed; and Hauser had brought an old spelling book with gnawed edges, which he held wide open on his knee, with his great spectacles askew.

While I was wondering at all this, Monsieur Hamel had mounted his platform, and in the same gentle and serious voice with which he had welcomed me, he said to us:

"My children, this is the last time that I shall teach you. Orders have come from Berlin to teach nothing but German in the schools of Alsace and Lorraine. The new teacher arrives tomorrow. This is the last class in French, so I beg you to be very attentive."

Those few words overwhelmed me. Ah! the villains! That was what they had posted at the mayor's office.

My last class in French!

And I barely knew how to write! So I should never learn! I must stop short where I was! How angry I was with myself because of the time I had wasted, the lessons I had missed, running about after nests, or sliding on the Saar! My books, which only a moment before I thought so tiresome, so heavy to carry—my grammar, my sacred history—seemed to me now like old friends, from whom I should be terribly grieved to part. And it was the same about Monsieur Hamel. The thought that he was going away, that I should never see him again, made me forget the punishments, the blows with the ruler.

Poor man! It was in honor of that last lesson that he had put on his fine Sunday clothes; and I understood now why those old fellows from the village were sitting at the end of the room. It seemed to mean that they regretted not having come oftener to the school. It was also a way of thanking our teacher for his forty years of faithful service, and of paying their respects to the fatherland which was vanishing.

I was at that point in my reflections, when I heard my name called. It was my turn to recite. What would I not have given to be able to say from beginning to end that famous rule about participles, in a loud, distinct voice, without a slip! But I got mixed up at the first words, and I stood there swaying against my bench, with a full heart, afraid to raise my head. I heard Monsieur Hamel speaking to me:

"I will not scold you, my little Frantz; you must be punished enough; that is the way it goes; every day we say to ourselves: 'Pshaw! I have time enough. I will learn tomorrow.' And then you see what happens. Ah! it has been the great misfortune of our Alsace always to postpone its lessons until tomorrow. Now those people are entitled to say to us: 'What! you claim to be French, and you can neither speak nor write your language!' In all this, my poor Frantz, you are not the guiltiest one. We all have our fair share of reproaches to address to ourselves.

"Your parents have not been careful enough to see that you were educated. They preferred to send you to work in the fields or in the factories, in order to have a few more sous. And have I nothing to reproach myself for? Have I not often made you water my garden instead of studying? And when I wanted to go fishing for trout, have I ever hesitated to dismiss you?"

Then, passing from one thing to another, Monsieur Hamel began to talk to us about the French language, saying that it was the most beautiful language in the world, the most clear, the most substantial; that we must always retain it among ourselves, and never forget it, because when a people falls into servitude, "so long as it clings to its language, it is as if it held the key to its prison." Then he took the grammar and read us our lesson. I was amazed to see how readily I understood. Everything that he said seemed so easy to me, so easy. I believed, too, that I had never listened so closely, and that he, for his part, had never been so patient with his explanations. One would have said that, before going away, the poor man desired to give us all his knowledge, to force it all into our heads at a single blow.

When the lesson was at an end, we passed to writing. For that day Monsieur Hamel had prepared some entirely new examples, on which was written in a fine, round hand: "France, Alsace, France, Alsace." They were like little flags, waving all about the class, hanging from the rods of our desks. You should have seen how hard we all worked and how silent it was! Nothing could be heard save the grinding of the pens over the paper. At one time some cock-chafers flew in; but no one paid any attention to them, not even the little fellows, who were struggling with their straight lines, with a will and conscientious application, as if even the lines were French. On the roof of the schoolhouse, pigeons cooed in low tones, and I said to myself as I listened to them:

"I wonder if they are going to compel them to sing in German too!"

From time to time, when I raised my eyes from my paper, I saw Monsieur Hamel sitting motionless in his chair and staring at the objects about him as if he wished to carry away in his glance the whole of his little schoolhouse. Think of it! For forty years he had been there in the same place, with his yard in front of him and his class just as it was! But the benches and desks were polished and rubbed by use; the walnuts in the yard had grown, and the hop vine which he himself had planted now festooned the windows even to the roof. What a heart-rending thing it must have been for that poor man to leave all those things, and to hear his sister walking back and forth in the room overhead, packing their trunks! For they were to go away the next day—to leave the province forever.

However, he had the courage to keep the class to the end. After the writing, we had the lesson in history; then the little ones sang all together the *ba, be, bi, bo, bu.* Yonder, at the back of the room, old Hauser had put on his spectacles, and, holding his spelling book in both hands, he spelled out the letters with them. I could see that he too was applying himself. His voice shook with emotion, and it was so funny to hear him, that we all longed to laugh and to cry. Ah! I shall remember that last class.

Suddenly the church clock struck twelve, then the Angelus rang. At the same moment, the bugles of the Prussians returning from drill blared under our windows. Monsieur Hamel rose, pale as death, from his chair. Never had he seemed to me so tall.

"My friends," he said, "my friends, I—I—"

But something suffocated him. He could not finish the sentence.

Thereupon he turned to the blackboard, took a piece of chalk, and, bearing on with all his might, he wrote in the largest letters he could:

"VIVE LA FRANCE!"

Then he stood there, with his head resting against the wall, and without speaking, he motioned to us with his hand:

"That is all; go."

# Knute Rockne

*Francis Wallace*

Great players and great coaches win with loyalty to team and school. No one knew it better than Knute Rockne.

From 1918 through 1930 Knute Rockne, that homely Norwegian with the well-splashed nose, had a phenomenal football coaching record at Notre Dame: 105 games won, 12 lost, 5 tied. Yet it wasn't what he did but how he did it that made him the greatest coach of all time. Like other coaches, he looked at his boys and saw weight, speed, and brains. But he went further: he looked into their hearts and minds, saw character and built on it. He used his keen insight to weld a sum of ordinary talents into extraordinary teams—mostly with talk. Advice, philosophy, wisecracks, caustic comment poured from him "like champagne from a battered oilcan," Westbrook Pegler once said.

There was no "secret" to the Rockne system of football. Once he put up a sign for visitors: "Secret Practice. Come and bring your notebooks." On another occasion, when an Army scout missed a train connection and didn't get to the Notre Dame game he was to cover, Rockne obligingly sent him the plays he planned to use against the West Pointers. Army figured that the diagrams were a ruse, and prepared to meet different plays. In the game Rockne used exactly the same plays he had sent—and won. "It isn't the plays that win," he said to me. "It's the *execution.*"

When Rockne began coaching, football was a game of brawn. He preached and proved that ingenuity, quick thinking, and teamwork could beat size and strength. His players often were not impressive physically (his famous "Four Horsemen" of 1922, 1923, 1924 averaged under 160 pounds), but they usually won because Rockne could inspire them to play above their natural ability.

His pregame pep talks were famous nationwide. In these he spared neither his team nor himself. I was a witness to one when Rockne, seriously ill with phlebitis, wanted so badly to beat Carnegie Tech that he accompanied the team to Pittsburgh against doctor's orders. The air in the locker room was thick with tension. The crippled Rockne sat glumly on a table, staring at his players. Behind the lockers, the team doctor whispered to me, "If he lets go, and that blood clot jumps from his leg to his heart or his brain, he may never leave this room alive."

Suddenly Rock let go. I had never heard such an outburst. His voice crackled as if charged with electricity. He thundered, he blustered, he exhorted with revival-meeting fervor. Gradually he wove his magic spell. Finally he dropped into the chanting line: "We are going out there and fight, fight, *fight*—and we're going to WIN!" As he finished his explosion, the team roared out onto the field—and Rock fell back in a cold sweat. Later he was helped to the field, where he watched in a wheelchair as his fired-up team won, 7–0.

Rock knew just when to deflate a player's incipient big head, when to give an encouraging pat on the back. If a star back seemed to be taking his publicity too seriously, Rock might pull out his best linemen in practice and let the star find out the hard way how far he could go without able players in front of him. Whenever the star protested, Rock would growl, "Show those tacklers your clippings!"

If Rockne had not gone into coaching, it is likely that he could have been a brilliant professor of chemistry—a subject which he did teach for a few years at Notre Dame. As a youngster brought to this country from Norway, he had shown an early hunger for knowledge. The Rocknes had a custom which permitted any member to dip into the family purse for money to buy gifts for other members; young Knute would buy books for his sisters—and then read them first.

There was no money to send him to college, so Knute worked four years in the Chicago post office to earn a thousand dollars toward his education. He went to Notre Dame because he heard it was a "poor boys' school" where he would have a good chance of getting a job. It was an unlikely-looking freshman who turned up in South Bend the autumn of 1910. He was overage (twenty-two), undersized (5 feet, 8 inches; 145 pounds) and already balding. He described himself as a "lone Norse Protestant" in a Catholic school. (He was converted to Catholicism fifteen years later.) Even though he was working his way through school he became captain of the football team (and third-string All America end), an editor of the yearbook, a star of the dramatic club. And, majoring in science, he achieved an average of over 90 for his four years and graduated *magna cum laude*!

As a player, as well as a coach, Rockne helped to revolutionize football. During summer vacations he worked as a lifeguard at a resort with a teammate named Gus Dorais. They whiled away their spare time throwing and catching the ball—which at that time was usually just kicked or carried. In the fall of 1913 the nationally unknown Notre Dame team went east to play mighty Army. The much bigger Army team outplayed Notre Dame on the ground. But when Notre Dame got the ball, Dorais would flip passes to Rockne and others for big gains. Rockne scored two touchdowns, and Notre Dame won, 35–13. With this victory came a change in the popular attitude toward football: instead of being considered a battering-ram contest of brute force, it became a game where skill and speed counted as much as bulk and strength.

As a coach, Rock was a stickler for physical conditioning. He hated softness and self-indulgence; his players were forbidden to smoke, and drinking was unthought of. Inside the rough exterior, however, he was a deeply kind man. He used to bring the youngsters outside the gate into home games. (One of these small fry, about five years old at the time, was Joe Kuharich, later to become Notre Dame's head coach.) He did some remarkable things for his players: not long ago I met one of his "old boys" who said, "My mother died of cancer; it wasn't until we opened the safe-deposit box that I found out Rock had been writing pep talks to her for years."

He helped me in scores of ways. When I was a young newspaperman I had to decide whether to stick with a salaried job or to strike out as a freelance writer. As I thought about it, I could almost hear Rockne's voice as he spoke these words on other occasions: "Be unorthodox. Don't be afraid to take chances. If you believe something, don't hesitate to try it just because no one else will."

I gave up the security of the newspaper job and soon was doing much better on my own. He helped me with my first magazine article. My first book, *Huddle,* was a fictional account of Rockne and Notre Dame.

Although Rock could always charm men and inspire boys, he was awed by women. On student dates he was such a tongue-tied blusher that the girls quickly gave up on him. Finally, however, at a resort near Sandusky, Ohio, where he had a summer job, he met a fellow employee named Bonnie Skiles. Bonnie was probably Rock's first and only girl. They married not long after his graduation and there was never a more devoted husband and family man than this father of three sons and a daughter.

Rockne preached loyalty, and he practiced it by remaining at

Notre Dame despite many attractive offers from other schools. His loyalty was cemented by an incident that happened in 1921. His team had won twenty straight games and was a big favorite to beat Iowa. However, Iowa upset Notre Dame 10–7. "There will be no alibi," Rockne snapped after the defeat.

It was a glum coach and team aboard the train as we pulled into South Bend at one o'clock Sunday morning. Suddenly, from out of the darkness, we heard the familiar Notre Dame cheer known as the Skyrocket—the victory yell. The student body had marched en masse three miles into town to meet the beaten team. Rockne slipped out on the far side of the train, but the crowd spotted him and hoisted him on top of a baggage truck.

A thousand boys stood in the darkness and cheered him. The hard-bitten coach, visibly touched, had trouble pulling himself together following the ovation. "After this," he said, "I will never leave Notre Dame as long as you want me." And he never left.

I last saw Rock in Florida in March 1931 on a short vacation. He left there for California, where Hollywood was trying to interest him in acting in a film. Passing over Kansas, his airplane crashed on a hilltop, killing all aboard. The nation was thunderstruck. "It takes a mighty big calamity to shock this country all at once," his friend Will Rogers wrote. "But, Knute, you did it."

Last rites for Rockne were held from the church on the broad campus he loved so well. The final tribute was spoken by the university president, the Reverend Charles O'Donnell. He said, "In an age that has stamped itself as the era of the 'go-getter'—a horrible word for what is all too often a ruthless thing—Knute Rockne was a 'go-giver'—a not much better word, but it means a divine thing."

The grave where Rockne is buried in South Bend is marked by only a small stone, and it is hard to find. Yet a hundred or more of his old players and friends go there every year after a memorial Mass. There are other monuments to his memory: the giant Notre Dame stadium, the glowing tradition he created, the warm place he still holds in the hearts of thousands of people who never even met him.

Before departing for California, Rock had left a pair of tan, high-topped shoes to be half-soled. No one ever called for those shoes. And nobody in football has ever come close to filling them.

# The Thousandth Man

*Rudyard Kipling*

This Kipling poem, which reminds us that loyalty and reliability can sometimes be rare commodities, echoes Ecclesiastes 7:28 in the Bible: "one man in a thousand have I found."

One man in a thousand, Solomon says,
Will stick more close than a brother.
And it's worth while seeking him half your days
If you find him before the other.
Nine hundred and ninety-nine depend
On what the world sees in you,
But the Thousandth Man will stand your friend
With the whole round world agin you.

'Tis neither promise nor prayer nor show
Will settle the finding for 'ee.
Nine hundred and ninety-nine of 'em go
By your looks, or your acts, or your glory,
But if he finds you and you find him,
The rest of the world don't matter;
For the Thousandth Man will sink or swim
With you in any water.

You can use his purse with no more talk
Than he uses yours for his spendings,
And laugh and meet in your daily walk
As though there had been no lendings.
Nine hundred and ninety-nine of 'em call
For silver and gold in their dealings;
But the Thousandth Man he's worth 'em all,
Because you can show him your feelings.

His wrong's your wrong, and his right's your right,
In season or out of season.
Stand up and back it in all men's sight—
With *that* for your only reason!
Nine hundred and ninety-nine can't bide
The shame or mocking or laughter,
But the Thousandth Man will stand by your side
To the gallows-foot—and after!

# 10

# Faith

Faith, Hope, and Love are formally regarded as "theological" virtues in traditional Christian doctrine. They mark dispositions of persons who are flourishing in life from that religious perspective. There is nothing distinctively Christian, however, in recognizing that religious faith adds a significant dimension to the moral life of humanity worldwide. Faith is a source of discipline and power and meaning in the lives of the faithful of any major religious creed. It is a potent force in human experience. A shared faith binds people together in ways that cannot be duplicated by other means.

Clashing faiths, on the other hand, divide people in sometimes the most violent ways. The history of the world's religions unfortunately gives ringing confirmation to what James Madison so brilliantly analyzed in *Federalist 10* as the natural human tendency toward faction. "So strong is this propensity of mankind to fall into mutual animosities that where no substantial occasion presents itself the most frivolous and fanciful distinctions have been sufficient to kindle their unfriendly passions and excite their most violent conflicts." A secular world stripped of all vestige of religion would assuredly have no "religious wars," but it by no means follows that it would be a world at peace. We do faith a disservice in laying at its doorstep the fundamental causes of faction.

Faith contributes to the form and the content of the ideals that guide the aspirations we harbor for our own lives, and it affects the way we regard and behave with respect to others. What Paul cites as "the fruit of the Spirit"—love, joy, peace, patience, kindness, generosity, faithfulness, gentleness, and self-control (Galatians 5:22–23)—has its parallels in all the major faiths; and the Golden Rule, expressed in one form or another, is recognized almost universally. The "Illustrations of the *Tao*," assembled by C. S. Lewis as an appendix to *The Abolition of Man*, represents a more extensive collection of such widely recognized "Natural Law."

A human being without faith, without *reverence* for anything, is a human being morally adrift. The world's major religions provide time-tested anchors for drifters; they furnish ties to a larger reality for people on the loose. Faith can contribute important elements to the social stability and moral development of individuals and groups.

Early in this century the American psychologist and philosopher William James conducted a pioneering study of the faith experience of religious persons historically and throughout the world. It was published under the title *The Varieties of Religious Experience.* He discovered among those who had experienced the most profound religious states a virtually universal tendency toward what he called "monism" and "optimism." Fundamental bedrock reality is both unified and good. If there are any universal articles of faith, these are prime candidates. In a world so fragmented and full of woe, faith in its underlying unity and goodness is a sustaining encouragement to those who are working on reality's "surface"—within any of the major religious traditions—for love, joy, peace, patience, kindness, generosity, faithfulness, gentleness, and self-control.

To parents who are themselves insecure in their faith and, like the nineteenth-century English radical John Thelwall, think it "unfair to influence a child's mind by inculcating any opinions before it should have come to years of discretion, and be able to choose for itself," there is an enlightening anecdote in Samuel Taylor Coleridge's *Table Talk* for July 27, 1830. "I showed [John Thelwall] my garden, and told him it was my botanical garden. 'How so?' said he, 'it is covered with weeds.'—'Oh,' I replied, '*that* is only because it has not yet come to its age of discretion and choice. The weeds, you see, have taken the liberty to grow, and I thought it unfair in me to prejudice the soil towards roses and strawberries.' "

## Now I Lay Me Down to Sleep

I have read that John Adams said this one every night throughout his adult years. The Bennett family says it every night, too.

Now I lay me down to sleep;
I pray the Lord my soul to keep.
If I should die before I wake,
I pray the Lord my soul to take.

---

## Sleep, My Babe

We parents know we cannot do our jobs all alone. From the beginning, we ask for aid.

Sleep, my babe, and peace attend thee,
  All through the night;
Guardian angels God will lend thee,
  All through the night;
Soft the drowsy hours are creeping,
Hill and vale in slumber sleeping,
Mother dear her watch is keeping,
  All through the night.

God is here, thou'lt not be lonely,
All through the night;
'Tis not I who guards thee only,
All through the night.
Night's dark shades will soon be over,
Still my watchful care shall hover,
God with me His watch is keeping,
All through the night.

## A Child's Prayer

Prayer, like all good habits, is best learned while we are very young.

Lord, teach a little child to pray,
And then accept my prayer;
For thou canst hear the words I say,
For thou art everywhere.

A little sparrow cannot fall
Unnoticed, Lord, by thee;
And though I am so young and small,
Thou dost take care of me.

Teach me to do the thing that's right,
And when I sin, forgive;
And make it still my chief delight
To serve thee while I live.

# Noah and the Ark

*Retold by Jesse Lyman Hurlbut*

Even today, every time they see a rainbow, millions of people are reminded of the story of how Noah's faith and righteousness saved him from the destruction of his generation.

By the time that Adam died, there were many people on the earth; for the children of Adam and Eve had many other children; and when these grew up, they also had children; and these too had children. So after a time that part of the earth where Adam's sons lived began to be full of people.

It is sad to tell that as time went on more and more of these people became wicked, and fewer and fewer of them grew up to become good men and women. All the people lived near together, and few went away to other lands; so it came to pass that even the children of good men and women learned to be bad, like the people around them.

And as God looked down on the world that he had made, he saw how wicked the men in it had become, and that every thought and every act of man was evil.

And God looked down on the earth, and said:

"I will take away all men from the earth that I have made; because the men of the world are evil, and evil continually."

But even in those bad times, God saw one good man. His name was Noah. Noah tried to do right in the sight of God. As Enoch had walked with God, so Noah walked with God, and talked with him. And Noah had three sons: their names were Shem and Ham and Japheth.

God said to Noah, "The time has come when all the men and women on the earth are to be destroyed. Every one must die, because they are all wicked. But you and your family shall be saved, because you alone are trying to do right."

Then God told Noah how he might save his life and the lives of his family. He was to build a very large boat, as large as the largest ships that are made in our time; very long and very wide and very deep; with a roof over it; and made like a long wide house in three stories, but so built that it would float on the water. Such a ship as this was called an "ark." God told Noah to build this ark, and to have it ready for the time when he would need it.

"For," said God to Noah, "I am going to bring a great flood of water on the earth, to cover all the land and to drown all the people on the earth. And as the animals on the earth will be drowned with the people, you must make the ark large enough to hold a pair of each kind of animal, and several pairs of some animals that are needed by men, like sheep and goats and oxen; so that there will be animals as well as men to live upon the earth after the flood has passed away. And you must take in the ark food for yourself and your family, and for all the animals with you, enough food to last for a year, while the flood shall stay on the earth."

And Noah did what God told him to do, although it must have seemed very strange to all the people around, to build this great ark where there was no water for it to sail upon. And it was a long time, even a hundred and twenty years, that Noah and his sons were at work building the ark, while the wicked people around wondered, and no doubt laughed at Noah for building a great ship where there was no sea. At last the ark was finished, and stood like a great house on the land. There was a door on one side, and a window on the roof, to let in the light. Then God said to Noah, "Come into the ark, you and your wife, and your three sons, and their wives with them; for the flood of waters will come very soon. And take with you animals of all kinds, and birds, and things that creep; seven pairs of those that will be needed by men, and one pair of all the rest; so that all kinds of animals may be kept alive upon the earth."

So Noah and his wife, and his three sons, Shem, Ham, and Japheth, with their wives, went into the ark. And God brought to the door of the ark the animals, and the birds, and the creeping things of all kinds; and they went into the ark, and Noah and his sons put them in their places, and brought in food for them all. And then the door of the ark was shut, so that no more people and no more animals could come in.

In a few days the rain began to fall, as it had never rained before. It seemed as though the heavens were opened to pour great floods upon the earth. The streams filled, and the rivers rose, higher and higher, and the ark began to float on the water. The people left their houses and ran up to the hills, but soon the hills were covered, and all the people on them were drowned.

Some had climbed up to the tops of higher mountains, but the water rose higher and higher, until even the mountains were covered and all the people, wicked as they had been, were drowned in the great sea that now rolled over all the earth where men had lived. And all the animals, the tame animals—cattle and sheep and oxen—were drowned; and the wild animals—lions and tigers and all the rest—were drowned also. Even the birds were drowned, for their nests in the trees were swept away, and there was no place where they could fly from the terrible storm. For forty days and nights the rain kept on, until there was no breath of life remaining outside of the ark.

After forty days the rain stopped, but the water stayed upon the earth for more than six months; and the ark, with all that were in it, floated over the great sea that covered the land. Then God sent a wind to blow over the waters and to dry them up: so by degrees the waters grew less and less. So, after waiting for a time, Noah opened a window and let loose a bird called a raven. Now the raven has strong wings; and this raven flew round and round until the waters had gone down, and it could find a place to rest, and it did not come back to the ark.

After Noah had waited for it awhile, he sent out a dove; but the dove could not find any place to rest, so it flew back to the ark, and Noah took it into the ark again. Then Noah waited a week longer, and afterward he sent out the dove again. And at the evening, the dove came back to the ark, which was its home; and in its bill was a fresh leaf which it had picked off from an olive tree.

So Noah knew that the water had gone down enough to let the trees grow once more. He waited another week, and sent out the dove again; but this time the dove flew away and never came back. And Noah knew that the earth was becoming dry again. And God said to Noah:

"Come out of the ark, with your wife, and your sons, and their wives, and all the living things that are with you in the ark."

So Noah opened the door of the ark, and with his family came out, and stood once more on the ground. All the animals and birds and creeping things in the ark came out also, and began again to bring life to the earth.

The first thing Noah did, when he came out of the ark, was to give thanks to God for saving all his family when the rest of the people on the earth were destroyed. He built an altar, and laid upon it an offering to the Lord, and gave himself and his family to God, and promised to do God's will.

And God was pleased with Noah's offering, and God said:

"I will not again destroy the earth on account of men, no matter how bad they may be. From this time no flood shall again cover the earth; but the seasons of spring and summer and fall and winter shall remain without change. I give to you the earth; you shall be the rulers of the ground and of every living thing upon it."

Then God caused a rainbow to appear in the sky, and he told Noah and his sons that whenever they or the people after them should see the rainbow, they should remember that God had placed it in the sky and over the clouds as a sign of his promise that he would always remember the earth and the people upon it, and would never again send a flood to destroy men from the earth.

So, as often as we see the beautiful rainbow, we are to remember that it is the sign of God's promise to the world.

---

# All Things Beautiful

*Cecil Alexander*

The miracle of ordinary things fills children's worlds. They sense, as Wordsworth phrased it, the "intimations of immortality" we too often neglect as adults.

All things bright and beautiful,
All creatures great and small,
All things wise and wonderful,
The Lord God made them all.

Each little flower that opens,
Each little bird that sings,
He made their glowing colors,
He made their tiny wings.

The purple-headed mountain,
The river running by,
The sunset, and the morning,
That brighten up the sky;

The cold wind in the winter,
 The pleasant summer sun,
The ripe fruits in the garden,
 He made them every one.

The tall trees in the greenwood,
 The meadows where we play,
The rushes by the water,
 We gather every day;

He gave us eyes to see them,
 And lips that we might tell
How great is God Almighty,
 Who has made all things well.

---

# Job

*Retold by Jesse Lyman Hurlbut*

The book of Job in the Bible is widely recognized as one of the world's great dramatic poems, both in the sublimity of its theme and the magnificence of its expression. Its main subject is straightforward but profound: why do righteous people suffer? The suffering of this "perfect and upright" man, his torment, his patience, and his final humility, have become a proverbial measure of faith.

Here is a simple prose version of the events in the book of Job.

At some time in those early days—we do not know just at what time, whether in the days of Moses or later—there was living a good man named Job. His home was in the land of Uz, which may have been on the edge of the desert, east of the land of Israel. Job was a very rich man. He had sheep, and camels, and oxen, and asses, counted by the thousand. In all the east there was no other man so rich as Job.

And Job was a good man. He served the Lord God, and prayed to God every day, with an offering upon God's altar, as men worshipped in those times. He tried to live as God wished him to live, and was always kind and gentle. Every day, when his sons were out in the field, or were having a feast together in the house of any of them, Job went out to his altar, and offered a burnt offering for each one of his sons and his daughters, and prayed to God for them; for he said:

"It may be that my sons have sinned or have turned away from God in their hearts; and I will pray God to forgive them."

At one time, when the angels of God stood before the Lord, Satan the Evil One came also, and stood among them, as though he were one of God's angels. The Lord God saw Satan, and said to him, "Satan, from what place have you come?" "I have come," answered Satan, "from going up and down in the earth and looking at the people upon it."

Then the Lord said to Satan, "Have you looked at my servant Job? And have you seen that there is not another man like him in the earth, a good and a perfect man, one who fears God and does nothing evil?" Then Satan said to the Lord: "Does Job fear God for nothing? Hast thou not made a wall around him, and around his house, and around everything that he has? Thou hast given a blessing upon his work, and hast made him rich. But if thou wilt stretch forth thy hand, and take away from him all that he has, then he will turn away from thee and will curse thee to thy face."

Then the Lord said to the Evil One, "Satan, all that Job has is in your power; you can do to his sons, and his flocks, and his cattle, whatever you wish; only lay not your hand upon the man himself."

Then Satan went forth from before the Lord; and soon trouble began to come upon Job. One day, when all his sons and daughters were eating and drinking together in their oldest brother's house, a man came running to Job, and said:

"The oxen were plowing, and the asses were feeding beside them, when the wild men from the desert came upon them, and drove them all away; and the men who were working with the oxen and caring for the asses have all been killed; and I am the only one who has fled away alive!"

While this man was speaking, another man came rushing in; and he said:

"The lightning from the clouds has fallen on all the sheep, and on the men who were tending them; and I am the only one who has come away alive!"

Before this man had ended, another came in; and he said:

"The enemies from Chaldea have come in three bands, and have taken away all the camels. They have killed the men who were with them; and I am the only one left alive!"

Then at the same time, one more man came in, and said to Job:

"Your sons and your daughters were eating and drinking together in their oldest brother's house, when a sudden and terrible wind from the desert struck the house, and it fell upon them. All your sons and your daughters are dead, and I alone have lived to tell you of it."

Thus in one day, all that Job had—his flocks, and his cattle, and his sons and his daughters—all were taken away; and Job, from being rich, was suddenly made poor. Then Job fell down upon his face before the Lord, and he said:

"With nothing I came into the world, and with nothing I shall leave it. The Lord gave, and the Lord has taken away; blessed be the name of the Lord."

So even when all was taken from him Job did not turn away from God, nor did he find fault with God's doings.

And again the angels of God were before the Lord, and Satan, who had done all this harm to Job, was among them. The Lord said to Satan, "Have you looked at my servant Job? There is no other man in the world as good as he; a perfect man, one that fears God and does no wrong act. Do you see how he holds fast to his goodness, even after I have let you do him so great harm?" Then Satan answered the Lord, "All that a man has he will give for his life. But if thou wilt put thy hand upon him and touch his bone and his flesh, he will turn from thee, and will curse thee to thy face."

And the Lord said to Satan, "I will give Job into your hand; do to him whatever you please; only spare his life."

Then Satan went out and struck Job, and caused dreadful boils to come upon him, over all his body, from the soles of his feet to the crown of his head. And Job sat down in the ashes in great pain; but he would not speak one word against God. His wife said to him,

"What is the use of trying to serve God? You may as well curse God, and die!"

But Job said to her, "You speak as one of the foolish. What? shall we take good things from the Lord? and shall we not take evil things also?" So Job would not speak against God. Then three friends of Job came to see him, and to try to comfort him in his sorrow and pain. Their names were Eliphaz, and Bildad, and Zophar. They sat down with Job, and wept, and spoke to him. But their words were not words of comfort. They believed that all these great troubles had come upon Job to punish him for some great sin, and they tried to persuade Job to tell what evil things he had done, to make God so angry with him.

For in those times most people believed that trouble, and sickness, and the loss of friends, and the loss of what they had owned, came to men because God was angry with them on account of their sins. These men thought that Job must have been very wicked because they saw such evils coming upon him. They made long speeches to Job, urging him to confess his wickedness.

Job said that he had done no wrong, that he had tried to do right; and he did not know why these troubles had come; but he would not say that God had dealt unjustly in letting him suffer. Job did not understand God's ways, but he believed that God was good; and he left himself in God's hands. And at last God himself spoke to Job and to his friends, telling them that it is not for man to judge God, and that God will do right by every man. And the Lord said to the three friends of Job:

"You have not spoken of me what is right, as Job has. Now bring an offering to me; and Job shall pray for you, and for his sake I will forgive you."

So Job prayed for his friends, and God forgave them. And because in all his troubles Job had been faithful to God, the Lord blessed Job once more, and took away his boils from him, and made him well. Then the Lord gave to Job more than he had ever owned in the past, twice as many sheep, and oxen, and camels, and asses. And God gave again to Job seven sons and three daughters; and in all the land there were no women found so lovely as the daughters of Job. After his trouble, Job lived a long time, in riches, and honor, and goodness, under God's care.

# I Never Saw a Moor

*Emily Dickinson*

Faith requires no proofs.

I never saw a moor,
I never saw the sea;
Yet know I how the heather looks,
And what a wave must be.

I never spoke with God,
Nor visited in heaven;
Yet certain am I of the spot
As if the chart were given.

---

# The Fiery Furnace

*Retold by Jesse Lyman Hurlbut*

The book of Daniel in the Bible is about the Jewish hero Daniel, who is taken captive to Babylon and, along with his friends Shadrach, Meshach, and Abednego, brought up in the court of King Nebuchadnezzar. The literal trial by fire we read about here is one of our most memorable examples of steadfastness in one's faith.

At one time King Nebuchadnezzar caused a great image to be made and to be covered with gold. This image he set up as an idol to be worshipped, on the plain of Dura, near the city of Babylon. When it was finished, it stood upon its base or foundation almost a hundred feet high, so that upon the plain it could be seen far away. Then the king sent out a command for all the princes, and rulers, and nobles in the land to come to a great gathering, when the image was to be set apart for worship.

The great men of the kingdom came from far and near, and stood around the image. Among them, by command of the king, were Daniel's three friends, the young Jews, Shadrach, Meshach, and Abednego. For some reason Daniel himself was not there. He may have been busy with the work of the kingdom in some other place.

At one moment in the service before the image all the trumpets sounded, the drums were beaten, and music was made upon musical instruments of all kinds, as a signal for all the people to kneel down and worship the great golden image. But while the people were kneeling there were three men who stood up and would not bow down. These were the three young Jews, Shadrach, Meshach, and Abednego. They knelt down before the Lord God only.

Many of the nobles had been jealous of these young men because they had been lifted to high places in the rule of the kingdom, and these men, who hated Daniel and his friends, were glad to find that these three men had not obeyed the command of King Nebuchadnezzar. The king had said that if anyone did not worship the golden image he should be thrown into a furnace of fire.

These men who hated the Jews came to the king, and said, "O king, may you live forever! You gave orders that when the music sounded everyone should bow down and worship the golden image; and that if any man did not worship he should be thrown into a furnace of fire. There are some Jews whom you have made rulers in the land, and they have not done as you commanded. Their names are Shadrach, Meshach, and Abednego. They do not serve your gods, nor worship the golden image that you have set up."

Then Nebuchadnezzar was filled with rage and fury at knowing that anyone should dare to disobey his words. He sent for these three men, and said to them, "O Shadrach, Meshach, and Abednego, was it by purpose that you did not fall down and worship the image of gold? The music shall sound once more, and if you then will worship the image, it shall be well. But if you will not, then you shall be thrown into the furnace of fire to die."

These three young men were not afraid of the king. They said, "O King Nebuchadnezzar, we are ready to answer you at once. The God whom we serve is able to save us from the fiery furnace and we know that he will save us. But if it is God's will that we should die, even then, you may understand, O king, that we will not serve your gods, nor worship the golden image that you have set up."

This answer made the king more furious than before. He said

to his servants, "Make a fire in the furnace hotter than ever it has been before, as hot as fire can be made, and throw these three men into it."

Then the soldiers of the king's army seized the three young Jews as they stood in their loose robes, with their turbans or hats on their heads. They tied them with ropes, and dragged them to the mouth of the furnace, and threw them into the fire. The flames rushed from the open door with such fury that they burned even to death the soldiers who were holding these men; and the men themselves fell down bound into the middle of the fiery furnace.

King Nebuchadnezzar stood in front of the furnace, and looked into the open door. As he looked he was filled with wonder at what he saw; and he said to the nobles around him:

"Did we not throw three men bound into the fire? How is it then that I see four men loose, walking in the furnace, and the fourth man looks as though he were a son of the gods?"

The king came near to the door of the furnace as the fire became lower, and he called out to the three men within it:

"Shadrach, Meshach, and Abednego, ye who serve the Most High God, come out of the fire and come to me."

They came out and stood before the king, in the sight of all the princes, and nobles, and rulers; and everyone could see that they were alive. Their garments had not been scorched nor their hair singed, nor was there even the smell of fire upon them. The king, Nebuchadnezzar, said before all his rulers:

"Blessed be the God of these men, who has sent his angel and has saved their lives. I make a law that no man in all my kingdoms shall say a word against their God, for there is no other god who can save in this manner. And if any man speaks a word against their God, the Most High God, that man shall be cut in pieces, and his house shall be torn down." And after this the king lifted up these three young men to still higher places in the land of Babylon.

# Daniel in the Lion's Den

*Retold by Jesse Lyman Hurlbut*

This story, also from the book of Daniel, takes place later in Daniel's life. His ability as a seer has led King Darius to give him a high government office.

The lands which had been the Babylonian or Chaldean empire now became the empire of Persia; and over these Darius was the king. King Darius gave to Daniel, who was now a very old man, a high place in honor and in power. Among all the rulers over the land Daniel stood first, for the king saw that he was wise, and able to rule. This made the other princes and rulers very jealous, and they tried to find something evil in Daniel, so that they could speak to the king against him.

These men knew that three times every day Daniel went to his room, and opened the window that was toward the city of Jerusalem, and looking toward Jerusalem made his prayer to God. Jerusalem was at that time in ruins, and the Temple was no longer standing; but Daniel prayed three times each day with his face toward the place where the house of God had once stood, although it was many hundreds of miles away.

These nobles thought that in Daniel's prayers they could find a chance to do him harm, and perhaps cause him to be put to death. They came to King Darius, and said to him:

"All the rulers have agreed together to have a law made that for thirty days no one shall ask anything of any god or any man, except from you, O king; and that if anyone shall pray to any god, or shall ask anything from any man during thirty days, except from you, O king, he shall be thrown into the den where the lions are kept. Now, O king, make the law, and sign the writing, so that it cannot be changed, for no law among the Medes and Persians can be altered."

The king was not a wise man, and being foolish and vain, he was pleased with this law which would set him even above the gods. So, without asking Daniel's advice, he signed the writing; and the law was made, and the word was sent out through the kingdom that for thirty days no one should pray to any god, or ask a favor of any man.

Daniel knew that the law had been made, but every day he went to his room three times, and opened the window that looked toward Jerusalem, and offered his prayer to the Lord, just as he had prayed in other times. These rulers were watching nearby, and they saw Daniel kneeling in prayer to God. Then they came to the king, and said, "O King Darius, have you not made a law that if anyone in thirty days offers a prayer, he shall be thrown into the den of lions?" "It is true," said the king. "The law has been made, and it must stand."

They said to the king, "There is one man who does not obey the law which you have made. It is that Daniel, one of the captive Jews. Every day Daniel prays to his God three times, just as he did before you signed the writing of the law."

Then the king was very sorry for what he had done, for he loved Daniel, and knew that no one could take his place in the kingdom. All day, until the sun went down, he tried in vain to find some way to save Daniel's life; but when evening came these men again told him of the law that he had made, and said to him that it must be kept. Very unwillingly the king sent for Daniel, and gave an order that he should be thrown into the den of lions. He said to Daniel, "Perhaps your God, whom you serve so faithfully, will save you from the lions."

They led Daniel to the mouth of the pit where the lions were kept, and they threw him in; and over the mouth they placed a stone; and the king sealed it with his own seal and with the seals of his nobles, so that no one might take away the stone and let Daniel out of the den.

Then the king went again to his palace, but that night he was so sad that he could not eat, nor did he listen to music as he was used to listen. He could not sleep, for all through the night he was thinking of Daniel. Very early in the morning he rose up from his bed and went in haste to the den of lions. He broke the seal, and took away the stone, and in a voice full of sorrow he called out, scarcely hoping to hear any answer except the roaring of the lions, "O Daniel, servant of the living God, has your God been able to keep you safe from the lions?"

And out of the darkness in the den came the voice of Daniel, saying, "O king, may you live forever! My God has sent his angel, and has shut the mouths of the lions. They have not hurt me, because my God saw that I had done no wrong. And I have done no wrong toward you, O king!"

Then the king was glad. He gave to his servants orders to take Daniel out of the den. Daniel was brought out safe and without harm, because he had trusted fully in the Lord God. Then, by the king's command, they seized those men who had spoken against Daniel, and with them their wives and their children, for the king was exceedingly angry with them. They were all thrown into the den, and the hungry lions leaped upon them, and tore them in pieces as soon as they fell upon the floor of the den.

After this King Darius wrote to all the lands and the peoples in the many kingdoms under his rule, "May peace be given to you all abundantly! I make a law that everywhere among my kingdoms men fear and worship the Lord God of Daniel, for he is the living God, above all other gods, who only can save men."

---

## The 23rd Psalm

The book of Psalms was the ancient hymnal of the Jewish people. Most of the psalms were probably written for use in worship; one finds among them songs of praise, thanksgiving, adoration, devotion, doubt, and complaint. Martin Luther called the Psalter "a Bible in miniature." Psalm 23, a hymn of trust in God, is probably the most widely loved.

The Lord is my shepherd; I shall not want.

He maketh me to lie down in green pastures: he leadeth me beside the still waters.

He restoreth my soul: he leadeth me in the paths of righteousness for his name's sake.

Yea, though I walk through the valley of the shadow of death, I will fear no evil: for thou art with me; thy rod and thy staff they comfort me.

Thou preparest a table before me in the presence of mine enemies: thou anointest my head with oil; my cup runneth over.

Surely goodness and mercy shall follow me all the days of my life: and I will dwell in the house of the Lord forever.

# The Healing of the Paralytic

*Retold by Jesse Lyman Hurlbut*

This story from the New Testament is a miracle story of physical healing brought about through tremendous faith. It is a good way to remember that faith heals spiritually as well.

After a time Jesus came again to Capernaum, which was now his home. As soon as the people heard that he was there they came in great crowds to see him and to hear him. They filled the house, and the courtyard inside its walls, and even the streets around it, while Jesus sat in the open court of the house and taught them. It was the springtime and warm, and a roof had been placed over the court as a shelter from the sun.

While Jesus was teaching, the roof was suddenly taken away above their heads. They looked up, and saw that a man was being let down in a bed by four men on the walls above.

This man was paralyzed, so that he could neither walk nor stand. He was so eager to come to Jesus that these men, finding that they could not carry him through the crowd, had lifted him up to the top of the house, and had opened the roof, and were now letting him down in his bed before Jesus.

This showed that they believed in Jesus, without any doubt whether he could cure this man. Jesus said to the man, "My son, be of good cheer; your sins are forgiven!"

The enemies of Jesus who were sitting near heard these words, and they thought in their own minds, though they did not speak it aloud, "What wicked things this man speaks! He claims to forgive sins! Who except God himself has power to say, 'Your sins are forgiven'?"

Jesus knew their thoughts, for he knew all things, and he said, "Why do you think evil in your hearts? Which is the easier to say, 'Your sins are forgiven,' or 'Rise up and walk'? But I will show you that while I am on earth as the Son of Man, I have the power to forgive sins."

Then he spoke to the paralyzed man on his couch before them, "Rise up, take up your bed, and go to your house!"

At once a new life and power came to the man. He stood upon

his feet, rolled up the bed on which he had been lying helpless, placed it on his shoulders and walked out through the crowd, which opened to make a way for him. The man went, strong and well, to his own house, praising God as he walked.

---

# The Captain's Daughter

*James T. Fields*

Sometimes the youngest inspire us the most by their trust in a higher power. This is a good poem to recite aloud.

We were crowded in the cabin,
Not a soul would dare to sleep—
It was midnight on the waters,
And a storm was on the deep.

'Tis a fearful thing in winter
To be shattered by the blast,
And to hear the rattling trumpet
Thunder, "Cut away the mast!"

So we shuddered there in silence—
For the stoutest held his breath,
While the hungry sea was roaring
And the breakers talked with Death.

As thus we sat in darkness,
Each one busy with his prayers,
"We are lost!" the captain shouted
As he staggered down the stairs.

But his little daughter whispered,
As she took his icy hand,
"Isn't God upon the ocean,
Just the same as on the land?"

Then we kissed the little maiden,
  And we spoke in better cheer,
And we anchored safe in harbor
  When the morn was shining clear.

---

# The Sermon to the Birds

*Retold by James Baldwin*

St. Francis was born in the latter part of the twelfth century in Assisi, Italy. The founder of the Franciscan order of the Roman Catholic church, he is still admired today for his simple life of poverty, his love of peace, and his respect for all living things. Here is one of the most famous stories about him.

Very kind and loving was St. Francis—kind and loving not only to men but to all living things. He spoke of the birds as his little brothers of the air, and he could never bear to see them harmed.

At Christmastime he scattered crumbs of bread under the trees, so that the tiny creatures could feast and be happy.

Once when a boy gave him a pair of doves which he had snared, St. Francis had a nest made for them, and the mother bird laid her eggs in it.

By and by, the eggs hatched, and a nestful of young doves grew up. They were so tame that they sat on the shoulders of St. Francis and ate from his hand.

And many other stories are told of this man's great love and pity for the timid creatures which lived in the fields and woods.

One day as he was walking among the trees the birds saw him and flew down to greet him. They sang their sweetest songs to show how much they loved him. Then, when they saw that he was about to speak, they nestled softly in the grass and listened.

"O little birds," he said, "I love you, for you are my brothers and sisters of the air. Let me tell you something, my little brothers, my little sisters: You ought always to love God and praise Him.

"For think what He has given you. He has given you wings

with which to fly through the air. He has given you clothing both warm and beautiful. He has given you the air in which to move and have homes.

"And think of this, O little brothers: you sow not, neither do you reap, for God feeds you. He gives you the rivers and the brooks from which to drink. He gives you the mountains and the valleys where you may rest. He gives you the trees in which to build your nests.

"You toil not, neither do you spin, yet God takes care of you and your little ones. It must be, then, that He loves you. So, do not be ungrateful, but sing His praises and thank Him for his goodness toward you."

Then the saint stopped speaking and looked around him. All the birds sprang up joyfully. They spread their wings and opened their mouths to show that they understood his words.

And when he had blessed them, all began to sing; and the whole forest was filled with sweetness and joy because of their wonderful melodies.

## The Honest Disciple

As this Jewish folk tale reminds us, faith is often the path to other virtues (in this case, honesty).

Once a rabbi decided to test the honesty of his disciples, so he called them together and posed a question.

"What would you do if you were walking along and found a purse full of money lying in the road?" he asked.

"I'd return it to its owner," said one disciple.

"His answer comes so quickly, I must wonder if he really means it," the rabbi thought.

"I'd keep the money if nobody saw me find it," said another.

"He has a frank tongue, but a wicked heart," the rabbi told himself.

"Well, Rabbi," said a third disciple, "to be honest, I believe I'd be tempted to keep it. So I would pray to God that He give me the strength to resist such temptation and do the right thing."

"Aha!" thought the rabbi. "Here is the man I would trust."

# St. Nicholas and the Golden Bars

Since the Middle Ages, St. Nicholas has been one of the most popular saints of the Christian church. He is the patron saint of merchants, travelers, sailors, bakers, and, of course, children, who seldom fail to be curious about the "ancestor" of Santa Claus (a name which comes from Sinter-Klaas, as St. Nicholas is known in Holland).

Long ago there lived a husband and wife who had more money than they knew what to do with, but more than anything else they wanted a child. They prayed to God for many years to give them their heart's desire, and at last when a son was born, they were the happiest people in the world. They named him Nicholas.

They thought there was no one like their boy, and indeed he was a kind and gentle child, and never gave them a moment's trouble. But while he was still a little boy, a terrible plague swept over the country, and his father and mother died, leaving him quite alone.

All the great riches which his parents had possessed were left to Nicholas, and among other things he inherited three bars of gold. These were his greatest treasure, and he thought more of them than all his other riches.

Now in Nicholas's town there lived a nobleman with three daughters. They had once been very wealthy, but great misfortunes had overtaken the father, and now they were all so poor they scarcely had enough to live on. The nobleman tried as hard as he could to find work, but when people saw his soft hands, which had never known any kind of hard labor, they took him to be lazy, and turned him away.

At last a day came when there was not even enough bread to eat, and the daughters said to their father: "Let us go out into the streets and beg, or do anything to get a little money, so we won't starve."

But the father answered: "Not tonight. I cannot bear to think of it. Wait at least until tomorrow. Something may happen to save us from such disgrace."

Just as they were talking together, Nicholas happened to be passing, and since the window was open he heard all they said. It seemed terrible to think that this family should be so poor and actually in want of bread, and Nicholas tried to plan a way to help them.

He knew they would be much too proud to take money from him, so he had to think of some other way. "I must ask God to show me how," he told himself.

So that night, before he climbed into bed, Nicholas prayed as hard as he could, and asked God to guide him. Suddenly he remembered the three golden bars, and at once an idea flashed into his head. He jumped up and took one of them, and quickly started out for the nobleman's house.

Just as he had hoped, Nicholas discovered that the same window was still open, and by standing on tiptoe he could barely reach it. So he lifted the golden bar and slipped it through, and didn't wait to hear what became of it, in case anyone should see him.

Inside the house, the poor father sat worrying as his children slept. He wondered if there was any hope for them anywhere, and he prayed earnestly that heaven would send help. "Tomorrow I will knock on every door in the city until I find work," he told himself. "God will help us through these hard times."

Suddenly something fell at his feet. The nobleman looked down, and to his amazement and joy, he found it was a bar of pure gold.

"My child," he cried as he showed his eldest daughter the shining gold, "God has heard our prayers and has sent this from heaven! Now we will have enough to eat and some to spare. Call your sisters, and I will go and change this treasure."

The precious golden bar was soon sold to a bank, and it brought so much money, the family was able to live in comfort and have all they needed. And not only was there enough to live on, but so much was left over that the father gave his eldest daughter a large dowry, and very soon she was happily married.

When Nicholas saw how much happiness his golden bar had brought to the poor nobleman, he decided the second daughter should have a dowry too. So he went as before and found the little window again open, and was able to throw in the second bar as he had done before. This time the father was dreaming happily, and did not find the treasure until he waked the next morning. Soon afterward the second daughter had her dowry and was married too.

Now, the father began to think that it was a bit unusual, to say the least, that not one but two golden bars should fall from heaven, and he wondered if by any chance human hands had placed them in his room. The more he thought about it, the more mysterious it seemed, and he made up his mind to keep watch every night, in case another bar should be sent as a dowry for his third daughter.

And so when Nicholas went the third time and dropped the last bar through the little window, the father came quickly out, and before Nicholas had time to hide, caught him by the cloak.

"O Nicholas," he cried, "are you the one who has helped us in our need? Why did you hide?" And then he fell on his knees and began to kiss the hands that had helped him so graciously. But Nicholas asked him to stand up, and give thanks to God instead, and begged him not to tell anyone the story of the golden bars.

---

# Hanukkah Hymn

The Hanukkah festival of lights commemorates the rededication of the Temple in Jerusalem. This Hanukkah hymn expresses the praise, joy, and hope appropriate in commemorating that historic event.

Rock of Ages, let our song
Praise Thy saving power;
Thou, amidst the raging foes,
Wast our sheltering tower.
Furious, they assailed us,
But Thine arm availed us,
And Thy word
Broke their sword
When our own strength failed us.

Kindling new the holy lamps,
Priest approved in suffering,
Purified the nation's shrine,
Brought to God their offering.
And His courts surrounding,
Hear, in joy abounding,
Happy throngs
Singing songs
With a mighty sounding.

Children of the martyr race,
Whether free or fettered,
Wake the echoes of the songs
Where ye may be scattered.
Yours the message cheering
That the time is nearing
Which will see
All men free,
Tyrants disappearing.

---

# A Child's Dream of a Star

*Charles Dickens*

Of all the virtues, faith best helps us bear the pain and uncertainty of life lost.

There was once a child, and he strolled about a good deal, and thought of a number of things. He had a sister, who was a child too, and his constant companion. These two used to wonder all day long. They wondered at the beauty of the flowers; they wondered at the height and blueness of the sky; they wondered at the depth of the bright water; they wondered at the goodness and the power of God who made the lovely world.

They used to say to one another, sometimes, Supposing all the children upon earth were to die, would the flowers, and the water, and the sky be sorry? They believed they would be sorry. For, said they, the buds are the children of the flowers, and the little playful streams that gambol down the hillsides are the children of the water; and the smallest bright specks playing at hide-and-seek in the sky all night, must surely be the children of the stars; and they would all be grieved to see their playmates, the children of men, no more.

There was one clear, shining star that used to come out in the sky before the rest, near the church spire, above the graves. It was larger and more beautiful, they thought, than all the others, and every night they watched for it, standing hand in hand at a window. Whoever saw it first, cried out, "I see the star!" And often they cried out both together, knowing so well when it would rise, and where. So they grew to be such friends with it, that, before lying down in their beds, they always looked out once again, to bid it good night; and when they were turning round to sleep, they used to say, "God bless the star!"

But while she was still very young, oh, very, very young, the sister drooped, and came to be so weak that she could no longer stand in the window at night; and then the child looked sadly out by himself, and when he saw the star, turned round and said to the patient pale face on the bed, "I see the star!" and then a smile would come upon the face, and a little weak voice used to say, "God bless my brother and the star!"

And so the time came, all too soon! when the child looked out alone, and when there was no face on the bed; and when there was a little grave among the graves, not there before; and when the star made long rays down toward him, as he saw it through his tears.

Now, these rays were so bright, and they seemed to make such a shining way from earth to heaven, that when the child went to his solitary bed, he dreamed about the star; and dreamed that, lying where he was, he saw a train of people taken up that sparkling road by angels. And the star, opening, showed him a great world of light, where many more such angels waited to receive them.

All these angels, who were waiting, turned their beaming eyes upon the people who were carried up into the star; and some came out from the long rows in which they stood, and fell upon the people's necks, and kissed them tenderly, and went away with them down avenues of light, and were so happy in their company, that lying in his bed he wept for joy.

But there were many angels who did not go with them, and among them one he knew. The patient face that once had lain upon the bed was glorified and radiant, but his heart found out his sister among all the host.

His sister's angel lingered near the entrance of the star, and said to the leader among those who had brought the people thither:

"Is my brother come?"

And he said, "No."

She was turning hopefully away when the child stretched out his arms, and cried, "Oh sister, I am here! Take me!" and then she turned her beaming eyes upon him, and it was night; and the star was shining into the room, making long rays down toward him as he saw it through his tears.

From that hour forth, the child looked out upon the star as on the home he was to go to, when his time should come; and he thought that he did not belong to the earth alone, but to the star too, because of his sister's angel gone before.

There was a baby born to be a brother of the child; and while he was so little that he never yet had spoken word, he stretched his tiny form out on his bed, and died.

Again the child dreamed of the opened star, and of the company of angels, and the train of people, and the rows of angels with their beaming eyes all turned upon those people's faces.

Said his sister's angel to the leader:

"Is my brother come?"

And he said, "Not that one, but another."

As the child beheld his brother's angel in her arms, he cried, "Oh, sister, I am here! Take me!" And she turned and smiled upon him, and the star was shining.

He grew to be a young man, and was busy at this books when an old servant came to him and said:

"Thy mother is no more. I bring her blessing on her darling son!"

Again at night he saw the star, and all that former company. Said his sister's angel to the leader:

"Is my brother come?"

And he said, "Thy mother!"

A mighty cry of joy went forth through all the star, because the mother was reunited to her two children. And he stretched out his arms and cried, "Oh, mother, sister, and brother, I am here! Take me!" And they answered him, "Not yet," and the star was shining.

He grew to be a man, whose hair was turning gray, and he was sitting in his chair by the fireside, heavy with grief, and with his face bedewed with tears, when the star opened once again.

Said his sister's angel to the leader, "Is my brother come?"

And he said, "Nay, but his maiden daughter."

And the man who had been the child saw his daughter, newly lost to him, a celestial creature among those three, and he said, "My daughter's head is on my sister's bosom, and her arm is around my mother's neck, and at her feet there is the baby of old time, and I can bear the parting from her, God be praised!"

And the star was shining.

Thus the child came to be an old man, and his once smooth face was wrinkled, and his steps were slow and feeble, and his back was bent. And one night as he lay upon his bed, his children standing round, he cried as he had cried so long ago:

"I see the star!"

They whispered to one another, "He is dying."

And he said, "I am. My age is falling from me like a garment, and I move toward the star as a child. And oh, my Father, now I thank Thee that it has so often opened, to receive those dear ones who await me!"

And the star was shining; and it shines upon his grave.

---

# Nearer Home

*Phoebe Cary*

This poem expresses the sentiments of John Greenleaf Whittier, who said that "the steps of faith fall on the seeming void, but find the rock beneath."

One sweetly solemn thought
  Comes to me o'er and o'er;
I'm nearer my home today
  Than I ever have been before;

Nearer my Father's house,
  Where the many mansions be;
Nearer the great white throne,
  Nearer the crystal sea.

Nearer the bound of life,
  Where we lay our burdens down;
Nearer leaving the cross,
  Nearer gaining the crown!

But lying darkly between,
  Winding down through the night,
Is the silent, unknown stream,
  That leads at last to the light.

Oh, if my mortal feet
  Have almost gained the brink;
If it be I am nearer home
  Even today than I think—

Father, perfect my trust!
  Let my spirit feel, in death,
That her feet are firmly set
  On the Rock of a living faith!

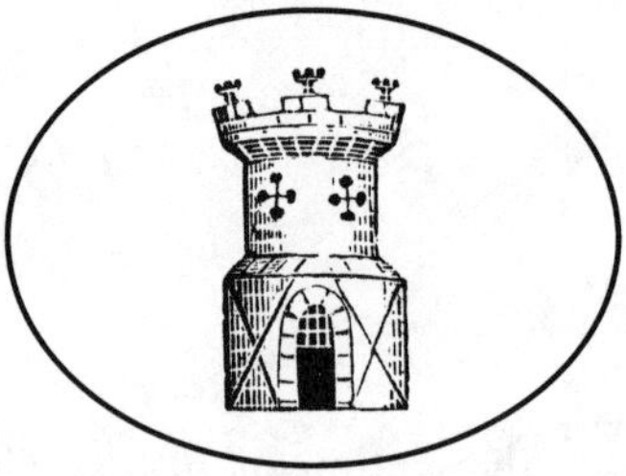

# A Mighty Fortress Is Our God

*Martin Luther*

This hymn, written by Martin Luther in 1529, has been characterized as "the Battle Hymn of the Reformation." One admirer has noted that "there is something in it like the sound of Alpine avalanches and the first murmur of earthquakes." It is based on Psalm 46.

A mighty fortress is our God,
A bulwark never failing;
Our helper he, amid the flood
Of mortal ills prevailing.
For still our ancient foe
Doth seek to work us woe;
His craft and pow'r are great,
And arm'd with cruel hate,
On earth is not his equal.

Did we in our own strength confide,
Our striving would be losing;
Were not the right man on our side,
The man of God's own choosing.
Dost ask who that may be?
Christ Jesus, it is he;
Lord Sabaoth his name,
From age to age the same,
And he must win the battle.

And though this world, with demons fill'd,
Should threaten to undo us,
We will not fear, for God hath willed
His truth to triumph through us.
The Prince of darkness grim,
We tremble not for him;
His rage we can endure,
For lo, his doom is sure—
One little word shall fell him.

God's word above all earthly pow'rs,
No thanks to them, abideth;
The Spirit and the gifts are ours
Through him who with us sideth.
Let goods and kindred go,
This mortal life also;
The body they may kill;
God's truth abideth still,
His kingdom is forever.

# Amazing Grace

*John Newton*

John Newton, the London-born author of this hymn, went to sea at age eleven, was later imprisoned on a man-of-war, escaped to work on a slave-trading vessel, and eventually became a slave ship captain. The hymn is a personal testimony to the "amazing grace" that turned Newton's life around (he later became an ardent abolitionist). After his ordination into the ministry of the Church of England in 1764, Newton and William Cowper produced the *Olney Hymns,* one of the greatest of the Anglican hymnals.

Amazing grace, how sweet the sound,
That saved a wretch like me!
I once was lost, but now am found,
Was blind, but now I see.

'Twas grace that taught my heart to fear,
And grace my fears relieved;
How precious did that grace appear
The hour I first believed!

Through many dangers, toils, and snares,
I have already come;
'Tis grace has brought me safe thus far,
And grace will lead me home.

The Lord has promised good to me,
His word my hope secures;
He will my shield and portion be
As long as life endures.

When we've been there ten thousand years,
Bright shining as the sun,
We've no less days to sing God's praise
Than when we'd first begun.

# Faith of Our Fathers, Living Still

*Frederick W. Faber*

This hymn makes us mindful of the millions of martyrs around the world who suffered dungeons, fire, and sword for their faith, including those who today know the insides of "prisons dark" so that they and others may be "in heart and conscience free." The original version of this hymn was first published in 1849.

Faith of our fathers, living still
In spite of dungeon, fire and sword,
O how our hearts beat high with joy
Whene'er we hear that glorious word!
Faith of our fathers, holy faith,
We will be true to thee till death.

Our fathers, chained in prisons dark,
Were still in heart and conscience free,
And blest would be their children's fate,
Though they, like them, should die for thee.
Faith of our fathers, holy faith,
We will be true to thee till death.

Faith of our fathers, faith and prayer,
Shall keep our country brave and free,
And through the truth that comes from God,
Our land shall then indeed be free.
Faith of our fathers, holy faith,
We will be true to thee till death.

Faith of our fathers, we will love
Both friend and foe in all our strife,
And preach thee, too, as love knows how
By kindly words and virtuous life.
Faith of our fathers, holy faith,
We will be true to thee till death.

# We Understand So Little

Our understanding of God's creation is imperfect, so our faith must fill in the gaps, as this old Jewish folktale reminds us.

Once there were two young brothers who had spent all their lives in the city, and had never even seen a field or pasture. So one day they decided to take a trip into the countryside. As they were walking along, they spied a farmer plowing, and were puzzled about what he was doing.

"What kind of behavior is this?" they asked themselves. "This fellow marches back and forth all day, scarring the earth with long ditches. Why should anyone destroy such a pretty meadow like that?"

Later in the afternoon they passed the same place again, and this time they saw the farmer sowing grains of wheat in the furrows.

"Now what's he doing?" they asked themselves. "He must be a madman. He's taking perfectly good wheat and tossing it into these ditches!"

"The country is no place for me," said one of the brothers. "The people here act as if they had no sense. I'm going home." And he went back to the city.

But the second brother stayed in the country, and a few weeks later saw a wonderful change. Fresh green shoots began to cover the field with a lushness he had never imagined. He quickly wrote to his brother and told him to hurry back to see the miraculous growth.

So his brother returned from the city, and he too was amazed at the change. As the days passed they saw the green earth turn into a golden field of tall wheat. And now they understood the reason for the farmer's work.

Then the wheat grew ripe, and the farmer came with his scythe and began to cut it down. The brother who had returned from the city couldn't believe it. "What is this imbecile doing now?" he exclaimed. "All summer long he worked so hard to grow this beautiful wheat, and now he's destroying it with his own hands! He is a madman after all! I've had enough. I'm going back to the city."

But his brother had more patience. He stayed in the country and watched the farmer collect the wheat and take it to his granary. He saw how cleverly he separated the chaff, and how carefully he stored the rest. And he was filled with awe when he realized that by sowing a bag of seed, the farmer had harvested a whole field of grain. Only then did he truly understand that the farmer had a reason for everything he did.

"And this is how it is with God's works, too," he said. "We mortals see only the beginnings of His plan. We cannot understand the full purpose and end of His creation. So we must have faith in His wisdom."

## Deucalion and Pyrrha

*Retold by Thomas Bulfinch*

Greek mythology describes a Golden Age of innocence and happiness, followed by the ages of Silver, Bronze, and finally Iron. The latter was a savage time when "crime burst in like a flood" and "modesty, truth, and honor fled." War sprang up; the guest was not safe in his friend's house; brothers and sisters, husbands and wives could not trust one another. Reverence toward the gods was neglected, and one by one they abandoned the earth. Only the piety of one couple, Deucalion and Pyrrha, saved the human race.

Jupiter, seeing the wicked state of the world, burned with anger. He summoned the gods to council. They obeyed the call, and took the road to the palace of heaven. The road, which anyone may see in a clear night, stretches across the face of the sky, and is called the Milky Way. Along the road stand the palaces of the illustrious gods; the common people of the skies live apart, on either side. Jupiter addressed the assembly. He set forth the frightful condition of things on the earth, and closed by announcing his intention to destroy the whole of its inhabitants, and provide a new race, unlike the first, who would be more worthy of life, and much better worshippers of the gods.

So saying he took a thunderbolt, and was about to launch it at the world, and destroy it by burning; but recollecting the danger that such a conflagration might set heaven itself on fire, he changed his plan, and resolved to drown it. The north wind, which scatters the clouds, was chained up; the south was sent out, and soon covered all the face of heaven with a cloak of pitchy darkness. The clouds, driven together, resound with a crash; torrents of rain fall; the crops are laid low; the year's labor of the husbandman perishes in an hour. Jupiter, not satisfied with his own waters, calls on his brother Neptune to aid him with his. He lets loose the rivers, and pours them over the land. At the same time, he heaves the land with an earthquake, and brings in the reflux of the ocean over the shores. Flocks, herds, men, and houses are swept away, and temples, with their sacred enclosures, profaned. If any edifice remained standing, it was overwhelmed, and its turrets lay hid beneath the waves.

Now all was sea, sea without shore. Here and there an individual remained on a projecting hilltop, and a few, in boats, pulled the oar where they had lately driven the plow. The fishes swim among the treetops; the anchor is let down into a garden. Where the graceful lambs played but now, unwieldy sea calves gambol. The wolf swims among the sheep, the yellow lions and tigers struggle in the water. The strength of the wild boar serves him not, nor his swiftness the stag. The birds fall with weary wing into the water, having found no land for a resting place. Those living beings whom the water spared fell a prey to hunger.

Parnassus alone, of all the mountains, overtopped the waves; and there Deucalion, and his wife, Pyrrha, of the race of Prometheus, found refuge—he a just man, and she a faithful worshipper of the gods. Jupiter, when he saw none left alive but this pair, and remembered their harmless lives and pious demeanor, ordered the north winds to drive away the clouds, and disclose the skies to earth, and earth to the skies. Neptune also directed Triton to blow on his shell, and sound a retreat to the waters. The waters obeyed, and the sea returned to its shores, and the rivers to their channels.

Then Deucalion thus addressed Pyrrha: "O wife, only surviving woman, joined to me first by the ties of kindred and marriage, and now by a common danger, would that we possessed the power of our ancestor Prometheus, and could renew the race as he at first made it! But as we cannot, let us seek yonder temple, and inquire of the gods what remains for us to do."

They entered the temple, deformed as it was with slime, and approached the altar, where no fire burned. There they fell prostrate on the earth, and prayed the goddess to inform them how they might retrieve their miserable affairs. The oracle answered, "Depart from the temple with head veiled and garments unbound, and cast behind you the bones of your mother."

They heard the words with astonishment. Pyrrha first broke silence: "We cannot obey; we dare not profane the remains of our parents."

They sought the thickest shades of the wood, and revolved the oracle in their minds. At length Deucalion spoke: "Either my sagacity deceives me, or the command is one we may obey without impiety. The earth is the great parent of all; the stones are her bones; these we may cast behind us; and I think this is what the oracle means. At least, it will do no harm to try."

They veiled their faces, unbound their garments, and picked up stones, and cast them behind them. The stones (wonderful to relate) began to grow soft, and assume shape. By degrees, they put on a rude resemblance to the human form, like a block half finished in the hands of the sculptor. The moisture and slime that were about them became flesh; the stony part became bones; the veins remained veins, retaining their name, only changing their use. Those thrown by the hand of the man became men, and those by the woman became women. It was a hard race, and well adapted to labor, as we find ourselves to be at this day, giving plain indications of our origin.

---

# A Name in the Sand

*Hannah Flagg Gould*

This poem reminds us that we should not overestimate our own importance—except in the eyes of God.

Alone I walked the ocean strand;
A pearly shell was in my hand:
I stooped and wrote upon the sand
  My name—the year—the day.
As onward from the spot I passed,
One lingering look behind I cast;
A wave came rolling high and fast,
  And washed my lines away.

And so, methought, 'twill shortly be
With every mark on earth from me:
A wave of dark oblivion's sea
  Will sweep across the place
Where I have trod the sandy shore
Of time, and been, to be no more,
Of me—my day—the name I bore,
  To leave nor track nor trace.

And yet, with Him who counts the sands
And holds the waters in His hands,
I know a lasting record stands
  Inscribed against my name,
Of all this mortal part has wrought,
Of all this thinking soul has thought,
And from these fleeting moments caught
  For glory or for shame.

---

## The Kids Can't Take It If We Don't Give It

*George Herman "Babe" Ruth*

We should not assume that disciplined faith springs from the heart of its own accord. We do not necessarily "find" such faith on our own. Baseball great Babe Ruth (1895–1948) reminds us that, like other virtues, it must be transmitted to the young by caring adults.

Bad boy Ruth—that was me.

Don't get the idea that I'm proud of my harum-scarum youth. I'm not. I simply had a rotten start in life, and it took me a long time to get my bearings.

Looking back to my youth, I honestly don't think I knew the difference between right and wrong. I spent much of my early boyhood living over my father's saloon, in Baltimore—and when I wasn't living over it, I was in it, soaking up the atmosphere. I hardly knew my parents.

St. Mary's Industrial School in Baltimore, where I was finally taken, has been called an orphanage and a reform school. It was, in fact, a training school for orphans, incorrigibles, delinquents, and runaways picked up on the streets of the city. I was listed as an incorrigible. I guess I was. Perhaps I would always have been but for Brother Matthias, the greatest man I have ever known, and for the religious training I received there which has since been so important to me.

I doubt if any appeal could have straightened me out except a Power over and above man—the appeal of God. Iron-rod discipline couldn't have done it. Nor all the punishment and reward systems that could have been devised. God had an eye out for me, just as He has for you, and He was pulling for me to make the grade.

As I look back now, I realize that knowledge of God was a big crossroads with me. I got one thing straight (and I wish all kids did) —that God was Boss. He was not only my Boss but Boss of all my bosses. Up till then, like all bad kids, I hated most of the people who had control over me and could punish me. I began to see that I had a higher Person to reckon with who never changed, whereas my earthly authorities changed from year to year. Those who bossed me had the same self-battles—they, like me, had to account to God. I also realized that God was not only just, but merciful. He knew we were weak and that we all found it easier to be stinkers than good sons of God, not only as kids but all through our lives.

That clear picture, I'm sure, would be important to any kid who hates a teacher, or resents a person in charge. This picture of my relationship to man and God was what helped relieve me of bitterness and rancor and a desire to get even.

I've seen a great number of "he-men" in my baseball career, but never one equal to Brother Matthias. He stood six feet six and weighed 250 pounds. It was all muscle. He could have been successful at anything he wanted to in life—and he chose the church.

It was he who introduced me to baseball. Very early he noticed that I had some natural talent for throwing and catching. He used to back me in a corner of the big yard at St. Mary's and bunt a ball to me by the hour, correcting the mistakes I made with my hands and feet. I never forgot the first time I saw him hit a ball. The baseball in 1902 was a lump of mush, but Brother Matthias would stand at the end of the yard, throw the ball up with his left hand, and give it a terrific belt with the bat he held in his right hand. The ball would carry 350 feet, a tremendous knock in those days. I would watch him bug-eyed.

Thanks to Brother Matthias I was able to leave St. Mary's in 1914 and begin my professional career with the famous Baltimore Orioles [at that time a minor league team]. Out on my own . . . free from the rigid rules of a religious school . . . boy, did it go to my head. I began really to cut capers.

I strayed from the church, but don't think I forgot my religious training. I just overlooked it. I prayed often and hard, but, like many irrepressible young fellows, the swift tempo of my living shoved religion into the background.

So what good was all the hard work and ceaseless interest of the Brothers, people would argue? You can't make kids religious, they say, because it just won't take. Send kids to Sunday School and they too often end up hating it and the church.

Don't you believe it. As far as I'm concerned, and I think as far as most kids go, once religion sinks in, it stays there—deep down. The lads who get religious training, get it where it counts—in the roots. They may fail it, but it never fails them. When the score is against them, or they get a bum pitch, that unfailing Something inside will be there to draw on.

I've seen it with kids. I know from the letters they write me.

The more I think of it, the more important I feel it is to give kids "the works" as far as religion is concerned. They'll never want to be holy—they'll act like tough monkeys in contrast, but somewhere inside will be a solid little chapel. It may get dusty from neglect, but the time will come when the door will be opened with much relief. But the kids can't take it, if we don't give it to them.

I've been criticized as often as I'm praised for my activities with kids on the grounds that what I did was for publicity. Well, criticism doesn't matter. I never forgot where I came from. Every dirty-faced kid I see is another useful citizen. No one knew better than I what it meant not to have your own home, a backyard, and your own kitchen and ice box. That's why all through the years, even when the big money was rolling in, I'd never forget St. Mary's, Brother Matthias, and the boys I left behind. I kept going back.

As I look back those moments when I let the kids down—they were my worst. I guess I was so anxious to enjoy life to the fullest that I forgot the rules—or ignored them. Once in a while you can get away with it, but not for long. When I broke training, the effects were felt by myself and by the ball team—and even by the fans.

While I drifted away from the church, I did have my own "altar," a big window of my New York apartment overlooking the city lights. Often I would kneel before that window and say my prayers. I would feel quite humble then. I'd ask God to help me not make such a big fool of myself and pray that I'd measure up to what He expected of me.

In December 1946 I was in French Hospital, New York, facing a serious operation. Paul Carey, one of my oldest and closest friends, was by my bed one night.

"They're going to operate in the morning, Babe," Paul said. "Don't you think you ought to put your house in order?"

I didn't dodge the long, challenging look in his eyes. I knew what he meant. For the first time I realized that death might strike me out. I nodded, and Paul got up, called in a chaplain, and I made a full confession.

"I'll return in the morning and give you Holy Communion," the chaplain said, "but you don't have to fast."

"I'll fast," I said. I didn't have even a drop of water.

As I lay in bed that evening I thought to myself what a comforting feeling to be free from fear and worries. I now could simply turn them over to God. Later on, my wife brought in a letter from a little kid in Jersey City.

"Dear Babe," he wrote. "Everybody in the seventh-grade class is pulling and praying for you. I am enclosing a medal which if you wear will make you better. Your pal—Mike Quinlan.

"P.S. I know this will be your 61st homer. You'll hit it."

I asked them to pin the Miraculous Medal to my pajama coat. I've worn the medal constantly ever since. I'll wear it to my grave.

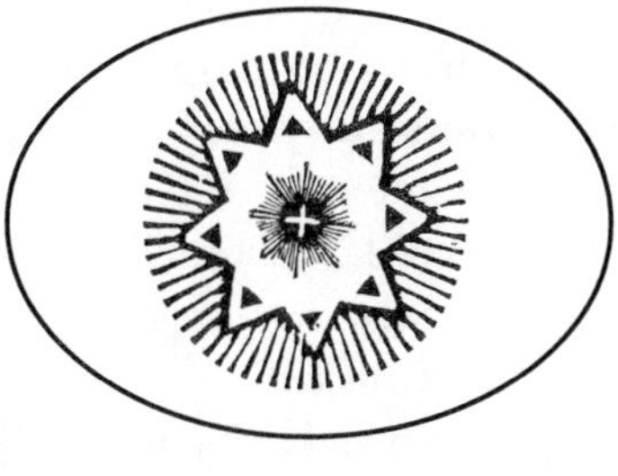

# Our Lady's Juggler

*Anatole France*

Faith leads us to employ our God-given talents in God's service.

In the days of King Louis there was a poor juggler in France, a native of Compiègne, Barnaby by name, who went about from town to town performing feats of skill and strength.

On fair days he would unfold an old worn-out carpet in the public square, and when by means of a jovial address, which he had learned of a very ancient juggler, and which he never varied in the least, he had drawn together the children and loafers, he assumed extraordinary attitudes, and balanced a tin plate on the tip of his nose. At first the crowd would feign indifference.

But when, supporting himself on his hands face downward, he threw into the air six copper balls, which glittered in the sunshine, and caught them again with his feet; or when throwing himself backward until his heels and the nape of the neck met, giving his body the form of a perfect wheel, he would juggle in this posture with a dozen knives, a murmur of admiration would escape the spectators, and pieces of money rain down upon the carpet.

Nevertheless, like the majority of those who live by their wits, Barnaby of Compiègne had a great struggle to make a living.

Earning his bread in the sweat of his brow, he bore rather more than his share of the penalties consequent upon the misdoings of our father Adam.

Again, he was unable to work as constantly as he would have been willing to do. The warmth of the sun and the broad daylight were as necessary to enable him to display his brilliant parts as to the trees if flower and fruit should be expected of them. In wintertime he was nothing more than a tree stripped of its leaves, and as it were dead. The frozen ground was hard to the juggler, and, like the grasshopper of which Marie de France tells us, the inclement season caused him to suffer both cold and hunger. But as he was simple-natured he bore his ills patiently.

He had never meditated on the origin of wealth, nor upon the inequality of human conditions. He believed firmly that if this life should prove hard, the life to come could not fail to redress the balance, and this hope upheld him. He did not resemble those thievish and miscreant Merry Andrews who sell their souls to the devil. He never blasphemed God's name; he lived uprightly, and although he had no wife of his own, he did not covet his neighbor's, since woman is ever the enemy of the strong man, as it appears by the history of Samson recorded in the Scriptures.

In truth, his was not a nature much disposed to carnal delights, and it was a greater deprivation to him to forsake the tankard than the Hebe who bore it. For whilst not wanting in sobriety, he was fond of a drink when the weather waxed hot. He was a worthy man who feared God, and was very devoted to the Blessed Virgin.

Never did he fail on entering a church to fall upon his knees before the image of the Mother of God, and offer up this prayer to her:

"Blessed Lady, keep watch over my life until it shall please God that I die, and when I am dead, ensure to me the possession of the joys of paradise."

Now on a certain evening after a dreary wet day, as Barnaby pursued his road, sad and bent, carrying under his arm his balls and knives wrapped up in his old carpet, on the watch for some barn where, though he might not sup, he might sleep, he perceived on the road, going in the same direction as himself, a monk, whom he saluted courteously. And as they walked at the same rate they fell into conversation with one another.

"Fellow traveler," said the monk, "how comes it about that you are clothed all in green? Is it perhaps in order to take the part of a jester in some mystery play?"

"Not at all, good father," replied Barnaby. "Such as you see me, I am called Barnaby, and for my calling I am a juggler. There would be no pleasanter calling in the world if it would always provide one with daily bread."

"Friend Barnaby," returned the monk, "be careful what you say. There is no calling more pleasant than the monastic life. Those who lead it are occupied with the praises of God, the Blessed Virgin, and the saints; and, indeed, the religious life is one ceaseless hymn to the Lord."

Barnaby replied—

"Good father, I own that I spoke like an ignorant man. Your calling cannot be in any respect compared to mine, and although there may be some merit in dancing with a penny balanced on a stick on the tip of one's nose, it is not a merit which comes within hail of your own. Gladly would I, like you, good father, sing my office day by day, and especially the office of the most Holy Virgin, to whom I have vowed a singular devotion. In order to embrace the monastic life I would willingly abandon the art by which from Soissons to Beauvais I am well known in upward of six hundred towns and villages."

The monk was touched by the juggler's simplicity, and as he was not lacking in discernment, he at once recognized in Barnaby one of those men of whom it is said in the Scriptures: Peace on earth to men of good will. And for this reason he replied—

"Friend Barnaby, come with me, and I will have you admitted into the monastery of which I am prior. He who guided St. Mary of Egypt in the desert set me upon your path to lead you into the way of salvation."

It was in this manner, then, that Barnaby became a monk. In the monastery into which he was received the religious vied with one another in the worship of the Blessed Virgin, and in her honor each employed all the knowledge and all the skill which God had given him.

The prior on his part wrote books dealing according to the rules of scholarship with the virtues of the Mother of God.

Brother Maurice, with a deft hand, copied out these treatises upon sheets of vellum.

Brother Alexander adorned the leaves with delicate miniature paintings. Here were displayed the Queen of Heaven seated upon Solomon's throne, and while four lions were on guard at her feet, around the nimbus which encircled her head hovered seven doves, which are the seven gifts of the Holy Spirit, the gifts, namely, of Fear, Piety, Knowledge, Strength, Counsel, Understanding, and Wisdom. For her companions she had six virgins with hair of gold, namely, Humility, Prudence, Seclusion, Submission, Virginity, and Obedience.

At her feet were two little naked figures, perfectly white, in an attitude of supplication. These were souls imploring her all-powerful intercession for their soul's health, and we may be sure not imploring in vain.

Upon another page facing this, Brother Alexander represented Eve, so that the Fall and the Redemption could be perceived at one and the same time—Eve the Wife abased, and Mary the Virgin exalted.

Furthermore, to the marvel of the beholder, this book contained presentments of the Well of Living Waters, the Fountain, the Lily, the Moon, the Sun, and the Garden Enclosed of which the Song of Songs tells us, the Gate of Heaven and the City of God, and all these things were symbols of the Blessed Virgin.

Brother Marbode was likewise one of the most loving children of Mary.

He spent all his days carving images in stone, so that his beard, his eyebrows, and his hair were white with dust, and his eyes continually swollen and weeping; but his strength and cheerfulness were not diminished, although he was now well gone in years, and it was clear that the Queen of Paradise still cherished her servant in his old age. Marbode represented her seated upon a throne, her brow encircled with an orb-shaped nimbus set with pearls. And he took care that the folds of her dress should cover the feet of her, concerning whom the prophet declared: My beloved is as a garden enclosed.

Sometimes, too, he depicted her in the semblance of a child full of grace, and appearing to say, "Thou art my God, even from my mother's womb.

In the priory, moreover, were poets who composed hymns in Latin, both in prose and verse, in honor of the Blessed Virgin Mary, and amongst the company was even a brother from Picardy who sang the miracles of Our Lady in rhymed verse and in the vulgar tongue.

Being a witness of this emulation in praise and the glorious harvest of their labors, Barnaby mourned his own ignorance and simplicity.

"Alas!" he sighed, as he took his solitary walk in the little shelterless garden of the monastery, "wretched wight that I am, to be unable, like my brothers, worthily to praise the Holy Mother of God, to whom I have vowed my whole heart's affection. Alas! alas! I am but a rough man and unskilled in the arts, and I can render you in service, blessed Lady, neither edifying sermons, nor treatises set out in order according to rule, nor ingenious paintings, nor statues truthfully sculptured, nor verses whose march is measured to the beat of feet. No gift have I, alas!"

After this fashion he groaned and gave himself up to sorrow. But one evening, when the monks were spending their hour of liberty in conversation, he heard one of them tell the tale of a religious man who could repeat nothing other than the Ave Maria. This poor man was despised for his ignorance; but after his death there issued forth from his mouth five roses in honor of the five letters of the name Maria, and thus his sanctity was made manifest.

Whilst he listened to this narrative Barnaby marveled yet once again at the loving kindness of the Virgin; but the lesson of that blessed death did not avail to console him, for his heart overflowed with zeal, and he longed to advance the glory of his Lady, who is in heaven.

How to compass this he sought but could find no way, and day by day he became the more cast down, when one morning he awakened filled full with joy, hastened to the chapel, and remained there alone for more than an hour. After dinner he returned to the chapel once more.

And, starting from that moment, he repaired daily to the chapel at such hours as it was deserted, and spent within it a good part of the time which the other monks devoted to the liberal and mechanical arts. His sadness vanished, nor did he any longer groan.

A demeanor so strange awakened the curiosity of the monks.

These began to ask one another for what purpose Brother Barnaby could be indulging so persistently in retreat.

The prior, whose duty it is to let nothing escape him in the behavior of his children in religion, resolved to keep a watch over Barnaby during his withdrawals to the chapel. One day, then, when he was shut up there after his custom, the prior, accompanied by two of the older monks, went to discover through the chinks in the door what was going on within the chapel.

They saw Barnaby before the altar of the Blessed Virgin, head downward, with his feet in the air, and he was juggling with six balls of copper and a dozen knives. In honor of the Holy Mother of God he was performing those feats, which aforetime had won him most renown. Not recognizing that the simple fellow was thus placing at the service of the Blessed Virgin his knowledge and skill, the two old monks exclaimed against the sacrilege.

The prior was aware how stainless was Barnaby's soul, but he concluded that he had been seized with madness. They were all three preparing to lead him swiftly from the chapel, when they saw the Blessed Virgin descend the steps of the altar and advance to wipe away with a fold of her azure robe the sweat which was dropping from her juggler's forehead.

Then the prior, falling upon his face upon the pavement, uttered these words—

"Blessed are the simplehearted, for they shall see God."
"Amen!" responded the old brethren, and kissed the ground.

---

# Mary Wollstonecraft on Faith

## *From* A Vindication of the Rights of Woman

English author Mary Wollstonecraft (1759–1797) was a pioneer of the women's rights movement. Her major work, *A Vindication of the Rights of Woman,* shocked many contemporaries by calling for equal education and the opening of professions to women. Here the reformer expresses her faith that we improve ourselves according to God's plan.

In the present state of society it appears necessary to go back to first principles in search of the most simple truths, and to dispute with some prevailing prejudice every inch of ground. To clear my way, I must be allowed to ask some plain questions, and the answers will probably appear as unequivocal as the axioms on which reasoning is built; though, when entangled with various motives of action, they are formally contradicted, either by the words or conduct of men.

In what does man's preeminence over the brute creation consist? The answer is as clear as that a half is less than the whole, in Reason.

What acquirement exalts one being above another? Virtue, we spontaneously reply.

For what purpose were the passions implanted? That man by struggling with them might attain a degree of knowledge denied to the brutes, whispers Experience.

Consequently the perfection of our nature and capability of happiness must be estimated by the degree of reason, virtue, and knowledge, that distinguish the individual, and direct the laws which bind society: and that from the exercise of reason, knowledge and virtue naturally flow, is equally undeniable, if mankind be viewed collectively. . . .

When that wise Being who created us and placed us here, saw the fair idea, He willed, by allowing it to be so, that the passions should unfold our reason, because He could see that present evil would produce future good. Could the helpless creature whom he called from nothing break loose from His providence, and boldly learn to know good by practicing evil, without His permission? No. How could that energetic advocate for immortality [Rousseau] argue so inconsistently? Had mankind remained forever in the brutal state of nature, which even his magic pen cannot paint as a state in which a single virtue took root, it would have been clear, though not to the sensitive unreflecting wanderer, that man was born to run the circle of life and death, and adorn God's garden for some purpose which could not easily be reconciled with His attributes.

But if, to crown the whole, there were to be rational creatures produced, allowed to rise in excellence by the exercise of powers implanted for that purpose; if benignity itself thought fit to call into existence a creature above the brutes, who could think and improve himself, why should that inestimable gift, for a gift it was, if man was so created, as to have a capacity to rise above the state in which sensation produced brutal ease, be called, in direct terms, a curse? A curse it might be reckoned, if the whole of our existence were bounded by our continuance in this world; for why should the gracious fountain of life give us passions, the power of reflecting, only to embitter our days and inspire us with mistaken notions of dignity? Why should He lead us from love of ourselves to the sublime emotions which the discovery of His wisdom and goodness excites, if these feelings were not set in motion to improve our nature, of which they make a part, and render us capable of enjoying a more godlike portion of happiness? Firmly persuaded that no evil exists in the world that God did not design to take place, I build my belief on the perfection of God.

# L'Envoi

*Rudyard Kipling*

This poem has long been a favorite because of its assertion of the individual's power of creativity and responsibility for self-development.

When Earth's last picture is painted, and the
 tubes are twisted and dried,
When the oldest colors have faded, and the
 youngest critic has died,
We shall rest, and, faith, we shall need it—lie
 down for an eon or two,
Till the Master of All Good Workmen shall set us
 to work anew!

And those who were good shall be happy: they
 shall sit in a golden chair;
They shall splash at a ten-league canvas with
 brushes of comet's hair;
They shall find real saints to draw from—
 Magdalene, Peter, and Paul;
They shall work for an age at a sitting and never
 be tired at all!

And only the Master shall praise us, and only
 the Master shall blame;
And no one shall work for money, and no one
 shall work for fame;
But each for the joy of the working, and each,
 in his separate star,
Shall draw the Thing as he sees It for the God of
 Things as They Are!

# Landing of the Pilgrim Fathers

*Felicia Hemans*

Faith has helped found nations—including the United States. This poem helps us remember that many of the first settlers to reach America from other lands came seeking religious freedom. People still come for that reason.

The breaking waves dashed high,
  On a stern and rock-bound coast,
And the woods against a stormy sky,
  Their giant branches tossed;

And the heavy night hung dark,
  The hills and waters o'er,
When a band of exiles moored their bark
  On the wild New England shore.

Not as the conqueror comes,
  They, the true-hearted came;
Not with the roll of the stirring drums,
  And the trumpet that sings of fame;

Not as the flying come,
  In silence and in fear—
They shook the depths of the desert gloom
  With their hymns of lofty cheer.

Amidst the storm they sang,
  And the stars heard, and the sea;
And the sounding aisles of the dim woods rang
  To the anthem of the free.

The ocean eagle soared
  From his nest by the white wave's foam;
And the rocking pines of the forest roared—
  This was their welcome home.

There were men with hoary hair
  Amidst that pilgrim band:
Why had they come to wither there,
  Away from their childhood's land?

There was a woman's fearless eye,
  Lit by her deep love's truth;
There was manhood's brow serenely high,
  And the fiery heart of youth.

What sought they thus afar?
  Bright jewels of the mine?
The wealth of seas, the spoils of war?
  They sought a faith's pure shrine!

Aye, call it holy ground,
  The soil where first they trod;
They have left unstained what there they found—
  Freedom to worship God.

---

# Jefferson Urges an Examination of Faith

*Thomas Jefferson*

In this 1787 letter to his nephew Peter Carr, whose own parents were dead, we find Thomas Jefferson urging the young man to scrutinize religion with an open yet thoughtful mind, and to accept it or reject it on his own terms. Faith, like other virtues, should be part of a self-examined life.

He who made us would have been a pitiful bungler, if he had made the rules of our moral conduct a matter of science. For one man of science, there are thousands who are not. What would have become of them? Man was destined for society. His morality, therefore, was to be formed to this object. He was endowed with a sense of right and wrong, merely relative to this. . . . The moral sense, or conscience, is as much a part of man as his leg or arm. It is given to all human beings in a stronger or weaker degree, as force of members is given them in a greater or less degree. It may be strengthened by exercise, as may any particular limb of the body. This sense is submitted, indeed, in some degree, to the guidance of reason; but it is a small stock which is required for this; even a less one than what we call common sense.

State a moral case to a plowman and a professor. The former will decide it as well, and often better than the latter, because he has not been led astray by artificial rules. In this branch, therefore, read good books, because they will encourage, as well as direct your feelings. The writings of Sterne, particularly, form the best course of morality that ever was written. Besides these, read the books mentioned in the enclosed paper; and above all things, lose no occasion of exercising your dispositions to be grateful, to be generous, to be charitable, to be humane, to be true, just, firm, orderly, courageous, etc. Consider every act of this kind, as an exercise which will strengthen your moral faculties and increase your worth.

Religion. Your reason is now mature enough to examine this object. In the first place, divest yourself of all bias in favor of novelty and singularity of opinion. Indulge them in any other subject rather than that of religion. It is too important, and the consequences of error may be too serious. On the other hand, shake off all the fears and servile prejudices, under which weak minds are servilely crouched. Fix reason firmly in her seat, and call to her tribunal every fact, every opinion. Question with boldness even the existence of a God; because, if there be one, he must more approve of the homage of reason, than that of blindfolded fear.

You will naturally examine first the religion of your own country. Read the Bible, then, as you would read Livy or Tacitus. The facts which are within the ordinary course of nature, you will believe on the authority of the writer, as you do those of the same kind in Livy and Tacitus. The testimony of the writer weighs in their favor, in one scale, and their not being against the laws of nature, does not weigh against them. But those facts in the Bible which contradict the laws of nature, must be examined with more care, and under a variety of faces. Here you must recur to the pretensions of the writer to inspiration from God. Examine upon what evidence his pretensions are founded, and whether that evidence is so strong, as that its falsehood would be more improbable than a change in the laws of nature, in the case he relates. For example, in the book of Joshua, we are told, the sun stood still several hours. Were we to read that fact in Livy or Tacitus, we should class it with their showers of blood, speaking of statues, beasts, etc. But it is said, that the writer of that book was inspired. Examine, therefore, candidly, what evidence there is of his having been inspired. The pretension is entitled to your inquiry, because millions believe it. On the other hand, you are astronomer enough to know how contrary it is to the law of nature that a body revolving on its axis, as the earth does, should have stopped, should not, by that sudden stoppage, have prostrated animals, trees, buildings, and should after a certain time have resumed its revolution, and that without a second general prostration. Is this arrest of the earth's motion, or the evidence which affirms it, most within the law of probabilities?

You will next read the New Testament. It is the history of a personage called Jesus. Keep in your eye the opposite pretensions: 1, of those who say he was begotten by God, born of a virgin, suspended and reversed the laws of nature at will, and ascended bodily into heaven; and 2, of those who say he was a man of illegitimate birth, of a benevolent heart, enthusiastic mind, who set out without pretensions to divinity, ended in believing them, and was punished capitally for sedition, by being gibbeted, according to the Roman law, which punished the first commission of that offense by whipping, and the second by exile, or death, *in furea*. . . .

These questions are examined in the books I have mentioned, under the head of Religion, and several others. They will assist you in your inquiries; but keep your reason firmly on the watch in reading them all.

Do not be frightened from this inquiry by any fear of its consequences. If it ends in a belief that there is no God, you will find incitements to virtue in the comfort and pleasantness you feel in its exercise, and the love of others which it will procure you. If you find reason to believe there is a God, a consciousness that you are acting under his eye, and that he approves you, will be a vast additional incitement; if that there be a future state, the hope of a happy existence in that increases the appetite to deserve it; if that Jesus was also a God, you will be comforted by a belief of his aid and love.

In fine, I repeat, you must lay aside all prejudice on both sides, and neither believe nor reject anything, because any other persons, or description of persons, have rejected it or believed it. Your own reason is the only oracle given you by heaven, and you are answerable, not for the rightness, but uprightness of the decision.

---

# The Farewell Address

*George Washington*

In his famous Farewell Address of September 19, 1796, given as he prepared to leave office, George Washington offered the new nation a guide for the future. In this excerpt we find his thoughts on the importance of religion and morality to the country's well-being.

Of all the dispositions and habits which lead to political prosperity, Religion and Morality are indispensable supports. In vain would that man claim the tribute of Patriotism, who should labor to subvert these great Pillars of human happiness, these firmest props of the duties of men and citizens. The mere politician, equally with the pious man ought to respect and to cherish them. A volume could not trace all their connections with private and public felicity. Let it simply be asked where is the security for property, for reputation, for life, if the sense of religious obligation *desert* the oaths, which are the instruments of investigation in Courts of Justice? And let us with caution indulge the supposition, that morality can be maintained without religion. Whatever may be conceded to the influence of refined education on minds of peculiar structure, reason and experience both forbid us to expect that National morality can prevail in exclusion of religious principle.

'Tis substantially true, that virtue or morality is a necessary spring of popular government. The rule indeed extends with more or less force to every species of free Government. Who that is a sincere friend to it, can look with indifference upon attempts to shake the foundation of the fabric? . . .

Observe good faith and justice toward all Nations. Cultivate peace and harmony with all. Religion and morality enjoin this conduct; and can it be that good policy does not equally enjoin it? It will be worthy of a free, enlightened, and at no distant period, a great Nation to give to mankind the magnanimous and too novel example of a People always guided by an exalted justice and benevolence. Who can doubt that in the course of time and things the fruit of such a plan would richly repay any temporary advantages which might be lost by a steady adherence to it? Can it be, that Providence has not connected the permanent felicity of a Nation with its virtue? The experiment, at least, is recommended by every sentiment which ennobles human Nature. Alas! is it rendered impossible by its vices?

---

# Second Inaugural Address

*Abraham Lincoln*

When Abraham Lincoln gave his second inaugural address on March 4, 1865, the end of the Civil War was in sight. Sherman was moving northward through the South after his march from Atlanta to the sea; Sheridan had pushed Confederate forces out of the Shenandoah Valley; and Grant was slowly tightening the Union vise around Lee's army at Petersburg. Lincoln's words are those of a victorious yet exhausted leader who is searching for the meaning of the vast struggle. The biblical quotes he uses are from Matthew and the book of Psalms.

At this second appearing to take the oath of the presidential office there is less occasion for an extended address than there was at the first. Then a statement somewhat in detail, of a course to be pursued seemed fitting and proper. Now, at the expiration of four years, during which public declarations have been constantly called forth on every point and phase of the great contest which still absorbs the attention, and engrosses the energies of the nation, little that is new could be presented. The progress of our arms, upon which all else chiefly depends, is as well known to the public as to myself, and it is, I trust, reasonably satisfactory and encouraging to all. With high hope for the future, no prediction in regard to it is ventured.

On the occasion corresponding to this four years ago all thoughts were anxiously directed to an impending civil war. All dreaded it, all sought to avert it. While the inaugural address was being delivered from this place, devoted altogether to *saving* the Union without war, insurgent agents were in the city seeking to *destroy* it without war—seeking to dissolve the Union, and divide effects, by negotiation. Both parties deprecated war, but one of them would *make* war rather than let the nation survive, and the other would *accept* war rather than let it perish, and the war came.

One eighth of the whole population were colored slaves, not distributed generally over the Union, but localized in the southern part of it. These slaves constituted a peculiar and powerful interest. All knew that this interest was somehow the cause of the war. To strengthen, perpetuate, and extend this interest was the object for which the insurgents would rend the Union even by war, while the government claimed no right to do more than to restrict the territorial enlargement of it. Neither party expected for the war, the magnitude or the duration which it has already attained. Neither anticipated that the *cause* of the conflict might cease with or even before the conflict itself should cease. Each looked for an easier triumph, and a result less fundamental and astounding. Both read the same Bible, and pray to the same God, and each invokes His aid against the other. It may seem strange that any men should dare to ask a just God's assistance in wringing their bread from the sweat of other men's faces, but let us judge not that we be not judged. The prayers of both could not be answered. That of neither has been answered fully. The Almighty has his own purpose. "Woe unto the world because of offenses for it must needs be that offenses come, but woe to that man by whom the offense cometh!" If we shall discern therein any departure from those divine attributes which suppose that American Slavery is one of those offenses which, in the providence of God, must needs come, but which, having continued through His appointed time, He now wills to remove, and that He gives to both North and South this terrible war as the woe due to those by whom the offense came, shall we discern therein any departure from those divine attributes which the believers in a Living God always ascribe to Him? Fondly do we hope, fervently do we pray, that this mighty scourge of war may speedily pass away. Yet, if God wills that it continue until all the wealth piled by the bondman's two hundred and fifty years of unrequited toil shall be sunk, and until every drop of blood drawn with the lash, shall be paid by another drawn with the sword, as was said three thousand years ago, so still it must be said "the judgments of the Lord, are true and righteous altogether."

With malice toward none, with charity for all, with firmness in the right as God gives us to see the right, let us strive on to finish the work we are in, to bind up the nation's wounds, to care for him who shall have borne the battle and for his widow and his orphan, to do all which may achieve and cherish a just and lasting peace among ourselves and with all nations.

---

# Battle Hymn of the Republic

*Julia Ward Howe*

Julia Ward Howe (1819–1910) wrote "The Battle Hymn of the Republic" in the predawn hours of November 18, 1861, when she was visiting Washington, D.C. She had recently watched Union army troops drilling to the strains of "John Brown's Body," and a companion suggested she compose new lyrics for the tune. The result was published in the *Atlantic Monthly* a few months later. Its assertion of faith that God was with the North's cause immediately appealed to the Union army, which adopted it as its marching song. After the war, its popularity spread to all parts of the country.

Mine eyes have seen the glory of the coming of the Lord;
He is trampling out the vintage where the grapes of wrath are stored;
He hath loosed the fateful lightning of His terrible swift sword:
His truth is marching on.

I have seen Him in the watch-fires of a hundred circling camps;
They have builded Him an altar in the evening dews and damps;
I can read His righteous sentence by the dim and flaring lamps:
His day is marching on.

I have read a fiery gospel writ in burnished rows of steel:
"As ye deal with my contemners, so with you my grace shall deal;
Let the Hero, born of woman, crush the serpent with his heel,
Since God is marching on."

He has sounded forth the trumpet that shall never call retreat;
He is sifting out the hearts of men before His judgment-seat;
Oh, be swift, my soul, to answer Him! be jubilant, my feet!
Our God is marching on.

In the beauty of the lilies Christ was born across the sea,
With a glory in his bosom that transfigures you and me:
As he died to make men holy, let us die to make men free,
While God is marching on.

---

# Going to Church

*Theodore Roosevelt*

Teddy Roosevelt offered his reasons for going to church in *Ladies' Home Journal* in 1917.

1. In this actual world a churchless community, a community where men have abandoned and scoffed at or ignored their religious needs, is a community on the rapid downgrade. It is perfectly true that occasional individuals or families may have nothing to do with church or with religious practices and observances and yet maintain the highest standard of spirituality and of ethical obligation. But this does not affect the case in the world as it now is, any more than that exceptional men and women under exceptional conditions have disregarded the marriage tie without moral harm to themselves interferes with the larger fact that such disregard if at all common means the complete moral disintegration of the body politic.

2. Church work and church attendance mean the cultivation of the habit of feeling some responsibility for others and the sense of braced moral strength which prevents a relaxation of one's own moral fiber.

3. There are enough holidays for most of us which can quite properly be devoted to pure holiday making. . . . Sundays differ from other holidays—among other ways—in the fact that there are fifty-two of them every year. . . . On Sunday, go to church.

4. Yes, I know all the excuses. I know that one can worship the Creator and dedicate oneself to good living in a grove of trees, or by a running brook, or in one's own house, just as well as in church. But I also know as a matter of cold fact the average man does *not* thus worship or thus dedicate himself. If he stays away from church he does not spend his time in good works or in lofty meditation. He looks over the colored supplement of the newspaper.

5. He may not hear a good sermon at church. But unless he is very unfortunate he will hear a sermon by a good man who, with his good wife, is engaged all the week long in a series of wearing and humdrum and important tasks for making hard lives a little easier.

6. He will listen to and take part in reading some beautiful passages from the Bible. And if he is not familiar with the Bible, he has suffered a loss. . . .

7. He will probably take part in singing some good hymns.

8. He will meet and nod to, or speak to, good, quiet neighbors. . . . He will come away feeling a little more charitably toward all the world, even toward those excessively foolish young men who regard church-going as rather a soft performance.

9. I advocate a man's joining in church works for the sake of showing his faith by his works.

10. The man who does not in some way, active or not, connect himself with some active, working church misses many opportunities for helping his neighbors, and therefore, incidentally, for helping himself.

# The Lamb and The Tyger

*William Blake*

In "The Lamb" and "The Tyger," William Blake (1757–1827) depicts creatures representing two very different worlds. As a pair, the poems ask us to come to grips with the proposition that both are God's creations.

## *The Lamb*

Little Lamb, who made thee?
Dost thou know who made thee?
Gave thee life and bid thee feed,
By the stream and o'er the mead;
Gave thee clothing of delight,
Softest clothing wooly bright;
Gave thee such a tender voice,
Making all the vales rejoice!
Little Lamb who made thee?
Dost thou know who made thee?

Little Lamb I'll tell thee,
Little Lamb I'll tell thee!
He is callèd by thy name,
For he calls himself a Lamb:
He is meek and he is mild,
He became a little child:
I a child and thou a lamb,
We are callèd by his name.
Little Lamb God bless thee.
Little Lamb God bless thee.

## *The Tyger*

Tyger! Tyger! burning bright
In the forests of the night,
What immortal hand or eye
Could frame thy fearful symmetry?

In what distant deeps or skies
Burnt the fire of thine eyes?
On what wings dare he aspire?
What the hand, dare seize the fire?

And what shoulder, and what art,
Could twist the sinews of thy heart?
And when thy heart began to beat,
What dread hand? and what dread feet?

What the hammer? what the chain?
In what furnace was thy brain?
What the anvil? what dread grasp
Dare its deadly terrors clasp?

When the stars threw down their spears,
And water'd heaven with their tears,
Did he smile his work to see?
Did he who made the Lamb make thee?

Tyger! Tyger! burning bright
In the forests of the night,
What immortal hand or eye
Dare frame thy fearful symmetry?

## The Loom of Time

According to one popular ancient Greek myth, human destiny lay in the hands of three goddesses named the Fates—Clotho, who spun the thread of life, Lachesis, who assigned each mortal his or her destiny, and Atropos, who with "abhorrèd shears" (as Milton put it) cut the thread at death. This poem elaborates on the theme, expressing the faith that God has a design for each of our lives, even though we may not understand it now.

Man's life is laid in the loom of time
  To a pattern he does not see,
While the weavers work and the shuttles fly
  Till the dawn of eternity.

Some shuttles are filled with silver threads
  And some with threads of gold,
While often but the darker hues
  Are all that they may hold.

But the weaver watches with skillful eye
  Each shuttle fly to and fro,
And sees the pattern so deftly wrought
  As the loom moves sure and slow.

God surely planned the pattern:
  Each thread, the dark and fair,
Is chosen by His master skill
  And placed in the web with care.

He only knows its beauty,
  And guides the shuttles which hold
The threads so unattractive,
  As well as the threads of gold.

Not till each loom is silent,
  And the shuttles cease to fly,
Shall God reveal the pattern
  And explain the reason why

The dark threads were as needful
  In the weaver's skillful hand
As the threads of gold and silver
  For the pattern which He planned.

# The Volunteer at Auschwitz

*Chuck Colson*

Between 1940 and 1945, as many as two million people were murdered at the Nazi concentration camp at Auschwitz and the neighboring extermination site of Treblinka in south-central Poland. Countless acts of courage and faith took place amid the horror there. This is the story of one of them.

Maximilian Kolbe was forty-five years old in the early autumn of 1939 when the Nazis invaded his homeland. He was a Polish friar in Niepokalanow, a village near Warsaw. There, 762 priests and lay brothers lived in the largest friary in the world. Father Kolbe presided over Niepokalanow with a combination of industry, joy, love, and humor that made him beloved by the plainspoken brethren there.

In his simple room, he sat each morning at a pigeonhole desk, a large globe before him, praying over the world. He did so, tortured by the fact that a pale man with arresting blue eyes and a terrifying power of manipulation had whipped the people of Germany into a frenzy. Whole nations had already fallen to the evil Adolf Hitler and his Nazis.

"An atrocious conflict is brewing," Father Kolbe told a group of friars one day after he had finished prayers. "We do not know what will develop. In our beloved Poland, we must expect the worst." Father Kolbe was right. His country was next.

On September 1, 1939, the Nazi blitzkrieg broke over Poland. After several weeks, a group of Germans arrived at Niepokalanow on motorcycles and arrested Father Kolbe and all but two of his friars who had remained behind. They were loaded on trucks, then into livestock wagons, and two days later arrived at Amtitz, a prison camp.

Conditions were horrible, but not horrific. Prisoners were hungry, but no one died of starvation. Strangely, within a few weeks the brothers were released from prison. Back at the friary, they found the buildings vandalized and the Nazis in control, using the facility as a deportation camp for political prisoners, refugees, and Jews.

The situation was an opportunity for ministry, and Father Kolbe took advantage of it, helping the sick and comforting the fearful.

While Kolbe and the friars used their time to serve others, the Nazis used theirs to decide just how to impose their will on the rest of Europe. To Adolf Hitler, the Jews and Slavic people were the *Untermenschen* (subhumans). Their cultures and cities were to be erased and their industry appropriated for Germany. On October 2, Hitler outlined a secret memorandum to Hans Frank, the governor general of Poland. In a few phrases he determined the grim outcome for millions: "The [ordinary] Poles are especially born for low labor . . . the Polish gentry must cease to exist . . . all representatives of the Polish intelligentsia are to be exterminated. . . . There should be one master for the Poles, the German."

As for Poland's hundreds of thousands of priests?

"They will preach what we want them to preach," said Hitler's memo. "If any priest acts differently, we will make short work of him. The task of the priest is to keep the Poles quiet, stupid, and dull-witted."

Maximilian Kolbe was clearly a priest who "acted differently" from the Nazis' designs.

In early February 1941, the Polish underground smuggled word to Kolbe that his name was on a Gestapo list: he was about to be arrested. Kolbe knew what happened to loved ones of those who tried to elude the Nazis' grasp; their friends and colleagues were taken instead. He had no wife or children; his church was his family. And he could not risk the loss of any of his brothers in Christ. So he stayed at Niepokalanow.

At nine o'clock on the morning of February 17, Father Kolbe was sitting at his pigeonhole desk, his eyes and prayers on the globe before him, when he heard the sound of heavy vehicles outside the thick panes of his green-painted windows. He knew it was the Nazis, but he remained at his desk. He would wait for them to come to him.

After being held in Nazi prisons for several months, Father Kolbe was found guilty of the crime of publishing unapproved materials and sentenced to Auschwitz. Upon his arrival at the camp in May 1941, an SS officer informed him that the life expectancy of priests there was about a month. Kolbe was assigned to the timber detail; he was to carry felled tree trunks from one place to another. Guards stood by to ensure that the exhausted prisoners did so at a quick trot.

Years of slim rations and overwork at Niepokalanow had already weakened Kolbe. Now, under the load of wood, he staggered and collapsed. Officers converged on him, kicking him with their shiny leather boots and beating him with their whips. He was stretched out on a pile of wood, dealt fifty lashes, then shoved into a ditch, covered with branches, and left for dead.

Later, having been picked up by some brave prisoners, he awoke in a camp hospital bed alongside several other near-dead inmates. There, miraculously, he revived.

"No need to waste gas or a bullet on that one," chuckled one SS officer to another. "He'll be dead soon."

Kolbe was switched to other work and transferred to Barracks 14, where he continued to minister to his fellow prisoners, so tortured by hunger they could not sleep.

By the end of July 1941, Auschwitz was working like a well-organized killing machine, and the Nazis congratulated themselves on their efficiency. The camp's five chimneys never stopped smoking. The stench was terrible, but the results were excellent: eight thousand Jews could be stripped, their possessions appropriated for the Reich, gassed, and cremated—all in twenty-four hours. Every twenty-four hours.

About the only problem was the occasional prisoner from the work side of the camp who would figure out a way to escape. When these escapees were caught, as they usually were, they would be hanged with special nooses that slowly choked out their miserable lives—a grave warning to others who might be tempted to try.

Then one July night as the frogs and insects in the marshy land surrounding the camp began their evening chorus, the air was suddenly filled with the baying of dogs, the curses of soldiers, and the roar of motorcycles. A man had escaped from Barracks 14.

The next morning there was a peculiar tension as the ranks of phantom-thin prisoners lined up for morning roll call in the central square, their eyes on the large gallows before them. But there was no condemned man standing there, his hands bound behind him, his face bloodied from blows and dog bites. That meant the prisoner had made it out of Auschwitz. And that meant death for some of those who remained.

After the roll call, Camp Commandant Fritsch ordered the dismissal of all but Barracks 14. While the rest of the camp went about its duties, the prisoners from Barracks 14 stood motionless in line. They waited. Hours passed. The summer sun beat down. Some fainted and were dragged away. Some swayed in place but held on; those the SS officers beat with the butts of their guns. Father Kolbe, by some miracle, stayed on his feet, his posture as straight as his resolve.

By evening roll call the commandant was ready to levy sentence. The other prisoners had returned from their day of slave labor; now he could make a lesson out of the fate of this miserable barracks.

Fritsch began to speak, the veins in his thick neck standing out with rage. "The fugitive has not been found," he screamed. "Ten of you will die for him in the starvation bunker. Next time, twenty will be condemned."

The rows of exhausted prisoners began to sway as they heard the sentence. The guards let them; terror was part of their punishment.

The starvation bunker! Anything was better—death on the gallows, a bullet in the head at the Wall of Death, or even the gas in the chambers. All those were quick, even humane, compared to Nazi starvation, for they denied you water as well as food.

The prisoners had heard the stories from the starvation bunker in the basement of Barracks 11. They said the condemned didn't even look like human beings after a day or two. They frightened even the guards. Their throats turned to paper, their brains turned to fire, their intestines dried up and shriveled like desiccated worms.

Commandant Fritsch walked the rows of prisoners. When he stopped before a man, he would command in bad Polish, "Open your mouth! Put out your tongue! Show your teeth!" And so he went, choosing victims like horses.

His dreary assistant, Palitsch, followed behind. As Fritsch chose a man, Palitsch noted the number stamped on the prisoner's filthy shirt. The Nazis, as always, were methodical. Soon there were ten men—ten numbers neatly listed on the death roll. The chosen groaned, sweating with fear. "My poor wife!" one man cried. "My poor children! What will they do?"

"Take off your shoes!" the commandant barked at the ten men. This was one of his rituals; they must march to their deaths barefoot. A pile of twenty wooden clogs made a small heap at the front of the grassy square.

Suddenly there was a commotion in the ranks. A prisoner had broken out of line, calling for the commandant. It was unheard of to leave the ranks, let alone address a Nazi officer; it was cause for execution.

Fritsch had his hand on his revolver, as did the officers behind him. But he broke precedent. Instead of shooting the prisoner, he shouted at him.

"Halt! What does this Polish pig want of me?"

The prisoners gasped. It was their beloved Father Kolbe, the priest who shared his last crust, who comforted the dying and nourished their souls. Not Father Kolbe! The frail priest spoke softly, even calmly, to the Nazi butcher. "I would like to die in place of one of the men you condemned."

Fritsch stared at the prisoner, No.16670. He never considered them as individuals; they were just a gray blur. But he looked now. No.16670 didn't appear to be insane.

"Why?" snapped the commandant.

Father Kolbe sensed the need for exacting diplomacy. The Nazis never reversed an order; so he must not seem to be asking him to do so. Kolbe knew the Nazi dictum of destruction: the weak and the elderly first. He would play on this well-ingrained principle.

"I am an old man, sir, and good for nothing. My life will serve no purpose."

His ploy triggered the response Kolbe wanted. "In whose place do you want to die?" asked Fritsch.

"For that one," Kolbe responded, pointing to the weeping prisoner who had bemoaned his wife and children.

Fritsch glanced at the weeping prisoner. He did look stronger than this tattered No.16670 before him.

For the first and last time, the commandant looked Kolbe in the eye. "Who are you?" he asked.

The prisoner looked back at him, a strange fire in his dark eyes. "I am a priest."

*"Ein Pfaffe!"* the commandant snorted. He looked at his assistant and nodded. Palitsch drew a line through No.5659 and wrote down No.16670. Kolbe's place on the death ledger was set.

Father Kolbe bent down to take off his clogs, then joined the group to be marched to Barracks 11. As he did so, No.5659 passed by him at a distance—and on the man's face was an expression so astonished that it had not yet become gratitude.

But Kolbe wasn't looking for gratitude. If he was to lay down his life for another, the fulfillment had to be in the act of obedience itself. The joy must be found in submitting his small will to the will of One more grand.

As the condemned men entered Barracks 11, guards roughly pushed them down the stairs to the basement.

"Remove your clothes!" shouted an officer. *Christ died on the cross naked,* Father Kolbe thought as he took off his pants and thin shirt. *It is only fitting that I suffer as He suffered.*

In the basement the ten men were herded into a dark, windowless cell.

"You will dry up like tulips," sneered one jailer. Then he swung the heavy door shut.

As the hours and days passed, however, the camp became aware of something extraordinary happening in the death cell. Past prisoners had spent their dying days howling, attacking one another, clawing the walls in a frenzy of despair.

But now, coming from the death box, those outside heard the faint sounds of singing. For this time the prisoners had a shepherd to gently lead them through the shadows of the valley of death, pointing them to the Great Shepherd. And perhaps for that reason Father Kolbe was the last to die.

On August 14, 1941, there were four prisoners still alive in the bunker, and it was needed for new occupants. A German doctor named Boch descended the steps of Barracks 11, four syringes in his hand. Several SS troopers and a prisoner named Brono Borgowiec (who survived Auschwitz) were with him—the former to observe and the latter to carry out the bodies.

When they swung the bunker door open, there, in the light of their flashlight, they saw Father Maximilian Kolbe, a living skeleton, propped against one wall. His head was inclined a bit to the left. He had the ghost of a smile on his lips and his eyes wide open, fixed on some faraway vision. He did not move.

The other three prisoners were on the floor, unconscious but alive. The doctor took care of them first: a jab of the needle into the bony left arm, the push of the piston in the syringe. It seemed a waste of the drug, but he had his orders. Then he approached No. 16670 and repeated the action.

In a moment, Father Kolbe was dead.

# Death, Be Not Proud

*John Donne*

John Donne's (1572–1631) famous lines insist that death is not the final sleep, but the final awakening.

Death, be not proud, though some have callèd thee
  Mighty and dreadful, for thou are not so;
  For those whom thou think'st thou dost overthrow
Die not, poor Death, nor yet canst thou kill me.
From rest and sleep, which but thy pictures be,
  Much pleasure—then, from thee much more must flow;
  And soonest our best men with thee do go,
Rest of their bones and soul's delivery.
Thou'rt slave to fate, chance, kings, and desperate men,
  And dost with poison, war, and sickness dwell;
  And poppy or charms can make us sleep as well,
And better than thy stroke. Why swell'st thou then?
  One short sleep past, we wake eternally,
  And death shall be no more. Death, thou shalt die.

---

# The Dying Christian to His Soul

*Alexander Pope*

Alexander Pope borrowed the last two lines of this verse from Paul's First Epistle to the Corinthians (15:55), which in turn echoes older passages from the Bible.

Vital spark of heavenly flame!
Quit, O quit this mortal frame!
Trembling, hoping, lingering, flying,
O! the pain, the bliss of dying!
Cease, fond nature, cease they strife,
And let me languish into life!

Hark! they whisper: angels say,
Sister spirit, come away!
What is this absorbs me quite?
Steals my senses, shuts my sight,
Drowns my spirit, draws my breath?
Tell me, my soul, can this be death?

The world recedes; it disappears!
Heaven opens on my eyes! my ears
With sounds seraphic ring!
Lend, lend your wings! I mount! I fly!
O Grave! where is thy victory?
O Death! where is thy sting?

---

# The Path of Virtue

*From the* Dhammapada

As the following passages help show, the world's great faiths are in accord in many fundamental moral principles. This is worth noting because sometimes people object to the teaching of values on the grounds that people of different faiths must have essentially different values. But as we see here, faiths of different names and histories often share common precepts.

The *Dhammapada* (Path of Virtue) is traditionally ascribed to the Buddha. The following selection from this Hinayana text is a collection of proverbial sayings on the spiritual life.

He who does not rouse himself when it is time to rise, who, though young and strong is full of sloth, whose will and thought are weak, that lazy and idle man never finds the way to knowledge.

What ought to be done is neglected, what ought not to be done is done; the desires of unruly, thoughtless people are always increasing.

But they whose whole watchfulness is always directed to their body, who do not follow what ought not to be done, and who steadfastly do what ought to be done, the desires of such watchful and wise people will come to an end.

He who says what is not goes to hell; he also who, having done a thing, says I have not done it. After death both are equal: they are men with evil deeds in the next world.

Better it would be to swallow a heated iron ball, like flaring fire, than that a bad unrestrained fellow should live on the charity of the land.

Four things does a reckless man gain who covets his neighbor's wife—demerit, an uncomfortable bed, thirdly, punishment, and lastly, hell.

As a grass blade, if badly grasped, cuts the arm, badly practiced asceticism leads to hell.

If anything is to be done, let a man do it, let him attack it vigorously! A careless pilgrim only scatters the dust of his passions more widely.

They who are ashamed of what they ought not to be ashamed of, and are not ashamed of what they ought to be ashamed of, such men, embracing false doctrines, enter the evil path.

They who fear when they ought not to fear, and fear not when they ought to fear, such men, embracing false doctrines, enter the evil path.

They who see sin where there is no sin, and see no sin where there is sin, such men, embracing false doctrines, enter the evil path.

They who see sin where there is sin, and no sin where there is no sin, such men, embracing the true doctrine, enter the good path.

A man does not become a Brahman by his plaited hair, by his family, or by birth; in whom there is truth and righteousness, he is blessed, he is a Brahman.

I do not call a man a Brahman because of his origin or of his mother. He is indeed arrogant, and he is wealthy; but the poor, who is free from all attachments, him I call indeed a Brahman.

Him I call indeed a Brahman who is free from anger, dutiful, virtuous, without appetites, who is subdued, and has received his last body.

Him I call indeed a Brahman who does not cling to sensual pleasures, like water on a lotus leaf, like a mustard seed on the point of a needle.

Him I call indeed a Brahman who without hurting any creatures, whether feeble or strong, does not kill nor cause slaughter.

Him I call indeed a Brahman who is tolerant with the intolerant, mild with the violent, and free from greed among the greedy.

Him I call indeed a Brahman from whom anger and hatred, pride and hypocrisy have dropped like a mustard seed from the point of a needle.

Him I call indeed a Brahman who utters true speech, instructive and free from harshness, so that he offend no one.

Him I call indeed a Brahman who takes nothing in the world that is not given him, be it long or short, small or large, good or bad.

Him I call indeed a Brahman who in this world has risen above both ties, good and evil, who is free from grief, from sin, and from impurity.

---

# Man's Nature Is Good

*Mencius*

Mencius was a Chinese Confucian sage roughly contemporary with Aristotle in the West. To him we owe much of our understanding of the thought of Confucius. Here he explains the Confucian perspective on human nature and its development.

The tendency of man's nature to good is like the tendency of water to flow downward. There are none but have this tendency to good, just as all water flows downward.

Now by striking water and causing it to leap up, you may make it go over your forehead, and, by damming and leading it, you may force it up a hill—but are such movements according to the nature of water? It is the force applied which causes them. When men are made to do what is not good, their nature is dealt with in this way.

In good years the children of the people are most of them good, while in bad years the most of them abandon themselves to evil. It is not owing to their natural powers conferred by heaven that they are thus different. The abandonment is owing to the circumstances through which they allow their minds to be ensnared and drowned in evil.

All things which are the same in kind are like to one another—why should we doubt in regard to man, as if he were a solitary exception to this? The sage and we are the same in kind.

The trees of the New mountain were once beautiful. Being situated, however, in the borders of a large state, they were hewn down with axes and bills—and could they retain their beauty? Still through the activity of the vegetative life day and night, and the nourishing influence of the rain and dew, they were not without buds and sprouts springing forward, but then came the cattle and goats and browsed upon them. To these things is owing the bare and stript appearance of the mountain, which when people see, they think it was never finely wooded. But is this the nature of the mountain?

And so also of what properly belongs to man—shall it be said that the mind of any man was without benevolence and righteousness? The way in which a man loses his proper goodness of mind is like the way in which the trees are denuded by axes and bills. Hewn down day after day, can it—the mind—retain its beauty? But there is a development of its life day and night, and in the calm air of the morning, just between night and day, the mind feels in a degree those desires and aversions which are proper to humanity, but the feeling is not strong, and it is fettered and destroyed by what takes place during the day. This fettering taking place again and again, the restorative influence of the night is not sufficient to preserve the proper goodness of the mind; and when this proves insufficient for that purpose, the nature becomes not much different from that of the irrational animals, which when people see, they think that it never had those powers which I assert. But does this condition represent the feelings proper to humanity?

Now chess playing is but a small art, but without his whole mind being given, and his will bent to it, a man cannot succeed at it. Chess Ts'ew is the best chess player in all the kingdom. Suppose that he is teaching two men to play. The one gives to the subject his whole mind and bends to it all his will, doing nothing but listening to Chess Ts'ew. The other, although he seems to be listening to him, has his whole mind running on a swan which he thinks is approaching, and wishes to bend his bow, adjust the string to the arrow, and shoot it. Although he is learning along with the other, he does not come up to him. Why?—because his intelligence is not equal? Not so.

I like fish and I also like bear's paws. If I cannot have the two together, I will let the fish go, and take the bear's paws. So, I like life, and I also like righteousness. If I cannot keep the two together, I will let life go and choose righteousness.

There are cases when men by a certain course might preserve life, and they do not employ it; when by certain things they might avoid danger, and they will not do them.

Therefore, men have that which they like more than life, and that which they dislike more than death. They are not men of distinguished talents and virtue only who have this mental nature. All men have it; what belongs to such men is simply that they do not lose it.

The disciple Kung-too said, "All are equally men, but some are great men, and some are little men—how is this?" Mencius replied, "Those who follow that part of themselves which is great are great men; those who follow that part which is little are little men. To the mind belongs the office of thinking. By thinking, it gets the right view of things; by neglecting to think, it fails to do this. Let a man first stand fast in the supremacy of the nobler part of his constitution, and the inferior part will not be able to take it from him. It is simply this which makes the great man."

# The Way to Tao

*Chuang-tzu*

Taoist thought traces itself to the author of the *Tao Te-ching,* traditionally identified as Lao-tzu. The following excerpt from *The Way to Tao* by Chuang-tzu is a passage in which Lao-tzu explains the Way (the Tao).

"Whatsoever is not said in all sincerity, is wrongly said. And not to be able to rid oneself of this vice is only to sink deeper toward perdition.

"Those who do evil in the open light of day—men will punish them. Those who do evil in secret—God will punish them. Who fears both man and God, he is fit to walk alone. Those who are devoted to the internal, in practice acquire no reputation. Those who are devoted to the external, strive for preeminence among their fellows. Practice without reputation throws a halo around the meanest. But he who strives for preeminence among his fellows, he is as a huckster whose weariness all perceive though he himself puts on an air of gaiety.

"He who is naturally in sympathy with man, to him all men come. But he who forcedly adapts, has no room even for himself, still less for others. And he who has no room for others, has no ties. It is all over with him.

"Birth is not a beginning; death is not an end. There is existence without limitation; there is continuity without a starting point. Existence without limitation is space. Continuity without a starting point is time. There is birth, there is death, there is issuing forth, there is entering in. That through which one passes in and out without seeing its form, that is the Portal of God.

"The Portal of God is nonexistence. All things sprang from nonexistence. Existence could not make existence existence. It must have proceeded from nonexistence, and nonexistence and nothing are one. Herein is the abiding place of the sage.

"Discard the stimuli of purpose. Free the mind from disturbances. Get rid of entanglements to virtue. Pierce the obstructions to Tao.

"Honors, wealth, distinction, power, fame, gain—these six stimulate purpose.

"Mien, carriage, beauty, arguments, influence, opinions—these six disturb the mind.

"Hate, ambition, joy, anger, sorrow, pleasure—these six are entanglements to virtue.

"Rejecting, adopting, receiving, giving, knowledge, ability—these six are obstructions to Tao.

"If these twenty-four be not allowed to run riot, then the mind will be duly ordered. And being duly ordered, it will be in repose. And being in repose, it will be clear of perception. And being clear of perception, it will be unconditioned. And being unconditioned, it will be in that state of inaction by which there is nothing which cannot be accomplished."

---

# Crossing the Bar

*Alfred Tennyson*

The literal "bar" of this poem is the kind of submerged sandbar that frequently stretches across the mouth of a river or entrance to a harbor. A ship "crosses the bar" when it puts out to sea.

Sunset and evening star,
  And one clear call for me!
And may there be no moaning of the bar,
  When I put out to sea,

But such a tide as moving seems asleep,
  Too full for sound and foam,
When that which drew from out the boundless deep
  Turns again home.

Twilight and evening bell,
  And after that the dark!
And may there be no sadness of farewell,
  When I embark;

For though from out our bourne of Time and Place
  The flood may bear me far,
I hope to see my Pilot face-to-face
  When I have cross'd the bar.

---

## Last Lines

*Emily Brontë*

Faith stands firmly rooted in all-pervading love and life, unshaken by doubt and death.

  No coward soul is mine,
No trembler in the world's storm-troubled sphere:
  I see Heaven's glories shine,
And faith shines equal, arming me from fear.

  O God, within my breast,
Almighty, ever-present Deity!
  Life—that in me has rest,
As I—undying Life—have power in Thee!

  Vain are the thousand creeds
That move men's hearts: unutterably vain;
  Worthless as withered weeds,
Or idlest froth amid the boundless main,

  To waken doubt in one
Holding so fast by thine infinity;
  So surely anchored on
The steadfast rock of immortality.

  With wide-embracing love
Thy Spirit animates eternal years,
  Pervades and broods above,
Changes, sustains, dissolves, creates, and rears.

Though earth and man were gone,
And suns and universes ceased to be,
And Thou were left alone,
Every existence would exist in Thee.

There is not room for Death,
Nor atom that his might could render void:
Thou—Thou are Being and Breath,
And what Thou art may never be destroyed.

# Acknowledgments

For permission to reprint copyrighted material, grateful acknowledgment is made to the following publishers, authors, and agents:

"To the Little Girl Who Wriggles" and "Alice's Supper" by Laura E. Richards. Used by permission of Little, Brown Co.

"The Magic Thread" from *Fairy Tales,* translation copyright 1985 by Hodder & Stoughton Ltd. Used by permission of Doubleday, a division of Bantam Doubleday Dell Publishing Group, Inc.

The Boy Scout Oath and the Boy Scout Law copyright © Boy Scouts of America. Used by permission.

The Girl Scout Promise and Law used by permission of the Girl Scouts of the United States of America.

"F. Scott Fitzgerald to His Daughter" reprinted from *F. Scott Fitzgerald: The Crackup*. Copyright 1945 by New Directions Publishing Corp. Reprinted by permission of New Directions Publishing Corp.

"Letter from Birmingham City Jail" by Martin Luther King, Jr., reprinted by arrangement with The Heirs to the Estate of Martin Luther King, Jr., % Joan Daves Agency as agent for the proprietor. Copyright 1963 by Martin Luther King, Jr., copyright renewed 1991 by Coretta Scott King.

"Men Without Chests" reprinted from *The Abolition of Man* by C. S. Lewis by permission of Collins Fount, an imprint of HarperCollins Publishers Limited.

*The Velveteen Rabbit,* by Marjery Williams, used by permission of Simon & Schuster.

"Childhood and Poetry" by Pablo Neruda reprinted from *Neruda and Vallejo: Selected Poems,* edited by Robert Bly, Beacon Press, Boston, 1971, copyright 1971 by Robert Bly. Reprinted with his permission.

"It's Plain Hard Work That Does It" by Charles Edison reprinted with permission from the December 1961 *Reader's Digest*. Copyright © 1961 by the Reader's Digest Assn., Inc.

"Kill Devil Hill" reprinted from *Kill Devil Hill: Discovering the Secret of the Wright Brothers* by Harry Combs (Houghton Mifflin Company/TernStyle Press, Ltd.). Courtesy of the author.

"Rosa Parks" reprinted from *Rosa Parks: The Movement Organizes,* by Kai Friese. Copyright © 1990 Silver Burdett Press. All rights reserved. Used with permission.

"The Iron Horse" reprinted from *They Rose Above It* by Bob Considine. Copyright © 1977 by Millie Considine as Executive of the Estate of Bob Considine. Used by permission of Doubleday, a division of Bantam Doubleday Dell Publishing Group, Inc.

"Instant Hero" by Blaine Harden reprinted from *The Washington Post,* January 15, 1982. Copyright © 1982, *The Washington Post.* Reprinted with permission.

"Prisoner of War" by Vice Admiral James Bond Stockdale reprinted courtesy of the author.

"The Long, Hard Way Through the Wilderness" reprinted from *The Bible Story for Boys and Girls, Old Testament,* by Walter Russell Bowie. Copyright renewed © 1980 by Mrs. James B. Evans, Mrs. Elizabeth Chapman, and W. Russell Bowie, Jr. Excerpted by permission of the publisher, Abingdon Press.

"I Have A Dream" by Martin Luther King, Jr., reprinted by arrangement with The Heirs to the Estate of Martin Luther King, Jr., % Joan Daves Agency as agent for the proprietor. Copyright 1963 by Martin Luther King, Jr., copyright renewed 1991 by Coretta Scott King.

"I Decline to Accept the End of Man" by William Faulkner reprinted from *Essays, Speeches, and Public Letters by William Faulkner* by William Faulkner. Copyright © 1965 by Random House, Inc. Reprinted by permission of Random House, Inc., the Estate of William Faulkner, and Chatto & Windus, publisher.

"The Indian Cinderella" reprinted from *Canadian Wonder Tales* by Cyrus Macmillan by permission of the Estate of the author and The Bodley Head, publisher.

"Thunder Falls" reprinted from *Fireside Book of North American Indian Folktales* by Allan A. Macfarlan (Harrisburg, Pa: Stackpole Books, 1974), by permission of Paulette J. Macfarlan.

"How Queen Esther Saved Her People" reprinted from *The Bible Story for Boys and Girls, Old Testament,* by Walter Russell Bowie. Copyright renewed © 1980 by Mrs. James B. Evans, Mrs. Elizabeth Chapman, and W. Russell Bowie, Jr. Excerpted by permission of the publisher, Abingdon Press.

"Loyalty to a Brother" reprinted from *The Scout Law in Action,* compiled by Walter Macpeek. Copyright © 1966 by Abingdon Press. Reprinted by permission.

"Nathan Hale" reprinted by permission of American Heritage Magazine, a division of Forbes Inc., © Forbes Inc., 1964.

"Flag Day" reprinted from *The New York Times.* Copyright © 1940 by The New York Times Company. Reprinted by permission.

"Ethical Loyalty" reprinted from *To Serve with Honor* by Richard A. Gabriel, pages 40–42, 196–97. Copyright © 1982 by Richard A. Gabriel. Published by Greenwood Press, an imprint of Greenwood Publishing Group, Inc., Westport, CT. Reprinted with permission.

"Knute Rockne" by Francis Wallace reprinted with permission from the October 1960 *Reader's Digest.* Copyright © 1960 by the Reader's Digest Assn., Inc.

"The Kids Can't Take It if We Don't Give It" by George Herman "Babe" Ruth reprinted with permission from *Guideposts Magazine.* Copyright © 1948 by Guideposts Associates, Inc., Carmel, New York 10512.

"The Volunteer at Auschwitz" reprinted from *The Body* by Charles Colson. Copyright 1992, Word, Inc., Dallas, Texas. Used with permission.

The editor also gratefully acknowledges the endeavors of scholars and collectors such as James Baldwin, Jesse Lyman Hurlbut, and Andrew Lang, who in a past age devoted their energies to preserving some of the best of our heritage, and whose works have supplied this volume with many truly great stories.

Reasonable care has been taken to trace ownership and, when necessary, obtain permission for each selection included.

# Index

WILLIAM J. BENNETT served as Director of the Office of National Drug Control Policy under President Bush and served as Secretary of Education and Chairman of the National Endowment for the Humanities under President Reagan. He has a bachelor of arts degree in philosophy from Williams College, a doctorate in political philosophy from the University of Texas, and a law degree from Harvard. Dr. Bennett is currently a co-director of Empower America, a Distinguished Fellow in Cultural Policy Studies at the Heritage Foundation, and a senior editor of *National Review* magazine. He, his wife, and two sons live in Chevy Chase, Maryland.